Advances in the Study of Societal Multilingualism

Contributions to the Sociology of Language

9

Editor
Joshua A. Fishman

MOUTON PUBLISHERS · THE HAGUE · PARIS · NEW YORK

Advances in the Study of Societal Multilingualism

Edited by
Joshua A. Fishman
Yeshiva University

MOUTON PUBLISHERS · THE HAGUE · PARIS · NEW YORK

ISBN 90-279-7742-9
© 1978, Mouton Publishers, The Hague, The Netherlands
Jacket design by Jurriaan Schrofer
Printed in Great Britain

אבֿרהמעלען
ער זאָל זיַבֿן דריַבֿשפּראַכיקייט
אָפּשאַצן און אָפּהיטן !

Preface

Societal multilingualism is in many respects the foundation field out of which all of the sociology of language grows and ramifies. This is necessarily so, given the fact that it provides easiest access to the data of intra-network as well as inter-network variation in language usage and in behavior directed towards language. However, its very centrality to the entire sociolinguistic enterprise makes it necessary that we approach our consideration of recent advances pertaining to it either via a well chosen subtopic that is more manageable than the whole, or alternatively, that we proceed directly from one subtopic to another in order to exhaustively examine the whole. Having already attempted the former approach on a previous occasion (Fishman 1972) I have undertaken the current volume in accord with the latter.

The progression of subtopics employed in this volume is more easily explained than defended. In a very global sense this progression follows that which often obtains in the 'real world', though the divisions there are less clearcut than they are on a table of contents page. Initially, societal multilingualism is reflected in the lexical, phonological, and grammatical *influences* that languages that have been brought into contact often have upon each other. Viewed normatively, from the point of departure of monolingual gatekeepers of language purity and correctness, these *influences* are *interferences*. However, evaluational judgements aside, these influences are the beginnings of varieties which may themselves undergo continuous conscious as well as unconscious development, depending on the language awareness and purposiveness of their users, and which enter into more or less normatively established situational and metaphorical variation in their own right. Studies focusing at least in part upon phononema of *degree* and *kind* of language influence in contact situations have therefore been placed in Part One.

So many are so accustomed to viewing societal multingualism as a problem, as a conflict indication, and as a concomitant of intergroup strife that it is still all too rare to recognize that stable within-group and between-group multilingualism is not now, nor has it been in the past, all that exceptional. However, since it is really not possible to say objectively whether the 'steady state' or the 'unsteady state' is the more 'natural' or 'pervasive' with respect to societal multilingualism (indeed since it is instructive to always see the one as a stage in the coming into being of the other), Part Two should be taken as presenting studies that are at least in part reflective of the societal search for a *modus operandi* between the language varieties present rather than necessarily the absence or erosion thereof.

Nevertheless, as has happened over and over again throughout world history, and particularly under modern conditions of rapid social and cultural change, the sociolinguistic foundations of society can be basically shaken. The third Part (Part III of the present Volume) concentrates on such situations or their consequences as reflected in the spread of languages of 'wider' communication (sometimes for quite specific or 'narrow' purposes) whether among elites, common folk, or both. However, even when language shift on a massive scale does occur and when one or another language comes into newfound regional, national, and even international prominence the results are not necessarily displacive throughout the repertoire. Languages of wider communication normally remain functionally specific languages and it takes extremely pervasive and disruptive dislocation indeed for them to become mother-tongues as well.

That being the case, societies are repetitively faced with the normative redefinition of functional allocations within their socio-behavioral and sociolinguistic repertoires. That indeed is the implication of Part Four. The storms pass but life goes on. Societal multilingualism in some form is usually here to stay. Languages of wider communication come and go. Their final upshot is as often to broaden repertoires as to narrow them. Social and societal behavior cannot proceed without normatively recognized means of making situational, metaphorical, and even demographic distinctions. Social and cultural change therefore leads inexorably to the establishment of new functional allocations just as definitely as it leads to the disestablishment of old ones.

The unity of mankind is a unity of fate and not a unity of face; it is a unity of ultimate interdependence, not of ultimate identity. From the beginning to the end of the nineteenth century the modern world slowly lost its faith in 'eternal progress' and in 'universal education' as processes that would necessarily lead to the solution of any and all social problems. The twentieth century has seen a quite similar steady disillusionment with respect to the achievement of phenotypic uniformation. Modernism is just one stripe in the cloak of many colors that every society wears. As a result, societal multi-lingualism will not merely 'linger on' in 'backward' corners of the globe but it will defend itself by modern methods (rather than merely give in to such methods) and will do so within the very heartland of western modernity *per se*. The 'new ethnicity' move-ments in the United States (Fishman 1974) will doubtlessly find counterparts in Great Britain, France, Spain, Germany, Italy, and the Soviet Union. Perhaps then it will become clearer than it is today that the 'unity of mankind' must be built upon a recognition and acceptance of mankind's diversity, and not merely upon the diversity of one social group from the other; upon the diversity that exists internally, in each group within itself. It is this diversity of both kinds that creates and recreates societal multilingualism and that makes it part and parcel not only of society but of humanity *per se*. It is an honorable task for the sociology of language (and for all who have joined in making this publication possible) to teach us to accept this diversity and finally to put it to creative, esthetic, and ethical use.

Jerusalem, Israel   Joshua A. Fishman
August 1973

REFERENCES

Fishman, Joshua A.
  1972 'Language Maintenance and Language Shift as a Field of Inquiry (Re-visited)', in *Language in Sociocultural Change*, ed. by Anwar Dil. (Stan-ford, Stanford University Press), pp. 76–134.
  1974 'The Third Century of Non-English Language Maintenance and Non-anglo Ethnic Maintenance in the USA', *TESOL Quarterly*.

Contents

PART THREE: THE SPREAD OF LANGUAGES OF WIDER
COMMUNICATION

PART FOUR: THE RE-ESTABLISHMENT OF FUNCTIONAL
ALLOCATION

ADDENDA

PART ONE

Language Contact

Bilingualism, Language Contact, and Immigrant Languages in the United States: A Research Report 1956–1970

PREFATORY NOTE

The following report might well be entitled 'Bilingualism Revisited', for it represents my return to a field with which I have had only intermittent contact in recent years. The immediate occasion was my course in Bilingualism and Language Contact at Harvard University; I am grateful to my students for discussion and comment and also to the Harvard University Research Committee for making available the services of Jack Fellman as a research assistant. The literature accumulated since 1956 was too vast to be covered completely; the reader should note the limitations described in section 1.0.

1. SCOPE OF THE PROBLEM

1.0. *Definition of the Field*

The dimensions of the field of bilingualism and language contact in the United States (and Canada) were established in the late 1940s and early 1950s by four scholars: Werner Leopold, Einar Haugen, Uriel Weinreich, and William F. Mackey.

Leopold's pioneering work, *Speech Development of a Bilingual Child*, was completed with the appearance of its fourth volume in 1949. Beginning in 1939 as a documented report on the acquisition of English and German by his daughter Hildegard, it provided in Volume 4 the materials for a description of her bilingual development (for the latest report see Leopold 1956–57). In contrast to this sharply focused case study stood my broad survey of the language experiences of an immigrant ethnic group, *The Norwegian Language in America: A Study in Bilingual Behavior* (1953: reprinted and revised 1969). The analysis was based on fieldwork going back to

1936, chiefly in rural Norwegian-speaking communities of Wisconsin and neighboring states, as well as readings in Norwegian-American literature and personal experiences in urban midwestern communities. The methods and theoretical framework were those of American and Scandinavian dialectology, influenced by American structuralism.

In 1953 appeared also Uriel Weinreich's classic monograph *Languages in Contact: Findings and Problems* (reprinted 1963), which offered a theoretical framework for the study of bilingualism. Weinreich was influenced by European structuralism as represented in America by André Martinet and Roman Jakobson. The book was a by-product of his fieldwork on Romansh-German bilingualism in Switzerland, the topic of his still unpublished Columbia dissertation (1951). Weinreich also drew heavily on his own Yiddish-American experiences. While the above three were all professors of Germanic languages in American universities, Mackey was an English-speaking Canadian professor of linguistics in a French-Canadian university (Laval) who found his stimulus for bilingual research in the special situation of French Canada. His earliest published studies appeared in 1952 and 1953; in an article of 1956 he called for a 'redefinition of bilingualism' which would be more comprehensive than the usual conception. He interested himself in the problem of measuring bilingualism (1962, 1965, 1966). It was therefore a natural development when he became in 1966 the founder and director of an International Center for Research on Bilingualism at Laval University, and in 1967 the organizer for Unesco of an International Seminar on the Description and Measurement of Bilingualism at Moncton University in New Brunswick (Kelly, ed. 1969). In later studies he addressed himself to the typology of bilingual education (1970a) and the development of tests for determining the relation between code and message in the case of bilingual usage (1970b).

The situation of American researches in bilingualism was summed up and critically surveyed by me in 1956 in my monograph *Bilingualism in the Americas: A Bibliography and Research Guide* (reprinted 1964 and 1968; review by Mackey 1958). Although limited to the western hemisphere, this study provided access to a large sector of the world's literature on bilingualism. It embodied many of the advances made by Leopold, Weinreich, Mackey, and others. When I was asked to update my 1956 work for *Current Trends in Linguistics* Volume 10, I felt that the best I could do would be to leave *Bilingualism in the Americas* (hereafter *BIA*) as it was and report on the further development of the field since that date. This report will therefore assume familiarity with *BIA* and may be regarded as its direct continuation. The framework of *Current Trends*, however, required the (virtual) exclusion of Latin America and Canada, which were treated elsewhere (the former by Robert J. Di Pietro in Volume 4 (1968) the latter by J. Rudnyćkyj Volume 10 (1972)); a corresponding survey for Europe by Els Oksaar was found in *Current Trends*, Volume 9 (1970).

The field defined by these writers, who were all linguists by training, was inevitably language-centered. They saw the bilingual individual as the locus of *language contact* (Weinreich 1953:1), a 'veritable laboratory for the interaction of competing linguistic patterns' (Haugen 1953:4). They emphasized the significance of language contact as a prerequisite for understanding *linguistic change* (diachrony) and *linguistic variation* (synchrony). They reinterpreted the long-studied phenomenon of *linguistic borrowing* (Haugen 1950, see *BIA* 3.44) in the light of their fieldwork among bilingual speakers and proposed that borrowing be considered a result of *linguistic interference,* defined as 'those instances of deviation from the norms of either language which occur in the speech of bilinguals as a result of their familiarity with more than one language' (Weinreich 1953:1). At the same time all of these linguists were deeply concerned with the psychological and sociological contexts of language contact. They provided ample observations and some suggestive guidelines to psychologists, sociologists, and educators interested in the problem. They furnished the most detailed and sophisticated linguistic analyses so far made of bilingualism and invited social scientists to consider the problem from their special points of view.

1.1. *The Theory of Bilingualism*

The popular view of a bilingual as having *native command* of two (or more) languages imposed so narrow a definition on the field that it led to virtual sterility. It put bilingualism in the paradoxical position of being either invisible or nonexistent: if a speaker is bilingual, he must then be indistinguishable from natives of each language; if he is distinguishable, he can not be a bilingual! However, when bilingualism surfaced as a social or personal problem, it was nearly always because of some disability or handicap imposed on one or the other of the languages in contact. The bilingual was observed to fall short of the norms in one or both languages, and his failure was rightly or wrongly attributed to his knowledge of the other.

It was therefore inevitable that the writers cited above should adopt a broad definition of bilingualism, since a limited, absolutistic conception could not do justice to the many and varied phenomena resulting from the coexistence of two or more languages in a single community or individual (Mackey 1956). By considering bilingualism as a *relative* rather than an *absolute* concept, they found it possible to classify bilinguals along several parameters and to study the correlation of various background factors with the observed variety of bilingual behavior. Weinreich's definition of bilingualism as 'the alternate use of two languages' by the same individuals deliberately left indeterminate such factors as *frequency of alternation, proficiency of use,* and *distance between the languages.* It even left the actual *number of languages* uncertain, since 'bi-' commonly subsumed more than two, i.e., each new language was assumed to enter into a bilingual relation with one or more of the old. Bilingualism thereby became a generic term, replacing the more precise *multilingualism* (or the somewhat pejorative *polyglossy*), *cf.* German *Mehrsprachigkeit* (Haugen 1970a, 1970b, 1972).

A bilingual was thus opposed to a *monolingual* (also called a *unilingual, cf.* French *unilingue*), although it was not established just how much he needed to know of a second language before he was called bilingual. I suggested (1953:7) that *ability to produce sentences* in the second language ought to be the minimum requirement, but it was clear that the ability to *understand* sentences might also qualify one (Diebold 1961b). Since it was possible for the same speaker to switch from one dialect of a language to another, and there was no clear border between dialect and language, even the user of two dialects might qualify as a bilingual of sorts, even though the term *bidialectal* was also coined for such a person. Those speakers whose mastery of both languages approached or equaled that of natives were called *equilinguals* (Raffler-Engel 1961) or *balanced bilinguals*, contrasting with those who were *dominant* in one or the other language. A contrast that was first suggested by Weinreich (1953:10) was that between *compound* and *coordinate* bilingualism, the former being one that supposedly resulted from having learned two languages in identical contexts, the latter in distinct contexts (see section 4). Since language could be independent of the culture, it was suggested that one should distinguish *biculturalism* from *bilingualism* (Soffietti 1955). Various typologies were proposed for describing the nature of the respective languages entering into contact, e.g. *standard/dialect, creole/standard,* etc. (Di Pietro 1968; an especially elaborate and insightful classification was that of Pohl 1965).

For linguists the primary interest of bilingualism was (as suggested above) the relationships entered into by the two languages themselves. How one looked at this symbiosis depended very much on the theoretical concepts with which one approached the study of language. Leopold saw the problem as an *ontogenetic* one, the building up of language patterns in a child faced with the task of distinguishing two sets of utterances. I saw it as *phylogenetic,* the struggle by a bilingual group to adapt its two languages to the novel situations faced by immigrants. In both cases it was possible to catch language history on the wing and to identify some of the variability in usage which eventually resulted in various kinds of pattern shifts. Weinreich applied doctrinal structuralism to the problem of how languages interpenetrate, distinguishing various kinds of transfers from one language to the other, e.g., *overdifferentiation, underdifferentiation, reinterpretation of distinctions,* and *substitution* (1953:18—19). He made a distinction between *phonemic* and *phonetic* interference which depended on one's acceptance of these as two distinct levels of phonology. He distinguished *speech* from *language* in the spirit of Saussure (*parole: langue*), comparing interference in speech to 'sand carried by a stream', in language to 'sand deposited on the bottom of a lake' (1953:11).

Among those who contributed to the continuing discussion of these problems was Kenneth Pike, who (together with Fries) proposed the term 'coexistence of systems' as a way of describing certain unorganic or incompletely adapted elements in some languages (Fries and Pike 1949). More recently he proposed a way of seeing bilingualism in the perspective of his tagmemic theory (1960). Like other students of bilingualism he saw the two languages as *contrastive systems,* made up of units which could be identified across their borders by speakers who mastered or were trying to master both. He saw the systems as in part 'topologically-same', i.e., as forming an elastic, relational system; if two systems had many identifiable items, they were historically the same and synchronically close. He suggested that two systems which shared speakers could constitute hypersystems, which included multiple styles or dialects at their core, bilingual speakers along the margins, and operated within a single cultural matrix. His views were incorporated into the definitive version of his theory (Pike 1967, chapter 15, especially 583 ff.), where he asked, without fully answering his own question: 'To what extent does the bilingual act as if he were using a hypersystem of language, in which the two languages that he speaks somehow fuse into one larger system?' (583).

The question was answered affirmatively by certain sociolinguists, notably Ferguson (1959), Hymes (1967), and Gumperz (1964a, 1964b, 1967). Gumperz concentrated on the study of stable bilingual or diglossic societies (e.g., in India and Norway) where two or more code varieties alternated according to the sociolinguistic situation, e.g., with one used in the home, another in official contexts. He proposed to call 'the totality of linguistic forms regularly employed in the course of socially significant interaction' a *verbal repertoire* (1964b:137); earlier he had used the term *code matrix* (1964a:1117). Using Lamb's stratificational approach to language description, he argued (without complete or conclusive demonstration) that in these cases the differences were 'almost entirely grammatical' and could be pinpointed to the 'representational rules translating morphemic class-symbols to the morphophonemic stratum and in the representational rules converting the morphophonemic into phonemic symbols' (1964a: 1121), i.e., in the morphemic stratum (1964b:147). This restated in novel terminology the well-known principle that grammar (in the narrow sense of morphology) was the most resistant part of language and the one traditionally used to establish cognacy in comparative linguistics. Gumperz also reinterpreted the usual studies of 'interference' in terms of an integrated communication matrix within a bilingual society: 'Code switching in everyday interaction sets up cross currents of diffusion which materially change the structure of local speech varieties' (1967:49). 'It can be shown that such interaction generates its own norms of correctness' (1967:50). The existence of 'bilingual norms' had been pointed out by me (first in 1938, in greater detail in 1953), who found among my American Norwegian informants a 'remarkably high degree of uniformity of practice with respect to the adoption of English materials' (Haugen 1953:60).

It was inevitable that the development of generative-transformational grammar would tempt some of its practitioners to integrate bilingualism into its theory. Chomsky's view of grammar as a set of rules to generate the sentences of a language excluded in principle all forms of variability: 'Linguistic theory is concerned primarily with an ideal speaker-listener, in a completely homogeneous speech-community' (Chomsky 1965:3). This limitation was obviously a strategic device to permit the linguist to operate in a logico-mathematical vacuum, abstracted from the concerns that have occupied most linguists working to describe natural languages operating in ordinary communicative situations. Chomsky's model resembled more closely the practices of traditional, speculative, and normative grammarians than those of linguists basing themselves on the empirical data collected in the field or on available texts of extinct or extant languages.

Granting the premise of grammar as a linearly ordered set of rules with an attached lexicon, it was obvious enough that linguistic variability required the insertion into a grammar of alternation rules. Weinreich pointed out the existence of what he called *automatic conversion formulas* between dialects (1953:2) and proposed setting up a *diasystem* for related dialects (1954a). I proposed (Haugen 1956:45) that interlingual identification be formalized as *diaphonic* and *diamorphic* formulas, with an arrow to mark the direction of identification, e.g., $_E$/-m, -n, -η>-n/$_S$ (read: all final nasals in English are identified by Spanish speakers as final /n/). Such formulas had the general shape of generative rules and could easily be translated into current terminology. In a 1961 paper DeCamp (published in 1969) proposed a method for doing so in the framework of generative grammar, adopting what he called *interstructural lexical conversion rules,* which would transform the structure of one idiolect, etc., into that of another, and illustrated his proposal with an analysis of three vowel systems of Jamaican English. In a later paper he proposed a set of *switching rules* to be inserted in the grammar wherever relevant, which would be activated by a feature in the base (e.g., [+ Low] characterizing a particular style of language within the competence of the speaker) (DeCamp 1969; 1970). While such rules could indeed be considered 'generative', they were clearly distinct from the usual transformational rules, since they represented an entirely different dimension from these (i.e., *horizontal* rather than *vertical, inter-* rather than *intralinguistic*).

Harris's proposal for a *transfer grammar* (Haugen 1956:49) was not followed up (except in a study by Dingwall 1966), but the concept entered into the practice of what is more commonly called *contrastive linguistics.* Dingwall (1964b) reviewed the attempts to apply generative grammar to this field and made some proposals for a *diaglossic grammar* along lines that were more fully developed in his thesis (Dingwall 1964a). Afendras (1969) proposed the use of mathematical models for the description of linguistic diffusion. These were promising developments, but at the moment they offered little that would interest a student of bilingualism. The only known application of these methods to an American immigrant language was a paper by Ureland (1970) on Texas Swedish. Gilbert (1970b) advocated the consideration of immigrant linguistics from the point of view of generative grammar, maintaining that both would profit from the confrontation. He suggested that the linguistic changes in immigrant languages could be seen as a form of restructuring the grammars by the American-born generations: what was optional for the first generation became obligatory for the second, etc. A further step toward integrating bilingual research with recent linguistic thinking about universals of language was taken by Di Pietro (1970; 1971).

1.2. *Bibliographies, Surveys, Symposia*

The bibliographies in Weinreich (1953) and Haugen (1956) were still the most complete and useful introductions to the field. At the Eighth International Congress of Linguists in Oslo in 1957, Weinreich and Haugen were invited rapporteurs to a section on 'Languages in Contact' (chaired by Mackey). In their reports (1958) they offered perspectives of past research and prospects for the future, incidentally revealing the similarities and differences in their respective approaches. Internationally speaking, the most important initiative toward greater depth of understanding of bilingualism was that undertaken in 1963 by the government of Canada in appointing its Royal Commission on Bilingualism and Biculturalism (popularly 'the B and B Commission'). Its *Preliminary Report* appeared in 1965, Book I: *The Official Languages* in 1967, Book II: *Education* in 1968. Book III: *The Work World* in 1969, Book IV: *The Cultural Contribution of the Other Ethnic Groups* in 1970, and others were expected in due course.

The nearest thing to such a comprehensive study in the United States was the Language Resources Project directed by Joshua A. Fishman, summarized as *Language Loyalty in the United States,* a three-volume mimeographed report (1964a) to the Language Research Section of the United States Office of Education, which supported the project. The report was published in edited and curtailed form under the same title (1966a; reviews by Gilbert 1967c, Rudnyćkyj 1968, Hasselmo 1969b). This survey was supplemented by an intensive study of a Puerto Rican community in Jersey City, New Jersey, summarized in a two-volume report entitled *Bilin-*

gualism in the Barrio (Fishman, Cooper, Ma, *et al.* 1968), most of which would eventually be printed. Fishman's studies will be discussed later in the section dealing with the bilingual community (5.2., etc); most of his work was of a sociolinguistic and psychological nature.

Fishman was one of the most active workers in developing *sociolinguistics* (or as he preferred to call it *the sociology of language*) as an interdisciplinary field in which bilingualism plays an important role. In 1963 the Social Science Research Council appointed a Committee on Sociolinguistics, chaired by Charles A. Ferguson, of which Fishman was a member. At the Center for Applied Linguistics a bibliography by Pietrzyk (1964) was prepared under Ferguson's direction for the use of a summer seminar on sociolinguistics at Bloomington, Indiana, in 1964. Some papers prepared by the members of this seminar appeared under the editorship of Stanley Lieberson as an issue of *Sociological Inquiry* (Spring 1966), entitled 'Explorations in Sociolinguistics' (also issued as Publication 44, *International Journal of American Linguistics* in October 1967). Many of the same persons had participated in a UCLA Sociolinguistic Conference in 1964, the proceedings of which (with full discussion) appeared as *Sociolinguistics,* edited by William Bright (1966). John MacNamara edited an issue of the *Journal of Social Issues* (April 1967) containing articles on 'Problems of Bilingualism'. Several of the same contributors, plus some others, were invited to address the International Seminar on the Description and Measurement of Bilingualism at the University of Moncton (1967: proceedings, Kelly, ed. 1969). Important publications by members of the same group were the sociolinguistic readers edited by Dell Hymes (1964) and Joshua Fishman (1968) in which there were special sections on bilingualism.

The Georgetown University Round Table Meeting on Languages and Linguistics devoted special sessions to bilingualism in 1954, 1962, and 1970 (published in their *Monograph Series on Languages and Linguistics* 7, 15, 23). J. Vernon Jensen, an educational psychologist, prepared a bibliographical survey on the *Effects of Childhood Bilingualism* (1962), summarizing the arguments for and against exposing children to a second language and making recommendations for educational policy. A review of the educational literature by Herschel T. Manuel appeared in the *Encyclopedia of Educational Research* (1960). English in Hawaii was the subject of an annotated bibliography by Tsuzaki and Reinecke (1966). A bibliography of

German dialect studies in North America was published by Viereck (1967), while Glenn G. Gilbert organized a symposium on the German language in America (Gilbert, ed. 1971) and edited a book on bilingualism in Texas, Louisiana, and Oklahoma (1970). A symposium on 'multilingualism and sociocultural organization' at the 1961 meeting of the American Anthropological Association was printed in *Anthropological Linguistics* (January, 1962). The related field of English teaching to bilingual populations in the United States won renewed interest with the organization of TESOL (Teaching of English to Speakers of Other Languages) in 1964 (Allen 1965). The *Modern Language Journal* for 1965 devoted the major part of two issues to a symposium edited by Robert F. Roeming on 'Bilingualism and the Bilingual Child'. Since 1962 the international *Linguistic Bibliography* published by Unesco under the auspices of the Permanent International Committee of Linguists (CIPL) established a special section on Bilingualism. Popular surveys of the topic were published by Mackey (1960, 1967).

   Kloss (1969b), while working for the International Center for Research on Bilingualism in Quebec, prepared a comprehensive and stimulating report on possibilities for research in group bilingualism, listing some fifty to sixty potential projects. While the report emphasized national problems (section 5.5.), there was virtually no field of sociocultural interaction which he had overlooked. Another important survey was a programmatic statement by Ornstein (1970) for a sociolinguistic study of Southwest Spanish based at the University of Texas at El Paso. Ornstein projected a broad approach based on contemporary sociolinguistics; he criticized current linguistic theory for failing to take linguistic variety into account.

   A conference on child language in Chicago on November 22–24, 1971, chaired by Theodore Andersson and R. W. Rutherford, devoted itself to dual language learning in young children.

2. LANGUAGES AND DIALECTS IN THE UNITED STATES

2.0. *Minority Language Research*

It is no longer true that 'linguists have rarely exploited the possibilities of immigrant bilingualism' (Haugen 1953:2). After 1956 a goodly number of articles and monographs appeared, though most of the latter were doctoral dissertations which still remain unpublished except in microfilmed or xeroxed form. Since we are here dealing only with the United States, we shall not divide the languages into *native, colonial, immigrant,* and *creole,* as was done in *BIA.* Within the United States the factual sociolinguistic situation imposed a dichotomy of *dominant* versus *dominated,* with English as dominant and all other languages of whatever source as dominated. As we shall see later, this imposed a *unilateral* bilingualism on the dominated groups. A common euphemism for a dominated group was *minority group,* and we might very well speak of *minority languages,* even though their speakers were in some areas an actual majority. In conformity with a more neutral usage we shall here divide the studies into those relating to the *English* language (as influenced by non-English languages) and *non-English* languages (as influenced by English). Another possible (but also faintly euphemistic) usage was that which called non-English languages 'other languages', as in the name of the organization TESOL (Teaching of English to Speakers of Other Languages).

It is one of the commonly observed facts about colonial languages that in certain respects they tend to be 'conservative'. This trait is noticeable chiefly to speakers of the vernacular in its original home, where the trend may have been different, due for example to the influence of the standard language. The hope of finding archaic dialect forms among American Swedes was one of the stimuli for the three field expeditions (1962—66) headed by Hedblom and sent over from Sweden. In a report (1969) on his experiences, however, he noted that such speakers (with 'frozen dialects') constituted only a tiny minority ('några tiotal') of the 500 recorded voices. All the rest showed a trend to leveling which in general favored the informal standard of the homeland, with occasional hypercorrections. The cause of the leveling was clearly association with fellow Swedes in America, where conspicuous dialect forms would lead to comments or even misunderstandings. Lance (1969:45) similarly found occasional archaisms in the Spanish of his Mexican informants in Bryan, Texas. Wacker in her study of the written German of immigrant newspapers (1964; reviewed by Gilbert 1967b) commented repeatedly on archaic words and word forms (pp. 23—5, 125—215, etc.), because the writers have been 'vom Kerngebiet der deutschen Sprache weitgehend isoliert' (175). But the number of such archaisms was not great, compared to the great infusion of English; and some of the archaisms could even be regarded as anglicisms (e.g., the retention of terms like *Fusz* and *Meile* for 'foot' and 'mile'). While the speech of the immigrants tended to be dialectal, thanks to their social origin, their written language showed little or no influence from the dialects.

2.1. *English and its Dialects*

We can here only allude in passing to the important studies by Labov on American social dialects; his studies on Martha's Vineyard (1963b) and New York City (1966) include some references to foreign influence. It continued to be apparent that standard American English had not been deeply influenced by non-English speech (Malmström and Ashley 1958; Mencken 1963:251—66). One of the most comprehensive (but unoriginal) attempts to collect such influences was Schonfelder's (1957) work on German words in American English. He proved to his own satisfaction that the influence was greater than commonly assumed, but his material showed how marginal most of the words were, being either regionally or topically restricted. The *regions* included such dense and long-enduring German settlement areas as Pennsylvania and the *topics* those domains in which Germans had been most influential, e.g., beer brewing, wurst making, and the celebration of Christmas. Along the margins of the language a few morphemes had detached themselves and became productive, e.g., *-fest* as in *gabfest* or *slugfest* and *-burger* (by false analysis of *hamburger*) as in *healthburger* or *lobsterburger*. Yiddish had a similar influence within its spheres, as shown by Feinsilver's (1958; 1962) collections of translated idioms and bilingual puns. Fischer (1965) collected German loanwords from a volume of *Time* magazine. Eichhoff (1971, to appear) studied the pronunciation and spelling of current German loans in American English. Texas English was combed for non-English influences, e.g., by Atwood (1962) who found loans from New Orleans French (*armoire, shivaree*). Mexican Spanish (*hacienda, mesquital, vaquero*), and German (*krebbel, smearcase*) (see Labov review, 1963). Sawyer (1958, 1970) and Johansen (1961) found Spanish and German influences respectively in the English pronunciations of some Texans. Lozano (1961) studied Spanish loanwords in the English of San Antonio, Texas, and concluded that they had mostly been mediated by spelling. Pilati (1969) found a community in Montana whose English was strongly marked by Finnish phonology.

The most interesting area for this kind of study was no doubt the state of Hawaii, where an indigenous Malayo-Polynesian language struggled to maintain itself alongside numerous immigrant languages, all of them gradually being replaced by the dominant English. Reinecke's work (going back to 1935, see *BIA*, and now published as Reinecke 1969) was supplemented by that of Tsuzaki. Jointly they published a valuable bibliography (1966) of English in Hawaii covering the period from 1818 to 1965. Hawaiian loanwords in English were discussed in joint articles by Reinecke and Tsuzaki (1967), by Tsuzaki and Elbert (1969), and by Tsuzaki (1968). M.A. theses on the English of the Japanese (Hayes 1958) and of Puerto Ricans (Kindig 1960) were written at the University of Hawaii. A detailed study of the 'pidgin' English spoken by older Japanese immigrants in Hawaii was presented as a Wisconsin dissertation by Susumu Nagara (1969). This 'case study in bilingualism' provided a thorough 'bilingual description' of the phonology, morphology, and syntax of this functional, but highly distorted, kind of English. Reinecke (1969) rejected the popular term 'pidgin' for this kind of speech, which he called 'creole' or 'makeshift language' and distinguished from the 'colonial dialect' or 'Hawaiian Island dialect' that sprang up among the descendants of the plantation workers. Harms (1969) discussed the problems of teaching successful communication to the linguistically complex communities of Hawaii, where 'there are only minority groups'.

Other studies were concentrated particularly on the phonology of immigrant English, i.e., the foreign 'accent', as this was related to the native languages of the speakers. Hungarian accent (in Louisiana) was analyzed by Nelson (Louisiana State, 1956), Hungarian (in New York) by Nemser (Columbia, 1961), Puerto Rican Spanish by M. E. Jones (Michigan, 1962), Greek by Alatis (1966), and Yiddish by Davis (1967). As will appear below, these were attempts to test the traditional linguistic theory of interlingual perception. A project directed by Lance to study Spanish-English bilingualism in a Texas community revealed few strictly Spanish-derived errors among Spanish-speaking children (G. M. Smith 1969 and Ward 1969, both in Lance 1969). A brief account of English learning problems of Navajo children by Cook and Sharp (1966) suggested further possible studies in this field.

An active program of research in 'Black' speech revealed traces of creolization and cast doubt on the usual opinion of American dialectologists, that this speech was identical with that of its white social counterparts (Stewart 1967). The extensive literature on social dialects will not be reported on here, since most of it falls outside the

present framework (see, e.g., Shuy, ed. [n.d.], Houston 1969,
Wolfram 1969; selective bibliographies by Stewart, ed, 1966, Shuy
1968). In 1969 a program for fast dissemination of papers on English
social dialect studies was established by the American Dialect Society
(Vol. 1, No. 3). De Camp (1968) surveyed the field of creole studies,
with a bibliography of recent contributions.

2.2. Non-English Languages and Dialects

Only those studies have been included that aimed at a deeper
understanding of the contact situation and were not just analyses of
isolated phenomena.

American Indian
It will be unnecessary to go into the acculturation of the Indian here,
since a competent survey of the literature is available by Dozier
(1967) for the Southwest, including many of the papers listed in *BIA*
2.1–2. He discusses two problems: (a) the distinction between linguistic and nonlinguistic evidence (citing among others Troike's 1956
critique of Casagrande's Comanche studies); (b) linguistic and nonlinguistic factors in promoting borrowing (he misreads *BIA* 66 as
advocating a primarily linguistic view of loanword resistance; I agree
with Dozier and with Bright 1960 that sociocultural factors may well
override the purely linguistic barriers). Another paper in the same
volume (edited by Hymes and Bittle) on 'Southwestern Ethnolinguistics' by the Voegelins and Schutz (1967) surveys the language
ecology of all the ethnic populations of the area. In a summary
discussion the authors find that the Indian languages are 'private and
conservative', 'links to the cultural past', while 'the English-language
culture is public and progressive' (449). Spicer devotes a chapter to
this topic in his book (1962) on the 'cycles of conquest' in the
Southwest and shows the functional changes in the role of the Indian
languages.
        Among the more scattered materials were Oswalt's (1958) inter-
esting discovery of a dozen Russian loanwords in Southwestern
Pomo; Wick Miller's (1959–60) study of phonological substitutions
in the Spanish loans of Acoma, the Brights (1959) for Patwin and
McLendon's (1969) for Eastern Pomo; and Kiddle's (1964) report on
the spread of Spanish words for 'cat' among Indian tribes. Kennard
(1963) studied Hopi suffixes on English stems in Hopi, Mierau
(1963) the phonemic differences between monolingual and bilingual

Yavapai-Apache speakers in Arizona, Bodine (1968) the changes in Taos names as clues to linguistic acculturation. Mary Miller (1970) investigated the language attitudes of fifty children of Indian background on a reservation near Phoenix: thirty of them were convinced that English was the 'best' language. Although they fall outside our present bailiwick, two studies of parallel Mexican phenomena by American scholars should be mentioned: Diebold's (1961a, 1961b) on Huave and Law's (1961) on Nahuat. A paper overlooked in *BIA* was a brief report by Waterhouse (1949) on an extraordinary situation among the Chontal Indians of Mexico: they teach their children Spanish first and their native Chontal later.

Immigrant Languages
Anyone who now wishes background information on the current status of these could turn to Joshua A. Fishman's report on *Language Loyalty in the United States* (1966a), on which more below (section 5.3.). The statistics and detailed analyses gathered in this work showed clearly enough the drastic decline in non-English speakers of virtually all languages except Spanish. Fishman emphasized the urgency of further study of these declining and soon to disappear immigrant tongues, as had Weinreich (1954b) in a plea for 'more intensive field studies in bilingualism' (with the purpose of studying the process of 'linguistic convergence').

There were some responses to these appeals, including the Texas symposia listed above (section 1.2.). For one state, Kansas, there was a purely demographic study of non-English language groups (Carman 1962) which one might have wished duplicated for every state of the Union. Dissertations were prepared, but for the most part unpublished, on American Finnish, German, Greek, Italian (Sicilian), Kashubian, Polish, Slovak, Spanish, Swedish, and Yiddish. Active research was known to be going on in German, Spanish, and Swedish. Below is a brief summary of the post-1956 work known at the time of writing (1970), arranged by languages, listed in alphabetical order (cf. *BIA* 29).

Armenian: Hewson (1963) reported on the adaptation of names to English patterns (rather less than expected).

Czech: Reference was made to the maintenance of Czech in Texas by Olesch (1970) and Perkowski (1970). According to the latter, an M.A. thesis on English loanwords in Texas Czech was written at the University of Texas in 1967 by Margaret Cunningham Kutac.

Danish: Paulsen (1967) noted the effect on folklore retention of the rapid disappearance of this language.

Dutch: A comprehensive program of collecting data from Dutch and Frisian settlements in the United States was initiated in 1966 by Jo Daan and reported in a preliminary paper (1969). Shetter studied Brabants dialect in Wisconsin (1957) and the sound system of Jersey Dutch (1958).

Finnish: Meri Lehtinen made a detailed study of one American Finnish informant in an Indiana dissertation (1966); Larmouth (1967) reported on some surname changes among the Finns of northern Minnesota.

French: A study of northern New England by Mary R. Miller (1970) showed that Canadian French was still solidly entrenched in many communities of the area. Sister Maris Stella (1959) published an analysis of New England French pronunciation (following up Locke's 1949 study, *BIA* 2.5.3.). Brault, who was then teaching at Bowdoin College, took an interest in utilizing the local French speech as a basis for French teaching: he prepared teaching materials (1960), organized a conference at Bowdoin for a discussion of the problems involved (1961a), and reported on the vocabulary of New England French (1961b). Theriault (1960) surveyed the problems of language maintenance among the New England French and offered a pessimistic prognosis. Tisch (1954, 1957) offered materials on the French of Louisiana and its social status. Diament (1962) collected a list of over 200 anglicisms casually overheard among foreign-born French speakers in the United States (primarily a list of classified loanshifts). Three short studies by Raleigh Morgan, Jr., offered information on the structure (1959), the lexicon (1960), and linguistic leveling (1970) in the French Creole spoken at St. Martin, Louisiana. LeCompte (1967) produced a word atlas of Grand Isle and Lafourche Parish in Louisiana.

German: The most active research in immigrant languages was that being pursued on German, as appeared clearly from the comprehensive bibliography by Viereck (1967). This included both the monolingual and the bilingual aspects of German speech and writing (as *BIA* 28–9 did not) from the beginning down to 1967, and listed a number of research projects in progress. (Two items from *BIA* were overlooked: Graham 1955 and Stine 1939; Tucker 1934 got his given names reversed.) As Viereck noted, research had been concentrated on Pennsylvania German (Reed 1961, 1967, 1971; Seifert 1967, 1971; Reed and Seifert 1954, overlooked in *BIA*), Texas (Gilbert 1963, etc.) and Wisconsin (Seifert 1963), while elsewhere research was spotty, particularly in urban areas. Viereck called for an 'immediate systematic survey of all the different German dialects still spoken' as a matter of extreme urgency (1967: 551). His bibliography made it superfluous to list anything but the most important studies here. Awaited was the appearance of Gilbert's *Linguistic Atlas of Texas German* (1972?) in the Deutscher Sprachatlas series; this was to have about 140 maps. Gilbert followed his Harvard dissertation (1963) on a Texas German dialect with several articles (1964, 1965a; 1965b; 1967a) discussing aspects of the development of German in Texas. He also took the initiative for a 1968 symposium on the German language in America (1971) and for a compilation of studies by eleven authors on bilingualism in the south central states (1970). Contributors on German in the latter were Gilbert, Pulte, and Wilson; in the former Eichhoff, Kloss, Reed, Seifert, and Yoder (these items will not be included in our bibliography). A European student of the subject, Helga Wacker, analyzed the German *Schriftsprache* overseas; her dissertation (1956) was revised for publication in two volumes, one of which dealt with the United States (1964). Since her book was done without benefit of fieldwork and showed no familiarity with the literature on other immigrant languages in the United States, it was chiefly concerned with deviations from standard German and became little more than a collection of anglicisms and archaisms. A Wisconsin newspaper was culled for English influences by Seeger (1970). Swiss dialect islands in Ohio and Indiana were described in an Ohio State dissertation by Marion R. Wenger (1965). English loanwords were garnered from Missouri Low German by Willibrand (1957b).

Greek: Macris (1957) extended his work on a 1955 dissertation dealing with New York Greek by comparing the loanwords listed in a 1926 study by Lontos with those he had found himself: there was a common core, but also considerable changes. Diebold (1963) studied the code-switching of Greek-Americans, finding that they often failed to change codes when they interlarded their speech with borrowed phrases. Seaman's (1965) Indiana dissertation was a most detailed and insightful study of Greek-American language contact. He based his work on tape-recorded interviews with forty-one bilingual informants and presented an abundance of material on language maintenance as well as carefully classified examples of phonological and morphological interference.

Hungarian: Short articles by Bako (1961, 1962) outlined a program of research on Hungarian in America. Fishman published a chapter from the mimeographed report on *Language Loyalty in the United States* (1964: chapter 17) as a separate monograph (1966b).

Icelandic: A comprehensive survey (chiefly Canadian) was undertaken by Bessason (1967), the only one since the pioneering work by Vilhjalmur Stefansson in 1903.

Italian: Di Pietro (1960) offered a structural description of a (New York State) Sicilian dialect in America as a Cornell dissertation. In articles he discussed the effects of borrowing as a mechanism of linguistic change (1961) and the learning problem of Italian /s/ and /z/ (1964). Correa-Zoli made a study of American Italian in San Francisco (1970).

Kashubian: In a Harvard dissertation Perkowski (1964) analyzed materials collected from a Kashubian speaker in Minnesota; he found that the amount of interference (English, Polish, German) varied with the speech partner.

Norwegian: Johansen contributed a paper on Texas Norwegian to Gilbert (1970).

Polish: Lyra (1962a) presented (in an Indiana dissertation) the results of a detailed investigation of American Polish speakers in various parts of the country. He demonstrated the effects of the contact situation of the immigrants on their Polish, including not only the bilingual effects, but also intralinguistic levelings and simple forgetting. He published two articles, one describing his research (1962b) and the other the acculturation of Polish surnames (1966). Olesch (1970) and Perkowski (1970) reported on Polish in Texas.

Russian: Benson collected Americanisms in the immigrant Russian press (1957) and in the speech of immigrants (1960) mostly located in New Jersey. He found the amount of English influence to be correlated with various social factors, including that of pride in their language.

Slovak: In a Michigan dissertation Goldie Piroch Meyerstein (1959) analyzed recordings of twenty-two Slovak speakers living in New York and Chicago. The results were compared with those of earlier studies on Czech and Norwegian. She made an interesting comparison of interference in first- and second-generation immigrants; some of this material was published as a long article (1966).

Sorbian: This West Slavic language (known as Wendish among its American speakers) is still spoken by a small number of descendants of Sorbian settlers in Serbin, Texas, whose language has been investigated by Vaněk (1967), Olesch (1970) and Perkowski (1970); see these for additional bibliography.

Spanish: As virtually the only non-English language with a growing number of speakers, Spanish excited a great deal of attention, much of it pedagogical in nature. The literature has become enormous, and the reader is referred to Ornstein's (1970) broad-based survey with its bibliography (section 1.2.). The language of the *Tirilones* in Texas was examined for English influence by Coltharp (1965, 1970). Mexican immigrants and their descendants were studied in San Antonio, Texas, by Lozano (1961), in Fort Worth and Dallas, Texas, by Poulter (1970), in Bryan, Texas, by Lance and co-workers Smith and Ward (1969), in Los Angeles by Phillips for a Wisconsin dissertation (1968), and in Detroit by Tsuzaki for a Michigan dissertation (1970). Each of these provided detailed analyses of English influences in phonology, morphology, and lexicon. Lance described his Mexican speakers as having, contrary to popular opinion, 'a highly versatile linguistic competence encompassing a dialect of English, a dialect of Spanish, and the ability to use a mixture of the two when the social situation is ambiguous as to the choice of language or dialect for etiquette purposes' (12). Puerto Rican Spanish was studied in Cambridge, Massachussetts, by Colette Grinevald-Craig in a Paris-Nanterre thesis (1968–69). Basing herself on half-hour interviews with 223 informants, she presented a sketch of the social background and selected examples of the various types of English interference in their speech. In Fishman's preliminary report (Fishman, Cooper, Ma, *et al.*, 1968) on his study of Puerto Ricans in Jersey City, New Jersey, there was a massive collection of data on the immigrant community, but the linguistic material was limited to sample criteria following the methods developed by Labov (section 4.3.). Hull (1963) analyzed the influence of English on the vocabulary of baseball in Puerto Rican Spanish.

Swedish: In a Harvard dissertation Hasselmo (1961) analyzed materials collected from the speech of elderly Swedish immigrants in Worcester, Massachusetts. He continued working on the problem and published (*inter alia*) a survey article (1963b), a paper on American-Swedish 'language poetry' (1963a), a paper (at the Moncton Seminar: Kelly, ed. 1969:122–41) on problems of measuring interference, and two on community norms in a Swedish settlement in Minnesota (1969c; 1970). His particular interest was in trying to establish principles for the often apparently irregular switching of bilinguals. He also worked with the tapes recorded by the three successive expeditions for the collection of Swedish dialect materials in America under the auspices of the Swedish Dialect Archives in

Uppsala, Sweden. These expeditions were conducted by Folke Hedblom in 1962, 1964, and 1966 (see reports in bibliography), who collected extensive samples from virtually every part of the United States where Swedes had settled. Beside his travel reports, Hedblom published articles on American-Swedish place names (1966), on early immigrants (1968), on dialects (1969a), plus texts (1969b). Most recently a report appeared of work being done on Swedish in Texas by Ureland (1970), who classified the interferences according to the principles of generative grammar.

Ukrainian: Zhluktenko (1964) published a study of Ukrainian speakers in Canada and the United States (review by Rudnyćkyj (1972).

Welsh: E. Jones (1958) studied language maintenance among Welsh speakers in Utica, New York, comparing them with corresponding settlements in Patagonia, South America.

Yiddish: Two dissertations provided extensive materials and analyses of the form of American Yiddish: Rayfield (1970), who studied East European immigrants in Santa Monica and Los Angeles, and Green (1962), who did his research for a Michigan dissertation among immigrant and native-born speakers in Detroit. Fishman surveyed the backgrounds and prospects of language maintenance (1965a) in relation to the 'attitudes, values, and aspirations' of Yiddish speakers.

3. LANGUAGE CONTACT

3.0. *Linguistics and Bilingualism*

Languages are *in contact* 'if they are used alternately by the same persons' (Weinreich 1953:1; the term, which I (in 1958:777) attributed to Martinet on information from Weinreich, was actually used even earlier, e.g., by W. von Humboldt in 1836 and Edgar Sturtevant in 1917, as pointed out by Lyra 1962a, 1962b). The definition was inadequate, since the languages need not be actually used: it is sufficient that they be known. By definition the 'ideal' bilingual is one who knows more than one language, i.e., who has internalized (made habitual) the productive patterns (rules of grammar) and the lexica of two distinct speech communities. In terms of ideal competence, he could be said to have a *dual competence*, i.e., that he has coded (tagged) every rule and every item in the lexicon for the proper language and kept their semantic values entirely apart. Since all languages possess some overlapping features, the ones that were so identified by the speakers tended to form a *confusion matrix* leading to innovative extension of identification and consequent breakdown of the distinction between codes. The key to bilingual performance is *code convergence:* under conditions of language contact the experiences of bilinguals are rarely so distinct that it is possible for them to keep the codes wholly apart. To save themselves effort, bilinguals in speaking to each other take shortcuts that collapse distinctions which have no communicatory value. The result is a more or less gradual shift from two codes towards one, with various intermediate codes in which elements from both of the other two are involved. An interpretation of certain bilinguals as having a single *langue,* with two *paroles,* was advanced by Ščerba as far back as 1926 for Sorbian-German bilinguals (Weinreich 1953:10); although rejected by Weinreich, it has been revived recently for the American Sorbians of Texas by Olesch (1970:162).

The traditional term for such interlingual influence has been *borrowing* (hence the many terms involving 'loan', German *Lehn*); specialists have elaborated the terminology at need (see discussions in *BIA* 39 ff.) The term *interference* was introduced by Weinreich and defined as 'a deviation from the norms of one language under influence from those of another' (actually the term had already been used in Europe, e.g., by K. Sandfeld at the Fourth Congress of Linguists in Copenhagen in 1938). This definition is elastic since any such deviation will, if repeated and accepted by the community, become part of the norm, whereupon it ceases to be a case of interference.

I insisted on a distinction between *borrowing* as a process of *code alternation* and *switching* as a process of *code preservation,* in which 'the two languages are not superimposed, but follow one another' (Haugen 1953:65). In 1956 I accepted from Weinreich the term *interference* for the simultaneous overlapping of two norms, as it occurs when bilinguals are unable or unwilling to keep the codes entirely separate. I therefore proposed that *code switching* be used to refer to the alternate use of two languages, including everything from the introduction of a single, unassimilated word up to a complete sentence or more into the context of another language. (This point appears to have been misunderstood by Birgit Stolt (1964, 294, footnote 1); in principle there is no difference between what she calls a 'Zitatwort' and a switch at the end of a sentence). A case of interference which has been accepted and shows by its form that the speaker has made it part of his language can then be said to have been *integrated*, which most nearly corresponds to the traditional concept of borrowing.

The whole topic of language contact from the linguistic point of view was given an integrative review by Hasselmo in his paper for the Moncton seminar (Kelly, ed. 1969: 122—41). Although devoted primarily to the problem of measurement, the paper reviewed the terminology of the field and proposed certain improvements. Together with the comments of the participants in the seminar, this paper now forms a useful starting point for the student of the subject: the author concluded with a set of research proposals which it was to be hoped might be implemented.

3.1. Contrastive Analysis

I originally proposed the term *bilingual description*, which was meant to designate a point-by-point comparison of two (or more) languages, in the same sense that a bilingual dictionary compares the lexicon of two languages. Weinreich's *differential analysis* suggested that the description be limited to the differences between languages, while the most widely used term, *contrastive analysis*, seemed even more confining. Perhaps the best term would have been Harris's *transfer grammar*, which was revived by Selinker (1966). I also put forth (very tentatively) the term *dialinguistics* (*BIA* 41); a similarly formed term was *diaglossic grammar* used by Dingwall (1964a), from which one would presumably derive *diaglossics*.

The popularity of the term *contrastive* was primarily due to its acceptance in the field of applied linguistics, where it was promoted by the Center for Applied Linguistics as a scientific technique to improve the quality of foreign language teaching. In 1959 a *Contrastive Structure Series* was launched under the editorship of Charles A. Ferguson, supported by a contract with the U.S. Office of Education. Volumes were projected on the phonology and grammar of each of the five foreign languages most commonly taught in the United States: French, German, Italian, Russian, and Spanish. Of these the following had appeared: Moulton's *The Sounds of English and German* (1962a), Kufner's *The Grammatical Structures of English and German* (1962), Stockwell and Bowen's *The Sounds of English and Spanish* (1965), Stockwell, Bowen and Martin's *The Grammatical Structures of English and Spanish* (1965), Agard and Di

Pietro's corresponding volumes on Italian (1965a,b). According to the general editor, these books were based 'on the conviction held by many linguists and specialists in language teaching that one of the major problems in the learning of a second language is the interference caused by the structural differences between the native language of the learner and the second language' (Ferguson in Moulton 1962a:v). They were designed for language teachers and textbook writers.

Similar studies were made for other languages, e.g., Alatis' dissertation (1966) on the English pronunciation of Greek immigrants, which bore the subtitle 'A Study in Language Contact with Pedagogical Implications'. Others were made on a less ambitious scale for a number of languages in the pages of the periodicals *Language Learning* and *International Review of Applied Linguistics.* Two collections of relevant articles from the former appeared: *English as a Foreign Language* (1953); *Theory and Practice in English as a Foreign Language* (1963). A good example is T. R. Anderson (1964), who spelled out a technique for helping teachers to make their own contrastive analyses, using English and Cebuano as an example. Since these have only a peripheral interest to our topic of bilingualism, we shall not attempt to list them, but refer the reader to the bibliographical checklist by Gage (1961) and the bibliography of Hammer and Rice (1965), which it was planned to update in 1969 (Lotz, *Linguistic Reporter,* February 1969, p. 7). Most recently this approach was projected into an international program of cooperation between the United States and Yugoslavia, in which Yugoslav and American scholars were jointly engaged in making contrastive studies of English and Serbo-Croatian, with the support of the respective governments and the Ford Foundation. According to the first Report (*Yugoslav . . .* 1969) of the project 'its primary aim is to facilitate the teaching of English as the second language to speakers of Serbo-Croatian'. The project was directed by Rudolf Filipović at Zagreb and coordinated by William Nemser representing the Center for Applied Linguistics. The results were to be presented in three series: *A. Reports, B. Studies; C. Pedagogical Materials;* of these *A1–6, B1–5,* and *C1* had appeared (1972). Similar projects were negotiated by the Center for Applied Linguistics with Romania and Hungary (Nemser 1970); see Nemser and Slama-Cazacu (1970) on the principles of contrastive linguistics.

A paper by Nemser (1969) in the first volume of the Yugoslav Serbo-Croatian-English Contrastive Project reflected ideas which were not only of interest to the academic teaching of language but also to the study of the behavior of bilinguals. They appeared to be based in part on work done by Nemser for his Columbia dissertation on the English pronunciation of Hungarian bilinguals (1961; Nemser and Juhasz 1964). He suggested that the learner who is faced with the task of acquiring a second language does not remain bound to the structures of his native language, so that one cannot at every point account for or predict his performance merely by a contrastive study of the two languages. Between L_T (the target language, i.e., the model, 'foreign' language) and L_S (the source language, i.e., the replica, 'native' language) there is a whole series of L_a (approximative systems), which reflect the learning experience step by step, but which are themselves systems, however transient they may prove to be. He called these *learner systems* and pointed out that when the learner reaches a plateau of learning, as is often the case with immigrants when they have reached a level adequate for communication, they are stabilized. Languages of limited communication, which he called *utility systems*, often characteristic of taxi drivers and bartenders, represent another type of stable learner systems. The ultimate in this type is of course pidgin and creole speech, which has elements in common with what he called *learner pidgin*, often a combination of L_S grammatical elements and L_T lexical elements. He advocated the study of L_a, not only for their pedagogical value but also for general linguistic theory. It was obviously relevant to the problems of language acquisition of children, since like theirs it could (in a generative approach) be interpreted as the addition of rules, some from the L_T and some from the L_S. Another critic of contrastive analysis was Upshur (1962) who found it in some respects 'impractical' and 'theoretically invalid', though his argument was only sketchily supported.

Nemser's discussion could be regarded as a valuable supplement to and extension of this writer's in *BIA* 43—50, where 'interlingual identification' was discussed. It was there suggested that tests be made by 'playing recordings of speech in one language to monolingual speakers of another and asking them to identify the sounds' (49). Such identification was the 'necessary condition for interference', but not 'the sufficient condition' (50). Weinreich wrote similarly that 'the forms and, particularly, the direction and extent of interference are determined in considerable measure by extralinguistic elements in the psychological and sociocultural situation in which the contact of languages takes place' (1957a:1). Nemser found that the makers of contrastive analyses had limited themselves too exclusively to the strictly linguistic comparison, assuming that this was sufficient for a prediction or explanation of the behavior of learners (the same point was made by Alatis 1966). Nemser called for study of *learner systems,* which would reflect the actual progress of students from ignorance to competence; he proposed a more detailed program in Nemser and Slama-Cazacu (1970). This had been the position of bilingual description all along, whose central concern it was to study the stabilized community languages resulting from incomplete learning of a second language. Here the various types of interference had been 'frozen' into a new system, and many individual variations had been leveled out. A useful study of such a system was Kelkar's analysis of 'Marathi English' (1957), which treated it as 'a language in its own right' and noted that any attempt by a Marathi to use Standard English consonants would be considered 'affected, if not incorrect'! Another important programmatic article was Diebold (1962), outlining the requirements that differential descriptions must meet if they were to have a value for linguistic theory and prediction: that it be possible to distinguish cognacy from interference, that a descriptive theory be evolved which would account for marginal utterances, and that a theory of assimilative linguistic change be found for the prediction of the form of linguistic interference. Such hypotheses could best be tested, he suggested, in an area like Mexico, where one intrusive language had influenced a multitude of different and unrelated native languages.

The theory of contrastive analysis was presented in a paper by Moulton (1962b), which summed up his experience with the first volume of the *Contrastive Analysis Series.* A similar classification was made by Stockwell and Bowen (1965). Moulton classified the interlingual contrasts into ten classes of four types: phonetic (1), phonemic (2–5), allophonic (6–7), and distributional (8–10). He distinguished each of these by formulas of the order O : A, meaning that a phoneme /A/ in the target language does not occur in the source language, e.g., German /x/ in *Nacht* does not occur in English. He suggested different types of drills according to whether the problem was one of distinguishing source from target L ('S/T drills') or two target phonemes ('T/T drills'). This discussion brought out very clearly the complication which was introduced into the problem by structural phonemic theory, which in my opinion did more to obscure than to clarify the situation. The resulting formulas were virtually identical with those suggested by me (1954a, cf. 1956:45)

and are called *diaphones,* except that the latter were given direction
by the use of an arrow (section 1.1.). There was reason to question
whether a phonemic transcription was likely to be the most useful in
a foreign language text; the primary data consist of the phones (=
Moulton's allophones) and the sequences in which they occur. Raun
(1968) even suggested that speakers reflected distinctive feature
analysis by replacing foreign phonemes (e.g., [y]) with sequences
(e.g., [iu]).

Now that the development of generative phonology freed linguists
from the necessity of pressing all the allophones into one or another
phoneme, perhaps it was time to take a new look at the problem. In
this case it seemed clear (at least to me) that the German examples
cited by Moulton were best classified as either (1) graphemic or (2)
phonemic, while the latter were either (a) paradigmatic or (b) syntagmatic (to use Hjelmslevian terms following Weinreich 1957a and
Green 1963: in more familiar terminology, phonetic or distributional). Some of Moulton's classifications produced pseudo-
problems, e.g., the analysis of English *ch* as a single phoneme /č/ vs.
German *tsch* as two /tš/, or of German *z* as a single phoneme /c/ vs.
English *ts* as two /ts/. The tendency of English learners to pronounce
German *z* as /z/ or *qu* as /kw/ or *r* as /r/ was surely due to the
spelling, to which they were trained to respond automatically. The
auditory replica of German *z* in English would be either /t-/ or /s-/,
not /z/; as for /kv-/ there are occasional loanwords in English like
kvas and *kvetch,* which have not as far as I know offered any
difficulties, so long as they are spelled *kv.* Learning German /ʀ/ was
a different matter, since it involved not only (as Moulton rightly
observed) suppressing the grapheme-to-phone response, but of replacing it with a new phone (which is different initially and medially
from finally, thereby making it a dual problem), and of teaching the
sequences in which it occurred. In teaching the paradigmatic possibilities in each position, there was of course a difference between the
simple (one-to-one) diaphone and the *divergent* (one-to-two) diaphone, with the former requiring s/ᴛ drills, the latter much more
difficult and probably requiring not only ᴛ/ᴛ, but also s/ᴛ drills. It
could be convenient to sum up the phones in phonemes, but this
could adequately be done in terms of the letters of the alphabet,
which would relieve us from the need of deciding, e.g., whether
German *z* is one or two phonemes.

This was also the conclusion of Brière (1966; 1968), who made an
experimental investigation of phonological interference in which

unfamiliar sounds were identified by American subjects. While the experiment was not sufficiently extensive to permit of absolute proof, the results were in full agreement with the informal observations on which my conclusions were based. Brière found that 'any prediction of a hierarchy of difficulty of learning phonological categories must be based on descriptions of these categories in terms of exhaustive information at the phonetic level rather than on description solely in terms of distinctive features or allophonic membership of phoneme classes' (1968:74). He found that 'T (target) sounds which are close equivalents of N (native) system sounds, whether phonemic or allophonic, are easier to learn than T sounds without such equivalents' (1968:73). Green (1963) suggested a scale for grading interference by difficulty, distinguishing exact (native) and approximate (non-native) reproduction of unfamiliar sounds (with the implication that the latter would be sufficient for most language learners).

We are reminded of Yao Shen's demonstration (1955, *cf. BIA*) that 'phonemic charts are not enough'. Di Pietro (1964) also emphasized the importance of distributional statements. In a full-length book (Di Pietro 1971) he gave the field its first generative textbook. Nemser's detailed studies of the interpretation of English stops and interdental fricatives by native speakers of Hungarian (1961) uncovered radical discrepancies between the perceptive and productive responses to the stimuli, which could not be accommodated by present contact theory. In my fieldwork with American-Norwegian speakers I identified what I called *erratic substitution* (Haugen 1953: 394), which Davis (1967) also found in his analysis of Yiddish-American English. *Reborrowing* (after a period of learning) could also account for some of the deviations from expected substitutions. In my review of Weinreich's book (1954:381—4) I offered a critique of the thoroughgoing structuralism of that period, questioning explanatory hypotheses that assumed the reality of the abstract phonemic pattern or the importance of phonemic burdening.

Much less was done in the way of bilingual analysis on the grammatical/syntactic level. To an even higher degree than in phonology this involved problems of typology and linguistic universals, which lie beyond the purview of this survey. Basing myself on the common uses of *morphemes* as a technical term, I suggested the use of *diamorphs* as a parallel to *diaphones* (1956:46). Again it was a question not of structural equivalence as identified by linguists, but of bilingual behavior as observed among actual users of the language.

As with the phones, the linguist had at his command two types of
information: (1) physical form (paradigmatic distinction) and (2) distribution (syntagmatic ordering). The second criterion was roughly
equivalent to 'meaning' but included also syntactic meaning, i.e., the
function of the morpheme within the grammatical/syntactic structure. Diamorphs could therefore be either *homophonous* (if they
were identified on the basis of form) or *synonymous* (if they were
identified on the basis of meaning); if both, they could be called
homologous. The bilingual, in switching from one language to the
other, should ideally match morphemes only if they were synonymous (e.g., plural suffix should match plural suffix regardless of the
phonological structure). Interference occurs when homophony in-
trudes, so that, e.g., a plural suffix in one language is interpreted as a
corresponding singular in another (e.g., *data* used as a singular by
many English speakers; *koks* 'coke' singular in Norwegian, from
English *cokes*).

Kufner's (1962) contrastive sketch of English and German structures was avowedly less complete than Moulton's corresponding
phonology. It could be described as a truncated German grammar
whose purpose it was to highlight those aspects of the structure of
German which had caused particular difficulty in teaching native
speakers of English. The ordering was from larger to smaller units of
syntax and grammar, with two final chapters on obligatory categories, grammatical and semantic. Since the learner/bilingual's main
problem was that of knowing how far he could (semantically) identify (formally) similar structures, such a sketch offered little for the
student of bilingualism. There were many informal remarks on German structures that offered problems for the English-speaking
learner, e.g., the case system, where the source language had at most
two case endings, the target language four (each with several allo-
morphs). This was a clear case of divergent structures, which regularly offer the greatest problem for a learner. The less-than-perfect
bilingual simplifies things for himself by mapping elements from the
target language on to rules of his source language.

As pointed out by this writer (*BIA* 48–9), the interlingual identification of whole utterances was identical with the process of translation. The learner had not acquired the language as long as he was still
only replacing one formally characterized structure with another that
was similarly characterized. 'The bilingual . . . is constantly compelled to identify items of extremely different structure' (Haugen
1956:48). This point was echoed in two papers published

(*Yugoslav . . .* 1969) for the Yugoslav Serbo-Croatian-English Project (*B. Studies* 1, 13—25, 26—35), where Ivic and Spalatin discussed two approaches to contrastive analysis, formal correspondence vs. translation equivalence, and unequivocally concluded that the latter was superior: 'In some cases, correspondences are impossible or unlikely, in others they are spurious' (Ivic, p. 24); 'our experience is that languages can be effectively contrasted only on a semantic basis, specifically, on the basis of translation equivalence' (Spalatin, p. 34). Levenston (1965) proposed just such a technique for making contrastive syntactic statements.

It was tempting to draw a parallel between the phonological and the semantic level of contrastive analysis: in each case the ultimately relevant units for interlinguistic comparison were found in the so-called 'extralinguistic' *substance*. Just as phonologies must be compared in terms of articulatory phones, so grammars must be compared in terms of semantic units, i.e., what some now were calling the underlying or 'deep structure' level. Similarities in the grammatical-phonological structure (whether of the base or the transformations) could be helpful as crutches in the process of learning, but like all crutches they could also lead to permanent disability. For example, the inevitable identification by a learner of German of the present participial -*end* (or French -*ant*) with English -*ing* would virtually compel the appearance of forms like 'ich bin singend', or 'Singend ist Spass', while the learning of the English 'progressive' as a form of continuous present on the part of a German could lead to his using it *ad nauseam*, as in 'the stairway is having six steps'. The chief problem was not to learn a rule, but to know when to stop using it.

Some attempts were made to formalize an approach to syntactic analysis on this level, e.g., by Dingwall (1964a; 1964b; 1966), but as the author admitted, one disadvantage of his logical model was 'the general complexity of the approach as a whole' (1966:60). An experiment by Selinker (1966; 1969) was more limited in its aims, having set out to test the principles of 'transfer' by experimental controls of a 'psycholinguistic' nature. After a critical and sophisticated introduction evaluating the contributions of linguists and psychologists to the field of psycholinguistics, Selinker described the procedure whereby he elicited English sentences from 132 native Hebrew speakers in Israel who had studied English for two years. All the 1,640 sentences counted consisted of a verb string followed by any one of the four combinations: Object — Time Adverb, Object — Place Adverb, Object — Adverb (degree), Place Adverb — Time

Adverb. Some of these are differently ordered in Hebrew and English, and the experiment was designed to test the extent to which these learners of English imported the Hebrew order into their learners' English. A control group of thirty American children reassured the experimenter that the English order was what he believed it to be, while the Israeli children also produced corresponding Hebrew sentences to establish the Hebrew order. The result showed a statistically valid replication of the Hebrew orders in the English sentences for all eight possible combinations, of which four were 'positive transfers' (correct), three were 'negative transfers' (errors), and one was a 'neutral transfer' (free variation). An example of negative transfer was 'I like very much movies'. This elaborate and time-consuming procedure would appall the average linguist, who would have 'predicted' the result on the basis of his differential analysis. It was still good to have this study as a reminder that no analysis is really validated unless it is confirmed in the behavior of actual speakers.

3.2. Switching

Having now considered the problems involved in predicting potential interference between languages in contact, we shall look at some studies that tried to catch interference on the wing. As proposed in section 3.0., we shall consider that interference occurs primarily in a matrix of switching, i.e., the interspersal into a speaker's utterance of one or more unadapted items from another language than the one which primarily characterizes it.

Following a tradition that is more honored in social sciences than in humanistic linguistics, Kolers manipulated bilingual speakers into switching and studied some of the results. In one of these studies (1966b) he asked subjects to read alternate versions of the same text, some of which were monolingual, others mixed. He found that they took no extra time in *decoding* the mixed texts, but if they were asked to read them aloud, the extra *encoding* required an average of 0.3–0.5 seconds for each switch, although many switches showed no actual pauses. In free speech the switching required three to five times more time, about 1.3 seconds. This marked increase of time, reflecting the 'plugging in' of a different set of rules, suggested that the *encoder* had to put extra effort into his production, which he would hardly do unless the effort brought a reward in the form of increased success in communication. For the *decoder* switching clearly brought no extra embarrassment and hence encountered little resistance (i.e., when the listener was not concerned with the form of language but with its content). It could also be that the extra time actually reflected the encoder's hesitation over what to say next, i.e., his momentary embarrassment at not recalling the word in the language he was currently using. This might not apply to reading aloud a prepared text, but even in this case the reader, when he had perceived the switch, had to go back and refocus the word where the switch began, which many of the subjects actually failed to do, with consequent overlapping (interference).

Another psychologist who stimulated switching in experimental subjects was MacNamara (1967c), in a test of the linguistic independence of bilinguals. Subjects who were asked to name as many words as possible in a given time fell to one-third of the number when they were asked to switch languages between each word, likewise when asked to translate each word. MacNamara concluded, not surprisingly, that 'to the extent to which linguistic independence is maintained, rapid changing of language appears to involve an upset to central thought processes' (p. 736). As the author granted, however, this would not be true of those bilinguals who made a habit of switching.

Most linguists preferred to study switching in natural rather than manipulated context, which was now made easier than before thanks to the growing refinement and availability of recording equipment. Among those who turned their attention to this particular phase of bilingual study were Rayfield (1970), Hasselmo (1961, 1966, 1970), and Clyne (1967). A fourth, who based herself on a remarkable collection of bilingual texts from the early sixteenth century, Luther's 'Table Talk' (*Tischreden*), was Birgit Stolt (1964). The two last-named strictly speaking fall outside the geographical limitations of this essay, but it is useless to speak of a theoretical advance as if it were limited to the United States, when both of the latter scholars had drawn freely from earlier American writings (especially Haugen and Weinreich).

Rayfield's study of Yiddish speakers in California (1970) offered a dual set of explanations for switching, (a) as a *response to the speech situation*, e.g., the entry of an outsider, the use of fixed phrases of greeting and parting, the quotation of utterances known only in one language (including proverbs), the carry-over effect of a single loan-word, change of topic, etc.; (b) as a *rhetorical device*, e.g., emphasis by repetition in another language, bringing out a contrast, pointing up an unexpected aspect, making a parenthetical remark, bringing in taboo words or topics, etc. She regarded the second explanation as the more important and found that the bilingual had a 'double stock of rhetorical devices' (119).

Hasselmo (1961:61) devoted himself to a study of the linguistic circumstances of switching, as recorded from speakers who had difficulty in maintaining a consistent discourse in their native Swedish, due in part to lack of practice. He found their conversation rich in examples of switching, and often lacking the 'phonological borders' which childhood bilinguals were more likely to master. Having virtually only a single (Swedish) sound system, they were prone to create replicas of English function words that were indistinguishable from corresponding colloquial Swedish ones (*an* > *en*; *that, it* > (*d*)*et; them* > *dem; we* > *vi,* etc.). To account for these and other observed phenomena he distinguished between such *ragged* switching and the more 'ideal' *clean* switching, with little or no interference. He also studied the units of discourse that were especially liable to be switched and the point of switching in relation to the sentence structure. Later he (Hasselmo 1966, 1970) distinguished between *limited* and *unlimited* switching, the latter being that which spilled over from one unit to the next. Within entire discourses he analyzed switching in terms of *content units* and *discourse markers.* By recording stories at intervals of some months he uncovered a tendency towards constancy of switching within such linguistic routines.

Stolt (1964:57–8, 292–8; 1969) similarly identified stretches of discourse which were 'linguistically neutral' and caused the speaker to lose his 'linguistic orientation' so that he continued in a different language from the one he started in. Clyne (1967:17; also 1969) introduced the term *triggering* for the effect such inserted items had on the formulation of a sentence and distinguished various kinds of triggering, among which one could mention his *anticipational* and *consequential* types. All of these discussions contributed to a refinement of the problem of sentence formation, suggesting that a sentence might be abstractly formed even before the speaker was sure which language it was going to come out in. The well-known phenomenon of 'macaronic' writing (or speech) was usually avoided in serious or formal discourse, but for bilingual communicators it could (as we shall see later) have an effect similar to that of slang or vulgar speech for monolinguals.

Diebold (1963) found that his (small) sample of Greek-Americans were unable to switch within a Greek context without carrying over

Greek phonology into their English loans. This finding was only tentative, but it raised questions about the validity of the distinction between clean and ragged switching. Finally, Lance (1969) reported his observations of switching (which he unfortunately called 'mixing') in a Spanish and English-speaking family in Bryan, Texas. The American-born generation did not hesitate to intercalate unassimilated items from English into their Spanish, ranging from single words to one or more sentences. Among the items selected for this treatment were technical terms, proper names, tag questions, interjections, parenthetical remarks, and direct quotations; but also grammatically interwoven parts of sentences (*'Te digo que este dedo* has been bothering me so much'). The investigator attributed the unabashed switching to the relaxed atmosphere of the conversations; but 'neither informant displayed the least awareness of when she was switching from. one language to the other' (p. 82). He rejected the idea that switching was due to inadequacy of linguistic competence, rather that the speakers simply used whichever expression 'was closer to the tip of the tongue'. The study was suggestive of further possibilities of research; as in the case of Stolt's study of Luther, there was a large area of inexplicable switching. Gumperz and Hernandez (1969) suggested that switching conveyed secondary meanings of formality or solidarity. Gumperz (1970) presented examples to show that switching serves definite communicative ends, calling it 'a metaphoric process'.

3.3. *Interference*

Linguists were censured by Fishman (1968) for their concern with 'interference', which he identified with an excessive interest in 'what (phonetic, lexical or grammatical) structures of language X have rubbed off on language Y and vice versa', and he compared their activity amusingly but irrelevantly to that 'of a housewife looking for smears of wet paint' (p. 27). This may indeed have been the position of many traditional grammarians as well as educated speakers of standard languages, who regarded bilingual dialects as 'corrupted' forms of the language. It was certainly not the view of the four scholars listed above (section 1.0.), who established the study of bilingual interference in North America. Weinreich, who introduced the term, made it perfectly clear that an established loan is no longer interference: 'What the historical linguist finds to be an effect of interference from another language may not be one to the user of the

language' (1953:11). In a section on the 'crystallization of new
languages from contact' he discussed the criteria which might permit
a linguist to say that a new norm had come into existence as the
result of interference (1953:69). I specifically rejected the notion
that immigrant speech was 'debased' (Haugen 1953:12), pointing out
that a 'confusion of tongues' did not mean 'confusion of communication' (1953: 72). I adduced evidence to show that an informal norm
existed among immigrant rural Norwegian speakers, a norm that
differed in specific ways from that of corresponding rural Norwegian
dialects. I called such modified norms *bilingual dialects*, of which
American Norwegian would be one (1953:60—63). To describe such
a norm in terms of its deviation from the monolingual norm of the
'same' language was not a denial of its status as an independent
variety; it was merely a descriptive convenience (Haugen 1970b).

The description of *phonic* interference was the subject of an
important article by Weinreich (1957a), written as a reply to my
review (1954) of *Languages in Contact* and amending some of his
own formulations in the book. He here distinguished the causes of
phonic interference as (1) phonic, (2) extraphonic, (3) extralinguistic, and (4) erratic. He made a basic distinction between *syntagmatic* and *paradigmatic* factors, i.e., sequential distribution vs. allophonic inventory, and proposed an analysis by distinctive features.
He extended also his treatment of prosodic features. Since 1956
detailed descriptions were made of the phonologies of speakers of
English whose native language was Japanese (Nagara 1969), Hunga-
rain (Nelson 1956; Nemser 1961), Yiddish (Davis 1967), and Spanish
(M. E. Jones 1962). An experiment to determine the loss of information caused by the beginning learner's 'accent' was made by Lane
(1963); he found that Serbian, Punjabi, and Japanese accents caused
about 36 percent more distortion than native speech.

Phonological adaptation of English materials in immigrant languages was studied for Dutch (Shetter 1958), Finnish (Lehtinen
1966), French (Stella 1959), German (Gilbert 1963, 1965b, etc.),
Greek (Diebold 1963; Seaman 1965), Icelandic (Bessason 1967),
Italian (Di Pietro 1960), Kashubian (Perkowski 1964), Polish (Lyra
1962a, 1962b), Slovak (Meyerstein 1959, 1966), Spanish (Lozano
1961; Tsuzaki 1970; Phillips 1968; Lance 1969); Swedish (Hasselmo
1961); Yiddish (Rayfield 1970; Green 1962). It would be impossible
to discuss in detail the results of these many studies, most of which
were not published except as dissertations. The general impression
was the expected one that immigrant speakers maintained the native

phonology well, even into the second generation, but that they vacillated between complete and partial adaptation of the numerous (and fairly uniform) loans which they made from English. Meyerstein (1966) found a major difference between immigrant and second-generation speakers in the greater incidence of unassimilated loans in the speech of the latter.

Problems of description and quantification were discussed and variously solved by these authors, but the printed studies were not particularly numerous or conclusive. Weinreich's paper (1957a) stimulated Saporta, Brown, and Wolfe (1959) to apply an experimental method developed by psychologists to determine whether foreign accent interfered with the communication of messages. Mackey (1962) offered a schema for the description of bilingualism, in which interference was included as one aspect; he set up rubrics for the cultural, semantic, lexical, grammatical, and phonological levels, the last named being broken down into intonation, rhythm, catenation, and articulation. On each level percentage measurements were envisaged for *importations* and *substitutions* with respect to units and structures analyzed by types and tokens. In a later article (1965) he proposed a somewhat different table, this time with a sample calculation. This technique remained to be validated through use on extensive populations, as did the applicability of the results of availability tests. Some of his results based on Acadian informants are presented in a theoretical article (1970b) which demonstrates the fluidity of the synchronic norm, especially among bilinguals. Meyerstein (1966) offered a suggestive format for counting the number of interferences in a text. The whole problem of measurement and description was surveyed by Hasselmo for the Moncton Seminar (Kelly, ed. 1969), with many useful suggestions for further research.

Lexical interference, which in most cases meant *loanwords* plus *loanshifts,* was the classical playground of dialinguistics. So-called 'necessary' loanwords, which quite simply filled lexical gaps in the borrowing language, were usually easy to identify, at least for the linguist, and mostly also for the bilingual speaker. For the dominated immigrant languages of the United States the studies listed above documented an almost monotonous parade of such words in all those domains which the immigrants shared with the dominant culture, such as government, trade, schools, amusements (*cf.* my word count, 1953:94). Even 'necessary' loanwords did not need to be borrowed outright but could be replaced by loanshifts made up of native material. This was common enough when there were available cognates (e.g., American English *corn* 'maize' being replicated by *korn* in American Norwegian), but apparently required extra effort when new words had to be created and was therefore unusual in the kind of informal speech with which we are here dealing. The so-called 'unnecessary' loanwords, which were more strongly condemned by purists (as when American immigrants adopted English words for 'fence' or 'river', for which native words were available), also reflected the law of least effort: objects that were named in contexts associated with the new culture were given the names used in that culture, without reflection on their greater or lesser likeness to objects already known from the homeland. This was not, as sometimes thought, 'snobbishness', but may be considered a form of cultural 'laziness', often associated with lack of ideological language loyalty.

Grammatical interference, on the other hand, was the classical battleground of dialinguistics. As Weinreich pointed out, 'that entirely contrary views could be held by such responsible scholars is apparently due to the lack of agreement between them on fundamental terms and concepts' (1953:29; see also *BIA* 63 ff.). The doctrine that grammar is the most tenacious and resistant part of a language and the one by which languages are classified, depends on a rather narrow definition of grammar. It is probably true that bound morphemes are less readily borrowed than free ones and that high frequency (form) words are less readily borrowed than low frequency (content) words, but these are more matters of availability than of structure. Words are usually borrowed in just one form, e.g., nouns are borrowed as either singulars or plurals, and are then fitted into the morphological system of the borrowing language. But not always, especially among bilinguals, whose awareness of the form system of both languages keeps them from adapting fully. In such cases, dual forms may result, as in the plural of English *index,* which vacillates between *indices* and *indexes.* If enough such forms enter the language, new morphological rules may be developed, as when *-ette* (from words like *cigar-ette*) developed into a productive suffix (*kitchen-ette, major-ette*). In the American immigrant languages it was common enough for English *-s* to have entered as a plural suffix, but for most part only in loanwords, and not always in these (e.g., *cars, keys, peas* were all singulars in American Norwegian).

In Lehtinen's (1966) analysis of a third-generation American-Finnish speaker's language, rules are set up for introducing English elements into the Finnish stream of speech and for accommodating them to the Finnish system. She found that severe nongrammatical restrictions applied to the switching of entire sentences, while shorter switches were best formulated in terms of 'surface grammar', with single words of pivotal significance. Morphological 'code-accommodation' preceded phonological in ordering the rules; in the latter the 'conversion' (i.e., the substitution) of phonemes was primarily based on phonetic similarity (as noted above) and only secondarily on structural correspondence.

Until such time as agreement would be reached on the best way of describing languages, it was hardly possible to establish overall measures of interference. But it was still possible to demonstrate correlations between interference and different kinds of psychological and social contexts.

As suggested earlier, one of the reasons for studying interference was to identify. potential learning problems. However, it was observed by several students that the learning problems went beyond those arising from interference. G. M. Smith (1969) studied the tape recordings of children in a Spanish-speaking family in Texas and found that most of the errors were 'language development problems' and could not be directly traced to their Spanish. Nemser (1961) also found that the interpretation of English obstruents by Hungarians did not coincide with those predictable from a differential description. Nemser has further developed his insights in relation to 'contrastive linguistics', criticizing the *hubris* prevalent in the field (Nemser and Slama-Cazacu 1970:115). Lehtinen (1966) found that beside the expected English influence in American Finnish there were deviations due to a combination of the informant's relatively low competence in Finnish and non-specific interference from the overall systemic differences of English from Finnish.

The *intermediate* systems that arose through bilingual contacts (this writer's *bilingual dialects*) could clearly be characterized by a combination of additions (innovative interferences) and deletions (amnesic reorderings). It might be worth exploring them as special cases of the learning process in reverse: as the learner builds new systems in the language he acquires, he dismantles and reorders the systems of the language he already knows.

3.4. Borrowing

The results of *integration* by bilingual speakers of loans into one or both of their languages concerned most of the investigators who dealt with bilingualism and its effects. Other terms were advocated, e.g., Harris's *transfer* (Selinker 1966; 1969) or *transference* (Clyne 1967). This had the advantage of being neutral and permitting a distinction between *positive* and *negative* transfer, the former being a reinforcement of the native language, the latter an 'interference' with its norms, a true 'borrowing'. Any kind of transfer assumed the presence of a *model* in the target language for which the speaker wished to find a *replica* in the source language, and this replica could be either an *importation* of the model or a *substitution* drawn from the native stock of items (my terminology, *BIA* 50 ff.). On the word level, importation resulted in a *loanword*, in which the phonemes could be replaced by native phonemes, but in an order imported from the model. Substitution of a native word or compound resulted in a *loanshift*, which could be a native word with shifted meaning or a combination of native words in shifted contexts. A *loanblend* combined the two processes (Haugen 1953). This terminology was adopted by Hockett in his *Introduction to Modern Linguistics* (1958, chapter 48). Weinreich (1953:50—51) made use of a terminology created by Betz, importing the latter's German compounds as calques or loan translations: *loan translation, loan rendition, loan creation*.

Theoretical problems relating to borrowing were discussed by Emeneau (1962), who questioned the possibility of developing a calculus that would explain past situations of bilingualism and predict results of future ones. He felt that each situation was a unique historical event. He pointed out that the general opinion of linguists which rejected the possibility of structural borrowing was falsified by observations he had made in India (see the discussion above, section 3.3.). Hoenigswald (1962), another leading student of historical linguistics, discussed the relation between socially 'downward' and 'upward' borrowings, suggesting that the latter were only 'need-filling', while the former were, in addition, 'prestigious'. In this connection one should remember Weinreich's warning against concluding that 'the direction of interference is exclusively from the dominant language to the non-dominant one' (1953:98). One can easily recall instances of lower-class and vulgar terms that have been diffused upwards through a kind of prestige attached to 'democracy' or 'masculinity' or 'sportsmanship'.

A great many of the theses and articles listed in section 2 brought extensive lists of loanwords and loanshifts noted in the various vernaculars studied. It had become clear to most investigators that such lists were uninteresting unless they were analyzed from either a linguistic or a sociolinguistic point of view (for an example see Willibrand 1957b). Gilbert (1965b) showed how German writings in Texas could be profitably used as a source for English loanwords. He also discussed the mechanisms of borrowing and applied them to categories developed by the investigators discussed above, as did most writers now discussing the problems. Among the most detailed and competent studies made of particular immigrant groups were the analyses of Lyra of Polish (1962a) and Seaman of Greek (1965).

What was sorely needed was some kind of synthesis of the results so far attained, a difficult problem since so many of the most important studies had not been published. Rayfield (1970) compared the amount and nature of interference in the Yiddish she observed in Los Angeles with that in Norwegian as described by me in the Middle West, as well as with earlier contact situations of Yiddish with Slavic and Hebrew in Europe. She found that there were great similarities in the development of American Yiddish and Norwegian, but that Yiddish went farther than Norwegian in the adoption of English function words and loanshifts. This comparison was not based on detailed or statistical comparisons and could only be regarded as an impressionistic hunch. It was vitiated by the fact that my study concentrated on the rather stable rural communities, Rayfield's on an unstable and recent urban community. As Hasselmo's analysis of urban Swedish speakers (1961) showed, Scandinavians in this situation were no different from Yiddish speakers in adopting what Rayfield described as 'unnecessary' loanwords. In an urban situation the constant need for switching would lead inevitably (at least among the less language-militant users) to 'unnecessary' borrowing (Green 1962:168; Benson 1957). Green's study of Yiddish in Detroit (1962) made more careful distinctions between various kinds of informants: recent immigrants (less than seven years), earlier immigrants (more than thirty years), and nonimmigrants (second generation). He found that the immigrants spoke a fairly uniform English, with marked Yiddish interference, the American-born a uniform American English; but there was wide variation in the kind of Yiddish spoken, 'from almost flawless mastery on the part of some speakers to a considerable use of English structures and lexicon on the part of others' (p. 246). However, the group of long-settled immigrants did represent 'a range of Yiddish likely to be heard in the community' (p. 247).

Di Pietro (1961) summarized the results of his studies of American Sicilian in an article on 'the effect of borrowing as a mechanism

of linguistic change'. He found that lexemes (which he called 'con-
tentives', following Hockett) were freely adopted from English,
mostly one-morpheme idioms, but also phrases and whole sentences
('Merry Christmas'; 'what do you want?'), functioning as idioms. No
functors were adopted, but the borrowed lexemes, even when fully
adopted, brought with them certain changes in the distribution of
phonemes and the frequency of certain patterns of word stress and
syntax: all in all, a quantitative rather than a qualitative change.
Interesting were certain 'folk-etymological' adaptations, whereby
breakfast > /béddaféšta/ 'beautiful feast' and *never mind* > /léva-
mánu/ 'remove the hand'. Loanshifts whereby *cornu* 'horn' acquired
the meanings of the homophonous 'corn' and 'corner' could be
interpreted in more than one way.

An observation made by a number of investigators (e.g., Haugen
1953:398) is that verbs were almost invariably given a native grammatical form, while nouns and adjectives could often occur without.
Benson (1960) noted that while English verbs were integrated into
American Russian, adjectives and nouns were not necessarily so.
Topping (1962) found the same for English verbs in Chamorro
(misleadingly called 'loanblends'), which often became quite un-
recognizable (*ha-li-li-yit* 'he leads', where *lead* > *-li . . . yit*). The
apparent universality of the phenomenon was confirmed by Stolt's
analysis of Luther's Table Talk (1964:121—66): 'Im verbalen Bereich
schliessen sich die beiden sprachlichen Systeme gegenseitig aus'
(166). The centrality of the verb in the sentence supplements the
fact that tense is an obligatory category in (at least) the Indo-
European languages.

Among the many valuable observations made in these studies was
one by Lance (1969:17) that violations of the usual norms by
bilinguals were not all due to interference. He called some of the
errors a result of 'arrested language development', which could of
course affect both languages in the case of childhood bilinguals (as
well as monolinguals). Seaman pointed out for American Greeks that
their Greek could lose some of its distinctions simply because of
their weakening knowledge of it through lack of practice
(1965:184). Bilinguals were as liable as other speakers to make false
analogies and ungrammatical sentences, but the evidence did not
point to the bilingual situation as such as having anything to do
with it. Problems arose when one was forced to account for certain
mergers of grammatical forms, e.g., the coalescence of oblique cases
of the German nouns in Texas (*mit den Mann* instead of *mit dem*

Mann). Eikel (1949, cf. *BIA* 2.5.3.) argued for English influence, while Gilbert (1965a) convincingly rejected this theory in favor of one that assumed it as a German dialect feature which was only reinforced by English influence. Seaman (1965:190) argued for influence from English in the tendency of Greeks to lose the aspect forms of Greek; but this, too, could be due to lack of practice of forms that were rather specialized in the original language. Final decisions on this problem would have to await a careful synthesis and review of the findings of these and future investigators.

Seen in a purely semantic light, the loanwords reflected the cultural differences between the borrowing and lending languages. This was amply brought out by a number of studies, in which full information was given on the historical and social circumstances of language contact: e.g., Nagara (1969), whose thesis included a 203-page appendix outlining the history of language contacts in Hawaii; M. E. Jones (1962), who told the story of the introduction of English into Puerto Rico. Borrowing in the dominant languages was used as an index of acculturation to the dominant culture: *cf.* Diament's collection of anglicisms in American French (1962). Tsuzaki (1970) showed how the acculturation of Mexicans in Detroit was correlated (a) to the incidence of borrowing, up to the time when the shift to English occurred and (b) after that time, to the use of English. Macris (1957) compared his own collection of loanwords among New York Greeks with those of Lontos (1926, see *BIA*) and found a considerable change over time. The adaptation of names was another clue to acculturation (Bodine 1968 on Taos names). Kennard (1963) showed Hopi acculturation in terms of adopted English loanwords; more of this in the section on the bilingual community (section 5.3.). Benson (1960) spelled out the various factors that entered into the concept of 'acculturation' and were reflected indirectly in borrowing (among Russian Americans): length of residence, knowledge of English, contact with English speakers, level of education in Russian, pride in the language, intensity of *Sprachgefühl*. Brief loanword studies for particular groups were Oswalt (1958) on Russian words in Pomo, Reinecke and Tsuzaki (1967) and Tsuzaki and Elbert (1969) on Hawaiian words in English, Wick Miller (1959—60) on Spanish in Acoma, and Feinsilver (1958, 1962) on Yiddish idioms in English. More elaborate, typically German studies, not based on fieldwork but on written texts, were Schönfelder's (1957) on German in English, and Wacker's (1964) on English in German; for comments see above (section 2.2.).

3.5. *Methods of Research*

While long-established dialects and standard languages allowed the
investigator a wealth of informants whose linguistic competence was
unquestioned, the student of bilingualism was dealing with a zone of
research that by definition lay between that of the established
norms. He was therefore faced with the problem of locating informants who exhibited the kind of phenomena in their performance
that made him suspect the presence of interference between norms.
At the same time he had to reassure these informants that interference was not (as often assumed) a mark of inferiority or incom-
petence. He had to gain their confidence so that they would not
consciously or unconsciously 'clean up' their language, but relax and
talk in their normal way. This situation was similar to that of the
student of social dialect, and similar methods were used to gain
access to informants.

The traditional dialectologist's way of structuring his interviews
with informants was to use a questionnaire: for an example see
Haugen 1953:645—53 (contrary to Clyne 1967:22 it was not administered in writing but orally, and it did permit comparability by
asking all informants the same questions). When arranged topically,
this made it possible to inverview the informant serially on the topics
involved, so that he could express himself on the subject while still
being controlled to the extent of providing the minimally necessary
forms. (Informants' names were suppressed in Haugen 1953 but were
added for the record in the reprinted edition, 1969). A combination
of comparability and flexibility therefore characterized the use of a
questionnaire (which of course also included data on the sociolinguistic background of the informant). Such questionnaires were
constructed by Seifert for German in Pennsylvania and Wisconsin
(Seifert 1946), by M. E. Jones for English in Puerto Rico (1962), by
Lyra for Polish (1962a), by Seaman for Greeks in Chicago (1965), by
Lozano for Spanish in San Antonio, Texas (1961), and by Green for
Yiddish in Detroit (1962). Green noted, however, that after starting
with a 250-item questionnaire, he gradually cut it down after experience with informants and stopped transcribing by hand. He went
over more and more to free conversations, which he tape-recorded
and later transcribed. He then listed the various kinds of interference
on punch cards, and in this way was able to work out his generalizations. A further step in this direction is announced by Perkowski
(1970:169), whose data on Sorbian are going to be coded in such a

way that a computer 'will produce all of the desired charts automatically', a procedure now being developed also at the University of
Wisconsin in Professor F. Cassidy's work on the *Dictionary of American Regional English.*

The trend among a number of investigators was certainly away
from the formal questionnaire in the direction of unstructured conversations. Attention was focused on small communities, e.g., Di
Pietro on Sicilians of a small area in upstate New York (1960, 1961),
Hasselmo on Swedes of Worcester, Massachussetts (1961), Rayfield
on the Jews of Venice and Santa Monica, California (1970). A
characteristic and interesting departure on the part of Rayfield was
her use of tests, e.g., a recollection test of forty-three common
loanwords in Yiddish, asking the informants to give the Yiddish
equivalent and timing their responses. Hasselmo developed the
methods used by Labov in New York for application to Swedes in
the Chicago Lake settlement, in an effort to establish the norms of
the community (1969c; 1970). Some even concentrated on a single
family, using the primary group as a cross-section of the community
by taking one with three generations living, e.g., Lance and his
co-workers in Bryan, Texas (1969). Their technique was the 'almost
totally unstructured conversation', to avoid the suggestion that the
informants were being tested; the small number of informants made
it possible to elicit a great deal of information from each.

Personal interviewing by the investigator himself allowed for many
informal observations and a kind of observer participation. It also
permitted the elicitation of alternate responses and could no doubt
be expanded (in the direction initiated by Hasselmo) towards a more
explicitly generative approach. At the opposite end of the scale stood
the use of written texts, as Benson's (1957) study of the American
Russian press, Schönfelder's of German loans in English (1957), and
Wacker's of English loans in German (1964). The tape-recorder even
permitted spoken language to be subjected to textual analysis, as
practiced, e.g., by Nagara (1969) in his study of Japanese English in
Hawaii, where recordings made by others formed the basis of his
dissertation. My recorded interviews (1953:479) were later transferred to tape and one copy was deposited with the Archives of the
Languages of the World at Indiana University in Bloomington.

No matter what the method, the important point was that the
investigator be clearly aware of the purpose for which he was
collecting his data. It was of little interest to collect facts if they did
not in some way throw light on the essential problems of the field.

4. THE BILINGUAL INDIVIDUAL

4.0. *Psycholinguistics and Bilingualism*

The *sine qua non* of bilingualism is individuals who are bilingual, i.e., who know more than one language (in whatever degree) and are therefore potential users of that language (in whatever mode). It is of course impossible to isolate the individual bilingual from his society, since without it he would neither have learned nor had any use for a second language, or even a first. Nevertheless it is practical to isolate in this section studies made by researchers who thought of themselves as primarily psychologists and therefore concentrated on the performance of the individual.

Fortunately it was no longer true that the interests of psychologists 'have touched bilingualism primarily at one point: the effects of bilingualism on the individual IQ' (*BIA* 69). The approach referred to in *BIA* under the name of *psycholinguistics* was followed up by several researchers, who made of it a lively field with a great deal of exciting work. The names we will meet most often in the following pages (which represent an attempt by a linguist to assimilate and understand the work of technical psychologists) are those of Lambert and his associates at McGill University, Susan Ervin-Tripp at Berkeley, Paul Kolers at M.I.T., and John MacNamara at Dublin, now McGill. This mixed bag of North American and European work cannot be reported piecemeal, since the work of each depended closely on that of the others. At a number of points they interacted also with sociologically oriented scholars under the rubric of *social psychology* and eventually the more special *sociolinguistics*, which will be surveyed in the next section.

Psychologists were interested in the performance of bilinguals as an index to such problems as *language acquisition, language storage,* and *language transfer* (positive or negative). We may explicate these terms by saying that they were trying to find (1) how one learns a second language, (2) how one maintains a second language, as distinct from a first, and (3) how one's other psychological functions are affected by a second language. While all of these were worth studying for their own sakes, they obviously had a very real relevance to the educational problems we shall discuss below. In the following account we shall follow the same general outline as in *BIA*, chapter 4, with some minor changes: 4.1. The Acquisition of Language (*BIA* 4.3.), 4.2. Motivational Stereotypes (*BIA* 4.4.), 4.3. Bilingual

Proficiency (*BIA* 4.5.), 4.4. Linguistic Independence (*BIA* 4.6.), 4.5. Effects of Bilingualism (*BIA* 4.7., 4.8.).

4.1. *The Acquisition of Language*

The account of language learning in *BIA* 4.3. was not falsified by later research, but new points of view were strongly asserted and much interesting research was undertaken. The whole question of how a language is learned was placed in a new light by the novel theories of Noam Chomsky (e.g., 1965:47—58) concerning language ('generative grammar'), which rejected behaviorism and returned to more traditional conceptions. Chomsky associated his point of view with the philosophical tradition of Cartesian *rationalism* and formulated it as a contrast to the *empiricism* which he detected not only in Bloomfieldian behaviorism, but also in the typical American structuralism of such scholars as Bloch, Trager, and Hockett. The problem was philosophical rather than linguistic, unless one accepted Chomsky's claim that linguistics was a branch of psychology. The shift in emphasis on the part of Chomsky and his followers could not have an immediate impact on methods of language teaching, but it might lead to a reduction of rote memorization in favor of the deliberate learning of rules. Since most language teachers had never accepted the behavioristic point of view of the learner as a learning machine with a *tabula rasa,* and had judiciously combined the teaching of rules with a program of memorization and variation, there was not a great deal that such an approach could change in teaching practices. Whatever 'innate ideas' might enable the child learner to acquire the grammar of a language presented to it in infancy, these would also operate (or fail to operate) in a second language so long as this was presented in infancy or childhood.

We may therefore disregard for the time being any effect that so-called 'language universals' might have on language acquisition, with the suggestion that such universals could well facilitate the learning of a second and third language by psychological transfer. The bilingual-to-be, however, faced the primary problem of acquiring all those language-specific differences that characterize each language in its uniqueness. Recent thinking on this topic emphasized the creativity of the user and hence of the learner. The reader of Chomskian linguistics was faced with a terminology that seemed baffling and inflated, because it attributed to the child capacities ordinarily associated with philosophers only: 'The child is presented with certain "primary linguistic data", data which are, in fact, highly restricted and degraded in quality. On the basis of these data, he constructs a grammar that defines his language and determines the phonetic and semantic interpretation of an infinite number of sentences. This grammar constitutes his knowledge of his language' (Chomsky and Halle 1968:330–1). As repeatedly pointed out by Hymes and supported by studies of language learning among Indians in Oregon (Philips 1970), knowing a language also includes 'the rules for appropriate speech usage in contexts where talking is necessary'.

The emphasis on the process of 'constructing a grammar', a metaphorical way of describing the observations and inductive generalizations which the learner made, left out of account the sheer memorization of lexical items, idioms, and even whole sentences, which was an obvious and inescapable part of learning any language, whether the first or second. In generative grammar the process of learning appeared to be thought of as somehow parallel to the linguist's way of constructing a grammar of an unknown language; but it was well-recognized that a linguist could 'construct' a grammar without being able to speak the language, and the same could be true if a child did no more than construct an intellectual edifice: what the child somehow 'constructs' was surely a set of habits that enabled him not only to 'know' a language but also to use it. The possibility of speaking of a child's learning as 'the construction of a grammar' resulted from the 'systematic ambiguity' with which Chomsky and Halle used the term 'grammar' to mean both the grammarian's 'description of the speaker's competence' and 'the competence itself' (Chomsky and Halle 1968:3). The implication that there was a one-to-one congruity between the two was, to say the least, premature. Since the grammarian's description referred only to 'the system of rules that specifies the sound-meaning correspondence' of a language, there was little place in it for the lexicon, without which no referential meaning could be conveyed.

While a certain amount of research on child learning resulted from generative grammar (e.g. Miller 1970), little of this was so far applied to bilingualism. One reason may be Chomsky's theoretical concern with 'an ideal speaker-listener, in a completely homogeneous speech-community' (1965:3), which left little room for the kind of heterogeneity that characterized bilinguals.

At the Moncton Seminar (in 1967) the topic was introduced by R. M. Jones (Aberystwyth), with discussions by Ervin-Tripp (Berkeley), Rivers (Monash), and Malherbe (Natal). There was general emphasis on the child's active acquisition of language: 'The child in learning a language is constructing a unified edifice, and not collecting an indiscriminate or infinite number of words' (R. M. Jones 1969:24). While Jones suggested that second-language learning duplicates first-language learning, Rivers categorically rejected this position: even at an early preschool age children show evidence of native-language interference (Kelly, ed. 1969:37).

Recent research on early language acquisition as it bore on bilingualism was summed up in a paper by Susan Ervin-Tripp (1968), a revision of the contribution she made to the discussion at the Moncton Seminar (Kelly, ed. 1969:26–35). She referred to experiments showing that children paid more attention to sound (as compared with sense) than adults did: 'They generalize more between words alike in sound, give more clang associations, confuse the meanings of similar-sounding words' (1968:1). They required more social support than adults to maintain a language, perhaps because they lacked the adult's 'rich inner speech' (p. 6), and they were readily affected by the values placed on language learning by their environment (p. 7). They constructed systems readily and changed them again as readily, learning with or without overt imitation, and often transferred morphs and rules from one language to the other (p. 12). Other recent studies were analyzed by her (1970) to demonstrate that 'many of the theoretical issues and concepts in psycholinguistic work on grammatical processing, and in child language research are relevant to studies of bilingualism'.

Empirical studies of language development in bilingual children did not yet approach Leopold's classic work (1939–49) in size or detail. Except for a brief summary article on his daughter's language development (1956–57), Leopold devoted himself chiefly to the study of similar phenomena in Germany, e.g., the language of children of occupation personnel (1960), or the influence of English and standard German on dialects and daily speech (1968). Burling (1959) reported on his son's simultaneous learning of English and Garo (a Tibeto-Burman language of Assam, India) during a two-year residence among Garo speakers. The paper offered many interesting observations and modified some generalizations made by Leopold, e.g., that the bilingual develops his syntax before his morphology or that bilingualism leads to greater freedom of linking between word and meaning. Brosnahan (1960) discussed factors likely to be involved in a child's second-language learning; he analyzed proficiency as success in falling within the 'field of dispersion' which Martinet

48   *Einar Haugen*

proposed. In an Indiana dissertation Contreras (1962) described the development of a bilingual child's speech between the ages of one and two, establishing eleven successive phonological states and evaluating various theories concerning language development. Valette (1964) reported briefly on the learning of French by a four-year-old American child in a French-speaking nursery school after nine months' immersion: the standard achieved was only that of a French three-year-old. Kinzel in a Washington dissertation (1964) described the language development of a six-year-old child in a French-speaking home in America: lexical and grammatical interference was common, due usually to interlingual identification and consequent transfer.

An experiment was devised by Lambert to simulate conditions of bilingual learning, in the hope that it might throw light on the often vexing question of whether it is better to learn a second language concurrently with the first or consecutively (Lambert and Witelson 1961). The highly simplified conditions of the experiment permitted only very tentative conclusions: concurrent order called for more time and experience to master two vocabularies (for the same referents), but it also resulted in much better retention and overall grasp. It was doubtful that this result could be generalized.

One of the most interesting problems in language acquisition was what we may call the *puberty threshold.* Prepuberty learners were known to have a capacity for exact reproduction of foreign sounds which was often the despair of older learners. Penfield, whose researches on the brain were reported in *BIA 73,* attributed this difference to a loss of neurological plasticity in the brain. A full account of this hypothesis is found in Penfield and Roberts (1959) and a popular article in *The Atlantic Monthly* (Penfield 1964). Penfield's views were based on the observation that a brain-damaged child could replace the functions of the left 'uncommitted cortex' with those of the right, while an older person was unable to make this switch. 'The secret of the child's success lies in the action of the switch mechanism, a conditioned reflex that works in his brain automatically' (1964:80). Consequently Penfield advised that a second language be learned before the hardening of the learning faculty: 'The uncommitted cortex must be conditioned for speech in the first decade' (1964:81).

Adult learners also offered interesting problems for psychological research. Some of these were explored by Ervin (-Tripp) in a series of articles on American Indian, French, Italian, and Japanese bilinguals in America. She found (1961a) that the categories of color naming differed systematically among bilingual Navajo speakers from those of monolingual ones. A test of recall based on pictures shown to Italian-English bilinguals (1961b) showed that pictures were recalled and named more often in the bilinguals' dominant language than in the other regardless of which language they had learned them in. Thematic Apperception Tests (TAT) administered to French bilinguals (1964) showed that they made significiantly different responses to the same pictures according to the language of response, especially along these dimensions: in French there was more rejection of overt aggression and higher evaluation of privacy and independence of feelings. Similar tests administered to Japanese war brides (1967) failed to show a consistent shift in attitude with language: they entertained both American and Japanese attitudes, but not always correlated with language. It was more a matter of 'set', self-instructions that led the subject to produce 'typical' responses. Skill in the second language (English) was found to be correlated to length of residence, while successful pronunciation proved to be correlated to reading ability.

4.2. *Motivational Stereotypes*

The basic motivations for language learning, as set forth in *BIA* 73–75, include the necessity of communication, function in social advance, emotional involvement, and religious or literary-cultural value. It has often enough been pointed out that the failure to learn foreign languages may be due to antipathy to one's immigrant background or fear of revealing an 'inferior' origin (Nida 1957–58). In Canada Lambert conducted a number of experiments, with the aid of students and associates, which explored the 'roles of attitudes and motivation in second-language learning'. These go back into the 1950s (Lambert, Hodgson, Gardner, and Fillenbaum 1960), but continued through the 1960s; the latest summary of results was Lambert, Gardner, Olton, and Tunstall (1968). This article extended the previous studies made in Canada to French-speaking communities in Louisiana, Maine, and Connecticut.

In brief, the Lambert-inspired studies used the technique of *matched guises*, i.e., the same person was recorded in two different languages, and subjects were asked to evaluate the personality characteristics of the speaker. By reducing the differences entirely to linguistic ones, it proved possible to get responses that reflected individual and community attitudes to the respective language groups. In French Canada it appeared clearly that adult English and French speakers agreed in rating the English more favorably, even on such traits as good looks, intelligence, dependability, ambition, and character. The English found that the French had a better sense of humor and the French rated themselves high on religiousness and kindness. These stereotypes, which (if a non-Canadian may comment) definitely reflect the power relationships in Canada, were absent in children at the age of ten (E. Anisfeld and Lambert 1964), but began appearing about the age of twelve (Lambert, Frankel, and Tucker 1966), especially among bilingual girls from the upper middle class attending private schools. Comment is unnecessary: the implantation of community stereotypes takes place about the same time as the development of personality at puberty! A similar study of voices taped with and without a Jewish accent reflected a devaluation in height, good looks, and leadership for those who had the accent, while Jewish subjects rated the Jewish-accented voices favorably on sense of humor, entertainingness, and kindness (Anisfeld, Bogo, and Lambert 1962).

One significant finding in connection with these stereotypes was that they correlated positively with the learning of language. Montreal high school students studying French as a second language did significantly better in the subject if their attitudes to French speakers were favorable (Gardner and Lambert 1959). By giving students also a battery of aptitude and intelligence tests the investigators found that there was a clear statistical independence between two determinants of achievement: (1) aptitude-intelligence, and (2) attitude-motivation. It was not possible to determine for certain whether attitude caused or was caused by achievement, but study of the backgrounds and family attitudes of the students suggested that the former was true (Lambert, Gardner, Olton, and Tunstall 1968). For those who went on to become experts in the other language (e.g., prospective French teachers), it was found (through observation of such students attending a six-week French summer school) that total immersion in another culture and language could lead to increased *anomie*, i.e., negative evaluation of oneself and one's own culture (Lambert 1963; Lambert, Gardner, Barik, Tunstall 1963). In an integrative review article (1967) Lambert summarized these results in the form of a 'social psychology of bilingualism'; such stereotypes, here elicited by an indirect technique, undoubtedly affect the predisposition of one group to imitate another and to accept its values. 'The bilingual can enjoy the fun of linguistic spying but must pay the price of suspicion from those who don't want him to leave his "own" domain' (1967:105). Other studies showed that 'the bilingual child may well start life with the enormous advantage of having a more open, receptive mind about himself and other people' (1967:106). This important and readable article leads into the topic discussed later when we get to the bilingual community (section 5).

4.3. *Bilingual Proficiency*

The term 'proficiency' will be retained here as a description of skill in performance, which in general implies a corresponding competence (in the sense that this term is used in generative grammar). The kinds of testing described in *BIA* 4.5. (pp. 75—8) continued, but will not be further analyzed here, since they were well summarized in Lado's book on *Language Testing* (1961). He there showed the complexities involved in composing tests of skills in a single language, and, as MacNamara pointed out, the complexities involved in establishing comparable measures of skills in two languages were 'far more than double' (1967a:61).

MacNamara's summary was the best available source for a survey of current thought among psychologists concerning the testing of bilingual proficiency. He devoted himself to six topics: degree of bilingualism, the distinction between coordinate and compound bilinguals, linguistic independence, linguistic interference, language switching, and translation. Only the first of these will be considered in this section.

A study directed by Lambert with Havelka and Gardner (1959) continued the work on dominance initiated earlier (*BIA* 77). After testing French-English bilinguals for word recognition, facility in word completion and word detection, response sets, and speed of reading, they found that these were correlated in such a way that they appeared to reflect a single dimension. Speed of translation, however, did not so correlate. Another investigation compared bilinguals with monolinguals for skill in perceiving phoneme sequences not familiar from their own languages (Cohen, Tucker, and Lambert 1967): bilinguals were superior in perceiving entirely new sounds.

Among the tests applied to bilinguals to establish their relative bilinguality (as summarized by MacNamara 1967a, but also at the Moncton Seminar in somewhat more detail, Kelly, ed. 1969:80—97) were language background questionnaires (LBQ), self-rating scales, fluency tests (word completion, speed of reading, and word naming),

flexibility tests (name as many synonyms as possible for some
popular concept, like 'getting drunk', or as many meanings as possible for a familiar word, or words detectable in a string of letters like
French DANSONODENT), and dominance tests (asking a subject to
choose among amibiguous signals, e.g., French/English *pipe*).
MacNamara found that the most powerful predictors of bilingual
proficiency were the self-rating scales and the speed of reading aloud.
Otherwise he advised psychologists to limit themselves to selecting
bilinguals for those precise skills they wished to manipulate: In a
critique (at Moncton) of MacNamara's paper, Jakobowitz (Kelly, ed.
1969:98–102) challenged the idea that fluency and flexibility tests
were 'indirect' measures of bilinguality, and he maintained that the
use of difference scores (score in language *A* minus that in *B*) was
inadequate, since bilingualism involved a much more profound shift
of personality than could be reflected in such tests. He also urged
advocates of bilingualism to emphasize and explore more extensively
the positive advantages of second-language learning, e.g., in the form
of 'greater cognitive flexibility in the child'.

In tests designed to compare the word associations of American
and French monolinguals with those of Canadian bilinguals and
monolinguals, Lambert and Moore (1966) found greater diversity
among the French and French-Canadian monolinguals than among
American and English-Canadian monolinguals; the French-Canadian
bilinguals responded according to the language they were using, with
an intermediary degree of response similarity. Harrison (1967) found
that among Mexican-American bilinguals in Texas, women responded
better to a (female) Spanish-speaking interviewer, men to an English-
speaking one.

Recent studies by the Anisfelds and Semogas (1969) were directed
at testing the responses of bilinguals (Lithuanian-English) to familiar
and unfamiliar phonological systems. Subjects were asked to listen to
initial clusters, some of which were permissible and some imper-
missible in each or neither of their languages. They were asked to
decide whether these would be acceptable in the name of a new
product, if they were pleasant or unpleasant, and if they actually
occurred. Older bilinguals showed cross-influences in both languages,
while younger ones showed only influence by English on their
Lithuanian. The conclusion was that 'even in their underlying representations – not only in their overt realizations – the two linguistic
systems of the bilinguals studied were not tightly sealed off from
each other'.

The most extensive proficiency testing of bilinguals so far was Fishman's study of Puerto Ricans in greater New York (Fishman, Cooper, Ma, *et al.* 1968), in which tests involving word naming, word association, listening comprehension, and linguistic usage were administered to a large number of speakers. Fishman and Cooper (1969) reported on the methods used, essentially a sampling of selected sociolinguistic criteria (section 5.2.). One of the studies performed on the results was reported by Fishman and Terry (1969): in an effort to determine how valid their informants' self-ratings were, they correlated these with the actual performance on the tests. They found that census claims were 'more akin to a respondent's substantially accurate overall self-perceptions as a bilingual than they are to his minute by minute sociolinguistic performance' (648). It was not clear to this writer exactly what they meant.

4.4. *Linguistic Independence*

This term, used as the title of an article by MacNamara (1967c), here replaces the one used in *BIA* 4.6 (pp. 78–80: 'Coexistence of systems') as a better designation for the basic problem of the bilingual, that of keeping his languages apart. Interference then becomes merely one part of the problem, defined as failure to maintain complete independence. The remarkable fact about bilinguals was the extent to which they actually succeeded in maintaining independence, as shown in successful switching, in spite of all temptations to the contrary. The interesting psychological problem was how to account for the separate storage and retrieval of two or more languages.

The early psycholinguists (Osgood and Ervin-Tripp 1954, *cf.* *BIA* 4.6.) approached the problem by suggesting that bilinguals differed with respect to their linguistic independence. Some bilinguals, known as *coordinate,* were relatively independent, while others, called *compound,* were relatively fused. The idea was derived from Weinreich, who suggested that 'there is need for experimental investigation of the possibility that some bilinguals interpret at least parts of the linguistic systems as merged rather than coexistent' (1953:9). He then demonstrated how a bilingual who had identified the meanings of Russian *kniga* and English *book* might be said to have a compound sign, while one who had not would have separate signs. He reported cases from the literature (Swadesh, Ščerba, Loewe) of bilingual groups said to 'have only one language with two modes of expression'. He pointed to experiments by Saer in Wales with bilingual association tests which, he believed, 'opened exciting prospects for further experimentation'.

It is important to keep in mind that in spite of his enthusiasm for this line of experimentation, Weinreich did not himself accept any such sharp dichotomy as that which the psycholinguists proceeded to develop. In the first place he wrote that 'it would appear off hand that a person's or a group's bilingualism need not be entirely of type A [separate] or B [compound], since some signs of a language may be compounded while others are not' (1953:10). In the second place, he pointed out a third interpetation of the sign (type C), 'which is likely to apply when a new language is learned with the help of another (by the so-called "indirect method")': in that case the word *kniga* would have only the English *book* as its referent and not a real book at all. He noted that the transition from this state to fluency 'also merits investigation as a problem in psycholinguistics' (1953:11).

Unfortunately, the psycholinguists picked up the idea without heeding Weinreich's warning and without fully appreciating what he was saying. Ervin-Tripp and Osgood translated Weinreich's Saussurean diagram into stimulus-response terminology, but they lumped his systems *B* and *C* into one, which they called 'compound' and described as 'typical of learning a foreign language in the school situation . . . obviously fostered by learning vocabulary lists', i.e., Weinreich's C. They added that it could 'also be characteristic of bilingualism acquired by a child who grows up in a home where two languages are spoken more or less interchangeably by the same people and in the same situations' (1954:140). These two situations were clearly different and should lead to different results, the former at best to a stiff, bookish, foreign sounding speech with no real fluency, the latter to a creolized, composite language with great fluency and variability. A further error was the assumption that these varying circumstances of initial learning would necessarily persist, so that the fluent adult user of a language should still retain traces of this initial learning situation.

Most of the experimentation performed to test the hypothesis that bilinguals can be divided into these two categories (or placed on a continuum with these two at the ends) was done by Lambert and associates. We cannot here report on all these studies, which fall somewhat outside our framework. The first study (Lambert, Havelka, and Crosby 1958) tested bilinguals on the Osgood semantic differential and found that 'coordinates' distinguished translation equivalents better than 'compounds', but a hypothesis that they would be poorer translators was not confirmed. Even the main hypotheses were not confirmed for 'coordinates' who learned their French in Montreal, suggesting that the cultural background was the main factor, not the method of learning. A study of aphasics (Lambert and Fillenbaum 1959) was inconclusive, giving only weak support to the hypothesis that 'coordinates' would be more likely to lose only one of their languages than 'compounds'. Application of the 'semantic satiation' test (Lambert and Jakobovits 1960; Jakobovits and Lambert 1961) confirmed the predicted difference, but with the old result that for 'coordinates' satiation *increased* the intensity of meaning in translation equivalents, which suggested that they were nevertheless associated interlingually. Further tests trying to show a closer interlingual association for 'compounds' than 'coordinates' were not especially revealing (Lambert 1961a, 1963). The next step was to apply the Stroop color-word test, a method of distracting subjects by asking them to name colors while being presented with conflicting color words (Preston 1965). The results showed clearly that 'bilinguals are unable to shut out the other language', but not that there was any difference between 'compounds' and 'coordinates'. As indicated above, one reason for poor results was certainly the confused definition adopted in the beginning, as admitted by Lambert (1969), where he granted that the compound category should not have included those who learned the language by 'supposedly indirect methods' (1969:108, footnote). The definition adopted in 1969 was only slightly improved: 'Compounds' were now redefined as 'those brought up in a thoroughly bilingual home environment from infancy on', i.e., *childhood bilinguals,* while 'coordinates' were 'those who had learned their second language at some time after infancy, usually after ten years of age and usually in a setting other than the family' (Lambert 1969: 108). In Lambert and Rawlings (1969) and Segalowitz and Lambert (1969) the compound 'must have learned both languages at the same time and have attained fluency in both by age 6'! One is not surprised to read that 'our own confidence in the compound-coordinate matter is still only lukewarm' (Lambert 1969:126).

Any attempt to find a simple dichotomy of this type among bilinguals was doomed to failure from the start, as Weinreich warned. There could be a continuum from the 'ideal' bilingual with two totally separated systems to the 'ideal' monolingual with only one, but it was a continuum with many dimensions, if that is conceivable. Fusion could take place in any part of the language; a truly 'coordinate' bilingual would be a schizophrenic, and a truly 'compound' bilingual would not be a bilingual at all. The coordinate-compound dichotomy was severely but justly criticized by Diller (1967), who argued (as we have here) that the terms were poorly defined concepts, that the experimental evidence did not support the concepts, and that there were strong linguistic reasons why these concepts could not be valid. These opinions were vigorously supported from a psychological point of view by MacNamara (1970), who rejected the distinction as totally irrelevant to the process of cognition.

If we turn to other psychological studies of bilingualism, we find confirmation of this view. Kolers conducted a number of tests at Massachusetts Institute of Technology and Harvard University in an attempt to determine how bilinguals stored their languages. Instead of categorizing his bilinguals, he tested the nature of their interlingual identifications by presenting the same list of words in each language and then asking alternatively for the first word association in each language. He distinguished (Kolers 1963) a language-independent storage (somewhat like the 'compound' system of Osgood), which he called the 'shared' hypothesis, and a language-specific storage ('coordinate' system) which he called the 'separate' hypothesis. The results, he felt, 'cast some doubt on the usefulness of these terms to describe psychological functions' and on 'the assumption in the dichotomy that linguistic performance is forever determined by the way a bilingual learned his second language initially' (1963:299). The range of associations showed that responses in two languages were more similar the more concrete and the less emotional their meanings were. Kolers (1965) experimented with recall of words under conditions of dual color and dual language coding: he found that mixed color coding was more confusing than mixed language coding, presumably because the latter was subject to deeply ingrained rules. In a test of short-term memory Kolers (1966a) showed that repeating a word in two languages had exactly the same effect on a bilingual's recall as repeating the word in one. Kintsch and Kintsch (1969) also devised a test to distinguish between primary (short-term) and secondary (long-term) memory: the former tended to store words by sound, the latter by meanings, so that bilinguals might well do both at various stages of their learning. Kolers (1966b) tested bilinguals on monolingual and mixed passages and found that decoding was unaffected by the mixture, but that encoding (reading aloud, or free composition) was markedly slowed down by the necessity of switching. In a popular summary of his experiments Kolers (1968) concluded that the bilingual had neither wholly separate nor wholly shared storage: some information was restricted to the language of encoding, while some was readily accessible in both languages. There was no either-or. The degree of semantic distinctness of two languages was a matter of the cultural distinctness of the speakers, not of the way they learned the language.

The problem of independence was closely allied to that of switching, a term that implied the existence of a 'switch' (Penfield and Roberts 1959) that turned one language off and the other on. Attempts to test this theory experimentally (Preston 1965) by asking subjects to name colors while being confused by conflicting color words suggested that both languages were turned on simultaneously: interfering stimuli were both being decoded at once. The suggestion was then advanced (MacNamara 1967a) that the speaker-listener has two switches, one for *production* (output) which keeps him speaking in the same language, one for *reception* (input) which enables him to understand the other language simultaneously. Kolers (1966b) and MacNamara (1967a) experimented with compulsory switching and found that receptive switching (decoding) was instantaneous, while productive switching (encoding) took a perceptible time interval (see section 3.2.). In later studies (MacNamara 1967c; MacNamara, Krauthammer, and Bolgar 1968) MacNamara found that the difference could be interpreted as examples of reduction of response uncertainty: times could be reduced if the bilingual anticipated the switch, up to as much as one-half. Lenneberg (1967) noted that the time for a regular switch approached the minimum threshold of speed for language operations (.18 seconds). It is quite apparent to me that the difference between encoding and decoding speed stems from the time required for formulation of semantically uncoded material, which is always a process of choice whether in one or more languages. Formulation in two languages increases the uncertainty of choice and the necessity of monitoring the language tags that identify the items and rules of each language. Even decoding requires extra time when the code is unexpectedly shifted, as anyone who has tried it knows: one can miss one or more words at the beginning of an utterance if one is 'set' for a different language from the one that actually comes. Rescanning the stored output may then permit decoding at a later point. As MacNamara pointed out, 'linguistic independence makes for smoother thought processes' (1967c:736).

Some psychologists sought to find answers to the problem of bilingual storage by studying aphasics. Lambert and Fillenbaum (1959) reviewed the European literature on this subject and gathered reports on cases in Montreal, in the hope of finding that 'coordinates' might be more prone to lose only one of their languages than the 'compounds'. The results were inconclusive, as pointed out by Charlton (1964) and Diller (1967), from different points of view. Charlton studied ten unselected cases seen at the Neurological Institute of New York, and found that 'it is usual for all languages to be affected to a similar degree' (1964:310). 'The "mother tongue" was as vulnerable as a more recently acquired language.' The aphasic bilingual's environment at the time of recovery was probably crucial in determining the language of his preference.

4.5. *Effects of Bilingualism*

As appeared clearly from the survey of American discussion on the 'good' or 'bad' effects of bilingualism in *BIA* 80—5, the participants were not invariably unbiased and objective. This was also the conclusion of J. Vernon Jensen, who prepared a survey of the literature on the 'Effects of Childhood Bilingualism' for the National Council of Teachers of English (1962). Unfortunately the survey did not attempt to weigh the contributions to the discussion, but was largely a pro-and-con listing of arguments. Jensen did note that 'since World War II the most fruitful studies have been the revolutionary contributions of the linguists' and that while 'earlier studies tended to emphasize disadvantages', 'investigations in the last two decades tend to stress the advantages' (1962:14). His study included items of specifically educational interest that have not been repeated here; the interested reader is referred to his 220-item bibliography. The conclusions were cautious, suggesting the need of 'taking into account many variables', and stating the objective of education as being 'to determine what is best for the "whole person" for his "whole life" '. It was obvious that the chief reason for even questioning the benefits of bilingualism in the United States was the availability of a choice to many parents. In those parts of the world where bilingualism is stable, its necessity has made its values obvious and unquestioned. In America, however, the dominance of English in national life made it a matter of conscience for parents whether they should expose their children to the concurrent learning of another language than English.

One of the bugbears held up before such parents was that their children would be handicapped in intelligence and consequent school achievement by learning a non-English language in the home. The literature on bilingualism and intelligence was surveyed by Darcy (1963), who found that most of the differences in performance by bilinguals were due to differing ages of learning, socioeconomic backgrounds, methods of testing or teaching, and differing definitions of bilingualism. Fishman (1965) explicitly analyzed the potential variables and pointed out that before the role of bilingualism in the formation of intelligence could be answered, it would be necessary to specify these variables. This was apparent enough in the studies of Chinese-speaking children in Hawaii (M. E. Smith 1957: monolinguals have greater word choice in English), bilinguals in Guam (J. Cooper 1958: means below standard), Jewish children (Levinson 1959: no difference between groups), Polish junior high school students in Milwaukee (Kosinski 1968: no difference in reading ability), third-grade children (Kittell 1959: no significant difference in total mental age), Spanish-speaking children in the Southwest (Cline 1961: socioeconomic differences more important than linguistic; Carrow 1957: no difference in reading skills, monolinguals advantaged in speaking; Knapp 1960: bilinguals slower in test performance; Fitch 1966: difference in English skills reduced for vocabulary by fifth grade), etc. MacNamara (1970) rejected all of these results (including his own for Irish) as irrelevant to an understanding of intelligence, because they concentrated on individual differences rather than common traits: they 'do not mean that bilinguals are more stupid than unilinguals, they have only been made to appear so'.

A more challenging study of the problem was initiated in Montreal by Peal and Lambert (1962; reprinted in Michel 1967). The subjects were monolingual and bilingual 10-year-old children drawn from six French schools in Montreal, matched for class, sex, and age. The results showed that the bilingual children did significantly better on every measure of intelligence, verbal or nonverbal. They also appeared to have greater mental flexibility, a superiority in concept formation, and a more diversified set of mental abilities. The investigators did not attempt to answer the question of why these results should be so unequivocally different from many of those undertaken earlier, except to point out that the latter had not matched the groups socioeconomically and had not made sure that they were dealing with real bilinguals. One may offer the further comment that the advantages of bilingualism must be more apparent in Montreal with its large bilingual population than in the United States; the brightest children would naturally respond to the opportunity. This will become even more apparent as we turn to the consideration of the bilingual community in the next section.

5. THE BILINGUAL COMMUNITY

5.0. Sociolinguistics and Bilingualism

In my report to the Eighth Congress of Linguists (Haugen 1958:772—3) I stressed the desirability of securing the cooperation of social scientists in investigating the setting of language contact. Linguists have long been aware of language as a *fait social,* to use Meillet's phrase, and none of the American students of bilingualism neglected its social contexts. Only the last decade, however, saw a concerted effort to bring the techniques of sociological research to bear on language problems, including bilingualism. The tender shoots of an American ethnolinguistics (*BIA* 87) did not develop, except as part of the usual anthropological linguistic research that relied primarily on individual participant-observation. Hymes's work (including his reader, 1964) was in this tradition, though it did not employ the term. Instead (as noted above, section 1.2.) sociologists joined with linguists, anthropological or otherwise, in a concerted effort to create the field of *sociolinguistics,* in which the social functions of language would be examined with novel techniques (Fishman 1968). These techniques can tentatively be summed up as a *reduction* in the number of *linguistic* features identified, in order to make possible an enormous *expansion* in the number of *speakers* investigated. Methods of mass sampling could only be applied if the number of linguistic features selected for study were reduced to variables that were socially *diagnostic.*

The difference between a more popular-discursive and a technical-investigative approach was exemplified by the two textbooks, Hertzler's *A Sociology of Language* (1965) and Fishman's *Sociolinguistics* (1970a), the former summing up the general assumptions of a preceding generation, the latter providing a novel terminology as well as programs for future research (both books had special chapters on bilingualism). The difference was marked by Fishman's (1967b) searching review of Hertzler, which was a summary and programmatic statement of the newborn discipline of sociolinguistics. Typical of the new approach was the emphasis in Fishman's work on the *interaction* of language varieties rather than on their rivalry or separation. This stemmed in turn from the concept of the *speech community* within which exist a multitude of functionally distinct varieties ranging all the way from idiolects to unrelated languages, together forming the *verbal repertoire* (Gumperz) of the community (*lingual repertoire* might be a preferable expression, since 'verbal' ordinarily suggests 'lexical' or even 'oral'). By thus shifting the meaning of Bloomfield's *speech community* from 'community speaking the same language' to 'community interacting through language(s)' certain advantages were gained (Fishman 1970a:29). All forms of linguistic *variability* could be regarded without prejudice under one angle of vision, and statistical methods could be applied to determine 'who speaks what variety of what language to whom, when and concerning what' (Fishman 1970a:2). Fishman's text sketched in a brief outline the methods by which linguists (as 'describers of the code') and sociologists (as 'describers of the community') could cooperate, in terms of the concepts which underlay the particular concerns of sociolinguists in the sixties (Fishman 1967b; ed. 1968; in Kelly, ed. 1969: 275–81).

The emphasis on *variability* and *interaction* contrasted with the usual assumption by (theoretical) linguists of a uniform code as the ideal condition of satisfactory description. The *free variation* of structural linguistics was given social correlates by sociolinguists (Labov) who saw in it not only an index of class and/or region, but also a major factor in linguistic change. This view was then extended from free variation within the framework of an otherwise rigid code to variations surpassing the framework in the form of 'other' dialects or languages. The change was beneficial to the study of bilingualism by giving it a status in linguistic research which had been denied it by traditional descriptive/structural linguistics. It also placed such concepts as 'switching', 'interference', 'code convergence', and 'borrowing' into a framework of social interaction where their functions became more apparent than before and more amenable to theoretical consideration.

It was apparent that explorations were going to be made in the techniques of appraising what may be called *variable systems*. On the sociolinguistic side this was foreseen in a theoretical article by Hymes (1967), calling for a taxonomy of sociolinguistic systems 'understood as the rules governing speaking in a community', every community

being 'characterized by a variety of codes and by rules for choosing
and switching among them'. On the more purely linguistic side
DeCamp (1970) was working similarly toward a method of applying
generative theory to the description by introducing sociolinguistic
features (e.g., [+ pompous]) into the base to mark items and rules
that had to be switched when the speaker passed from one style (or
language) to another.

Some of the researches conducted under these and other theories
will be considered below; the headings run roughly parallel to those
of *BIA* (in parentheses): 5.1. Linguistic Relativity (*BIA* 5.1.1.); 5.2.
Language Functions (*BIA* 5.3.); 5.3. Language Loyalty: Shift and
Maintenance (*BIA* 5.2., 5.4., 5.5.); 5.4. Education and Bilingualism
(*BIA* 5.7.); 5.5. National Bilingualism (*BIA* 5.6.).

5.1. *Linguistic Relativity*

As noted in *BIA* (pp. 87–89) the 'Weltanschauung' hypothesis,
which assigned different 'world views' to different languages, has a
certain relevance to the study of bilingualism, since the bilingual by
definition will 'partake in two distinct modes of interpreting experience'. Although associated with the names of Boas, Sapir, and Whorf
in the United States, the hypothesis was an old one, as appeared
from the historical sketches by Brown (1967), Christmann (1967),
and R. L. Miller (1968). German philosophers of language published
books dealing with the theme, e.g., Herder in 1768 and Humboldt in
1812 and 1820. Although it was sometimes referred to as the
principle of 'linguistic relativity' (Whorf), it was more appropriately
called 'linguistic determinism', since it held that language determines thinking, as expressed, e.g., in the Swedish linguist Esaias
Tegnér's title: *The Power of Language over Thought* (*Språkets makt
över tanken*, Stockholm, 1880). American linguists like Boas and
Sapir, who were familiar with the European tradition, found this
concept fruitful in interpreting the great diversity of grammatical and
semantic systems in American Indian languages. The purely cognitive
aspect of the problem became for them a social fact: 'The world in
which different societies live are *distinct* worlds, not merely the same
world with different labels attached' (Sapir 1929:209).

Sapir's student Benjamin Whorf sought the evidence for his 'linguistic relativity' in the gross differences in modes of expression
between such languages as Hopi and English. The theory won great
attention among anthropologists, as one can see by the sympathetic

consideration given it in Hymes' collection of readings on *Language in Culture and Society* (Hymes, ed. 1964:115—63). In *BIA* I pointed out that any pair of languages would serve (Haugen 1956:88—9), since bilinguals often reported a sense of moving from one world into another when switching languages, even if the languages were closely related. It soon became evident, however, that Whorf's formulations were more challenging than demonstrable, since his methods and assumptions were ill-defined and circular, as pointed out by Lenneberg (1953). In an attempt to 'systematize' the hypothesis, Fishman (1960) concluded that in its most acceptable form it applied only to the lexicon. It was little more than a truism which said that 'what is easily expressible in one language is not necessarily easily or accurately expressible in another' and that the difference was easily relatable to 'gross cultural differences: obviously. Eskimos are more interested in snow, and Arabs in horses, than are most English speakers' (Fishman 1960:327; for references in the next paragraph see his bibliography). Hymes (1966) suggested that Whorf's relativity could be extended from language structure to language use and presented American Indian materials to show a correlation between ethnographic and linguistic data.

Lenneberg pointed to the possibility of experimental evidence which would support the relevance to behavior of differential coding. He found that colors were more easily named and remembered if simple words existed in the language for naming them, and of course that languages differed widely in their coding of colors (Lenneberg 1953:470). He also showed (1967) that codeable colors assisted learners in memorizing nonsense syllables. Whorf's claims, however, went well beyond lexicon: he maintained that 'formulation of ideas is not an independent process, strictly rational in the old sense, but it is part of a particular grammar and differs, from slightly to greatly, between grammars' (1940:231). One of his illustrations was the claim that the absence of tense forms in Hopi was associated with an outlook on life that was 'timeless' and ahistorical. Hoijer (1954) argued that the overlapping of actor, action, and object in a Navajo sentence reflected the 'passivity' and 'fatefulness' of Navajo life and mythology. Glenn (1959) held that the 'inductive' order of adjective-noun in English corresponded with an 'inductive' quality in English life, as compared with French 'deductive' noun-adjective order. The only serious effort to test this conception on informants was Carroll and Casagrande's (1958) experiment with Navajo and American children, who were asked to classify objects by color, size, shape, form, number, etc. It was predicted that the Navajo speakers would more often classify objects by shape because verb forms have overt expression of this category. When compared with Navajo children who were dominant in English, the hypothesis was confirmed; but white middle-class children in Boston agreed better with the Navajo-dominant speakers! Fishman in his review of the hypothesis concluded that 'linguistic relativity, where it does exist, is not necessarily an awesomely powerful factor in cognitive functioning' (1960:336).

Later research did not prove fruitful in establishing the Sapir-Whorf hypothesis in its stronger form. The development of an interest in linguistic universals caused linguists to grow more excited by what languages had in common than by what kept them apart. Carroll, who had done more to promote Whorf's ideas than anyone else, reconsidered the issues (1963) and found that the theory could be accepted only in a developmental sense: the learning child could well be dominated by the categories of his language, but maturation consisted in transcending them. Hopi children whose language 'predisposed' them to classify objects by shape rather than color had lost this trait by the age of ten. He concluded that 'mental operations are largely independent of the language in which they take place' and no world view is 'inextricably bound with any particular language' (Carroll 1963:19). Fishman (1970a) also reconsidered his earlier more favorable view by pointing out that newer linguistic thought emphasized '(a) that languages primarily reflect rather than create socio-cultural regularities in values and orientations and (b) that languages throughout the world share a far larger number of structural universals than has heretofore been recognized' (1970a:69). His own researches in bilingualism had shown him that 'two languages may co-exist in a stable diglossic pattern throughout the speech community and yet be as structurally different as any two languages chosen at random' (1970a:73). Sociolinguistic concepts like 'linguistic repertoire', he now felt, would prevent the typing of languages and societies as wholes and make students more aware of the independent variability of both.

This eminently sensible conclusion did not alter the fact that speakers of different languages speak about different things and that the differences are often reflected in the interferences of bilingual speakers. Wherever imperfect bilinguals import items or rules from other languages, they demonstrate that their linguistic and societal worlds are different, but to some extent overlapping and therefore fusable. Their sense of being different persons, i.e., of belonging to different cultures, when speaking one rather than another language, is a confirmation of the principle of bilingual relativity, but only in what for Whorf would have been a trivial sense. The automaticity and comparative semantic emptiness of grammatical structures make it possible for bilinguals to master more than one language and guarantee that as a vehicle of thinking one language will perform as well as another.

Two further remarks on this discussion are worth making: (a) The idea, hinted at by Whorf, that one language is necessarily more suited for certain types of thinking ('relativity could be better expressed in Hopi than in English') is patently false, since advanced scientific thinking is not done in any natural language, but in mathematics, a language devised to avoid the pitfalls of the former; and (b) the distinction of 'coordinate' and 'compound' bilingual proposed by the psychologists is almost certainly one between bilinguals who, thanks to their distinct experiences of two languages (say in France and the United States), are able to keep them apart not only linguistically but also culturally, and bilinguals who have grown up (say in Montreal) with partially fused competencies, in which the 'world views' of the two languages have been more or less approached to one another.

In the end the whole discussion of the bilingual's two world views boiled down to a realization of the fact that bilinguals were normally bicultural, although the two did not necessarily coincide in all respects. Soffietti (1955) first called attention to the distinction. Diebold (1961a) investigated the relationship of language and culture in a Huave community in Mexico, suggesting that linguistic change resulting from contact was conditioned by cultural factors of the contact stituation. He showed (1961b) how an Indian community could be only receptively bilingual and yet share extensively in the culture of the dominant Spanish community. It was the conclusion of R. Miller's (1968) survey and critique that the 'Whorfians' have failed to produce sufficiently objective criteria to substantiate their claims, that they have shown an inadequate regard for the context in which language is used, and that they have relied too completely on linguistic data alone. MacNamara (1970) pointed out some of the disastrous implications of the theory for the functioning of bilinguals.

5.2. *Language Functions*

The term 'function' here refers to those services which language performs for the individual in his interaction with other individuals within the framework of his lingual community. We are here concerned only with those functions that characterize the bilingual community, and that determine the bilingual speaker's choice of language (whether for learning or for performance). Monolinguals have, by definition, no choice, except of varieties within their language, and bilinguals speaking to them are similarly constrained, except when they succumb to the temptation of displaying their wider repertoire by introducing heterolingual elements. It is therefore redundant to speak of language ,functions in communities consisting of monolingual groups, since the functions of the languages will coincide with those of the groups themselves. However, it is difficult to conceive of a community of monolingual groups; they can become a community only by virtue of becoming at least in part bilingual. As soon as two or more individuals are bilingual, they may constitute a bilingual community among themselves and will have a choice of language in their communication.

The references in *BIA* 92—3 to the functions that determine language choice in bilingual communities were supplemented by a number of special studies. Weinreich (1957b) reported on some 'functional aspects' of bilingualism in India. An important theoretical article was Herman (1961) reporting on studies in the social psychology of language choice among immigrants to Israel. While the setting was not American, the profile drawn by Herman was fully applicable to American immigrant languages and was adopted by American researchers. Herman showed that immigrants went through stages of 'anticipatory socialization', 'over-conformity', 'vacillation', 'retreat and withdrawal', and finally 'adjustment and integration'. In each of these situations he inferred a varying potency of three major factors, *personal needs* (aspiration, insecurity, skill), the *immediate situation* (face-to-face interaction) and the *background situation* (norms involving group identification). The last named had the highest potency (a) when the language was used in a public (nonprivate) setting, (b) when the language identified the speaker as member of a nonprestigious group, in a situation of intolerance, and (c) when the speaker was committed to a specific group identification, or a particular level of skill.

Studies that followed in the wake of Herman's article included Hunt (1966), who queried graduate student/teachers in a Philippine university on their language experiences and provided illustrations from their multilingual experience for most of Herman's categories.

Hunt noted that 'the immediate situation' was difficult to distinguish from 'personal needs' and 'the background situation', but did not otherwise generalize. A comparison of multilingualism in New Mexico (Pueblo Indians speaking Keresan) and Ireland (Tory Islanders speaking Gaelic) by Robin Fox (1968) outlined the domains of the respective languages and estimated the fluency of speakers at various ages. Fox concluded that 'language is more than just a mirror of reality but is an effective part of the reality of social change' (1968:464). Gumperz (1964a, 1964b) reported on fieldwork in Khalapur, India, and Hemnesberget, Norway, in terms of the 'verbal repertoire' and 'social organization' of each, in an effort to show that the compartmentalization of the one corresponded to that of the other. The novelty consisted in adopting 'repertoire' as an elastic term accommodating whatever varieties of language functioned within the community, characterized by a 'common core' and an 'inventory of structural variants from which speakers selected in accordance with situational and co-occurrence restraints' (1964b:143). To describe these restraints he introduced a contrast between *transactional switching* (in formal or impersonal situations) which reflected the social status of the variants and *personal switching* (in informal or personal situations), which reflected stylistic and topical status, with a consequent likelihood of changes in the co-occurrence restrictions (Gumperz 1966).

The implications of these views for bilingualism were developed by Gumperz in later papers (1967, 1969, 1970; Gumperz and Hernandez 1969), in which he noted the existence of stable bilingual communities and claimed that in such communities at least some bilinguals 'alternate between the two languages for much the same reasons that monolinguals select among styles of a single language' (1967:48). This alternation in everyday interaction 'sets up cross currents of diffusion which materially change the structure of local speech varieties' (1967:49). The illustrations offered were secured by asking bilinguals to translate a story from one language to the other; the results were predictably sentences which read like calques of one another, even when the languages were unrelated (e.g., Kannada and Marathi). It was claimed that 'the two languages differ only in their morphophonemics', i.e., these bilingual dialects of the respective languages approached that popular conception wherein two languages differ only in the 'words that are inserted in the slots'. (For further details see Gumperz 1964a; Blom and Gumperz 1968.) The merging observed here appeared to be an extreme instance (found

only in informal situations) of the structural fusion pointed out by
this writer for his American Norwegian immigrants (Haugen
1953:72—3 *et passim*). In both cases we were dealing with 'compound' bilinguals in the psychologists' sense, with partially fused
systems which reduced the language distance and the speakers' effort
in switching (section 3.0.). The overall implications of these findings
for linguistic theory were developed by Labov in his commentary on
Gumperz' Moncton paper (Kelly, ed. 1969:250—5); we shall not
enlarge further on this topic.

One particular type of bilingualism in which the two languages had
clearly delimited functions was isolated by Ferguson and given the
name *diglossia* (1959). This was the situation found in some countries where, 'in addition to the primary dialects of the language
(which may include a standard or regional standards) there is a very
divergent, highly codified (often grammatically more complex)
superposed variety, the vehicle of a large and respected body of
written literature, either of an earlier period or in another speech
community, which is learned largely by formal education and is used
for most written and formal spoken purposes but is not used by any
sector of the community for ordinary conversation'. The *superposed*
varieties he called *H* (for High) and exemplified them by Classical
Arabic, Katharevousa Greek, Standard German (in Switzerland), and
Standard French (in Haiti). The *primary* varieties he called *L* (for
Low): Spoken Arabic, Dhimotiki Greek, Schweizerdeutsch, and
Haitian Creole. Ferguson made a special point of distinguishing
diglossia from the usual *standard-with-dialects* by defining as *H* only
a variety with an exalted function in the community and not used in
familiar speech by any sector of the community. Ferguson's *H* was in
every case a superposed literary standard which differed from other
standards only in not having a spoken counterpart, i.e., the gap
between the received *H* and the actual (spoken) *H* was greater than
with most standards. In part the similarity of these communities
depended on the definition of the communities: the German and
French *H* did have spoken counterparts, but not within the political
unit in question. Except for this difference it was hard to tell
Ferguson's *H* apart from any other more or less artificially received (or
newly created) standard.

It was therefore tempting to apply the term *diglossia* to any
situation in which two language varieties stood in a similar functional
relationship of *H* to *L*, including standard-with-dialect. Fishman did
not resist the temptation and extended the term to include any

socially established split between languages, even when these were historically unrelated, as in the case of Hebrew and Yiddish. The perspective here was entirely sociological, with *diglossia* the 'societal counterpart' of *bilingualism*, now limited to 'individual competence' (Fishman 1967a). This dichotomy made it possible to distinguish communities with or without each, making four possibilities (Fishman 1967c): diglossia with bilingualism (e.g., Hebrew/Yiddish) and without (English/African languages in new African countries), no diglossia with bilingualism (immigrant communities) and without bilingualism (tribal communities). Since Fishman (following Gumperz) made no distinction between languages and dialects or even registers and styles of one language, this made for an extremely broad set of generalizations leading to such predictions as the following: if the functions ('roles') of the languages ('varieties') were not 'kept separate by dint of association with quite separate (though complementary) values, domains of activity and every day situations, one language (or variety) would displace the other as role and value distinctions merged and became blurred' (Fishman 1967a:32). In other words, if a language serves no function, it disappears; but how can we know that it served no function except by the fact that it disappeared?

The linguistic diversity of communities attracted a number of studies of this kind, in which various criteria were used to type the communities. Gumperz (1962) made a preliminary categorization according to complexity of code matrices (later he used the term 'repertoires'), from the least complex (bands of hunters and gatherers) through the somewhat more diverse (tribal communities) to the most diverse (intermediate communities, with mixed strata), which with modernization tended to simplify around the standard. Kloss, whose activity in this field dated back a number of years, presented ten variables for the determination of types of multilingual communities (1967a) and advanced further data on the topic at the Moncton seminar (1969a), as well as discussing various special types of bilingualism. His distinction between *Abstand* and *Ausbau* languages (again in Kloss 1967c) had become familiar to all students in the field as a precision of the term *language.* Mackey (1966) was another who worked out a typology of functions, applying it to a still unpublished material from the bilingual communities of Acadia.

The chief attempts to provide statistical data on the functions of language in a bilingual community were those initiated by Fishman among Puerto Rican speakers in greater New York. The basic scheme was presented in an article entitled 'Who Speaks What Language to Whom and When?' (Fishman 1965c). Here he categorized the sources of variance in language choice as including (a) *media:* writing, reading, speaking; (b) *role:* inner speech, decoding, encoding; (c) *situation:* more formal, less formal, intimate; (d) *domain:* family, friends, organizations, occupations, etc. By combining these into a single table he was able to show the *dominance configuration* of the two languages in contact. A full report of the data secured was presented in *Bilingualism in the Barrio* (Fishman, Cooper, Ma, *et al.,* 1968), but a survey of the methods and some of the results was prepared by Cooper for the Moncton Seminar (Kelly, ed. 1969:192–208). The tests administered included tests of word naming, picture naming, word association, recall, and word frequency rating. It was difficult for the non-psychologist to judge these reports, which seemed excessively indirect in their attempts to measure bilingual behavior (as noted by commentators at the Moncton Seminar, pp. 209–27).

Much more appealing was the work done by Fishman and associates on determining the linguistic dimensions' of the Puerto Rican neighborhood. The theory of this approach was presented by Fishman and Herasimchuk (1969; also in Fishman and Cooper 1969), essentially an adaptation of Labov's method. A limited number of phonological features were selected for study in each language (e.g., loss of plural-*s* before a consonant in Spanish). The frequency of each feature was then determined in each of several speech contexts varying in degree of formality and correlated with the sex, age, education, and birthplace of each informant. Fuller results of this technique were presented in Ma and Herasimchuk (1968:638–835). By mathematical analysis of the data they were able to isolate six speech styles by the co-occurrence of phonological variables, and to divide the speakers into four linguistic subgroups: native adult bilinguals, American-born or childhood bilinguals, monolinguals with strong interference, and highland-born Puerto Ricans. Kimple *et al.* (1969) tested informants on the naturalness of using each of the two languages in given settings.

In summing up recent work on bilingual functions, MacNamara (1967d) made the point that 'both bilingualism and diglossia should be considered not in isolation, but rather as salient examples of a capacity for code variation which is also found among monolinguals'.

5.3. *Language Loyalty: Shift and Maintenance*

Language attitudes were shown to be powerful factors in promoting or retarding the use of languages (*BIA* 5.4), leading alternatively to partial or total language displacement (*BIA* 5.5.). The most elaborate and insightful investigation of this development among American ethnic language groups was undertaken by Fishman, who produced in his book *Language Loyalty in the United States* (1966a) a monumental study of the 'self-maintenance efforts, rationales, and accomplishments of non-English speaking immigrants on American shores' (p. 15). The research underlying this work was supported by the Language Research Section of the United States Office of Education, the first instance known to this writer of official support for activities promoting an interest in non-English languages in the United States. (For a discussion of its contents see Fishman 1965d; also reviews by Gilbert 1967b; Rudnyćkyj 1968; Hasselmo 1969b.)

The term *language loyalty* was first used as a technical term in American linguistic discussion by Weinreich (1953:99 ff.), who defined it as 'a state of mind in which the language (like the nationality), as an intact entity, and in contrast to other languages, assumes a high position in a scale of values, a position in need of being "defended" '. He noted the possible effects of such loyality 'in counteracting language shifts' and called for careful study of the relationship between them (1953:108). Fishman's study followed up this theme by gathering into one volume an integrated review of the situation in which non-English immigrant (and colonial) languages have found themselves in the United States and the efforts their users have made to prevent or retard extinction. He adopted the term *language maintenance* as the opposite of *language shift* (Fishman 1964b), thereby emphasizing the active, self-conscious aspects of the process somewhat more than I, who had used the *index of retention* (Haugen 1953:283) as a cover term for both the loyalistic and the purely traditional persistence of language under pressures of American acculturation. The difference between the intellectual leaders and the masses in such groups was often one of linguistic *ideologization,* which stressed the cultural and symbolic values of maintenance in the face of the obvious economic and political advantages of shift. The difference was interestingly reflected in a study of Puerto Rican intellectuals in New York by Fishman: when asked 'what makes you a Puerto Rican', ordinary people simply pointed to the facts of birthplace and parentage, but the intellectuals stressed their attitudes, knowledge, sentiments, and behaviors (Fishman 1969b:224). A special study was made by Hesbacher and Fishman (1965) of the loyalist attitudes and practices prevalent among Yiddish and Polish leaders in two Pennsylvania communities.

The whole field of what has been called 'minority group research' in the United States received its bibliography by Francis (1957–58), all sociological with precious little attention to the linguistic aspects. Most of this research was oriented to measuring the degree of assimilation (also known as 'acculturation' in sociological circles) to white, Anglo-Saxon, protestant (WASP) culture. The fact that even language shift did not automatically result in acculturation was the concern of a number of students. One writer (Gordon 1961) noted that all the current rival theories of American assimilation, which he called 'Anglo-Conformity', 'The Melting Pot', and 'Cultural Pluralism', missed the point, which was that groups could become more or less acculturated to WASP norms without being structurally integrated into WASP society, due in part to mutual resistance to 'structural assimilation', expressed as social and marital taboos. The problem was well posed in an essay by Nahirny and Fishman (1965) on the development of ethnic identification among the American-born generations of non-English immigrants. Fishman adopted the term *ethnic group* to characterize groups having in common ethnic traditions from non-English backgrounds, therewith replacing the more usual *minority group*, previously also known as *national* or even *racial* groups. These later terms were of course difficult of definition and tended to be pejorative, while *ethnic group* and its abstract derivative *ethnicity* were sufficiently abstruse to remain relatively neutral. For a frank and critical discussion of the term and its limitations see Fishman (1965b).

Most of the studies listed above in section 2.2. contained background materials outlining not only some of the history, but also the ethnic outlook and its development for each group. Language shift and maintenance was the special theme of such articles and books as Nyholm's study on the Danish Lutheran churches (1963), Hasselmo's description of Swedish (1963b), E. Jones on the Welsh settlements in Utica, New York (1958), Tisch on French in Louisiana (1954), Graham on Spanish language radio in northern Colorado (1962), Sawyer on the social aspects of bilingualism in San Antonio, Texas (1964) and the aloofness from Spanish influence in Texas English (1959), and Grinevald-Craig (1968–69) on the linguistic situation of the Puerto Rican community of Cambridge, Massachusetts, and Oliver

(1970) on Spanish in New Mexico. Nagara's Wisconsin dissertation (1969) on the Pidgin English of Japanese immigrants in Hawaii included a detailed survey of the language history of the island. The development down to 1935 was sketched by Reinecke (1969). Some attention was even paid to bilingualism as an 'index of acculturation' in island legislatures of American possessions in the Pacific (Meller 1959); the study was based on the assumptions that (a) bilingualism was an evidence of acculturation and (b) that the further progress of this acculturation would lead to the disappearance of the native languages, assumptions which might apply within an American context but were otherwise of dubious universality.

The peculiarly American situation of *permissive ethnicity* (as opposed to *promotive ethnicity*) was the subject of a German study by Heinz Kloss (1963; review by Gilbert 1969), who also contributed a chapter ·on German-American maintenance efforts to Fishman's volume (1966a:206–52). Kloss's book, which was updated and translated as *The Bilingual Tradition in the United States* (in press), made the point (as adumbrated already in this writer's *BIA* 106–7) that official tolerance was not to be confused with an encouragement of ethnic identities. This survey of the legal constraints under which non-English languages operated in the United States was a commendable pioneer effort in the field. The importance of the common school in the anglicization of the immigrant emerged clearly from this study, as it had from several of the others mentioned above. The speaking of a language not consecrated by scholastic support produced in its practitioners something like a sense of shame and personal abasement or at best a benevolent indifference (E. Jones 1958:248; Grinevald-Craig 1968–69).

One of the interesting indices of the anglicization of the non-English immigrant (discussed in *BIA* 104–6) was the adaptation of given, family, and place names to English customary practice. A few studies of this phenomenon were added to the ones already available, but no integrative study of the whole phenomenon was made. Lyra (1966) found that Polish names were subjected to formal changes, or semantically recreated, or dropped entirely (Kaczmarzewski > Kasmarski; Bialkowski > White; Styczkowski > Martin). Hewsen (1963) discussed Armenian names, Hedblom (1966) Swedish place names, and Larmouth (1967) Finnish surname changes in northern Minnesota. Without more detailed information about the motivations for these changes from the persons concerned, it was difficult to interpret the data except in general terms.

Fishman's book (1966a), to which we now return, represented (in
its own phrase) 'an attempt to provide basic data and to review
integrative concepts' (32). In chapters that were organized more like
separate essays or monographs, the author and his associates provided statistical information on mother-tongue and nativity in the
American population (chapter 2, with John E. Hofman), the non-
English and the ethnic group press, 1910–60 (chapter 3, with Robert
G. Hayden and Mary E. Warshauer; on this see also Fishman and
Fishman 1959), foreign language broadcasting (chapter 4, by Mary
E. Warshauer), the ethnic group school and mother tongue maintenance (chapter 5, with V. C. Nahirny), mother-tongue maintenance
in ethnic parishes (chapter 6, by John E. Hofman), organizational
and leadership interest in language maintenance (chapter 7, with
V. C. Nahirny), some community dynamics of language maintenance
(chapter 8, by Robert G. Hayden), followed by four chapters on the
maintenance effort of specific groups: the Germans (H. Kloss),
the French (H.-B. Lemaire), the Spanish in the Southwest (Jane
M. Christian and Chester C. Christian, Jr.), and the Ukrainians (V. C.
Nahirny and J. Fishman). The remaining chapters were more theoretical and summarizing: the process and problems of language maintenance (chapter 13, by Nathan Glazer), planned reinforcement of
language maintenance (chapter 14 by Fishman), and a summary on
language maintenance in a supraethnic age (Chapter 15, by Fishman).
Appendices included methodological notes and an article on the field
published elsewhere (Fishman 1964b) and referred to above. One
chapter in the original version of the book, that on Yiddish, was
published separately (Fishman 1965a). Fishman had discussed
American Jewry earlier (1958–59); in a later lecture (1967d) he
summarized the differences between the Yiddish language maintenance problem and that of other American languages.

The work as a whole was a monumental effort to bring to the
American consciousness some awareness of the interest and importance of the ethnic self-maintenance efforts. The implied purpose (at
least in chapter 14) of rescuing for American use the 'resource' of
foreign-language competence seemed unrealistic, however, in view of
the acknowledged shift by second- and third-generation descendants
to English and — worse yet — the well documented drift of the immigrant languages away from their original bases including the *dialecti-
zation* of their structure and the *anglicization* of their semantic
content. To put it bluntly: not one in a thousand American-born
language learners could impress their European colinguals as an

adequate speaker or writer of the national standard. Their 'ethnic' language therefore remained for most of them an in-group American medium, functionally limited and doomed to wither on the vine. Its interest was overwhelmingly historical, excepting only for those groups who were still being allowed to immigrate, above all the Spanish-speaking groups from Mexico and Puerto Rico. A study by Hayden and Fishman (1964) showed that while half of the foreign-language teachers in American high schools and colleges had ethnic backgrounds for their learning of the language, only a few of these translated their background into 'overt, supportive behavior' in relation to their own language group. While one might therefore doubt that a scholarly study would actively contribute to language maintenance, one could indeed hope that the interest it stirred up would at least spread to the school system and create some new currents in educational circles.

5.4. *Education and Bilingualism*

The first and most immediate expression of language loyalty naturally comes with the education of children in the home. In previous sections we have reported on various studies that have explored the conditions favoring or disfavoring such education; on the one hand continuity of family traditions and cultural pride, on the other community and peer group pressures when the family was isolated from its colinguals. On the level of parents' decision to use or discontinue the non-English language there were such discussions as the enthusiastic report on home Swedish by Totten (1960) and the pro-and-con opinions of Hofmann, Brandt, Leopold, and Vent on home German (1957–58). When I am asked by parents for advice, I can only say that I am not aware of any evidence that establishes the supposedly harmful effects of bilingualism, but that of course it requires sympathetic determination and intelligent methods on the part of American parents to overcome the natural resistances of children to making efforts that find no support in their peer group. The American-Chinese linguist Yuen Ren Chao offered some good advice on bilingual home training in his textbook on linguistics (1968:144–8). For a view of the problem in reverse one could study the learning of English by the children of Americans living in France (Metraux 1965; Marie *et al.* 1967).

Beyond the family the maintenance of a non-English language required the support of a school system, and the history of American ethnic groups is littered with the débris of language schools (Fishman and Nahirny in Fishman 1966a:92—126; on German see also Kreye 1961 and Willibrand 1957a). Brault (1964) scotched some misconceptions about teaching children their ethnic language and sadly noted the low status of mother-tongue teachers. By the 1960s the number of groups who were financially able and willing to maintain such schools were few indeed. Official support of non-English schools was discussed in a symposium on 'subsidized pluralism in American education', compiled by Fishman and edited by Brickman and Lehrer (1959; see *BIA* bibliography): as Fishman pointed out in his summary, it was hard to find a formula that would support foreign language schools without at the same time violating the bans on state-supported religion and racial segregation. Such schools were either sectarian or (like the Bilingual — French-English — School in Belmont, Massachusetts) supported by parents determined to inculcate a particular culture in their children.

To some extent the other alternative *could* benefit the languages, viz., that embodied in the Bilingual Education Program, adopted by the U.S. Congress as Title VII in the Elementary and Secondary Education Act of 1968. It was obvious from the wording of this act, however, that it grew out of concern with the educational problems of disadvantaged children in learning English and not out of tenderness toward their native heritage. In a broader perspective one could see it as part of a general concern with disadvantaged children, including those whose English could be described as 'substandard', i.e., ineffective in securing them well-paid jobs. The opportunity for

Two alternatives were proposed and won some support during the fifties and sixties, both involving the introduction of foreign language (*FL*) teaching into the established American school system. One was the movement toward earlier *FL* teaching in the schools, sustained by America's growing involvement abroad since World War II and by the widespread conviction that languages were best learned before puberty (Stern 1967). This educational wave was known as FLES (Foreign Languages in the Elementary School) and has its own bibliography, which will not be included here (see Kloss 1967d; Andersson 1969). It naturally favored the major world languages (French, Spanish, German, Russian, etc.), or as the phrase ran, 'languages of wider communication'. In general, it was also limited to the teaching of the language as a subject and did not include its use as a medium of teaching. It could therefore not benefit the 'ethnic' languages or their maintenance.

involvement on the part of sociolinguists in both programs came by virtue of the need for basic information and research in bilingual and bidialectal performance (above, section 1.2.). The novel and startling departure from traditional American policy (Kloss, in press) was the recognition 'that the use of a child's mother tongue can have a beneficial effect upon his education'. The first goal was still 'to develop greater competence in English'; but this was followed by that of becoming 'more proficient in the use of two languages' and thereby 'to profit from increased educational opportunity'. The program envisaged the use of both languages 'as mediums of instruction for the same pupil population' and 'the study of the history and culture associated with a student's dominant language'. The limitations of the program were apparent in its emphasis on populations of 'families with incomes below 3,000 dollars'. It was a kind of poor relief available to school systems applying for the aid dispensed under the act, so that once again 'bilingualism' was associated in the popular mind with poverty and alienation, a 'problem' to be 'solved' by its gradual elimination. There was no change in the official policy of 'Anglo-Conformity', only a transitional toleration of 'linguistic Pluralism' (section 5.3.). The methods and goals of the program were ably presented in a *Handbook of Bilingual Education* by Saville and Troike (1970). A two-volume manual designed to provide inspiration and guidelines for the program was written by Theodore Andersson and Mildred Boyer (1970). This included definitions, samplings, and a rationale of bilingual programs, as well as concrete plans for making non-English languages not only subjects of school instruction, but also part-time media to give 'every child in America a better chance to touch his outermost limits', in the words of the Act. Twenty-five appendices provide an abundance of detailed information about the Act itself and about the use of non-English languages in the United States in and out of school. Leibowitz (n.d.) offered a critique of the Act and of American language policy in general. A more skeptical view of bilingualism was held by Roeming (1971), who refused to believe that 'the desperation of whole groups of people' could be alleviated 'through romantic attachment to an undefinable heritage'. Fishman (1970b) analyzed the politics behind the Act with some asperity.

The Bilingual Education Act was only one expression of the new interest in the teaching of 'bilingual' children. Educational testers continued to find deficiencies in their English achievement whether their mother-tongue was Chamorro (J. G. Cooper 1958) or Spanish

(Johnson 1962) or Chinese (Chen 1964). The educational problems
were well summed up by Manuel (1960), as he had done a decade
before. Carroll prepared a succinct list of research problems concerning the teaching of foreign or second languages to younger
children (1963; published in Stern 1967:94—109). Theodore Andersson, who headed a major project in the field, called for the introduction of local non-English languages into the schools in order to
restore the children's pride in themselves and their heritage (1957;
1965). Modiano (1968) studied the situation in Mexico and found
that Indian children who first learned to read in their mother tongue
surpassed markedly those who were introduced to reading in Spanish.
Manuel's (1965) book on the Spanish-speaking children of the Southwest and their education stressed the dual handicap of knowing
neither language well. Abraham (1957) showed the importance for
the teachers of understanding the children's heritage and cultural
background. Christian (1965) called for the development of a bicultural personal identification in the children. A conference 'for the
teacher of the bilingual child' was held at the University of Texas in
1964; the papers were printed in the *Modern Language Journal* and
edited by Roeming (1965). Gaarder, who was director of the Language Section in the Office of Education, reported on research and
policy at the conference (1965a); elsewhere (1965b) he wrote on
'the challenge of bilingualism' for the profession and on the organization of the bilingual schools (1967), describing in some detail the
Coral Way Elementary School in Miami, Florida, where English and
Spanish were given equal time and equal treatment. A planning
conference organized by Ohannessian (1968) devoted itself to plans
for a bilingual kindergarten program for Navajo children, an innovation for the Bureau of Indian Affairs. *The Florida Foreign Language
Reporter* took an active interest in bilingual problems, for understandable reasons, and published a special anthology issue of articles
(many of them by authors mentioned elsewhere in this report) on
'Linguistic-Cultural Differences and American Education' (Aarons *et
al.* 1969). Many of the papers at the Twenty-first Annual Georgetown Round Table (Alatis 1970) were devoted to these problems,
some of which are reported on here.

In neighboring Canada the educational problems were in part the
same as in the United States, at least for the 'other' languages, while
in part they were radically different, thanks to the size and developing power of the French 'minority'. Book II of the Report of The
Royal Commission on Bilingualism and Biculturalism was an exhaus-

tive summary of the historical and social backgrounds of the problem. The importance of the school in providing citizens with 'an education which allows them to participate in either society' was underlined, and it was recommended that 'all children must be given an introduction to the second language through the school system' (Royal Commission, Book II, 1968:269). The active interest of Canadian scholars in the topic was reflected in the work of Mackey and Lambert, reported above. Mackey prepared (1970a) a 'typology of bilingual education', in which he outlined all the possible variations in a scheme relating the variables of home language (unilingual vs. bilingual) with those of school language (same as home vs. not same), curriculum (single-medium vs. dual-medium), direction (acculturation vs. irredentism), distribution (different vs. equal), change (complete vs. gradual), and finally the relation of the school to the area and the nation (same vs. different language). He pointed out that each of these factors might affect the nature of the curriculum. Lambert was consultant to a major educational experiment in teaching the grade school subjects in French to children from English-speaking homes from the start. The results of the first two years (Lambert and MacNamara 1969; Lambert, Just, and Segalowitz 1970) were 'extremely encouraging in that the pilot class of experimental children demonstrated high level skills, relative to native speaking control classes, in all aspects of both French and English as well as in mathematics' (1970:1). While the results showed that they did not equal unilingual French children in French, they did not suffer in English by comparison with unilingual English-speaking children or in mathematics or intelligence. The situation was obviously somewhat different from that which had led MacNamara (1966, 1967b) to conclude that Irish children of English-speaking background who were taught mathematics did suffer in comparison with those who were not. In the *McGill Journal of Education* Barkman (1969; see also his 1968) surveyed some of the research results in the field in the hope that these 'will eventually open the avenues of communication between the two major language and culture groups in Canada' (p. 57).

5.5. *National Bilingualism*

We discussed briefly the policy of American officialdom toward bilingualism in the preceding section: it became evident that the United States did not have a political problem similar to that of the so-called bilingual countries, only an educational and social problem. Nevertheless a number of American and American-connected scholars took an interest in the problems of national bilingualism in other countries, either as disinterested scholars or as consultants to various agencies and governments. Ferguson as director of CAL pointed the way by drawing up national sociolinguistic profiles at the Center (1966) and by his studies in diglossia (5.2. above). Weinreich (1957b) contributed crucially by his studies of 'functional aspects of Indian bilingualism', in which be used the census figures of India to work out the geographical and social incidence of bilingualism, the relative functional importance of the languages, the linguistic diversity, and the significance of this diversity for communication. Stewart (1962; rev. 1968) followed up Ferguson's approach by devising a typology for describing national multilingualism in terms of seven typical varieties: standard, classical, artificial, vernacular, dialect, creole, and pidgin, which could be characterized by being plus or minus *standardized, autonomous, historical,* and *vital.* Discussions of other variables were published by Kloss (1967a; 1967b) and Fishman (1967a), both theoretical in nature, calling for more adequate data from national censuses. Kloss (1969b) presented a comprehensive survey of potential research projects in the field (section 1.2.).

In outlining the profile of a multilingual nation one was frequently confronted with the inadequacy of the statistical data available concerning language competence. Lieberson, a sociologist with statistical training, interested himself in the kind of information that could be extracted from the various national censuses. He showed that data on the number of speakers of each language could be used (following a paper by Greenberg) to calculate a linguistic diversity index for the nation and for its regions (1964, 1969a). This was simply a measure of the probability that any two members of the nation spoke the same language; as Hughes pointed out in his commentary at the Moncton Seminar (Kelly, ed. 1969:321), 'the probability that two randomly chosen persons could talk to each other would be more useful somewhere where there is some randomness in the probability that any one person will meet any other'. Lieberson also found many inadequacies in the language questions asked in the national censuses and proposed an improved schedule which would really meet the needs of scholars (1966). In his survey of the problems for the Moncton Seminar he called for better census techniques and for better definitions of bilingualism and greater statistical sophistication on the part of linguists (1969a; 1969b).

Lieberson (1970) and others were keeping their eyes trained primarily on our neighbor Canada, where the problems of national bilingualism were unfolding rapidly before their eyes. Not only were the Canadian census data more informative than those of the United States, but the growing library of reports from the Royal Commission on Bilingualism and Biculturalism offered unlimited possibilities for new insights (for a sympathetic summary see Vinay 1969). But there were of course similar problems in many nations of the world in which Americans took an interest; it is sufficient to refer to the fundamental studies of Karl Deutsch on 'national mobilization' (which fall somewhat outside our framework here). Others worked on the problems of 'developing nations', e.g., Fishman (1969a) in a paper delivered at a Seminar on the Social Implications of Multilingualism in Eastern Africa at Dar es Salaam, Tanzania, 1968. Fishman, with Ferguson and Das Gupta, organized a conference on the language problems of developing nations at Warrenton, Virginia, November 1–3, 1966. The resulting volume (1968) offered a galaxy of papers relating more to language and nationhood than to bilingualism as such (see also Haugen 1966). But the nations in question were precisely the ones where political developments had housed many languages in one mansion and thereby created the basic necessity for bilingualism, not only in daily life, but in education and government as well. On the solution of this problem rested perhaps the future peace and welfare of the world.

6. SUMMARY AND CONCLUSIONS

The period surveyed in this report showed a gratifying interest in every aspect of bilingualism and language contact, with a great expansion of research and publication. Most striking was the development of psycholinguistics and sociolinguistics as ancillary disciplines in which psychologists and sociologists could cooperate with linguists. The immediate and urgent task appeared to be the coordination of their insights with those of newer trends in linguistic thinking, so that progress could be made under a unified theory of bilingual competence and performance. This would in turn affect the kind of data to be collected.

Since much of the data existed only in the form of residual bilingualism, the urgency of collection could not wait for such a unified theory. In a country increasingly committed to total geo-

82   *Einar Haugen*

graphical and social mobility, with only theoretical tolerance of
regional and local segregation by language or 'ethnic' group, it was
obvious that the number of informants for this kind of research was
rapidly diminishing. In this situation one could only hope that more
projects would be undertaken similar to that of the Swedish Dialect
Archives (section 2.2.) or the *Texas Studies in Bilingualism* (Gilbert,
ed. 1970). Meanwhile one awaited a bibliography of worldwide
bilingualism being worked on at the International Center for Research on Bilingualism at Laval University. Perhaps the most useful
and totally neglected possibility was that of issuing in a common
series as many as possible of the doctoral dissertations on American
immigrant languages now lying unpublished in the archives of major
American universities.

REFERENCES*

The numbers in brackets following each reference indicate the paragraph to
which the reference relates.

Aarons, Alfred C., Barbara Y. Gordon, and William A. Stewart, eds.
    1969 'Linguistic-Cultural Differences and American Education', *Florida For-
          eign Language Reporter* 7:1 (November) (Tallahassee, Florida). [5.4.]
Abraham, Willard
    1957 'The Bilingual Child and His Teacher', *Elementary English* 34:474—478
          (Champaign, Illinois). [5.4.]
Afendras, Evangelos A.
    1969 'Sociolinguistic History, Sociolinguistic Geography and Bilingualism',
          unpublished paper (Université Laval). [1.1.]
Agard, Frederick B., and Robert J. Di Pietro
    1965a *The Sounds of English and Italian* (= *Contrastive Structure Series*).
          (Chicago, University of Chicago Press). [3.1.]
    1965b *The Grammatical Structures of English and Italian* (= *Contrastive Struc-
          ture Series*) (Chicago, University of Chicago Press). [3.1.]
Alatis, James E.
    1966 'The American English Pronunciation of Greek Immigrants: A Study in
          Language Contact with Pedagogical Implications', dissertation (Ohio
          State University). [*Dissertation Abstracts* 27.3027—A] [2.1., 3.1.]
Alatis, James E., ed.
    1970 'Report of the 21st Annual Round Table: Bilingualism and Language
          Contact: Anthropological, Linguistic, Psychological, and Sociological
          Aspects', *Monograph Series on Language and Linguistics* 23 (George-
          town University, Washington, D.C.). [1.2., 5.4.]

* See p. 111 for several addenda to this references-list.

Allen, Virginia French, ed.
1965 *On Teaching English to Speakers of Other Languages, Papers Read at the TESOL Conference,* Tucson, Arizona, May 8—9, 1964 (National Council of Teachers of English, Champaign, Illinois). [1.2.]

Anderson, Tommy R.
1964 'A Case for Contrastive Phonology', *International Review of Applied Linguistics in Language Teaching/Internationale Zeitschrift für angewandte Linguistik in der Spracherziehung 2:219—230* (Heidelberg). [3.1.]

Andersson, Theodore
1957 'Foreign Languages and Intercultural Understanding', *National Elementary Principal* 36:32—35. [5.4.]
1965 'A New Focus on the Bilingual Child', *Modern Language Journal* 49:156—160 (Ann Arbor, Michigan). [5.4.]
1969 *Foreign Languages in Elementary Schools: A Struggle Against Mediocrity* (Austin, University of Texas Press). [5.4.]

Andersson, Theodore, and Mildred Boyer
1970 *Bilingual Schooling in the United States,* 2 Volumes (Austin, Texas, Southwest Educational Development Laboratory). [5.4.]

Anisfeld, Elizabeth, and Wallace R. Lambert
1964 'Evaluational Reactions of Bilingual and Monolingual Children to Spoken Languages', *Journal of Abnormal and Social Psychology* 69:89—97 (Washington, D.C.). [4.2.]

Anisfeld, Moshe, Elizabeth Anisfeld, and Ruta Semogas
1969 'Cross-Influences between the Phonological Systems of Lithuanian-English Bilinguals', *Journal of Verbal Learning and Verbal Behavior* 8:257—261 (New York). [4.3.]

Anisfeld, Moshe, Norman Bogo, and Wallace E. Lambert
1962 'Evaluational Reactions to Accented English Speech', *Journal of Abnormal and Social Psychology* 65:223—231 (Washington, D.C.). [4.2.]

Atwood, E. Bagby
1962 *The Regional Vocabulary of Texas* (University of Texas Press, Austin). [2.1.]

Bako, Elemer
1961 'Hungarian Dialectology in the United States of America, *Hungarian Quarterly* 1:48—53 (New York). [2.2.]
1962 *American Hungarian Dialect Notes,* Volume 1 (American Hungarian Studies Foundation, New Brunswick, New Jersey). [2.2.]

Barkman, L. Bruce
1968 'Bilingualism and the Teacher of English as a Foreign Language', in *Applied Linguistics: A Survey for Language Teachers,* ed. by Monika Kehoe, 58—72. [5.4.]
1969 'Some Psychological Perspectives on Bilingualism and Second Language Teaching', *McGill Journal of Education* 4:48—58 (Garden City, Ste. Anne de Bellevue, P.Q., Canada). [5.4.]

Benson, Morton
1957 'American Influence on the Immigrant Russian Press', *American Speech* 32:257—263 (New York). [2.2., 3.4., 3.5.]

84   *Einar Haugen*

1960 'American-Russian Speech', *American Speech* 35:163—174 (New York). [2.2., 3.4.]
Bessason, Haraldur*
1967 'A Few Specimens of North American-Icelandic', *Scandinavian Studies* 39:115—146 (Menasha, Wisconsin). [2.2., 3.3.]
Bilingual Education Program, Title VII, Elementary and Secondary Education
1965 *Act of 1965, as Amended* (Mimeographed version, published by the United States Office of Education). [5.4.]
BIA, see Haugen 1956.
Blom, Jan-Petter, and John J. Gumperz
1968 *Some Social Determinants of Verbal Behavior* (= *Working Paper 4. Laboratory for Language-Behavior Research*) (University of California, Berkeley). [5.2.]
Bodine, John J.
1968 'Taos Names: A Clue to Linguistic Acculturation', *Anthropological Linguistics* 10:5: 23—27 (Bloomington, Indiana). [2.2., 3.4.]
Brandt, Thomas O.
1957- 'Reply to Margaret Hofmann', *American German Review* 24:40 (Phila-
58   delphia). [5.4.]
Brault, Gerard J.
1960 'I. A Manual for Franco-Americans. II. A Workbook for Franco-Americans. III. A Transcript of Interviews with Franco-Americans', mimeographed materials (Brunswick, Maine). [2.2.]
1961a *Les conférences de l'Institut franco-américain de* Bowdoin College (Brunswick, Maine). [2.2.]
1961b 'New England French Vocabulary', *The French Review* 35:163—175 (Baltimore). [2.2.]
1964 'Some Misconceptions about Teaching American Ethnic Children Their Mother Tongue', *Modern Language Journal* 48:67—71 (Ann Arbor, Michigan). [5.4.]
Brière, Eugène J.
1966 'An Investigation of Phonological Interference', *Language* 42:768—796 (Baltimore). [3.1.]
1968 *A Psycholinguistic Study of Phonological Interference* (= *Janua Linguarum series minor* 66) (The Hague, Mouton). [3.1.]
Bright, William
1960 'Animals of Acculturation in the California Indian Languages', *University of California Publications in Linguistics* 4:215—246 (Berkeley and Los Angeles). [2.2.]
Bright, William, ed.
1966 *Sociolinguistics: Proceedings of the U.C.L.A. Sociolinguistics Conference, 1964* (= *Janua Linguarum series major* 20) (The Hague, Mouton). [1.2.]
Bright, William, and Elizabeth
1959 'Spanish Words in Patwin', *Romance Philology* 13:161—164 (Berkeley and Los Angeles). [2.2.]

Brosnahan, L. F.
1960 'Some Aspects of the Child's Mastery of the Sounds in a Foster Language', *Studia Linguistica* 14:85–94 (Lund). [4.1.]
Brown, Roger Langham
1967 *Wilhelm von Humboldt's Conception of Linguistic Relativity* (= *Janua Linguarum series minor* 65) (The Hague, Mouton). [5.1.]
Burling, Robbins
1959 'Language Development of a Garo and English Speaking Child', *Word* 15:45–68 (New York). [4.1.]
Carman, J. Neale
1962 *Foreign-Language Units of Kansas, Historical Atlas and Statistics* (Lawrence, University of Kansas Press). [2.2.]
Carroll, John B.
1963 'Linguistic Relativity, Contrastive Linguistics, and Language Learning', *International Review of Applied Linguistics in Language Teaching/ Internationale Zeitschrift für angewandte Linguistik in der Spracherziehung* 1:1–20 (Heidelberg). [5.1.]
Carrow, Mary A.
1957 'Linguistic Functioning of Bilingual and Monolingual Children', *Journal of Speech and Hearing Disorders* 22:371–380 (Ann Arbor, Michigan). [4.5.]
Chao, Yuen Ren
1968 *Language and Symbolic Systems* (Cambridge University Press). [5.4.]
Charlton, M. H.
1964 'Aphasia in Bilingual and Polyglot Patients — A Neurological and Psychological Study', *Journal of Speech and Hearing Disorders* 29:307–311 (Ann Arbor, Michigan). [4.4.]
Chen, Martin K.
1964 'Intelligence and Bilingualism as Independent Variates in a Study of Junior High School Students of Chinese Descent', dissertation (University of California, Berkeley). [*Dissertation Abstracts* 25.1779–1780] [5.4.]
Chomsky, Noam
1965 *Aspects of the Theory of Syntax* (Cambridge, Massachusetts, M.I.T. Press). [1.1., 4.1.]
Chomsky, Noam, and Morris Halle
1968 *The Sound Pattern of English* (New York, Harper and Row). [4.1.]
Christian, Chester C., Jr.
1965 'The Acculturation of the Bilingual Child', *Modern Language Journal* 49:160–165 (Ann Arbor, Michigan). [5.4.]
Christmann, Hans Helmut
1967 *Beitrage zur Geschichte der These vom Weltbild der Sprache* (= *Akad. der Wissenschaften und der Literatur, Abh. der Geistes- und Sozialwissenschaftlichen Kl.*, Jahrgang 1966. Nr. 7) (Mainz). [5.1.]
Cline, Marion
1961 'Achievement of Bilinguals in Seventh Grade by Socioeconomic Levels', dissertation (University of Southern California). [*Dissertation Abstracts* 22.3113–3114] [4.5.]

Clyne, Michael G.
  1967 *Transference and Triggering* (The Hague, Mouton). [3.2., 3.4., 3.5.]
  1969 'Switching between Language Systems', in *Proceedings of the Tenth
        International Congress of Linguists*, (Bucharest, 1967) (Bucharest, Aca-
        demie) Vol. 1, 343—349. [3.2]
Cohen, Stephen P., G. Richard Tucker, and Wallace E. Lambert
  1967 'The Comparative Skills of Monolinguals and Bilinguals in Perceiving
        Phoneme Sequence', *Language Sciences* 10:159—168 (Bloomington,
        Indiana). [4.3.]
Coltharp, Mary Lurline
  1965 *The Tongue of the Tirilones: A Linguistic Study of a Criminal Argot* (=
        Alabama Linguistic and Philological Series 7) (University, Alabama)
        [2.2.]
  1970 'Invitation to the Dance: Spanish in the El Paso Underworld', in
        Gilbert, ed. 1970:7—17. [2.2.]
Contreras, Heles W.
  1962 'The Phonological System of a Bilingual Child', dissertation (Indiana
        University). [4.1.]
Cook, Mary Jane, and Margaret Amy Sharp
  1966 'Problems of Navajo Speakers in Learning English', *Language Learning*
        16:21—29 (Ann Arbor, Michigan). [2.1.]
Cooper, James G.
  1958 'Predicting School Achievement for Bilingual Pupils', *Journal of Educa-
        tion and Psychology* 49:31—36 (Washington, D.C.). [4.5., 5.4.]
Cooper, Robert
  1969 'How Can We Measure the Roles which a Bilingual's Languages Play in
        his Everyday Behaviour?', in Kelly, ed. 1969:192—208. [5.2.]
Correa-Zoli, Yoli
  1970 'Lexical and Morphological Aspects of American Italian in San Fran-
        cisco' dissertation (Stanford University). [*Dissertation Abstracts*
        31:2365—A] [2.2.]
Daan, Jo
  1969 'Bilingualism of Dutch Immigrants in the U.S.A.', in *Proceedings of the
        Tenth International Congress of Linguists*, Bucharest, 1967 (Bucharest,
        Academie) Vol. 1, 759—763. [2.2.]
Darcy, Natalie T.
  1963 'Bilingualism and the Measurement of Intelligence: Review of a Decade
        of Research', *Journal of Genetic Psychology* 103:259—282 (Province-
        town, Mass.). [4.5.]
Davis, Lawrence M.
  1967 'The Stressed Vowels of Yiddish-American English', *Publications of the
        American Dialect Society* 48:51—59 (Gainesville, Florida, and Univer-
        sity, Alabama). [1969] [1.2., 2.1., 3.1., 3.3.]
DeCamp, David
  1968 'The Field of Creole Language Studies', *Latin American Research
        Review* 3:25—46 (Latin American Studies Association, Hispanic Foun-
        dation, Library of Congress, Washington, D.C.). [2.1.]

1969 'Diasystem vs. Overall Pattern: The Jamaican Syllabic Nuclei', in *Studies in Language, Literature, and Culture of the Middle Ages and Later*, ed. by E. B. Atwood and A. Hill (Austin, Texas) 3—12. [1.1.]

1970 'Is a Sociolinguistic Theory Possible?' *Twentieth Georgetown Roundtable, Monograph Series on Language and Linguistics* 22:157—173 (Georgetown University, Washington, D.C.). [1.1., 5.0.]

Diament, Henri

1962 *Anglicisms in the Speech of French Bilingual Immigrants in the United States* (Mexico City). [2.2., 3.4.]

Diebold, A. Richard, Jr.

1961a 'Bilingualism and Biculturalism in a Huave Community', dissertation (Yale University). [2.2., 5.1.]

1961b 'Incipient Bilingualism', *Language* 37:97—112 (Baltimore). [1.1., 2.2., 5.1.]

1962 'A Laboratory for Language Contact', *Anthropological Linguistics* 4:41—51 (Bloomington, Indiana). [3.1.]

1963 'Code-Switching in Greek-English Bilingual Speech', *Monograph Series on Language and Linguistics* 15:53—62 (Georgetown University, Washington, D.C.). [2.2., 3.2., 3.3.]

Diller, Karl C.

1967 ' "Compound" and "Coordinate" Bilingualism — A Conceptual Artifact', paper presented to Linguistic Society of America, December 29, 1967. [4.4.]

Dingwall, William Orr

1964a 'Diaglossic Grammar', dissertation (Georgetown University). [1.1., 3.1.]

1964b 'Transformational Generative Grammar and Contrastive Analysis', *Language Learning* 14:147—160 (Ann Arbor, Michigan). [1.1., 3.1.]

1966 'Morpheme Sequence Classes, a Taxanomic Approach to Contrastive Analysis', *International Review of Applied Linguistics in Language Teaching/Internationale Zeitschrift für angewandte Linguistik in der Spracherziehung* 4:39—61 (Heidelberg). [3.1.]

Di Pietro, Robert J.

1960 'The Structural Description of an Alcamese Sicilian Dialect in America', dissertation (Cornell University). [*Dissertation Abstracts* 21.1945] [2.2., 3.3., 3.5.]

1961 'Borrowing: Its Effect as a Mechanism of Linguistic Change in American Sicilian', *General Linguistics* 5:30—36 (Lexington, Kansas City). [2.2., 3.4., 3.5.]

1964 'Learning Problems Involving Italian [s], [z] and English /s/, /z/', in *Proceedings of the Ninth International Congress of Linguists*, Cambridge, Mass., 1962 (The Hague, Mouton) 224—227. [2.2., 3.1.]

1968 'Bilingualism', in *Current Trends in Linguistics*. Volume 4, *Ibero-American and Caribbean Linguistics*, ed. by Thomas A. Sebeok (The Hague, Mouton): 399—414 [1.0.]

1970 'The Discovery of Universals in Multilingualism', *Monograph Series on Language and Linguistics* 23:13—24 (Georgetown University, Washington D.C.). [1.1.]

1971 *Language Structures in Contrast* (Rowley, Mass., Newbury House).
       [1.1., 3.1.]
Dozier, Edward P.
1967 'Linguistic Acculturation Studies in the Southwest', in Hymes and
       Bittle, eds. 1967:389–402. [2.2.]
Eichhoff, Jürgen
1971 'German in Wisconsin', in Gilbert, ed. 1970:43–57. [2.2.]
       To appear 'Zur Aussprache und Rechtschreibung von Wörtern deutscher Her-
       kunft im amerikanischen Englisch'. [2.1.]
Emeneau, Murray B.
1962 'Bilingualism and Structural Borrowing', *Proceedings of the American
       Philosophical Society* 106:430–442 (Philadelphia). [3.4.]
English as a Foreign Language, Selected Articles from *Language Learning* 1
1953 (Ann Arbor, Michigan), [3.1.]
Ervin, Susan M.*
1961a 'Semantic Shift in Bilingualism', *American Journal of Psychology*
       74:233–241 (Urbana, Illinois). [4.1.]
1961b 'Language and Recall in Bilinguals', *American Journal of Psychology*
       74:446–451 (Urbana, Illinois). [4.1.]
1964 'Language and TAT Content in Bilinguals', *Journal of Abnormal and
       Social Psychology* 68:500–507 (Washington, D.C.). [4.1.]
Ervin-Tripp, Susan
1967 'An Issei Learns English', *Journal of Social Issues* 23:78–90 (Ann
       Arbor, Michigan). [4.1.]
1968 *Becoming a Bilingual* (= *Working Paper 9, Language Behavior Research
       Laboratory*) stencilled (University of California, Berkeley). [4.1.]
1970 'Structure and Process in Language Acquisition' *Monograph Series in
       Language and Linguistics* 23:313–353 (Georgetown University,
       Washington, D.C.). [4.1.]
Feinsilver, Lilian M.
1958 'Like Influences from Yiddish and Pennsylvania German', *American
       Speech* 33:231–232 (New York). [2.1., 3.4.]
1962 'Yiddish Idioms in American English', *American Speech* 37:200–206
       (New York). [2.1., 3.4.]
Ferguson, Charles A.
1959 'Diglossia', *Word* 15:325–340 (New York). [1.1., 5.2.]
1966 'National Sociolinguistic Profile Formulas', in Bright, ed. 1966:309–
       324. [5.5.]
Fischer, Heinz
1965 'Kulturelle Sprachverwandtschaft zwischen dem Englischen und dem
       Deutschen. Deutsches Wortgut in einem Halbjahr des amerikanischen
       Nachrichtenmagazins TIME, 1964–1965', *Deutschunterricht für Aus-
       länder* 15:103–111 (Goethe-Institut, Munich). [2.1.]
Fishman, Joshua A.
1958- 'American Jewry as a Field of Social Science Research', *YIVO Annual
1959   of Jewish Social Science* 12:70–102 (New York). [5.3.]
1960 'A Systematization of the Whorfian Hypothesis', *Behavioral Science*
       5:323–339 (Ann Arbor, Michigan). [5.1.]

1964a 'Language Loyalty in the United States: The Maintenance and Perpetuation of Non-English Mother Tongues by American Ethnic and Religious Groups', 3 volumes, mimeographed. Report to U.S. Office of Education. [1.2., 5.3.]

1964b 'Language Maintenance and Language Shift as a Field of Inquiry: A Definition of the Field and Suggestions for its Further Development', *Linguistics* 9:32—70 (The Hague). [Also in Fishman 1966a:424—458] [5.3.]

1965a *Yiddish in America: Socio-Linguistic Description and Analysis* (Bloomington, Indiana University) (*International Journal of American Linguistics* 31:2, Part II [Baltimore]). [2.2., 5.3.]

1965b 'Varieties of Ethnicity and Varieties of Language Consciousness', *Monograph Series on Language and Linguistics* 18:69—79 (Georgetown University, Washington, D.C.). [5.3.]

1965c 'Who Speaks What Language to Whom and When?', *Linguistique* (1965):67—88 (Paris). [5.2.]

1965d 'The Status and Prospects of Bilingualism in the U.S.', *Modern Language Journal* 49:143—155 (Ann Arbor, Michigan). [5.3.]

1965e 'Bilingualism, Intelligence, and Language Learning', *Modern Language Journal* 49:227—237 (Ann Arbor, Michigan). [4.5.]

1966a *Language Loyalty in the United States: The Maintenance and Perpetuation of Non-English Mother Tongues by American Ethnic and Religious Groups* (The Hague, Mouton). [1.2., 2.2., 5.3., 5.4.]

1966b 'Hungarian Language Maintenance in the United States', *Uralic and Altaic Series* 62 (Bloomington, Indiana, and The Hague). [2.2.]

1967a 'Some Contrasts between Linguistically Homogeneous and Linguistically Heterogeneous Policies', *International Journal of American Linguistics* 33:4. 18—30 (Baltimore). [Also in *Indiana University Publications in Anthropology, [Folklore], and Linguistics* 44:18—30 [Bloomington, Indiana] Reprinted from Lieberson, ed. 1966]. [5.2., 5.5.]

1967b Review of Hertzler 1965, *Language* 43:586—604 (Baltimore). [5.0.]

1967c 'Bilingualism with and without Diglossia; Diglossia with and without Bilingualism', *Journal of Social Issues* 23:29—38 (Ann Arbor, Michigan). [5.2.]

1967d 'Language Maintenance and Language Shift: Yiddish and Other Immigrant Languages in the United States', *Research Conference, YIVO Institute* (New York, Yeshiva University). [5.3.]

1968 'Sociolinguistic Perspective on the Study of Bilingualism', *Linguistics* 39:21—49 (The Hague). [Also in Fishman, Cooper, *et al.* 1968:952—999] [3.3., 5.0.]

1969a 'National Languages and Languages of Wider Communication in the Developing Nations', *Anthropological Linguistics* 11:111—135 (Bloomington, Indiana). [5.5.]

1969b 'Puerto Rican Intellectuals in New York: Some Intragroup and Intergroup Contrasts', *Canadian Journal of Behavioural Science/Revue canadienne des sciences du comportement* 1:215—266 (Ottawa). [Also in Fishman, Cooper, *et al.* 1968:124—145]. [5.3.]

90   Einar Haugen

1969c 'The Description of Societal Bilingualism', in Kelly, ed. 1969:275—281.
      (Title only: 'Chairman's Summary') [Also under the above title in
      Fishman, Cooper, et al. 1968:1029—1040] [5.0.]
1970a Sociolinguistics (Rowley, Mass., Newbury House) [5.0., 5.1.]
1970b 'The Politics of Bilingual Education', Monograph Series in Language
      and Linguistics 23:47—58 (Geogetown University, Washington, D.C.).
      [5.4.]
Fishman, Joshua A., ed.
1968 Readings in the Sociology of Language (The Hague, Mouton). [1.2.,
      5.0.]
Fishman, Joshua A., W. Brickman, and S. Lehrer, eds.
1959 'Subsidized Pluralism in American Education', Supplement to School
      and Society, May 23 (New York). [5.4.]
Fishman, Joshua A., and Robert L. Cooper
1969 'Alternative Measures of Bilingualism', Journal of Verbal Learning and
      Verbal Behavior 8:276—282 (New York). [Reprinted from Fishman,
      Cooper, et al. 1968:880—928]. [4.3., 5.2.]
Fishman, Joshua A., Robert L. Cooper, Roxana Ma, et al.
1968 Bilingualism in the Barrio, 2 volumes (= Final Report, U.S. Department
      of Health, Education and Welfare) (Yeshiva University, New York).
      [1.2., 2.2., 4.3., 5.2.]
Fishman, Joshua A., Charles A. Ferguson, and Jyotirindra Das Gupta
1968 Language Problems of Developing Nations (New York). [5.5.]
Fishman, Joshua A., and Eleanor Herasimchuk
1969 'The Multiple Prediction of Phonological Variables in a Bilingual Speech
      Community', American Anthropologist 71:648—657 (Menasha, Wis-
      consin). [5.2.]
Fishman, Joshua A., and Charles Terry
1969 'The Validity of Census Data on Bilingualism in a Puerto Rican Neigh-
      borhood', American Sociological Review 34:636—650 (Washington,
      D.C.). [Also in Fishman, Cooper, et al. 1968:300—329]. [4.3.]
Fitch, Michael J.
1966 'Verbal and Performance Test Scores in Bilingual Children' (= Research
      Study 1) dissertation (Colorado State University). [Dissertation Ab-
      stracts 27.1654A—1655A]. [4.5.]
Fox, Robin
1968 'Multilingualism in Two Communities', Man 3:456—464 (London).
      [5.2.]
Francis, E. K.
1957- 'Minderheitsforschung in Amerika', Kölner Zeitschrift für Soziologie
1958 und Sozialpsychologie 9:517—548, 10:116—133, 233—247, 401—417.
      [5.3.]
Fries, Charles C., and Kenneth L. Pike
1949 'Coexistent Phonemic Systems', Language 25:29—50 (Baltimore).
      [1.1.]
Gaarder, A. Bruce
1965a 'Teaching the Bilingual Child: Research, Development and Policy',
      Modern Language Journal 49:165—175 (Ann Arbor, Michigan). [5.4.]

1965b 'The Challenge of Bilingualism', in *Foreign Language Teaching: Challenges to the Profession*, ed. by G. Reginald Bishop, Jr. (Princeton) 54–101. [5.4.]
1967 'Organization of the Bilingual School', *Journal of Social Issues* 23:110–120 (Ann, Arbor, Michigan). [5.4.]

Gage, William W.
1961 *Contrastive Studies in Linguistics. A. Bibliographical Check-List* (Washington, Conference on American Language). [3.1.]

Gardner, Robert C., and W. E. Lambert
1959 'Motivational Variables in Second Language Acquisition', *Canadian Journal of Psychology/Revue canadienne de psychologie* 13:266–272 (Toronto). [4.2.]

Gilbert, Glenn Gordon
1963 'The German Dialect Spoken in Kendall and Gillespie Counties, Texas', dissertation (Harvard University). [*Dissertation Abstracts* 25.6609]. [2.2., 3.3.]
1964 'The German Dialect of Kendall and Gillespie Counties, Texas', *Zeitschrift für Mundartforschung* 31:138–172 (Wiesbaden). [2.2.]
1965a 'Dative Versus Accusative in the German Dialects of Central Texas', *Zeitschrift für Mundartforschung* 32:288–296 (Wiesbaden). [2.2.]
1965b 'English Loanwords in the German of Fredericksburg, Texas', *American Speech* 40:102–112 (New York). [2.2., 3.4.]
1967a 'Linguistic Atlas of Texas German', *Jahresbericht 1966, Forschungsinstitut für deutsche Sprache* 9–10 (Marburg, Lahn). [2.2.]
1967b Review of Wacker 1964, *Zeitschrift für Mundartforschung* 34:83–86 (Wiesbaden). [2.0.]
1967c Review of Fishman 1966a, *Orbis* 16:572–577 (Louvain). [1.2., 5.3.]
1969 Review of Kloss 1963, *Language* 45:218–224 (Baltimore). [5.3.]
1970a 'The Linguistic Geography of Non-Official Languages in the United States', in *Proceedings of the Tenth International Congress of Linguists*, Bucharest, 1967 (Bucharest, Academie) Volume 2, 203–208.
1970b 'Linguistic Change in the Colonial and Immigrant Languages in the United States', in *Studies . . . Presented to Lee M. Hollander*, ed. by John Weinstock (Austin, Texas, Pemberton Press). [1.1.]
1972 *Linguistic Atlas of Texas German* (Marburg, Elwert Verlag, and Austin, Texas, University of Texas Press). [2.2.]

Gilbert, Glenn Gordon, ed.
1970 *Texas Studies in Bilingualism: Spanish, French, German Czech, Polish, Sorbian, and Norwegian in the Southwest*, with a concluding chapter on code-switching and modes of speaking in American Swedish (Berlin, Walter de Gruyter). [1.2., 2.2., 6.0.]
1971 'The German Language in America', *Symposium* (1968) (University of Texas). [1.2., 2.2.]

Gordon, Milton M.
1961 'Assimilation in America: Theory and Reality', *Daedalus* 90:263–285 (American Academy of Arts and Sciences, Boston, Mass.). [5.3.]

Graham, Robert Somerville*
1962 'Spanish Language Radio in Northern Colorado', *American Speech*
37:207—211 (New York). [5.3.]
Green, Eugene
1962 'Yiddish and English in Detroit: A Survey and Analysis of Reciprocal
Influences in Bilinguals' Pronunciation, Grammar, and Vocabulary',
dissertation (University of Michigan). [*Dissertation Abstracts* 23.629].
[2.2., 3.3., 3.4., 3.5.]
1963 'On Grading Phonic Interference', *Language Learning* 13:85—96 (Ann
Arbor, Michigan). [3.1.]
Grinevald (-Craig), Colette
1968- 'La situation linguistique de la communauté porto-ricaine de Cam-
1969 bridge, Massachusetts', thesis, stencilled (Faculté des Lettres de Paris —
Nanterre, Departement d'espagnol). [2.2., 5.3.]
Gumperz, John J.
1962 'Types of Linguistic Communities', *Anthropological Linguistics* 4:28—
40 (Bloomington, Indiana). [5.2.]
1964a 'Hindi-Punjabi Code-Switching in Delhi', in *Proceedings of the Ninth
International Congress of Linguists*, Cambridge, Mass., 1962 (The
Hague, Mouton) 1115—1124. [1.1., 5.2.]
1964b 'Linguistic and Social Interaction in Two Communities', in *The Ethnography of Communication*, ed. by John J. Gumperz and Dell Hymes (=
American Anthropologist 66/6, Part 2:137—153) (Menasha, Wisconsin).
[1.1., 5.2.]
1966 'On the Ethnology of Linguistic Change', in Bright, ed. 1966:27—38.
[5.2.]
1967 'On the Linguistic Markers of Bilingual Communication', *Journal of
Social Issues* 23:48—57 (Ann Arbor, Michigan). [1.1., 5.2.]
1969 'How Can We Describe and Measure the Behavior of Bilingual Groups?',
in Kelly, ed. 1969:242—249. (Commentaries by William Labov, Felix
Kahn, P. Pandit). [5.2.]
1970 'Verbal Strategies in Multilingual Communication', *Monograph Series
on Language and Linguistics* 23:129—148 (Georgetown University,
Washington, D.C.). [3.2., 5.2.]
Gumperz, John J., and Edward Hernandez
1969 *Cognitive Aspects of Bilingual Communication* (= *Working Paper* 28,
Language-Behavior Research Laboratory (University of California,
Berkeley). [3.3.]
Hammer, John H., and Frank A. Rice, eds.
1965 *A Bibliography of Contrastive Linguistics* (Washington, D.C., Center for
Applied Linguistics). [3.1.]
Harrison, Helene
1967 'A Methodological Study in Eliciting Linguistic Data from Mexican
American Bilinguals', dissertation. (*Disseration Abstracts* 28.4157A).
[4.3.]
Harms, L. S.
1969 'Social Dialect and Speech Communication Proficiency' in *Proceedings*

of the Tenth International Congress of Linguists Bucharest, 1967 (Bucharest, Academie) Volume 1, 663—668. [2.1.]

Hasselmo, Nils*

1961 'American Swedish: A Study in Bilingualism', dissertation (Harvard University). [2.2., 3.2., 3.4., 3.5.]

1963a 'Language in Exile. The Swedish Immigrant Community in Transition', in *Essays in Honor of Dr. Conrad Bergendoff*, ed. by Dowie and Espelie (= *Augustana Historical Society, Publication* 20) (Rock Island, Illinois) 121—146. [2.2.]

1963b 'Language Displacement and Language Influence in Swedish America', *The Swedish Pioneer Historical Quarterly* 14:62—84. [2.2., 5.3.]

1966 'Linguistic Routines and Code-Switching: Some Comments on an American-Swedish Speech Economy', unpublished paper (MLA Meeting). [3.2.]

1969a 'How Can We Measure the Effects which One Language May Have on the Other in the Speech of Bilinguals?', in Kelly, ed. 1969:122—141. [2.2., 3.2., 3.3.]

1969b Review of Fishman 1966a, *Lingua* 22: 261—266 (Amsterdam). [1.2., 5.3.]

1969c 'On Diversity in American-Swedish', *Svenska landsmål och svenskt folkliv* 92:53—72. [2.2., 3.5.]

1970 'Code-Switching and Modes of Speaking', in Gilbert, ed. 1970:179—210. [2.2., 3.2., 3.5.]

Haugen, Einar*

1953 *The Norwegian Language in America: A Study in Bilingual Behavior*, 2 Volumes (Philadelphia). [Second Printing, revised, 1969. 1 volume, Bloomington, Indiana]. [1.0. *et passim*.]

1954 Review of Weinreich 1953, *Language* 30:380—388 (Baltimore). [1., 3.1., 3.3.]

1956 *Bilingualism in the Americas: A Bibliography and Research Guide* (= *Publications of the American Dialect Society* 26) (University of Alabama). [Reprinted 1964 and 1968]. [1.0. *et passim*].

1957 'The Phoneme in Bilingual Description', *Language Learning* 7:17—24 (Ann Arbor, Michigan). [3.1.]

1958 'Language Contact', *Proceedings of the Eighth International Congress of Linguists*, Oslo, 1957 (Oslo, Oslo University Press) 772—785. [1.2., 5.0.]

1966 'Dialect, Language, Nation', *American Anthropologist* 68:922—935 (Menasha, Wisconsin). [5.5.]

1970a 'On the Meaning of Bilingual Competence', in *Studies . . . Presented to Shiro Hattori . . .*, ed. by R. Jakobson and S. Kawamoto (Tokyo, Japan) 221—229. [1.1.]

1970b 'Linguistics and Dialinguistics. 21st Annual Round Table, Bilingualism and Language Contact: Anthropological, Linguistic, Psychological and Sociological Aspects', *Monograph Series on Language and Linguistics* 23 (Georgetown University, Washington, D.C.).

1972 'Bilingualism as a Social and Personal Problem', in *Active Methods and Modern Aids in the Teaching of Foreign Languages*, ed. by R. Filipović

(London) 1—14. [1.1.]

Hayden, Robert G., and Joshua A. Fishman
1964   'The Impact of Exposure to Ethnic Mother Tongues on Foreign Language Teachers in American High Schools and Colleges', *Modern Language Journal* 48:262—274 (Ann Arbor, Michigan). (Also in Fishman 1964a, chapter 13). [5.3.]

Hayes, Robert W.
1958   'A Phonological Study of the English Speech of Selected Japanese Speakers in Hawaii', M. A. thesis (University of Hawaii). [2.1.]

Hedblom, Folke
1962   'Om svenska folkmål i Amerika. Från Landsmåls- och Folkminnesarkivets bandinspelningsexpedition 1962', *Svenska Landsmål och Svenskt Folkliv* 85:281.113—157 (with English summary). [2.2.]
1963   'The Swedish Speech Recording Expedition in the Middle West', *The Swedish Pioneer Historical Quarterly* 14:47—61. [2.2.]
1965a   'Bandinspelningsexpeditionen till Svensk-Amerika 1964. En reserapport', *Svenska Landsmål och Svenskt Folkliv* 88:286.1—34 (with English summary). [2.2.]
1965b   'Swedish Speech and Popular Tradition in America: A Report from the Uppsala Tape Recording Expedition 1964', *The Swedish Pioneer Historical Quarterly* 16:137—154. [2.2.]
1966   'Ortnamn i emigrantsamhälle', *Namn och Bygd. Tidskrift för nordisk ortnamnsforskning* 54:127—140 (Uppsala). [2.2., 5.3.]
1967a   'Research of Swedish Speech and Popular Traditions in America 1966: A Report of the Third Uppsala Expedition Sponsored by the American-Scandinavian Foundation', *The Swedish Pioneer Historical Quarterly* 18:76—92. [2.2.]
1967b   'Den tredje inspelningsexpeditionen till Svensk-Amerika', *Svenska Landsmål och Svenskt Folkliv* 89:287.97—115 (with English summary). [2.2.]
1968   'Om de första Halsingarna i Minnesota. Från en dialektinspelning 1966', *Hälsingerunor* (1968): 148—157. [2.2.]
1969a   'Svenska folkmål i nya världen: Fran 1960-talets fältundersökningar i Amerika', *Saga och Sed* (1968): 38—49 (Uppsala). [2.0., 2.2.]
1969b   Amerikasvenska texter i fonogram 1. Hälsingland. Bergsjömal', Svenska Landsmål och Svenskt Folkliv 92:1—52 [2.2.]

Herman, Simon N.
1961   'Explorations in the Social Psychology of Language Choice', *Human Relations* 14:149—164 (New York, London). [Reprinted in Fishman 1968a:492—511]. [5.2.]

Hertzler, Joyce O.
1965   *A Sociology of Language* (New York). [5.0.]

Hesbacher, Peter, and Joshua A. Fishman
1965   'Language Loyalty: Its Functions and Concomitants in Two Bilingual Communities', *Lingua* 13:145—165 (Amsterdam). [5.3.]

Hewson, Robert H.
1963   'Armenian Names in America', *American Speech* 38:214—219 (New York). [2.2., 5.3.]

Hockett, Charles F.
1958   *A course in Modern Linguistics* (New York, Macmillan). [3.4.]
Hoenigswald, Henry M.
1962   'Bilingualism, Presumable Bilingualism, and Diachrony', *Anthropological Linguistics* 4/1:1—5 (Bloomington, Indiana). [3.4.]
Hofmann, Margaret Schultze
1957   'Can the Mother Tongue be Retained for Children of German Immigrants?', *American German Review* 23:15—17 (Philadelphia). [5.4.]
Houston, Susan H.
1969   'A Sociolinguistic Consideration of the Black English of Children in Northern Florida', *Language* 45:599—607 (Baltimore). [2.1.]
Hull, Adrian L.
1963   'The Linguistic Accommodation of a Cultural Innovation as Illustrated by the Game of Baseball in the Spanish Language of Puerto Rico', dissertation (Columbia University). [2.2.]
Hunt, Chester L.
1966   'Language Choice in a Multilingual Society', *Sociological Inquiry* 36:240—253 (Toronto). [5.2.]
Hymes, Dell
1966   'Two Types of Linguistic Relativity', in Bright, ed. 1966:114—158. [5.1.]
1967   'Models of the Interaction of Language and Social Setting', *Journal of Social Issues* 23:8—28 (Ann Arbor, Michigan). [1.1., 5.0.]
Hymes, Dell, ed.
1964   *Language in Culture and Society: A Reader in Linguistics and Anthropology* (New York, Harper & Row). [1.2., 5.0., 5.1.]
Hymes, Dell H., and William E. Bittle, eds.
1967   *Studies in Southwestern Ethnolinguistics* (= *Studies in General Anthropology* 3) (The Hague, Mouton). [2.2.]
Jakobovits, Leon, and W. E. Lambert
1961   'Semantic Satiation among Bilinguals', *Journal of Experimental Psychology* 62:576—582 (Washington, D.C.). [4.4.]
Jensen, J. Vernon
1962   'Effects of Childhood Bilingualism', *Elementary English* 39:132—143, 358—366 (Champaign, Illinois). [1.2., 4.5.]
Johansen, Kjell
1961   'The English of Kendall and Gillespie Counties, Texas', M. A. thesis (University of Texas). [2.1.]
1970   'Some Observations on Norwegian in Bosque County, Texas', In Gilbert, ed. 1970:170—178. [2.2.]
Johnson, Bruce Edward
1962   'Ability, Achievement and Bilingualism: A Comparative Study Involving Spanish-Speaking and English-Speaking Children at the Sixth-Grade Level', dissertation (University of Maryland). [*Dissertation Abstracts* 23.2792] . [5.4.]
Jones, Emrys
1958   'Welsh-Speaking in the New World', *Norsk Tidsskrift for Sprogvidenskap Supplement,* Bind V (Lochlann, Volume 1):241—260 (Oslo). [2.2., 5.3.]

96   *Einar Haugen*

444
Jones, Morgan Emory
  1962 'A Phonological Study of English as Spoken by Puerto Ricans Contrasted with Puerto Rican Spanish and American English', dissertation (University of Michigan). [*Dissertation Abstracts* 23.2127–2128] [2.1., 3.3., 3.4., 3.5.]
Jones, R. M.
  1969 'How and When Do Persons Become Bilingual?', in Kelly, ed. 1969:12–25. [4.1.]
Kelkar, Ashok R.
  1957 ' "Marathi English": A Study in Foreign Accent', *Word* 13:268–282 (New York). [3.1.]
Kelly, L. G. ed.
  1969 *Description and Measurement of Bilingualism: An International Seminar*, University of Moncton, June 6–14, 1967 (Toronto). [1.0., 1.2., 3.3., 4.1., 4.3., 5.0., 5.2., 5.5.]
Kennard, Edward A.
  1963 'Linguistic Acculturation in Hopi', *International Journal of American Linguistics* 29:36–41 (Baltimore). [2.2., 3.4.]
Kiddle, Lawrence B.
  1964 'American Indian Reflexes of Two Spanish Words for Cat', *International Journal of American Linguistics* 30:229–305 (Baltimore). [2.2.]
Kindig, Maita M.
  1960 'A Phonological Study of the English Speech of Selected Speakers of Puerto Rican Spanish in Honolulu', M.A. thesis (University of Hawaii). [2.1.]
Kintsch, Walter, and Eileen
  1969 'Interlingual Interference and Memory Processes', *Journal of Verbal Learning and Verbal Behavior* 8:16–19 (New York). [4.4.]
Kinzel, Paul Fred
  1964 'A Description of Lexical and Grammatical Interference in the Speech of a Bilingual Child', dissertation (University of Washington) [*Dissertation Abstracts* 25.7257]. [4.1.]
Kittell, Jack E.
  1959 'Bilingualism and Language – Non-Language Intelligence Scores of Third-Grade Children', *Journal of Educational Research* 52:263–268 (Madison, Wisconsin). [4.5.]
Kloss, Heinz
  1963 *Das Nationalitätenrecht der Vereinigten Staaten von Amerika* (= *Ethnos, Schriftenreihe der Forschungsstelle für Nationalitäten- und Sprachfragen*, Kiel, Band 1) (Vienna, Stuttgart). [5.3.]
  1967a 'Types of Multilingual Communities: A Discussion of Ten Variables', *International Journal of American Linguistics* 33:4.7–17 (Baltimore). [5.2.] [Reprinted from Lieberson, ed. 1966].
  1967b 'Bilingualism and Nationalism', *Journal of Social Issues* 23:39–47 (Ann Arbor, Michigan). [5.5.]
  1967c ' "Abstand Languages" and "Ausbau Languages" ', *Anthropological Linguistics* 9/7:29–41 (Bloomington, Indiana).

1967d *FLES. Zum Problem des Fremdsprachenunterrichts an den Grund-schulen Amerikas und Europas* (Godesberg, Wissenschaftliches Archiv). [5.4.]

1969a Commentary on Lieberson 1969, in Kelly, ed. 1966: 296—316. [5.2.]

1969b *Research Possibilities on Group Bilingualism: A Report* (Quebec, International Center on Bilingualism). [1.2., 5.5.]

1971 'German as an Immigrant, Indigenous, Foreign, and Second Language in the United States', in Gilbert, ed. 1971: 106—127.

In press 'The Bilingual Tradition in the United States' (Rowley, Massachusetts, Newbury House) (an updating and translation of Kloss 1963). [5.3., 5.4.]

Knapp, Robert R.

1960 'The Effects of Time Limits on the Intelligence Test Performance of Mexican and American Subjects', *Journal of Educational Psychology* 51:13—20 (Washington, D.C.). [4.5.]

Kolers, Paul A.

1963 'Interlingual Word Associations', *Journal of Verbal Learning and Verbal Behavior* 2:291—300 (New York). [4.4.]

1965 'Bilingualism and Bicodalism', *Language Sciences* 8:122—26 (Bloomington, Indiana). [4.4.]

1966a 'Interlingual Facilitation of Short-Term Memory', *Journal of Verbal Learning and Verbal Behavior* 5:314—319 (New York). [4.4.]

1966b 'Reading and Talking Bilingually', *American Journal of Psychology* 79:357—376 (Urbana, Illinois). [3.2., 4.4.]

1968 'Bilingualism and Information Processing', *Scientific American* 218:78—86 (New York). [4.4.]

Kosinski, Leonard Vincent

1968 'Bilingualism and Reading Development: A Study of the Effects of Polish-American Bilingualism upon Reading Achievement in Junior High School', dissertation (University of Wisconsin). [*Dissertation Abstracts* 24.2462—2463]. [4.5.]

Kreye, George W.

1961 'German Instruction in Kansas', *The American German Review* 27:9—11 (Philadelphia). [5.4.]

Kufner, Herbert L.

1962 *The Grammatical Structures of English and German: A Contrastive Sketch* (= *Contrastive Structure Series*) (Chicago, University of Chicago Press). [3.1.]

Labov, William

1963a Review of Atwood 1962, *Word* 19:266—272 (New York). [2.1.]

1963b 'The Social Motivation of a Sound Change', *Word* 19:273—309 (New York). [2.1.]

1966 *The Social Stratification of English in New York City* (Washington, D.C., Center for Applied Linguistics). [2.1.]

Lado, Robert

1961 *Language Testing* (New York). [4.3.]

Lambert, Wallace E.

1961a 'Behavioral Evidence for Contrasting Forms of Bilingualism. Twelfth

Georgetown Roundtable', *Monograph Series on Language and Linguistics* 14:73—80 (Georgetown University, Washington, D.C.). [4.4.]

1961b 'Aspects psychologiques de l'étude d'une deuxième langue', in *Les Conférences de l'Institut Franco-Americaine de Bowdoin College,* Gerard L. Brault, Director (Brunswick) 29—38. [4.4.]

1963 'Psychological Approaches to the Study of Language, Part II: On Second-Language Learning and Bilingualism', *Modern Language Journal* 47:114—120 (Ann Arbor, Michigan). [Reprinted in Michel, ed. 1967:215—50]. [4.2., 4.4.]

1967 'A Social Psychology of Bilingualism', *Journal of Social Issues* 23:91— 109 (Ann Arbor, Michigan). [4.2.]

1969 'Psychological Studies of the Interdependencies of the Bilingual's Two Languages', in *Substance and Structure of Language,* ed. by Jan Puhvel, 99—126. [4.4.]

Lambert, Wallace E., and S. Fillenbaum
1959 'A Pilot Study of Aphasia among Bilinguals', *Canadian Journal of Psychology/Revue canadienne de psychologie* 13:28—34 (Toronto). [4.4.]

Lambert, Wallace, E. Hannah Frankel, and G. Richard Tucker
1966 'Judging Personality through Speech: A French-Canadian Example', *The Journal of Communication* 16:305—321 (Athens, Ohio). [4.2.]

Lambert, Wallace E., R. C. Gardner, H. C. Barik, and K. Tunstall
1963 'Attitudinal and Cognitive Aspects of Intensive Study of a Second Language', *Journal of Abnormal and Social Psychology* 66:358—368 (Washington, D.C.). [4.2.]

Lambert, Wallace E., R. C. Gardner, R. Olton, and K. Tunstall
1968 'A Study of the Roles of Attitudes and Motivation in Second-Language Learning', in Fishman, ed. 1968:473—91. [4.2.]

Lambert, Wallace E., J. Havelka, and C. Crosby
1958 'The Influence of Language-Acquisition Contexts on Bilingualism', *Journal of Abnormal and Social Psychology* 56:239—244 (Washington, D.C.). [4.4.]

Lambert, Wallace E., J. Havelka, and R. C. Gardner
1959 'Linguistic Manifestations of Bilingualism', *American Journal of Psychology* 72:77—82 (Urbana, Illinois). [4.3.]

Lambert, Wallace E., R. C. Hodgson, R. C. Gardner, and S. Fillenbaum
1960 'Evaluational Reactions to Spoken Languages', *Journal of Abnormal and Social Psychology* 60:44—51 (Washington, D.C.). [4.2.]

Lambert, Wallace E., and Leon A. Jakobovits
1960 'Verbal Satiation and Changes in the Intensity of Meaning', *Journal of Experimental Psychology* 60:376—383 (Washington, D.C.). [4.4.]

Lambert, Wallace E., M. Just, and N. Segalowitz
1970 'Some Cognitive Consequences of Following the Curricula of Grades One and Two in a Foreign Language', to appear. [5.4.]

Lambert, Wallace E., and J. MacNamara
1969 'Some Cognitive Consequences of Following a First-Grade Curriculum in a Second Language', *Journal of Educational Psychology* (Washington, D.C.).

Lambert, Wallace E., and Nancy Moore
1966 'Word-Association Responses: Comparisons of American and French Monolinguals with Canadian Monolinguals and Bilinguals', *Journal of Personality and Social Psychology* 3:313–320 (Washington, D.C.). [4.3.]
Lambert, Wallace E., and Chris Rawlings
1969 'Bilingual Processing of Mixed-Language Associative Networks', *Journal of Verbal Learning and Verbal Behavior* 8:604–609 (New York). [4.4.]
Lambert, Wallace E., and S. Witelson
1961 'Concurrent and Consecutive Orders of Learning Two "Languages" ', mimeographed (McGill University). [4.1.]
Lance, Donald M.
1969 *A Brief Study of Spanish-English Bilingualism: Final Report* (= Research Project Orr-Liberal Arts-15504) (College Station, Texas). [2.0., 2.1., 2.2., 3.2., 3.3., 3.4., 3.5.]
Lane, Harlan
1963 'Foreign Accent and Speech Distortion', *Journal of the Acoustical Society of America* 35:451–454 (Lancaster, Pa., and New York). [3.3.]
Larmouth, Donald W.
1967 'Finnish Surname Change in Northern Minnesota', *American Speech* 42:31–37 (New York). [2.2., 5.3.]
Law, H. W.
1961 'Linguistic Acculturation in Isthmus Nahuat', in *A William Cameron Townsend en el vigésimoquinto aniversario del Instituto Lingüístico de Verano* (Mexico City) 555–561.
Le Compte, Nolan Philip, Jr.
1967 'A Word Atlas of Lafourche Parish and Grand Isle, Louisiana', dissertation (Louisiana State University). [2.2.]
Lehtinen, Meri
1966 'An Analysis of a Finnish-English Bilingual Corpus', dissertation (University of Indiana). [*Dissertation Abstracts* 27:4224–4225–A] . [2.2., 3.3.]
Leibowitz, Arnold H.
[n.d.] *Educational Policy and Political Acceptance: The Imposition of English as the Language of Instruction in American Schools* (Distributed by ERIC, Clearing House for Linguistics, Center for Applied Linguistics, Washington, D.C.). [5.4.] .
Lenneberg, Eric
1953 'Cognition in Ethnolinguistics', *Language* 29:463–471 (Baltimore). [5.1.]
1967 *The Biological Foundations of Language* (New York). [5.1.]
Leopold, Werner F.
1939- *Speech Development of a Bilingual Child*, 4 Volumes (Evanston,
1949 Illinois). [1.0]
1956- 'Ein Kind lernt zwei Sprachen', *Sprachforum* 2: 248–252 (Münster.
1957 [1.0., 4.1.]
1957- 'American Children Can Learn their German Mother Tongue', *American*

1958   *German Review* 24:4—6 (Philadelphia). [5.4.]
1960   'Bilingualism of Occupation Children in Germany', in *Festschrift für Hermann M. Flasdieck,* ed. by W. Iser and H. Schabram (Heidelberg) 166—179. [4.1.]
1968   *English Influence on Postwar German* (= *University of Nebraska Studies, New Series* 36) (Lincoln, Nebraska). [4.1.]

Levenston, E. A.
1965   'The "Translation-Paradigm", a Technique for Contrastive Syntax', *International Review of Applied Linguistics in Language Teaching/ Internationale Zeitschrift für angewandte Linguistik in der Spracher-ziehung* 3:221—225 (Heidelberg). [3.1.]

Levinson, Boris M.
1959   'A Comparison of the Performance of Bilingual and Monolingual Native Born Jewish Preschool Children of Traditional Parentage on Four Intelligence Tests', *Journal of Clinical Psychology* 25:74—76 (Brandon, Vermont). [4.5.]

Lieberson, Stanley
1964   'An Extension of Greenberg's Linguistic Diversity Measures', *Language* 40:526—531 (Baltimore). [Reprinted in Fishman, ed. 1968:546—553]. [5.5.]
1966   'Language Questions in Censuses', *Sociological Inquiry* 36:262—279 (Toronto). [5.5.]
1969a 'How Can we Describe and Measure the Incidence and Distribution of Bilingualism?', in Kelly, ed. 1969:286—295. [Commentaries by H. Kloss, K. D. MacRae, E. C. Hughes, E. G. Malherbe]. [5.5.]
1969b 'National and Regional Language Diversity', *Proceedings of the Tenth International Congress of Linguists,* Bucharest, 1967 (Bucharest, Academia), Volume 1, 769—763. [5.5.]
1970   *Language and Ethnic Relations in Canada* (New York, Wiley). [5.5.]

Lieberson, Stanley, ed.
1966   'Explorations in Sociolinguistics', *Sociological Inquiry* 36:2. [Also published in 1967 as Publication 44, Part II, of *International Journal of American Linguistics* 33.2 (Baltimore)]. [1.2.]

Lozano, Anthony G.
1961   'Intercambio de español y inglés en San Antonio, Texas', *Archivum: Revista de la Facultad de Filosofía y Letras (Universidad de Oviedo)* 11:111—138 (Oviedo, Spain). [2.1., 2.2., 3.3., 3.5.]

Lyra, Franciszek
1962a 'English and Polish in Contact', dissertation (Indiana University). [2.2., 3.0., 3.3., 3.4., 3.5.]
1962b 'The Polish Language in the United States: Some Problems and Findings', *The Polish Review* 7/2.81—95 (New York). [2.2., 3.0., 3.3.]
1966   'Polish Surnames in the United States', *American Speech* 41:39—44 (New York). [2.2., 5.3.]

Ma, Roxana, and Eleanor Herasimchuk
1968   'The Linguistic Dimensions of a Bilingual Neighborhood', in Fishman, Cooper, *et al.,* eds. 1968:638—835. [5.2.]

Mackey, W. F.

1956 'Toward a Redefinition of Bilingualism', *Journal of the Canadian Linguistic Association/Revue de l'Association canadienne de linguistique* 2:4—11 (Edmonton, Alberta). [1.0., 1.1.]

1958 Review of Haugen 1956, *Journal of the Canadian Linguistic Association/Revue de l'Association canadienne de linguistique* 4:94—98 (Edmonton, Alberta). [1.0.]

1960 'Bilingualism, *Encyclopedia Britannica,* Fourteenth Edition, Volume 3, 562. [1.2.]

1962 'The Description of Bilingualism', *Journal of the Canadian Linguistic Association/Revue de l'Association canadienne de Linguistique* 7:51—85 (Edmonton, Alberta). [Reprinted in Fishman, ed. 1968a:554—584]. [1.0., 1.1., 3.3.]

1965 'Bilingual Interference: Its Analysis and Measurement', *Journal of Communication* 15:239—249 (Athens, Ohio). [1.0., 3.3.]

1966 'The Measurement of Bilingual Behavior', *The Canadian Psychologist Psychologie canadienne* 7:75—92 (Ottawa). [1.0., 1.1., 5.2.]

1967 'Bilingualism as a World Problem', in *E. R. Adair Memorial Lectures* (Harvest House, Canada). [Also in French: 'Le bilinguisme: phénomène mondial'] . [1.2.]

1970a 'A Typology of Bilingual Education', *Foreign Language Annals* 3:596—608.

1970b *Language and Ethnic Relations in Canada* (New York, Wiley. [5.5.]

1970c 'Interference, Integration and the Synchronic Fallacy', *Monograph Series in Language and Linguistics* 23:195—227 (Georgetown University, Washington, D.C.). [1.0., 3.3.]

McLendon, Sally
1969 'Spanish Words in Eastern Pomo', *Romance Philology* 23:39—53 (Berkeley, Los Angeles). [2.2.]

MacNamara, John
1966 *Bilingualism and Primary Education* (Edinburgh). [5.4.]

1967a 'The Bilingual's Linguistic Performance — A Psychological Overview', *Journal of Social Issues* 23:58—75 (Ann Arbor, Michigan). [4.3., 4.4.]

1967b 'The Effects of Instruction in a Weaker Language', *Journal of Social Issues* 23:121—35 (Ann Arbor, Michigan). [5.4.]

1967c 'The Linguistic Independence of Bilinguals', *Journal of Verbal Learning and Verbal Behavior* 6:729—736 (New York). [3.2., 4.4.]

1967d 'Bilingualism in the Modern World, Introduction', *The Journal of Social Issues* 23:1—7 (Ann Arbor, Michigan). [1.2., 5.2.]

1969 'How Can One Measure the Extent of a Person's Bilingual Proficiency?', in Kelly, ed. 1969:80—97. [Commentaries by A. Tabouret-Keller, E. Nuytens, L. Jakobovits] . [4.3.]

1970 'Bilingualism and Thought', *Monograph Series on Language and Linguistics* 23:25—45 (Georgetown University, Washington, D.C.). [4.4., 4.5., 5.1.]

MacNamara, John Marcel Krauthammer, and Marianne Bolgar
1968 'Language Switching in Bilinguals as a Function of Stimulus and Response Uncertainty', *Journal of Experimental Psychology* 78:208—215 (Washington, D.C.). [4.4.]

102   Einar Haugen

Macris, James
1957 'Changes in the Lexicon of New York City Greek', *American Speech*
32:102–109 (New York). [2.2., 3.4.]
Malmstrom, Jean, and Annabel Ashley
1958 *Dialects – U.S.A.* (National Council of Teachers of English, Champaign,
Illinois). [2.1.]
Manuel, Herschel T.
1960 Bilingualism', *Encyclopedia of Educational Research*, Third Edition
(New York) 146–150. [1.2., 5.4.]
1965 *Spanish-Speaking Children of the Southwest: Their Education and the
Public Welfare* (Austin, Texas). [5.4.]
Marie, Judith H., Harriet R. Frankel, and Nancy Le Floch
1967 'A Study of Bilingualism among Franco-American Children', unpublished paper (= *Association of American Wives of Europeans* 9) (Avenue
Franklin Roosevelt, Paris 8e). [5.4.]
Meller, Norman
1959 'Bilingualism in Island Legislatures of the Pacific as an Index of Acculturation – An Hypothesis', *Sociology and Social Research*
43:408–414 (Los Angeles). [5.3.]
Mencken, Henry L.
1963 *The American Language*, One-Volume Abridged Edition, ed. by Raven
I. McDavid, Jr. (New York). [2.1.]
Metraux, Ruth W.
1965 'A Study of Bilingualism among Children of U.S.-French Parents', *The
French Review* 38:650–665 (Baltimore). [5.4.]
Meyerstein, Goldie Piroch
1959 'Selected Problems of Bilingualism among Immigrant Slovaks', dissertation, (University of Michigan). [*Dissertation Abstracts* 20.1774]. [2.2.,
3.3.]
1966 'Bilingualism among American Slovaks', *Publications of the American
Dialect Society* 46:1–19 (Gainesville, Florida, and University, Alaska).
[2.2., 3.3.]
Michel, Joseph, ed.
1967 *Foreign Language Teaching, an Anthology* (New York). [4.5.]
Mierau, Eric
1963 'Concerning Yavapai-Apache Bilingualism', *International Journal of
American Linguistics* 29:1–3 (Baltimore). [2.2.]
Miller, Mary R.
1969 'Bilingualism in Northern New England', *Publications of the American
Dialect Society* 52:1–23 (Gainesville, Florida, and University, Alaska).
[2.2.]
1970 'The Language and Language Beliefs of Indian Children', *Anthropological Linguistics* 12/2.51–61 (Bloomington, Indiana).
Miller, Robert L.
1968 *The Linguistic Relativity Principle and Humboldtian Ethnolinguistics*
(The Hague). [5.1.]
Miller, Wick R.
1959- 'Spanish Loanwords in Acoma', *International Journal of American*

1960 *Linguistics* 25:147—153, 26:41—49 (Baltimore). [2.2., 3.4.]

Modiano, Nancy
  1968 'Bilingual Education for Children of Linguistic Minorities', *América Indígena* 28:405—414 (Mexico, D.F., Mexico). [5.4.]

Morgan, Raleigh, Jr.
  1959 'Structural Sketch of Saint Martin Creole', *Anthropological Linguistics* 1/8:20—24 (Bloomington, Indiana). [2.2.]
  1960 'The Lexicon of Saint Martin Creole', *Anthropological Linguistics* 2/1:7—29 (Bloomington, Indiana). [2.2.]
  1970 Dialect Leveling in Non-English Speech of Southwest Louisiana', In Gilbert, ed. 1970:50—62. [2.2.]

Moulton, William G.
  1962a *The Sounds of English and German* (= *Contrastive Structure Series*) (Chicago, University of Chicago Press). [3.1.]
  1962b 'Toward a Classificiation of Pronunciation Errors', *Modern Language Journal* 46:101—109 (Ann Arbor, Michigan). [3.1.]

Multilingualism and Socio-Cultural Organization. A Symposium Presented
  1962 at the 1961 Meetings of the American Anthropological Association', *Anthropological Linguistics* 4/1 (Bloomington, Indiana). [1.2.]

Nagara, Susumu
  1969 'A Bilingual Description of Some Linguistic Features of Pidgin English used by Japanese Immigrants on the Plantations of Hawaii: A Case Study in Bilingualism', dissertation (University of Wisconsin). [2.1., 3.3., 3.4., 3.5., 5.3.]

Nahirny, Vladimir C., and Joshua A. Fishman
  1965 'American Immigrant Groups: Ethnic Identification and the Problem of Generations', *Sociological Review* 13:311—326 (Keele, Staffordshire). [5.3.]

Nelson, Agnes
  1956 'A Study of the English Speech of the Hungarians of Albany, Livingston Parish, Louisiana', dissertation (Louisiana State University) [*Dissertation Abstracts* 17.694—695]. [2.1., 3.3.]

Nemser, William Joseph
  1961 'The Interpretation of English Stops and Interdental Fricatives by Native Speakers of Hungarian', dissertation (Columbia University) [*Dissertation Abstracts* 22.1168—1169]. [2.1., 3.1., 3.3.]
  1969 'Approximative Systems of Foreign Language Learners', in *Yugoslav Serbo-Croatian — English Contrastive Project*, B1 (Zagreb) 3—12. [3.1.]
  1970 'Contrastive Linguistics at the Center for Applied Linguistics' Center for Applied Linguistics Newsletter 12/3:1—5 (Washington, D.C.). [3.1.]

Nemser, William Joseph, and F. Juhasz
  1964 'A Contrastive Analysis of Hungarian and English Phonology,' *ACLS* Project 70:163—216. [3.1.]

Nemser, William Joseph, and T. Slama-Cazacu
  1970 'A Contribution to Contrastive Linguistics (A Psycholinguistic Approach: Contact Analysis'), *Revue roumaine de Linguistique* 15:101—128 (Bucharest). [3.1., 3.3.]

Nida, E. A.
1957-   'Some Psychological Problems in Second-Language Learning', *Language*
1958   *Learning* 8:7–15 (Ann Arbor, Michigan). [4.2.]
Nyholm, Paul C.
1963   *The Americanization of the Danish Lutheran Churches in America*
         (Institute for Danish Church History, Copenhagen). [5.3.]
Ohannessian, Sirarpi
1968   *Planning Conference for a Bilingual Kindergarten Program for Navajo
         Children. Conclusions and Recommendations, October 11–12, 1968*
         (Washington, D.C., Center for Applied Linguistics). [5.4.]
Oksaar, Els
1970   'Bilingualism', in *Current Trends in Linguistics,* Volume 9, *Linguistics
         in Western Europe,* ed. by Thomas A. Sebeok (The Hague, Mouton)
         476–511. [1.0.]
Olesch, Reinhold
1970   'The West Slavic Languages in Texas with Special Regard to Sorbian in
         Serbin, Lee County', in Gilbert, ed. 1970:151–162. [2.2.]
Oliver, Joseph D.
1970   *Social Determinants in Communication Events in A Small Bilingual
         Community in New Mexico* (ERIC Clearing House for Linguistics,
         Center for Applied Linguistics, Washington, D.C.). [5.3.]
Ornstein, Jacob
1970   'Sociolinguistics and Southwest Spanish', in *Studies in Language and
         Linguistics,* ed. by Ralph W. Ewton, Jr., and Jacob Ornstein (El Paso,
         Texas, Texas Western Press) 127–184. [1.2., 2.2.]
Oswalt, Robert L.
1958   'Russian Loanwords in Southwestern Pomo', *International Journal of
         American Linguistics* 24:245–247 (Baltimore). [2.2., 3.4.]
Paulsen, Frank M.
1967   'Danish-American Folk Traditions, A Study in Fading Survivals', disser-
         tation (Indiana University). [*Dissertation Abstracts* 28.4069–A].
         [2.2.]
Peal, Elizabeth, and Wallace E. Lambert
1962   'The Relation of Bilingualism to Intelligence', *Psychological Mono-
         graphs: General and Applied* 76:1–23. [Reprinted in Michel
         1967:143–191]. [4.5.]
Penfield, Wilder
1964   'The Uncommitted Cortex: The Child's Changing Brain', *The Atlantic
         Monthly* (July): 77–81 (Boston, Mass.). [4.1.]
Penfield, Wilder, and Lamar Roberts
1959   *Speech and Brain Mechanisms* (Princeton). [Chapter on 'The Learning
         of Languages' reprinted in Michel 1967:192–214]. [4.1., 4.4.]
Perkowski, Jan Louis
1964   'A Kashubian Idiolect in the United States', dissertation (Harvard
         University) (LSM 2, 1969). [2.2., 3.3.]
1970   'A Survey of West Slavic Immigrant Languages in Texas', in Gilbert, ed.
         1970:163–169. [2.2., 3.5.]

Philips, Susan U.
1970 'Acquisition of Rules for Appropriate Speech Usage', Monograph Series on Language and Linguistics 23:77—101 (Georgetown University, Washington, D.C.). [5.1.]
Phillips, Robert Nelson, Jr.
1968 'Los Angeles Spanish: A Descriptive Analysis', dissertation (University of Wisconsin). [*Dissertation Abstracts* 28.2667]. [2.2., 3.3.]
Pietrzyk, Alfred, ed.
1964 'Selected Titles in Socio-Linguistics', mimeographed (Washington, Center for Applied Linguistics).
Pike, Kenneth L.
1960 'Towards a Theory of Change and Bilingualism', *Studies in Linguistics* 15:1—7 (Buffalo, New York). [1.1.]
1967 *Language in Relation to a Unified Theory of the Structure of Human Behavior* (The Hague, Mouton). [1.1.]
Pilati, Leona Lampi
1969 'The Fox Dialect: The Influence of Finnish on a Local American English Dialect', *Neuphilologische Mitteilungen* 70:145—158 (Helsinki). [2.1.]
Pohl, J.
1965 'Bilinguismes', *Revue Roumaine de Linguistique* 10:343—350 (Bucharest). [1.1.]
Poulter, Virgil L.
1970 'A Comparison of Voiceless Stops in the English and Spanish of Bilingual Natives of Fort Worth, Dallas', in Gilbert, ed. 1970:42—49. [2.2.]
Preston, M. S.
1965 'Inter-Lingual Interference in a Bilingual Version of the Stroop Color-Word Test', dissertation (McGill University). [4.4.]
Raffler-Engel, Walburga von
1961 'Investigation of Italo-American Bilinguals', *Zeitschrift für Phonetik, Sprachwissenschaft und Kommunikationsforschung* 14:127—130 (Berlin). [1.1.]
Raun, Alo
1968 'Native Speaker and Distinctive Features', *Lingua* 21:346—350 (Amsterdam). [3.1.]
Rayfield, Joan R.
1970 *The Languages of a Bilingual Community* (= *Janua Linguarum series practica* 77) (The Hague, Mouton). [2.2., 3.2., 3.3., 3.4., 3.5.]
Reed, Carroll E.
1961 'Double Dialect Geography', *Orbis* 10:308—319 (Louvain). [2.2.]
1967 'Loan-Word Stratification in Pennsylvania German', *German Quarterly* 40:83—86 (Appleton, Wisconsin). [2.2.]
1971 'The Dialectology of American Colonial German', in Gilbert, ed. 1971:3—13.
Reed, Carroll E., and Lester W. Seifert
1954 *A Linguistic Atlas of Pennsylvania German* (Marburg/Lahn). [2.2.]

Reinecke, John E.
1969 *Language and Dialect in Hawaii: A Sociolinguistic History to 1935*, ed. by Stanley M. Tsuzaki (Honolulu, University of Hawaii Press). [2.1., 5.3.]
Reinecke, John E., and Stanley M. Tsuzaki
1967 'Hawaiian Loanwords in Hawaiian English of the 1930s', *Oceanic Linguistics* 6:80—115 (Honolulu). [2.1., 3.4.]
Roeming, Robert R., ed.
1965 'Bilingualism and the Bilingual Child — a Symposium', *Modern Language Journal* 49:143—174, 220—239 (Ann Arbor, Michigan). [1.2., 5.4.]
1971 'Bilingualism and the National Interest', *Modern Language Journal* 55:73—81 (Ann Arbor, Michigan). [5.4.]
Royal Commission on Bilingualism and Biculturalism. 1965—, Ottawa. [1.2., 5.4., 5.5.]
1965 *Preliminary Report.*
1967 Book I: *The Official Languages.*
1968 Book II: *Education*
1969 Book III: *The Work World.*
1970 Book IV: *The Cultural Contribution of the Other Ethnic Groups.*
Rudnyćkyj, J. B.
1968 Review of Fishman 1966a, *Language* 44:198—201 (Baltimore). [1.2., 5.3.]
1972 'Immigrant Languages, Language Contact and Bilingualism in Canada', in *Current Trends in Linguistics*, Volume 10: *Linguistics in North America*, ed. by Thomas A. Sebeok (The Hague, Mouton) 592—652. [1.0., 2.2.]
Sandfeld, Kristian
1938 'Problèmes d'interférences linguistiques', in *Proceedings of the Fourth International Congress of Linguists*, 59—61. [3.0.]
Sapir, Edward
1929 'The Status of Linguistics as a Science', *Language* 5:207—214 (Baltimore). [5.1.]
Saporta, Sol, Robert E. Brown, and W. Dean Wolfe
1959 'Toward the Quantification of Phonic Interference', *Language Sciences* 2:205—210 (Bloomington, Indiana). [3.3.]
Saville, Muriel R., and Rudolph C. Troike
1970 *A Handbook of Bilingual Education*, revised edition. (Washington, D.C., TESOL, Center for Applied Linguistics). [5.4.]
Sawyer, Janet Beck Moseley
1958 'A Dialect Study of San Antonio, Texas: A Bilingual Community', dissertation (University of Texas). [*Dissertation Abstracts* 18.586]. [2.1.]
1959 'Aloofness from Spanish Influence in Texas English', *Word* 15:270—281 (New York). [5.3.]
1964 'Social Aspects of Bilingualism in San Antonio, Texas', *Publications of the American Dialect Society* 41:7—15 (Gainesville, Florida, and University, Alabama). [5.3.]

1970 'Spanish-English Bilingualism in San Antonio, Texas', in Gilbert, ed. 1970:18—41. [2.1.]

Schönfelder, K.-H.
1957 *Deutsches Lehngut im amerikanischen Englisch: Ein Beitrag zum Problem der Völker- und Sprachmischung* (Halle). [2.1., 2.2., 3.4., 3.5.]

Seaman, Paul David
1965 'Modern Greek and American English in Contact: A Socio-Linguistic Investigation of Greek-American Bilingualism in Chicago', dissertation (Indiana University). [2.2., 3.3., 3.4., 3.5.]

Seeger, Mary A.
1970 'English Influence on the Language of the Dodge County Pioneer, Mayville, Wisconsin', dissertation (University of Wisconsin). [2.2.]

Segalowitz, Norman, and Wallace E. Lambert
1969 'Semantic Generalization in Bilinguals', *Journal of Verbal Learning and Verbal Behavior* 8:559—566 (New York). [4.4.]

Seifert, Lester W. J.
1946 'Wisconsin German Questionnaire', typescript (Madison, Wisconsin). [3.5.]
1963 'Stress Accent in Dane County (Wisconsin) *Kölsch*', *Monatshefte für Deutschen Unterricht* 55:195—202 (Madison, Wisconsin). [2.2.]
1967 'Word Atlas of Pennsylvania German', *Forschungsinstitut für deutsche Sprache* 8—9 (Marburg/Lahn). [2.2.]
1971 'The Word Geography of Pennsylvania German: Extent and Causes', in Gilbert, ed. 1971:14—42. [2.2.]

Selinker, Larry
1966 'A Psycholinguistic Study of Language Transfer', dissertation (Georgetown University). [*Dissertation Abstracts* 27.2518A]. [3.1., 3.4.]
1969 'Language Transfer', *General Linguistics* 9:67—92 (Lexington, Kentucky). [3.1., 3.4.]

Shetter, William Z.
1957 'Brabants dialekt in Wisconsin', *Taal en Tongval; Tijdschrift voor de Studie van de Nederlandse Volks- en Streektalen* 9:183—190 [2.2.]
1958 'A Final Word on Jersey Dutch', *American Speech* 33:243—251 (New York). [2.2., 3.3.]

Shuy, Roger, ed.
[n.d.] *Social Dialects and Language Learning. Proceedings of the Bloomington, Indiana, Conference 1964* (National Council of Teachers of English, Champaign, Illinois). [2.1.]
1968 *A Selective Bibliography on Social Dialects* (Washington, D.C., Center for Applied Linguistics). [2.1.]

Smith, Gail McBride
1969 'Some Comments on the English of Eight Bilinguals', in Lance, ed. 1969:17—24. [2.1., 2.2., 3.3.]

Smith, Madorah E.
1957 'Word Variety as a Measure of Bilingualism in Preschool Children', *Journal of Genetic Psychology* 90:143—150 (Provincetown, Mass.). [4.5.]

108   *Einar Haugen*

Soffietti, James P.
1955 'Bilingualism and Biculturalism', *Journal of Educational Psychology* 46. 222—227 (Washington, D.C.). [Reprinted in *Modern Language Journal* 44 (1960):275—277]. [1.1., 5.1.]

Spicer, Edward M.
1962 *Cycles of Conquest. The Impact of Spain, Mexico, and the United States on the Indians of the Southwest, 1533—1960* (Tucson, University of Arizona Press). [2.2.]

Stella, Sister Maris
1959 'A Note on the Pronunciation of New England French', *French Review* 32:363—366 (Baltimore). [2.2., 3.3.]

Stern, H. H.
1967 *Foreign Languages in Primary Education* (London). [Originally published in 1963 as one of the International Studies in Education of the Unesco Institute for Education, Hamburg] . [5.4.]

Stewart, William
1962 'An Outline of Linguistic Typology for Describing Multilingualism', in *Study of the Role of Second Languages in Asia, Africa, and Latin America*, ed. by F. A. Rice (Washington, D.C., Center for Applied Linguistics) 15—25.
1967 'Sociolinguistic Factors in the History of American Negro Dialects', *The Florida Foreign Language Reporter* 5:2.1—4 (Tallahassee, Florida). [2.1.]
1968 'A Sociolinguistic Typology for Describing National Multilingualism', in Fishman, ed. 1968:531—545. [5.5.]

Stewart, William, ed.
1966 *Clearinghouse for Social Dialect Studies* (= *Current Social Dialect Research at American Higher Institutions. Report 2*, Nov. 15). [2.1.]

Stockwell, Robert G., and J. Donald Bowen
1965 *The Sounds of English and Spanish* (Chicago). [3.1.]

Stockwell, Robert G., J. Donald Bowen, and John W. Martin
1965 *The Grammatical Structures of English and Spanish* (Chicago). [3.1.]

Stolt, Birgit
1964 'Die Sprachmischung in Luthers Tischreden. Studien zum Problem der Zweisprachigkeit', *Stockholmer germanische Forschungen* 4 (Stockholm).
1969 'Luther sprach "mixtim vernacula Lingua" ', *Zeitschrift für deutsche Philologie* 88:432—435 (Berlin). [3.0., 3.2., 3.4.]

Theory and Practice in English as a Foreign Language (Ann Arbor,
1963 Michigan). (Selected articles from *Language Learning* 2 [Ann Arbor, Michigan]). [3.1.]

Theriault, George F.
1960 'The Franco-American of New England', in *Canadian Dualism*, ed. by Mason Wade (Toronto) 392—411. [2.2.]

Tisch, Joseph Le Sage
1954 *French in Louisiana: A Study of the Historical Development of the French Language of Louisiana* (New Orleans). [2.2., 5.3.]

1957   *Des expressions courants en Louisiane aujourd'hui* (Alexandria, Louisiana). [2.2.]
Topping, Donald M.
1962   'Loanblends, a Tool for Linguists', *Language Learning* 12:281–287 (Ann Arbor, Michigan). [3.4.]
Totten, G. O.
1960   'Bringing up Children Bilingually', *American-Scandinavian Review* 48:42–46 (New York). [5.4.]
Troike, Rudolph C.
1956   'Comanche Linguistic Acculturation: A Critique', *International Journal of American Linguistics* 22: 213–215 (Baltimore). [2.2.]
Tsuzaki, Stanley Mamoru
1968   'Common Hawaiian Words and Phrases Used in English', *Journal of English Linguistics* 2:78–85 (Bellingham, Washington). [2.1.]
1970   *English Influences on Mexican Spanish in Detroit* (= *Janua Linguarum series practica* 107) (The Hague, Mouton). [2.2., 3.3., 3.4.]
Tsuzaki, Stanley Mamoru, and Samuel H. Elbert
1969   'Hawaiian Loanwords in English', *General Linguistics* 9:22–40 (Kansas City). [2.1., 3.4.]
Tsuzaki, Stanley Mamoru, and John E. Reinecke
1966   *English in Hawaii: An Annotated Bibliography* (= *Oceanic Linguistics, Special Publication* 1 [1966]) (Honolulu, Pacific and Asian Linguistics Institute, University of Hawaii). [1.2., 2.1.]
Upshur, J. A.
1962   'Language Proficiency Testing and the Contrastive Analysis Dilemma', *Language Learning* 12:123–127 (Ann Arbor, Michigan). [3.1.]
Ureland, Sture*
1970   'Preliminary Report on Texas-Swedish Research 1968–1969', in *The Nordic Languages and Modern Linguistics*, ed. by H. Benediktsson (Reykjavík) 540–550. [1.1., 2.2.]
Valette, Rebecca M.
1964   'Some Reflections on Second-Language Learning in Young Children, *Language Learning* 14:91–98 (Ann Arbor, Michigan). [4.1.]
Vaněk, Anthony L.
1967   'The Hierarchy of Dominance Configuration in Trilingualism', *Letopis* A 14/2 (Bautzen). [2.2.]
Vent, Henriette
1957-   'Reply to Margaret Hofmann', *American German Review* 24:39–40
1958   (Philadelphia). [5.4.]
Viereck, Wolfgang
1967   'German Dialects Spoken in the United States and Canada and Problems of German-English Language Contact Especially in North America: A Bibliography', *Orbis* 16:549–568 (Louvain). [1.2., 2.2.]
1968   'Supplement to Viereck 1967', *Orbis* 17:532–535 (Louvain).
Vinay, J.-P.
1969   'Problèmes de bilinguisme au Canada', in Kelly, ed. 1969:367–401. [5.5.]

Voegelin, C. F., F. M. Voegelin, and Noel W. Schutz, Jr.
  1967 'The Language Situation in Arizona as Part of the Southwest Culture
        Area', in Hymes and Bittle, eds. 1967:403—451. [2.2.]
Wacker, Helga
  1956 'Untersuchungen zur Gestalt der deutschen Schriftsprache beim
        Deutschtum der Vereinigten Staaten, Kanadas und Australiens sowie
        Südafrikas, Palästinas und Südamerikas: auf Grund der Sprache der
        überseeischen deutschen Zeitungen', Ph.D. dissertation (Tübingen).
        [2.2.]
  1964 *Die Besonderheiten der deutschen Schriftsprache in den USA*
        (= *Duden-Beiträge, Herausgegeben von Hugo Moser* 14) (Mannheim).
        [2.0., 2.2., 3.4., 3.5.]
Ward, Barbara Taylor
  1969 'Analysis of the English of Four Spanish-Speaking Foreign Students', in
        Lance, ed. 1969:25—45. [2.1., 2.2.]
Waterhouse, Viola
  1949 'Learning a Second Language First', *International Journal of American
        Linguistics* 15:106—109 (Baltimore). [2.2.]
Weinreich, Uriel
  1953 *Languages in Contact: Findings and Problems* (= *Publications of the
        Linguistic Circle of New York* 1) (New York). [Reprinted 1963, The
        Hague]. [1.0. *et passim.*]
  1954a 'Is a Structural Dialectology Possible?', *Word* 14:388—400 (New York).
        [Reprinted in Fishman, ed. 1968:305—319]. [1.1.]
  1954b 'Linguistic Convergence in Immigrant America'. Fifth Georgetown
        Roundtable, *Monograph Series on Language and Linguistics* 7:40—49
        (Georgetown University, Washington, D.C.). [2.2.]
  1957a 'On the Description of Phonic Interference', *Word* 13:1—11 (New
        York). [3.1., 3.3.]
  1957b 'Functional Aspects of Indian Bilingualism', *Word* 13:203—233 (New
        York). [5.2., 5.5.]
  1958 'Research Frontiers in Bilingualism Studies', *Proceedings of the Eighth
        International Congress of Linguistics,* Oslo, 1957 (Oslo, Oslo University
        Press) 786—797. [1.2.]
Wenger, Marion R.
  1965 'Swiss Dialect Islands in Ohio and Indiana', dissertation (Ohio State
        University). [2.2.]
Willibrand, W. A.
  1957a 'When German was King: A FLES Program around 1900', *German
        Quarterly* 30:254—261 (Appleton, Wisconsin). [5.4.]
  1957b 'English Loan Words in the Low German Dialect of Westphalia,
        Missouri', *Publications of the American Dialect Society* 27:16—21
        (Gainesville, Florida and University, Alabama). [2.2., 3.4.]
Wolfram, Walter A.
  1969 *A Sociolinguistic Description of Detroit Negro Speech* (= *Urban Lan-
        guage Series, Center for Applied Linguistics* 5) (Washington, D.C.).
        [2.1.]

Yugoslav Serbo-Croatian — English Contrastive Project, A. Reports 1—6, B. 1969-1972 Studies 1—4, C. Pedagogical Materials 1. (Zagreb). [3.1.]
Zhluktenko, Iurii Oleksiiovych
1964 *Ukrains'ko-anhliis'ki mizhmovni vidnosyny; ukrains'ka mova u SShA i Kanadi* (Kiev). [2.2.]

ADDENDA

Bessason, Haraldur
1971 'Isländskan i Nordamerika'. *Språk i Norden* 1971: 57—77 (Oslo).
Currie, Eva G.
1950 'Linguistic and Sociological Consideration of Some Populations of Texas'. *The Southern Speech Journal* 11:286—96.
Ervin-Tripp, Susan, and C. E. Osgood
1954 'Information Transmission with Code Translation', *Journal of Abnormal and Social Psychology* 20: 185—192.
Graham, Robert Sommerville
1955 'The Anglicization of German Family Names in Western Canada', *American Speech* 30: 260—265.
Hasselmo, Nils
1971 Det svenska språket i Amerika. *Språk i Norden* 1971: 125—62 (Oslo).
Haugen, Einar
1971 'Norsk i Amerika: Studier og status'. *Språk i Norden* 1971: 111—23 (Oslo).
Kimple, James, Robert Cooper, and Joshua A. Fishman
1969 'Language Switching and the Interpretation of Conversation', *Lingua* 23: 127—134.
Stine, Clyde S.
1939 'Bilingualism in the Pennsylvania Schools', *Pennsylvania School School* 87: 339—340.
Tucker, R. W.
1934 'Linguistic Substrata in Pennsylvania and Elsewhere', *Language* 10: 1—6.
Ureland, Sture
1971 'Report on Texas-Swedish Research'. *SLSE* 1971:27—74.
Virtaranti, Pertti
1971 'Finskan i Amerika'. *Språk i Norden* 1971:79—109 (Oslo).

Reprinted with permission from *Current Trends in Linguistics*, ed. by Thomas A. Sebeok, Volume 10, *Linguistics in North America*. (The Hague, Mouton, 1973).

Some (German-English) Language Contact Phenomena at the Discourse Level

As very little investigation has taken place so far of discourse phenomena in monolingual corpuses, it is natural that language contact
studies have been restricted almost entirely to units up to and
including the sentence.[1] For the purpose of this article, we shall
regard each of our taped interviews with German-English bilinguals in
Australia as one *discourse*. In the interviews the 330 informants (first
to fourth generation Australians living in urban 'melting pot' situations or in rural former *Sprachinseln*) were required to describe
pictures, relate experiences, and retell stories of books or television
programs. (Each informant was interviewed on one occasion only.) A
change of topic could mark the start of a new paragraph (*cf.*
Longacre 1969; Young and Becker 1965). We shall use the term
'sentence' informally and characterize it with Glinz (1952:74) as
'kleinste Sprecheinheit ... die kleinste Atemeinheit der normal
dahinfließenden Rede'.

   In his pioneering article Hasselmo (1970) considers the role of
preformulated discourse segments ('linguistic routines') such as
jokes, daily exchanges on the weather, health and neighbors, greeting
and leave-taking routines, and of *discourse markers*. Under the
latter heading Hasselmo includes (from his study of Swedish in
America, 1961):
(1) Sentence-initial (linking) sequence signals such as *and, but, however, anyway, consequently;*
(2) Those markers keeping the channel open between interlocutors,
e.g., *listen, you know, I tell you;*
(3) Markers signalling specific types of content units, e.g., *for instance*
(exemplification), *that is* (amplification), *something like that* (approximation), *and so on* (unspecified inclusion).
There are three other matters which I would like to raise:

Reference, i.e., the relationship between a *morphosemantic transfer* (word transferred in form and meaning) in one sentence and items from either code (German, English) in other sentences.

Quotation, i.e., how what the speaker or another interlocutor has said is *cited*, and its effects on transference, integration, and switching.

Switching within the discourse, i.e., how and where switching is likely to occur beyond the sentence level.

It is hoped that these considerations will enable us to propose a discourse model for bilingual corpuses and to suggest similarities and differences between language contact phenomena at the discourse level and in smaller units.

DISCOURSE SEGMENTS

The nearest to Hasselmo's 'preformulated discourse segments' in our corpus are stories of migration and first impressions of Australia (among the first generation) and 'old times', including school stories and grandfather stories (among descendants of pioneer settlers). Of the shorter routines, thanking and greeting would be relevant as sociolinguistic indices of the assimilation of German-speaking migrants. (*Cf.* Neustupny's [1968] speech patterns.) On leaving a shop after making a purchase a German will say: *Danke schön, auf Wiedersehen!* The unassimilated migrant will integrate this as *Thank you, goodbye!* when the Australian English equivalent would be Ø or simply *Thank you!* Similarly, unassimilated migrants transfer German *please — thank you* patterns to reply to offers — i.e., *please* for an affirmative reply, *thank you* for a negative one. In Australian English the answer to *How are you (going)?* is normally *How are you (going)?* but many migrants transfer the German routine of actually answering the question. On the other hand, very assimilated migrants transfer Australian English routines into German contexts. Direct investigations of such patterns among migrants of different language backgrounds in Australia could produce some interesting data on a discourse problem beyond the purely linguistic level.

DISCOURSE MARKERS

Hasselmo demonstrates how such 'signals' as *and, but,* and *of course* are transferred into 'American-Swedish' discourse. Both within 'sentences' and between them in a stretch of discourse *and* and *but* characterize the speech of our German-English bilinguals, e.g.,

Wir haben eine Farm in Rosebury /*and*/ in neunzehnhundertsixty-three haben wir / die Farm verkauft. Oh / nich' man kann nich' / ist ein deutsches Wort für das /*but*/ what's 'gum' in German?[2]

In the German of bilinguals in Australia *but* is frequently tagged on to the end of a sentence, e.g.,

Ich weiß nicht, wieviele Tausend's kost' / ich hab' vergessen / *but* . . .

and functions as a sort of 'filled pause' (Maclay and Osgood 1969:24). *And* and *und* are employed alternately by most of the informants who transfer *and*.[3] *Und* then usually retains its cumulative function within a sentence, while *and* acts as a 'sentence-initial sequence signal' or more prominently as a marker keeping open the channel, e.g.,

Das sind mehrere Taxen / *and* [ɛnd] Lieferwagen / *and* [ɛnd] eine Menge Personenkraftwagen auf der Straße geparkt.
Cf. by the same informant: Wir cutten Gras *und* harken es zusammen.

Das les' ich die 'Konstanze' / das ist eine deutsche Frauenzeitung *and* // Oder wenn es ein schöner Tag is', geh' ich 'raus in'n Garten *und* arbeit' ich im Garten.

Ich arbeit' an der Monash University / *and* / in dem German Department / *and* / what else do you want to know?
Cf. by the same informant: Schafe *und* Stockman auf sein Pferd.

While *well* can also be a rhetorical device to add an element of caution to the following statement, it, like *and* and *but*, serves to keep open the communication channel and can be regarded as a lexicalized filled pause. It often opens a new section of discourse (paragraph), e.g.,

Well / dieses Bild ist in einer Stadt.

Well, morgens um 7 Uhr steh' ich auf . . .

The frequency of *well* in German discourse may be attributed to the absence of an 'equivalent' in German. *You know,* in addition to giving a note of caution to a preceding statement, may serve to keep the speaker in control of the conversation. *Just a minute!* and *Wait on!* unambiguously fulfil the latter function. *Anyway* and *anyhow* which, like *and* are given by Hasselmo as examples of sequence signals, could also fit into the second category of discourse markers, e.g.,

Dann wasch' ich ab und zieh' meinen Sohn an. *Anyway,* was mach' ich dann?

'Markers signalling specific types of content units' (e.g., *for instance, and so on*) are rarely transferred in our corpus:

... je nachdem wie man gespart hat, *of course*

although there are occasional *semantic* transfers (sememe from one code transferred to lexeme of other code), e.g.,

Er jagt die foxes und rabbits *und alles.*

We thus have one group of transferred discourse markers which *refer back* to a previous sentence of the discourse, producing either a link (*but, and*) or a break with it (*Rubbish!, Sorry!, O.K. then!*), and another that keep the channel open for the next part of the discourse to follow (*well, you know, just a minute!*). The second group and many examples of the first group are very similar to, or forms of, hesitation phenomena. (They also correspond largely to the interjection tagmemes in Longacre 1969.)

   A link with a question posed by the field worker is expressed in the corpus by *Sorry!, Alright!, O.K. then!, Oh boy!, Oh my goodness!* and *Jees!* and a link with the speaker's own previous sentence(s) by *Gosh!, Sorry!, Oh blow!, That's wrong!, Rubbish!, Doesn't matter!, That's about all!, That's it!, let's scrap that!, What else!* and *is it?* (or the semantic transfer *is' es?*), e.g.,

... und haben schöne Spaziergänge gemacht / *Ah, what else did we do?* Dann / dann sind wir einkaufen gewesen.

Field Worker: Könnten Sie mir bitte den Verlauf eines typischen

Tages beschreiben?
Interviewee: Eines hübschen Tages?
Field Worker: Eines typischen Tages!
Interviewee: Ah. Typischen. *Sorry!*

However, the first-person and second-person-orientated markers are generally interchangeable.

Anyway can be used as an 'erasing' hesitation phenomenon at the discourse level, e.g.,

Wie ich gesehen habe, dieses particular Bild ist / *Anyway*, dies' Bild zeugt nicht von einem sehr fruchtbaren Boden.

Another example of this kind:

Ich habe eine colourfulle / *I'm sorry!* (*I'm sorry!* 'erases' the false start.)

Such discourse markers as *Sorry!*, *Jees!*, *Oh my goodness!* and *Oh blow!* are late lexicalizations which may be explained as deleted performatives (Ross 1970).

The markers *Excuse me!*, *Oops!* and to some extent *Sorry!* can refer to extra-linguistic (non-verbal) factors (e.g., treading on someone's foot) as well as to linguistic (verbal) ones. It is at the discourse level, especially in relation to *reference*, that it is perhaps most difficult to isolate purely linguistic factors. (This is borne out by the model, symbols, and examples proposed in Isenberg 1968.) That the English 'equivalents' are preferred to *Entschuldigung!* (*Verzeihung!*) and *Oppla!* may be attributed to habitual English lexicalization of the (*apologize*) sememe. The speaker usually apologizes to English-speaking interlocutors or to bilinguals and the planning of the apology becomes automatic and inflexible (*cf.* Miller, Galanter, and Pribram 1960:82).

So far we have considered discourse markers mainly from the speaker's point of view, although we have shown how some of the markers connect the field worker's and interviewee's speech. Hasselmo cites *uh-huh, yes,* and *is that so* as examples of receiver's signals which indicate that 'he is indeed attentive' (Hasselmo 1970:185). Owing to the nature of our corpus (interviews) we have not recorded many instances of this. However, some of our informants do transfer *yes* and *no* as sentence-initial discourse signals. What factors induce an interlocutor to respond with a *yes* or *no* rather than with the corresponding interjection in the 'migrant language' has interested scholars working on Norwegian, Swedish, and Dutch in the United States. Haugen, in his *The Norwegian Language in America* (1953:92) writes: 'The interjection *nå* 'no' has largely replaced the N *nei,* but the N *ja* has rarely been replaced by *jess.* Since *yah* is the usual midwestern word for *yes* in Am Eng., possibly through German-Scandinavian influence, the result is that the yes-no system in Am N is exactly like that of Am Eng.' Hasselmo has found a similar pattern in his 'American Swedish' corpus.[4] Daan (1970) is also struck by '. . . the almost complete lack of Dutch *nee* beside Eng. *no* as opposed to the high frequency of Dutch *ja* beside Eng. *yes* . . .' However, she attributes this to the difference in function between English *yes* and Dutch *ja.*

In 'Australian German' it is only in the old German settlements that there is any tendency worth reporting. Among our 250 first-generation migrant informants, *yes* was recorded twelve times from one speaker and once from another, and one speaker employed *no* once. However, in the Tarrington area — one of the old German settlements in Victoria — there was a clear tendency towards the use of *no* rather than *nein,* and in other former *Sprachinseln* — the Victorian Wimmera and the Barossa Valley-Hahndorf-Lobethal district of South Australia — there was a considerable occurrence of *no.* *Yes* was also transferred but much less frequently in proportion to instances of *ja.* (In the calculations below we are not including *ja* as an expletive, *Er ist ja nicht gekommen,* or as a question marker, *Also? Sie kommen morgen wieder, ja?,* both peculiarly German uses.) The presence of the transferred *yes* in 'Australian German' may prove Haugen's explanation about its absence in 'American Norwegian'. (This would also apply to 'American Swedish' and 'American Dutch'. Incidentally, the use of *yah* is widespread in informal Australian English.) It is more the *no-nein* relationship that needs to be elucidated in our corpus.

Different settlements produced somewhat varying results (see Table I). The Barossa Valley and the other South Australian settlements studied are noted for their 'retentiveness' and 'purism' and there are indications of revitalization (Clyne 1968; Paul 1965:136). This accounts for the great predominance there of *ja* and *nein.* Many of our informants employed both sets of interjections in their German but very few used *ja* or *nein* in English discourse. Some speakers followed the interjection from one code by that from the other code

for emphasis in German discourse: *yes ja, ja yes, nein no, no nein.*
Where emphasis was placed on the affirmative, *ja* was employed,
often preceded by [ɔx], [ɔ:], or [ɛ·ω], or repeated twice or three
times. (*Oh yes* occurred rarely, if so, mainly interrogatively or as an
attention marker with appropriate intonation.) Emphasis may partly
explain the high frequency of *ja* as opposed to *yes.* We can thus
derive *ja* from

      Es ist (± emph.) der Fall

      daß X

and *yes* from

      Es ist (– emph.) der Fall

      daß X (Cf. Lakoff 1968:111ff.)

For negative emphasis *no* or *nein* was generally repeated or preceded
by *oh.* While some of the informants, especially in Tarrington, did
not employ *nein* at all, the majority of our 'settlement' bilinguals
showed free variation between *no* and *nein* with *no* becoming a sort
of stylistic variant of *nein,* both being derived from

      Es ist (± emph.) nicht der Fall

      daß X

REFERENCE

Any word (or group of words) can evoke not only a use of the same
word earlier in the discourse but the whole section of experience
surrounding previous parts of the discourse by reminding the hearer
of the statement of which the word was part. It can refer back to

Table I.

	Tarrington (Western Victoria) 25 informants	Barossa Valley, Hahndorf, Lobethal (South Australia) 68 informants	Murtoa-Minyip (Wimmera, N.W. Victoria)[a] 30 informants	Total (123)
yes	35	23	118	176
ja	125	286	417	828
yeah	7	6	69	82
[jas]	–	2	–	2
nein	15	41	139	195
nee	–	1	–	1
no	60	22	97	179

[a] We are omitting the figures for two informants, – one a compulsive *yes* user (61 instances) and one a compulsive *yeah* user (50 instances), as they were not typical in this respect.

something expressed by a synonym (*Auto* referring back to *Wagen*) or an 'implying word' (*Hochzeit* implies *Braut* so that word can be employed without any previous explicit reference; similarly *Blume* implies *Pflanze*). This is formalized by Isenberg (1968) for nouns in consecutive sentences. How much reference is made between items from the two languages in contact depends on the individual speaker. He may use the German lexeme and the corresponding English one in more or less *free variation* in a stretch of discourse, e.g.,

Das ist ein Bild von ein' *Strand,* wo Leut' schwimmen oder sich sonnen. Im Hintergrund ist ein Berg und Gebüsch und ein paar Häuser am Abhang. Man sieht die Fahne von den life-savers, die in Australien fast an jeder *beach* zu finden sind. Leut' haben Sonnenschirm' und der hitzt ein bißchen, ein Schatten zu gebilden (*sic!*) und / das ist eigentlich friedlich. Sonst sind die *Stränder* in Australien ein bissele überfüllt.

Viele *Schafe* / wenig Menschen / 's ungefähr die right rechte Proposition (= *Proportion*), die man hier hat / bevölkerungsmäßig zu den *sheeps* / Sagen wir, ungefähr hundert *Schafe* zu einem Mann.

He may on the other hand contrast semantically the morphosemantic transfer (word transferred into another code in form and meaning) with the corresponding German lexeme, e.g.,

... die zwei *Hirten*, wie man auf deutsch sagt. Aber natürlich sind das eigentlich *drovers*.

Das ist ein Foto, gemacht an der *beach* / ... the scenery is' / nearly dasselbe, wie wir in Deutschland haben / an der / am *Strand*. (Cf. Australian *beach*; German *Strand*).

In the second type semantic integration has taken place.

CITATION

In bilingual discourse there are three possibilities of communication which we should account for in our analysis:
(1) The interlocutors *A* and *B* employ both codes (English and German) in communication;
(2) *A* speaks German to *B*, and *B* speaks English to *A*, while *A* and *B* understand both codes, and this form of communication is effective;
(3) *A* speaks and understands two codes, one of which *B* does not speak and understand.
In all these cases it is necessary to quote 'across codes'. If one of the interlocutors wishes to refer to something in the same or another discourse in the other code he has the following means of doing it:
    (a) *A quotation-phrase clause or sentence,* i.e., within a stretch of discourse in one code the speaker switches into the other for the phrase clause or sentence cited, e.g.,

... hat sie gesagt / es gehört doch ein *carpet* dazu / a Teppich[5] / '*a old, faded carpet*' / And she said'*Don't* / *Watch that nobody treads on my old, faded carpet!*' (Original speech situation: 3, converted to interview situation: 1.)

Dann später kriegte ich ein' Brief von England / von Mrs. Borgers / und die schrieb zu mir: '*Do you remember? You're coming to visit us!*' (Situation 1.)
Mrs. Reher said to him: '*Wer sind denn doch die Männer do her?*' / And she answered / Oh, Hannah / that was her daughter / answered: '*Berger und Wenschmute!*' / Yes, they were over in the paddock. (Original speech situation: 3, converted to interview situation: 1.)

This issue was raised by Haugen (1953). He mentions that one of his informants switches in order to quote an English speaker (*cf.* also Hasselmo 1970:201).

(b) *Lexical replacement in the quotation,* i.e., the lexemes of the quotation are in the code of the discourse but the syntax is still that of the code of the original. This amounts to a syntactic transfer or 'loan idiom'. The category is negligible as far as our corpus is concerned, occurring only in one example:

Unser Sohn sitzt für Examen morgen. (Original speech situation: 2, converted to 'ideal' interview situation: 3.)

(c) *Lexicosyntactic replacement in the quotation,* i.e., the construction and all or some of the lexemes of the original are replaced, e.g.,

'That's not good' and *'Das is' no good'* and *'He has to have that'* und 'Er hat das und jenes zu haben.' (Original speech situation: 2; interview situation: 2. The speaker speaks mainly at home.)

The interchange of *and* and *und* may be explained by consequential and anticipational triggering (see Clyne 1967:84—89.)
Original: 'What's going on here?'
Quotation: 'Was geht denn hier an?'
    When either the interlocutor or a third person is cited in the other code (i.e., not the code of the discourse) a quotation-word may be inserted merely as a morphosemantic transfer, e.g.,[6]

A: 'Habt Ihr einen Löffel?'
B: 'We'll share a *löffel*'.
C: 'Ein sehr schöner Mann. Er's ganz schwarz. Schwarz wie Kohl'.
D: 'But he's not so *schwarz!*'

Original: 'Kommt zum deutschen Gottesdienst!'
Quotation: Ich sagte: 'No, now you come to the *deutschen Gottes-dienst!'* (All situation 2).

As situation 2 is very prevalent in migrant homes as the pattern of communication between parents and children, it is desirable that as many 'normal' conversations in the home as possible be recorded.

DISCOURSE SWITCHING

Some attention has been given to switches within a sentence (Hasselmo 1961, Clyne 1967, Chapter V; Stolt 1964). A switch within a stretch of discourse may sometimes be triggered by a quotation-clause or sentence (one instance is the *And she said* in the first example under [a]).
A switch may accompany the use of a transferred discourse marker, e.g.,

Das is' irgendeine beach. Welche das is' / das kann ich nicht sagen. *It doesn't matter. I think so.*

Wenn ich mich so fühle, geh' ich 'raus in den Garten und / *well* / *look after my flowers.*

A previous investigation (Clyne 1969) showed that in speech marked by an abundance of switching the phenomenon occurred most frequently after discourse markers of Hasselmo's second class; *and, anyway,* and especially *well.* These can be regarded as 'lexicalized filled pauses' (see above) which, as they are used in both the English and the German discourse of the speakers and represent a time gap since the last lexeme of unambiguous affiliation, produce a triggering effect.
In his article 'How Do We Measure the Effects which One Language May Have on the Other in the Speech of Bilinguals?' Hasselmo recommends that configurations of codeswitching be examined at the discourse as well as the sentence level (1969:140). In my corpus I have found that where a switch occurs between two sentences within a stretch of discourse — even one 'internally conditioned' by a trigger-word — it may take place between *textual topic* and *comment*, e.g.,

Topic: Wir haben jedes Jahr a camp; sechs Tag.[7]
Comment: I only came back from it last week.

Topic: Das ist ein Foto, gemacht an der beach.
Comment: Could be, kann be / kann sein in Mount Martha.

Topic: Aber Mutti laßt mi net an ihrem Auto schaffe.
Comment: I wonder why.

Topic: Trockenes Land.
Comment: Northern Territory, perhaps.

Topic: Ich kann nicht kegeln oder Squash spielen.
Comment: Only fifth and sixth formers can do that.

Topic: Ein typisches Melbourne-Bild.
Comment: Melbourne in Collins Street or Bourke Street.

Topic: Er was Mr. Fred Berger / Der wohnte da in Gnadenthal.
Comment: And he went down there one day.

Such switches between topic and comment occur also within a
sentence, e.g.,

That's an Australian gum-tree and das ist was dieses Bild so typisch
australien landscape macht.

though they may be more frequent and more easily discernible at the
discourse level.

   A switch within the speech of one interlocutor can be conditioned
by a previous switch on the part of his speech partner when introducing a new 'discourse routine'. In nearly all our interviews informants were asked to describe a picture in English or to talk in
English. Most of them were able to switch automatically into
English. A more voluntary variation on this is where the interlocutor
reads an extensive quotation in, say, *L1* after speaking *L2*, and a
subsequent question or statement from the speaker is then in *L1*, e.g.,

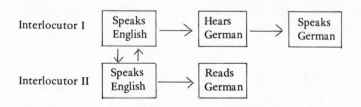

By the end of the quotation (or statement) the interlocutor no
longer remembers that the previous sections of the discourse were in
L2.

INTEGRATION

Just as with the transference of smaller units, integration and stabilization varies. Hasselmo (1970:207) suggests that at least some of the English discourse units introduced into Swedish discourse are used with such regularity that they may be regarded as 'integrated'. Some of the German (English) exchange routines (e.g., greeting, accepting offers) are integrated linguistically into English (German) discourse but remain foreign in pattern and can cause confusion in communication. The more limited availability of discourse markers in one language — especially of those which have the function of keeping the channel open — together with a spontaneous habitual lexicalization of certain hesitation and apology routines lead to integration and merger of discourse markers among bilinguals. The same applies to *no* in some idiolects. In others *yes* and *no* are apparently integrated as stylistic variants to avoid too much repetition. We have attempted to show above how quotations can be integrated in varying degrees into discourse in the other code. Contrast of normally 'synonymous diamorphs' (Haugen 1956:47) in reference at the discourse level is indicative of semantic integration. Whether a speaker switches for the quotation or integrates it lexically and/or grammatically may depend on the speaker's and hearer's attitude to the 'mixing' of codes at the discourse level: see Figures 1 and 2.

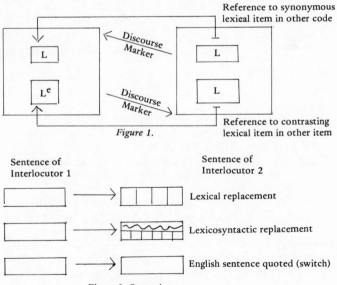

Figure 1.

Figure 2. Quotation.

DISCOURSE AND LOWER LEVELS

The use of morphosemantic transfers, the semantic integration of a
transfer (Clyne 1967:74) so that it contrasts with a 'native' item, and
the partial integration of a sentence by means of lexical and lexicosyntactic replacements (Clyne 1970) have been observed in the study
of language contact at other levels. So has the phenomenon of
switching. At the sentence level we have attempted to distinguish
between internally and externally conditioned switching though in
some cases, as in the lower levels, it is not clear whether a trigger-
word or a concept is anticipated. Discourse markers-cum-hesitation
phenomena can function as 'trigger-elements', though it may be
hesitation itself or 'interference between modes of speaking' (Hasselmo 1970:208) that sets off the switch. While the introduction of a
new routine by the interlocutor may be regarded as an externally
conditioned switch at the lower level, at the discourse level it is really
internally conditioned, for the passage or quotation acts as a 'trigger-
element' within the discourse.

More investigations into monolingual and bilingual discourse
would make possible a refined model to replace these preliminary
remarks on German-English contact phenomena at the discourse
level.

BIBLIOGRAPHY

Clyne, Michael G.
 1967   *Transference and Triggering* (The Hague, Nijhoff).
 1968   'Decay, Preservation, and Renewal: Notes on Some Southern Australian
        Settlements', *AUMLA* 29:33–43.
 1969   'Switching Between Language Systems', in *Actes du Xe Congrès Inter-
        national des Linguistes,* Bucharest, 1967 (Bucharest. Academy),
        pp. 343–349.
 1970   'German-English Bilingualism and Linguistic Theory', in *Dichtung,
        Sprache, Gesellschaft*. Proceedings of the 4th International Ger-
        manists' Congress, Princeton, 1970, forthcoming.
Daan, J.
 1970   'Bilingualism of Dutch Immigrants in the U.S.A.', in *Dichtung, Sprache,
        Gesellschaft*. Proceedings of the 4th International Germanists' Congress,
        Princeton, 1970, forthcoming.

Glinz, Hans
1952 *Die innere Form des Deutschen* (Bern, Francke).
Harris, Zellig S.
1952 'Discourse Analysis', *Language* 28:1—30 (Baltimore).
Hasselmo, Nils
1961 'American-Swedish: A Study in Bilingualism', unpublished Ph.D. thesis (Harvard University).
1969 'How Can We Measure the Effects Which One Language May Have on the Other in the Speech of Bilinguals?', in *Description and Measurement of Bilingualism: An International Seminar,* ed. by L. G. Kelly (Toronto, University of Toronto Press) pp. 121—141.
1970 'Code-Switching and Modes of Speaking', in *Texas Studies in Bilingualism* (= *Studia linguistica Germanica* 3), ed. by G. Gilbert (Berlin, de Gruyter) pp. 179—210.
Haugen, Einar
1953 *The Norwegian Language in America: A Study in Bilingual Behavior* (Philadelphia, University of Pennsylvania Press; Oslo, Gyldendal Norsk Forlag).
1956 *Bilingualism in the Americas: A Bibliography and Research Guide* (University, Alabama, American Dialect Society; University of Alabama Press).
Isenberg, H.
1968 'Überlegungen zur Texttheorie', mimeographed (Berlin, Arbeitsstelle für strukturelle Grammatik).
Koch, W. A.
1965 'Preliminary Sketch of a Semantic Type of Discourse Analysis', *Linguistics* 12:5—30 (The Hague).
Lakoff, Robin
1968 *Abstract Syntax and Latin Complementation* (Cambridge, Mass., M.I.T. Press).
Longacre, R. E.
1969 'Discourse, Paragraph and Sentence Structure in Selected Philippine Languages', mimeographed.
Maclay, H., and C. E. Osgood
1969 'Hesitation Phenomena in Spontaneous Speech', *Word* 15:19—44 (New York).
Miller, G. A., E. Galanter and K. H. Pribram
1960 *Plans and the Structure of Behavior* (New York, Holt, Rinehart, and Winston).
Neustupný, J.
1968 'Some General Aspects of "Language" Problems and "Language" Policy in Developing Societies', in *Language Problems of Developing Nations,* ed. by J. A. Fishman, C. A. Ferguson, and J. Das Gupta (New York, Wiley) pp. 285—294.
Paul, P.
1965 'Barossadeutsch', unpublished M.A. thesis (University of Adelaide).
Ross, John R.
1970 'On Declarative Sentences', in *Readings in Transformational Grammar,*

ed. by R. A. Jacobs and P. S. Rosenbaum (Waltham, Mass., Blaisdell) pp. 222–272.

Stolt, Birgit
1964   *Die Sprachmischung in Luthers 'Tischreden': Studien zum Problem der Zweisprachigkeit* (= *Stockholmer Germanistische Forschungen* IV) (Stockholm: Almqvist & Wiksell).

Young, R. E., and A. L. Becker
1965   'Toward a Modern Theory of Rhetoric: A Tagmemic Contribution', *Harvard Educational Review* 35:450–468.

NOTES

Reprinted with permission from *Studies for Einar Haugen*, ed. by Evelyn Firchow *et al.* (The Hague, Mouton, 1971).
The Research project on German-English Bilingualism in Australia is supported by a grant from the Australian Research Grants Commission.

1. I agree with Hasselmo (1970: footnote 5; 181) that the procedures for discourse analysis proposed by Harris (1952) and Koch (1965) have no direct bearing on this type of analysis.
2. / denotes *short pause.*
3. Hasselmo (1970:187) also reports alternation among his bilinguals.
4. Nils Hasselmo in personal communication: 'E *no* has replaced Sw *nej* in all environments . . . E *yes* alternates with Sw *ja* . . . but has not replaced the Sw item in any community or informant.'
5. Speaker is of Swabian descent.
6. See also the first example under (a).
7. Speaker is of Swabian descent.

Triglossia and Swahili-English Bilingualism in Tanzania

This article addresses itself to the study of the sociological correlates of speech behavior among bilingual speakers of English and Swahili in Tanzania. Factors influencing language maintenance, code-switching, and code-mixing are discussed. Four main phases of language acquisition are considered: the pre-primary school phase, the primary school phase, the secondary school phase, and the post-secondary school phase.

Three languages with both varying and overlapping roles interact, creating a triglossia situation: first the vernacular or mother-tongue of each particular ethnocultural group; second Swahili, the local *lingua franca* and national language; third English, the predominant language of higher learning and to a certain extent of official and commercial business.

This paper also discusses the diglossia relationship between the vernacular and Swahili on the one hand and Swahili and English on the other. The developmental state of the languages is dealt with in terms of socially 'restricted' and 'elaborated' codes.

Urban life tends to impose its own sociocultural influences on the bilinguals. There is free shifting and mixing between Swahili and English interlocutors, topics, and setting.

Lastly the article raises questions of the sociological and linguistic consequences of the multilingual situation. (Multilingualism, diglossia; code-switching; code-mixing; Swahili; English, national language problems.)

In the last ten years a great deal of attention has been given to the study of the psychological and sociological correlates of speech behavior. Theoretical frameworks have been suggested within which functional roles of language or codes in bilingual and diglossia situations can be assessed. It is refreshing to see that most of these studies are oriented towards problems of practical import such as the relationship between acquisition of a particular language or code to learning processes; the psychological and sociocultural consequences of bilingualism; and the linguistic or structural effects (maintenance, code-switching, and interference) resulting from situations of sustained contact between languages.

Factors affecting language maintenance and code-switching are multi-dimensional and vary from situation to situation (not to mention individual to individual). That is why it is essential to study as many different situations as possible if only to test the present hypotheses as to what phenomena are likely to be present when certain situational factors obtain.

This article attempts a preliminary study of the variables affecting language maintenance, code-switching and language mixing among bilingual speakers of Swahili and English in Tanzania in the context of the general situation of triglossia that prevails for such speakers.[1]

Three related and overlapping factors seem to influence the mode of language maintenance and code-switching among the bilinguals discussed here: the sociological context of language acquisition (the sociocultural settings[2] in which the languages have been acquired and used); the communicative function of each language (for what purpose each language now is used, when speaking what, and to whom); the communicative capacity of each of the languages involved (the state of development of each language in terms of its adequacy in a situation of modernization).[3]

In all, fifteen respondents were interviewed to determine language acquisition patterns and subsequent language behavior. The cases were characteristic of the general modes of language acquisition and use in the country. They comprised people with varying educational and socioeconomic backgrounds. Eight were university graduates employed in professional or executive occupations, six had the equivalent of secondary or high school education with middle type white-collar or skilled jobs, and one had only primary school education but through experience had acquired very good control of English.

The respondents interviewed were all then living in Dar-es-Salaam, the capital city. Having lived in the same city continuously for nearly three years and having mixed freely with all social groups, and particularly those who are often referred to as the western-educated 'elite', I came to the conclusion that the respondents represented fairly well the linguistic behavior of urban Tanzanians, particularly of the age group of thirty and over. Interviews were restricted to those of this age group who had received their formal primary and secondary school education before the 1960s (i.e., before the country's independence) because patterns of language acquisition are bound to change gradually as more emphasis is put on the development of Swahili as the primary national, official language. For example, at the present time the language is used as the only medium of instruction in primary schools, and there is official intention of gradually introducing it as a medium of teaching in the secondary school system. Also, there is now a deliberate policy of using Swahili as the official language of correspondence within the civil service and parastatal bodies, in the armed forces, the police, the National Youth Service, and even as the primary language of parliamentary debating. This is greatly enhancing the prestigious status of Swahili at the national level *vis-à-vis* English and the vernacular languages, with a possible consequent effect of gradually altering patterns of language acquisition and behavior among people of younger generations. Thus the particular age group studied here serves as a sort of central or baseline for later developments; it would seem that up to the time of the conclusions here drawn they defined quite reliably the outlines of the general language behavior of those entering urban life.

PATTERNS OF LANGUAGE ACQUISITION

Four main phases of language acquisition and use were found. These were (1) pre-primary school, (2) primary school, (3) secondary school, and (4) post-secondary school (including present situation).

(1) In the pre-primary school phase three groups could be distinguished. The first group (three respondents) comprised those who knew no other language apart from the mother-tongue vernacular. The parents, relatives, friends, and generally the ethnocultural community of respondents in this group either knew no Swahili or, if they did, insisted on speaking only in the vernacular in situations of intragroup communication. The second group of respondents, besides having a vernacular as the first and primary language of socialization and communication in their area, also knew some Swahili. Both parents (and especially the father) knew and used Swahili at home as a secondary medium of communication. This was also true of the immediate community. Almost all the respondents in this group (ten) said that before going to the primary school they did not

realize that they were speaking (or mixing) two distinct languages.[4] Respondents in the third group (two) had Swahili as their first and only language of communication and socialization in the pre-primary school phase. These were people born in urban areas on the coast.

(2) Phase two of language acquisition context was characterized by primary school environment. All the respondents said that the primary school was situated within their own mother-tongue area. All school contacts (with the possible exception of some of the teachers) were speakers of the same mother-tongue as themselves. However, Swahili was the medium of instruction throughout primary school life for all but three respondents. In the case of the three, who came largely from monolingual rural areas, instruction in the first two standards was in the vernacular but Swahili was introduced right from the beginning as a subject. Swahili then took over as a medium of teaching in the rest of the primary school. So in all cases Swahili was the primary language of learning and in most cases alternated with the vernacular as playground language.

The main feature of the primary school phase in the case of most vernacular-speaking respondents was that Swahili became the language both of learning and of a wider (national) and more varied sociocultural orientation. It afforded them a comparatively more sociologically elaborate code than the vernacular. The two languages were in a complementary kind of relationship, giving rise early to the phenomenon of code-switching as the sociocultural contexts based on the vernacular and Swahili alternated. First literacy (facility for reading and writing) for all but three was gained in Swahili. English was taught as a subject from the fourth standard in many schools. The teachers of English, however, were non-native speakers of English; most of them were themselves primary school leavers (with or without teacher-training background).

It was in the secondary school phase that major changes in patterns of acculturation, language acquisition, and use occurred. In all cases the secondary schools were situated outside the vernacular areas.[5] The secondary school was a meeting place of children from diverse linguistic and cultural backgrounds. For all of them Swahili was the primary language of communication and the basis of acculturation into the wider sociocultural norms and values of the country. Swahili was taught as a subject at this level (i.e., in the period before the 1960s). The pupils were introduced to the more advanced written forms of the language including literary styles. By the time they had completed secondary school they had developed a very good control of Swahili partly because they had now been exposed to the more formal school teaching of the subject, but perhaps even more because the language now had become the primary language of face-to-face interaction especially outside the school compound. They could now use it creatively in its various registers including slang and colloquial forms.

A significant factor in the secondary school phase was that English was not only taught seriously but also functioned as the medium of learning (often even in the teaching of Swahili). Throughout secondary school great emphasis was laid upon the teaching of English and acquisition of it was vital to the successful completion of secondary school education. (In fact it has been the belief of many educationists that total academic performance of a pupil varies proportionally with his degree of control of English; though no testing has been done to prove this I think it is reasonable to assume that this might be true, everything else being equal, as long as the medium of instruction and examination remains English.) Most of the teachers, if not all, were English-speaking expatriates, although there might have been a few African teachers with university or equivalent education. English language and literature were taught mostly by native speakers of English.

There was great enthusiasm on the part of the pupils to acquire as good a control of English as possible because of its socioeconomic prestige. All respondents said that there were regulations (breach of which resulted in school-type punishment) requiring pupils to use only English in the school compound. As all secondary schools were boarding schools, pupils were exposed to a great deal of English in the four or five years of secondary education. However, the English that was learned was rather 'bookish', taught with little reference to its sociocultural matrices. There was little opportunity at this level for free socialization with native speakers of English. Schools were segregated due to the policy of racial compartmentalization, and on most occasions contact of African pupils with native speakers of English was limited to their teachers and missionaries. The contact was essentially a formal contact restricting language use to formal pupil-teacher-priest forms. The type of English acquired, therefore, though adequate for school topics, could not cover all the sociocultural settings in which the pupils found themselves, especially those settings requiring informal, slang, colloquial, or affective usages. Consequently Swahili continued to be the basis of affective socialization inside and outside school in spite of the regulations insisting on the use of only English, except perhaps where the respondents were speakers of the same mother-tongue. English, however, had now established itself very strongly as a language of learning, in which the cognitive aspects of the new cultural world were based. Swahili and English were in a complementary relationship giving rise to code-switching between them as cultural settings shifted.

(4) In the post-secondary school phase the respondents spent most of their lives outside mother-tongue or vernacular areas (apart from occasional visits). All of them were now living in areas in which Swahili and English alternated as primary languages depending on the interlocutors and/or the topics being discussed. The vernacular now had become a weak tertiary language. Of the fifteen respondents, eight had received a university-type education in East Africa and/or abroad. These had greater facility in using English in its various registers and said that they had no problem in maintaining English both in .written and spoken forms. But they admitted that their fluency was frequently reduced in slang and idiomatic usages. They also found it difficult to use English effectively in deeply affective and humor settings especially when talking to English speakers.[6] Among Swahili interlocutors English could be used to function in certain sociocultural contexts normally associated with Swahili.[7]

TRIGLOSSIA

These cases of language acquisition reflect the general language situation of Tanzania, a situation of intersection between two developing diglossia situations, one involving Swahili and some vernacular and the other involving Swahili and English. From the standpoint of most of the individuals just described, the situation might be called one of triglossia, nor is triglossia here a term simply for trilingualism. As in the original classic definition of diglossia by Ferguson (1959), there are differences between the language varieties not only in external circumstances of use but also in internal characteristics, in this case communicative capacity. The relations between the language varieties are not such as to maintain strict segregation: there is code-mixing in conversation as well as code-switching. Such mixing is facilitated between the vernaculars and Swahili by their common base (over 90 percent of the population speak languages which belong to the Bantu family) although code-mixing between Swahili and non-Bantu vernaculars would seem equally common (in the latter case there might be significant structural differences in the way the two languages are mixed, as there are between Swahili and English, but this is not the subject of this article). As between Swahili and English, such mixing seems to be due to the present overlap of the functional ranges of the two languages, and also to habit perhaps arising from lack of constraint to language mixing. In the speech behavior of the respondents code-mixing involving the vernacular, Swahili, and English also occurred within one utterance.

Vernacular and Swahili

A certain diglossia situation exists between the vernacular and Swahili. The vernacular is used as intragroup language (often mixed with Swahili) of ethnocultural identification and solidarity. Typically, the vernacular manifests a rural African sociocultural life characterized by a subsistence peasant/pastoral socioeconomic organization. It is learned and used almost wholly in face-to-face situations. Although the vernacular is adequately expressive of its own sociocultural contexts it may be considered in a sociological sense 'a restricted code' (to use Bernstein's term):

> The most general condition for the emergence of this code is a social relationship based upon a common extensive set of closely shared identifications and expectations self-consciously held by the members. It follows that the social relationship will be one of an inclusive kind. The speech is here refracted through a common cultural identity which reduces the need to verbalize intent so that it becomes explicit, with the consequence that the structure of the speech is simplified, and the lexicon will be drawn from a narrow range. The extra-verbal component of the communication will become a major channel for transmitting individual qualifications and so individual difference. The speech will tend to be impersonal in that it will not be specially prepared to fit a given referent . . . The meanings are likely to be concrete; descriptive or narrative rather than analytical or abstract. In certain areas meanings will be highly condensed. The speech in these social relations is likely to be fast and fluent, articulatory clues are reduced; some meanings are likely to be dislocated, condensed, and local (there will be a low level of vocabulary and syntatic selections; *the unique meaning of the individual is likely to be implicit*) (Bernstein 1965:127–8).

Swahili is based on a more urban type of African culture and, although it has a greater range of syntactic and lexical differentiations than the vernacular, it is still in its basic form representative of a pre-industrialized non-technological culture. In this sense it is somewhat a restricted code in that it does not yet adequately cover all the sociocultural domains introduced by the adoption of facets of modern technological culture (although great efforts are being made now in Tanzania to develop it into a working modern language of the nation). Swahili is considered the language of culture and communication at the national level. There would seem to be no conflict or competition between the vernacular and Swahili except that when speaking to elders it is considered good manners to maintain the vernacular, which manifests in a better way the role and value systems of the vernacular culture. Among the younger and more detribalized speakers there is a merging of role and value distinctions based on Swahili and the vernacular, with Swahili systems often dominating. For example, eleven of the respondents said that they maintain the vernacular completely only when speaking to people who do not understand Swahili (and there are now few of these, perhaps less than 10 percent). A commoner situation is to switch between the vernacular and Swahili as topics change or even in the middle of a sentence. The vernacular is not much used in writing; letters to vernacular speakers who do not understand English are often written in Swahili. The reason would seem to be that it was in Swahili that literacy in most cases was first introduced at the primary school phase. Also Swahili has fairly well standardized written forms.

Swahili and English: Code-Choice and Code-Capacity

A different diglossia situation exists between Swahili and English. English is generally the dominant language of official business, commercial and legal transactions, and higher education. It is also a language through which almost all world literature and technological and scientific information is acquired. It is an elaborated code in a complementary relationship with Swahili. Of the elaborated code Bernstein says:

> The verbal planning here, unlike the case of a restricted code, promotes a higher level of syntactic organization and lexical selection. The preparation and delivery of relatively explicit meaning is the major function of this code. This does not mean that these meanings are necessarily abstract, but abstraction inheres in the possibilities. The code will facilitate the *verbal*

transmission and elaboration of the individual's unique experience (1965:128).

An elaborated code, through its regulation, induces in its speakers a sensitivity to the implications of separateness and difference and points to the possibilities inherent in a complex conceptual hierarchy for the organization of experience (1967:128).

However, English is still spoken effectively by only a small percentage of the population (perhaps 15 percent). There is still no socioeconomic class of Tanzanian speakers who operate only in English. For almost all bilinguals Swahili remains the effective language of socialization and communication within the broad community.[8]

Most respondents said they write and listen to the radio in English even if equivalent information is available in Swahili. For example, eleven of the respondents never bought Swahili newspapers or magazines or listened to radio news bulletins in Swahili (except in the case of important information presented only in Swahili). Four read and listen to both English and Swahili materials. They do this mainly because of a personal or professional interest in Swahili materials. As to writing, eleven of the respondents did it mostly in English. Swahili was used in writing only to relatives who do not understand English at all or not very well. Three respondents said that they did their writing in both English and Swahili. However, as will be shown below, code-mixing occurs even in writing.

Reasons given by bilinguals as to why they prefer to read and listen to materials in English when the information is also available in Swahili are (1) they can read English faster than Swahili, (2) it is easier to understand what *exactly* is meant when material is in English than when it is in Swahili. The first reason would seem to be due to the fact that most of their reading habits and skills were developed through reading materials in English. Also there is little material in Swahili that appeals to people with secondary or higher education. Most of the available literary materials are likely to have been read at school. The second reason is of a more linguistic nature: there are certain lexical and structural reasons why bilinguals prefer to read and listen to materials in English. English possesses a greater range than Swahili of lexical differentiations to cope with modern settings requiring precise or technical terminologies.

A few examples will illustrate this: the English sentence 'he died of an acute alcoholic poisoning' was translated in a first radio news

bulletin as *alifariki kwa kutokana na mvinyo mkali aliokunywa*
(literally 'he died as a result of drinking alcohol with a very high
alcoholic content'); in the second news bulletin the same sentence
was translated *alikufa kwa kunywa pombe nyingi* (literally 'he died
as a result of drinking too much alcohol'). The word 'kidnap' was
rendered in Swahili as *kutorsosha* which in Swahili connotes the
meaning of 'eloping' of a boy and a girl, or generally of helping
someone to escape (i.e., with his own connivance). The legal phrase
'hostile witness' was once rendered *shahidi mjeuri* (literally 'insolent
witness'). Such Swahili equivalents of English terms are coined *ad hoc*
by bilingual translators and news editors who are under immediate
pressure to translate into Swahili news originally conceived and
written in English. Present English-Swahili dictionaries are inadequate and innovators have to rely on the genius of Swahili readers
or listeners to disambiguate the referential contents of the new terms
through hearing them frequently in contextual usages. Ironically it is
the bilingual speakers who are likely to guess correctly the intended
meaning of a new term the first time they hear it, as they might have
earlier read or heard the same information in English. Also, translators are often in the habit of transferring from English to Swahili
complex sentence structures in journalistic style when translating
English sentences into Swahili. The result frequently is long and
tedious Swahili sentences that are difficult to follow because of their
oddity. For example, the sentence below is a translation of the
English sentence above it, both taken from a bilingual news bulletin.
It has an almost identical structure to the English sentence:

> For the first time in his long sojourn on earth, man was able —
> in the words of U.S. poet Archibald Macleish — 'to see the earth
> as it really is, small, blue and beautiful in that eternal silence
> where it floats', and men could also 'see ourselves as riders on
> the earth together'.

> *Kwa mara ya kwanza katika safari yao hiyo ya mwezini,*
> *mwanadamu aliweza kuona — chambilecho cha mshairi wa*
> *Kiamerika Archibald Macleish — 'dunia kama ilivyo, ndogo, ya*
> *baluu na nzuri katika upekwe ule wa kipekee ambako inaelea',*
> *na wanadamu 'tukaweza kujiona wenyewe kama ni wapandaji*
> *wa pamoja wa ardhi hii'.*

As a result of the structural borrowing the above Swahili sentence is
odd and extremely vague.

In the case of formal written forms it would seem that it is easy to
predict what language choice will be made, given the nature of the

topic, the interlocutors, and the setting; the same is true of spoken forms in formal settings such as university lectures, religious services, political speeches, meetings, court situations, and ceremonial occasions. For example, at the time of this research official correspondence between different ministries was mostly in English; there was a good deal of Swahili used in correspondence with regional administration. In such parastatal bodies as the national banks and insurance agencies English was the primary and almost the only language used. On official forms of application there was a tendency for both English and Swahili versions although the English versions predominated. Ordinances and other legal documents were in English.

The medium of university lecturing was English, as were general academic activities except in the teaching of Swahili. Religious services were conducted in English and Swahili at different times to give the participants a choice of language they preferred in this setting. In the case of Moslem congregations prayers were conducted in Arabic while sermons were usually in Swahili (this was in the capital city). Political meetings involving the masses or within the ruling party were conducted in Swahili. High courts conducted their business in English although interpreters might be used if one or more of the participants did not understand this language.

Predictability is possible here because to a large extent one must, out of considerations of efficiency of communication and of appropriateness in a country with a clear-cut national policy, use as much Swahili as possible, except where not yet possible for some technical or linguistic reasons. But in formal letter writing code-mixing would seem to occur. For example, one of the respondents kindly allowed me to quote a relevant part of his letter below (Swahili in italics):

Dearest . . .

Wajionaje siku hizi? Mi Mzima wa afya; hofu kwako, pole na shughuli . . . ama kwa kweli nina hamu yakuwa . . . imeniishia . . . and I think I have sound reasons for doing so — personal rather than indoctrinated — but may be prejudiced, I don't know . . . My stay there might be a problem (and it is a problem, for it isn't a visit), but I do hope you will in time inform me of any inconveniencies you envisage, and why not, your own suggestions are also welcome . . . *tafadhali huo ni msaada wako ambao nakuomba. Nadhani nisiseme zaidi ya hapo na natumai tumeelewana . . .*

With love from . . .

CODE-CHOICE AND CODE-MIXING IN FACE-TO-FACE SITUATIONS

What is extremely difficult to predict is language choice between
bilinguals in face-to-face situations. In most cases there is constant
and unpredictable code-switching and language-mixing even when
discussing highly technical subjects such as zoology, medicine, or
engineering. It is not a simple case of lexical borrowing to fill lexical
gaps in given English or Swahili sentences. Frequently this happens
even if equivalent Swahili-English lexical items exist. A few examples
of sentences actually uttered will illustrate this phenomenon of
mixing Swahili and English in sentences (Swahili in italics).

Mlikuwa mna different classes (you had different classes).

Wanalay wapi foundation (where are they laying the foundation).

Ile accident *Ilitokea alipolose* control *Na Aka*overturn and
landed in a ditch (the accident occurred when he lost control
and overturned . . .).

Wambie wakupe up-to-date image *ya yaltiyotokea* so that you
can go ahead with it, *si mambo madogo haya* (tell them to give
you an up-to-date image of what happened so that you can go
ahead with it. These are not small matters.) *Hii* cultural contact,
*wako waafrika wanao*enjoy Indian songs, they even sing them,
wanavyozipenda. (This cultural contact, there are Africans who
enjoy Indian songs, they even sing them so much do they like
them.)

Zile hormones *za uvyazi za* tilapia *zategemea zile* environmental
factors *zinazowaathiri hawa* tilapia. (The reproductive hormones of tilapia depend upon how the environmental factors
have been impinging on tilapia.)

The following is an extract from a tape-recorded verbal report by a
research assistant (Swahili in italics).

Inakuwa maana yake they go against their own wishes *ku*standardize, *maana wengi sana katika* legal affairs *hawaja*standardize
*bwana, matatizo haya wameweze kuya*solve *kwa kutumia* dictionary *mpya* published by the legal Research Bureau of the
University. *Umeiyona bwana? na wanao* legal translators
wanaweza kutumia maneno katika legal terms *za kiingereza* but
they cannot use them as they wish. *Barua* of everyday colloquial Swahili *wanaweza kuandika lakini ile* typical *maana
yake* typical *mambo wanayotumia katika* legal affairs *tu kama
wanavyoji*repeat *yaani katika ile* correspondence *yao wana*

translators *wao wenyewe* except *maana yake* tourism, information, high court *na* justice division. *Wengi katika* ministries *wana*
tendencies *za kutumia hizi* bilingual expressions *za kiswahili.*
Kisha nikaenda kwa bwana he's been there for some time. *Barua*
za ministry *Katika wizara wana* tendency *kuandika kiingereza*
maana medium *ilikuwa kiingereza. Sasa ndio wameanza kutu-*
mia direct approach to *masomo ya kiingereza na anasema kuwa*
inadequacy *anasema kuwa* amount of materials and tests for
students' use *hapa* university *anasema ni ndogo sana, anasema*
hii ni complaint often voiced by the students themselves *labda*
materials *zenyewe kiasi* it's enough *maana yake* again *hawana*
textbooks *za kiswahili iko* inadequacy compared *uki*compare *na*
English Department . . . *lakini* of course *wanasema ni kitu kipya*
but . . .

In urban situations, in which this enquiry was mainly made, Swahili
and English function in a bicultural situation of great complexity.
There has been rapid modernization in the past ten years through the
introduction of new styles of living. Bilinguals of the type we are
considering here have suddenly found themselves assuming new
socioeconomic roles as executives, academics, businessmen, tech-
nologists, officers in the forces, and politicians, roles that the colonial government did not in their education system specifically train
them to assume. Cultural adjustments have to be made constantly as
roles change. These often require switches between Swahili and
English. For example, one of the respondents was an economist who
worked mostly with English speakers (expatriates). During most of
his working hours he was compelled to maintain English. His wife
was bilingual in the vernacular and Swahili (but did not have English)
with the vernacular as her primary and Swahili her secondary language of communication with the husband. His young daughter went
to a mainly expatriate primary school where the medium of teaching
was English. She was bilingual in Swahili and English with English as
her primary language at school and when speaking to some of her
playmate neighbors. When speaking to his wife the respondent
switched between the vernacular and Swahili or mixed them depending on the topic. With his child he spoke mostly in English as he
wanted her to improve her knowledge of this language so that it
might help her at school. The child normally maintained English
when talking to her father and Swahili when talking to the mother.
She did not normally mix English and Swahili.

Certain social-psychological situations seem to influence language maintenance among the bilinguals. One of the respondents said that whenever he argued with his bilingual wife he would maintain Swahili as much as possible while she would maintain English. A possible explanation is that Swahili norms and values assign different roles to husband and wife (socially more clear-cut?) from the English norms and values (socially less clear-cut or more converging?). Maintaining one language or the other could then be a device for asserting one's desired role. Swahili is thus often an exponent of one set of roles and English of another and generally (since overlappings occur) those for Swahili are more informal. For example, one could create a situation of social distance by just maintaining English with a bilingual stranger. In Swahili, roles are based on national values, and it would be more difficult to create a feeling of distance without appearing rude or arrogant (or too much of a 'black Englishman'). Also due to less established hierarchical power structures in local cultures (so far) where authority is based on occupational seniority as found in industrialized societies, English is in a better position for asserting authority. (During the colonial days an African policeman would deliberately speak to monolingual suspects in broken European-type Swahili with English intonation and rhythmic beat in order to intimidate the latter or create a feeling of complete alienation between them.)

It was most interesting to observe that there were sociolinguistic constraints in code-switching and mixing as between the local vernacular, Swahili, and English. The more prevalent pattern was the vernacular + Swahili, Swahili + English, but rarely the vernacular + English, although the vernacular + Swahili + English also occurred. For example, the following sentences were recorded (the vernacular parts of the utterance are in small capitals; Swahili is italicized. The vernacular in the case of the first four utterances is Kinyakyusa, a language spoken in the southwestern highlands of Tanzania on the eastern shores of Lake Nyasa. The last three examples involve Kipare, a language spoken on the northern highlands near Mount Kilimanjaro. The orthography in both cases is standard and non-phonetic):

TWAGANILE NABALINDWANA NUINJILA, BIKUSEKA, BAFUMIBE *nikupiga* AMALYFU (We met girls laughing on the road having been enjoying themselves.)

NALONDAGA UKUTI LINGA TUULILE AMAG*odoro po tunaweza kutafuta vitanda baadaye.* (I was thinking that we buy mattresses and then look for beds later.)

MWANGELE NABO GONJWA NDAGA; TULINI *tabu lijo ukaja mumo bila madawa.* (How are you doing with the sick, we are in difficulties in these rural areas without medicine.)

Kaka John alipiga simu, BATI KALI *tuende* outing *naye, nikamwambia kuwa mwenzake* not available; *akajibu: vipi nawe kujifanya* so expensive NGATI ULINDALAMA. (John rang me asking if we could go out. I told him I was not available and he answered that I was making myself as expensive as if I were gold.)

TWEKIFIKA HENE Bus Stop *tulikuta* bus completely full up. (When we reached the Bus Stop we found the bus full.)

KANGI NERI *tena* proper information about the matter. (Moreover he has proper information about the matter.)

TUMANYIJE MHAHA *wa majeshi yote ya Tanzania.* (Don't you know the commander of all the armed forces in Tanzania.)

A possible explanation is that the order in which the three languages were learned (or the habit of switching developed) is relevant to the nature of the code-switching pattern. It is also possible that the pattern is influenced by the complementarity of the sociocultural functions of the vernacular, Swahili, and English. In the sociocultural setting of the vernacular, Swahili is more adjacent to the vernacular than English. One might suggest the existence of a hierarchy of social distance: everything being equal the vernacular expresses least social distance, English most and Swahili in between. If this hypothesis is true one could venture a statement to the effect that a multilingual speaker switches and mixes between varieties adjacent in implicit degree of social distance expressed by the three codes. Theoretically at least the vernacular + Swahili + English is the most comprehensive system for the multilinguals, given the appropriate setting.

Tolerance to code-switching and language mixing is very high among bilinguals and might even be considered stylistic in certain situations. In fact Swahili English would seem to be the easiest system to maintain in face-to-face encounters among bilinguals; while one might grope for words and structures in Swahili or English, mixed Swahili English flows much more easily. Is this a case of shifting bidirectional lexical interference? Or could it be that the lexical/syntactic system of English and Swahili are merged in certain interlocutory situations so that interlocutors are free to choose between 'synonyms' of an English-Swahili lexical system? One bilingual speaker uttered the sentence *'umenunua* fruit?' 'have you bought fruit?'. When asked why he did not use the Swahili word *matunda* 'fruit' he answered that *matunda* is fruit on trees which you go and pick and fruit is *matunda* you buy in the market.

An important linguistic development in this shifting diglossia situation is that English is greatly influencing the development of Swahili both at the structural and lexical levels. Innovators of new structural (syntactic) styles and new lexical terms are people with English as their language of reference. Such innovations take the form of extending the meanings of existing terms or giving them new meanings altogether to match terms in English. Many new political, economic, and scientific terms have been added to Swahili in this way.

Loan translations provide particularly interesting examples of this unstable bicultural situation. Sometimes even idioms get translated. For example, a speaker came out with: 'As the English say: Love is grass, it grows anywhere'. In fact this is a Swahili idiom equivalent to the English 'love is blind'. Often bilinguals, including radio news readers, mix up Swahili and English time systems. In Swahili the day begins at dawn and one o'clock is equivalent to the English 7.00 a.m. Often people say in Swahili or English seven o'clock when they really mean one o'clock. The Swahili *chukua dawa* (take medicine) is a loan translation. To a Swahili monolingual it could only mean 'get, or carry the medicine'. Some of the loan translations are misleading and ridiculous, like the case of an announcer who translated 'cocktail party' as *karamu ya mkia wa jogoo* (literally 'feast of the tail of a cock' on the analogy of ox-tail soup). The impression given by the Swahili phrase is that there is a feast at which tails of cocks are served.

PROSPECTS FOR SWAHILI AND ENGLISH

What are the linguistic and social-psychological consequences of such random code-switching and language mixing in mixed urban areas? Could it affect proficiency in Swahili and/or English? Or will this behavior result in the emergence of a new Swahili English mixed language?

It is questionable whether such language behavior would lead to loss of proficiency in English or Swahili. There is a school of thought which believes that in a situation like that obtained in Tanzania the multilinguals concerned fail to master perfectly one of the languages they operate in. In my view this is not in all cases true, although in a complex transitional triglossia such as this it is likely that certain individuals would be so affected. Most of the bilinguals seem to be able to maintain well either English or Swahili where the setting demands the use of one or the other. Proficiency would appear to depend upon the individual bilingual's aptitude and his linguistic and sociocultural experiences in English and Swahili. But it is often observed that those who can maintain English proficiently can also maintain Swahili well and vice versa. Might the reason lie in the bilingual's psychological ability to separate the codes?

It is very unlikely that a new spoken language in the form of Swahili-English pidgin or creole will emerge in Tanzania. At the moment bilinguals of Swahili and English constitute a very small percentage of the total population (although their influence as an 'elite' group occupying the top and middle positions in the civil service, parastatal and commercial bodies, and institutions of higher learning is out of proportion to their numbers, at least at present, in spite of the fact that the workers and peasants would seem to gradually influence the sociopolitical system at the base). Also there are social constraints working against the development of such a code. Swahili is gaining tremendous prestige as the national language. There is now a conscious effort on the part of bilinguals to improve their proficiency in Swahili as its functions in the national life widen. Great effort is being made to develop Swahili as a modern national language. It is the only medium of teaching in primary school and is soon to be introduced as the medium in the secondary school for the teaching of at least some subjects. It is the official language of government business (together with English), and the language of parliamentary debates. Speaking Swahili well is a symbol of full national acculturation and identification. Already the tendency of separating the two languages is very noticeable among the younger generations: in schools, youth camps, and even streets. Also English is no longer the only language of socioeconomic prestige. While a national of Tanzania can get by and even assume a leadership role in the ruling party or become a member of the country's parliament without knowledge of English, lack of knowledge of Swahili for him would be a very big handicap if he were seeking a national role.

What is likely to happen in time is that the functions of Swahili and English will be more and more clearly demarcated until the two languages reach a stable functional relationship. We might then get a more defined 'triglossia' situation in the country, and perhaps increasingly a simple diglossia for many who will be bilingual in Swahili and English. It is conceivable that English in larger urban multiracial areas might develop as a language of social integration among speakers of different ethnic and national backgrounds who belong to a certain socioeconomic class, while Swahili grows as the language of national integration among Tanzanians as a whole.

It would be interesting to know what social-psychological adjustments are made as one switches from one language to the other. Are the thought processes affected? For example, when discussing such notions as agnosticism and democracy a bilingual might hold slightly varying views depending on whether the discussion is in English or Swahili, as if each language imposes its own thought framework or the sociocultural setting demands a certain verbal behavior.

As the functional role of Swahili broadens what would be the sociological consequences? Will Swahili develop an elaborated code learned at school and the university that will not be available to the masses of the peasants and workers? It would be ironical if this happened because one of the reasons for adopting Swahili was to democratize the sociopolitical system. Perhaps it will not, with the great efforts being made to make education universal and to expand adult literacy and education programs.

REFERENCES

Bernstein, B.
  1958 'Some Sociological Determinants of Perception', *British Journal of Sociology* 9:159—174. [Reprinted in Bernstein 1971:23—41.]
  1965 'A Sociolinguistics Approach to Social Learning', in *Penguin Survey of the Social Sciences* (Harmondsworth, Penguin Books) pp. 144—168. [Reprinted in Bernstein 1971:118—139.]
  1967 'Elaborated and Restricted Codes: An Outline', in *Explorations in Sociolinguistics*, ed. by S. Lieberson (= *International Journal of American Linguistics* 33 [4]) (Bloomington, Indiana, Indiana University) pp. 126—133.
  1971 *Class, Codes, and Control*, Vol. 1 (London, Routledge and Kegan Paul).
Bram, J.
  1966 *Language and Society (Studies in Sociology)* (New York, Random House).
Ervin-Tripp, S.
  1964 'An Analysis of the Interaction between Language, Topic, and Listener', in *The Ethnography of Communication*, ed. by J. Gumperz and D. Hymes (= *American Anthropology* 66 [6], part 2) (Washington D.C., American Anthropological Association) pp. 86—102.

Ferguson, C. A.
  1959 'Diglossia', *Word* 15:325–340 (New York).
  1968 'Language Development', in *Language Problems of Developing Nations,*
       ed. by J. A. Fishman, C. A. Ferguson, and J. Das Gupta (New York,
       John Wiley).
Fishman, J. A.
  1967 'Bilingualism With and Without Diglossia, Diglossia With and Without
       Bilingualism', *Journal of Social Issues* 23:29–38 (Ann Arbor, Michi-
       gan).
  1968 *Bilingualism in the Barrio,* Vols. 1–2 (Washington, D.C., U.S. Depart-
       ment of Health, Education, and Welfare).
Gumperz, J. J.
  1966 'On the Ethnology of Linguistic Change', in *Sociolinguistics,* ed. by
       W. Bright (The Hague, Mouton) pp. 27–49.
  1967 'On the Linguistic Correlates of Bilingual Communication', *Journal of
       Social Issues* 23:48–57 (Ann Arbor, Michigan).
Hall, R. A., Jr.
  1966 *Pidgin and Creole Languages* (Ithaca, New York, Cornell University
       Press).
Hymes, D.
  1964 *Language in Culture and Society* (New York, Harper and Row).
Labov, W.
  1964 'Phonological Indices to Social Stratification', in *The Ethnology of
       Communication,* ed. by J. Gumperz and D. Hymes (= *American
       Anthropologist* 66 [6], part 2) (Washington, D.C., American Anthro-
       pological Association) pp. 86–102.
Lambert, W. E.
  1967 'A Social Psychology of Bilingualism', *Journal of Social Issues*
       23(2):91–109 (Ann Arbor, Michigan).
Lawton, D.
  1969 *Social Class, Language and Education* (London, Routledge and Kegan
       Paul).
Le Page, R. B.
  1964 *The National Language Question* (London, Oxford University Press).
Weinreich, U.
  1963 *Language in Contact* (The Hague, Mouton).
Whiteley, W. M.
  1969 *Swahili — the Rise of a National Language* (London, Methuen).
Whorf, B. L.
  1956 Selected essays in *Language, Thought and Reality.,* ed. by J. B. Carroll
       (New York, John Wiley).

NOTES

Reprinted with permission from *Language and Society* 1(1972):197–213 (Cambridge University Press).

I am greatly indebted to my many Tanzanian friends without whose cooperation and help I would have found it extremely difficult to write this article. I am also indebted to Professor A. Mazrui, Professor Dell Hymes, and Professor Whiteley with whom I discussed this paper: they raised a number of useful points which made me rethink the organization of the original version that I read at the Conference of the Seventh World Congress of Sociology, Varna, September 1970.

1. The term 'triglossia' is modelled on Ferguson's (1959) 'diglossia' to refer to a language situation whereby three languages are involved, having in some areas well-defined complementary functional ranges, and in others overlapping functional ranges because of their varying sociocultural bases, and also varying stages of development. A typical example of a triglossia situation would be found where there exist side-by-side (a) regional (or vernacular) languages whose basic role is in oral intragroup communication; (b) a local standardized *lingua franca* which is used extensively in the education system, mass media, and in government administration but which is not developed enough to cover all settings of a modern urban technological culture; and (c) a world language. The situation would give rise to intersecting diglossia on the one hand between the regional language and the local *lingua franca* and on the other between the local *lingua franca* and the world language, giving rise to code-switching and code-mixing involving two or three of the languages concerned.

2. Ervin-Tripp (1964) describes the term setting thus: 'We shall use the term setting here in two senses, that of locale, or time and place, and that of situation, including the "standing behaviour patterns . . . social situations may be restricted by cultural norms which specify the appropriate participants, the physical setting, the topics, the functions of discourse, and the style".'

3. On features of development, C. A. Ferguson (1968) says: 'The view adopted here is that there are at least three dimensions relevant for measuring language development; graphization — reduction to writing; standardization — the development of a norm which overrides regional and social dialects; and, for want of a better term, modernization — the development of intertranslatability with other languages in a range of topics and forms of discourse characteristic of industrialized, secularized, structurally differentiated, 'modern' societies.'

4. All the respondents were speakers of Bantu languages. Languages of this family (of which Swahili is one) have similar structural organization at all the linguistic levels. In addition they share a core of common basic vocabulary.

5. There were then less than five secondary schools in the country, all of them situated in linguistically and culturally heterogeneous areas where Swahili dominated as a language of communication and socialization.

6. Two respondents (other than the fifteen) who came from a former French colony said that they went to racially mixed schools in their country. The medium of instruction throughout the education system was French. There was also a deliberate effort to acculturate the children to the French way of life. The language was taught as part of French culture. The two French-speaking African respondents stated that they had no difficulty in separating

the function of their vernacular from French and that they very rarely mix the vernacular and French when speaking to other bilinguals, except perhaps when speaking to relations whose French is very poor.

7. Spoken and written forms recognized as East African English are developing. It is not certain if this development will eventually correct the register deficiency among the bilinguals.

8. Spoken and written forms recognized as East African English are emerging. It is not yet certain if this development will eventually correct the register deficiency among the bilinguals. It may be relevant also to note that an English based pidgin or creole has not yet developed as a form spoken by any community.

PART TWO

Language Maintenance and Language Shift

LILIAN A. BRUDNER-WHITE

4

Occupational Concomitants of Language Variability in Southern Austrian Bilingual Communities

Studies on bilingual and multilingual communities have been lacking in metatheoretical orientation related to language decision-making. The main research focus in decision-making studies should be upon the content and characteristics of behavior related to language usage and cognition. This orientation would describe the kinds of information needed to construct and compare models of language choice and usage in a single society and across societies. In particular, before such models could be formalized, further information would be needed to pay attention to variability in individual choice of language affiliation, to describe the reward structure which enters into choice behavior involving decisions about language choice, and to provide a description of cultural constraints on language affiliation. Such a model would take into account different types of relational structures involving language decisions. Eventually it would include certain methods which are sensitive to individual differences in cognitive and behavioral structure. This article will describe a particular bilingual situation in terms of some descriptive elements mentioned above.

It is assumed that a bilingual situation is a consequence or outcome of a series of individual choices about language usage or a selection among two or more alternate languages. These selections are in some way part of larger strategies for status and role maintenance and enhancement that are made with consideration of the bounds placed on decision-making by local norms or other constraints on action. We take the view that individuals maintain a language given that there are alternative languages, only if there is more reward in speaking two languages than one and hence that for some individuals at least the structure of rewards favors the adaptation or perpetuation of second and third languages. In consequence the language behavior of people in aggregates is influenced by rewards to particular groups of persons who have specific sociodemographic characteristics and who are linked to the political and economic structure of the society in a common way.

Language choice is thus an epiphenomenon of more complex relationships among ecology, economics, politics, and other institutional aspects of human relationships such as marriage rules and rules of inheritance and other formal relationships that influence group membership and the allocation of goods and services. The study of such choices requires a theory about what is being maximized by which members in what social contexts. Such a theory can only be derived from extended analysis of how native respondents make decisions in which language choice is directly or indirectly involved. The study of language decision-making also requires a theory about how each language articulates with the reward structure of a community, as well as some account of how people make decisions involving language that influence their daily behavior. The reward structure is assumed to include culturally valued goods and economic allocation of scarce resources over people and services. Viewed in this framework, language choice behavior in a two or n-language situation is assumed to be maximizing behavior and to be amenable to general anthropological theories about maximization.

Two further assumptions are made: first, that sharing in language choice-making activities in a population is problematic and cannot be assumed and thus some attempt must be made to account for differences in language orientation and usage patterns related to major sociodemographic characteristics (e.g., age, sex, occupation, etc.) and second, that language choice is dynamic and highly responsive to change in more fundamental social, economic, and political relationships. These assumptions will be tested in the case study that follows.

The sociodemographic variable that will be controlled for is occupation. It has been noted that occupation is 'the most obvious and most effective predictor of differential location within the structure of social inequalities' (Runciman 1968:55). Therefore, should language choice be related to economic maximization, occupational differences within a social aggregate should be the best predictors of language choice, and change in occupational structure should lead to change in language patterns.

The discussion which tests this assumption in particular has three parts: section 1 presents a summary discussion of the adaptive history of the area and focuses on the economic causes of language shift over time; section 2 presents a more detailed discussion of the occupational structure and reward systems in bilingual villages; section 3 presents some examples of cultural prescriptions for different occupations relating to marriage and language choice and also data on actual decisions involving language made by members of the population in spouse selection.

Carinthia, Austria, is an alpine region with richly contrastive topography divided by the Drau River into a rugged mountainous area in the north, an area of rolling countryside in the southeast, and an area of swampy and mountainous river valleys in the southwest. It is a federal southern province of Austria bordering on Yugoslavia and Italy to the south, the Tirol to the west, Salzburg to the northwest, and Styria to the east. Stable bilingualism persists today only in the mountainous southwestern area where communication in the past was poor, where the soil is swampy and rocky, and where relatively little land is available for intensive cultivation, namely, at the crests of the Karawanken and Carnic Alps in the Rosenthal, Drau, and Gail valleys.

Slovene and German have coexisted since the ninth century here and in the entire southern portion of the province until some two centuries ago. From the early period Slovene has been associated with a rural agrarian and dairying people and German has been associated with trade and commerce. Over the course of time Slovene remained embedded in the reward structure of the rural peoples and was particularly associated with the ownership and control of agrarian resources and with the perpetuation of an agrarian way of life.

1. HISTORICAL ASPECTS OF PRESENT LANGUAGE LOYALTY

The traditional association between Slovene and particular subsistence practices may be demonstrated through an examination of the four major language shifts that have occurred. During a period of over one thousand years there have been at least four major language shifts. First, Germans moved into Slovene lands as colonists and in many cases assimilated to Slovene although they also built towns and cities that were entirely German. Second, Germans were excluded from Slovene communities although Slovenes began moving into the towns and cities and adopting German. Third, some Slovene communities shifted from exclusive Slavic monolingualism to a stable

156 *Lilian A. Brudner-White*

pattern of Slovene-German bilingualism. Fourth, in other communities the Slovene populations became rapidly assimilated to German, superceding a period of transitional bilingualism. The third and fourth shifts were initiated at the same period, being generated by the same agents of change.

Each language shift was related to a fundamental change in the organizational basis of local political and economic institutions. The first occurred as a German feudal society encroached upon a stock-raising Slovene population and absorbed it politically. The second occurred as the feudal Slovene communities developed sufficient political autonomy to constrain access to their territories. The third and fourth shifts occurred as the feudal Slovene communities began to be incorporated more fully into the centralized nation-state; it was associated with the decline of feudalism and the emergence of a modern national economic system.

1.1. The Early Language Shift: Linguistic Polarization With Two-Way Assimilation of Populations

Before it was conquered by the Romans, Carinthia was part of the Celtic kingdom of Noricum. After Roman rule Slovenes penetrated the area and were followed by Bavarians. Before the end of the ninth century the German populations, reinforced by waves of subsequent migrations, had established trade centers and subjugated the indigenous Slovene populations. In this period of language contact German was spoken only in trade and market centers. By the eleventh century the nobility of the province was entirely German (Leeper 1941:98–99) and effective control of the territory was held by the Catholic church and the local lords or *Grundherren* (Leeper 1941:111). The Slovenes became absorbed into an increasingly stratified system of social organization. Their leaders were replaced by German lords and Slovene remained the language of the peasants.

1.2. The Second Language Shift: Slavic Exclusiveness in Rural Communities

Some time after the thirteenth century Slovene villages became corporate communities in the sense that the concept is used by Wolf (1957; 1966:4–5). Villagers were obligated to the local German lords for services that they performed and for revenues in produce and taxes but Slovene communities were free to build their own administrative structures.

The peasants were in villeinage to the local lord who owned the land on which they worked and the household in which they dwelt; he also had various legal rights over them. But in the typical village more than one *Grundherr* owned land and had peasants dwelling and working on it. Thus a village's lands were parceled out not only to many peasants but also to several lords.

In most cases the local lords did not live on or near village lands. Peasants lived in the village, had multiple kin ties there, and worked cooperatively. There is no doubt that many decisions were made on the basis of informal transactions between them. By the fifteenth century powerful cliques developed among them. The local community or *Nachbarschaft* established many practices that later assured the autonomy of local communities. These included procedures for determining rights in land use, for the organization and allocation of tasks relating to land use, and for the local settlement of disputes.

It is quite clear that the local lords had the authority to make decisions regarding land transfers on their holdings, but the *Nachbarschaft* gradually developed as an important political group dedicated to the protection of villager's lands. Michor's (n.d.) history of a typical village indicates that the community resisted immigration from outsiders as well as struggling with the local lords to obtain greater property rights. The Slovene peasants were powerful enough to exclude incoming German peasants from their villages although as land became more scarce Slovene peasants emigrated to the towns and cities and became assimilated to German.

1.3. The Third Language Shift: From Slovene to Bilingualism

The third and fourth language shifts were brought about by the Hapsburgs who initiated major political and economic transformations in the Austro-Hungarian empire. In 1335 Carinthia became part of the Hapsburg possessions, and it remained with them until 1918 when the Republic of Austria was established. The Hapsburgs brought about the decline of the feudal lords. They were particularly successful in increasing their political power at the expense of local lords in the eighteenth century. In 1773 tenant servitude was ended by proclamation, and proclamations of 1770 and 1785 granted the peasant freeholder full ownership of land without obligation to the lord as well as rights of sale and purchase.

With the breaking of feudal bonds and the creation of new social and economic privileges many communities were opened to further economic and social change. In communities that continued to practice subsistence agriculture with small-scale dairying the third major language shift from Slavic to bilingualism occurred. Although emigration to urban areas increased, the remaining population retained Slovene but also adopted German.

1.4. *The Fourth Shift: From Slovene to German Monolingualism*

By the mid-nineteenth century Hapsburg land easement policy encouraged the distribution of the property of many of the village commons to individual peasants. In most communities where this occurred the fourth language shift from Slovene to German monolingualism was initiated.

In the areas where common lands were distributed the *Nachbarschaft* disappeared or was weakened and many of its political functions were absorbed by the *Gemeinde* or elected village council. With the distribution of village lands to individuals, neighborhood and kin ties were also weakened and corporate groups were replaced by individual-centered coalitions. In these, according to recent data, 'the individual is "freed" to enter into individual coalitions and maximize his resources both in the economic field and in the marriage market'.

Common lands had been important in that they provided pasturage for cattle and horses. A traditional function of the *Nachbarschaft* was to integrate village pastoral activities and to control lands devoted to the growing of fodder. The economic organization of traditional villages required the practice of stock raising since actual plowlands were quite small, often under forty acres, and arable land in the southwest was swampy with relatively low productivity. Most holdings were located above the valley floor on rugged terrain with sharp inclines. Holdings in the southeast were productive and the terrain was not rugged.

In the swampy and mountainous valleys of the southwest, today as in the past, agrarians cultivate in four ecological zones to achieve maximum use of all available land. Each zone is used in a rotating pattern largely determined by the customary yearly cycle. The first zone lies on the valley floor: administrative offices, shops, residences, gardens, orchards, plowlands, and some common grazing lands are located here. The second zone lies some hundred feet above the valley floor and is largely meadow and some scrub brush; the meadows are used for livestock grazing and for the growing of fodder, depending largely on topographic conditions. The third zone is entirely alpine, rugged terrain with mountain vegation interspersed in an area of woodlands. The fourth zone, lying above the tree line, is the area referred to as the *Alm,* and it is used for grazing.

The alienation of *Alm* lands was particularly important in destroying the power of the *Nachbarschaft* or weakening its power in some communities. Honigmann (1964:278) has described the complex economic, social, and psychological importance of the *Alm* to traditional life: it 'efficiently conserved most of the two annual crops of valley hay for the stalled cattle to consume in winter' and it was suited to stock raising because 'calves and heifers intended for autumn sale could be raised cheaply through the summer on the mountain meadows, leaving valley hay for the more productive milk cows'. In daily life the *Alm* was a social and psychological focus of community life (Honigmann 1964:279–281).

Due to local topographic conditions many villages had no *Alm* lands. This was particularly true in east central Carinthia where the terrain was less rugged and where only one or two ecologically distinct zones existed. In this area, from the beginning, stock raising was less important to communal life. In some areas farmsteads lay widely dispersed from each other; in others, once common lands were distributed, much of the basis for traditional community life disappeared.

A fourth language shift from bilingualism to German monolingualism has tended to accompany the abandonment of *Alm* land. The structural features associated with *Alm* lands and traditional agriculture and dairying will be discussed in section 2.

2. STRUCTURAL ASPECTS OF LANGUAGE ADAPTATION

This section focuses on the social, economic, and political factors that have retarded a fourth language shift, namely, those local conditions that led to the persistence of bilingualism in some communities. Although national political and economic policies have been major factors initiating recent language shifts, the immediate cause of language shift in some communities is found in local patterns of adaptation. Communities with good means of communication located near industrial and market centers became assimilated to German more rapidly than other communities in the nineteenth

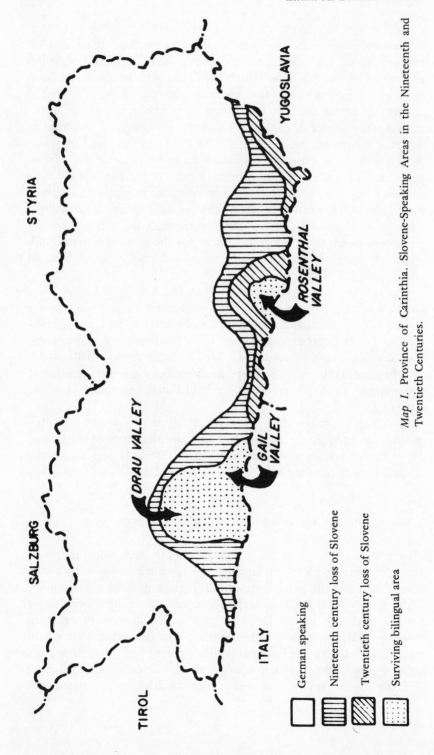

Map 1. Province of Carinthia. Slovene-Speaking Areas in the Nineteenth and Twentieth Centuries.

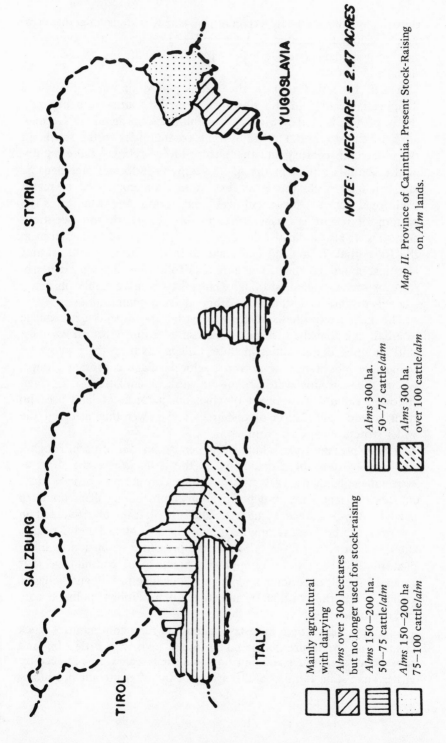

Map II. Province of Carinthia. Present Stock-Raising on. *Alm* lands.

NOTE: 1 HECTARE = 2.47 ACRES

STYRIA

SALZBURG

TIROL

ITALY

YUGOSLAVIA

☐ Mainly agricultural
with dairying

▨ *Alms* over 300 hectares
but no longer used for stock-raising

▥ *Alms* 150—200 ha.
50—75 cattle/*alm*

☐ *Alms* 150—200 ha
75—100 cattle/*alm*

▥ *Alms* 300 ha.
50—75 cattle/*alm*

▨ *Alms* 300 ha.
over 100 cattle/*alm*

century. But by the twentieth century, as new systems of transportation developed, remoteness became less important as a factor retarding assimilation to German, particularly with the spread of national education.

It can be noted that in the initial period of contact Slovene disappeared earlier in the north than in the south, probably as a result of the fact that Slovene communities bordered on German areas to the north but other Slovene communities to the south. In the nineteenth century and thereafter Slovene receded more rapidly in the southeast than in the southwest, as the former area became industrialized while the latter by comparison continued to retain traditional patterns of agricultural organization. Map I indicates the pattern of recent language shifts in the nineteenth and twentieth centuries. It also indicates the present major areas of bilingualism in the Rosenthal, Drau, and Gail valleys. In that these valleys are not identical much of the discussion that follows is most particularly relevant to Gail valley, although Gail valley is more similar in many respects to these valleys than to other adjacent communities.

The major hypothesis relating to structural aspects of language retardation is that the specific mechanism retarding a fourth language shift in some communities in these valleys has been the practice of impartible inheritance supported by local village corporate groups; where these groups were absent or weak, assimilation to German followed rapidly as a result of changing patterns of land use and transfer and reallocation of resources and power that affected the wider structures of communities.

At the present time bilingualism persists in Carinthia in roughly the same pattern of distribution as the *Alm*. Where the *Alm*, or commonage lands used for transhumance, continues to be important to the local economy and political structure bilingualism tends to persist. Map II indicates the size and distribution of *Alm* land in Carinthia at the present time. A comparison of Maps I and II reveals the co-occurrence of the *Alm* and the present distribution of bilingualism. But it was not simply the presence of commonage that retarded social, economic, and linguistic change in bilingual villages; rather it was the continued importance of traditional political control over resources.

In many areas where industry penetrated rural communities stock raising and agriculture decreased. In other areas with little *Alm* land subsistence agriculture and dairying on a small scale were replaced by either large-scale farming and dairying or by other income producing activities. Where a village community had a great deal of arable land, sale and consolidation of holdings often followed. Many communities were absorbed into the market system and in these communities the fourth language shift followed.

But many communities did not alter their system of adaptation. Villagers sought instead to maximize the holdings that they had and to continue to practice traditional small-scale dairying and agriculture. Rather than attempting to develop new modes of social and economic adaptation, some communities utilized their traditional social resources and political alliances to protect their holdings and where possible to expand them by discouraging outsiders from buying land or from moving into their communities.

In an adaptive strategy of this type Slovene played an important role, as it does at the present time for agrarian members of bilingual communities. Presently, Slovene plays an important part in daily social transactions in bilingual villages, particularly in the conduct of business related to agrarian and dairying activities. Political meetings are conducted in both Slovene and German, giving a decided advantage to Slovene speakers. Informal political and economic decision-making occurs in settings where drinking and ritual singing in Slovene are a part of the social transaction. Major economic and political discussions are undertaken after meetings of the *Nachbarschaft* or commonage holding unit.

Bilingualism is an important concomitant to the political power of the *Bauern*. It delimits membership in the core sector of the agrarian community within the villages. Its use focuses social activities on community activities which are of specific interest to the *Bauern* and of which they are the dominant participants. In these and other ways Slovene becomes an important strategic weapon for the *Bauern* in their struggle for power and prestige in a gradually urbanizing area. Slovene thus has an important association with the traditional agrarian way of life. The retardation of a fourth language shift in some Carinthian communities is thus in large part the result of the maximization of traditional social and cultural resources by the *Bauern*.

2.1. *The Function of the* Nachbarschaft *in the Distribution of Resources and Power.*

In most Austrian villages, as Honigmann (1963:40) noted, the major social categories are *Bauern* and *Arbeiter*.

Bauern are subsistence agrarians and dairy farmers who have inherited a freehold estate. Traditionally, in most villages, they form an exclusive endogamous group with a narrow range of social relationships and economic ties. *Arbeiter* in traditional villages are often the sons of *Bauern* who, being disinherited from major agrarian resources, are members of the working class. Their children generally remain in the *Arbeiter* class and emigrate from rural villages to urban areas.

These categorical distinctions suggest the principal social, economic, and political lines of cleavage in Austrian village structure. As reported by Powell (1970) many Austrian communities show marked political hostilities between agrarians and working-class groups. Hostility is often played out in the arena of major national political parties. In many villages *Bauern* and *Arbeiter* are two separate and hostile political factions. The *Bauern* tend to be members of the Austrian People's Party (ÖVP) and the *Arbeiter* to be members of the Austrian Socialist Party (SPÖ).

Rivalry between *Bauern* and *Arbeiter* is rooted in economic competition but factionalism is not equally pronounced in all villages. Honigmann (1964:44—45) reports that factionalism appears to be weakly articulated in Altirdning where market transactions assume great importance for all members of a village, but the reverse is true in bilingual villages which are for the most part agriculturally marginal and where *Arbeiter* tend to compete with *Bauern* for village resources in goods, services, and personnel.

In bilingual villages the *Bauern* are the dominant political faction. Their strength is based on the fact that they there form an elite group with exclusive membership and widespread control over the major village resources in land. Membership in the *Nachbarschaft* is restricted to shareholding members. Shares in the *Nachbarschaft* are limited in number and they are obtained through inheritance.

The *Nachbarschaft* regulates the use of village common lands and herd size. Both are important to the maintenance of a viable standard of living for agrarians since the sale of milk is the major cash product. It also regulates the cutting and sale of lumber on communal lands. It allocates various tasks to shareholding members and settles many disputes relating to land use. There is a growing tendency for its functions to be pre-empted by other agencies, which is a change that would be highly favored by the *Arbeiter* since it diminishes the power of the *Nachbarschaft* considerably. But most *Nachbarschaft* organizations in bilingual villages have been able to resist major challenges to their authority, both from the *Arbeiter* and from other agents threatening their control over village resources.

In bilingual villages the *Nachbarschaft* is the most influential faction in the village *Gemeinde*. In turn the authority of the *Gemeinde* extends to the control of all lands and buildings not privately owned or directly controlled by the authority of the *Nachbarschaft*. The *Nachbarschaft* directly or indirectly influences all major transactions affecting agrarian resources in land; it is also indirectly responsible for the fact that village lands are not sold to outsiders and only infrequently to *Arbeiter*. Compared to urban elites *Bauern* resources, wealth, and skills of an economic nature are limited. But in the arena of the village the *Bauern* have major control of resources in land, personnel, goods, and services. Their strategy is to preserve this monopoly, first by regulating the size of their own membership and, second, by limiting the resources that are transferred to *Arbeiter* through inheritance. In this way they protect both the monopoly of their small elite group and the resources through which their power is maintained.

Through limiting their own number the *Bauern* are able to divide amongst themselves the available resources in lands and through time to consolidate and increase their holdings. This strategy becomes increasingly important in marginal areas where it is only through resources in land that local personnel can obtain prestige and power. But the traditional value placed on land continues to be important only where the participation of outsiders can be constrained. As Honigmann's (1963:45) study indicated, where nonagrarian resources are brought into play in local competition, prestige is often derived from wealth rather than from traditional esteemed-class membership.

2.2. *The Distribution of Land Through Inheritance*

Inheritance in bilingual villages, as elsewhere in Austria, favors transmission of land and other major resources to male heirs. Land is generally transmitted through the patriline from father to son. Property inherited from a father is referred to as *Vatergut* and that inherited from a mother as *Muttergut*. As Wolf (1970:101) reported in the Tirol, these categories 'tend to remain conceptually separate'. Since property is generally transmitted through the patriline the major resources of an estate are *Vatergut*. Women can inherit property, although in bilingual villages transmission of property has a distinct agnatic bias. The dowry of a woman, if it is substantial, gives her important control over resources and major decisions made with respect to their use.

Until the nineteenth century the traditional inheritance pattern was ultimogeniture, but after 1900 there was a shift to primogeniture. As greater opportunities arose for villagers in neighboring towns and cities, sons eligible to inherit homesteads — particularly small estates — frequently migrated. Migration was at a peak before 1920 and even after that time there was less assurance that an heir would be available to inherit homesteads. As the number of heirs and the value of homesteads diminished, primogeniture was increasingly favored; it encouraged an earlier decision on the part of fathers and their eligible sons and provided greater assurance that at least one son would inherit and work the land.

In the period between World Wars I and II the pattern of desertion and the sale of small homesteads became more common; many households lost sons in the wars as well. With growing industrialization many village estates were abandoned and their lands sold and consolidated into holdings of other villagers.

By World War II there was a decrease in population as a result of the emigration at earlier periods. This decline improved man-land ratios. Destruction of some homesteads permitted remaining villagers to increase the relative size of their holdings and to enhance their standard of living. More recently the government also took steps to discourage emigration. These included price supports on various crops and assistance in developing local marketing cooperatives. Governmental intervention served to appreciably diminish the rate of emigration. Land once again became a valued resource and important in local economic competition.

Distribution of Property at Marriage
Carinthian laws of inheritance of freehold estates are similar in many respects to those of the Tirol described by Pospisil (1971). The most crucial distinction is that between freehold property (*Freier Grundbesitz*), connected with farms or *Geschlossener Höfe*, and all other property.

The major property of an estate is generally allotted during the lifetime of a testator, although its actual transfer may be delayed until after the death of the latter. Property allotments are made at the time of the marriage of heirs. Table I indicates the classification of property in the distribution of an estate to children as quitclaim and dowry payments, showing the exact way in which it is related to patterns of land holdings in various ecological zones. A binary contrast is made between the portion of the main coheir or *Anerbe* and the portions of other coheirs. In bilingual villages impartibility is modified by codified law in the direction of partibility: the bulk of an estate is intended to go to the main coheir and the remainder to other coheirs. As Pospisil (1971:324) reported in his study of the Tirol: 'Coheirs are not main heirs and therefore do not inherit the same *absolute* amount of property as the "main coheir" — the *Anerbe.*'

Table I. *Classification of Property*

Classes I and II: Homestead property

  Class I; Freehold property (*Freier Grundbesitz*)
    A. Impartible core
      Ecozone 1 (Valley floor)
                    Hof (house and auxiliary buildings)
                    Gemüsegarten (vegetable garden)
                    Obstgarten (orchard)
                    Acker (grain field)
                    Feldwiese (hay fields)
                    Koppelweide (enclosed pasture)
    B. Partible   (Homesteads may have duplicate items)
      Ecozone 2 (low-lying meadows)
                    Wiese (meadows)
                    Weide (pasture)
      Ecozone 3 (Alpine woodlands)
                    Privatwald (woodlands)
      Ecozone 4 (Alpine meadows above treeline)
                    Wiese (meadows)

  Class II: Impartible communal land shares (*Nachbarschaftsanteile*)
      Ecozone 1 *Sumpfwiese* (swampy hay-growing area)
                    Moosweide (grazing area for horses)
      Ecozone 3 *Gemeinschaftswald* (woodlands)
      Ecozone 4 *Almwiese* (hay meadow above treeline)
                    Almweide (pasture area above treeline)

Classes III and IV: Private property
  Class III: additional farm resources
    Cattle and other livestock
    Farm equipment
    Cash

Class IV: Personal property

Under customary interpretation at the village level, property is divided into an impartible core and partible residual shares. The impartible core includes the major land holdings that are required for the practice of subsistence agriculture and stock raising. Items in classes IA and II are transferred to the main coheir or *Anerbe*. Items in class IB are partible. If there is only one heir this property is also transferred to him. If there is more than one eligible coheir they divide it. Partible items are those customarily traded or sold to other village households. Items in this class are transferred principally through inheritance to the *Anerbe* and coheirs and are supplemented by dowries, quitclaim payments, and land purchase through transactions with other households.

Some items in class IB are given to coheirs other than the *Anerbe* who marry into neighboring households. Lands are rarely sold except to meet a family crisis. The partible portion may be transferred with other items in property class III through quitclaim payments or *Ausbezahl* to sons or as dowry or *Mitgift* to daughters.

The items in property class III are additional farm resources some of which are utilized for quitclaim payments. Items in this class represent fluid capital or capital investments. However, the individual is morally constrained to provide for the economic future of heirs and to protect investments represented by this class of items. They are traded or transferred only for important economic reasons.

Items in class IV are personal property which are transferred after the death of a testator and connote esteem, prestige, and sentiment. Other items may also be transferred *causa mortis* or after the death of a testator but customarily a disposal of items in classes I to III is supposed to be made before death or specified in a legally valid will.

In summary, payment to heirs at the time of their marriage is allocated in the following manner:

1. To the *Anerbe*: items in property classes I and II. If there are other coheirs remaining in the village items in class IA remain with the *Anerbe* but items in class IB are divided among the coheirs.
2. To the female coheirs remaining in a neighboring household: items in class IB or more commonly livestock (an item in class III).
3. To male coheirs remaining in a neighboring household: items in class IB or farm equipment (an item in class III).
4. To emigrating children of either sex: cash, advanced education, or training for a vocation (items in class III).

Inheritance Practices and Substantive Law
In Carinthia as in the Tirol (see Pospisil 1971:322—327 for comparative and fuller discussion) the transmission of freehold property is partially regulated by codified law and various bureaucratic agencies. First, freehold property is registered with the *Hofabteilung des Hauptbuches* of the *Grundbuch* or 'the farm section of the main land register' (Pospisil 1971:324). Second, its transmission is regulated by a set of codified laws. Third, all changes in the land connected with a farmstead are registered with the *Hofbehörde* or farm office. Finally the value of an estate is determined on the premises by a locally appointed appraiser or *Sachverständige*. The intent of the law is to modify inheritance toward partibility to achieve greater equality of distribution among coheirs and at the same time to assure that the main coheir has sufficient land to practice agriculture. In bilingual villages where land holdings are small these two goals are incompatible and the former, that of providing a major coheir with sufficient land to practice agriculture and dairying, takes precedence over the latter, the ideal of equality in distribution. All decisions made at the local level serve to intensify impartibility.

Modifications at the Local Level Related to Substantive Laws
Laws of inheritance establish classes of inherited property and of obligatory and optional heirs and specify procedures of allotment and classes of obligation in apportioning an estate. These have been described by Pospisil (1971) for the Tirol and need not be discussed here. Although codified laws delimit classes of heirs and classes of allotments of property the laws concerning them in cases of intestacy are modified at the local level by the land appraiser. The interpretation of codified laws within the village takes into account the general policy of members of the *Nachbarschaft* that unnecessary alienation of land contravenes the interests of the agrarian members of the community.

The provision that a local land appraiser be appointed by the *Gemeinde* to make decisions in cases of death without testament gives a village important control over property distribution. Many *Bauern* die intestate, having made only an informal partition of an estate. In such cases the land appraiser, who is himself a *Bauer* and member of the *Nachbarschaft*, determines what an estate is actually worth. Low appraisals influence the size of shares for minor heirs and are beneficial to the major heir. It is common practice for the appraiser to evaluate an estate well below its actual market value to protect the impartibility of the estate (see Pospisil 1971:325 for comparative discussion).

In some cases the appraiser is also authorized to determine whether a major heir is competent (*bauernfähig*) to inherit a farm and whether the land allocated to him is of sufficient size to provide a living through full-time subsistence agriculture. If an appraiser is not satisfied with the informal partitioning of an estate he may suggest another method of partitioning, contingent on subsequent approval by the courts. If a potential *Anerbe* has been managing a freehold estate his claims are strengthened. The appraiser judges the claims of all concerned parties as well as the size of the holding and may in effect disinherit an *Anerbe* with a poor reputation, e.g., for drunkenness or extravagance.

Other aspects of the substantive law are open to manipulation. For example, the shares of an heir may be reduced by *Anrechnung* or accountability. As Pospisil (1971:323) noted, this reduction may be legally made by parents 'only to the extent that it is used for upkeep and education to the beneficiary's minor siblings'. Accountability may be reckoned in such a manner that the value of a coheir's share in the estate has been exhausted before the time when he can claim his allotments. Thus claims of minor and major heirs may be weakened if an heir does not meet local expectations with regard to the choice of a mate and the choice of an occupation. The claims of minor heirs may be weakened to permit the resources of a freehold to be kept intact for the major heir. Thus despite the presence of a complex set of codified laws and the existence of governmental agencies to oversee property transaction, the abstract ideal of the law is modified at the village level, given the cooperation of the parties concerned.

Inheritance, Marriage, and Occupational Expectations
The normal sequence of patrilineal inheritance may be modified if an heir does not meet the expectations of his kin and community. In bilingual villages the *Anerbe* is expected to devote himself to full-time agriculture. The distribution of property according to substantive law takes this commitment into account (see Pospisil 1971:324). The portion of an estate going to the *Anerbe* may be drastically reduced if he does not become a full-time *Bauer*. In fact he is likely to be bypassed entirely.

The *Anerbe* is expected to marry a girl from a neighboring farmstead (see Honigmann 1963:45—47 for a comparative discussion on this practice in Styria). Power in the village is directly related to the place of the individual in various local kinship coalitions. Families that restrict their affinal bonds to persons who are already close kinsmen are best able to maximize their social and economic resources and their access to goods and services. Restriction of the marriage market to local personnel provides an additional advantage to members of the *Bauern* faction. By marrying a person from a neighboring farmstead a major heir brings additional resources in land into a household through quitclaim and marriage payments. In this way existing kin ties are also often strengthened, thereby providing a household with increased potential for future mobilization of resources. Given the power structure of bilingual villages a *Bauer* with a monolingual spouse would be severely handicapped in daily social transactions in which personal influence plays an important part. Male minor coheirs attempt to marry females in their own or neighboring villages who have inherited a freehold estate. Others become *Arbeiter* whose access to local resources is regulated by patron-client relationships with the *Bauern*. Such relationships are important to the *Arbeiter* for the majority of disputes are settled informally at the village level and access to minor goods and services is obtained through informal personal contacts. The majority of minor coheirs do not inherit land and many choose to emigrate and thereby become absorbed into German-speaking Austrian society.

3. CULTURAL PRESCRIPTIONS AND MODAL BEHAVIOR

All communities probably have some self-regulated mechanisms that determine or control competition for resources that may limit population size and density and influence the structure of group composition. In any society where linguistic diversity exists there will probably be orderly procedures that directly or indirectly channel behavior in the population, leading to the maintenance of significant social distinctions.

Language loyalty for the most part in southern Carinthia is viewed in terms of loyalty to a particular regional sub-unit. The procedures that maintain loyalty to Slovene, as we have seen, are part of the larger adaptation patterns of the rural community. Similarly, the cultural prescriptions of folk beliefs that support the use and perpetuation of Slovene in some segments of the local population are generally coded in nonlinguistic terms. The prescriptions which generally are used to make decisions related to marriage and occupational choice are also in some cases prescriptions which tend to support the perpetuation of Slovene. However, it should be noted that statements about behavior cover a wide range of occupational choices and marriage possibilities.

The body of folk beliefs or prescriptions affects behavior both in the bilingual and monolingual sector of the rural communities. In bilingual villages Slovene is incorporated into folk prescriptions for persons in agrarian professions only. With the exception of a relatively small pan-Slovene nationalist group, the beliefs which are expressed that actually perpetuate Slovene are associated with major life-cycle decisions of the individual and focus not on Slovene directly but on appropriate behavior related to neighborhood and locality.

The general hypothesis offered in this section states that language usage patterns are part of a larger set of features or attributes associated with particular occupations. Marriage choice is also associated with job selection in that persons in specific kinds of occupations are expected to marry females with specific significant traits or attributes. Briefly, persons who are in occupations where use of Slovene is reinforced by multiplex role-ties continue to marry bilinguals and to perpetuate Slovene in the home. Those who are not in occupations where multiplex role-ties associated with subsistence agriculture and dairying exist do not regularly select marriage partners who are Slovene-speaking and as a consequence Slovene probably will not be transmitted to offspring or be perpetuated in the home in such marriages.

To explore the relationships described here I will consider first the folk statements about marriages as they are commonly expressed by residents of bilingual villages. These statements or folk prescriptions are widely shared by both monolingual and bilingual speakers. They indicate the extent to which language choice by Ego is part of a larger strategy of identity maintenance associated with fundamental socioeconomic decision-making. Table II summarizes statements of informants in the left column, and the implication for culturally appropriate behavior is presented in the right column. It should be noted that rules of appropriate behavior with linguistic corollaries are stated in terms of occupational prescriptions:

Table II. *Folk Statements About Marriage and Their Consequences for* Bauern

Folk Statements: English Gloss	Consequences
1. '*Bauern* should marry a sensible wife who knows how to work hard and how to do farm work.'	1. A 'sensible wife' for a *Bauer* is the daughter of a *Bauern* family.
2. '*Bauern* should marry a girl who brings land to the marriage.'	2. *Bauern* should marry a girl from the village or as close to home as possible to make the use of any land brought to the marriage practical.
3. 'A girl who is educated is not a fit wife for a *Bauer*, that is, she will be spoiled and extravagant.'	3. *Bauern* should marry girls whose character and capacity for work and thrift are known; girls with education are spoiled.
4. 'It is of the greatest importance that if a girl inherits, her husband's character be known.'	4. *Bauern* daughters who inherit should marry local men to keep land within the village and to make sure it is intact for future heirs.
5. 'All women should marry men who are as well-off or better-off than their fathers.'	5. Hypergamy: Uneducated men with little land are not good prospects for girls from families with land.

Folk Statements About Marriage and their Consequences for Men with Local Businesses (Geschäftsleute *and* Werden)

	Consequences
1. 'A businessman's wife should know how to work hard, to save money.'	1. There is no mention made as to whether such a girl need be local, although a girl from a *Bauern* family is assumed to be sensible and hard-working.
2. 'The wife of a businessman should be able to keep books and to socialize with important business contacts.'	2. Keeping books involves schooling and is associated with education; socializing with customers is defined as ability to speak with poise and to appear dignified. A wife from a wealthy family or from an urban area is assumed to be more worldly and suitable than a local girl for a wealthy businessman.

In examining the examples for *Bauer* and *Geschäftsman* of how bilingual villagers conceive of an ideal spouse it can be noted that each occupation has its own requirements. Cultural prescriptions are not formulated directly in terms of linguistic identity, as can be noted, but their components ('from a family that is well-known', 'living close by', etc., as contrasted with 'education' and 'worldliness') have important implications for selection of spouse by linguistic criteria. If we examine the consequences of such rules the characteristics of the idealized marriage for persons in various occupations lead to the following selections:

1. *Bauern* marriages should be endogamous within the bilingual circle of villages where families tend to know each other and to be previously related by kin ties. *A bilingual spouse is mandatory.*
2. *Geschäftsleute* (businessmen generally) and *Werden* (pub owners) should marry daughters of wealthy *Bauern,* but not from the same village, and the girls should have advanced education. Whether the girl is from a nearby bilingual village or from a monolingual family in a more distant or urban area is *optional* — thus a *bilingual spouse is optional.*
3. *Arbeiter, Tischler, Schneider,* and *Ampter* (i.e., workers, carpenters, tailors, clerks) are limited in their choice by the hypergamy of the local girls: they are limited to choice of girls from similar backgrounds to their own or else must marry girls from outside the area who are monolingual German. *A bilingual spouse for this category is optional but unlikely.*

To what extent do marriage choices actually match the verbalized cultural prescriptions? To what extent are certain occupations more endogamous than others and hence more likely to perpetuate bilingual households? Before examining modal behavior related to language choice and choice of a spouse it is important to note that there is one occupational category that must be further examined in detail. This is the *Bauern-Arbeiter* category.

Many men who have inherited some small parcels of land also have full-time jobs outside the village. Such persons generally view themselves as part-*Bauer* and part-*Arbeiter* or as *Bauer-Arbeiter.* In ranking the various professions in the village they always rank the *Bauern* above the *Arbeitern* (Brudner and White 1972). *Bauern Arbeiter* form a distinct transitional occupational category between *Bauern* and *Arbeiter,* but for the most part they attempt to develop patron-client relationships with the *Bauern* and to be regarded as *Bauern*. Given that persons in this category view themselves as distinct from other *Arbeiter* it is useful to examine their behavior distinct from both the *Bauern* and *Arbeiter* pattern.

To examine modal behavior three persons from bilingual villages were selected to judge whether or not persons in the village were bilingual. Villages were then placed in one of two categories. Persons were placed in the first category (bilingual) if they used Slovene at least as much as German in a bilingual village. They were placed in the second category (monolingual) if they did not speak Slovene or only ocasionally used a Slovene phrase or spoke in Slovene.

A complete classification of persons, using household census data, was made in one village. More than ninety percent of persons in this census could be categorized in a two-way distinction. Persons who could not be easily categorized were omitted from the final sample. Also omitted from the final sample were unmarried persons, including minors as well as bachelors and spinsters.

Table III provides information on over ninety percent of the married residents of one bilingual village. The rows of the table classify the husbands by occupation, by language, and by whether or not they grew up within the village. The columns of the table classify the wives by their father's occupation by language and by whether or not they grew up within the village.

Table III. *Marriage Data from One Bilingual Community*

Key to Table
Terms   Gloss

Bauer	subsistence agrarian
Bauer-Arbeiter	subsistence agrarian and laborer
Arbeiter	unskilled laborer
Ampter	office worker
Geschäftsman	owner of business
Tischler	carpenter
Schneider	tailor
Wirt	innkeeper
Lehrer	teacher
Zollampter	toll keeper or border guard
Polizist	policeman

WIFE:

WIFE: daughter of ....

HUSBAND:	From Village BILINGUAL				From Village MONO-LINGUAL	Not from Village BILINGUAL			Not from Village MONO-LINGUAL		
	Bauer	*Bauer-Arbeiter*	*Geschäftsman*	*Arbeiter*		*Bauer*	*Bauer-Arbeiter*	*Arbeiter*	*Bauer*	*Arbeiter*	*Urban*
	1a.	1b.	2.	3.		1a.	1b.	3.	1a.	3.	5.
From Village											
BILINGUAL											
1a. *Bauer*	24	8	0	0	0	7	9	1	1	0	0
1b. *Bauer-Arbeiter*	13	3	0	0	0	6	4	4	0	0	0
2. *Geschäftsman, Wirt*	0	0	0	0	0	4	0	0	1	0	2
3. *Arbeiter, Tischler, Schneider, Ampter*	1	0	0	0	0	0	0	2	0	5	3
4. *Lehrer* (Teacher)	1	0	1	0	0	0	0	2	0	1	0
MONOLINGUAL											
3. *Arbeiter*	0	0	0	0	0	0	0	0	0	3	0
Not from Village											
BILINGUAL											
1. *Bauer*	3	0	0	0	0	0	0	0	0	0	0
3. *Arbeiter Ampter*	4	1	0	0	0	0	0	0	0	1	1
MONOLINGUAL											
1a. *Bauer*	0	0	0	0	0	0	0	0	0	1	0
1b. *Bauer-Arbeiter*	2	0	1	0	0	0	0	0	0	0	0
3. *Arbeiter*	2	1	1	0	0	0	0	0	0	1	0
5. Urban: *Zollampter* (tollkeeper) *Polizist* (policeman)	0	0	0	0	0	0	0	0	0	0	10

Note that there are no monolingual wives from within the village and that there are monolingual wives from urban areas married to men from the village but no husbands from urban areas married to women from the village. Note also that not everyone from the village is bilingual — there are some *Arbeiter* men who are monolingual Germans yet who were brought up in the village.

Examining the correspondence between the idealized 'marriage rules' for occupational groups and the actual data of Table III, we note the following.

Occupational Group 1a: 98% of Bauern men from the village marry bilingual husbands. Exceptions to the general trend of bilin- this class a bilingual wife is mandatory; 92% of *Bauern* daughters marry billingual husbands. Exceptions to the general trend of bilingual endogamy in this case are a result of a few families where there is no male heir and the female heir (with no male siblings to act as a control) marries a male monolingual from outside the village (four cases out of fifty).

Occupational Group 1b: 100% of Bauern-Arbeiter men and 92% of the daughters of *Bauern-Arbeiter* marry other bilinguals. As predicted this group has the same marriage pattern as the *Bauern.*

Occupational Group 2: approximately half of their *Geschäftsman-Wirt* males marry bilinguals and all of these are from outside the village. Daughters of men in this category (from the village) also show a mixed pattern of marriage choice consistent with optional choice of a bilingual spouse.

Occupational Group 3: 79% of the *Arbeiter* men from the village (including *Tischler, Schneider* and *Ampter*) marry monolingual German wives, and no daughters of *Arbeiter* from the village have married and remained in the village.

Our overall hypothesis is that the occupational structure, which is governed by resource distribution, is in turn a major criterion of both language affiliation and marriage decisions. If this is true then the degree of endogamy should be higher when people are classified by occupation than when they are classified by language affiliations. Romney (1971) has developed a measure of the amount of endogamy for marriage data like that presented in Table IV. In order to test the hypothesis that marriage choice is more strongly related to occupation than it is to language affiliation the data in Table III have been summarized twice. Table IV shows the summary data for language affiliation. It shows the number of marriages where both spouses are bilingual, where both are monolingual, where husband is monolingual and wife bilingual, and where husband is bilingual and wife is monolingual.

Table IV. *Marriage Data Classified by Language Affiliation*

		WIFE		
		Bilingual	Monolingual	Sub-totals
HUSBAND	Bilingual	98	16	114
	Monolingual	7	15	22
	Subtotals	105	31	136 = Grand Total

Table V is the summary table for occupation. It shows the extent to which *Bauern* and *Bauern-Arbeiter* form an endogamous group.

Table V   *Marriage Data Classified by Occupation ·*

		WIFE: daughter of		
		Bauer or *Bauer-Arbeiter*	All other occupations	Sub-totals
HUSBAND	*Bauer* or *Bauer-Arbeiter*	80	7	87
	All other occupations	15	34	49
	Subtotals	95	41	136 = Grand Total

The Romney endogamy measure separates the influence of marriage preferences from the influence of differences in group sizes. To accomplish this the tables are transformed into percentages and normalized by a procedure whereby the sum of each row and column in the table must be 100% (for a description of the procedure see Romney 1971). The results are given in Tables IV and VII.

Table VI. *Normalized Marriage Data: Language Affiliation*

		WIFE	
		Bilingual	Monolingual
HUSBAND	Bilingual	78.4%	21.6%
	Monolingual	21.6%	78.4%

Table VII. *Normalized Marriage Data: Occupation*

		WIFE: daughter of	
		Bauer or *Bauer-Arbeiter*	All other occupations
HUSBAND	*Bauer* or *Bauer-Arbeiter*	83.6%	16.4%
	All other occupations	16.4%	83.6%

From these tables, where the effect of differences in the number of persons in each classification has been removed, it is seen that occupational endogamy is more likely than language endogamy. The Romney index of endogamy is computed by taking the difference between the percent of endogamous and exogamous marriages for a classification. The coefficient for occupational endogamy is .67 while the coefficient for language affiliation endogamy is .57. These are consistent with the hypothesis that occupation is the direct influence on marriage choice and that language affiliation is correlated with marriage choice because both of the latter variables are influenced by occupation.

The data presented here strongly indicate that language variability is generated by the occupational system in Carinthia. Occupational differences lead to the perpetuation of older linguistic forms for speakers in traditional agrarian jobs. Persons in other occupations tend to use and perpetuate German through marriage with German speakers.

4. CONCLUSION: THE FUNCTION OF BILINGUALISM

If language choice is the product of aggregate decisions of members
of a population, then one strategy in identifying such rules as are
related to decision-making is to identify an aggregate of persons who
make decisions related to language in a common way and to contrast
them with other members of the population. We assume that a
theory of language decision-making must lie outside sociolinguistic
variables proper although some rules relating to sociolinguistic behavior are obviously involved. However, in an examination of the
various functions that languages play in the lives of aggregates of
persons in the population a more detailed examination of priorities
in maximization becomes important for comparative purposes.

We know that following radical changes in political and economic
relationships and processes in the eighteenth, nineteenth, and
twentieth centuries many European nations experienced major language shifts or alterations in patterns of habitual language and dialect
usage (Tabouret-Keller 1968; Fishman 1970). Changes at the national level led to the formation of new kinds of political and
economic ties between rural communities and national governments,
to the development of new social and economic opportunities for
rural peoples as well as urban populations, and to the strengthening
of standard languages in the schools and other local-level public
forums. With developments of this type, which had ramifications
throughout national societies, the semi-isolation of many communities came to an end. Yet in certain kinds of communities, despite
these changes, stable patterns of bilingualism and multilingualism
persist — i.e., it is still the norm for the linguistic competence of
individuals to extend to two or more languages and to be transmitted
from one generation to the next.

We have seen in this case study that occupational variables appear
to be significant in accounting for linguistic diversity in one community; however, it is also clear that this is a result of the way the
second language is embedded in the reward and subsistence structure
of bilingual communities. This relationship between language and
subsistence practices is probably important in other communities as
well. Examining comparative data from another Austrian community
we find an important relationship between impartible inheritance
and community resistance to change.

Although inheritance laws are similar in all parts of Austria,
inheritance practices, the composition of productive units, and fac-

tors of land use and sale vary widely. Honigmann's (1963, 1964) study of a monolingual village of Austria, Altirdning in neighboring Styria, provides some indirect evidence of an association between impartible inheritance and other boundary maintaining mechanisms. At the present time inheritance practices in Altirdning favor impartible inheritance less than those in bilingual villages. In Altirdning all heirs to a farmstead receive equal portions as their share in an estate although only one sibling actually takes possession of it. The heir to whom the farmstead is transferred compensates all the others for their interests, even to the extent of going into debt in order to make a monetary settlement (Honigmann 1963:46). In bilingual villages, as we have seen, the bulk of an estate goes to a single heir and only a minimal residual payment is made to other siblings and of these only a small portion are payments in cash. In Altirdning the traditional patrilineal extended family appears to be less important than in bilingual villages. Land is sold more often. Transhumance is no longer practiced (Honigmann 1964). At the present time prestige is derived from wealth rather than from 'category membership' (Honigmann 1963:45). Despite the fact that some of the traits of traditional social organization persist in Altirdning, at a more fundamental level of adaptation there has been less resistance to change generally than in bilingual villages in Carinthia.

One cannot generalize in any direct way from these comparisons but there are indications that local structural organizations may have an important part to play in making some communities more resistant to change than others and that resistance to change generally is an intervening variable influencing language maintenance. For example, inheritance practices in a monolingual village in the Tirol described by Pospisil (1971) are more similar to those of Altirdning than they are to bilingual villages in Carinthia. Both monolingual villages show greater partibility of a farmstead and more equitable distribution of shares to all heirs than is customary in bilingual villages. Comparison with Altirdning and the Tirol indicates that the social organization of bilingual villages conforms to an older pattern. All bilingual villages in this area of Carinthia are of a single type in which subsistence agriculture and dairying are importantly related to the maintenance of a preindustrial social order where prestige and power are derived from category membership and from resources in land held by a corporate group.

Reporting on two villages in the Alpine region of Italy — one bilingual (German-Italian) with impartible inheritance and the other

monolingual with partible inheritance — Wolf (1970:11) suggests
that in a system of social organization with impartible inheritance,
productive resources can be maintained as the monopoly of the
principal heir and kept from entering into a market economy: 'I
would suggest that we need to interpret impartible inheritance not
merely as a strategy for economic ends; it is also a strategy which
creates and maintains a social order, a distribution of rights and
disabilities, hence a structure of power.'

Broader comparative evidence on other European societies supports an important association between impartibility and general
community resistance to change (Habbakuk 1955). Impartible inheritance creates and sustains a particular type of power and decision-making structure: one which is related to permanent migration
of disinherited sons, is highly resistant to land sale, and effectively
consolidates resources in the hands of the few. It is quite clear that
language maintenance in bilingual and multilingual situations is related to larger patterns of resource control and distribution. It is for
this reason that models of language selection need focus on the use
of language in the maximization of other social, economic, and
political utilities. On the basis of this evidence we can make the
stronger claim that it is not possible to assess values associated with
language maintaince by analysis only of behavior associated directly
with language choice because there are often a number of indirect
linkages between economic structure and language maintenance that
are important to the survival of second and third languages.

There is every reason to believe that different groups of individuals
in a society will hold different notions about the value of a second
and third language and also possibly incompatible representations
about the functions of a second and third language. It becomes
important to understand the reward structure that generates different cognitive representations related to language choice. The conventional sociolinguistic approach is to ignore the fact that problems
of variability are important to our understanding of how and why
second and third languages persist. Too often data on bilingual
communities are aggregated in a summative way and then a 'normative' or 'collective representation' model is constructed. Such a
model based on an impressionistic formulation not only provides a
limited amount of information about second and third language
maintenance but also gives the often false impression that second and
third languages are maintained only because certain individuals in a
population like or dislike a particular language or set of languages or

are conscious or unconscious of the part language plays in their daily strategies. In actual fact, as we have seen, language decision-making is often deeply embedded in other important economic and political relationships and processes, and the belief structure that maintains a second or third language may take into account a wide variety of other features that typify or differentiate a particular category of persons such that language affiliation is the result not of individual choice but of larger selection processes.

REFERENCES

Brudner, L.
1972 'The Maintenance of Bilingualism in Southern Austria', *Ethnology* 6:1, 39—54 (Pittsburgh).
Brudner, Lilian, and Douglas R. White
1972 'Rank Order Utilities in Occupational Preference Data', paper presented at the Mathematical Social Science Board, Conference on Decision Making, Palo Alto, Calif., December.
Fishman, Joshua A.
1968 'Nationality-Nationalism and Nation-Nationalism', in *Language Problems of Developing Nations,* ed. by J. Fishman *et al.* (New York) pp. 34—52.
1970 *Sociolinguistics: A Brief Introduction* (Rowley, Mass., Newbury House Language Series).
Habbakuk, H. J.
1955 'Family Structure and Economic Change in Nineteenth Century Europe', *Journal of Economic History* 15:1—12.
Honigmann, J. J.
1963. 'Bauern and Arbeiter in a Rural Austrian Community', *Southwestern Journal of Anthropology* 19:40—53 (Albequerque, New Mexico).
1964 'Survival of a Cultural Focus', in *Explorations in Cultural Anthropology,* ed. by W. Goodenough (New York) pp. 277—292.
Leeper, A. W. A.
1941 *A History of Medieval Austria* (London).
Leopold, W. O.
1959 'The Decline of German Dialects' *Word* 15:130—153 (New York).
Michor, H.
n.d. 'Geschichte des Dorfes Feistritz a.d. Gail', unpublished manuscript (Carinthia).
Pospisil, L.
1971 *Anthropology of Law: A Comparative Theory* (New York).
Powell, G. B.
1970 *Social Fragmentation and Political Hostility: An Austrian Case Study* (Stanford).

Romney, A. Kimball
1971 'Measuring Endogram', in *Explorations in Mathematical Anthropology,*
ed. by P. Kay (Cambridge, Massachusetts, M.I.T. Press) pp. 191–214.
Runciman, W. G.
1968 'Class, Status and Power', in *Social Stratification,* ed. by J. A. Jackson
(Cambridge, Cambridge University Press).
Tabouret-Keller, A.
1968 'Sociological Factors of Language Maintenance and Shift: A Methodological Approach Based on European and African Examples,' in *Language Problems of Developing Nations,* ed. J. Fishman *et al.* (New
York) pp. 107–118.
Wolf, E. R.
1957 'Closed Corporate Peasant Communities in Mesoamerica and Central
Java', *Southwestern Journal of Anthropology* 13:1–18 (Albequerque,
New Mexico).
1966 'Types of Latin American Peasantry', *American Anthropologist*
57:452–471 (Menasha, Wisconsin).
1970 'The Inheritance of Land Among Bavarian and Tyrolese Peasants',
Anthropologica 7:99–113 (Ottowa).

NOTE

Revised and expanded from *Ethnology* 6(1972):39–54. Reprinted with permission.
The descriptive portion of this article contains large sections of the discussion
that are taken directly from 'The Maintenance of Bilingualism in Southern
Austria' (Brudner 1972). I am grateful for the assistance of Dr. George Peter
Murdock, Dr. Douglas R. White, and Dr. Michael Burton for their comments and
suggestions regarding various drafts of this article.

Yiddish in Israel: A Case Study of Efforts to Revise a Monocentric Language Policy

רעד צו מיר ײדיש, מעֶן ײדיש לאַנד,
און איך וועל צו דיר רעדן עבֿרית ממילא.

INTRODUCTION

There is no doubt that with respect to language planning in Israel, questions of basic policy (e.g., selection of the national/official language), at least vis-à-vis the Jewish population per se, are no longer widely believed to be at issue. In accord with the mainstream of Zionist ideology, which antedates the State by almost half a century, Hebrew is the national and official language of the country (with Arabic also being recognized for certain functions, see Fisherman 1972). To the extent that any other languages are widely believed to have nationwide roles these are English' and Arabic.[1] Other languages, especially Yiddish, are widely spoken in the country, particularly by adults and most particularly by adults who have emigrated from eastern Europe. Indeed at this time, after a quarter century of statehood, Hebrew is the mother-tongue of only roughly 40 percent of the Jewish population and the primary spoken language of only three-quarters of that same population (Hofman and Fisherman 1971; Schmelz and Bachi 1972).[2] However, all other mother-tongues are commonly referred to collectively as loazit 'foreign' and, as mother-tongues, are felt to merit little attention and less support. Indeed even as second or 'additional' languages only English, French, and Arabic have received organized attention aimed at fostering and retaining them.

The general topic of this article is the extent to which a purportedly monolingual-monocultural polity such as Israel's (referred to elsewhere as engaged in implementing Type B self-definitions and decisions, see Fishman 1969b) can be influenced to move toward greater contextualized acceptance of at least some other languages and cultures at a time when its basic language policy-making stage has passed. Given that several 'other-language' communities within a linguistically monocentric polity may seek to effect a change or reconsideration of basic policy, which groups among them (if any) are likely to be better able to do so and why? Specifically, if some of the languages in question are also *world languages* but are spoken by small groups within the country, others are *small languages* on the world scene but are spoken by substantial minorities within the country, and others still are *in-group languages* not previously allocated any public functions (not withstanding their many speakers), do all three of these tend to fare similarly or differently in the struggle for maintenance and recognition, when their advocates assume that the operational and sociocultural integrity of the polity is not to be endangered? While data from one country alone cannot hope to provide adequate answers to such questions, trend data across several languages even for a single country can go far toward suggesting dimensions worthy of more definitive exploration on a comparative basis. This is the basic premise of the data presented in this article *vis-à-vis* the further sociolinguistic study of language policy revision in purportedly monocentric speech communities.

YIDDISH AS A SPECIAL PROBLEM IN ISRAEL

Israel in general, and more specifically Yiddish in Israel, would seem to afford a particularly advantageous context for exploring the above-mentioned general question. As in all countries with large and recent immigrant populations, official policy and declared ideology must be tempered by the practical compromises required for daily functioning in all walks of life. However, more than all other immigrant languages, Yiddish in Israel presents a special claim for special consideration by the government: it is a Jewish language; it is the mother-tongue of a high proportion of the adult population of European extraction and a language-in-common with Ashkenazim the world over; it was considered a worthy handmaiden to Hebrew by various Zionist parties and ideologists during the first third of this century (some, for example Bialik, even admitting that Yiddish kept Hebrew alive during the many centuries of its nonvernacular use by incorporating into itself numerous Hebraic elements); it developed a large and first-rate belletristic literature and a sizable body of modern scholarship during the very period in which modern Hebrew was being revived and modernized; and it was the primary language of most of the hallowed six million exterminated by the Nazi war machine and its confederates.

On the other hand, some of the very factors which give Yiddish a distinctly advantaged claim over other immigrant languages in Israel are also associated with unique disadvantages: it was once a powerful ideological and massive functional rival of Hebrew and as such was long officially downgraded and 'discouraged' by most Zionist ideologists and activists; it is associated with the diaspora powerlessness and entrepreneural 'nonproductivity' which Zionism sought to correct; it has never been as diffused with sanctity among Jews, nor as respected by non-Jews, as has Hebrew, even though it is popularly associated with ultra-orthodoxy; it is particularly associated with eastern European Jewry (and with its branches in western Europe, the New World, South Africa, and Australia) and therefore is generally unknown to Sefardi, African, and Asian Jews (some of whom have learned it but many of whom consider it part of an Ashkenazi plot to limit upward social mobility for non-Ashkenazim).[3]

Thus the basic question *vis-à-vis* Yiddish in Israel is which of three differing approaches to it will triumph. One approach (the 'official' approach adopted by governmental agencies on various occasions) is to consider Yiddish as no more and no less than a kind of immigrant *loazit*. Its adherents demand for it more favorable treatment than that given to varieties of *loazit*, primarily on the basis of its special status as a Jewish language. Its detractors demand for it less favorable treatment than that given to other varieties of *loazit* primarily on the grounds of its past rivalry with Hebrew, its purported inappropriateness for the task of unifying a people scattered throughout the world (a sizeable minority of whom are not even Ashkenazim[4]), its increasing abandonment by most Ashkenazim themselves since the end of World War II, and the increasing demographic (if not cultural) 'orientalization' of the Jewish population of Israel *per se*.

YIDDISH AS A FIELD OF SPECIAL SOCIOLINGUISTIC INTEREST

Yiddish *per se* is also of interest to us in this study because of its value for the sociology of language more generally. To a large extent this is due to the fact that the language and its networks of users have been the subject of several previous sociolinguistic investigations (Fishman 1965a, 1965b, 1965c, 1969a, 1972a, 1972b; Doroshkin 1969; Poll 1965; Weinreich 1953, 1967; in press; Ronch *et al.* 1969)

סגן ראש הממשלה

ירושלים, ס"ז אלול תשכ"ד

24 באוגוסם 64.

לכבוד
עורך ה"לצטע נייעס".
תל-אביב

אדוני העורך,

בשובי מחו"ל עיינתי בקטעי עתונות שציצטברו על שולחני בשבועות האחרונים
והופתעתי לקרוא דברי חרעומת על שחיארתי את שפת האידיש, כביכול, כ"שפה זרה".
(א: פרעמדה שפראך).

די לעיין ב"דברי הכנסת" מיום 3.6.64 ומיום 8.7.64 - כדי לוהיוונוה כי מעולם
לא השתמשתי בניסוי כזה. להנך, הדגשתי בדברי תשובתי לח"כ משה סבה את המעמד
המירחד של שפת יידיש בתולדותיו, בתרבותו ובמערכת זכרונותיו של עמנו.

מסתבר כי אין מקום לתרעומת נגדי על דברים שלא אמרתי. לי יש יסוד
לתרעומת שה נגד עתונים שאיבם מדייקים במסירת דברים על דיוקם ; ואת התרעומת
הזאת אני מביע בפניך במלוא המרץ.

כפי שהסברתי בכנסת הקושי גער במצוקה תקציבית ובעיקרון השוויוני
שהיה מחייב הגדלת מיכסת הזמן העומדת לרשותן של שפות יהודיות אחרות, ובעיקר
לאדינו, אילו הורחב הזמן המיועד לתוכנית השידור היידיש.

מותר להתווכח על בעיות מעשיות כאלה אך אין רשות לשים בפי דברים שלא
אמרתי. אני מקווה כי תואיל לתקן את הדרוש המטעה שהנקט לקוראיך על ידי
פירסום מובלט של מכתב זה.

ב ב ר כ ה,

Fig. 1. Letter by Abba Eban (August 24, 1964) to the editor of the Yiddish daily *Letste Nayes*, claiming to having been misrepresented and misquoted in the Yiddish press. Not only did he not refer to Yiddish as 'a foreign language' but he stressed in his remarks in the Knesset (June 3 and July 8 1964) 'the special status of Yiddish in our history, in our culture and in the entire system of memories of our people'. However, any increase in the (radio) budget for Yiddish would have to be at the expense of 'another Jewish language, particularly Ladino'. (Note: the two Yiddish phrases in the letter are misspelled, in both cases Hebrew rather than Yiddish orthographic conventions being used.)

several of which have raised issues and presented data of general significance. Any continuity in social research is sufficiently rare to make the few instances of this kind within the sociology of language noteworthy in and of themselves. However, it must be recognized that this scholarly interest is due, at least to a substantial extent, to the fact that Yiddish speech (or, more accurately, speech and writing) networks have lent themselves so easily to investigations of several topics that are of basic importance to the sociology of language, e.g., the differentiation of sociolects along cultural and religious experiential lines, the detachment of varieties initially functioning in a diglossic relationship to a classical language, the success and failure of language nationalism, the standardization and planning of languages with recently expanded functions, etc.

In the present case our interest in Yiddish itself, other than in the Israeli context of pressures for greater public recognition and support, will be a comparative one, largely *vis-à-vis* Yiddish in the United States. In both instances huge immigration movements have carried major contingents of Yiddish speakers to locales far distant from and far different than those from which they came. However, in the one case (the United States) Yiddish can obviously appeal only to the democratic ideal of cultural pluralism and freedom of cultural continuity, whereas in the other (Israel) it can also appeal on a more particularistic basis as well. In both instances the context is one of urbanization, industrialization, and national cultural consolidation. In one case (the United States), however, the process is far advanced and immigration from eastern Europe is long past its apex; in the other case (Israel) the immigration of Yiddish speakers is both more recent as well as still very much in the offing insofar as immigration from the Soviet Union is concerned. Thus basically we will be looking to see whether the trends *vis-à-vis* Yiddish language maintenance in the United States (if possible in comparison with other immigrant languages there) are similar to or different from those pertaining to Yiddish in Israel (if possible also in comparison with other languages of relatively recent immigrants there). Once again our goal — the study of a larger speech community in two different contexts — will be a study which is suggestive in nature rather than definitive in the hope that our work can be used as a stepping-stone for future investigation.

1. BASIC DEMOGRAPHICS

1.1. On the basis of the latest census figures available (those for 1961; 1971 data are expected shortly) Hebrew is the 'main language spoken' for some three-quarters of the Jewish population of Israel. All in all 87.5% of the entire Jewish population claim to speak Hebrew but for some 12.2% of the Hebrew claimants it is only a secondary or additional language rather than their major claimed vehicle of spoken communication. If these figures are accurate then Israel is not yet as linguistically homogeneous from the point of view of usage as is the United States (where 94.1% of the population as of 1969 claimed English to be their current usual 'home language') but it is well advanced in that direction, given the fact that it is both much younger as a sociopolitical entity and that its immigrational period is still so close at hand.[5] Nevertheless, the numerical position of Yiddish, both absolutely and relatively, is very different in these two contexts. In Israel Yiddish is the immigrant-based principal language with the highest number of speakers (only Hebrew and Arabic being claimed more frequently) with 101,110 persons (aged two or older) claiming it as their 'main spoken language' (Table I).[6]

Table I. *Yiddish in Israel and the United States: Basic Numerical Status*

	Israel 1961[a]	U.S.A. 1969[b]
Mother-tongue	—	1,620,000
Principal spoken language	101,110 (36.46%)	126,000
Additional spoken language	176,375 (63.54%)	—
Percent of total Jewish population for whom it is the principal spoken language	5.6%	2.1%
Percent of total Jewish population for whom it is the principal *or* additional spoken language	13.4%	—

[a] Israeli data in this and subsequent tables are based upon a Jewish population aged two years or older of 2,072,630 in 1961 and are derived from various tables reported in *Languages, Literacy and Educational Attainment*, Part III (= *Central Bureau of Statistics, Population and Housing Census 1961, Publication 29*).

[b] United States data in this and subsequent tables are based upon a total population of 198,214,000 in 1970 and are derived from various tables reported in *Current Population Report, Series P-20*, No. 221, 'Characteristics of the Population by Ethnic Origin: November 1969' (U.S. Bureau of the Census).

In the United States Yiddish is claimed as 'language usually spoken at home' by only 126,000 individuals and, as such, is outclaimed by Spanish, Italian, German, Polish, and French (Table IV). Indeed Yiddish in Israel (as of 1961) was the principal spoken language of 5.6% of the total Jewish population and was claimed as an *additional* spoken language by an even larger proportion, 7.8%. While no accurate comparable figures are available for the United States the proportions claiming Yiddish as either principal or additional spoken language (assuming a Jewish population of 6,000,000) must be much smaller (approximately 2.1%).

1.2. If there is any similarity between Israel and the United States *vis-à-vis* the demographic bases of Yiddish it is that it is overwhelmingly the language of an older foreign-born population in both settings (Tables II and IIIA). With respect to the age factor alone, and from the point of view of maintaining Yiddish, the situation is probably better in Israel than it is in the United States. Although the data are not, strictly speaking, comparable (the United States only reporting on mother-tongue claimants in this connection and Israel

Table II. *Nativity of Yiddish Claimants*

	Israel 1961	U.S.A. 1969
Mother-tongue		
native-born	–	1,142,000 (70.52%)
foreign-born	–	478,000 (29.48%)
total	–	1,620,000
Principal spoken language		
native-born	3,325 (2.7 %)	20,000 (15.88%)
foreign-born	97,140 (97.3 %)	106,000 (84.12%)
total	100,865[a]	126,000
Principal or additional spoken language		
native-born	35,740 (12.88%)	–
foreign-born	241,745 (87.12%)	–
total	277,485	–

[a] In other tables this total is reported as 101,110.

העתק

סגן ראש הממשלה
ירושלים, ל' בשבט תשכ"ה . 2 פברואר 1965

לכבוד
ח"ה מ. גרוס-צימרמן, ב. הלר, מ. חלמיש
אגודת סופרי ועתונאי יידיש
רחוב דב הוז 25
תל-אביב

נכבדי,

בהמשך לשיחתנו בלשכתי ב-19 בינואר, ברצוני לסכם את המצב ולענות על מכתבכם
שהשארתם בידי בסוף הפגישה.

אני שותף להערכתכם ללשון יידיש ולעמדתכם ששפה זו אינה רק אחת הלשונות
שאותן יש לנצל כאמצעי לקליטת עולים חדשים. דבר זה בא לביטוי בפגישתחנו כשהודגש
ש"קול ישראל" רואה בשידורים בלשון יידיש דבר שאינו תלוי אך ורק בזרם העליה של דוברי
יידיש. לפיכך ימשיך שירות השידור לטפח ולפתוח את השידורים ביידיש בהתאם לאפשרויות
התקציביות העומדות לרשותו.

ביודעי כמה כנה דאגתכם לענין זה זימנתי את הפגישה בהשתתפות מנהל "קול
ישראל", על מנת לשתף אתכם בבעיות המעשיות והכספיות העומדות בפנינו. יחד עם זאת אני
שמח להודיעכם כי שירות השידור מחפש אפשרות להוסיף שידור חדשי נוסף של שירה ביידיש.
השרות אוסף כעת את החומר הדרוש לכך ואני מקווה שיפעיל תכנית זו בחדשים הקרובים.

כאשר לייצוג במליאת רשות השידור, עלי להודיעכם כי החוק קובע כיצד תורכב
המליאה. כאשר יתקבל החוק בכנסת, תהיו רשאים לדאוג לייצוג האינטרסים המיוחדים שלכם
באמצעות הנציגות של הסופרים ברשות.

בכבוד רב,

אבא אבן

Fig. 2. Deputy Minister Abba Eban's letter (February 2, 1965) to representatives of the
Yiddish Writers and Journalists Association of Israel indicating his agreement with their
view that Yiddish was not merely a tool to be used for the adjustment of immigrants and
that radio broadcasting in Yiddish should not depend only on the number of new Yiddish-
speaking immigrants. Given the new Broadcasting Authority, Yiddish writers may seek to be
represented on the Plenary Committee among the literary representatives who will serve on
it. (To this day no such representation has been granted, although many other interest
groups are represented on the Plenary Committee.)

only reporting on principal-/additional-use claimants), it seems probable that the average native-born speaker of Yiddish in the United States (in his early fifties) and the average foreign-born speaker of Yiddish in the United States (in his late sixties) are each fifteen to twenty years older than their counterparts in Israel (Table IIIA).[7] However, the same underlying factor, most probably responsible for the foregoing (namely, far greater recency of immigration), is also responsible for the fact that there are currently proportionally fewer native-born claimants of Yiddish in Israel than in the United States (Table II). Many foreign-born claimants of Yiddish in Israel were still of childbearing age in 1961 (certainly proportionally more so than in the United States) and if their Israeli-born offspring will also be Yiddish-speaking (either primarily or additionally) a rise in native-born claimants of Yiddish may be expected in Israel during the years immediately ahead.

Table IIIA. *Nativity and Age of Yiddish Claimants*

1. Mother-tongue (U.S.A.)   (1969)

	Native-born	Foreign-born
under 14	.4%	.2%
14–24	7.0%	1.5%
25–44	29.4%	4.6%
45–64	50.6%	30.7%
65+	12.7%	63.1%
(median	50.2	65+)
(total number	1,142,000	478,000)

2. Principal/additional spoken language (Israel)

	Native-born		Foreign-born	
	age 2–14	age 15+	age 2–14	age 15+
Principal	1,955	1,880	2,145	94,995
	(51.5%) →	(48.5%)	(2.2%) →	(97.8%)
Additional	13,400	18,465	10,885	133,720
	(42.0%) →	(58.0%)	(7.5%) →	(92.5%)
	(13.0%)	(9.2%)	(16.3%)	(41.5%)
	↓	↓	↓	↓
	(87.0%)	(90.8%)	(83.7%)	(58.5%)

Table IIIB

1. *Main Language Spoken at Home by Age (for Jewish Israelis Aged Eighteen or Older)*[a]

			LANGUAGE				
Age	Hebrew	Yiddish	Arabic or Turkish	Eastern European	Western or central European	Latin American or Balkan	%
18–24	18	2	26	16	7	3	16
24–29	12	1	10	4	7	7	10
30–34	13	2	5	1	9	7	10
35–39	12	3	2	4	4	17	10
40–44	11	5	8	2	20	3	11
45–49	10	9	8	19	9	13	10
50–54	7	16	10	10	4	13	8
55–64	13	39	12	22	29	23	16
65+	4	24	14	13	11	13	8
total	100%	100%	100%	100%	100%	100%	100%
X%	71	7	8	5	4	2	

2. *Main Language Spoken at Home by Ethnic Origin (for Jewish Israelis Aged Eighteen or Older)*

			LANGUAGE				
Ethnic origin	Hebrew	Yiddish	Arabic or Turkish	Eastern European	Western or central European	Latin American or Balkan	%
Born in Asia or Africa	41	1	94	3	50	44	42
Born in Europe or America	37	97	0	95	44	44	42
Sabra: father born in Asia or Africa	7	0	5	0	4	4	5
Sabra: father born in Europe or America	12	1	0	3	2	7	8
Sabra: father born Sabra	4	1	1	0	0	0	3
X%	70	7	8	5	4	2	

[a] Tables generated by Liz Nadel from the data bank of *Tarbut Yisrael 1970* (Katz *et al.* 1972).

1.3. All in all the striking difference between the demographic position of Yiddish in Israel and in the United States seems to be
explainable on demographic grounds *per se*. Israel has experienced a
far more recent major wave of Yiddish-speaking immigrants than has
the United States (and more such are expected from the Soviet
Union). As a result a much higher proportion of the Jewish population is Yiddish-speaking, and Yiddish claimants are both younger and
more commonly foreign-born than they are in the United States.

2. YIDDISH AND OTHER RECENT IMMIGRANT LANGUAGES: DEMO-GRAPHIC COMPARISONS

2.1. In both Israel and the United States Yiddish is one of the six top languages — as far as numbers of speakers are concerned — derived from relatively recent immigrant stock.[8] The other five languages in question are only partially the same, however, with Polish, French, and German being of substantial importance in both countries. Spanish and Italian, however, are of such importance only in the United States (although an increasing *aliya*/immigration from Latin America is now expected in Israel) and Hungarian and Rumanian are of importance only in Israel (Table IV). Over and above the foregoing it is quite clear that Yiddish is first among the 'top six' in Israel (or second if Arabic is included) whereas it is last in rank in the United States. The comparative precariousness of Yiddish in the United States is quite evident. Not only is its total number of mother-tongue claimants lowest among the 'top six' but so is its proportion of native-born claimants and its claimed *rate of use as principal language* among those for whom it was the mother-tongue. Only German is proportionately less claimed as principal language by the foreign-born for whom it was the mother-tongue; no other language is so little claimed as principal language among the *native-born* for whom it was the mother-tongue as is Yiddish.

The situation in Israel is appreciably more favorable. Not only is Yiddish clearly numerically stronger than any of the other 'top six' languages of recent immigrants but its rate of claimed use as principal language (among all that claim to speak it) is by no means weak. If we examine the *total number of claimants* Yiddish is in the company of Polish, German, and French in that in each case some 37% of all its claimants also claim it as their principal spoken language (Table IV).[9]

If we examine only native-born claimants the position of Yiddish also appears to be relatively good. Although, in general, major use of languages other than Hebrew is rather low among native-born Israelis (but not yet as low as is major use of languages other than English in the United States), Yiddish is claimed as the principal spoken language by some 11% of those native-born Israelis who claim to speak it at all (Table IV), a percent which is somewhat larger than that which pertains to either German (5%), Hungarian (8%), or Rumanian (10%), while somewhat smaller than that for Polish (14%) or French (17%).

מ. מדן

נדמה לי שצריך להאמר בצורה ברורה ביותר, שתהיה מובנת גם לעתונים הלועזיים
ולה ועורכיהם, שיש הבדל גדול מאד בין ה"ג׳רוסלם פוסט" ובין כל עתון לועזי אחר היוצא
ארץ. ה"ג׳רוסלם פוסט" אינו עתון המיועד לציבור העברי, הוא בעיקר בטאון של המדינה
פי חוץ, והוא צריך להביע דבריו של הישוב העברי ושל מדינת-ישראל כלפי חוץ, והשפה
בגלית היא אחד מאמצעי התקשורת היעילים שמביאים דברינו כלפי חוץ. לכן יש מעמד מיוחד
תוך זה, לא פחות מאשר לעתונים עבריים אחרים.

העתונים הלועזיים השונים אין להם זכות להיות יותר מאשר אמצעי עזר ארעי
ולה כל זמן שהוא לא רכש לעצמו את היכולת לקרוא עתון עברי. בתור כאלה הם חייבים
אות עצמם כדבר ארעי שמשרת ומסייע. אם נאמר להם שעליהם לתת מאמר ראשי בעברית, כדי
ביע את דעתם ולקנות להם זכות להכלל בסיקור היומי, אין ה"לעצטע נייעס" מיוחס יותר
"וויאצה נועסטרא" או עתון פולני. האידיש לא תהיה ואינה דבר מיוחס במדינה ששפתה
שמית עברית, לא יותר מהצרפתית או הרומנית. עתון יהודי צריך לדעת שתפקידו כלפי
ראיו להכשיר אותם להיות אזרחים של המדינה ולרכוש את השפה העברית. אם האידישיסטים
השלימו עם זה ובאים כאן לצעוק את צעקתם של התנועה הזאת המתפגרת בכל העולם כולו,
חנו לא ניתן להם סיוע זה. "ג׳רוסלם פוסט" זה דבר אחר וה"לעצטע נייעס" זה דבר אחר,
את הם חייבים לדעת.

Fig. 3. From the stenographic record of a meeting of the *Meliah* (Plenary Committee) of *Reshut Ha-Shidur* (The Broadcasting Authority), September, 1970.

Mr. M. Madan [Representative of the Academy of the Hebrew Language]:

'The various foreign language periodicals have no other justification than that of temporary auxiliary means for immigrants as long as they have not acquired the ability to read a Hebrew newspaper. . . . The *Letste Nayes* is not more privileged than (the Rumanian) *Viata Noastra* or a Polish periodical. Yiddish will not be and is not a privileged commodity in this country, whose official language is Hebrew, no more than French or Rumanian. . . . If the Yiddishists cannot make peace with this fact and they come here to cry their lament of this backward movement that is dying out all over the world, we will give them no help. The *Jerusalem Post* is one thing and *Letste Nayes* is another and they should know that.'

Table IV. The Top Six Immigrant Based Languages: U.S.A. 1969

Language	Mother-tongue		Principal language		Additional language	
	Native-born	Foreign-born	Native-born	Foreign-born	Native-born	Foreign-born
Spanish	4,878,000	1,822,000	3,104,000 (63.6)ᵃ	1,581,000 (81.2)		
German	4,809,000	1,025,000	256,000 (3.2)	159,000 (15.5)		
Italian	3,147,000	1,218,000	165,000 (5.2)	493,000 (40.5)		
French	1,801,000	378,000	254,000 (14.1)	160,000 (42.2)		
Polish	1,982,000	399,000	66,000 (3.3)	163,000 (40.7)		
Yiddish	1,142,000	478,000	20,000 (1.8)	106,000 (35.8)		
Israel 1961						
Yiddish			3,875 (10.8)	97,140 (40.5)	31,865	144,605
German			532 (4.8)	27,675 (42.2)	10,650	37,845
Rumanian			400 (9.6)	39,580 (59.1)	3,775	27,400
French			1,150 (17.3)	23,405 (38.0)	5,495	38,240
Polish			160 (14.7)	19,365 (37.0)	995	33,015
Hungarian			327 (8.2)	20,163 (50.2)	3,645	20,000

ᵃ Percentages are based upon the number of mother-tongue claimants of each language.

198   *Joshua A. Fishman and David E. Fishman*

2.2. Another glimpse of the relative staying power of Yiddish in Israel and in the United States is gained through examination of how its claimants behave with respect to the national languages of the countries under consideration (Table V). It has already been pointed out that very few claimants of the 'top six' mother-tongues in the United States continue to utilize them as their principal languages, least of all in the case of Yiddish. Only in the case of Spanish mother-tongue do less than an overwhelming proportion of the native-born and a distinct majority of the foreign-born employ anything but English as their principal language of everyday use.

In Israel the picture is still far different from the foregoing. On the average, speakers of the top six immigrant languages use Hebrew only about half of the time, Yiddish speakers included, and in the case of

Table V. *Use of Yiddish and the National Language: U.S.A. 1969*

Mother-tongue	Total claimants	Native-born; current language English	Foreign-born; current language English
Spanish	6,700,000	1,774,000 (36.4)	341,000 (18.7)
German	5,835,000	4,653,000 (96.8)	866,000 (84.5)
Italian	4,364,000	2,982,000 (94.8)	725,000 (59.5)
French	2,179,000	1,547,000 (85.9)	218,000 (57.7)
Polish	2,382,000	1,916,000 (96.7)	236,000 (59.2)
Yiddish	1,620,000	1,122,000 (98.2)	372,000 (77.8)

Israel 1961

Major 'other' language (other than Hebrew)	Index of Hebrew-speaking[a]	Speaking no Hebrew	Speaking mother-tongue only	Total claimants
Yiddish	51.5	58,950 (21.2)	27,025 (9.3)	277,485
German	52.1	13,885 (18.1)	7,540 (9.8)	76,700
Rumanian	38.0	25,275 (35.5)	6,305 (8.9)	71,155
French	54.0	8,390 (12.3)	3,050 (4.4)	68,290
Polish	52.8	8,550 (16.0)	2,030 (3.8)	53,535
Hungarian	45.2	11,610 (26.3)	4,770 (10.8)	44,135

[a] Index roughly indicates percent of time spent speaking Hebrew and is based upon *all* claimants of any particular 'other' language rather than only upon those knowing some Hebrew. In 1948 the corresponding indices were 29.7, 37.0, 28.1, 37.1, 39.4, 30.0 (Hofman and Fisherman 1971).

Hungarian and Rumanian even less than that. Yiddish claimants are also no less likely than are others to speak no Hebrew at all (about 20% of all claimants) and even to speak their mother-tongue *only* (about 10% of all claimants). Indeed in this last respect Yiddish claimants tend to be on a par with Hungarian and Rumanian claimants (even though they do not tend to be as recent in their immigration as are the latter two) and to reveal a substantially higher rate of mother-tongue monolingualism than either Polish or French claimants.[10] This latter fact is probably attributable to the existence of ultra-orthodox communities in which only Yiddish is employed. No similar Jewishness-committed communities function in the other top six languages of recent immigrants (nor, indeed, among the speakers of any other immigrant languages in Israel). In this connection then we begin to note factors that point to Yiddish not *only* as an immigrant language (as it is in the United States). In Israel Yiddish is also a special language of Jews and Jewishness (i.e., it represents a stream within the *majority* group and an element of its culture) for at least some of its claimants, although it is such *at the expense of Hebrew* among only a small (and possibly shrinking) minority, for some of whom Hebrew is ideologically unacceptable for everyday purposes.

2.3. A final explanatory dimension with respect to the differential staying power of Yiddish in Israel and in the United States may be that of settlement pattern. Jews are apparently the most urbanized immigrant group in the United States (Fishman 1966). This factor is, in turn, related to far greater exposure to English media, to English as a *lingua franca* among immigrants of different origins (Lieberson and Curry 1971), and to social mobility or cultural discontinuity. All of these processes have had a greater joint impact on Jews and on Yiddish mother-tongue claimants than on other relatively recent immigrants to the United States.

The Israeli setting reveals a far less definite picture as far as the differential impact or rurality is concerned (Table VI). Yiddish claimants *are* among the more urbanized of claimants of the top six languages but they are *not* the most urbanized (as they are in the United States), nor are they more urbanized than Rumanian claimants who, it will be remembered, are highly retentive. Indeed more powerful than rurality is the factor of place of settlement, in this case 'new settlements' (in which newcomers of a single background are often a sizeable minority if not a majority) vs. 'old settlements'.

„רק עברית"

אין א סעריע ארטיקלען האם
אייער מיסארבעטער יוסף גאיד־
קארן באהאנדלט פארשידענע אס־
פעקטן וואס שייך דער קליטה פון
די רוסישע יידן, אויף וועזכע מיר
האבן געוואַרט צענדליקער יארן,
ביז מיר האבן זיך דערוואַרט. און
הרבוואי וייטער נישט ערגער. איך
וויל זיך דא אפשטעלן אויף איין
אספעקט פון דער פראגע, וועגן
דעם עגין „רק עברית". וואס ביר
הערן אפט אין אונדזערע אמט.
איך האב זיך שוין אויך אַנע־
טראַסן אויף אזעלכע פאקטן, און
דאס דוקא מצד אנגשטעלטע.
וועלכע רעדן א גאנץ גוטן יידיש.
די דאזיקע מענטשו מיינען, אז

מיט אזא דעמאנסטראַציע רגבי א
נייעם עולה פירן זיי אויס א
גרויסע פאטריאָטישע מיסיע. פאק־
טיש אין דאס גראד פארקערט.
אזא האנדלונג קען נאר גורם זיין
פאַרדרוס און אפילו מארביטערונג
צווישן די עולים. דאָס איז פשוט
הפקרות. וואָס טאָר נישט פאָרע־
רירם ווערן. איך וויל אבער זאָגן.
אז א גרויסע צאל באאמטע. דוו־
קא פון משרד הקליטה. רעדן מיט
די עולים אין יידיש און אפילו
אין רוסיש.

מ. שליטנער,
קרית אונו

וואָס פאַר א תירוץ
האָבן זיי דערפאַר?

אויף אַלע פראָטעסטן און פאַ־
דערונגען וועגן איינפירן יידיש
אויף דער טעלעוויזיע, אָדער
פאַרלענגערן די האַלבע שעה אויף
דער ראַדיאָ האָט די פאַרוואַלטונג
א פאַרטיקן תירוץ — נישטא קיין
געלט אָדער קיין צייט. און אַלע
וויסן דאָך, אז אין אונדזער מלו־
כהשער אַדמיניסטראַציע איז מען
זייער שפּאָרעוודיק אין געלט און
צייט...

אַלע פאַרנאַכט, אַזייגער 1, גיט
דער ראַדיאָ (ב) אַ 15־מינוטיקן
פראָגראַם „עברית לעם". חוץ ביי־
עם פון טאַג אין אַן „עברית קלה",
גיט מען אַ 5־מינוטיקע לעקציע
אין עברית פון אַנפאַנגערס. טרעפט
זיך אין דער לעקציע אַ וואָרט,
וואָס מען דאַרף דערקלערן, פאַר־
טייטשט מען עס אין דריי שפּראַ־
כן: אין עגגליש, אין פראַנצױ־
זיש און אין רוסיש. אבער חלילה
נישט אין יידיש, כאָטש די צאָל
צוהערערס, וואָס רעדן און פאַר־
שטייען יידיש איז פיל גרעסער
ווי די פון די אַנדערע שפּראַכן.
און עס איז נישט צופעליק אזוי,
נאָר שטענדיק און אויסגעהאַלטן.

צי דען זשע קאָן די לערער־
קע, וואָס איז אַזאַ מומחה אין
שפּראַכן, קיין וואָרט יידיש נישט,
אָדער וייסט נישט, אַז עס זענען
דאָ ווערטערביכער, וואָס מען קאָן
אַ קוק טאָן דעם טייטש פון אַ
העברעאיש וואָרט אין יידיש. מעג
לעך אבער, אַז די לערערקע איז
דאָ נעבעך גאָרנישט שולדיק. עס
איז אַן אָנזאָג און אַ פאַרבאָט פון
דער דירעקציע.

ביילע מאַרק, נתניה

Fig. 4. Two letters to the editor concerning problems of recent immigrants. The first is
entitled 'What is their excuse?' (June 5, 1973).

During the twice daily radio broadcasts, in which new immigrants are taught Hebrew,
new words 'are explained in three languages: English, French and Russian. However, they are
never explained in Yiddish, although the number of listeners that speak and understood
Yiddish is greater than those of other languages. This is not done intermittently but
always .... it is probably not the teacher's fault. It is an indication that the radio administration has forbidden her to use Yiddish' (*Letste Nayes,* July 5, 1973).

The second letter (July 8, 1973) is entitled 'Hebrew only' and complains about
government employees who serve new immigrants and who can speak Yiddish well. 'The
people believe that by answering "only in Hebrew" they are engaging in a great patriotic
mission. Actually the case is just the opposite. Such behavior results in feelings of insult and
even bitterness among immigrants. Such behavior is really irresponsible and should not be
tolerated' (*Letste Nayes,* June 8, 1973).

Table VI. *Settlement Patterns: U.S.A. 1960 (Fishman 1966)*

Mother-tongue	% rural
Spanish	15
German	10
Italian	7
French	16
Polish	10
Yiddish	2

Israel 1961

Major 'other' language claimed (other than Hebrew)	Total	Rural	%	New settlements	%
Yiddish	277,155	23,600	9	44,335	16
German	76,700	9,050	12	7,485	10
Rumanian	71,110	6,125	9	23,390	33
French	68,315	11,295	16	33,385	49
Polish	3,970	3,970	6	10,485	19
Hungarian	7,625	7,625	17	12,270	28

Rumanian and Hungarian claimants (as well as French claimants most of whom actually hail from North Africa) are clearly most congregated in new settlements. Yiddish speakers on the other hand are most similar in their settlement pattern to such old timers as the German claimants in that they live overwhelmingly in old settlements. Thus it is the combination of urbanness plus old-settlement residence that particularly typifies Yiddish claimants. Given this pattern, Yiddish claimants (like German and even Polish claimants) are much exposed to Hebrew speaking media and neighbors and as such may be all the more dependent on separate districts, institutions, and organizations for mother-tongue maintenance. In a subsequent section we will examine whether or not they have such.

2.4. The census data reviewed in this section indicate that not only is the condition of Yiddish in Israel stronger than it is in the United States (this much was also clear from section 1) but that it is also in a relatively favorable condition *vis-à-vis* the other top six European-based languages of relatively recent substantial immigration in Israel itself. It is claimed as a principal or additional language by vastly more people (indeed by almost as many as the next remaining five languages combined); the degree to which it is claimed as only language or as principal language by foreign-born and native-born Israelis compares favorably with the others; and the substantial degree of urbanization and old-settlement residence of its claimants does not seem to have weakened its retentivity appreciably, although it has undoubtedly contributed to the dramatic growth in the extent to which its claimants have also acquired Hebrew in the period 1948–1961.

3. DIACHRONIC TRENDS IN RELATIVE RETENTIVITY

Two approaches have thus far been used in attempting to gauge the robustness of Yiddish in Israel today. The first was a direct comparison between Israel and the United States *vis-à-vis* Yiddish *per se*. The second was a relative comparison, again in both locales, but *vis-à-vis* the other languages of relatively recent major immigration. The final approach to be utilized here will be to reconsider the latter comparisons *over a period of time*, normally over the 1940 to 1960 (or 1969) span of years. Proceeding in this fashion it should become clear whether it has changed more or less, in the same or in different directions, than the other languages primarily dependent upon relatively recent large-scale immigration to the United States and Israel.

3.1. In this connection the American census provides interesting information particularly in the light of the continued decrease in the absolute and relative extent to which non-English mother-tongues have been claimed ever since 1920. It is clear from Table VIIA that this decrease must reflect processes that are particularly characteristic of former claimants of mother-tongues *outside* of the ranks of the big six. *Within* this fold, however, the decline has generally been very slow, limited to the foreign-born, and indeed often reversed. Only in the case of Polish and Yiddish has the decline been unrelenting. This is particularly noteworthy because it not only highlights the crucial importance of truly huge numerical concentrations if language maintenance is to be insured in American urban, industrialized, non-traditional surroundings, but it also highlights the difference between mother-tongue communities that are truly and

Table VIIA. *U.S.A.: Total Number of Claimants of Top Six Non-English Mother Tongues, 1940—1969*[a]

Mother-tongue	1940 total	1969	% change
Spanish	1,861,400	6,700,000	259.4
German	4,949,780	5,835,000	17.9
Italian	3,766,820	4,364,000	15.7
French	1,412,060	2,179,000	54.3
Polish	2,416,320	2,382,000	− 1.4
Yiddish	1,751,100	1,620,000	− 7.5

Foreign-Born Claimants of Top Six Non-English Mother Tongues, 1920—1969[a]

Mother-tongue	1920	1940	1960	1969	% change 1960—1969
Spanish	556,111	428,360	766,961	1,822,000	137.4
German	2,267,128	1,589,040	1,278,772	1,025,000	− 19.8
Italian	1,624,998	1,561,100	1,226,141	1,218,000	− 0.7
French	466,956	359,520	330,220	378,000	14.5
Polish	1,077,392	801,680	581,963	399,000	− 31.4
Yiddish	1,091,820	924,440	503,605	478,000	− 5.1

[a] All data for years prior to 1969 are from Fishman 1966.

completely recent immigrant-based and those that go back to colonial times. It is clear that the latter have continually been more retentive than the former and, moreover, that they continue to be such today, for were this not the case their total number of claimants would continue to drop as the number of their foreign-born claimants drops. Spanish is the most obvious case where this is not happening;[11] neither is it happening for German or French. (In the latter case in fact a minor resurgence of foreign-born strength may be noted.) However, not only are the fully immigrant mother-tongue communities differently retentive than those that can also draw upon colonial roots but, within the former category, Italians seem to have been far more successful in implanting their mother-tongue in the younger generation than either eastern European Jews or Poles, although the emigrations of all three groups were practically simultaneous. The reasons for this difference are not clear but it is obvious

Table VIIB. *Index of Speaking Foreign Languages among the Jewish Population*[a]

| 1948 | | 1961 | | Change |
Language	Index	Language	Index	in rank
1. Bulgarian	79.5	1. Turkish	55.5	+ 2
2. Rumanian	71.9	2. Persian	51.1	+12
3. Turkish	70.5	3. Hungarian	50.9	+ 2
4. Yiddish	70.3	4. Kurdish	49.6	+ 9
5. Hungarian	70.0	5. Bulgarian	48.6	− 4
6. Czech and		6. Greek	47.5	+ 4
Slovak	66.8	7. Spanish (including		
7. Italian	66.0	Dzudezmo)		+ 4
8. German	63.0	8. Rumanian	46.5	− 6
9. French	62.9	9. German	45.8	− 1
10. Greek	62.3	10. Yiddish	45.6	− 6
11. Spanish (including		11. Arabic	45.3	+ 6
Dzudezmo)	61.2	12. Russian	44.3	+ 6
12. Bukharian	57.5	13. Polish	44.2	+ 2
13. Kurdish	55.7	14. French	44.1	− 5
14. Persian[b]	51.8	15. Dutch	43.8	+ 1
15. Polish	50.6	16. Bukharian	43.0	− 4
16. Dutch	48.6	17. Italian	41.8	−10
17. Arabic	46.4	18. Czech and		
18. Russian	45.5	Slovak	41.3	−12
19. English[c]	43.4	19. English[c]	33.7	−

[a] From Hofman and Fisherman 1971.
[b] Many claimants of Persian are really speakers of Farsic/Parsic and many claimants of Greek are really speakers of Yevanic (my footnote: J.A.F.).
[c] Low index because heavily weighted as 'additional' language.

that some purely immigrant groups have been more retentive than others and that Yiddish speakers must not only be counted among the least retentive ones today but that they have a thirty- to forty-year history of such in the United States.

3.2. No directly comparable historical data are available for Israel (but note Table VIIB). However, some pertinent historical clues are not without interest. Table VIII indicates that the Yiddish mother-tongue share in the eastern European migration was beginning to run dry in 1955. Today, when a small additional migration can be expected from Rumania and a much larger one from the Soviet

Table VIII. *The Relative Share of Yiddish and Mother-Tongue among Foreign-Born Speaking a Language Other than Hebrew, by Period of Immigration (1961)*[a]

Mother-tongue	Soviet Union Russian		Poland Polish		Rumania Rumanian		Germany/ Austria German		Czechoslovakia Czech and Slovak		Hungary Hungarian	
	N	%	N	%	N	%	N	%	N	%	N	%
Up to 1947												
Yiddish	30,615	64.2	57,990	71.7	6,130	39.0	1,550	5.0	2,090	26.0	1,075	16.7
Mother-tongue	7,640	16.0	12,765	15.8	4,880	31.0	27,360	88.5	590	7.3	4,605	71.4
Other languages	9,430	19.8	10,080	12.5	4,715	30.0	1,990	6.5	5,370	66.7	765	11.9
Total	47,685	100.0	80,835	100.0	15,725	100.0	30,800	100.0	8,050	100.0	6,445	100.0
1948–1954												
Yiddish	16,210	64.6	56,245	74.9	35,185	39.8	5,140	57.6	3,495	30.1	1,950	17.5
Mother-tongue	2,575	10.3	15,785[b]	21.0	41,740	47.2	2,940	32.9	2,715	23.4	8,745	78.3
Other languages	6,295	25.1	3,065	4.1	1,445	13.0	845	9.5	5,395	46.5	470	4.2
Total	25,080	100.0	75,095	100.0	88,370	100.0	8,925	100.0	11,605	100.0	11,165	100.0
1955 on												
Yiddish	6,325	37.9	12,825	42.7	6,405	23.2	140	15.1	150	—	—	7.6
Mother-tongue	5,275	31.6	15,660	52.1	16,805	60.9	555	59.7	60	9.2	6,015	89.2
Other languages	5,095	30.5[c]	1,575	5.2	4,395	15.9	235	25.2	440	67.7[d]	220	3.2
Total	16,695	100.0	30,060	100.0	27,605	100.0	930	100.0	650	100.0	6,745	100.0

a From Hofman and Fisherman 1971.
b Mainly German.
c Mainly Polish.
d Mainly Hungarian.

Union the proportions of Yiddish speakers among these immigrants are very likely to be somewhat smaller (by 20 percent according to recent estimates) than what they were in 1955. A similar picture probably applies to immigration from the United States and Latin America. That immigration is also likely to be larger than it was in the recent past but, once again, the proportion of Yiddish speakers is likely to be smaller than was formerly the case. Thus, all in all, Yiddish in Israel is likely to be thrown back increasingly upon its own resources rather than being able to depend upon transfusions from outside, even though some such transfusions may well continue for another decade or so.

As Table IX reveals, and as we have seen heretofore, the resources of Yiddish in Israel are very considerable. In the capacity of principal or sole language it has far more claimants than any other of the 'top six', indeed almost as many as all others combined. However, its position as principal or sole language has deteriorated very rapidly over the past quarter-century. Since 1954 it has lost nearly 30 percent of its claimants in this particular respect, an indication of the ease and enthusiasm with which its claimants acquire (or also acquire) Hebrew. Rumanian and German too are marked by declining numbers of claimants as principal languages but their declines are far more gradual. French, Hungarian, and Polish on the other hand all show increased numbers of claimants between 1954 and 1961. Of course all of these trends reflect recency of immigration, foreign-born Yiddish claimants tending to have been in Israel somewhat longer than have claimants of Rumanian, French, Hungarian, or Polish.

If we could examine similar time-trend figures for claimants of Yiddish as a second or *additional* language our understanding would be much enhanced. (Unfortunately there are no Israeli time-trend statistics on *additional* language claiming.) There is no reason to expect that the number of claimants of Yiddish as an *additional* language has declined in Israel in recent years (rather there are many reasons — social, psychological, and demographic — to expect this number to have increased); but whether this is indeed true, and, if so, whether or not it is differentially so for Yiddish relative to others of the top six group, remains to be seen when the necessary 1971 data become available. In the meantime it seems possible that among the bulk of its claimants Yiddish runs the risk of more rapidly becoming nonretentive that do the other top six non-Hebrew mother-tongues. This is a possibility that deserves careful attention if only for reasons of contrastive analysis *vis-à-vis* Yiddish in the United States.

מעמאָראַנדום

מיר אונטן געחתמעטע, פאָרשטייער פון אַ געזעלשאַפטלעכן קאָמיטעט, אין וועלכן ס'זענען אַנגעשלאָסן:

דער געזעלשאַפטלעך־ליטעראַרישער קולטור־קרייז „המשך"
דער קולטורקרייז ביי דער י.ל. פרץ ביבליאָטעק אין נתניה
רעדאַקציע „יידישע צייטונג" — תל־אביב
רעדאַקציע „פריי ישראל" — תל־אביב
רעדאַקציע „פראָבלעמען" — תל־אביב
ביכערפאַרלאַג „ניי לעבן"
קרייז פאַר יידיש — רחובות
קרייז פאַר יידיש — חולון
שרייבער, אַרטיסטן, קינסטלער און קולטור־טוער —

מיר, וואָס רעפּרעזענטירן צענדליקער טויזנטער יידן, ישראל־בירגער, און נייע עולים, ווענדן זיך צו אייך מיט דער ביטע, נאָכצוקומען דעם פאָרלאַנג פון הונדערטער טויזנטער יידיש־ריידנדיקע יידן אין ישראל, אַז אין די אוידיציעס פון דער ישראל־טעלעוויזיע זאָל איינגעפירט ווערן אַ טעגלעכער פּראָגראַם פון מינימום אַ האַלבע שעה און אַז אין די אוידיציעס פון קול ישראל (ראַדיאָ) זאָל דער פּראָגראַם אין יידיש אויסגעברייטערט ווערן לכל הפּחות אויף אַנדערהאַלבן שעה טעגלעך. אונדזער ביטע באַזירט זיך אויף פאָלגנדיקע מאָטיוון:

1. אַ האַלבער מיליאָן ישראל־בירגער, וואָס רעדט יידיש, איז פאַראינטערעסירט צו הערן טעגלעך ראַדיאָ און טעלעוויזיע־אוידיציעס אין יידיש און אויף אַ הויכן ניוואָ;

2. דער גרעסטער טייל נייע עולים, ווי אַ גרויסער טייל פון אַלטע תושבים, („וותיקים") באַהערשן נישט גענוג די העברעישע שפּראַך און עס וועט נאָך לאַנג דויערן, ביז די דאָזיקע מענטשן וועלן קענען פאַרשטיין די פּראָגראַמען אין העברעיש;

3. הונדערטער טויזנטער יידיש רעדנדיקע קאַנדידאַטן פאַר עלייה, אין דער גאַנצער וועלט, פאַרהאַלטן זייער עולה זיין אין לאַנד, צוליב דעם חשש, אַז זיי וועלן ליידן אַ לאַנגע צייט אין פּראָצעס פון זייער קולטורעלער אינטעגראַציע, ווייל סוועלן יאָרן פאַרגיין, ביז זיי וועלן באַהערשן די העברעישע שפּראַך, אין אַ פולקאָמענער פאָרם — באַזונדערס צוליב זייער עלטער.

4. דערפאַר גלויבן מיר, אַז אויסגעברייטערטע פּראָגראַמען אין יידיש, אין ראַדיאָ און טעלעוויזיע (פון ישראל) וועלן זיין וויכטיקע פאַקטאָרן אין זייער גייסטיקער פאַרוואָרצלונג אין ישראל־היימלאַנד.

5. דער נאַציזם און דער סטאַלין־רעזשים אין רוסלאַנד האָבן צעשטערט דעם גרעסטן טייל פון די יידישע קבוצים אין אייראָפּע און מיט זיי אומגעבראַכט דעם גרויסן רוב פון די יידיש ריידנדיקע יידן;

דער ציל פון ביידע פּאָליטישע סיסטעמען איז געווען צו פאַרניכטן די טויזנט־יאָריקע יידישע קולטור.

דערפאַר איז אונדזער טיפסטע איבערצייגונג, אַז אויפהאַלטנדיק יידיש, ווערט גלייכצייטיק אויפגעהאַלטן די גאַנצע גייסטיקע ירושה פון אומגעקומענעם אייראָפּעישן יידנטום (נוסח אשכנז) און בתוכם די גרויסע אוצרות פון דער יידישער ליטעראַטור.

6. גוט־אָרגאַניזירטע, אויסגעברייטערטע און הויכקוואַליפיצירטע ראַדיאָ־ און טעלעוויזיע־אוידיציעס אין יידיש, וועלן מיטהעלפן דערציען די ישראל־יוגנט און איר דערמעגלעכן, כאָטש טיילווייז צו באַקענען זיך מיט דער שפּראַך און פאָלקלאָר און מיט די קולטור־ווערטן פון מזרח־אייראָפּעישן יידנטום אין עבר, פאַרטיפן איר פאַרבונדקייט מיטן וועלטיידנטום און פאַרשטאַרקן איר פאַרשטענדעניש פאַר די פּראָבלעמען און נויטן פון יידישן פאָלק היינט און בויען אַ בריק פאַר דער גאַנצקייט פון אַלע פאָלקס־טיילן אין דער צוקונפט.

7. גוטע יידישע פּראָגראַמען אין ראַדיאָ און טעלעוויזיע וועלן שטאַרקן אונדזערע שטרעבונגען פאַר אַ נאָרמאַלן קולטורלעבן פון די יידישע פאָלקס־מאַסן אין רוסלאַנד און אין די מערב־תפוצות און זיי דערמוטיקן צו אַ גרויסער עלייה אין ישראל.

8. מיר גלויבן, אַז יידיש איז געווען און איז נאָך היינט דער מעכטיקסטער כוח קעגן אַסימילאַציע און גייסטיקן שמד אין אַלע דיאַספּאָרע־לענדער;

יידיש פאַראייניקט אומעטום יידן פון פאַרשיידענע לענדער, וואָס רעדן פאַרשיידענע שפּראַכן און האַלט זיי צוזאַמען, ווי אָרגאַנישע טיילן פון יידישן פאָלק.

9. די מחלוקת פון די פאַרטייען וועגן יידיש און העברעיש און זייער ראָל אין לעבן פון יידישן פאָלק, איז שוין לאַנג פאַרשטומט וואָרן — זייט לעצטן גרויסן יידישן חורבן.

אין אונדזער איצטיקער תקופה איז נישט פאַראַן קיין שום אַנטאַגאָניזם צווישן יידיש און העברעיש, וועלכע זענען צווייגן פון איין קולטור. ביידע שפּראַכן האָבן דערפילט און דערפילן ווייטער זייערע נאַציאָנאַל־היסטאָרישע פונקציעס און זיי דערגאַנצן זיך.

דער קיום פון יידיש בילדעט נישט קיין שום סכנה פאַר העברעיש אין דער נייער אין העברעיש געשאַפענער קולטור און ער ברענגט זיי נישט קיין שום שאָדן.

10. די ערשטע חלוצים־בויערס האָבן גערעדט און געזונגען לידער אין יידיש; אין רוסלאַנד און אין אַמעריקע — היינט — ריידן די סאַמע וואָרצלדיקע יידן, פאַרבונדענע מיט חסידות און בית מדרש־קולטור, יידיש און זיי האַלטן אויף די המשכדיקייט פון אונדזער נאַציאָנאַל־קולטורעלן קיום אין דער וועלט.

יידיש איז אין משך פון הונדערטער יאָרן געווען דער בולטסטער אויסדרוק פון אונדזער נאַציאָנאַלער קולטורשעפערישקייט.

11. אַלס געטרייע ישראל־בירגער, אַפּעלירן מיר צו אייער געוויסן, צו פאַריכטן די עוולה, וואָס איז אָפּגעטאָן געוואָרן ביז איצט, אין ראַדיאָ און טעלעוויזיע פון ישראל לגבי די מאַסן יידן, וואָס ריידן יידיש, אין ישראל און אין גלות;

מיר דערקלערן מיט פולן באַוווסטזיין, אַז די צוהערער פון ראַדיאָ און טעלעוויזיע, וואָס צאָלן אָפּ דעם געזעצלעכן שטייער דערפאַר, האָבן די לעגיטימע רעכט ווי אין יעדער דעמאָקראַטישער מדינה, צו הערן די פּראָגראַמען אין ראַדיאָ און טעלעוויזיע פון זייער לאַנד, אין דער שפּראַך, אין וועלכער זיי ריידן און וואָס זיי פאַרשטייען.

מיר בעטן אייך דערמיט, אָנצונעמען די אויסדרוקן פון אונדזער טיפסטער הויכאַכטונג:

אין נאָמען פון געזעלשאַפטלעכן קאָמיטעט
פאַר יידיש־אוידיציעס אין ישראל־ראַדיאָ
און טעלעוויזיע, (שידורי ישראל) —

ישראל גורטמאַן — פאָרזיצער

אלטער אייזנבערג — סעקרעטאַר

Fig. 5. The 'memorandum' (petition) of the 'Public Committee for Yiddish Radio and Television Programs' to the 'Respected Administration of Israeli Radio and Television - "Shidurey Yisrael" ', drawn up by representatives of eight organizations and periodic publications and signed by tens of thousands, 'including artists, writers, and cultural activists, on behalf of hundreds of thousands, requesting more and better Yiddish programs'.

Table IX. *Number of Claimants of 'Top Six' Languages in Israel as First or Only Languages, 1948, 1950, 1954, 1961*[a]

Language	1948	1950	1954	1961	% change 1954–1961
Yiddish	78,141	174,492	153,678	101,110	−34.2
German	28,271	41,396	38,696	28,107	−37.4
Rumanian	6,486	35,108	43,118	39,980	− 7.3
French	4,324	15,720	13,820	24,555	77.7
Polish	4,989	29,868	16,031	19,525	21.8
Hungarian	6,818	21,484	18,242	20,490	12.3

[a] Derived from *Population and Housing Census*, 1961, Vol. I, p. xxxv (as given by Hofman and Fisherman 1971), with changes as amended in Vol. II, p. 46.

If the acquisition of Hebrew is to be considered an inevitable and direct indicator of nonretentivity (which it is not as a rule) then Yiddish is roughly in the same boat as Rumanian (Table VIIB) and not far different from Hungarian for the period 1948–1961. However, as we have noted before, neither Hungarian nor Rumanian has changed greatly in the extent to which they are claimed as principal languages. The fact that their claimants, like those of Yiddish, also show a fairly steep rate of acquiring Hebrew strengthens our suspicion that, on the one hand, the acquisition of Hebrew in Israel is not necessarily immediately displacively related to the original non-Hebrew mother-tongue, and, on the other hand, that the relationship between Hebrew and Yiddish is more likely to be *sui generis* than that between Hebrew and other mother-tongues. Just as there are relatively more claimants of 'Yiddish only' (i.e., of 'no Hebrew at all') among Yiddish speakers, there may also be relatively more claimants who have switched from Yiddish as a *principal* language to Yiddish as an *additional* language. After all is said and done this bimodality among Yiddish speakers (Yiddish speakers revealing both the largest proportion of language shift *as well as* the largest proportion of exclusive or principal language maintenance) may be the most typical and unique characterization of Yiddish speakers in Israel.

3.3. In summary, there is some reason to suspect that Yiddish speakers have been relatively less retentive in Israel over the past quarter-century than have claimants of the other top six languages based upon recent European immigration.

Unfortunately, there is no way to fully confirm or disconfirm this suspicion on the basis of Israeli census data since the available information is also compatible with a hypothesis of bimodality (namely, greater retentivity on the part of some and lesser retentivity on the part of others). If the decline from 1948 to 1961 in the number of claimants of Yiddish as *principal* language is indicative of a more widespread decline in Yiddish claiming (i.e., of a decline also in the number of claimants of Yiddish as an *additional* language) then the overall decline would be even greater than that of Yiddish mother-tongue claiming in the United States during a roughly similar period. While this does not seem to be likely on either demographic or socio-psychological grounds it certainly merits further careful attention in connection with the data presented in the sections that follow.

4. NUMERICALLY MAJOR CHANNELS OF LANGUAGE MAINTENANCE

4.1. *The Yiddish Press*

4.1.1. Although only approximately a fifth of all Jewish-sponsored periodical publications outside of Israel are in Yiddish (according to a November 1971 release of the World Association of Jewish Journalists) it is clear that the Yiddish component of the diaspora Jewish press is still one of its strongest pillars. All seven Jewish dailies published outside of Israel are in Yiddish and a very substantial proportion of the biweeklies and triweeklies. Seemingly, Yiddish publications appeal to those who desire more frequent (more intense) contact with Jewish concerns. Most of these readers are by now comfortably biliterate and therefore not at all dependent on the Yiddish press for sole (or even for predominant) contact with the printed word. Thus the fact that Yiddish speakers *do* maintain publications that publish more often than weekly (in the United States, Canada, Mexico, Argentina, France, etc.), whereas Jews who do not speak Yiddish *do not,* is indicative of Jewish orientational (affective, cognitive, and overt behavioral) differences of some importance *vis-à-vis* the centrality of Jewishness for the populations involved.

In 1960 (the last year for which exhaustive data are available; see Fishman 1966) the American Yiddish press by itself consisted of twenty-two publications with four more being partially in Yiddish

Joshua A. Fishman and David E. Fishman

מאת: ארי אבנר, יועץ למנהל הכללי

רשות השידור

ירושלים, ט"ז בחמוז תשל"ג
16 ביולי 1973
מספרנו...240...

לכבוד
פרופ' יהושע (שיקל) פישמן
בית הספר לחינוך
האוניברסיטה העברית
ירושלים

(handwritten Hebrew greeting)

תודה על מכחביך למנכ"ל רשות השידור ואלי מיום
.8.7.73

לצערי אין לנו עותקים של ספר התקציב להפצה
בציבור אבל אשמח אם תחקשר איתי ואשיב ברצון על שאלותיך.
תוכל להחקשר איתי בטלפון 536431.

(handwritten signature)

חלני המלכה 9, ירושלים

Fig. 6. The (Advisor to the General Manager of the) Israel Broadcasting Authority (IBA)
refuses to provide the senior author of this report with a copy of the newly adopted budget
for 1973−74 (in which funds for Yiddish broadcasting were cut notwithstanding increases
for other foreign languages). 'To my disappointment we have no copies of the budget for
distribution to the public. But I will be happy if you will get in touch with me and I will
reply with pleasure to your questions'. The IBA is an independent, 'non-partisan', civil
service agency not directly controlled by the legislative or executive branches of government
and therefore not easily influenced by public opinion. However, the members of its plenum
have frequently been critized for their 'party politics' approach to the IBA's programming,
particularly in connection with coverage of news and sensitive public issues. Thus on the
one hand the IBA is well insulated from public sentiment on behalf of Yiddish. On the
other hand its policy with respect to Yiddish reflects unofficial (Labor) party views and
could be altered, as are other IBA program practices, via (Labor) party pressure.

and partially in English. The total circulation of all of the foregoing was some 300,000. A reasonable estimate for 1970 would be that while considerably more than half of the 1960 publications were still in operation (perhaps 75 percent in all) their combined circulation was only approximately half of what it was in 1960. The Israeli picture in 1970 is rather close to (or even better than) the American picture with respect to the number of Yiddish publications but the combined circulation of these publications in Israel is necessarily much lower than it is in the United States, given the smaller population base involved.

4.1.2. However, fuller understanding of the condition of the Yiddish press, both in the United States and in Israel, is not attainable merely by comparing absolute magnitudes such as the foregoing (number of publications and readers) in the two countries. At least two other dimensions are necessary to round out the picture: comparisons with other minority languages and developmental trends over time. In the United States of 1960 the Yiddish press stood in fifth place relative to the other 'big six' immigrant-based minority languages, both with respect to number of non-English publications as well as with respect to combined number of readers that these publications could boast (Table X). Only French was in a poorer position than Yiddish in these two respects, but in its case increasing reliance on nearby (and rapidly expanding) Canadian publications was a mitigating circumstance. In addition, the position of the Yiddish press was deteriorating more rapidly than was that of any of the remaining top five

Table X. *Total Number of Non-English Periodical Publications and Their Combined Circulations for the Six Largest Non-English Mother-Tongue Groups in the United States, 1960*[a]

Mother-tongue	Number of periodical publications	Combined circulation
Spanish	49	507,000
German	54	343,000
Italian	26	298,000
French	15	87,000
Polish	43	739,000
Yiddish	22	239,000

[a] From Fishman *et al.* 1966.

immigrant-based minority languages. Even French, which had also
suffered a 35% drop in number of publications between 1950 and
1960, experienced a 17% *increase* in the total number of readers
during that period. No such compensating development appeared in
the case of Yiddish. Instead we find a 55% drop in combined
circulations if we follow the official statistics and a 40% drop if we
follow those of the Language Resources Project (Fishman 1966).

By contrast to the United States the general position of the
Yiddish press in Israel seems relatively firm. As befits the largest
non-Hebrew mother-tongue in the country, Yiddish had more
publications in 1970 than did any other of the top six immigrant-
based languages in the country (Table XI). However, even here it is
clear that the Yiddish press does not enjoy the predominance that
one would expect on the basis of the numbers or the proportions of
its claimants as principal or additional language. Furthermore, the
Yiddish press in Israel seems to be past its peak (reached in 1960).

4.1.3. In view of the fact that the Yiddish press outside of Israel is
particularly noteworthy for its dailies the fact that only one Yiddish
daily is published in Israel is deserving of some comment. Newsprint
is governmentally controlled in Israel, most particularly newsprint
for dailies. For many years after the establishment of the State of
Israel no newsprint was allocated for a daily in Yiddish even though
such allocations had already been made for a few dailies in other

Table XI. *Non-Hebrew Publications in Israel: 1940–1970 (Total
Number for Top Six Languages)*[a]

	1940	1945	1953	1955	1960	1965	1970
Yiddish	2	2	19	18	25	22	18
German	5	6	11	11	9	8	11
Russian			9	10	6	8	7
French	1	4	15	17	21	22	18
Polish	1	8	7	4	7	6	4
Hungarian	1	1	12	6	4	4	3
Multilingual		1	1	1	4	5	5
	10	21	72	66	76	75	66

[a] Compiled from various editions of *The Jewish Press of the World*, edited by
Joseph Fraenkel (London, Cultural Department of the Jewish Congress,
January 1972) and other standard references.

recent immigrant languages. This was interpreted as an expression of particular opposition in certain governmental circles to Yiddish and its press. This opposition at a less restrictive level is felt to continue to this very day and to express itself in the denial of any 'privileges for Yiddish'.

Those circles most actively favoring Yiddish in Israel today (various Yiddish writers, singers, actors, and organizational activists) advocate for it a special status on the basis of its being (currently and/or recently) the major Jewish language in the world today, the link-language between Israel and its most dedicated Ashkenazic supporters abroad, the language of the hallowed six million martyrs during the Nazi holocaust, the language of a huge portion of Soviet Jewry, etc. The latent purpose of all of these claims is to convince Israeli public opinion that Yiddish is not *loazit* (not 'a foreign language') and therefore that it should be favored governmentally rather than either disfavored or lumped together with culturally *foreign* languages. This view has led the one Israeli Yiddish daily (privately owned in part but with definite Labour Party support, if not outright control, during election campaigns[12]) to refuse to be classified as *loazit* by the governmental information office responsible for distributing excerpts from the nation's press to foreign press services. As a result the Yiddish daily is never mentioned in the releases of that office, *neither* under the indigenous nor under the *loazit* classification. Thus of all the dailies in the country only the Yiddish one is never publicized or dignified by governmental citation during the daily 'reviews of the press' prepared for the radio and for the wire services.

All of the privately owned Yiddish publications in Israel have complained on various recent occasions that they are not given a fair share of governmental and quasi-governmental advertising. Most Yiddish publications, however, are party-affiliated and therefore cannot reasonably expect much advertising from governmental or 'other party' sources. As a result of both of the factors mentioned above (restriction on newsprint for more frequent periodicals and restriction of advertisement revenue) most Yiddish publications are not only small and infrequent (see Table XII) but they are maintained by political groups and parties or are organizational organs for in-house purposes. Unlike Yiddish periodicals in the diaspora they do not generally attempt to marshal public opinion or to reach the most diversified and largest possible audiences, precisely because of their more focused party missions.

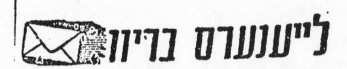

וייס 4.

ליעזערס בריוו

אין בענקשאפט
נאָרא יידיש וואָרט.

איך בין א נייער עולה פון רא־
טנפארבאנד. דער גורל האָט מיר
פאַרמשפט דאָרט צו לעבן 32 יאָר.
פון 1940 ביז 1972. אלע יאָרן האָב
איך געלעבט אין בענקשאפט נאָך
א יידיש וואָרט. לי־יענען עפעס
וואָס אױף מאַמע ־ לשון איז נישט
געווען. ביז איז אין די לעצטע יאָרן,
ווען עס האָט אנגעהויבן צו דער־
שיינען דער זשורנאַל „סאָוועטיש
היימלאַנד", וועלכן עס איז שווער
אין דער פולער. מאַכ צו באסטראכ־
טן אַלס יידישן, נישט געקוקט דע־
רױף וואָס ער איז געדרוקט מיט
יידישע אותיות. עס איז שווער צו
ליײענען די באשמוציקונג   פון
ישראל און פון יידישן פאָלק וואָס
ווערט   פארעפנטלעכט אױף די
שפאַלטן פון דאָזיקן זשורנאַל, וועל
כער געפינט אפילו א תירוץ פאַר
די רוצחים פון אומשולדיקע מענ־
טשן, כדי צו באַרעכטיקן די אַפי־
ציעלע אַנטי ־ ישראל פאָליטיק
פון דער סאָוועטישער פארטיי ־ און
רעגירונג. אפילו אין דעם פאָל פון
דעם מאָרד   איבער די ישראל־
ספאָרטלער אין מינכען. ווען דער
אפיציעלער סאָוועטישער אָרגאן
„איזוועסטיא" אין געווען געצווונ־
גען אויסצודריקן באדוי ערן צוליב
דעם „אינצידענט" אין מינכען, ווי
זײ האָבן דאָס באַצײכנט. האָבן
זײ אױך נישט געהאָט דעם מוט
אָן צו מאָדלען די מערדער.

און אט איז רעאַלײירט געווארן
מײן טרוים. איך געפין זיך אין
ישראל. פאַרשטײט זיך, אַז דאָ
האָב איך א מעגלעכקײט צו רעדן
און ליײענען אין מײן מאַמע־לשין.
אבער עס טוט ווי דאָס הארץ ווען
איך טרעף א סך יונגע מעַנטשן,
דער עיקר די יוגנט אין ישראל.
מיט וועלכע איך קען זיך נישט
דערעדן אין יידיש. דאָס איז פאר
מיר נישט פארשטענדלעך. פאַר־
שטײט זיך, אז קײנער צווייפלט
נישט אין דעם, אַז עברית איז די
אפיציעלע מלוכה ־ שפראך. אבער
אױך יידיש, די יידישע שפראך
וואָס איז אױך להכעיס אונדזערע
שונאים אַרויס   פון אלע פײיערן,
דאַרף   קולטיווירט ווערן אין אונ־
דזער יידישער מדינה און   מען
טאָר נישט דערלאָזן אַז זי זאָל
פארגעסן ווערן.

אשר זיגלבוים
חולון

Fig. 7. Two typical letters to the editor of the Tel Aviv Yiddish daily *Letste Nayes* protesting discrimination against Yiddish. The letter of March 20, 1973 (left) is by a recent immigrant from the Soviet Union. 'As if to spite our enemies Yiddish came out of the (crematorium) fires alive and must be cultivated in our Jewish State and not forgotten'. The letter of March 21 (right) states that the writer is heartbroken that television programs are broadcast in Hebrew, Arabic, English, and French but not in Yiddish. 'If such an injustice were to occur in any other country we would organize demonstrations and petitions for the whole world to hear. . . . It is high time for us to show our organized strength here and not to permit discrimination against Yiddish'.

נייַ ס ●

לייענערס בריוו

וועגן ייִדיש אין אונדזער טעלעוויזיע

פארוואס באאוולט מען די ייִדיש-רעדנדיקע

ווען איך זיך אין אוונט ביי מיין טעלעוויזיאר סוט ממש ווי דאס האַרץ. מצן הערט דאַרט, א חן עברית, אראביש, ענגליש, פראנ־צויש. אבער נישט קיין ייִדיש ווארט. פארוואס דארמן מיר ליידן אזא דיסקרימינאציע פון אונדזער מאמע־לשון אין אונדזער ייִדי־שער מדינה. עס האנדלט זיך ניט בלויז אין א פרינציפיעלן ענין, כאטש דאס איז נישט ווייניקער וויכטיק. עס זענען דאך אבער דא אין לאנד א גרויסע צאל ייִדן וואס פארשטייען נישט קיין עב־רית און נישט געקוקט דערויף וואס די דאזיקע מענטשן האבן אויס געגעבן גרויסע סומעס אויף איין קויפן די טעלעוויזארן און צאלן דעם שטייער פאר דער. טעלע־וויזיע, קענען זיי אבער פון דעם נישט געניסן. דאס זעט אויס ממש ווי א להכעיס, ווייל אויב עס מאכט זיך אמאל, אז די טעלעוויזיע איז געצוווונגען איבערצוגעבן א פאר ווערטער אין ייִדיש ווערן זיי פאר שריגן דורכן ספיקער, אז מען הערט נישט קיין איין ווארט. ווען אזא עוולה וואלט געשען אין א וועלכן עס איז גלות־לאנד וואלטן מיר ארגאניזירט פראטעסט־אק־ציעס. דעמאנסטראציעס און פע־טיציעס און געשריגן פאר דער גאנצער וועלט. איז פארוואס דער־לויבן מיר אויף אזא דיסקרימינא־ציע פון אונדזער ייִדישער שפראך אין אונדזער ייִדישער מדינה. ווע־גן כוח פון ייִדיש אין ישראל זאגט צווישן אנדערן דער פאקט, אז

בעת א רעספעראט אין ייִדיש זענען די זאלן כמעט שטענדיק איבער־פולט. דאקעגן בעת א רעפעראט אין עברית קומען געציילטע מענ־טשן. עס איז דעריבער די העכסטע צייט, אז מיר זאלן אין באוויזן דעם דאזיקן כוח אין אן אָראנגזירטער פאָרם און נישט סאלעריין מער די דאזיקע דיסקרימינאציע וואס ווערט אָנגעוואנדן לגבי טויזנטער בירגער אין אונדזער מדינה.

משה פייגע, בת״ים

Table XII. *Non-Hebrew Publications in Israel, 1955–1970*[a] *(Number by Frequency of Publication for Top Six Languages*[b]*)*

	1955						1960						1965						1970					
	Y	G	R	F	P	H	Y	G	R	F	P	H	Y	G	R	F	P	H	Y	G	R	F	P	H
Daily	–	2	–	1	–	1	1	2	1	1	1	1	1	2	1	1	1	1	1	1	1	1	1	1
Weekly	6	3	10	1	4	4	8	2	3	1	5	3	7	1	5	3	2	2	6	2	6	3	2	–
Monthly	6	5	–	3	–	–	9	4	1	3	1	–	4	4	–	3	3	1	4	6	0	7	1	2
Quarterly or less	6	1	–	12	–	1	7	1	0	16	–	–	10	1	1	15	–	–	7	2	0	7	–	0
Total	18	11	10	17	4	6	25	9	5	21	7	4	22	8	7	22	6	4	18	11	7	18	4	3

a   Derived from various editions of *The Jewish Press of the World*, edited by Joshua Fraenkel (London, Cultural Department of the World Jewish Congress, January 1972) and other standard references.
b   Y = Yiddish; G = German; R = Russian; F = French; P = Polish; H = Hungarian.

Two other by-products of the greater party dependence of the Israeli Yiddish press also deserve mention: (a) as a whole the periodicals are less assertively oriented toward Yiddish than is the Yiddish press anywhere else in the free world since, for most Israeli political parties, Yiddish is a vehicle of communication, a means rather than a symbol or value in its own right; (b) Yiddish periodicals of infrequent appearance are established and discontinued in accord with higher-order party purposes and priorities rather than in accord with popular interest.

4.1.4. *Conclusions* – The Yiddish press in Israel is stronger than that in the United States when comparisons in both cases are with the presses of other recent immigrant language groups. In the United States the Yiddish press is among the weakest and most rapidly weakening non-English presses of the top six immigrant language groups. In Israel, on the other hand, the Yiddish press is the strongest (or certainly among the strongest) non-Hebrew press(es) in the country and boasts a readership of great-loyalty-by-preference, since it could most easily switch entirely to the Hebrew press (from the point of view of literacy considerations alone) but does not choose to do so.

Nevertheless the Yiddish press in Israel reaches a much smaller public than does that in the United States (even if we compare total circulations with total numbers of claimants of Yiddish as principal language); it is more concentrated in the lower frequencies of publication and is more dependent on party whims. As the only substantial press in another Jewish language[13] it suffers under multiple handicaps: it is denied indigenousness (just as is the other non-

Table XIII. *Non-Hebrew Publications in Israel: 1965 and 1970 (Number, Frequency of Appearance, and Circulation for Top Six Languages)*[a]

Language	Year	Daily	Weekly	Monthly	Quarterly or less	Total
Yiddish	1965	1 (1) 16,000	7 (5) 28,600	4 (3) 9,700	10 (6) 15,000	22
	1970	1 (1) 23,000	6 (3) 11,400	4 (2) 6,500	7 (2) 7,000	18
German	1965	2 (1) 18,000	1 (1) 5,000	4 (1) 5,000	1 –	8
	1970	1 (1) 18,000	2 – –	6 – –	2 –	11
Rumanian	1965	1 (1) 16,500	5 (1) 10,000	– –	1 –	7
	1970	1 (1) 16,500	6 –	– –	– –	7
French	1965	1 (1) 5,000	3 –	3 –	15 (10) 53,000	22
	1970	1 (1) 7,000	3 –	7 (1) 20,000	7 –	
Polish	1965	1 (1) 17,000	2 (1) 10,000	3 –	– –	6
	1970	1 (1) 10,000	2 –	– –	– –	4
Hungarian	1965	1 (1) 14,000	2 –	1 –	– –	4
	1970	1 (1) 20,000	– –	2 –	– –	3

[a] From publication self-reports (i.e., the information on circulation figures were reported to us by the publications themselves). Figures in parentheses show the number of responding publications.

Hebrew press); it refuses the label of *loazit;* and it has had to withstand 'special handling' designed to restrict its growth. It is hard to tell to what extent all of these factors are responsible for the fact that the Yiddish press in Israel is not as clearly predominant in comparison to the presses of the other major languages of recent immigration as one would expect on the basis of a comparison between the number of *speakers* of these several languages (see Table XIII). The fact that immigrant Yiddish speakers have also learned Hebrew more rapidly than have most others, and the fact that those most likely to maintain the spoken language (the ultra-orthodox) are also most distant from the modern Yiddish literary tradition, must also be examined in viewing the future of the Yiddish press in Israel. All in all, its roots in print have not reached out as far as have its roots in other media.

4.2. *The Yiddish Radio*

Whereas the press in Israel is merely governmentally 'regulated' (by the control of. newsprint) and 'subsidized' (by making newsprint available at less than cost as well as by the placement of government and related advertising) rather than governmentally owned or controlled, radio and television are government monopolies. Thus what government policy has attempted and effected *indirectly* with respect to publications in languages of relatively recent immigration, it has been able to undertake directly in conjunction with radio and television. As a result the restrictions on Yiddish are more noticeable and attributable here than in conjunction with the press.

4.2.1. There is a total of three-and-a-half hours a week of Yiddish broadcasting in Israel, i.e., a half-hour a day every day of the week. The evening time-slot allocated to Yiddish broadcasting places it immediately before the even briefer periods allocated for other languages of recent immigrants (Dzudezmo, Yahudic/Arabic ['Mugrabi'], Hungarian, Rumanian, Polish, Russian, etc.) and immediately after the daily half-hour in 'simple Hebrew' (for immigrants).[14] This amount of time is the maximum ever made available to Yiddish in Israel and reflects considerable public pressure to overcome earlier restrictions. Nevertheless, neither this amount of time (no more than the average amount of Yiddish broadcasting in the United States today, when the *average program/hour* is lower than it has been in the past fifteen years, Hutchinson 1970), nor this *context* of time (the immigrant slot) is consonant with the demands of those interested in Yiddish in Israel.

Two mitigating factors are often referred to by the Broadcasting corporation's spokesmen called upon to defend the limitation of broadcast time for Yiddish. One is that Israeli broadcasting as a whole has only two stations available to it (five, if the stations largely reserved for Arabic, the armed forces, and broadcasts beamed to Europe and America are counted) and therefore three-and-a-half hours per week of Yiddish broadcasting is a larger fraction of the total internal broadcasting time than might otherwise be imagined (certainly far larger than it is in the United States). Plans are now presumably underway to increase the number of general stations to three, four, or even five and there is a 'possibility' (no promise and most certainly no definite plan) of increased Yiddish broadcasting time 'when and if'. Another mitigating factor is that Yiddish songs are also broadcast during times other than those reserved for Yiddish programs *per se*. Indeed there is currently a biweekly twenty-minute (formerly thirty-minute) program conducted in Hebrew of 'Songs in Yiddish'[15] and Yiddish songs can also be heard from time to time, unpredictably, in the context of other musical programs.

These two mitigating factors have done little to satisfy those most actively concerned for the status of Yiddish in Israel. It has been pointed out that neither French nor English (not to mention Arabic), both spoken by far fewer Israeli residents than is Yiddish, have had to wait until such time as more stations might be established before

Yiddish in Israel 219

being allocated double and triple the amount of time awarded to Yiddish broadcasting. In addition, neither French nor English broadcasting is presented in the context of immigrant programs[16] although its Israeli speakers are even more likely to be recent immigrants than are Yiddish speakers in Israel. Finally, as far as intermittent and irregular songs are concerned, there are obviously incomparably more such in French and in English throughout any week of broadcasting than there are in Yiddish. To add insult to injury the program 'Songs in Yiddish' is broadcast on the Sabbath, i.e., at a time when many of its potential listeners will not turn on their radio sets. All in all, therefore, Israeli broadcasting policy is viewed as being not only *anti-Yiddish* (and therefore anti-democratic *vis-à-vis* a widespread 'language of the people' as well as anti-Jewish-cultural-values) but also as *pro-French and English* (and therefore, fawning toward world languages that have no Jewish cultural values to transmit).[17]

4.2.2. The objective basis of insistence for more and better Yiddish radio program time in Israel is the demonstrated size of the actual

Table XIVA. *Hebrew Language Proficiency of Israeli Radio Listeners (Jews)*[a]

Kol Yisrael programs	Speak only	Read only	Speak read	Speak, read write	None	
Hebrew	15%	0%	6%	79%	0%	100%
Arabic	31	0	9	59	0	100
English	6	0	3	91	1	100
French	22	0	8	69	1	100
Yiddish	19	0	10	69	2	100
Other languages	23	0	9	66	3	100
Average in total population	16	0	6	77	1	100

[a] Derived by Liz Nadel from *Tarbut Yisrael, 1970* data bank (Katz *et al.* 1972). Other runs of the same data reveal that Hebrew is the 'main language' at home of only 45% of listeners to Yiddish radio programs. The comparable proportions for listeners to Arabic, English, and French programs are 62%, 64%, and 56%. Still other runs reveal that the upper educational level of listeners to Yiddish programs is comparable to that of listeners to the French programs. Thus the Yiddish programs appeal to Yiddish speakers most of whom *are* also literate in important world languages but who *nevertheless* are retentive of Yiddish as their home language.

220   Joshua A. Fishman and David E. Fishman

Table XIVB. *Israeli Radio Listening 1965: Selected Immigrant-Based Languages*[a]

Language	(1) 1965: % listeners	(2) 1965: % listeners 4 to 7 days per week	(3)[b] 1969: % of radio listeners that understand	(4) 1969: % of (3) that listen in listed language
Yiddish	24.3	12.7	42.0	48.1
French	9.1	3.6	20.6	40.4
Rumanian	8.3	5.4	12.2	64.0
Hungarian	2.5	1.4	5.3	42.7
Mugrabi	5.2	3.1	9.5	56.5
Judesmo	4.4	2.6	7.6	41.5

(1) Percentages of total population
(2) Percentages of total population
(3) Percentages of radio listeners
(4) Percentages of radio listeners who *understand* the particular language

[a] From *Radio Listening Survey*, June 1965, *Kol Yisrael*, and *Radio Listening and Television Watching*, January 1969 (Central Bureau of Statistics, 1969 [part I], 1970 [part II]).
[b] The Jewish population aged fifteen or older = 1,689,286. The number of listeners to *Kol Yisrael* = 1,574,356 during the week prior to the survey, or 92% of the total Jewish population aged fifteen or older.

Table XIVC. *Language Programs Broadcasted Abroad and for Immigrants: Channels 2, 3 and 4 Weekly Schedule, 1972–73*[a]

Language	Channel 2	Channel 3	Channel 4	Total
Hebrew	3:30 hours per week	3:30 hours per week	–	7:00 hours per week
English	–	5:15	7:00	12:15
French	–	3:30	7:00	10:30
Russian	1:30	21:00	–	22:30
Yiddish	3:30	7:00	–	10:30
Ladino [sic]	1:45	–	–	1:45
Mugrabi	1:45	–	–	1:45
Rumanian	1:45	3:30	–	5:15
Hungarian	0:15	1:45	–	2:00
Persian	–	3:30	–	3:30
Georgian	–	1:45	–	1:45

[a] From the 1972–73 budget report of *Shidurey Yisrael*. Arabic broadcasting is not shown. Except in the cases of English and French, channel 3 is primarily utilized for broadcasting abroad. In the cases of English and French channel 4 is utilized for broadcasting abroad whereas channel 3 broadcasts are heard abroad as well as locally. During the 1972–73 year Georgian began to be broadcast for one-and-three-quarters hours a week also on channel 2 (i.e., for local listeners).

Table XIVD. Radio Listeners[a] According to Languages Understood and Extent of Listening to Particular Languages[b] (January.–March, 1973)[c]

Language	Understand the language: total	Do not listen to programs in this language	Extent of listening in particular languages				Total number of listeners/ total number of people who understand[d]	Usually or often/ total listeners[d]	Extent of listening in particular languages to		
			Total	Usually or often	Sometimes	Rarely			Shidurey Yisrael alone	Foreign broadcasts alone	Both Shidurey Yisrael and foreign broadcasts
Yiddish	31.3	12.4	18.9[e]	8.2	6.9	3.8	.60	.43	18.1	(0.2)	(0.6)
French	18.5	7.3	11.2	3.8	4.9	2.5	.62	.34	6.6	(1.3)	3.3
Rumanian	10.1	4.2	5.9	2.8	2.1	(1.0)	.58	.48	4.4	(0.2)	(1.3)
Hungarian	4.0	2.9	(1.1)	(0.4)	(0.6)	(0.1)	.28	.36	(0.8)	(0.0)	(0.3)
Mugrabi	7.3	2.9	4.4	2.3	(1.3)	(0.8)	.60	.52	3.9	(0.1)	(0.4)
Judesmo	6.1	2.5	3.6[f]	(1.1)	(1.3)	(1.2)	.59	.30	2.9	(0.2)	(0.5)
English	34.6	17.6	17.0	3.9	7.6	5.5	.50	.23	5.4	5.7	5.9
Russian	10.1	4.3	5.8	(1.5)	(2.4)	(1.9)	.57	.26	5.2	(0.2)	(0.4)
Arabic	24.8	8.2	16.6	6.5	6.7	3.4	.67	.40	8.2	(0.9)	7.5

a Radio listeners constitute 88.2% of the (non-institutionalized) Jewish population aged fourteen or older (1972: $n = 1,970,642$).
b Figures in parentheses have a relative sampling error greater than 25%.*
c From 'Radio Listening Survey', unpublished. (Central Statistical Agency, January–March 1973).
d Computed by J.A.F. and D.E.F.
e Of those listening in Yiddish
2.4% replied that these programs were their only source of radio news
3.8% replied that these programs were an additional source of radio news
11.0% replied that they do so because they love the language and literature
1.7% replied that they do so for other reasons
f Of those listening in Judesmo
(0.2%) replied that these programs were their only source of radio news
(0.9%) replied that these programs were an additional source of radio news
2.1% replied that they do so because they love the language and literature
0.3% replied that they do so for other reasons

Table XIVE. *Recent Budgets of the 'Israel Broadcasting Authority' for 'Programs for New Immigrants and Foreign Broadcasting'*[a]

	1971–72	1972–73	1973–74
Yiddish	I £ 33,298	I £ 40,000	I £ 41,000
Judeo–Español (Judesmo)[b]	24,273	12,000	20,000
Easy Hebrew	28,381	40,000	40,000
Mugrabi	2,269	4,000	4,000
Rumanian	31,595	33,000	38,000
English	69,522	50,000	80,000
French	91,881	75,000	130,000
Russian	314,248	250,000	460,000[c]
Arabic	–	–	2,707,000[d]
'Songs of the Communities'	30,340	40,000	58,000[e]

The (semi-secret) budgets of the Israeli Broadcasting Corporation (*Shidurey Yisrael*) penalize Yiddish by (a) not being proportional to listenership, (b) not providing Yiddish broadcasting with the increases provided almost all other programs, and (c) requiring 'Songs in Yiddish' to be budgeted out of the general budget for Yiddish rather than being budgeted separately as is the case for 'Songs of the Communities' *vis-à-vis* Judeo-Español and Mugrabi.

[a] Figures pertain only to 'honorariums' for special performers and technicians rather than to salaries for permanent personnel. 1971–72 figures are *actual* expenditures whereas 1972–73 and 1973–74 figures are *allocations*. The total radio budget for 1973–74 was I £ 38,574,000 and for television I £ 54,806,000.

[b] The sharp drop in 1972–73 is attributable to additions to the budget for full-time personnel for programs in Judeo–Español.

[c] Of the total amount for Russian broadcasting, a minor sum is actually allocated for Georgian. In 1973–74 the Georgian allocation was I £ 54,570. No separate figures for Russian and Georgian are available for previous years.

[d] Of the total amount for Arabic broadcasting a minor sum is actually allocated for Persian. No separate figures are available for Arabic and for Persian in 1973–74 and no figures at all are available for the two previous years.

[e] 'Songs of the Communities' presents Sephardic/Oriental songs exclusively. The budget for 'Songs in Yiddish' (twenty minutes every other week) is included in the general budget for Yiddish, see above.

and potential listening audience in Yiddish. In 1969 fully 42 percent of Israeli radio listeners reported that they understood Yiddish (Table XIVA) and nearly half of these (i.e., some 300,000 listeners) listened to at least one broadcast per week in Yiddish. This proportion (of understanders to all listeners) is far greater (roughly double) than is the proportion of all Israelis for whom Yiddish is either principal or additional spoken language to all Israelis. Further, of those who understand Yiddish a very substantial proportion, whether in relative or in absolute terms, actually listens to broadcasts in Yiddish. Indeed many Yiddish devotees have commented that it is precisely the fact that such a huge population segment is both potentially and actually available for Yiddish radio programs that prompts the authorities to so severely limit the time available to it. Even after the initial drop in radio listening, which occurred soon after 1970 with the meteoric rise of television watching, the Yiddish broadcasts remained *the most listened to broadcasts of the entire week* (with the exception of the weekly news summary in Hebrew)[18] and, as such, a severe embarrassment to the authorities interested in limiting such broadcasts. Indeed the *Tarbut Yisrael 1970* data reveal that the Yiddish radio programs have substantial audiences among those whose 'major home languages' are Hebrew (12% of whom listen to the Yiddish programs), Russian-Polish-Ukrainian (43%), English-German (24%), and Spanish (17%).

By 1973, together with the overall recovery of radio listening and overall increase in Jewish population (relative to 1969–70), the number of people who listened to Yiddish programs was 372,451 (Table XIVC: 18.9% of 1,970,642), or at an all-time high in absolute terms, even though the *proportions* of Yiddish 'understanders' and listeners were lower than they had been (relative to 1969–70). Data for this same year (1973) confirm both the low rate or absence of Hebrew among Yiddish listeners (see Table XIVA) as well as the frequently claimed high emotional attachment to the language among listeners to Yiddish broadcasting. Note also the high proportion of *frequent* listenership to Yiddish programs, particularly in comparison with English, French, or Russian.

In 1964 the Israeli Broadcasting Corporation (then *Kol Yisrael*) broadcasted in ten 'foreign' languages daily for a total of seventeen-and-a-half hours of non-Hebrew programming. Of this total fourteen hours of daily broadcasting were conducted in Arabic and one hour each in English and in French. Thus only an hour-and-a-half per day remained for seven additional languages, among these Yiddish. It is this classification of Yiddish among the 'additional foreign languages' of purportedly lesser importance that so rankles in the hearts of Yiddish devotees, even more so now that the total amount of broadcasting has increased (Table XIVC). By 1970, 60 percent of all language-related letters of protest published in the Yiddish press

מאירועי הפסטיבל הישראלי

בוקר טוב, אליהו!

בברית־מילה (כסא אליהו). אצל בני
עדות המזרח רווחות כמה אמונות טפלות
הקשורות בכסא אליהו הנביא.

הערב הוא רב־לשוני. מרביתו בעברית,
כרבעו באידיש, יש בו קטעים בלדינו,
בתימנית, בכורדית וכו'.

○ נושא יהודי חם

"אליהו הנביא הוא נושא יהודי חם,
הקשור בזכרונות בית אבא של כל יהודי
מכל עדה", אומר דן. "היו לנו הרבה
היסוסים לגבי האידיש. פחדתי שחלק
מהקהל לא יבין, ויש גם הרבה אנשים
שהאידיש מרגיזה אותם. אבל החליטו
להשאיר את האידיש, כדאי שהקהל ידע
על כך ואולי יהיה זה מבחן לבגרותו
של הקהל. הכוונה היא לאירוע עממי,
שנועד לקהל האוהב פולקלור, תרבות
יהודית ומסורת".

משורר איציק מאנגער

אומר דן: "ההצגה אינה בנויה כ־
פרקים ואפיזודות אלא כמיקשה אחת.
מדי פעם מקיפים אספקט מסויים ה־
קשור באליהו — הולדת האגדה, הפר־
צופים השונים שלו, שפע התחפושות
(פעם הוא מופיע כרופא, פעם מתגלה
כעני, פעם ככלייזמר ופעם כנווד), פסח
ועלילות דם, כוס אליהו, ביקוריו, פולק־
לור הילדים, אליהו מלאך הברית, מיטיב
הבדלה, מיטיב השואה, הגsgועים אל

מיצד ומלחין גיל אלדמע

Fig. 8. (Maariv, August 8, 1973). From the interview with the producer of a new theater performance 'Elija the Prophet': 'Elija the Prophet is a warm Jewish theme associated with every Jew's memories from his "father's home" no matter of what communal origin he may be', says Dan Almagor. 'We had many doubts concerning (including material in) Yiddish. I was afraid that some of the audience would not understand Yiddish. There are also many people who are annoyed/upset by Yiddish. But it was decided to leave the Yiddish (material) in. It's better that the audience knows about it, and perhaps this will be a test of their maturity. . . .'

Subsequently it became evident that the audience attracted to a program of this type was Yiddish-speaking, understanding, and appreciating it to such a degree that the proportion of program material *in* Yiddish or translated *from* Yiddish was increased to more than half. The total program was both a qualitative and financial success.

dealt with this single issue.[19] While many admit that attention to Arabic may be justified on the basis of national security considerations they claim that the slighting of Yiddish cannot be justified in any democratic or Jewish context. As for the relative discrimination against Yiddish *vis-à-vis* English and French, neither of which is a Jewish language, that too is clear to Yiddish devotees since both of the latter languages have far fewer listeners and a lower proportion of listeners-to-understanders than in the case of Yiddish. Obviously, the amount of time devoted to English and French broadcasting in Israel does not depend on the sizes of their local audiences (the presence of sizeable numbers of English- and perhaps French-speaking tourists in Israel should not be overlooked; however, if that is done, then the interests of Yiddish-speaking tourists must also be considered).

4.2.3. Since radio and television are under one and the same governmental authority it comes as no surprise that there is no Yiddish telecasting at all in Israel. The arguments for and against this policy are identical to those pertaining to radio broadcasting (but are even more extremely put, since there is only one television channel for the entire country and a truly huge proportion of total telecasting time is inevitably in English). The only difference, then, with respect to these two media is that television represents a more active area of grievance, perhaps because of its *completely* exclusionist policy *vis-à-vis* Yiddish. As a result, the 1970–71 calendar year witnessed organized efforts to collect signatures petitioning for Yiddish on television, hundreds of letters to the editors of the private and anti-government Yiddish publications,[20] organized visits to officers in charge of Israeli television, mass meetings in Tel-Aviv, and interpolation by opposition members of Knesset, etc.

Thus far these protests have produced no reliable results[21] and it may well be that the protests themselves have now passed their peak. Political (and financial) pressure has been exerted upon the only Yiddish daily to tone down or discontinue its formerly active campaign for Yiddish telecasting and increased broadcasting. Overnight, during the spring of 1972, this publication practically ceased referring to these matters at all, leaving the campaign in much weaker and less experienced hands. In early 1973 the Yiddish daily once more began to publish letters of protest by its readers but at this writing it did not seem that they would have any effect whatsoever on the broadcasting corporation (now called *Shidurey Yisrael*).

4.2.4. The full story of Yiddish broadcasting in Israel cannot be told without referring to the considerable time devoted to it in connection with programs beamed to the Soviet Union. Such programs were recently offered four times a day, for half an hour each time, but now they are offered only twice a day for half an hour each time. Much evidence is available that these programs have had and continue to enjoy a very wide and faithful listenership in the Soviet Union. Indeed one frequent complaint of recent Soviet *olim* (immigrants) is that they heard *more* Israeli broadcasting in Yiddish before escaping from Soviet oppression than since arriving in their new-found homeland. This anomaly has also been referred to by others, including Yiddish and Russian periodicals in the Soviet Union *per se.* How, they ask, can the Israeli government criticize Soviet policies *vis-à-vis* press, radio, education, etc, in the Soviet Union when its own internal policy is so negative in each of these connections? It is obvious that the Israeli government is much more inclined to recognize Yiddish for the purposes of self-serving propaganda abroad than it is to recognize it for internal functions in Israel proper.[22] Israeli representatives who do not deign to speak or publish in Yiddish when 'at home' do not at all hesitate to do so on fund-raising or opinion-molding missions to Jewish communities abroad. When they return to Israel they either ignore or even distort the role of Yiddish in their successful fund-raising or *aliyah*-stimulating missions.

4.2.5. *Conclusions* — Yiddish broadcasting is severely restricted both as to time and as to content, while Yiddish telecasting is entirely denied in Israel, notwithstanding considerable public interest to the contrary. While Yiddish is recognized as a valuable medium in broadcasting to and motivating Jews abroad (particularly in the Soviet Union but also in South and North America) it is grudgingly allocated minimal and transitional immigrant orientational functions in broadcasting beamed for internal Israeli consumption. As of the present time all efforts to change policy in this connection have led to refusals that vary in politeness but not in firmness. Half-hearted suggestions by Yiddish protagonists to organize politically or to boycott the annual radio-television tax payments have thus far not gotten beyond the *'letter to the editor'* stage.

4.3. *The Yiddish Theater*

Since the rise of modern theater in Yiddish approximately a century

„איך שעם זיך וואס יידיש איז
אַ פרעמדע שפראַך אין ישראל"

דערקלערט דער גענעראַל-קאָנסול פון ישראל אין אויס־
טראַליע, אויף אַ גרויסער קולטור-אימפרעזע אין מעל־
בורן. — רעדאאקטאָר יצחק רובינשטיין, ווערקער איז גע־
קומען אויף אַ באַזוך אין ישראל, דערצײילט וועגן דער
יידישער „קולטור-אָפענסיווע". וואָס ווערט אונטערגענו־
מען דורכן יידישן ישוב אין אויסטראַליע

(פון אינגזער קאָרעספאָנדענט)

„קיין שום יידישע קולטור-שאַפונג ה' מרמור האָט די אויבן-ציטיר־
— און זיכער נישט די גײיסטרײיכע טע ווערטער געזאָגט נאָך דעם ווי
יידישע קולטור — קאָן נישט אויס־ ער האָט געהערט וועגן דעם. אַז
געשלאָסן ווערן פון דעם אוצר פון יידיש ווערט קלאסיפיצירט אין יש־
דער אויפגעלעבטער אלגעמײנער ראל ווי אַ פרעמדע שפראַך. דאָס
יידישער ציוויליזאציע. דעריבער אין אויך געוווען דאָס ערשטע מאל
בין איך אַזוי שטארק אויפגעצײ־ ווי דער ישראל קאָנסול איז אויפ־
טערט געוואָרן ווען איך האָב גע־ געטראָטן פאַרן יידישן עולם אין
הערט, אַז נאָך ביים הײינטיקן טאָג אויסטראַליע מיט אַ רעדע אין
ווערט יידיש קלאַסיפיצירטס אין יש־ יידיש, און אין דער דאָזיקער רע־
ראל אלס אַ „פרעמדע שפראַך". דע האָט ער ארויסגעהויבן די וויכ־

„עס ראָט זיך ממש נישט גלוי־ טיקייט פון קאַמף קעגן דער אסימי־
בן, אָבער אויב עס איז טאַקע יאַ לאַציע און האָט אַנגעוויזן אויף אַ
אַזוי, איז עס אַ חרפה און אַ בושה, רע מוראדיקע רעוולטאַסן סיי
און איך שעם זיך שטארק דערפון". פאַרן יידישן יחיד און סיי פאַרן

אַזוי האָט דערקלערט דער אסי־ גאַנצן פאַרק. צום סוף האָט ער צו־
ציעלער פאַרשטייער פון ישראל, געזאָגט, אַז ביי דער ערשטער בעס
דער גענעראַל-קאָנסול אין אויס־ געלעגנהייט וועט ער זען אויס
טראַליע, ה' דוד מרמור, אויפ־ צונוצן זיין השפעה, אַז דער דאָזי־
טרעטנדיק מיט אַ חדש צוריק קער פלעק זאל אָפגעוווישט ווערן.
אויף אַ גרויסער קולטור־ אימפרע־
זע, וואָס איז פאַרגעקומען אין מעל־
בורן און וואָס האָט מיט זיך פאַר־
געשטעלט דעם אָנהויב פון אַ גרוי־
סער אַקציע קעגן דער שפראַכלע־
כער אַסימילאַציע פון יידישן ישוב.

Fig. 8. 'I am ashamed that Yiddish is a foreign language in Israel' declares the General Consul of Israel in Australia, Mr. David Marmor, at a mass meeting in Melbourne at which a campaign against linguistic assimilation was announced. 'No single Jewish cultural creation - and certainly not the spiritually rich Yiddish culture - should be excluded from the treasury of the revived Jewish civilization. That is why I was so shocked to hear that even today Yiddish is classified in Israel as a "foreign language". At the first opportunity I will use my influence to see to it that this injustice will be corrected'. (*Letste Nayes*, May 21, 1973).

ago the theater has become an uncommonly popular recreational avenue as well as art form among eastern European Jews. Thus the well-nigh complete absence of Yiddish theater in Israel in former days was experienced as a particularly severe deprivation among Yiddish speakers, particularly among those for whom the flourishing Hebrew theater was inaccessible. Since the 1950s, however, a definite upturn has occurred in the number of Yiddish performances (see Table XV). While the expansion of the Yiddish theater in Israel may now be past its apogee it is clearly the major (and some would say the only substantial) non-Hebrew theater in the country.

Nevertheless, the condition of the Yiddish theater in Israel is far from being a satisfactory one, primarily because of governmental restrictions placed in its path. The same petty policy which once denied permission for a single Yiddish daily (although two publications, owned by the same publisher and published every other day, were permitted), today renders it logistically difficult (if not impossible) for a single permanent Yiddish theater company to perform daily in any given locale. Theoretically all non-Hebrew companies labor under this same disadvantage; practically speaking, however, only the Yiddish theater is affected since it alone would be capable of sustaining one or more permanent theaters.

As a result of the above policy of petty harassment and exclusion from the governmental and quasi-governmental subsidies available to the Hebrew theater the entire Yiddish theater in Israel 'wanders'.

Table XV. *Yiddish Theater in Israel 1945–1970*[a]

Year	Number of different titles	Number of performances					Total of titles by performances
		1-5	6-10	11-20	21-30	31+	
1940	0	0	0	0	0	0	0
1945	1	1	–	–	–	–	1
1950	10	8	1	2	–	–	43
1955	20	7	3	3	6	1	277
1960	19	5	2	2	6	2	274
1965	29	3	1	8	15	2	597
1970	22	12	7	1	0	2	226
total	101	35	14	16	27	8	1718

[a] Based upon a 25 percent count of Israeli Yiddish newspapers for the years indicated.

Since it is restricted to one- or two-day stands in any one place, it travels from town to town with more frequent returns to those cities (Tel Aviv, Haifa) in which its major audience is concentrated. However, even this costly solution does not fully extricate Yiddish theater in Israel from the disadvantages under which it labors. Much of the Hebrew theater is viewed as a national cultural-educational asset and therefore is both excused from tax levies on box office revenue as well as heavily subsidized. Yiddish theater has available to it neither of these avenues of support. As a result Yiddish theater tickets are correspondingly more expensive than their Hebrew counterparts and audience size is correspondingly reduced.

The financial difficulties faced by Yiddish theater in Israel have qualitative consequences as well. Since only those plays that can attract a larger-than-average audience are financially viable, Yiddish theater in Israel is very largely restricted to broad musical-comedy and burlesque-vaudeville. The lack of an artistic theater in Yiddish (at the same time that only large subsidies make such a theater in Hebrew possible) not only reduces the importance of Yiddish theater in the eyes of many Yiddish speakers *per se* but it also helps foster among Hebrew speakers the view of Yiddish as a humorous, touching, but obviously uncultured patois.

4.3.1. *Conclusions* — Yiddish theater in Israel grew dramatically during the 1950s and 1960s after most of the formal and informal restrictions imposed against it were removed or mitigated. At the present time, however, it would seem to have passed its numerical highpoint, partially as a result of the somewhat decreased size of the Yiddish speaking population but also as a result of the particular financial penalties to which Yiddish theater in Israel is exposed and as a result of the inevitable qualitative repercussions that these have had. To this very day there is no permanent Yiddish theater in Israel, nor an art theater, although the size of the Yiddish theater-going audience is still very substantial.

5. NUMERICALLY MINOR LANGUAGE MAINTENANCE EFFORTS: CULTURAL, EDUCATIONAL, AND ORGANIZATIONAL ENDEAVOR

5.1.1. *Yiddish Book-Publishing in Israel* — The Yiddish book, particularly the serious book (whether prose or poetry), still strikes many Jews — in Israel and elsewhere — as an oddity. Yiddish is most firmly

Federation to include
non-Hebrew writers

Jerusalem Post Reporter

TEL AVIV. — The Hebrew Writers Union yesterday decided by 85 votes to 11 to establish a "federation of Israeli authors."

Earlier, the union defeated by 70 to 33 a motion to open its own membership to "all writers who are citizens of Israel." However, it decided to lay the groundwork for the creation of associations of authors writing in Yiddish, Arabic, or other languages, and to form an overall federation. This motion was put forward as a compromise between a proposal that the union open its ranks to all Israeli writers and another calling for the group to retain its Jewish character.

Mr. Aharon Megged is to head a committee which will prepare the founding convention of the federation to be held not later than October.

The resolution was adopted at a meeting held at Beit Tchernikhovsky here under the chairmanship of Abba Kovner. It was proposed by a committee headed by Hanoch Bartov.

Fig. 9. The Hebrew Writers Union was shamed into admitting Yiddish writers into its broadened organizational structure, adopted due to the political advisability of admitting Arabic writers. During the debate on this topic the Hebrew writer Aharon Megged claimed not to know whether there was an association of Yiddish writers in Israel. He is answered by a Yiddish writer, recently arrived from the Soviet Union, that 'it is hardly a compliment (to one's self) "not to know" or to advocate that the Hebrew Writers Union be concerned only for Hebrew and Arabic'. (*Jerusalem Post*, March 22, 1972; *Letste Nayes*, March 23, 1973).

א בריוו צום שרייבער אהרון מגד

מיט א באַווונדערונג אינטערעס האָב
איך איבערגעלייענט אייער אינטער-
וויו אין „קול העם" נוב. 10 פון דעם
כ'ם מיט א סך פון אייערע פאָרמו-
לירונגען און אייספּירן. איך קאָן א-
בער בשום אופן נישט פאַרשטיין איי-
ער גרינגשעצונג צו דער יידישער לי-
טעראטור, וואָס פילט זיך אין דעם
אונטערטעקסט פון אייַערע רייד. איר
שטעלט זי אַוועק אין אײך ריי מיט
דער ליטעראטור, וואָס איז געשריבן
געוואָרן פון יידן אין אנדערע שפּרא-
כן (שוועביש, פּוֹיליש, רוסיש). נישט
פאַרמינערנדיק די באַדייטונג פון אַט
דער ליטעראטור, וועט איר דאָך מיזן
מסכים זיין אַז דאָס איז, אין תּוך, א
ליטעראטור וועגן יידן און אַז דער
קרייז פון איר איינפלוס איז א באַ-
גרענעצטער. בעת די יידישע ליטעראַ-
טור איז אין איר עצם וועזן דאָס
יידישע לעבן גופא, איך משך פון א
לאַנגן היסטאָרישן פעריאָד, און איז
כולל אין זיך די גייסטיקע געאַגראַפיע
פון דעם ווייט גרעסטן טייל פון דעם
יידישן פאָלק, אייגשליסלעך ישראל.

צום כבוד און שטאָלץ פון דער
יידישער ליטעראטור, דאָרף פאָרציי-
כנט ווערן, אַז דער רענעסאַנס-פּרא-
צעס פון דעם יידישן ישוב אין ישר-
אל, אין משך פון די לעצטע הונדערט
יאָר, איז צוערשט קינסטלעריש פאַר-
מולירט געוואָרן אין דער יידישער,
א סך פריער ווי אין דער העברעאי-
שער ליטעראטור.

צווישן אנדערן האָט איר אויך גע-
זאָגט, אַז איר ווייסט נישט צי אין
ישראל איז פאַראַן א פאַרייַן פון
יידישע מערק ד. י. אין איך וויים נישט
צי נישט ווּכן אין אזא געהוֹיבענע
מידה. איך וויל אָבער אָבער האָפן, אַז איר
ווייסט, אַז היינט צו טאָג איז אין אין
ישראל פאַראַן א גרוֹיסע יידישע
שרייבער-פלעיאַדע, וואָס שאַפט אן
אינטערעסקט פון אייַגנאַרטיקע און אינטערעסאַנטע לי-
טעראטור. א ליטעראטור, וואָס שפּיגלט
אָפּ אַלע עטאַפּן אין אַספּעקטן פון אונ-
זער ישראלאדיקער ווירקלעכקייט; א
ליטעראטור, וואָס האָט געווירקט און
איז בכוח אויך להבא צו מאָביליזירן
און פאָרמולירן קינסטלעריש די גייס-
טיקע ווערטן פון דעם פאָלק אין פון
דער מדינה. האָט איר דאָך אליין, זײַ-
נער-צייט, אַזוֹי באַפליגלדיק א זאָג
געטאָן, אַז דאָס הארץ פון יידיש
קלאַפּט אין דעם היינצײטיקן עברית
(לבה המה בה). איז פאַרוואָס-זשע
האַלט איר, אַז מען דאַרף פאַר דער
יידישער ליטעראטור זאָרגן
ווי וועגן דער אראביש(ער? וואָס שייך
שרייבער און זייערע באַדערפענישן
האָט איר געזאָגט אין דעם דערמאָנ-
אינטערוויויו, דאַרף זיין א גלייכע רעכט
כאַר אַלע, אָבער וואָס שייך ליטעראַ-
טורן, איז די דער שרייבער-פּאַרייַן, אַלם
אזעלכער, מחויב צו זאָרגן נאָר פאַר
דער העברעאישער אין אראבישער.
הײַתכן, פאַרוואָס??

ל. פּאָדריאַטשיק

established as a vernacular — as an informal spoken medium — and as such its association with radio, theater, and even the daily press is not hard to fathom. Even the semi-technical tradition of Bible translations and prayer book translations into stylized Yiddish, particularly for women but also for the unlearned more generally, follows from the role of Yiddish as the language of everyday life. Finally, humorous books in Yiddish for popular consumption have also had quite a vogue for more than a century. However, books of modern Yiddish poetry, novels, dramas, short stories, essays, literary criticism, as well as Yiddish books in the social sciences or humanities have rarely reached beyond a very small and select circle of *aficionados* anywhere in the Jewish world. The 150 to 175 Yiddish books of this type now published annually[23] generally have printings of one or two thousand copies and even these copies are distributed only with great difficulty. All in all, the modern Yiddish book is a by-product of the modern, secular, sociocultural movements that viewed Yiddish as a value and as a medium in its own right. These movements generally reached and influenced only a relatively small segment of Ashkenazic Jewry when they were at their height, from the mid 1920s to the late 1930s, in Poland, the Soviet Union, and the United States. Since then they have vanished or weakened to such an extent that their functioning, whether currently or in the past, is very often unknown to the Jewish 'man in the street'. However, even the dedicated few who are aware of and devoted to the continuation of good Yiddish literature face serious problems with respect to its future. One aspect of the problem is the dwindling number of writers. Tables XVI and XVIIA reveal different but related facets of this phenomenon: the age of Yiddish writers and the numbers of Yiddish books published.

5.1.2. Table XVI shows the age distribution for 221 Yiddish writers by country of residence and major literary genre. In most categories the average age is close to seventy, the geographic 'lows' being sixty-three and sixty-four (in Israel and in Argentina) and the literary-type 'low' being sixty-one (for children's literature). It is obvious from distributions such as these that the next decade will be an extremely critical one for Yiddish literature, particularly in the United States, its largest center. While the average age of Yiddish writers in Israel is somewhat younger than it is in the United States it is clear that there too the next few decades may well see the well-nigh complete cessation of Yiddish literary activity. Although a

Table XVI. Average Age of Yiddish Writers (as of 1970)[a] by Country/Region of Residence and Literary genre[b]

Country/region	Genre							Total
	1	2	3	4	5	6	7	
Argentina	75 (1)		72 (3)	66 (1)	70 (2)	62 (4)	54 (3)	64 (13)
Latin America			66 (1)	67 (1)		70 (2)	63 (1)	68 (6)
Soviet Union		72 (1)	62 (3)	62 (1)	78 (1)	75 (4)	56 (1)	69 (11)
Poland			76 (1)	61 (3)	85 (4)	73 (3)		74 (11)
France			62 (1)	70 (4)		67 (3)		69 (10)
British Commonwealth		61 (1)	73 (1)	62 (6)	78 (1)	73 (11)	68 (2)	69 (20)
West Europe		62 (1)		70 (8)	57 (2)			61 (4)
United States	70 (5)	69 (4)	70 (8)	70 (19)	69 (6)	70 (30)	75 (3)	70 (75)[c]
Israel		65 (3)	66 (13)	60 (10)	62 (15)	68 (28)	55 (2)	63 (71)
Total	71 (6)	67 (10)	66 (32)	66 (45)	67 (31)	68 (85)	61 (12)	68 (221)

1. traditional texts and commentaries
2. language and literature: research and criticism
3. novels, short stories
4. poetry
5. history and current events
6. journalism
7. children's literature and texts

[a] Derived from entries in Lexikon fun der nayer yidisher literatur [Lexicon of Modern Yiddish Literature], Volume 5 (New York, Congress for Jewish Literature, 1971).

[b] Numbers in parentheses indicate the number of cases on which each average is based.

[c] Compare with the last line of Table 3 in Fishman 1965c for the 1960 average.

dozen or so Yiddish writers have recently arrived in Israel from the Soviet Union, their average age is not strikingly different than that of other Yiddish writers in the country (although they may well be younger than their counterparts remaining in the Soviet Union) and it is also not at all evident whether their literary activity will find the material and moral support necessary for continuation in Israel. Thus far several of them have been helped to publish one or more books since arriving in Israel and a modest journal has been begun for their benefit, but none of them has been provided with the subsidized positions to which they were accustomed in the Soviet Union and which are indispensable if they are to have the peace of mind needed in Israel (and made available there to good Hebrew writers) for steady literary activity.[24]

5.1.3. Given the precarious age distribution shown in Table XVI the literary output revealed in Table XVIIA is little short of prodigious. It should be stressed, therefore, that Yiddish book publication in Israel also serves Yiddish authors and readers living elsewhere. In 1960, for example, 17 percent of the books published by American Yiddish authors were published in Israel (Fishman 1965c). This percentage has undoubtedly grown in the dozen years since then as the difference between what it costs to publish Yiddish books in the two countries has increased. On the other hand, the proportion of books by Israeli authors among all of the Yiddish books published in Israel has correspondingly decreased. At present this percentage is likely to be less than 25 percent. Nevertheless, the very fact that a relatively large number of Yiddish books is published annually in Israel is bound to have some impact on the Israeli scene. Such Yiddish books are more likely to be purchased by local Israeli libraries, to be reviewed or at least listed by local Hebrew and Yiddish publications, and even to be displayed in bookstore windows (a rare occurrence!) than are Yiddish books published elsewhere. Indeed, even visitors to Israel are more likely to buy such books than Yiddish books published in their own or in other countries. Thus the size of the Israeli Yiddish book publishing enterprise, even though it is not dependent primarily on Israeli manpower or financial resources, is a highly significant factor in the worldwide and in the Israeli position of the Yiddish language as a modern and serious literary vehicle. Yiddish book publication is still on the increase in Israel, the last twenty-five years (since the establishment of the State) revealing a five-fold increase in this respect, at the very same

Table XVIIA. *Non-Hebrew Book Publication in Israel, 1940–1970 (Top Six[a] Languages, as registered in Kiryat Sefer)*

Language	Type[b]	1940	1945	1950	1955	1960	1965	1970
Yiddish	1	–	–	1	1	4	1	2
	2	1	1	–	3	21	17	36
	3	2	3	2	4	8	12	14
	4	1	–	4	2	4	3	3
	5	–	–	–	–	–	–	1
	6	–	–	–	–	1	3	1
	T	4	4	7	10	38	36	54
German	1	–	–	1	–	1	–	1
	2	3	1	–	–	–	–	1
	3	2	2	2	–	4	6	4
	4	2	–	1	1	1	4	–
	5	–	1	–	–	–	–	–
	6	4	–	–	–	–	2	–
	T	11	4	4	1	6	12	6
French	1	–	–	1	–	2	–	1
	2	–	–	–	–	3	1	2
	3	–	2	–	1	1	–	1
	4	–	2	3	4	8	3	4
	5	–	–	–	–	–	–	–
	6	1	–	–	–	3	2	–
	T	1	4	4	5	17	6	8
Rumanian	1	–	–	–	–	–	–	–
	2	–	–	–	–	1	9	1
	3	–	–	–	–	1	1	1
	4	–	–	–	–	–	2	1
	5	–	–	–	–	–	–	–
	6	–	–	–	–	–	3	–
	T	–	–	–	–	2	15	3
Hungarian	1	–	–	–	–	–	–	–
	2	–	–	–	1	2	1	–
	3	–	–	–	–	–	1	3
	4	–	1	–	–	1	–	1
	5	–	–	–	–	–	–	–
	6	–	–	–	–	–	–	–
	T	–	1	–	1	3	2	4

236   Joshua A. Fishman and David E. Fishman

Table XVIIA. (continued)

Language	Type	1940	1945	1950	1955	1960	1965	1970
				Years				
Multilingual	1	–	–	–	1	1	–	1
(Hebrew plus	2	–	–	–	–	–	1	1
one or more of	3	–	–	–	2	7	9	14
the above	4	–	–	–	–	–	–	1
languages)	5	–	–	–	–	–	–	–
	6	4	–	2	1	3	3	–
	T	4	–	2	4	11	13	17

a Only one Polish book was located (1970).
b Types: 1 religious; 2 belles-lettres; 3 history; 4 Israel; 5 children's literature; 6 other.

time the number of books published in the other five major European mother tongues utilized by the Jewish population have remained very small (although these numbers too have grown). Indeed, even the official governmental register (which tends to *under-report* the number of Yiddish — as well as other non-Hebrew — books published in Israel in comparison with the number reported in *Kiryat Sefer,* the bibliographic journal of the National Library) reveals (note Table XVIIB) twenty-seven books published in Yiddish[25] in the Jewish years (i.e., dated from Rosh Hoshana, in September) 1969–70 and 1970–71, while at the same time only approximately five books are indicated as having been published in French, five in Russian (not

Table XVIIB. *New and Reprinted Books by Language of Original and Language of Publication*[a]

Language of publication	Total	Hebrew	Yiddish	English	French	Russian	German	other
		1969–70 to 1970–71 Language of original						
	1889	1246	44	312	41	132	36	78
1. Hebrew	1527	1185	15	225	32	16	31	23
2. English	224	46	4	54	1	111	5	3
3. Other languages	89[b]	6	25	8	5	5	–	40
4. Multilingual	39	7	–	22	1	–	–	9
5. Dictionaries	10	2	–	3	2	–	–	3

a From *Supplement, Monthly Bulletin of Statistics* 3, 16, (1973) 23. Table 7 (Israel Central Bureau of Statistics).
b 'Of these, 44 books were published in Arabic and 27 in Yiddish' (p. 15, Table 6). These Yiddish books are classified topically as 'largely belletristic' (p. 17, Table 9).

a major-tongue), and none in German. However, 224 books were published in English and (from yet another governmental table) forty-four in Arabic. Yiddish book publication, even according to governmental records, is fourth in size and may very well be third.[26] Obviously this relative position is unparalleled anywhere else in the world today, nor has it probably been equalled anywhere else at any time.

Nevertheless the Yiddish book market and literary scene are hardly known to Israelis outside of specialized circles. In addition, those most involved (both writers and readers) have the definite self-concept of being among the 'last of the Mohicans'. Writers try to make sure that their works will also appear in Hebrew or English (and indeed there is a substantial amount of translation from Yiddish into Hebrew, only a fraction of which is identified as such). They rarely see any future for themselves in Yiddish, although their fidelity to and creativity in Yiddish may even be all the greater in the twilight. Called upon, again and again, to provide leadership to the clamor among their readers for Yiddish on the radio, on the television, and in the schools, they have responded guardedly and even fearfully. In some respects their objective situation is no different than is that of the Yiddish writer in America. Subjectively, however, the context is different. Not only does the American Yiddish author feel himself to be part of the general Jewish struggle for diaspora survival but he also sees the upsurge in Jewish studies and in ethnic interests to encourage him in his belief that 'the worst is over' and better days are on the way. Most important of all, the Yiddish author in America knows that he is not 'at home' in a Jewish polity and therefore his expectations are accordingly lower at the same time that his public prominence (at least in New York) is better than is that of his counterpart in Israel.

Thus the Yiddish writer and Yiddish literature in Israel must cope with studied neglect and opposition, a situation much harder to accept than the lack of concern for Yiddish that sometimes marks Jewish life in the United States, Canada, France, etc., both because this occurs in a Jewish state and because it is often with malice aforethought. Examples are legion and are presented at every gathering of writers and cultural leaders.[27] Most recently the spotlight has been focused upon the new *Encyclopedia Judaica,* highly subsidized by Israeli cultural authorities, which not only utilizes many of the same anti-Yiddish articles that previously marked its much earlier Hebrew counterpart but which in addition noticeably updates the policy of ignoring or playing down the Yiddish literary scene in

יום א׳ 10.6.73 — י׳ בסיון תשל״ג

דיגשת לשון - וקצת יותר מזה

. ראש ממשלתנו, הגברת גולדה מאיר, נרשאת דברים
גייריש בארחה חגינית ממעם „סרם מאנגרי״.
„שני ילדי יודעים יידיש. דאגתי לכך, שילמדו את
השפה הזאת. עתה הבמחתי לנכדי, שברגע שאתפנה
מעבודתי הנוכחית אלמד גם אותם יידיש״: נאום ראש
הממשלה.
ואילו נשיאנו החדש, הפרופסור אפרים קציר, מוסיף,
באותו מעמד, משלו: „עד היום אני מתרגש כשאני קורא
סיפור ביידיש מאשר בעת
שאני קורא בעברית״.
מדוע ?

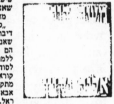

„כי יידיש היא השפה שבה
דיברו אבי ואמי כאשר רצו,
שאנו הילדים לא נבין על מה
הם משוחחים, ואנו השתדלנו
ללמוד את השפה כדי לחדור
לסודותיהם. ועד היום, כשאני
קורא או מדבר יידיש, כאילו
מתקרב אני בכך שוב אל
אבא ואמא״. נאום נשיא יש־
ראל.

   ✳ ✳ ✳

אל מה שקשור בפסיכולוגיה אישית, אני מתייחס תמיד
בדרך־ארץ. לעיקר, אם כבד לנשיא מצהיר שהוא מתרגש
כשהוא קורא סיפור ביידיש, יותר משהוא מתרגש כשהוא
קורא סיפור בעברית, משום שמתקרב בכך, כביכול, אל
הוריו המנוחים — אני מתנגד על מרי־הנגשה כסופר עברי
ועל יצר־הסארקאזם של עיתונאי המשרבב בלשוני־הקרתא
ושותק. בדל״ת אמותי שלי אני יכול לסבר, כי גם בביתי,
כשרצו הורי, יבדלו לחיים ארוכים, שהילדים לא יבינו את
אשר הם מדברים, שוחחו ביניהם לועזית, קרי : רוסית.
אני מצטער לומר, כי אינני מרגיש משום כך שום רגש חם
במיוחד לשפה הרוסית. אין זאת, כי אטימותי־לבו של ילד
הארץ היא בעוכרי, אבל כשאני נתקל באותיות קיריליות, אין
דוק של דמעות מלחלח את עיני, וכשאני שומע את צלצולה
הדשן של הרוסית, גם אז אינני יוצא מגדרי מחמת התפעמות.
אין ספק, גם זה ענין של פסיכולוגיה פרטית.
אולם כאשר הפסיכולוגיה הפרטית מתחייבת להשבע על
תפיסת־עולם כוללת, — לא פעם בלא שהגוגע־בדבר חש
בכך — ולהטביע את חותמה במהלכים עקרוניים, החייבים
להיות משוחררים מסימפאטיות או מפוביות אישיות, זה כבר
נושא הצריך להשיב את הרבים ולא רק את הפרט.
הגברת מאיר דאגת, שילדיה ינדעו יידיש ועתה היא
מתעתדת להקדיש מזמנה גם להוראות שפה זו לנכדיה.
טוב ויפה. אלא שאליו וקוץ בה. חוששני, שאהבתה
היידיש שבשבח אצל ראש־ממשלתנו — ולא רק אצלה לבדה
— את סולם־העדיפויות, שבמקרה דנן הוא לשונו, אך לא רק
לשונו בלבד.
מאושר הייתי, דרך משל, אילו היתה ראש הממשלה
שוקדת, בשעתו, על רכישת השפה העברית על־בוריית,
שבמקום לייחד את זמנה היקר עם אשת־ציבור לשונן היידיש
לילדיה, היתה מקדישה אותו לשיפור שליטתה בלשון העברית,
שפתנו הלאומית, שפת עברנו ותחיתנו, כדי שכולנו ניחנה
לא רק מחרישות שלכה אלא גם מצחות לשונו.
ובכל הצניעות אני גם סבור, כי מנהיגים ועסקנים אחרים
שלנו, לדרגיהם השונים, יפה היו עושים אילו נהגו כך.

   ✳ ✳ ✳

איני ירא מפני היידיש ואינני חושש להתלקחות מחודשת
של פולמוס־הלשונות. זאת ועוד : אינני מתלם — חלילה
לי — משושאי האוצרות המשוקעים ביידיש, במורשתה העממית
ובסטרותה, אף לא מהילת־הטראגיות ההורתה לראשה. יכולני

   ✳ ✳ ✳

גם להבין את הכאב שבו מלווים אוהביה את הצטמקות
מספר־דוברים. אבל אני מרהיב עוד להחזיק בדעה, כי סוב־טוב
היתה ראש הממשלה עושה אילו עודדה את ילדיה ואת נגדיה
ללמוד ...עברית.
תנגעת־שיחרורנו הלאומית החזירה אותנו לארץ־ישראל
והציבתנו כשפנינו אל המזרח. ההיסטוריה היא שגזרה, כי
בצד העברית תהיה העברית לשפתה השנייה של ארץ־ישראל
— הערבית ולא היידיש, לא הלאדינו, לא האנגלית, הצרפתית
וכיו״ב.
העברית היא גם השפה הרשמית השנייה של מדינת
ישראל — בצוותא עם העברית.
הערבית היא לשונם של תושבי ארץ־ישראל מבני האומה
השכנית, שרשרושיה לפותחים ואחוזים בעברה. היא לשונם של
שכנינו הסובבים אותנו, ואשר ביום מן הימים — אנו תקוה
— יהיו שכנינו־בשלום ולא שכנינו־באויבה.
לערבית יש לה מקום נכבד בתולדותינו הרוחניים. הואיל
וראש הממשלה מרבה להתרפק, בשנים האחרונות, על מסורת
אבות, אל נכון גם היא יודעת, כי יהודה הלוי כתב „כוזרי״
בערבית ואילו הרמב״ם נזקק לאותה לשון בהעלותו על הכתב
את „מורה נבוכים״ ואת פירושו למישנה.
אבל אפילו נתעלם לרגע מדברי־ימינו, — כלום אין די
בשכל הישר להשעים גם החיונית הצעותים שבוראה הערבית
לבני־הנוער שלנו, אפילו הרבה לסני שניגשים להגמיל
להם את היידיש ? הרי הערבית, היא השפה
שבלעדיה יכבד עליהם לבוא בדברים עם שכניהם, אלה שהם
אזרחי מדינתנו ואלה היושבים במדינות הסמוכות לנו, הבין
לנפשם ולתהות על מקורותיהם ותרבותם, מנהגיהם והליכו־
תיהם.
רק עכשיו, כ״ה שנים לאחר קום מדינת ישראל, מתעורר
משרד־החינוך לצרכים האובייקטיוויים של הוראת הערבית
לתלמידי בתי־הספר העבריים בישראל. אני מדגיש : מת־
עורר, — בלא לגרוע מן החיוב שבעצם התהדרותה, ובלא
מחלוקת אהשרה ההשתהות שבהדבנה הצורך האלמנטארי הזה.
אבל ראש הממשלה מתעתדת ללמד את נגדיה יידיש,
ואילו נשיאנו החרש מתרגש מסיפור ביידיש יותר מאשר
מסיפור בעברית.
ומה על אותם חלקי־ציבור יהודים — והם הרוב
בקרב אוכלוסינו — שאינם יכולים להיות שותפים לנהייה זו
ולהתרגשות זו, מפני שבאו לעולם, או צמחו ונתחנכו על רקע
לשוני־תרבותי שונה לגמרי מזה של מזרח־אירופה היהודי
דוברי־היידיש ?
האם גם עליהם ללמוד יידיש ?
לשם מה ?
כדי לחוג את זיקתם לתרבות עמם ?
הלא גם בתפוצות הרוב איננו נזרך לייידיש אלא
ללשונות אחרות, שבהן האנגלית היא הדומיננטית. היידיש
נעשית והולכת לשפת העבר של חלק מעמנו. תמונה
נפשם ותרבותם של אחדים מחשובי מנהיגינו אמנם משותחת
עליה, וכל אל לעובדה זו להעצים על צלילות דעתם ולהפוך
את הנוסטאלגיה הפרטים — הטבעיות והמובנות — למקור־
השראה מחמדד, שכבר שיבש די והותר את מערכות החינוך
בישראל, ואולי, בהשלכותיו הרחבות יותר, בולם אף תנופה
מדינית ומסלף חזון לימים יבואו.

   ✳ ✳ ✳

לשון אחת ויחידה עשווייה כיום לשמש דבק לאחות פרצות
ולאמר בדלים, ולהיות המפח אשר ילבה את אהבת
הארץ והעם : העברית, שפתנו ההיסטורית, שפת שיח־
רורנו ותחיתנו. אמת זו היא כזו אמיתיות, שהן כה פשוטות
וכה יסודיות, עד כי יש שאין משגיחים בהן.
אך כלום אותה אמת פחות פה חות אמיתית היא משום כך ?

Fig. 10. An attack (June 10, 1973) on Prime Minister Golda Meir for revealing that she plans
to teach her grandchildren Yiddish. 'History has decreed that besides Hebrew, Arabic shall
be the second language of the land of Israel, Arabic and not Yiddish, Ladino, English,
French or others....One should not attempt to transfer here disturbing particularistic
nostalgias'. (*Maariv*, June 10, 1972). A similar letter-essay (by Amnon Shamush) appeared
in *Davar* on June 22, 1973. Several replies were published to both letters, some of which
pointed out that not Yiddish but economic exploitation was splitting the population: 'On
the contrary, Yiddish has the potential of elevating both groups in the spirit of one of the
greatest ages of the Jewish people'.

Israel, while presenting that abroad as being over and done with. Several articles in the Israeli Yiddish press have pinpointed the *Encyclopedia's* rejection of favorable commissioned articles concerning Yiddish literature, particularly that in Israel, the substitution of negative and much abbreviated articles in their place, and the omission of any mention of dozens of Israeli Yiddish writers. This 'rewriting of history' has been labelled '1984-ish' and *'Yevsektsia-*like' (the latter reference being to the Soviet Jewish falsifiers and annihilators of Jewish life of the 1930s), the 'primary implementor' (which is not the same as being the 'ultimately responsible authority') being a professor at the Hebrew University.

5.2.1. *Yiddish in Israeli Education*
5.2.1.1. If one examines governmentally recognized and supported elementary and secondary education in Israel it is clear that Yiddish is almost entirely absent in that entire area of Israeli life. With the exception of three classes in a single high school (in Kiryat Khaim, a suburb of Haifa) no school under official auspices teaches Yiddish. On the other hand, Jewish children begin studying English in the fifth year of instruction and from then on this language remains a required subject of study throughout elementary and secondary school. In the ninth year (which is equal to the first year of senior high school study) students are permitted to select a second foreign language. The usual two options are French and Arabic, with the latter being selected primarily by those planning to major in Near Eastern Studies in their final two years of high school study.[28] The 'daring innovation' introduced three years ago in Kiryat Khaim was to permit students to choose among French, Arabic, and Yiddish at this point. Notwithstanding the popularity of Yiddish in Kiryat Khaim (it has regularly been selected by about a quarter of the students there[29]), no other high school has followed suit and there seems to be no organized sentiment in that direction among any body of parents, students, or teachers in Israel. Even the Kiryat Khaim 'daring innovation' has recently been subject to ridicule and criticism in an Israeli youth magazine (*Maariv LaNoar,* February 5 and 19, 1973).
5.2.1.2. There is a more significant role for Yiddish in two types of non-government-supported schools in Israel, namely, in those conducted by the ultra-orthodox on the one hand and by the Bundists on the other. Since both of these groups are often viewed as representing extreme ideological opposition to Zionism and to the State of Israel their espousal of Yiddish places it in the context of hostility

to *the* basic integrating loyalty shared by the vast majority of the Israeli population.

Of the above-mentioned schools those conducted by the Bundists are by far the least important numerically. They are Yiddishist-secularist as to orientation and supplementary as to organizational type. Roughly 100 children in all attend these schools (one in Tel Aviv and another in Beer Sheva), coming to them after regular public school hours for a total of five hours per week during a four-year period of elementary school age. The pupils are largely the children of eastern European Jewish parents who arrived in Israel subsequent to the end of World War II, although a sizeable minority are from Sefardic homes in which Yiddish is viewed as a status symbol. The former children frequently hear Yiddish spoken at home and their Yiddish school attendance thus reinforces their active use of spoken Yiddish while adding Yiddish literacy to their repertoire. The two schools in question concentrate on modern Yiddish literature, integrating the study of literature with holiday and laborite festivities.

The schools of the ultra-orthodox are much more numerous as well as of older vintage. They are referred to rather loosely as *Talmetoyres* and *Yeshives* and while not supported by the government are recognized *de facto* as fulfilling the requirements of compulsory school attendance. Bentwich (1965) reports 5,000 pupils to be in attendance at elementary schools of this type in 1962—63 and 2,500 more in secondary schools. Both of these numbers are probably underestimated and would be appreciably higher (perhaps doubled) by 1972—73. Even so, such children probably account for less than 5 percent of the total school attendance at either level. These schools serve children of many long-time residents in Israel/Palestine although, once again, a majority of their pupils are children of post-World-War-II arrivals. In these schools Yiddish is used as the language of oral instruction, the language of printed translation and commentary with respect to traditional texts, and the language of printed texts pertaining to whatever secular studies these schools offer (arithmetic, geography, etc., but not of course Yiddish literature). Very much like most of their counterparts in the United States (Poll 1965; Goldstein and London 1970) the pupils attending these schools most frequently live in compact religious neighborhoods in which Yiddish is the common language of everyday life for old and young alike. Thus these schools add Yiddish literacy to their pupils' repertoires and link Yiddish to formal Jewish studies in a way that the home alone could not accomplish.

בית הספר התיכון בקרית־חיים הנהיג את לימוד האידיש כשפה
זרה שניה, בצד הצרפתית והערבית. לדברי התלמידים, קל יותר
ללמוד אידיש, מה גם שמתבלים את השיעורים בבדיחות יהודיות

Fig. 11. Illustration accompanying an article in a youth magazine: 'Kiryat Haim High School offers instruction in Yiddish as a second foreign language besides French and Arabic. According to the students Yiddish is very easy to learn, particularly since the lessons are garnished with Jewish jokes'. Note that all of the words on the black-board ('Here the mother-tongue is spoken') are misspelled *Maariv Le Noar* (February 5, 1973).

5.2.1.3. At the adult level Yiddish is taught to an insignificant degree in local adult education centers in Tel Aviv, in a few other urban centers, and much more significantly at the major universities of the country. First introduced at the Hebrew University (Jerusalem) in 1952, Yiddish studies at that university are now available at both the undergraduate and graduate levels and appeal to a small but constantly growing number of (largely foreign-born) students. In 1972, twenty students with *majors* in Yiddish were registered in the Bachelor of Arts program and three in the Master's program. Several times that many students were enrolled in the *courses* in Yiddish language and literature, while a small number of doctorates were also being written in this field.

The Yiddish programs at Haifa, Tel Aviv, and Beer Sheva Universities are all much younger and smaller than at the Hebrew University. Given the availability of instructors their slow but steady growth in the years immediately ahead would seem to be assured if such growth is permitted (tacitly and overtly) by those in charge of the Hebrew University Yiddish program and by the cultural and fiscal authorities on whom the latter, in turn, are dependent. The most certain supply of instructors will probably be the Hebrew University program, although at least a modicum of American and other diaspora-trained instructors could also be attracted (even in view of the rapid growth of university-based Yiddish studies in the United States and Canada and their greater ability to pay young instructors decently and to promote them). Indeed it has often been claimed that the expansion of Yiddish studies at the secondary school level is stymied by the lack of trained teachers. Critics of the Yiddish program at the Hebrew University point out that it does not appear to be concerned about filling this need in cooperation with the university's School of Education (as do other language departments); rather it seems to question the need for the expansion of Yiddish studies into Israeli secondary schools by its very aloofness from the social scene.

The true significance of Yiddish studies at Israeli universities, and particularly at the Hebrew University, is at the moment neither numerical nor quantitative but, rather, attitudinal and emotional. However, the various university Yiddish programs have thus far operated on a strictly 'hands off' basis *vis-à-vis* ties to Yiddish literary, journalistic, theatrical, or organizational activity in Israel or elsewhere. The programs define themselves strictly as *academic* program for *Hebrew-speaking* pupils and appear to be extra careful not to be associated with any activities that imply that Yiddish is a living language of millions of Jews and therefore a language with claims for recognition and support by Israeli authorities and institutions. While Yiddish devotees in Israel are delighted and encouraged by the growth (actual and potential) of Yiddish studies in Israeli universities, the latter keep their distance from the former for fear of being suspected of ideological complicity. Given this self-imposed self-denial, as well as the denial of special interest or contacts with students coming from Yiddish-interested circles in the diaspora, the long-range impact of Yiddish studies on improving Israeli views and behaviors toward Yiddish is likely to be limited indeed. Thus this lack of impact is much different from that of the Bundist or *Talmetoyre* schools. The latter would dearly *like* to influence Israeli society but *cannot*. The university Yiddish programs, on the other hand, *could* probably influence Israelis to admit Yiddish into more widespread roles (e.g., in education, radio/television, and cultural life more generally). They *could* but as of now they *will* not, largely because of fear of being regarded as nonacademic on the one hand and anti-establishment on the other. Although excessively proud of the fact of their existence and excessively 'superior' in manner *vis-à-vis* academic Yiddish studies in the diaspora, Yiddish studies at the Hebrew University in particular and in Israel as a whole are as yet quantitatively miniscule, qualitatively generally unexceptional, and emotionally quite insecure when compared with those in the United States.[30]

5.3.1. *Yiddish in Israeli Organization Life* — There is practically no organizational base for Yiddish in Israel. In comparison to the United States, where the number of Yiddish speakers is declining rapidly but where the organizational bases established half a century ago (fraternal orders, camps, cultural organizations, etc.) still continue to operate, the Israeli picture is an odd inversion. Spoken Yiddish is much more in evidence than in the United States but institutional organization on its behalf is extremely weak. The organizational groups that were formative in the 1920s and 1930s were destroyed by force, terror, and antipathy by the time World War II began and no major additions have come into being since. As of today the only organizations with primarily Yiddish goals are the Yiddish Writers and Journalists Association (Tel Aviv, with smaller and largely dormant branches in Haifa and Jerusalem), its active Leyvik House in Tel Aviv, the Sholem Aleichem House (Tel Aviv), the Menora

עמ' 3 „מעריב לנוער" 19.2.73

האידיש מגדילה את הפער התרבותי

בתגובה לרשימתו של צבי שטיין על לימוד האידיש (גל. 22) : איך יתכן שבארץ לומדים שפה גלותית ? הטיעונים בעד לי־ מוד השפה בבית הספר הם כה חסרי־ערך, כמו : „מספר דוברי האידיש הולך ופוחת...", חרף זו בדיוק המטרה ! אנו תגענו לארץ על־מנת לדבר עברית ולא את שפת הגלות, שנכפתה עלינו.

מה משקל הטיעונים של התל־ מידים הלומדים שפה זו ? נמצא שהם מגוחכים : אנו לומדים שפה זו בגלל חבריחות העסיסיות שבה,

משום העזרה בבית, או בגלל ש־ האב מכין את עבודת־הבית של התלמיד, וכדומה.

האם לשם כך אנו נמצאים ב־ ארץ, כדי שכל אחד יוכל ללמוד את שפת האם — את השפה הזרה שאינה שייכת לו ? לשם מה קיים מיזוג־גלויות בישראל ?

בבתי־הספר התיכוניים נוהגים ללמד שפות זרות אחרות, כמו אנגלית וצרפתית. לדעתי, הצו־ רך ללמוד שפות בינלאומיות אלה הוא צורך מעשי (טיולים בחו"ל,

קריאת ספרי־מדע והכרת עולמנו המתפתח).

האידיש היא שפה השייכת אך ורק ליהדות אשכנז. מה בנוגע לקיבוצי יהודים אחרים ? היא אפילו לא שפת היהודים כאז ומתמיד, כפי שנאמר בכתבה. עברית היא שפתנו, אפילו אם אינה מהווה את שפת האם של כל אחד ואחד באה"י, על לי־מוד שפה זרה זו יש למחות, כיים שהיא מחזקת פער־הרבותי, שאה־ רים כיתדלים למחוק אותי.

שלום ראובנס, עכו

Fig. 12. 'Yiddish Increases The Cultural Gap'. A letter to the editor attacking the few students studying Yiddish at the one high school in Israel where it is available as an elective second foreign language. 'Is that why we find ourselves in this country, so that everyone should study his mother-tongue, the foreign language that has no relationship to him (sic)? For what purpose did the ingathering of exiles occur in Israel?....Yiddish is a language which is relevant only to Ashkenazic Jewry...The study of this language should be suppressed because it strengthens the cultural gap that others are trying to overcome' (*Maariv Le Noar*, February 19, 1973).

Publishing Company (Tel Aviv), the Kursky Library (Tel Aviv), the
I. L. Peretz Library and Publishing Company (Tel Aviv), the Workmen's Schools (Tel Aviv and Beer Sheva), and a handful (three to
five) of independent Yiddish culture clubs in Tel Aviv, Jerusalem,
and one or two other points.[31] It is noteworthy that none of the
above organizations operates on a truly national scale and that, all
told, they involve approximately 1,000 active members and reach a
periphery of some 5,000–10,000 others, almost all of whom are
elderly and East European-born. A sign of their combined impotence
is the fact that rarely, if ever, is any of their activity reported in the
general Hebrew press.[32] Yiddish organizations, Yiddish literature,
Yiddish culture, and Yiddish language have a far larger and better
'press' in English in New York than they have in Hebrew in Israel.

6. QUALITATIVE AND ANECDOTAL EVIDENCE AND IMPRESSIONS

The most popular Israeli humorist has quipped that in Israel 'one
speaks Yiddish, reads English and writes Hebrew'.[33] In a sense this is
true not only for the foreign-born eastern European generation but
also for their children and grandchildren. The latter do *not* speak
Yiddish, of course, but many can still follow a song and a story in
Yiddish with real enjoyment. There are also sufficiently many cases
of non-Ashkenazim (and even Arabs) who have learned Yiddish for
almost everyone to have met or heard of such 'oddities'. A Yiddish
expression – whether sweet, sad, or diminutive – is part of almost
everyone's stylistic repertoire, much to the chagrin of Hebrew
purists. Once in a while a Yiddish song will even rise into the hit
parade, a Yiddish play will 'really catch on', a Yiddish writer will be
more than merely mentioned by the Hebrew press. Generally
speaking there is a very widespread though low-key positiveness (or
receptiveness) toward 'a little Yiddish' at the level of vernacular
entertainment and nostalgia. Gone are the days of burning kiosks for
selling Yiddish papers, smashing Yiddish printing presses, and publicly ridiculing those who speak Yiddish. The martyred six million
are everyone's kith and kin (particularly the kith and kin of the
Israeli establishment). Had they not perished the Yiddish that most of
them spoke (certainly five out of six million were Yiddish speakers)
might have been a threat to Hebrew. Having perished, their Yiddish is
also hallowed as part of the 'dear, dead days beyond recall'.
A little Yiddish cannot hurt but too much might still be dangerous

246 Joshua A. Fishman and David E. Fishman

('the Orientals/Sefardim might go wild').³⁴ The Sefardim have never widely demanded recognition for their post-exilic vernaculars (Judesmo, Mugrabi, etc.) but the theoretical possibility of such demands is constantly advanced as a main reason for not responding to the demands for Yiddish in the mass media and in education as outlined above. *Vis-à-vis* authentic Jewish cultural diversity (as distinct from the diversity imported from non-Jewish sources) Israel is still at the stage of centrally ideologized cultural dictatorship for the purpose of cultural uniformity. Thus it is presumably still not desirable to identify as being of Yiddish origin the ghetto songs translated into Hebrew which are widely taught to honor 'the six million'. Incoming Russian immigrants are provided with orientational materials in Russian (as are others in English, French, Spanish, etc.) but very rarely is such material made available in Yiddish — whether to Russians (of whom 20 percent are Yiddish speakers) or to others. The English language *Jerusalem Post* (read largely by tourists as by Americans and Canadians in Israel) *regularly* comments upon the Israeli Yiddish stage, major Yiddish authors, and outstanding Yiddish publications — particularly those that have some relevance to Israel. Not a single Hebrew publication does anything of the kind. A large proportion of all Yiddish books published in Israel are subsidized by the President's Fund (under his personal control) for the encouragement of good literature, but the current President is likely to be 'the last Mohican' in this respect. Both the current President (Shazar) and the Prime Minister (Meir) are known as 'friends of Yiddish' (indeed President Shazar is still a Yiddish writer and a former editor of Yiddish publications), but they have never been known to intervene on behalf of Yiddish *vis-à-vis* radio/television, educational or other public recognition. Presumably 'friendship' has its limits.³⁵ A Yiddish-speaking tourist experiences no difficulty or unpleasantness in being served in Yiddish in restaurants, hotels, and stores throughout the country, but a Yiddish-speaking immigrant is 'encouraged' to shift to Hebrew as soon as he can. English-speaking immigrants are encouraged/expected to keep their children's knowledge of English as fluent as possible. The Ministry of Education helps local schools set up special English classes for such children so that they will not lose facility in English. Immigrants attempting to do likewise with respect to their children's Yiddish are viewed as oddballs or as religious extremists.

All in all Yiddish is associated with the eastern European past, with older eastern European immigrants, with sectarian opposition to the modern State, with vernacular humor, and with the tenderness of *gemeinschaft* lost. These constitute the major dimensions of Israeli ambivalence toward Yiddish. The most common feature to all of these associations is their vernacular focus. Any other level of Yiddish than the folk-popular is either unknown, unbelieved, or rejected as possibly disruptive. At great psychic cost a European elite rejected all of its European languages — those borrowed as well as those reshaped — and persuaded itself and its followers that one could build a new and interethnically united Jewish people only by so doing. The self-rejection and parental rejection that this signified for the European-derived state-building elite was justified on the ground of the greater absorptive possibilities that their self-denying sacrifice would make available to socially disadvantaged African, Middle Eastern, and Asian Jewries. To dignify Yiddish, to permit it into the sphere of national symbols, to accept it as fitting for higher functions and official public functions, thus runs counter to the ideological and emotional roots of the basic, modern, Zionist-Israeli enterprise. The notions of diglossia, of cultural pluralism, of bilingualism and biculturalism, so common in culturally multiple democracies the world over, are unknown or disregarded in *self*-reference, however much Israeli experts may recognize them in dealings with others.

Israel is creating a new Jewish people unlike any which *ever* existed before, even including the period before the destruction of the First Temple: a culturally unified, secular nationality. However little progress is being made along these lines practically, it is still the official line 'ideologically'. In this connection Yiddish at the level of vanishing vernacular, still accompanied by a few jokes, songs, and expressions, cannot do too much damage or elicit too much Oedipal guilt. Yiddish is reluctantly related to one of the high points attained by Jewish diaspora creativity by dint of great devotion and despite great suffering. It is openly related to continuity with the recent eastern European Jewish past but is viewed positively in this light mostly by Ashkenazim (and particularly by religious Ashkenazim) rather than non-Ashkenazim (see Tables XVIIIA and XVIIIB). It is sometimes related to the justice strivings of the powerless (and not only to the powerlessness of justice). Finally, it is related to sentiment and softness. To the extent that all of these associations are contradicted by a variety of modern Israeli trends and styles Yiddish is a reminder of things that many modern Israelis would rather forget. 'High Yiddish', the Yiddish of literature of the highest quality and worldwide repute, the Yiddish of immortal philosophy and

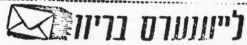

לעזערס בריוו

לאָמיר פאַרשטאַרקן
אונדזער קאַמף פאַר ייִדיש

לעצטנס האָבן זיך ווידער באַ־
וויזן אויף די שפּאַלטן פון "לעצ־
טע נייעס" א גרעטערע צאָל בריוו
פון לייענער אין יעלכע ס׳ווערן
באַנײַט די פאָדערונגען פאַר אינ־
פירן ייִדישע פראַגראַמען אין דער
טעלעוויזיע און אויסברייטערן די
ייִדישע אוידיציעס אין ראַדיאָ. עס
זענען גערעכט די רייצנער ווער־
כע זאָגען בײַ דער מיינונג, אז
איצט. מיט דערעצנטערן זיך פון
די וואַהלן צו דער כנסת, איז א
גינסטיקער מאָמענט פאַר אויס־
קעמפן גלײַכבאַרעכטיקונג פאַר
דער ייִדישער שפּראַך אין דער
ייִדישער מדינה. עס איז שוין
די העכסטע צײַט צו באַוויזן אינ־
דער כּוח. דעריבער איז כדאי
אונטערהאַלטן דעם פּאַרטלאַג וועגן
אָפגעבן אונדזער שטימע נאָר פאַר
די קאַנדידאַטן וואָס ווערן זיך
בפירוש פאַרפליכטן צו קעמפן פאַר
דער גלײַכבאַרעכטיקונג פון דער
ייִדישער שפּראַך. די מאַכן ־ עליה
פון רוסלאַנד האָט געבראַכט צו
אונדז טויזנטער אין טויזנטער
מענטשן פאַר וועלכע ייִדיש איז
דערווייל די איינציקע שפּראַך אין
וועלכער זיי קענען זיך אויסלעבן
און וואָס קאָן זיי העלפן אײַנגלי־
דערן זיך אין אונדזער לאַנד. די
דאָזיקע עליה האָט געבראַכט צו
אונדז אויף א באַדײַטנדיקע צאָל
ייִדישע קולטור ־ טעשפֿער. שרײַ־
בער, זשורנאַליסטן, אַקטיאָרן און
קולטור ־ טוער. צום באַדויערן.
זענען מיר נישט די געהעריקע אק־
טיוויטעט מצד אינדזערע ייִדישע
שרײַבער, ייִדישע קולטור ־ טוער
וועלכע דאַרפן שטיין אין שפּיץ
פון דאָזיקן קאַמף, איך מיין, אז
מיר האָבן איצט אַלע מעגלעכקייטן
צו שאַפן א געאיניקטן פראָנט פאַר
דער גלײַכבאַרעכטיקונג פון אונ־
דזער מאַמע לשון.
גריגאָרי לאַבלאָו, פתח־תקווה

עס פאָדערט זיך מער
ענערגישע מיטלען

איך האָב געלייענט אין "לעצטע
נייעס" דעם בריוו פון ה' בור־
שטיין בשייכות מיט אונדזער
קאַמף פאַר אײַנפירן ייִדישע פּראַ־
גראַמען אין דער טעלעוויזיע. ה'
בורשטיין לייגט פאָר צו שיקן
מאַסנווייז בריוו אין דער אַפּירונג
פון דער טעלעוויזיע אָן דער
פּראַגע. די ביז איצטיקע פּראַקטיק
האָט אָבער באַוויזן, אז די דאָזיקע
לייט נעמען זיך נישט איבער מיט
די דאָזיקע בריוו. עס פאָדערן זיך
מער ענערגישע מיטלען. איך מיין,
אז מער ווירקזאַמער וואָלט געווען
צו רעאַליזירן דעם פאָרשלאַג.
וועלכער איז שוין נישט איינמאָל
אַרויסגערוקט געוואָרן, און נעמ־
לעך: עס דאַרף געשאַפן ווערן א
קערפערשאַפּס וואָס זאָל עפענען א
ספּעציעלע קאָנטע אין א באַנק
אויף וועלכער עס זאָל איבערגע־
שיקט ווערן דער אָפּצאָל פאַר דער
טעלעוויזיע ביז עס וועלן נישט
אײַנגעפירט ווערן ייִדישע פּראַ־
גראַמען. מיר האָבן זיך אין גלות
נישט געשעמט מיט אונדזער מאַ־
מע־לשון. פּאָרקערטס. מיר האָבן
זיך ענערגיש געשלאָגן אין גע־
קעמפט פאַר דער ייִדישער שפּראַך
און ייִדישער קולטור. איז פאַר־
וואָס זאַרן מיר נישט פאָדערן על
כל פּנים רעספּעקט פאַר ייִדיש אין
אונדזער ייִדישער מדינה.
ר. מ. רחובות
(גענומער נאָמען און אַדרעס אין
רעדאַקציע)

ליענערס בריוו

וועגן הונדערטער בריוו,
וואָס פאָדערן רעכט
פאַר יידיש

עס דאַרף דערבײַ אױך געזאָגט
װערן, אַז אין אַ נישט קלײנער
מאָס טראָגן די פאַראַנטװאָרטלעכ־
קײט פאַר דעם צושטאַנד די אינ־
סטיטוציעס און געזעלשאַפטן,
וועלכע זענען געבױט געװאָרן כדי
צו פאָפולאַריזירן און אונטערשטי־
צן די יידישע קולטור־שאַפונג. זײ
האָבן נישט געפונען אין זיך גע־
נוג כּוח און מוט, כדי אױפצוצװינ־
גען צו פאַריכטן די דאָזיקע עװלה,
װוּ זענען אונדזערע יידישע שרײַ־
בער אין ישראל, װעלכע זענען
דאָך פון די ערשטע, װאָס װערן
דיסקרימינירט ? פאַרװאָס זעט מען
נישט די פירנדיקע ראָל אין דאָ־
זיקן קאַמף פון אַזעלכע אינסטיטו־
ציעס װי דאָס לײװיק־הױז, פֿראַנץ
קורסקי ־ ביבליאָטעק, פּרץ־פֿאַר־
לאַג, די יידישע אַקטיאָרן, — די
אַלע, װעלכע ציען זײער יניקה
פון יידיש.
כּל זמן עס װעט נישט געשאַפן
װערן קײן אײנהײטלעכער געזעל־
שאַפטלעכער כּוח, װאָס זאָל אַרום
נעמען די אַלע פאַראינטערעסירטע
אינסטיטוציעס, װעלן מיר גאָר־
נישט דערגרײכן. איצט איז די
געהאַריקסטע צײַט צו שאַפן אַזאַ
אײנהײטלעכן קאָמיטעט. מיטן
דערנענטערן זיך פון די װאַלן צו
דער כּנסת, דאַרף דער ענין גע־
שטעלט װערן אױפן טאָג־אָרדע־
נונג מיט דער גאַנצער שאַרפקײט.
יעדער קאַנדידאַ, אומ־אָפּהענגיק
פון װעלכער פּאַרטײ עס זאָל נישט
זײַן, דאַרף פיכן, אַז זײַן באַציאונג
צו יידיש, צום רעאַליזירן אונדזע־
רע גערעכטע פּאָסטולאַטן, װעט
האָבן אַ גרױסע השפּעה אױף דער
צאָל שטימען פון די װײלער.
יעקב בעניעס, חולון

די ליענער פון „לעצטע נייעס"
טרעפֿן זיך כּמעט יעדן טאָג אָן
אױף בריװ פון פאַרביטערטע מענ־
טשן, װעלכע דריקן אױס זײער
פֿאַרדרוס לגבי דער דיסקרימינאַציע
פון דער יידישער שפּראַך אין מדי־
נת ישראל, װאָס דװקא אין אונ־
דזער מדינה װערט צוגענומען בײַ
טױזנטער בירגער, נײַע עולים און
װתיקים, די מעגלעכקײט אױסצו־
לעבן זיך קולטורעל אין דער
שפּראַך אין װעלכער זײ זענען
דערצױגן געװאָרן. קײנער באַ־
צװײפֿלט נישט דעם פֿאַקט, אַז
העברעאיש איז די אָפֿיציעלע
שפּראַך פון דער מדינה. אָבער לײַ־
דער זענען פֿאַראַן טױזנטער און
טױזנטער מענטשן, פֿאַר װעלכע
עס איז שפּעט איבערצו־
שטעלן זיך, צו דערלערנען עברית
אין אַזאַ מאָס, װאָס זאָל קענען בא־
פֿרידיקן זײערע קולטור־באַדער־
פֿענישן. צום באַדױערן פֿאַרבלײַבט
דער װײן־געשרײַ ביז איצט אָן אַן
ענטפֿער.
פֿאַראַן בײַ אונדז פֿיל פֿירנדיקע
פּערזענלעכקײטן, מיניסטאָרן, כּנ־
סת ־ דעפּוטאַטן, װעלכע דעקלאַ־
רירן זיך אַפֿט מאָל אַלס פֿרײַנט
פון יידיש, װעלכע „זינדיקן" אַלײן
מיט אַ יידיש װאָרט. װעלכע װאָל־
טן געקענט אפֿשר העלפֿן אין לײַזן
דעם דאָזיקן אַנגעװײטיקטן פּראָב־
לעם, אָבער װעלכע נעמען זיך
נישט דעם ענין צו פֿיל צום
האַרצן. די דאָזיקע פּערזענלעכ־
קײטן גיבן זיך גאָרניט נישט אַפּ
קײן גענױער דין וחשבון. װיפֿל
שאָדן דער דאָזיקער חרם אױף
יידיש האָט געבראַכט נישט נאָר
דעם טײל יידיש ־ רעדנדיקע ביר־
גער פֿון אונדזער לאַנד, נאָר אױך
דעם נײַעם, אינטערװאָאַקסנדיקן
דור, אין נישט נישט אין אַ קלענערער
מאָס אױך די יידן אין די תּפֿו־
צות.

Table XVIIIA. *Attitudes toward Yiddish among High School Students of Ashkenazi Parentage (Herman 1972)*

	All respondents	Religious	Traditionalist	Non-religious
1. Very positive	7%	9%	9%	6%
2. Positive	28	47	31	18
3. No particular feeling	52	39	46	60
4. Negative	10	4	13	10
5. Very negative	3	1	1	6
Total %	100	100	100	100
n	577	115	147	315

insight, is rejected both cognitively and affectively. 'Low Yiddish' is shrugged off with a wry smile. Until Israel passes beyond its current adolescent nationalism and arrives at a more relaxed and pluralistically permissive nationalism that honors rather than disavows other and previous Jewish civilizations, the Yiddish advocate must find a middle ground that is neither threatening and unbelievable nor laughable and pitiful. This middle ground must escape from the Israeli's totalitarian cultural mentality and yet not be subject to the designation of kitsch and camp. The true mission of Yiddish in Israel is simultaneously more Jewish and more universal than can openly be avowed. Undoubtedly Israel will some day be sufficiently mature, secure, and accepting of Jews and Jewishness, of all times and in their own right, to accept Yiddish as well. The question is 'when?' and 'how does one manage till then?'

Table XVIIIB. *Attitudes toward Yiddish among High School Students of Oriental/Sefardi Parentage (Herman 1972)*

	All respondents	Religious	Traditionalist	Non-religious
1. Very positive	1%	1%	—%	—%
2. Positive	7	1	10	8
3. No particular feeling	69	84	62	74
4. Negative	10	7	13	5
5. Very negative	13	7	15	13
Total %	100	100	100	100
n	200	46	116	38

7. SUMMARY AND CONCLUSIONS

In Israel an ideologized classical language was first enabled and then required to function as a *lingua franca* and, as such, it ultimately displaced the ethnically more restricted vernaculars that preceded it. Although several of the latter are still strong and creative in Israel, Yiddish being first and foremost among them, none is being significantly maintained by native-born Israelis. Both the ideology of the Israeli State and the forces of modern, urban Israeli technology are proceeding along the path of producing a new monolingual, national-secular culture that is significantly discontinuous with the recent Jewish past. Even Arabic, a language officially protected and needed for very practical purposes, is largely being neglected if not curtailed (see Fisherman 1972) in the process of sociocultural and political-operational integration. It is little wonder then that Yiddish, lacking any of the legal guarantees available to Arabic and having once been linked to several anti-Zionist and anti-modern formations, should be viewed with misgivings in connection with any level other than the passing, the humorous, and the informal. Any efforts toward influencing Israel to experiment with and to foster the cultural multimodality needed (within the Jewish fold) if Yiddish is to find a place for itself there might therefore do well to exploit the permissiveness and even the sympathy that exists for Yiddish at these levels. Conversational Yiddish, Yiddish theater, and Yiddish song would seem to be the least threatening as well as the most influential avenues of keeping Yiddish alive (if a massive nodding acquaintance can be considered 'alive'). An organized and integrated approach to familiarizing the public with the world of Yiddish at this level might be the best way to gradually further the receptivity that already exists, while adding to it slowly and selectively at higher levels.

The current study has revealed that even in modern society widespread, informal speech networks can persist in the absence of well-established (recognized), written, formal functions and notwithstanding official repression of linguistic diversity. Such repression may take the shape of exclusion from public and higher functions and therefore from all broader, symbolic functions. Such controls can on occasion be counteracted by vigorous counterorganization around alternative elites and on behalf of a different distribution of power. Both between-group bilingualisms and within-group diglossias have commonly been displaced in this fashion in the past. Where, as in Israel, such counterorganization is politically and ideologically

למה אין מלמדים 'אידישקייט' בכרמיאל?

עולים שואלים את הרב הראשי שלמה גורן

קורו בכרמיאל בעת שנפגש עם העולים במקום.

הרב גורן, שבא ביוזמתו לכרמיאל כדי לקדם את נושא הקליטה הרוח־נית של העולים, הו־יע שבכרמיאל ובמרכזי קליטה אחרים, יעשו הכל כדי שהעולים יקבלו לימודי יהדות מפי מרצים ורבנים השולטים בשפ־תם של העולים. כן ביקש מכל אותן המשפחות המעורבות לחקדים ככל שניתן את הגיור ומילת הילדים כ־די למנוע בעזות יותר חמורות בע־תיד. לצורך הגיור ינתנו שיעורים ב־כרמיאל כדי שהעולים לא יצטרכו לנסוע לשם כך לחיפה. אולם ביחס למילת הילדים לא יוכל הרב גורן לשנות דבר, היות ובמקום אין בית־חולים. הרב ישתדל למצוא הסדר כדי שהאמהות יוכלו לשהות עם יל־דיהן אחר המילה בבית־חולים בחי־פה או בנהריה. כן קרא הרב גורן לעולים להיות ערים ולהודיע מיד על כל מקרה של הופעת מיסיונר המבקש לצוד נפשות כדי שאפשר יהיה לפעול בצורה המתאימה.

בשיחה עם הרב גורן נכחו כ־80 עולים אולם לא כולם יכלו להבין את המדובר ולכן גם לא יכלו לש־אול, היות והשיחה התנהלה כולה באידיש וקצת בתרגום לרוסית, בעוד שהיו במקום גם דוברי אנגלית ו־ספרדית.

למה אין קובעים מזוזות בדירות הניתנות לעולים? ה־אם בונים כאן שיכונים עבור גויים? למה לא מלמדים אידישקייט ולא מביאים פעם חזן לתפילה לבית הכנסת או, להבדיל, תיאטרון באידיש או ברוסית עבור העולים? למה אי אפשר לימול את ילדי ה־עולים בכרמיאל ועל ההורים לנסוע לבתי חולים מרוח־קים? — אלה השאלות ש־נשאלו אתמול באזני הרב ה־ראשי, הרב שלמה גורן, בבי־

Fig. 14. (Maariv, August 6, 1973) Unhappy new Soviet immigrants in the village of Carmiel (many of whom have since left for Canada and other countries) ask 'Why aren't *mezuzot* [small parchment scrolls containing Deuteronomy 6, 4–9, 11 and 13–21, fixed to the doorpost in wooden or metal cases] fixed to the doorposts of apartments for immigrants? Are the apartment complexes built for gentiles? Why don't they (i.e., government immigration and absorption authorities) teach *Yidishkeyt* ["Jewishness"] in the schools and why don't they sometimes bring a cantor to the services in the synagogue or, on the other hand, why don't they bring us theater in Yiddish or Russian? Why is it impossible to circumcise the sons of new settlers in Carmiel and the parents must travel great distances to hospitals to make their own arrangement. . .?' New immigrants from the Soviet Union (and from Europe and the Americas more generally) tend to view Yiddish as part of the entire constellation of Jewish traditional life (*Yidishkeyt*) and are disturbed by the wide-spread Israeli disregard, if not rejection, of it outside of organized Orthodox circles.

unacceptable to the adherents of minority languages there is no other defense against cultural monocentrism than the slow branching out from widespread, informal, vernacular functions (which incite less opposition) to more serious ones for a limited group of participants. Yiddish in Israel is now in a position such that if both of these last-mentioned directions are not followed by organized means in the reasonably near future its vernacular status too will increasingly weaken, thereby rendering much more difficult, if not impossible, any future serious development on behalf of its overt cultivation and functional re-allocation. Under such circumstances Yiddish still will not disappear from the Israeli scene since it is too institutionalized (albeit in small religious and academic spheres) for that to happen. It will merely withdraw increasingly into the attitudinal twilight zone to which modern societies assign those values and behaviors that are simultaneously too positive to be abandoned but also too conflicted to be implemented.

Additional perspective on the Israeli Yiddish case may be gained by comparing it briefly with the Hindi-Regional Vernaculars case on the one hand and with the Bahasa Indonesia-Javanese case on the other. In both cases hopefully high-status *linguae francae* were adopted (and systematically codified and elaborated) for modern, nation-wide, integrative purposes by nationalist elites who themselves were native speakers of what came to be viewed as regional vernaculars at best or as foreign (imperialist) western tongues at worst. In both cases the elites divested themselves of their own mother-tongues (just as so many nationalist elites had done in the nineteenth century European nationalist movements) in order to thereby foster the symbolically integrative 'national' languages that are now consistently gaining users and mother-tongue claimants, more slowly in India and more rapidly in Indonesia.

In India, however, local patriotism has been strong enough to require guarantees that the symbolically integrative national language not be assigned local functions that the regional vernaculars themselves desire. In addition, English has been maintained, at least temporarily, in a special national status so that anti-Hindu sentiments in certain regions might be assuaged even in conjunction with national functions. This is exactly the type of 'solution' that the Israeli establishment classically feared and that is still spuriously invoked in conjunction with discussions as to a possible special status for Yiddish.

In Indonesia regional languages of great status, such as Javanese, have received no special consideration and indeed are little used and less recognized for any official purposes such as radio, education, publications, etc. The young, particularly in urban areas, increasingly and displacively use Indonesian and its growth as a mother-tongue (from its uniform position as a special purpose 'other tongue' merely a generation ago) has been every bit as miraculous, widespread, and rapid as is the case of modern Israeli Hebrew. To the extent that the original nationalist elite was itself Javanese (not to mention those of other less prestigious regional origins) it has sacrificed its mother-tongue, seemingly quite willingly and without ambivalence, on the altar of Indonesian national integration, thus effectively foretelling the demise of one of the world's great literary and artistic traditions. This is the 'solution' that the Israeli establishment adopted for itself *vis-à-vis* Yiddish and the solution against which Yiddish-interested circles are struggling.

Obviously, what may be called for in Israel is a solution which is neither the Indian one (with its entrenched and troublesome poly-centrism) nor the Indonesian one (with its callous disregard of Javanese language and culture in order to foster the thirty-year-old [or, at most, fifty-year-old] language and culture of modern Indonesia). What may be needed, indeed, is a view of 'Yiddish as an (optional) additional language' for optional, internal (i.e., Jewish) functions, somewhat similar to that currently in vogue *vis-à-vis* 'English as a (required) additional language' for external (i.e., touristic and technical) functions. If required English will not displace Hebrew as the younger generation's mother-tongue then optional Yiddish for special Jewish functions will certainly not do so. If differential exposure to English will not split the Israeli population assunder culturally or economically then differential voluntary exposure to Yiddish will certainly not do so. An *encouraged or supported* special 'optional' status for Yiddish is every bit as possible and certainly less threatening than an encouraged or supported 'required' status for English.

Israeli cultural security is growing apace and with this growth and the increased appearance of a third generation on the scene (a generation that did not itself betray Yiddish nor make pogroms against Yiddish speakers on behalf of the cultural solidarity of the new Jewish people), there will doubtlessly come about a new willingness to recognize the validity of the plea for a special status for Yiddish. From the status of being especially prohibited, despised, or ignored, Yiddish may yet achieve the widespread status among Israeli

Circassians get U.S. expert, to teach them their language

Jerusalem Post Reporter

KAFR KAMA. — An American world expert in the Circassian language, Prof. John Catford of Michigan, has arrived in this village for a stay of up to two months to instruct teachers and intellectuals of the Circassian community of Israel how to read and write their own native language.

The Circassians, who are Moslems, left Russia about 100 years ago to escape the oppression of the Czarist regime, after their country was taken from the Turks. They speak their language among themselves but have never learn to write it. At their (state) schools, Arabic, Hebrew and English are the only languages taught.

In their quest for instruction they tried to learn from Circassion radio broadcasts in the Soviet Union. But when this failed, they turned to a neighbour, Education Minister Yigal Allon of Ginossar. The Ministry of Education found Prof. Catford, who was invited to help.

If this experiment succeeds, Circassian will be taught in schools here and at Rehaniya, in Upper Galilee.

The number of Circassians in Israel is about 3,500. They serve in the army and in the police.

Circassian uses Cyrillic script, as does Russian.

הצ'רקסים ילמדו
צ'רקסית —
מאמריקאי

כאבק, הנמשך זה 25
שנה, על זכות ללמד ה־
שפה הצ'רקסית בבתי־הס־
פר של הצ'רקסים בגליל
הגיע השבוע לסיומו והחל
כשנת הלימודים הבאה
ילכדו תלמידי שני הכפ־
רים, רחניה וכפר־כבא, גם
את שפת עדתם.
אילם על אף היענות
משרד החינוך לבקשה תו־
בעי שני הכפרים, הגודב־
רים כיום רק ערבית, לא
הצליחו זקני שני הכפרים
לבצוא מושחה לשפתם. רק
לאחר חיפוש במשך כבה
חודשים, נמצא ב... ניו־
יורק בארה"ב פרופסור
מובחתה לשפת הצ'רקסים,
שידע כמה כידוע, הוא ה־
יחיד במערב, היודע שפה
זו על בוריה.
האיש נאות לבוא ארצה
וללמד את הילדים בהתנד־
בות, לאחר שהבטיצה ה־
מקומית כפר־כבא הודיעה
לו, כי היא מוכנה לממן
את נסיעתו לישראל.

Canada opts for 'cultural diversity'

Jerusalem Post Reporter

TEL AVIV. — The Canadian authorities have adopted a policy of encouraging "cultural diversity" in an effort to achieve greater national unity. This was stated yesterday by Mr. Gerard Pelletier, Canadian Minister of Communications, who is visiting Israel as guest of Shimon Peres.

Addressing the Ministry's department heads, Mr. Pelletier noted that the Canadian authorities had had two choices when immigrants began to arrive in great numbers. "Either they could work towards cultural conformity or encourage cultural diversity."

Canada chose the latter way, believing that it not only enriched the entire cultural life of Canada, but also gave the newcomers — and "we have literally a hundred ethnic groups which have been grafted on the original bi-lingual French and English base" — a feeling that their former way of life was appreciated and worthy of appreciation.

Fig. 15. The long road toward non-Hebrew/non-Arabic mother-tongue recognition begins in Israel with a small non-Jewish population: *Jerusalem Post,* July 11 (left) and August 9 (right), 1973. The corresponding item in the Hebrew press, (*Maariv,* June 7, 1973) reports that the Circassians began to 'struggle for the right to teach Circassian in the schools of Circassians' twenty-five years ago. The possible benefits of cultural diversity for the Jewish population are beginning to be explored with distinguished foreign visitors.

256   *Joshua A. Fishman and David E. Fishman*

Ashkenazim (and even among Sefardim) of being a key to one of the
most creative and innovative cultures of the Jewish people, indeed a
culture that also provided (among its more minor accomplishments)
the major impetus to mass Zionism, the major source of the state-
building second *aliya*, and the major urgency for postwar recognition
of a Jewish state. The third generation will doubtlessly realize that
none of these things should be held against Yiddish in Israel but, on
the contrary, that Yiddish should be helped to find its way into
Israeli education, radio, theater, journalism, and literature as 'an
additional language' for those who understand its value – past,
present, and future.[36]

REFERENCES*

Bentwich, Joseph S.
  1965 *Education in Israel* (London, Routledge and Kegan Paul).
Doroshkin, Milton
  1969 *Yiddish in America* (Rutherford, Madison, Teaneck, N.J. Fairleigh
         Dickenson University Press).
Fisherman, Haya
  1972 'The "Official Languages" of Israel; Their Status in Law and Police
         Attitudes and Knowledge Concerning Them', *Language Behavior Papers*
         1:2–21 (Jerusalem) (mimeographed). [Also in *Multilingual Polities*, ed.
         by G. Savard (Quebec City, CIRB and Laval University Press) 1975
Fishman, Joshua A.
  1965a 'Language Maintenance and Language Shift in Certain Urban Immigrant
         Environments. The Case of Yiddish in the United States', *Europa
         Ethnica* 22:146–158.
  1965b 'U.S. Census Data on Mother Tongues: Review, Extrapolation and
         Prediction', in *For Max Weinreich on His Seventieth Birthday* (The
         Hague, Mouton) pp. 51–62.
  1965c *Yiddish in America* (Bloomington, Indiana, Indiana University Re-
         search Center in Anthropology, Folkore and Linguistics).
  1969a 'Language Maintenance and Language Shift. Yiddish and Other Immi-
         grant Languages in the United States', *Yivo Annual of Jewish Social
         Science* 16:12–26.
  1969b 'National Languages and Languages of Wider Communication in the
         Developing Nations', *Anthropological Linguistics* 2:111–135 (Bloom-
         ington, Indiana).
  1972a 'Yiddish in amerike: 1960–1970 un vayter [Yiddish in America:
         1960–1970 and Thereafter] ', *Goldene Keyt* 75:110–127 (in Yiddish).

* Standard references and governmental statistical publications cited as sources
  in the text are not listed in the bibliography but immediately after the tables
  for which they were utilized.

1972b 'Hasotsiologia shel yiddish be'artsot habrit; 'avar, hove ve'atid [The Sociology of Yiddish in America: Past, Present and Future]'. *Hug L'yidiot Am Yisrael Batfutsot* 8.3. (in Hebrew).

Fishman, Joshua A., *et al.*
1966 *Language Loyalty in the United States* (The Hague, Mouton).

Goldstein, Anne and London, Bernice
1970 'Yiddish Usage and Attitudes among Yeshiva Students', in *Seminar on the Sociology of Yiddish in America,* term paper (Yivo Institute for Jewish Research).

Herman, Simon
1972 *Israelis and Jews; A Study in the Continuity of an Identity* (New York, Random House). [See Tables 44 and 45, pp. 250–251, and discussion on pp. 82–83.]

Hofman, John and Fisherman, Haya
1971 'Language Shift and Language Maintenance in Israel', *International Migration Review* 5:2.204–226. [Also in *Advances in the Sociology of Language,* Vol. II, ed. by J. A. Fishman (The Hague, Mouton) 1972.]

Hutchinson, Mary
1970 'The Message's Medium', in *Seminar on the Sociology of Yiddish,* term paper (Yivo Institute for Jewish Research).

Katz, Elihu, *et al.*
1972 *Tarbut Yisrael 1970* [The Culture of Israel, 1970]. (Jerusalem, Israel Institute of Applied Social Research, and Communication Institute, Hebrew University) (in Hebrew).

Lieberson, Stanley, and Curry, T. J.
1971 'Language Shift in the United States: Some Demographic Clues', *International Migration Review* 5:125–137.

Poll, Solomon
1965 'The Role of Yiddish in American Ultra-Orthodox and Hasidic Communities', *Yivo Annual of Jewish Social Research,* 13:125–152.

Ronch, Judah, *et al.*
1969 'Word Naming and Usage for a Sample of Yiddish-English Bilinguals', *Modern Language Journal* 53:232–235.

Schaier, Barbara, and Hoffman, Karen
1972 'English, Hebrew and Arabic as Objects of Affective, Cognitive and Conative Behavior among Arab School Children in East Jerusalem and in a West Bank Village', in *Seminar on the Sociology of Bilingual Education,* term paper (Hebrew University).

Schmelz, U. O. and Bachi, R.
1972 [Hebrew as the Everyday Language of the Jews in Israel] *Leshonenu* 37:1.50–68 (in Hebrew).

Starr, Brenda, and Laster, Beverly
1971 'Attitudes Toward English and Hebrew among Middle and Lower Class Jewish Israeli Elementary School Pupils', in *Seminar on Language and National Identity,* term paper (Hebrew University).

Weinreich, Max
1953 'Yidishkayt and Yiddish: On the Impact of Religion on Language in Ashkenazic Jewry', in *Mordecai M. Kaplan Jubilee Volume* (New York,

Jewish Theological Seminary) pp. 481–514. [Also in *Readings in the Sociology of Language*, ed. by J. A. Fishman (The Hague, Mouton) 1968, pp. 382–413.]

1967   'The Reality of Jewishness vs. the Ghetto Myth; The Sociolinguistic Roots of Yiddish', in *To Honor Roman Jakobson* (The Hague, Mouton) 211–221.

1973   *Geshikte fun der yidisher shprakh* [History of the Yiddish Language] (New York, Yivo Institute) (in Yiddish; English and Hebrew translations are being prepared).

NOTES

Full text published for the first time in the volume.
The research reported in this article and the preparation of this report were supported by the Foundation for Jewish Culture, the Ford Foundation (International Division), and The Language Behavior Section, Hebrew University. Sincere thanks are due to David L. Gold, Brenda Bogush, Robert Cooper, Morris Goldwasser, David Roskies, Dina Roskies, Lee Strunin, and Ruth Debel for their helpful comments and corrections to an earlier draft of this article.

1. English is obligatory in all Israeli schools (whether for Jewish or Arabic children) from the fifth grade onward. Arabic is optional in schools for Jewish children from the ninth grade onward and there are plans for its obligatory introduction into earlier grades in the near future (Fisherman 1972). For attitudes toward English in a sample of Israeli school children see Starr and Laster 1971. For attitudes toward English and Arabic in a sample of Israeli policemen (Jews and Arabs) and for the legal statuses of both of these languages see Fisherman 1972. Correspondingly, for attitudes toward Hebrew, English, and Arabic in a sample of urban and rural Israeli-Arab school children see Schaier and Hoffman 1972.

2. No exact figure is available due to the fact that Israeli statistics deal with use of Hebrew rather than Hebrew as a *mother-tongue,* given the fact that the former always yields a higher proportion of the total population than the latter.

3. A 1971 newspaper photo of a 'Black Panther' (lower-class, radical, Afro-Asian) protest demonstration in Tel Aviv showed one placard that read 'Golda Teach Us Yiddish!'

4. While Sefardim and Eydot Hamizrakh account for some 20% of world Jewry they account for nearly 50% of Israeli Jewry and 60% of the elementary school population in the country.

5. Unlike Israel the United States regularly reports data on 'mother-tongue claiming' rather than on 'principal language claiming' only. Thus in 1969 84.9% of the native-born and 26.0% of the foreign-born population in the United States claimed English as their mother-tongue. Hebrew was probably the mother-tongue of 40% or so of the Israeli population in 1961.

6. To this figure should be added an estimated 1,000 to 1,200 Neturey Karta (ultra-orthodox Yiddish speakers who do not recognize the State) whose

non-cooperation with census authorities leaves them entirely unreported in the decennial Israeli censuses.

7. As Table IIIB reveals for the Jewish Israeli population aged eighteen or older, those for whom Yiddish is the main language spoken at home (which is by no means the same as all speakers of Yiddish) are rather easily typified with respect to age and ethnic origin.

8. Arabic will not be considered in this study, even though it is the most frequently claimed principal language (besides Hebrew) among Jews in Israel (with 366,570 claimants as principal or additional spoken language), because of its very special legal as well as its non-Jewish and non-immigrant status. Many of the Jewish claimants of Arabic are in fact Yahudic/Arvic ('Judeo-Arabic') speakers but this distinction is not made by the Israeli census. A related factor is responsible for our not reviewing the status of Spanish in this report, namely, that Spanish is unfortunately combined with Judesmo/Dzhudesmo (at times also referred to as Dzudezmo, Ladino, or 'Judeo-Español') in all government statistics.

9. The rate of such claims is higher for Hungarian (46%) and Rumanian (56%), in both cases probably due to more recent immigration and settlement patterns.

10. However, it should be noted that the continuity of the 'Yiddish only' or 'Yiddish primarily' ultra-orthodox communities must now be examined more carefully than heretofore in view of the fact that the generation born *after* the creation of the State is now well within its childbearing years. Whether their children too will be 'only' or 'mainly' Yiddish speaking remains to be seen. Preliminary observation in ultra-orthodox sections of Jerusalem reveals that almost all children of elementary school age do speak Hebrew when interacting with 'outsiders' and many do so when speaking to each other. Nevertheless knowledge and use of Yiddish among them still seem to be widespread.

11. For Spanish the large number of recent immigrants, and therefore of first generation American-born claimants, should be noted.

12. As of the pre-election months of spring 1973 the Yiddish daily was sold outright to the Labor Party with the proviso that the current editor be given tenure for life.

13. The Dzudezmo *La Luz de Israel* appears twice a week and there may be a few less frequent publications in this language as well as in Farsic/Parsic ('Judeo-Persian').

14. Early in 1973, with the need for Georgian broadcasting, the daily half hour of 'simple Hebrew' was split into two separate fifteen minute periods (one coming before the Georgian broadcast [placed immediately before the Yiddish broadcast] and the other coming earlier in the day and on another station).

15. In contrast to 'Songs in Yiddish' the program 'Tunes of the East' is broadcast for thirty minutes every week. The regular Yiddish broadcasts are strictly limited as to the amount of time they may devote to Yiddish songs. Currently only one song a month is permitted (as well as only one ten-minute program per month devoted to Yiddish literature), leading to the recent resignation of the long-time director of these programs who had struggled for their improvement and 'liberation'.

16. The two-hour time slot in which 'immigrant programs' (Easy Hebrew, Yiddish, Judeo-Español, Mugrabi, etc.) are broadcasted are merely identified as such ('Immigrant Programs'), rather than by language, in the radio schedules published by the Hebrew press. In addition the station on which they are broadcasted notifies its listeners, just before the 'immigrant programs' begin, that it is about to discontinue broadcasting and will resume after two hours. Both of these policies are calculated to minimize the number of non-immigrants who might be attracted to these programs. Nevertheless, as Table XIVA clearly indicates, those listening to the Yiddish programs do *not* do so because they know no Hebrew and they are *not* primarily new *olim*.

17. Paragraph 1 of the Broadcasting Law (*Hok Ha-Shidur*), requiring the broadcasting corporation 'to strengthen the bond with Jewish tradition and its values and to deepen the understanding thereof' as well as 'to present the life and the cultural treasures of all the branches of the Jewish people from various lands', is pointed to repeatedly as the statutory basis for claims that Yiddish is being slighted *vis-à-vis* English and French.

18. *Survey of Radio Listening and Television Viewing in the Jewish Population; October – December 1972, Preliminary Findings* (Jerusalem, Central Statistical Agency, 1973).

19. Most recently many protest letters have dealt with the newly instituted deletion of five minutes of the 'precious thirty' for advertisement of other than cultural items. This is viewed as a governmental effort to derive funds from Yiddish and at the same time to weaken Yiddish culture. It should be pointed out, however, that similar advertising has recently been introduced into other-language broadcasts as well. Overlooked is the fact that every three minutes of advertising pays the complete costs of thirty minutes of broadcasting. This fact, as well as the special funds for Yiddish (and other immigrant-directed) broadcasting received by the broadcasting corporation from the Jewish Agency (*Sokhnut*) indicates that on a strict cost-accounting basis the Yiddish programs are income-*producing* for the broadcasting corporation.

20. In 1972 a few letters on this subject were also published in the English language *Jerusalem Post*. No such have appeared in the Hebrew press, in whose radio schedules the Yiddish programs *per se* are not mentioned.

21. From 1970 to 1973 there were a total of three television programs partially in Yiddish, each of them greeted by numerous expressions of thanks in the Yiddish press.

22. The preparation of 'canned' radio programs in Yiddish for re-broadcasting on North American, European, and Latin American stations, once regularly undertaken, has recently been practically discontinued for 'lack of funds'. At the same time the broadcasting corporation's budget was increased by 40 percent from 1972 to 1973. A series of articles by Y. Kutler in the daily *Haaretz* (Winter-Spring 1972–73) has stressed the corporation's mismanagement of funds and resources.

23. Dina Abramowicz lists ninety-nine Yiddish books ('Yiddish Literature' *The Jewish Book Annual*, volume 30, New York, Jewish Book Council, 1972) for the period April, 1971–April, 1972. Only publications received by the Yivo Institute for Jewish Research (New York) are listed in her annual reports. For the period April, 1970–April, 1971, 125 books were listed.

24. The newly organized Committee for Yiddish Culture in Israel has announced a fund for the short-term support of newly arrived Yiddish writers and a worldwide book club to guarantee the sale of at least 2,000 copies of a few selected Yiddish books each year.

25. Unreported here, at this juncture, as well as probably not fully reported in government statistics, is the Israeli world of Yiddish religious publications (and republications), scholarly, semi-scholarly, and popular. Such eighteenth and nineteenth century Yiddish (*Ivre-taytsh*) classics as the *Tsene-Rene*, the *Korbn-Minkhe*, the *Beys-Yehude*, the *Makhzer Kol-Boy*, etc., are constantly being reprinted, albeit in unknown quantities and at unknown intervals. In addition new Yiddish commentaries and translations are not infrequently announced in the religious press (in Hebrew and in Yiddish) often without being subsequently 'clocked in' by *Kiryat Sefer*. Another unreported area is that of books about Yiddish in conjunction with eastern European Jewish folklore, history, literature, political movements, etc. Although their number is small and their impact limited to intellectual circles they should not be entirely overlooked as an information and opinion-molding channel.

26. Yiddish is also fourth as 'source language', Arabic being credited with only forty-two original titles subsequently translated into other languages (*Supplement: Monthly Bulletin of Statistics* 23 [1973] : 3. 14, Table 5).

27. On March 22, 1973, the Hebrew Writers Association, that had long excluded Yiddish writers from membership, finally voted to admit them to a newly planned Federation of Israeli Writers which had become politically 'advisable' due to pressures to recognize the existence of Arabic writers in Israel.

28. A June 1972 announcement of the Ministry of Education indicated a decision to pursue the goal of making spoken Arabic a *compulsory* subject in all Israeli schools from the sixth year of study and onward. A December 1972 announcement reported that 'an experiment in teaching spoken Arabic to fifth graders will begin next fall in 10 Israeli schools. If the pilot project succeeds the plan will be extended to all Israel's elementary schools . . . to enable Jewish children to converse with Arab children' rather than devote their attention to literary Arabic alone. The compulsory aspect of the above-mentioned program was dropped, as announced by Minister of Education Yigat Allon in June 1973, due to the already overcrowded curriculum and absence of the necessary personnel (*Maariv Le Noar*, June 11, 1973, p. 16).

29. In 1972 nine students took matriculation examinations in Yiddish as compared to 7 in Rumanian, 10 in Turkish, 21 in Persian, 37 in Russian, 1,012 in French, 1,603 in Arabic, and 12,155 in English.

30. The much-touted Yiddish chair and graduate program at Tel Aviv University, announced in March 1973, has regrettably fallen victim to internal intrigue inspired by competitive scholarly interest in Jerusalem, before it has had a chance to materialize. The two eminent and young literary scholars originally mentioned in connection with this chair have had to make other arrangements.

31. The newly organized Committee for Yiddish Culture in Israel includes a number of prestigious names outside of strictly Yiddishist circles and has begun to publish a Yiddish quarterly and a primarily press service organ

devoted to news of life in Israel more generally and to the Yiddish and Hebrew literary scenes in particular. It sponsors infrequent Yiddish and Hebrew lectures on the literature related to these two languages and publishes occasional volumes for 'newly arriving' Yiddish writers. The Committee's responsibilities toward Yiddish writers after a few years of residence in Israel and *re* the status of Yiddish as such in Israel (particularly in connection with Israeli youth and educational endeavors) remains undefined.

32. The major exception of recent date was the privately and commercially sponsored Yiddish Song Festival (Spring 1972), now to become an annual event, which was widely advertised in the Hebrew (as well as Yiddish and English) press in Israel, partially rebroadcasted on radio and television, and an obvious commercial and artistic success notwithstanding the absence of Hebrew reviews. More recently (Winter, 1972—73), a newly arrived Yiddish chorus from the Soviet Union has experienced similar success and recognition. A government-supported Yiddish Art Theater for Russian *olim* is also under consideration.

33. Other well-known quips about Yiddish and Hebrew, stemming from an earlier period, include Bialik's claim that although 'one *should* speak Hebrew; one speaks Yiddish automatically', and that when busy he spoke Yiddish because he had 'no time to speak Hebrew'. For details concerning Bialik's ambivalence toward Yiddish, see Yitskhak Avineri's reminiscences in *Maariv* December 15, 1972, p. 37.

34. The references to Sefardi/Oriental Jews as possible loci of violent protest if Yiddish were given 'too much' public recognition (such as an hour rather than half an hour of radio time per day) are based upon their purported identification of Yiddish with the current Ashkenazic establishment. Thus prior to the 1973 election campaign an Israeli humorist quipped that '(The) State of Israel invites applications for the position of Prime Minister. Applications in Yiddish (are) to (be) submitted to the Trade Union Executive Committee' (*Maariv* December 15, 1972).

35. The committee for Yiddish Culture in Israel has announced an annual prize for a Yiddish writer to be awarded under the patronage of the Prime Minister's office beginning in 1973.

36. The most noteworthy Yiddish-related, Israeli-sponsored event since the completion of this paper was the World Congress for Yiddish Culture, held in Jerusalem in August 1976. For my analysis of this largely public-relations and tourism-inspired event, see *Yidishe Shprakh* 1977. It remains to be seen whether the Congress's significant resolutions, or the government's promises anticipating it, will be realized. J.A.F.

Migration and the Decline of the Welsh Language

1. FACTORS WHICH HAVE CONDUCED TO THE DECLINE

1.1. *The Present Position*

The population of Wales according to the 1961 census was slightly over 2,500,000, a 1.6% increase over 1931, that is, an increase of 40,000. Of this total 26% (659,000) claimed to be able to speak Welsh to some extent, a decline of 27% in thirty years. In 1961 1.0% (26,000), the great majority of which was under the age of five, were able to speak Welsh only, a decline of 73.5% since 1931. These are the very bare outlines of the demographic status of the Welsh language at present: this study is intended to present a more detailed analysis of the present position and to trace the curve of the decline; to identify and describe the contributory causes, the most crucial of which has been rapid industrialization and migration in some key areas; as well as to suggest some of the social and linguistic conse-quences. Industrialization has helped to deplete the countryside and to encourage very large numbers of immigrants, both Welsh and English, into South and Northeast Wales. Even before the period of industrialization this movement was facilitated by the geography of the principality. Three points of easy access and communication have invited penetration from across the border while the moorlands and highlands have frustrated the consummation of the ultimate design of the invaders. Easy access is ensured along the northern and southern low-lying seaboard as well as in the center along the upper reaches of the Severn River. At the same time the central, rugged, mountainous heartland has provided safeguards against total collapse before the overwhelming flood of English influences. In these central areas agriculture and sheep farming have been the traditional occupa-

Map I. Areas of Wales

tions. South Wales — except for the rich agricultural area of the Vale of Glamorgan, the eastern parts of Monmouthshire, and parts of Carmarthenshire and South Pembrokeshire — is characterized by narrow valleys and long defiles reaching into the foothills and fringes of the central massif. The geographic and topographic variety has contributed to a complex distribution of the two languages as well as great regional differences in social and economic development.

1.2. The Industrial Age and its Consequences

Even when the problems arising from extremely rapid industrialization and movement of population became acute the Welsh language was still strong demographically although depressed culturally, opposed politically and administratively, as well as restricted to less prestigious uses. Between the end of the sixteenth and the beginning of the nineteenth centuries there had been little change in the 'Welsh way of life' among the independent peasantry. Even in areas which eventually became almost completely anglicized, such as Monmouthshire, the population was predominantly Welsh-speaking. In the middle of the eighteenth century those responsible for creating circulating schools found that Monmouthshire was a suitable area for Welsh as well as English instruction. 'In the three reckoned English counties, viz Monmouthshire,[1] Hereford and Shropshire . . . most of the inferior people speak Welsh' (E. T. Davies 1957:59). Well into the nineteenth century the western valleys of that county were entirely Welsh and the use of the language extended to the seaport villages and towns. In 1849 it was claimed that over two-thirds of the

Table I. *Competence in English and Welsh Among Pupils in Areas of North and South Wales (1858)*[a]

	Total	Total Welsh-speaking	Welsh-speaking children under ten years of age			Total	Total Welsh-speaking	Welsh-speaking children ten years or older		
			Good English	Imperfect English	Welsh only			Good English	Imperfect English	Welsh only
North Wales	1,115	903 (90%)	110 (12%)	437 (46%)	356 (39%)	640	557 (87%)	239 (43%)	244 (44%)	74 (13%)
South Wales	513	374 (75%)	111 (29%)	160 (44%)	103 (28%)	320	212 (70%)	133 (63%)	67 (32%)	12 (5%)

[a] From *Commission of Enquiry* 1858, vol. II: 631, Appendix D.

total population of Wales still spoke Welsh and of these more than half were monolingual (Phillips 1849:341). The Commissioners of 1844 spoke of South Wales as exhibiting the 'phenomenon of a peculiar language isolating the mass from the upper portion of society' (Commission of Enquiry ... 1847, vol. I:80). In 1858 in a representative area of North Wales with a population of 52,000 there were 'probably from 44 to 47 thousands who may be said to speak and know Welsh only, while of the remaining 5,000 a large proportion amounting to at least two thirds though conversant to a greater or lesser extent with English use Welsh as their vernacular language' (Commission of Enquiry ... 1858, vol II:452). Even in South Wales the same Commission estimated that 74% to 77% spoke Welsh habitually. The schools serving these areas maintained a high level of Welsh though they reflected the increasing influence of English on the older children and a growing disparity between the incidence of the language in North and South Wales (Table I).

Among the children under ten years of age the level of Welsh language maintenance was high, though appreciably higher in North

Table II. *Population of Wales in Thousands: 1801–1961. County*

Year	Total Wales	% Diff. Wales	Total Anglesey	% Diff. Anglesey	Total Brecon	% Diff. Brecon	Total Caernarvon	% Diff. Caernarvon	Total Cardigan	% Diff. Cardigan	Total Carmarthen	% Diff. Carmarthen	Total Denbigh	% Diff. Denbigh
1801	587		34		32		42		43		67		60	
1811	674	13	37	9	38	18	49	17	50	15	77	15	64	6
1821	771	17	45	22	44	16	58	18	58	16	90	16	77	19
1831	904	12	48	8	48	9	66	13	65	12	101	12	84	17
1851	1163	14	57	9	61	2	68	3	71	4	111	5	93	5
1871	1413	10	51	−3	60	0.5	106	28	73	1	116	2	109	8
1901	2013	13	51		54	−1	123	6	61	−5	135	5	138	10
1911	2421	20	51		59	9	125	−0.5	60	−2	160	19	145	10
1921	2656	9.6	52	1	61	3	130	4.5	61	2	175	9	155	8
1931	2593	−2	49	−3	58	−4	121	−7	55	−8	179	3	155	1
1951	2599	0.2	57	7	57	−.5	124	3	53	−3	172	−2	171	4
1961	2644	2.0	52	−8	55	−3	122	−2	54	1	168	−3	174	2
1971	2726	3.0	60	15	53	−4	123	1.0	55	2	162	−4	185	5

[a]From *Census of England and Wales* 1801–1971.

Wales than in the South where the shift to English is more rapid. Among the older children the decline amounted to a loss of 66% in North Wales and 82% in the South due no doubt to the influence of exclusively English instruction in the schools and increasing contact with English outside school.

1.3. *General Population Trends*

Estimation of the size of the population prior to 1801 is a hazardous enterprise. Widely differing accounts have been offered but it is now generally accepted that by about the middle of the sixteenth century the inhabitants of Wales numbered approximately 278,000. By 1600 this number had risen to 379,000, by 1700 to 419,000, and by 1800 to 587,000. During the period 1801–31 the increase in population in Wales alone kept pace with the general increase in England and Wales together, although the counties of Monmouth and Glamorgan were beginning to forge ahead, the former increasing from 46,000 to 98,000 and the latter from 72,000 to 126,000. In slightly more than

Distribution of Population of Wales and Percentage Decennial Differences[a]

Total Flint	% Diff. Flint	Total Glamorgan	% Diff. Glamorgan	Total Merioneth	% Diff. Merioneth	Total Monmouth	% Diff. Monmouth	Total Montgomery	% Diff. Montgomery	Total Pembroke	% Diff. Pembroke	Total Radnor	% Diff. Radnor
40		72		28		46		48		56		19	
47	17	85	19	31	10	62	4	52	8	61	5	21	15
54	14	102	20	34	9	72	15	60	16	74	16	22	5
60	5	126	24	36	6	98	35	66	9	81	9	25	14
68	6	232	46	39	4	157	29	67	1.5	94	7	25	–
76	12	398	36	47	10	195	13	68	1.5	92	–1	24	–2
84	11	860	41	49	1	297	17	55	–5.0	88	–1	22	–3
93	14	1121	30	46	–6.0	396	33	53	–4	90	2	21	–3
107	15	1254	12	45	–1.0	450	14	51	–4	92	2	22	4
113	6	1226	–2.0	43	–2.0	435	–3.0	48	–6	87	–5	21	–4
146	15	1203	–1.0	41	–1.0	426	–1.0	46	–1	91	2.5	20	–2.5
150	3	1230	2.2	38	–6.0	445	2.0	44	–1	94	1.5	18	–5
175	17	1256	2.0	35	–8.0	461	4.0	43	–2	99	5	18	–

fifty years — from 1800 to 1851 — the population of Wales doubled, something it had taken 250 years to do prior to 1800. During the nineteenth century it tripled. During the first twenty years of this century the decennial increases for Wales alone were nearly double those of England and Wales together — 20.3% and 9.5% compared with 10.9% and 4.9%. During the forty years thereafter the size of the population was relatively stable, while that of England and Wales together rose at an average of 4.3%. In fact between 1921 and 1931 Wales suffered a decline to one-fifth of its growth rate in the previous decade. This decline intensified during the nine years previous to 1940. The present growth rate is positive but it is less than a third of that of England and Wales together. Both of these facts have significance from the standpoint of language.

The abnormal growth of the population of Wales is a reflection of the development of industry especially in South Wales. Before 1750 the economy of Wales was pastoral and depressed; only in a few lowland areas was it possible to cultivate sufficiently large arable acreages. Industrial activity was fitful and isolated. It was not until toward the beginning of the nineteenth century, with the acceleration of the development of the iron industry in the higher reaches of the valleys and hills, did any ambitious industrial development reach Wales. Between 1850 and 1914 the iron industry increased in importance and tended to move into the coastal strip. The period 1914–1939 is remarkable for the decline of the extracting industries leading to economic depression and emigration which is characteristic of South Wales. Finally, during the past thirty years the Welsh economy has become more diversified and sophisticated.

These industrial changes were made possible by and have led to large increases of population in a few areas. This geographically selective increase has been based on considerable migration, first within Wales and later from England in far greater numbers (Table III).

The rural counties — Anglesey, Caernarvon, and Merioneth in North Wales; Radnor (which was largely English by the middle of the last century), Brecon, and Montgomery in Central Wales; Cardigan, Pembrokeshire, and Carmarthen in South West Wales — have been regarded traditionally as the main bulwarks of the Welsh language. All have been heavy population losers: some consistently from the beginning of the industrial era and others, like Anglesey, from the time when industrialization was intensified. As we shall see they contributed considerably to the satisfaction of the early labor needs

Table III. *Net Population Change per Thousand Due to Migration in Each Welsh County: 1851–1961* [a]

County	1851–61	1861–71	1871–81	1881–91	1891–1901	1901–11	1911–31 (20 years)	1931–51 (20 years)	1951–61
Anglesey	+25	+96	+58	-32	-31	-35	+13	+49	+4
Brecon	+35	-46	-98	-47	-48	-21	-34	-11	+4
Caernarvon	-19	+33	+18	-32	-9	-43	-15	-2	-2
Cardigan	-62	-45	-99	-133	-63	-21	-34	-11	+4
Carmarthen	-58	-48	-33	-45	-43	+67	+10	-65	0
Denbigh	-6	-44	-27	-22	-16	+1	-9	-4	+7
Flint	+158	-24	-51	-83	-24	+21	+132	+120	+40
Glamorgan	+133	+45	+144	+166	+54	+92	-131	-109	0
Merioneth	-61	+106	-12	-62	-54	-104	+14	-14	+13
Monmouth	-32	+35	-65	+59	-4	+119	-123	-111	+3
Montgomery	-72	-75	-96	-118	-90	-80	-50	-64	-11
Pembroke	-54	-74	-81	-99	-64	-73	-35	-24	-5
Radnor	-115	-83	-146	-118	-90	-80	-50	-64	-11

a From *Census of England and Wales 1851–1961.*

Map II. Study of Internal Migration in England and Wales: 1851–1951. (Reprinted with permission from Friedlander and Roshier 1966.)

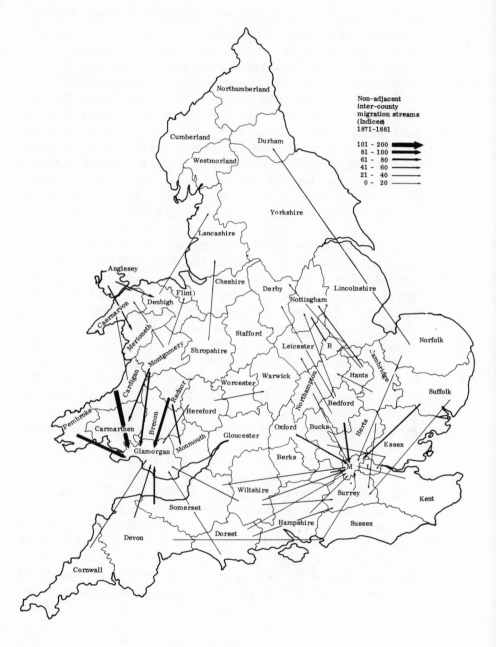

Map III. Study of Internal Migration in England and Wales: 1851–1951. (Reprinted with permission from Friedlander and Roshier 1966.)

of the industrial growth areas such as Flintshire in North Wales and Glamorgan in the South. The period of general industrial depression between 1920 and 1936 made only a slight contribution to the reversal or halting of emigration from the rural Welsh-speaking areas. The depression accelerated this process in the industrial areas.

We can distinguish four periods of migration. Up to 1850 the needs of Welsh industry were met by migration largely from the neighboring Welsh counties with some support from the southwestern counties of England. During this first phase iron and copper smelting, which made far smaller demands on labor than the second phase, were the most important industries. The second phase lasted from 1850 to 1900; during this period the southwest counties of England became the main source of labor, the change being greatly facilitated by the new railway network. The third phase, from 1910 onward, saw the emigration of Welshmen partly to England and partly to the United States. Within the short period of ten years at most the long-term process of immigration to Wales was reversed. But the damage to the demographic condition of the language had been done: the linguistic homogeneity of South Wales was completely disrupted by immigration to Wales and emigration only aggravated the disease. The fourth period, from the end of World War II to the present, has seen the retardation of the process of emigration, the stabilization of the industrial population, and a change in the nature of immigration, the composition of which has become extremely selective and professional. For these reasons the new immigrants are more mobile than the earlier immigrants had been.

These phases characterize the industrial areas. *Vis-à-vis* the rural counties — those in central Wales and the isolated North and Southwest, Anglesey, Brecon, Cardigan, Montgomery, Pembroke, and Radnor — whatever fluctuations have occurred have been only slight compared with a process of continuous emigration at a fairly consistent rate, as Table III shows for almost all areas except Glamorgan and Flintshire. Emigration in the latter counties leaped forward at the beginning of the industrial era and then declined until the beginning of this century when its second industrial phase began. The greatest percentage of these emigrants have been Welsh-speaking.

1.4. *Geographical Distribution of the Population*

1.4.1. *Trends in the Whole of Wales*

Without exception the predominantly rural counties manifest regular and continuous emigration. Among all the counties in England and Wales which belonged to the 'losing group' throughout the period 1851–1951, the Welsh rural counties ranked among those with the highest proportion of emigration. Apart from Merioneth and Caernarvon (which reached their population peaks in 1901 to 1921, respectively) the rural population peak was achieved before 1871 (Table II).

Since 1801 the rate of increase of the population of these counties has been comparatively slight. In 1801 all the counties other than those which became centers of industry aggregated 359,000. In 1971 the figure was 834,000 — an increase of 130% — while the total increase was 364%. The industrial counties of Glamorgan, Monmouth, and Flintshire had an elevenfold increase. The rural counties made their highest contribution to the total population at the beginning of the last century. In 1845 Carmarthenshire had a larger population than Glamorgan (34,300 and 29,400, respectively) while Brecon and Denbigh were only slightly below the Glamorgan total. By 1871, when the industrialization of Wales was being vigorously pursued, Glamorgan had increased its population twelve times, Denbigh five times, and Carmarthen and Brecon only three times. In 1801 Merioneth contributed 5% of the total population of Wales, approximately a third of Glamorgan's share. In 1961 the disparity was 1 to 32 and in 1971 1 to 36. Montgomeryshire's share declined from 8% in 1801 to 1.5% in 1971 and in Pembrokeshire it declined from 10% to 4%. The agricultural depression of the middle of the last century together with the shortage of labor in the iron industry, combined to make the Welsh-speaking areas of West Wales an attractive recruiting ground for the ironmasters of Glamorgan who paid their agents in Pembrokeshire £5 for every fifty workmen they secured (John 1960:69). It has been suggested that the depopulation of these areas occurred in ever-widening circles with Merthyr at the center (John 1960:69). The neighboring parishes made their greatest contribution to the industries of Merthyr up to the 1820s, while the almost completely Welsh-speaking areas of West Carmarthen and Pembrokeshire did not begin to make theirs until 1845.

During this century up to 1971, while the total for the whole of Wales has increased by 73,000 (4.1%), the population of rural Wales has declined by 53,000 (−8.2%). The most intensely Welsh of the rural areas has had even more serious losses: Montgomery, 12,000 (22%); Cardigan, 6,000 (10%); and Merioneth, 14,000 (28%) (Table II). When we look at very small parishes which have been and still are taken to represent traditional Wales the losses in fifty years have been severe: Penllyn (Merioneth), 36%; Edeyrnion (Merioneth), 20.5%; Hiraethog (Denbigh), 28.5%, and Tregaron (Cardigan), 37.7%. It is true that losses of comparable dimensions have been suffered in English-speaking rural areas: Builth (Brecon), 35%; New Radnor (Radnor), 31.2%; and Knighton (Radnor), 33%. But nothing that has happened in these English areas has helped to stanch the wound inflicted on the Welsh language.

During the last 100 years the population of rural central Wales has decreased by over 25%; during this century alone it has decreased by more than 17% compared with a 50% increase in Wales as a whole (Table II). The recognized pool of Welsh speech has become increasingly shallow. In terms of both actual numbers and proportions of the population the balance has shifted progressively to South Wales. After 1911, and contrary to what characterized the first phase of industrialization, the rural emigrants have tended to move to England. Consequently, the loss of Welsh in the rural areas has not benefited the urban areas of Wales. However, the decline in rural Wales cannot be attributed exclusively to emigration. The rate of natural increase has almost invariably been unfavorable to the rural areas, and this disadvantage has tended to increase. The rate of natural increase for England and Wales from 1951 to 1961 was 4.5% and for Wales alone 3.4%. During the same period in the central Wales rural counties it was only 0.4%. In the two most thoroughly Welsh-speaking counties, Merioneth and Cardiganshire, deaths exceeded births. In three counties, Caernarvon, Cardigan, and Merioneth, the decline in natural growth rates has been greater than the rate of emigration by 8.5%, 14.8%, and 6.6%, respectively.

The depopulation of the Welsh-speaking rural counties was not always a total loss to the Welsh language. The period 1851–71 was characterized by short-distance migration largely, much of it to and from adjacent counties. The condition of the language in South Wales at present would be very much poorer than it is if the migration from England had not been offset in previous years by the deployment of the internal resources of Wales. During the period 1850 to 1871 about 70% of the migrants into Glamorgan came from the neighboring Welsh-speaking counties. A large proportion of these immigrants were monolingual Welsh or nearly so. Between 1871 and 1881 long-distance migration set in and only 38% came from the five neighboring counties, while migration from the southwest counties of England rose rapidly to 37%. One feature of early short-distance migration from Welsh areas which census figures cannot reveal, but which was of great importance, was its occasional character. Farm workers and owners of small holdings in Carmarthenshire and Breconshire were accustomed to move into the iron works and mines of Monmouthshire and Glamorgan during the slack farming seasons and return home when the pressure of farm work required their presence. This constant mobility produced two contradictory results: it helped regularly to reinforce the existing Welsh character of the industrial area and at the same time it contributed to the disintegration of the settled traditional Welsh pattern of rural life. It promoted the acceptance of novel ideas and prepared the way for the forces tending toward the anglicization of even the remote rural areas. This aspect of migration assumed greater importance in the short period between 1876 and 1879 when temporary recession drove large numbers of short-distance migrants back to the farms. This oscillatory mobility, which took place between censuses, is not reflected in the census returns.

The rural areas have consistently received a certain number of immigrants and because these are concentrated in well-defined and limited areas their influence in eroding the Welsh character of those areas is more easily and immediately observed. For instance, the increase in the population of Cardiganshire between 1951 and 1971 is due largely to the inclusion of the expanded and predominantly English-speaking members, staff and students of the University of Wales at Aberystwyth. The hydroelectric construction project in the same county, manned by migrant labor (English and Irish), was responsible for an increase in the county population. Similar large construction projects in Merionethshire have inflated the local populations with non-Welsh elements as have military establishments in Breconshire, Cardiganshire, and other Welsh-speaking rural counties. In Anglesey the rise between 1961 and 1971 is due entirely to the expansion of a military base, the construction of a large nuclear electric generating plant, and the establishment of a large nonferrous industry — all of these being entirely alien to the rural character of the county. Where the populations of other rural areas have shown signs of natural increase between 1951 and 1961 — in Welshpool (5%), in Newtown (4%), and the borough of Montgomery (7%) — the locations of the increases have been close to the English border or along the Severn River and therefore within easy access to the English Midlands. Such rises in the population have not favored the maintenance of the Welsh language.

1.4.2. Trends Specific to Glamorgan

The history of industrialization in Wales is the history of changes in the economy of Glamorgan and Monmouthshire, the latter being one of a dozen counties in England and Wales which does not show simple migration patterns. Monmouthshire developed its own industries by drawing on English-speaking labor from across the border as well as from the same Welsh resources in Glamorgan. But it also contributed greatly to Glamorgan's population growth. In the 1840s, as the coal deposits of Merthyr and its neighborhood, together with those of the Rhondda, began to be exploited intensively, colliers in the valleys of Monmouthshire moved into Glamorgan to promote the exploitation. In the three decades 1851–61, 1871–81, and 1891–1901 a combination of immigration mainly from England and emigration to Glamorgan ensured a net negative migration balance for Monmouthshire (Table III). Not only did the number of immigrants fail to offset the number of Glamorgan-bound emigrants but the rate of decline of the Welsh language in Monmouth accelerated because the immigrants were almost all English and a large proportion of the emigrants were Welsh-speaking.

Glamorgan has a 'special place in the history of internal migration in Britain and belongs to a group of English and Welsh counties which experienced a net positive gain in the first period (beginning in 1851) and net losses thereafter' (Friedlander and Roshier 1966:263). Between 1801 and 1851, when the population of Glamorgan more than tripled from 71,000 to 232,000, the county was still largely agricultural with a lower population density at the end of that period than even Cornwall or Somerset – 253 compared with 259 and 289 per square mile. During the next sixty years, while the population of England and Wales as a whole rose by only 80%, there was more than a fivefold rise in Glamorgan. Over half a million of this increase was accounted for by immigration (Table III). Using their 'migration index', Friedlander and Roshier (1966) estimate that between 1851 and 1861 Glamorgan, of all counties in England and Wales, witnessed a flow of migrants second in its strength only to that of another Welsh county in process of industrialization, Flintshire. In the next decade, from 1861 to 1871 it was second only to

London and its neighboring counties. During this phase in addition to those from Monmouthshire (2,300) well over 70% of the Glamorgan immigrants were recruited from neighboring Welsh counties — Cardiganshire (1,500), Pembrokeshire (3,700), Carmarthenshire (5,700), and Brecon (2,100).

Thus, having been second in the list of gaining counties from 1851 to 1871, Glamorgan reached the top in 1871—81 when over 57% of the immigrants came from England (Table V). The flow continued until 1911. This was due to the greatly increased production of coal requiring more than 116,000 additional miners between 1871 and 1911. Of these 67% were recruited from neighboring English counties — Somerset, Gloucester, Devon, Wiltshire, and Hereford. There was therefore both a massive rise in the number of immigrants and an equally important decisive shift in the areas of origin. (Table V). When the total number of immigrants was held to no more than 21,000 (1861—1871) three quarters of them were Welsh. As the numbers increased to 74,000, then to 108,000, 105,000, and finally, in 1911 to 128,000, the Welsh contribution fell to a half. Between 1861 and 1911 the number of nonnative-born inhabitants of Glamorgan increased to 390,000, representing the residuum of nearly 430,000 immigrants, over 55% of them English monolinguals. The ratio of nonnative- to native-born remained constant between 1861 and 1911 at around 35% and in view of the rapid rise in the total population the constancy of this ratio must be attributed to the equally constant reinforcement already described. After 1911 the ratio fell to 21% because of the cessation of immigration (Table IV).

Table IV. *Total Number Born Outside Glamorgan and the Proportion of the Total Population: 1861—1951*[a]

Date of census return	1861	1871	1881	1891	1901	1911	1921	1931	1951
Total in thousands	116.8	117.9	180.8	260.6	297.8	390.9	280	261	254
Proportion of native population	36%	34%	35%	38%	34%	35%	22%	21.5%	21%

[a] From *Census of England and Wales, General Reports,* 1894, Table 8; 1901, Table 36; 1921, Table 22; for the other years, Tables 39, 40.

Table V. *Glamorgan Immigrants 1861–1911: Numbers (in Thousands) and Percentages According to Areas of Origin*[a]

Date of census return	Grand total of migration to Glamorgan	Welsh counties												Total of Welsh migrants	Welsh migrants % of grand total	Migration from England Total	%
		a. Anglesey	b. Brecon	c. Caernarvon	d. Cardigan	e. Carmarthen	f. Denbigh	g. Flint	h. Merioneth	i. Monmouth	j. Montgomery	k. Pembroke	l. Radnor				
1861–71	21.0	–	2.1	–	1.5	5.7	.1	–	.1	2.3	.4	3.7	.4	16.3	78	4.7	22
1871–81	74.7	–	3.6	.3	4.1	4.9	.2	.1	.2	10.1	1.4	5.8	.7	31.4	43	43.3	57
1881–91	108.8	.6	4.3	1.9	7.6	9.3	.7	.4	1.6	10.5	4.1	5.5	1.4	48.2	44	60.6	56
1891–1901	105.0	.4	4.2	1.0	3.8	11.6	.3	.3	1.1	13.5	1.4	7.1	.7	55.4	53	49.6	47
1901–1911	128.5	1.0	3.8	3.9	2.9	6.8	1.1	.3	2.5	11.6	2.2	5.5	1.3	42.9	33	85.6	67

a   From *Census of England and Wales,* see source for Table IX.

But from the standpoint of Welsh language maintenance the decline in the ratio is no consolation because the second- and third-generation migrants, though native-born, were predominantly if not exclusively English-speaking.

The fate of the Welsh language in Glamorgan has depended on the interaction of two factors. First, industrialization began in the strongest Welsh-speaking areas, the hills, and was fed by immigrants from other Welsh-speaking areas. This occurred during the first phase. During the second phase the labor supply was predominantly English; it was massive and exploited over a relatively short period. The first phase gave the Welsh language an opportunity to adapt to change. During the second phase immigration was too intense and too rapid to allow for the assimilation of the English. This fact was stressed by the Commission of Enquiry into Industrial Unrest (1917). Until 1895 'the inhabitants, in many respects, showed a marked capacity for stamping their own impress on all newcomers, and communicating to them a large measure of all their own characteristics; of more recent years the process of assimilation had been unable to keep pace with the continuing influx of immigrants'.

The changes did not occur uniformly throughout Glamorgan: the rate of population growth and of migration varied from district to district. The most rapid changes occurred in Merthyr and the Rhondda Valleys. The former, at one time the center of Britain's iron industry and the latter an area truly representative of the coalfield, are situated almost within the mountainous Welsh heartland. In 1851 Merthyr had a population of over 50,000: less than 28% were native-born; over 40% came from other Welsh counties; and 12% came from the neighboring Welsh-speaking districts of Glamorgan. Only a small portion of the remaining 20% came from England. It is at this point that the significance of the historical isolation of the uplands of Glamorgan from the effects of the Norman and Tudor occupation of Wales and consequent anglicization came to be felt. The Rhondda Valleys and Merthyr, unlike the low-lying areas of the county, had remained Welsh-speaking. Consequently, of the immigrants to Glamorgan the Welsh-speaking element was almost invariably attracted to the coalfields in the hills. In 1808 it was claimed that 'the workmen of all description at these immense works (at Merthyr) are Welshmen. Their language is entirely Welsh' (John 1960:62). It was not unnatural therefore that Welsh-speaking agricultural workers seeking industrial employment would favor Merthyr. The English migrants were drawn to the more linguistically

congenial agricultural lowlands: for example, by 1891 the 252,000
permanent or lifetime immigrants in Glamorgan as a whole were
divided almost equally between the Welsh and the English. However,
as far as the coalfields were concerned Welsh immigrants outnum-
bered the English by four to three. Outside the coalfield the ratio of
English to Welsh immigrants was reversed – it was nearly five to
two. Of the total of Welsh immigrants into Glamorgan as a whole
80% went into the coalfields. Their primary motivation naturally was
the prospect of relatively high wages; but the choice of their area of
employment was influenced considerably by its linguistic and cultural characteristics.

   If it was the traditional linguistic and cultural character of Merthyr
and the Rhondda which drew Welsh-speaking immigrants to those
areas, their presence in turn reinforced that tradition. In a period of
rapid transition they ensured that the inevitable process of anglicization was delayed and that the Welsh were able to adapt. In 1840,
before long-distance migration began to affect Merthyr but at a time
when because of short-distance movement the population of the
town and surrounding villages had increased from 13,000 to 85,000
in less than forty years, the religious situation (reflecting the linguistic division between the Established Church and nonconformist
sects) was highly favorable to the latter, there being nine times as
many chapels as churches. In one small but typical area of the town,
consisting of two very long rows of tenement houses 'standing
behind each other, close to the works and a fair average of the whole,
17 of the 20 families were Welsh; ten of the husbands could read
Welsh and four of the wives could read the Welsh Bible' (Tremenheere 1840:160). In 1846 only 12.3% of the population were English
and even this small proportion declined to 9% within five years.
Twenty years later the position had not altered greatly though the
children were rapidly becoming bilingual.

   In such towns as Merthyr, Aberdare and others where the different
   races converge, large numbers speak English for the purpose of
   necessary intercourse with their neighbours, who beyond the very
   scanty nomenclature used for this end are entirely ignorant of that
   language. Welsh is their vernacular for the fireside, for general conversation and for all the ordinary purposes of life . . . They would be
   recent emigrants from the agricultural western districts of Wales.
   However, among the children knowledge of English is in advance of
   the population. In these instances the parents have been longer

located in the district and the children are native to or brought here very young, and from intercourse with companions of their own age and other sources they not only are habituated to English in their earliest years but acquire and make more use of English abroad than they do of Welsh at home (Jenkins 1861:453).

In assessing and acknowledging the value to Welsh language maintenance of the concentration of Welsh migration on Merthyr and the Rhondda we should not ignore the fact that the same concentration deprived other areas in Glamorgan of similar much needed Welsh language support. Consequently, outside the coalfield the language collapsed very rapidly. From whatever angle it is examined the consequences of this early reinforcement of the Welsh population of Merthyr and the Rhondda Valleys at the beginning of its industrial expansion were apparent for many generations and have not yet completely disappeared.

2. THE RELATIVE DECLINE OF THE WELSH-SPEAKING POPULATION

2.1. *National Trends*

So far we have tried to analyze the process of population change and especially migration flows in the whole of Wales and in the critical localities. It has been suggested that changes in the demographic status of the Welsh language have paralleled these national and local changes. See Table VI.

With the exception of the period 1911—21 the proportion of the population which was bilingual rose consistently until 1951. It has been falling since so that in 1961 the percentage was only slightly greater than in 1891 — 25% and 24%, respectively. The continuous decline in the proportion of monolingual speakers of Welsh has been very much steeper; from 29% in 1891 to 1% in 1961. The rise in the proportion of monolingual English is continuous: from 41% in 1891 to 74% in 1961. It is clear that the bilinguals are becoming English monolinguals very rapidly and the Welsh monolinguals are becoming, but only temporarily, bilingual. The only decade when this process of complete transference of language loyalty was retarded was 1921 — 31. These years of depression in Wales produced the highest rate of emigration especially in South Wales. Since the areas most affected were the more highly industrialized, the proportion of monolingual

Table VI. *English- and Welsh-Speaking Populations of Wales: 1891–1961*[a]

		b Welsh only			c English and Welsh			d Total Welsh-speaking: b + c			e English only		
a Year of census	Total population in thousands	Total in thousands *1*	*l* as % of *a* *2*	Percentage decennial difference *3*	Total in thousands *1*	*l* as % of *a* *2*	Percentage decennial difference *3*	Total in thousands *1*	*l* as % of *a* *2*	Percentage decennial difference *3*	Total in thousands *1*	*l* as % of *a* *2*	Percentage decennial difference *3*
1891	1813	508	29	–	402	24	–	910	51	–	759	41	–
1901	2013	281	14	−45	649	32	+61	930	46	+ 2	928	54	+22
1911	2421	190	8	−36	786	32	+21	976	39	+ 5	1108	46	+30
1921	2656	153	6	−19	746	29	– 5	900	36	– 8	1467	63	+33
1931	2593	98	4	−36	820	32	+10	909	36	+ 1	1552	64	+ 5
1951	2472	41.1	2	−57	673	27	−18	714	28	−22	1758	72	+13
1961	2518	26.1	0.7	−38	629	25	– 7	656	26	– 8	1862	74	+ 6
1971													

[a] The totals of the language categories *d* and *e* do not, as they should, equal the totals in *a* because of omissions in language data returns. No census was taken in 1941. From *Census of England and Wales, General Reports*, 1891, Table 24; 1901, Tables 39 and 40; 1921, Table 25; 1931, Table 17; 1911, 1951, 1961, Table 102.

English and dominant bilingual English among the emigrants was exceptionally high. Consequently, the comparative though not the substantive demographic status of Welsh improved. With the almost complete disappearance of Welsh monolingualism, except among children between the ages of three and five, there remained after 1931 (4% monolingual Welsh) no pool from which bilinguals could be produced. From that time onward the curve of bilingualism has declined from 32% in 1931 to 25% in 1961. While the population of Wales increased from 1,800,000 in 1891 to 2,600,000 in 1961, the number of monolingual Welsh dropped from 540,000 to 26,000. The population increase represented a rise of almost 44% but the number of speakers of Welsh, bilingual and monolingual, dropped by 16%. Looked at nationally the picture of the Welsh language situation has no varied pattern and no light and shade: it is a simple picture of unrelieved gloom.

2.2. *Regional Differences in the Density and Distribution of the Welsh Language*

The description of the national trends in the demographic situation of the Welsh language cannot do justice to the complexity of the changes that occurred. The analysis needs to be pursued according to the type of locality (whether urban or rural) as well as according to the age and sex composition of the population. Consideration must also be given to two dimensions of the local incidence of the Welsh language. The first of these is the proportion of the total population of any locality which is Welsh-speaking. This is the measure of the intensity or density of Welsh and is referred to as the *intensity index*. The second dimension refers to the proportion of the national total of speakers of Welsh which is represented in any one area. This is what is designated as the *distributional index*. The two indices represent different aspects of the demographic status of the Welsh language, and as we shall see in Table VII they are negatively correlated in almost every locality.

In 1891 the thirteen counties, in terms of the intensity of Welsh, organized themselves into three clearly distinguishable groups. There were five with percentages of 90 and over (Group 1): Cardigan, Anglesey, Carmarthen, Merioneth, and Caernarvon. Next there are four counties which range between 51% and 68%, the highest being 20% below the lowest of the first five; those in Group 2 are Flint, Denbigh, Montgomery, and Glamorgan. Then there are four counties

Table VII. Welsh-Speaking Population of Each County in Thousands, Expressed as Percentage of Total Population of the County and as Percentage of the National Welsh-Speaking Total: 1891 and 1961

	Wales	Anglesey	Brecon	Caernarvon	Cardigan	Carmarthen	Denbigh	Flint	Glamorgan	Merioneth	Monmouth	Montgomery	Pembroke	Radnor
1891														
Total Welsh-speaking	910	40	29	107	73	100	52	27	320	58	39	32	24	1
Intensity index[a]	52	94	40	90	95	90	66	68	51	95	20	52	37	10
Distribution index[b]	–	4.4	3.2	12.0	8.0	11.0	5.7	3.0	35.0	6.3	4.4	3.5	2.6	1.0
1961														
Total Welsh-speaking	656	37	14	80	39	121	58	27	201	28	14	14	22	1
Intensity index	26	75	28	68	75	75	35	19	17	76	3	32	24	4
Distribution index	–	5.7	2.1	12.0	5.8	17.4	8.6	4.2	31.0	4.3	2.2	2.2	2.9	0.1

a *Intensity index* is the Welsh-speaking total expressed as percentage of total population of each county.
b *Distribution index* is the Welsh-speaking total of the county expressed as percentage of national Welsh-speaking total.

ranging between 10% and 51%: Brecon, Pembroke, Monmouth, and Radnor. It is not insignificant that the first group, the high intensity areas, were heavily if not exclusively agricultural in 1891 while the second group was either dominantly industrial or leaning in that direction. Group 3 with the lowest intensity, was either on the English border or as in the case of Pembrokeshire had an English enclave, 'little England beyond Wales'. Monmouth, which is in the third group, was both an industrial county and on the English border, and thus its intensity index was nearly the lowest of all. It is also noticeable that counties in the high intensity group all appear to behave in an identical fashion during the period 1891–1961 – their respective rates of attenuation of Welsh appear to be synchronized exactly. The four counties with medium intensity ratings also behave consistently as a group from 1891 to 1961 though less uniformly than the first group. In Group 2 Glamorgan and Flint suffer 66% and 60% loss of intensity between 1891 and 1961, while the two counties in the same group Denbigh and Montgomery, who retain a considerable agricultural character, suffer losses of only 40% each. Monmouth is an interesting case in the sense that the combination of its high industrial development and its vulnerability as a border county brought a loss of 85% intensity in seventy years.

There is thus a closely knit group of counties which have come to be identified increasingly with relatively high intensity of Welsh. They had achieved this status by the middle of the last century. As is the case with all other counties their 'Welshness' has diminished, but to nothing like the same extent as in other areas. Furthermore, the 'Welshness' of the whole of Wales has declined at a much sharper rate (from 52% in 1891 to 26% in 1961) than in the high-intensity counties. To that extent they have been less characteristic of Wales than they were when the level of Welsh in the whole of Wales was higher. The very sharp distinction in 1891 between the high-intensity areas and the two other groups has been accentuated consistently and increasingly in the last seventy years so as to produce a polarization, in terms of intensity of the incidence of Welsh, between the agricultural and the heavily industrial and semi-industrial areas.

This polarization has been aggravated by another characteristic of the demographic status of Welsh. The five counties in the high-intensity group, when judged on the intensity index, have a mean of 92% in 1891 and 75% in 1961 but they are low in the distribution index, contributing only 41.7% to the national total in 1891 and 45.2% in 1961. The industrial counties in 1891 had a relatively low

mean intensity index, 50% in 1891, and a very low mean in 1961 of
18%, but they contributed far more than 50% of the total number of
Welsh speakers in 1891 and 1961. However intense the incidence of
Welsh may be in the rural counties this is not reflected in the size of
their contribution to the national total.

Generally speaking increasing industrialization is correlated with a
declining intensity of use of Welsh. At the same time, if we exclude
Monmouth which is a special case, increasing industrialization is
correlated with an increasing proportion of the national Welsh-
speaking total. The great majority of speakers of Welsh live in highly
industrialized communities and though they maintain the Welsh
language their attachment to the traditional cultural associations of
the language becomes very much less assured. The polarization we
have already noted between the agricultural and the industrial counties is unlikely to be purely demographic. The minority who live in
the intensely Welsh-speaking areas are still closely attached to the
traditional associations of the Welsh language and its folk ethos and
they consistently seek to promote the preservation of that ethos. The
majority of Welsh speakers, those who live in the industrial areas,
though they are equally concerned to maintain the language as we
shall see in our discussion of attitudes, are in the process of developing a nontraditional, urbanized Welsh consciousness. They tend to
see the language as an expression of a different Welsh ethos from that
favored by the minority.

2.3. Within-County Urban and Rural Language Differences

Within most counties the rural areas are more intensely Welsh-
speaking than the urban areas of the same counties, reflecting the
between-county dichotomy. For instance, in 1901 the urban and
rural intensity indices for Anglesey were 85% and 93%; for Brecon,
20% and 87%; Caernarvon, 80% and 96%. The only counties where
the intensity of Welsh was greater in the urban areas were Merioneth
and Monmouth but in each case the difference was not great, 95%
and 93% and 13% and 12%, respectively. The same kind of relationship was continued until 1961 and Merioneth is now no exception —
69% and 77%. Furthermore, the gap between rural and urban areas
has increased. For instance, the disparity in Carmarthen rose from
17.5% in 1901 (the percentage difference between 79% and 93%) to
33% in 1961 (the percentage difference between 61% and 81%). In
Glamorgan the disparity rose from 22% (51% and 62%) to 25% (20%

and 25%). These increases in the difference between the intensity of Welsh in urban and rural areas are repeated in all other counties. Consequently, the polarization we noted as existing between counties is equally evident *within* counties.

When we analyzed the national pattern we found that the majority of speakers of Welsh lived in the industrial counties. This is not the case within each county. For instance, 72% of the total of Welsh speakers in Anglesey lived in the rural areas in 1901 and 64% in 1961. The figures for some other representative counties are: Brecon, 88% and 87%; Cardigan, 78% and 72%; Carmarthen, 70% and 62%; Merioneth, 54% and 59%. In 1901 Monmouth was an exception, with only 14% of its Welsh speakers living in the rural areas. It remained an exception in 1961 with a very low percentage of 8%. However the within-county disparity between the distribution of Welsh in rural and urban areas has decreased between 1901 and 1961 so that a far greater number of Welsh speakers in each county now live in the urban areas than did before. In Anglesey the percentage in urban areas in 1901 was 28% and in 1961 it was 36%. In other counties the significant increases have ranged from 6% in Cardigan to 14% in Denbigh, the mean increase being 7.5%.

Glamorgan, like Monmouth, was an exception to the general pattern between 1901 and 1961 in having a higher proportion of Welsh in urban areas — 66% and 65%. In Glamorgan as a whole there was therefore very little change between 1901 and 1961 in the disparity between urban and rural areas both in terms of the intensity of Welsh and in the proportion of the total number in the two types of area. But this was because Glamorgan, like Monmouth, was already very heavily industrialized in 1901 and could not therefore reflect, as the agricultural counties could, the increasing tendency towards the urbanization of the majority of Welsh speakers. This overall picture of the stability of Glamorgan is deceptive, however, and an analysis of the key urban areas and three representative rural areas reveals that the intensity of Welsh in urban and rural areas alike has decreased very considerably over the last seventy years. As far as the incidence of Welsh is concerned the increased industrialization of Glamorgan has virtually cancelled the differences between urban and rural areas which we have noticed elsewhere. Because of the size of its Welsh-speaking population, and its central role in the administration of Welsh affairs and in all aspects of education, Glamorgan is the key to the maintenance of the Welsh language. It is also the most intensely industrialized and urbanized community. Due to a conjunc-

Table VIII.   *Welsh-Speaking Population of Selected Areas of Glamorgan. Numbers in Thousands and as Percentage of Total Population: 1891—1961*[a]

	Cardiff (urban)		Merthyr (urban)		Swansea (urban)		Rhondda (urban)		Gower (rural)		Cardiff (rural)		Bridgend (rural)	
	nos.	%	nos.	%	nos.	%	nos.	%	nos.	%	nos.	%	nos.	%
1891	22	15	68	63	50	46	85	72	2	26	6	27	9	52
1901	12	8	36	55	28	54	66	64	2	35	5	23	8	54
1911	11	6	34	50	28	27	76	54	3	38	5	26	9	45
1921	9	5	30	40	42	22	68	47	3	39	4	12	9	39
1931	11	5	27	39	43	27	62	46	3	33	10	9	10	39
1951	10	5	15	36	31	20	31	30	3	27	6	8	7	21
1961	11	5	11	18	28	17	23	24	1.7	14	3.2	7	6	15

[a] From *Census of England and Wales*, 1891—1961 (see source of Table IV).

tion of these considerations — the size of its Welsh population, its key administrative and educational role, and the level of urbanization — the Welsh language is tending more and more to be identified with a contemporary and urban ethos rather than with a folk tradition as in the past.

Within Glamorgan the Cardiff urban area in 1901 as well as in 1961 had more in common linguistically with its rural neighboring area than with other urban areas such as Merthyr, Swansea, and Rhondda. The urban areas of Merthyr, Swansea, and Rhondda have more in common with central Glamorgan and the adjacent rural area of Bridgend than they have with other urban areas. The rural area of Bridgend has closer affinities linguistically with urban areas than with other rural areas. In fact the determining factor in these important cases within Glamorgan is not so much the urban or rural distribution of the populations as the geographical location and its place in the history of the Norman and English occupation eight centuries ago. The Welsh-speaking areas of Glamorgan, whether urban or rural, are situated outside the *historically* anglicized vale — either in the western or the northern valleys. Historically the English areas remained rural and industry developed in the Welsh areas. The rural district of Gower, for instance, comprises a thinly populated, almost exclusively English-speaking area to the south and within the same administrative district a densely populated industrial coal and steel producing district to the north. But the language division in Gower has hardly anything at all to do with industrialization or urbanization. It is still situated almost exactly along the boundary of the

Norman occupation of the peninsula in the thirteenth century (D. T. Williams 1934; 1935). The growth of industry in the Welsh-speaking part of Gower between 1891 and 1921 is reflected in the increased intensity in the Welsh-speaking population of Gower but this was confined to historical limits of Welsh language usage. Similarly decline of Welsh in Gower after 1931 is a result of the closing of mines and steel producing plants and consequent emigration. The area of Gower where the decline occurs is determined by the history of the area. Neither industrialization nor emigration has moved the historical-geographical division between the two languages.

It cannot be denied that outside Glamorgan the urban/rural factor is significant in considering the maintenance of Welsh but it is difficult to estimate the degree of that significance. This is partly because the method by which the urban/rural factor is calculated in the census returns is no longer a reflection of the true character of a given area. It is also due to the fact that on the one hand industrialization has not progressed far enough in most of the rural counties to permit of a substantive as opposed to an administrative demarcation between urban and rural areas. On the other hand in South Wales and in Glamorgan especially industrialization has proceeded so far as to obliterate that distinction for all intents and purposes.

3. MIGRATION AND CHANGES IN THE AGE AND SEX COMPOSITION OF THE WELSH-SPEAKING POPULATION

3.1. *Age*

Migrants are not likely to be a truly representative sample of the total population. As far as age is concerned they are a highly selective set. They are drawn from a fairly constant age group characterized by an excess of adolescents and young adults (D. Thomas 1938). In 1911 22% of the Glamorgan immigrants from Somerset were under 24 years of age, 22% were between 25 and 34 years, and 21% between 35 and 44. In other words 66% were younger than 45 years and 83% were younger than 55 years. Of the new arrivals from Devon 24% were younger than 35 and 67% were younger than 45. Those who came from Gloucestershire were even younger: 35% were younger than 24 and 81% were younger than 45. Roughly the same age pattern characterizes Welsh rural emigrants whatever their destination.

In consequence of the age distribution of immigrants to the industrial areas and of emigrants from the rural counties, the proportion of children aged 14 or younger, and of those between 15 and 24 years of age in the counties of Caernarvon, Cardigan, Carmarthen, and Merioneth (the 'constant losing' and rural counties), is generally speaking below the average for the whole of Wales and for England and Wales together. The proportion of children aged 15 or younger in 1961 is below the average for the whole of Wales by between 4% and 8% in Caernarvon, Cardigan, Carmarthen, and Merioneth, and above the average by 5% in Glamorgan. The counties of Brecon, Caernarvon, Carmarthen, and Merioneth are below the Welsh average by between 8% and 24%. Glamorgan is 10% above the national average of 13% in the 12 to 24 years of age group. In 1961 37.7% of the population of the central Wales rural counties were between the ages of 15 and 44 compared with 39.5% for England and Wales. The proportion of old people was very much higher than the national figure: 14.3% older than 65 years of age compared with 11.9% for England and Wales. The small proportion of children and young adults and, conversely, the high proportion of older age groups in these counties is the result of the continuous emigration of adolescents and young adults from the beginning of the nineteenth century together with a low birth rate in the rural counties.

The industrial counties on the other hand show the opposite tendencies (Table IX).

For instance, the 1911 census showed that the percentage of each group aged 45 years or younger was higher in Glamorgan than in Wales as a whole; for the group aged 14 years or younger the difference was very great: 29.6% to 24.3%. The bias in favor of youth still

Table IX. *Comparison of Age Composition of Populations of Wales, Glamorgan, and Key Industrial Areas in Glamorgan: 1911 and 1961*[a]

Age groups	1911				1961			
	Wales	Glamorgan	Merthyr	Rhondda	Wales	Glamorgan	Merthyr	Rhondda
0–14	24.3	29.6	28.2	28.0	19.0	24.0	20.0	19.1
15–24	18.0	21.0	21.0	21.0	13.0	13.2	13.6	14.0
25–44	32.1	32.5	34.0	32.8	27.0	27.0	28.0	27.0
45–65	16.4	14.5	13.1	12.6	27.2	25.1	28.1	27.0
65+	5.3	3.6	3.2	3.1	11.2	9.2	12.0	12.1

[a] From *Census of England and Wales, Report on the Welsh-Speaking Population*, 1911, 1961, Tables 1, 2.

Migration and the decline of the Welsh language 291

exists in the county though the difference at each age level has diminished and ceases at age 24. Conversely the population of Glamorgan has a lower percentage in the groups aged between 45 and 65+ than is the case for the whole of Wales. When we analyze the age composition of the key industrial and immigration areas of Merthyr and Rhondda in 1911 the bias in favor of youth is even more marked. But when we move forward to 1951 and 1961 the emigration of the young which has characterized the period 1921–31 produced a radical shift in the age composition of those areas towards a far greater proportion of the older age groups compared with the rest of Glamorgan.

3.1.1. The Age Structure of the Welsh-Speaking Population: General
The changes in the age composition of the population of Wales as a whole and of the several counties inevitably affected the maintenance of the language. The old were more conservative and less open to a new experience so that they clung to the familiar language, but the continuance of their contribution to the maintenance of the language was predictably limited. The young were not imbued with the same loyalties and were able to learn a new language quickly – the educational system ensured that they did. In shifting the age bias of the industrial population towards youth and of the agricultural population to the older age groups migration exercised a highly selective influence on the decline of the Welsh language.

3.1.2. Monolingual Welsh
An analysis of Table X permits us to draw the following conclusions. From 1901, when age statistics are first made available, the proportion of monolingual speakers of Welsh in any group declines without exception. As might be expected this decline is least steep in the groups aged 3 to 10 years, 15.1% in 1901 and 10.1% in 1961. The share which the older age groups have in the total of Welsh monolinguals rises significantly between 1901 and 1961. In 1901 the proportion of Welsh monolinguals in the group aged 15 to 24 years (10.4) was approximately one-third of the 65-year-old group (29.6). In 1911 it was one-fifth and in 1961 it was one-sixth. There is a similar difference between the very young and the adult groups. For instance, in 1901 the percentage of the group aged 5 to 9 years who were monolingual Welsh (12%) was slightly more than 2% greater than the 15 to 24 age group percentage (10.4%). In 1911 it was more than double (7.8% and 3.6%) and in 1961 the ratio was seven times

Table X.   *Welsh-Speaking Population: Percentage of Each Age Group which is Welsh-Speaking: 1901–1961*[a]

	Language spoken																	
	Welsh only						Both English and Welsh						Welsh-speaking (monolingual and bilingual)					
	1901	1911	1921	1931	1951	1961	1901	1911	1921	1931	1951	1961	1901	1911	1921	1931	1951	1961
3–4	16	13.0	11.2	9.6	6.0	4.7	20	17.4	15.5	12.5	8.5	8.3	36	30.4	26.7	22.1	14.5	13.0
5–9	12	9.7	7.8	6.1	4.2	2.1	28	26.5	21.6	20.5	15.9	14.7	44	36.2	29.4	26.6	20.1	16.8
10–14	8	6.0	4.7	2.9	1.6	.6	35	33.7	27.5	27.5	20.6	18.9	46	39.7	32.2	30.4	22.2	19.5
15–24	10.4	4.6	3.6	2.0	0.9	.3	37.4	36.0	30.9	31.5	21.9	20.4	47.8	40.6	34.5	33.5	22.8	20.9
25–44	12.6	6.2	4.2	2.1	0.8	.5	38.2	37.8	32.7	35.3	26.6	22.7	50.8	44	36.9	37.4	27.4	23.2
45–64	19.9	12.6	8.3	4.6	1.4	1.0	38.7	40.3	36.6	39.6	34.2	31.7	58.6	52.9	44.9	44.2	35.4	32.7
65+	29.6	22.6	16.6	10.8	2.8	1.8	34.7	37.8	35.3	39.1	37.9	35.4	64.3	60.2	51.9	49.9	40.7	37.2
3+	15.1	8.5	6.3	4.0	1.7	1.0	34.8	35.0	30.8	32.8	27.2	25.0	49.9	43.5	37.1	36.8	28.9	26.0

a   From *Census of England and Wales, Report on the Welsh-Speaking Population 1901–1961* (see source of Table VI).

the 15 to 24 years age group percentage (2.1. and 0.3). The rate of decline is faster among young adults than it is among the very young or the old. Thus Welsh monolingualism is increasingly becoming a characteristic of extreme youth and old age. However, higher proportions of Welsh speakers characterize the older groups in the industrial areas and the younger groups in rural areas. For instance, of the total monolingual Welsh population of Glamorgan in 1901 28% were between the ages of 3 and 15 years. In 1961 the figure was 3%. The proportion of the group aged 45 to 65 years during the same period rose from 20% to 45%, and in the 65+ group from 8% to 24%. In the rural county of Cardigan the groups aged 15 to 45 years accounted for 36% of the monolingual Welsh population in 1901 but by 1961 there had been shifts towards the very young and the very old, respectively. Only 12% of the monolingual Welsh were in the group aged 15 to 45 years but the 3 to 15 age group had increased its representation from 33% in 1901 to 42% in 1961 and the 45 to 65+ group from 34% to 40%. The same is true of Anglesey where we observe a decline in the proportion of monolinguals in the middle age groups (from 37% to 16%) and a rise in the proportion in the young and the old age groups − from 33% to 41% in the former and from 27% to 40% in the latter.

When, therefore, we consider the predominantly rural and the predominantly industrial counties separately, taking Cardiganshire and Anglesey as instances of the former and Glamorgan of the latter, we find that they exemplify opposing tendencies. In both sets of counties there is a marked decline but in the industrial areas the proportion shifts in favor of the very old while in the rural areas it shifts in favor of the very young. Opportunities for contact with a second language from birth are difficult to avoid in the industrial south so that what remains of Welsh monolingualism is a vestige of the past. In the rural areas contact with English is less frequent and less necessary so that monolingualism persists longer among children as well as among the older generation. It is becoming more and more evident that only the rural counties and the remote areas within them provide the demographic possibility of survival for the monolingual Welsh. Just as the intensity of the incidence of the Welsh language, though not its distribution throughout Wales, is being increasingly identified with the rural areas, so ignorance of English is becoming increasingly the characteristic of extremes of age − the very young and the very old.

3.1.3. Bilinguals

In every age group the proportion who are bilingual declined regularly except for the years 1921--31, but even in that period the retardation affected only the older age groups. The decline is invariably greater in the youngest age groups. Thus while the 1961 proportion is 40% of that of 1901 in respect to the group aged 3 to 5, it is 52% in respect to the group aged 5 to 10, 54% in the group aged 10 to 15 and 55%, 60%, and 80% for the groups aged 15 to 25, 25 to 45, and 45 to 65 years, respectively (Table X).

Therefore bilingualism is increasingly a characteristic of increasing age in Wales generally. If we compare the rural and the industrial counties there is very little difference. In both types of counties in successive decades there is a decrease in the proportion of bilinguals in the groups aged 25 years or younger. The position is relatively stable for the groups aged 25 to 45 and thereafter up to the age of 65+ the proportion who are bilingual increases with each decade (Table X). Bilingualism, like monolingualism (Welsh), is becoming increasingly a characteristic of the older age groups and tends to disappear as a characteristic of the younger groups. This is as true of rural as of industrial areas.

Between 1901 and 1961 bilingualism had been characterized by an age polarization. Command of the Welsh language, whether it is spoken exclusively or in conjunction with English, is a possession of the older men and women; the young, once they are old enough to have contact outside the family, rely on the English language more and more. This age polarization, though it reinforces the urban rural polarization, is a characteristic of both types of area. Furthermore, since the general age composition of the urban areas favors the young the decline is bound to be most rapid in such areas because there is no psychological or attitudinal resource to replenish the losses which occur when the older groups die off. In the rural areas, though the psychological or attitudinal resources favorable to Welsh exist among the young, the paucity of young people makes such a favorable attitude increasingly less productive. For instance, in rural Cardiganshire the greatest decline is among the group aged 15 to 25 years. In 1901 24% of the bilingual population were of this age; in 1961 the figure was 14%. The next highest loss was in the group aged 25 to 45 years — 31% to 25%. There was an increase of the proportion of bilinguals in the 45 to 65 and 65+ groups from 17% to 30% and from 5% to 17%, respectively. The age shift in favor of the older groups is also evidenced in Anglesey. Among the group aged 3 to 15 years the proportion declines from 19% to 16%; among the 15 to 25 age group the proportion decreases from 24% to 13%; among the 25 to 45 age group the decrease is from 33% to 26%. However, the two older groups, 45 to 65 and 65+, represent increasing proportions of the bilingual speakers of the county — 19% to 28% and 6% to 14%. This tendency for the older groups to have a greater proportion of bilinguals is not limited to the rural areas. In Glamorgan the proportion of bilinguals who are in the group aged 3 to 15 declines from 24% to 8%; the proportion in the group aged 15 to 25 falls from 22% to 8%; in the group aged 25 to 45 it falls from 32% to 22%. But the proportion of bilinguals who are in the older group rises even more steeply than in the rural areas — from 15% to 40% (the group aged 45 to 65) and from 4% to 21% (the 65+ group).

3.1.4. *Expected and Actual Survival of Speakers of Welsh and English: All Ages*

It may be argued that the age structure of the immigrant population is not strictly relevant to these considerations because the younger the migrant the more likely he is to be assimilated and learn the native language, while the older he is the less time he has to exert an influence. If we consider individuals only this is a cogent argument. But the phenomenon of migration into and out of Wales in the period from 1861 to 1911 was not a case of the movement of isolated individuals but of considerable mass mobility. The native Welsh were unable to assimilate the new arrivals while, because of their large numbers and concentrated areas, the immigrants did not need to adapt. The massiveness is exemplified when we analyze the relationship of *expected* to *actual*[2] survival of proportions of the population in each of the linguistic categories between 1911 and 1921, i.e., at the end of the period of maximum immigration. It is impossible to make a precise computation for the reasons we have advanced in section 2.2. but since the language changes are so great an otherwise unacceptable margin of error will not invalidate our tentative conclusions.

No comparison can be made between the two decades in respect to the youngest children since a very large proportion of them would have been too young to be included in 1911 even if they had already been born. But it is important to note that after the age of 15 to 25 the number of those speaking Welsh only amounts to less than half of the survivors of those who were stated to be able to speak Welsh only at ages 5 to 15 in 1911, the majority, about 21,000, having become

Table XI. Populations in Thousands in Each Language and Age Group in 1921 Compared with Expected Survivors from Corresponding Groups in 1911 at Ages 10 Years Younger[a]

Age in 1921	Welsh only			English and Welsh			Welsh-speaking			English only		
	Ex-pected	Actual	+/−	Ex-pected	Actual	+/−	Ex-pected	Actual	+/−	Ex-pected	Actual	+/−
3 to 5	–	10.7	–	–	15	–	–	25.7	–	–	62	–
5 to 15	–	34.2	–	–	134	–	–	168.2	–	–	353	–
15 to 25	37.8	17.0	−20.8	141	147	+6	178.8	164	−14.8	274	294	+20
25 to 45	37.1	32.1	− 5.0	272	248	−24	309.1	280.1	−29	413	452	+39
45 to 65	39.8	39.1	− 0.7	186	173	−13	225.8	212.1	−13.7	241	244	+ 3
65+	26.0	22.9	− 3.1	53	49	− 4	79	71.9	− 7.1	59	61	+ 2

[a] From Census of England and Wales. Language spoken in Wales and Monmouthsire 1921: 184–187.

bilingual.[3] Among the population who were bilingual at ages 15 to 25 the excess over the projection of survivors is, however, only 6,000, though that category must have included at least the full complement of the 21,000 deficiency in the monolingual Welsh category. Concurrent with the increase among bilinguals due to the acquisition of English by monolingual Welsh speakers, bilinguals were filtering off in 1911 into the monolingual English category in 1921. We can infer that about 10% of the bilingual category in 1911 claimed no knowledge of English ten years later. The transference of this proportion to the monolingual English category is suggested by the excess of the actual over the expected survivors in that category. The number (shown in Table XIX as 20,000) is in excess of the transferred bilinguals. This must have come from some external source, namely, immigration.

Among the population aged 25 to 45 years or the survivors of their counterparts aged 15 to 35 years in 1911, the direction of the language shift was the same and equally significant. The Welsh monolinguals were 5,000 less than the expected number, a loss of 14% compared with the earlier age group loss of over 50%. The bilingual group aged 24 to 25 showed a deficit of 24,000 so that if we add the number of transferred monolinguals (5,000) the loss of bilinguals must have amounted to nearly 30,000. Here again the loss of Welsh among bilinguals was only part of the reason. Immigration in conjunction with the loss of population in rural areas to England must account for a considerable portion of the decline of bilingualism in Wales.

3.1.5. *Those Aged 5 to 11 Years*
We have another source of information concerning the shift from Welsh to English among the group aged 5 to 11. In 1951 the linguistic competence of all children in the schools of Wales between the ages of 5 and 15 was recorded by their teachers. The mother-tongue of the children, whether English or Welsh, was specified and in each case their acquaintance with the second language, ranging from very little knowledge (Category *A*) to near native competence in the second language (*D*), was categorized. This information was recorded again in 1961 to coincide with the census. Table XII shows the percentage of children in each of the categories and a comparison of the situation in 1951 and 1961. The categories *A, B, C* and *D* were defined as:

Table XII^a. *Maintenance of Welsh and English Among All School*

	Total number of pupils in thousands		Percentage of totals		Level of competence					
Area					First language Welsh					
					% in each category (to the nearest whole					
					A		B		C	
	1951	1961	1951	1961	1951	1961	1951	1961	1951	1961
Anglesey	6.6	7.6	79	67	9	5	13	12	22	20
Brecon	6.9	7.7	18	12	0.2	4	5	3	15	5
Caernarvon	15.0	15.5	74	67	10	7	13	10	20	19
Cardigan	6.7	7.0	76	67	12	9	11	9	20	22
Carmarthen	20.7	22.2	62	53	10	10	14	9	19	18
Denbigh	22.1	24.9	25	19	6	4	8	6	14	11
Flint	19.0	22.4	8	6	0.1	–	0.1	1	0.8	5
Glamorgan	92.0	113.0	7	4	8	1	9	3	17	7
Merioneth	4.8	5.2	83	75	4	5	10	10	22	22
Monmouth	43.2	51.5	0.2	0.1	–	–	10	–	20	–
Montgomery	6.0	6.5	25	19	10	4	12	8	22	14
Pembroke	11.9	14.0	20	16	14	3	12	8	24	20
Radnor	2.7	2.6	1	0.6	3	–	36	–	10	–
Cardiff	30.7	40.2	0.4	0.3	70	⟶	2	0.5	8	3
Merthyr	8.2	8.9	1.0	1	1	–	–	–	5	–
Newport	12.4	16.1	0.1	0.1	–	–	–	–	–	1
Swansea	19.7	23.4	5	3	–	0.5	–	2	6	1
Wales	355.4	389.5	18	13	9.0	6	11	8	19	17

^a From *Central Advisory Council. . . Wales* 1953, Table III; Welsh Joint Education Committee 19

A Children who have no knowledge of the second language.
B Children who can understand but are unable to speak the language.
C Children who understand elementary lessons given in history or geography, etc., in the second language and can maintain simple conversations in it.
D Children who express themselves freely in the second language.

It should be noted that Category A (children who have no knowledge of the second language) is likely to reflect the position of the children whose mother-tongue is English far more correctly than that of the children whose mother-tongue is Welsh. As far as the latter are concerned the category will inevitably include children with some though a very low level of acquaintance with English. As far as the English-speaking children are concerned Category A will include some bilinguals but these are not likely to affect the total in that category significantly.

Pupils Aged 5 to 15 Years in 1951 and 1961

				First language English							
				Level of competence							
number)		Percentage of totals		% in each category (to the nearest whole number)							
D				A		B		C		D	
1951	1961	1951	1961	1951	1961	1951	1961	1951	1961	1951	1961
53	63	25	28	32	25	28	27	73	33	22	12.0
82	88	86	90	70	52	15	35	6	11	4	3
57	64	33	44	23	22	35	3	20	21	20	21
58	61	28	42	40	31	3	22	19	3	13	19
58	63	44	57	28	32	36	40	16	14	17	14
70	79	78	84	64	53	19	33	8	9	5	5
99	95	93	96	83	56	12	32	3	6	2	1
66	88	95	97	64	78	30	18	4	3	2	1
52	62	25	37	20	28	26	18	27	22	28	27
70	100	99	99	97	99	2	0.3	0.5	.07	0.1	0.03
56	74	79	84	82	66	12	28	4	4	3	3
50	70	80	87	87	88	7	6	3	3	2	3
50	100	99	99	99	99	0.5	0.5	0.25	0.3	0.1	0.1
80	97	99	99	98	42	0.25	54	1.0	3	0.1	0.2
93	100	99	99	95	91	4	6	0.8	2	0.4	0.8
100	90	99	99	99	99	–	–	–	–	–	–
98	97	98	99	75	70	–	23	–	4	–	0.1
61	69	84	87	78	69	2	20	9	4	3	2

The rapid movement away from Welsh monolingualism as the child grows older, common to both surveys, and the change in the overall position between 1951 and 1961 are very apparent. In 1951 only 9% of Welsh children were monolingual compared with 79% of the English children. In 1961 the figures were 6.1% and 70%. In 1951 11% of the Welsh and 15% of the English were included in the lowest bilingual rating (*B*). In 1961 the figures were 8% and 22%. The Welsh were ascending and the English were descending the scale of bilingual competence. In 1951 and 1961 among the Welsh-speaking children there were nearly twice as many moderate bilinguals (19% and 17%) as there were poor bilinguals (11% and 8%). The percentage of moderate bilingual Welsh-speaking children was also very much greater than the percentage of English children in the same category: 19% to 9% in 1951 and 17% to 4% in 1961. There was over 60% effective bilingualism (*D*) among Welsh children in 1951 and 1961 and little more than 2.5% among English children, who moved very reluctantly towards bilingualism as they grew older and showed even less inclination to do so in 1961 than in 1951. In the county of Caernarvon, for instance, where support for Welsh might be expected to make possible an equitable and reasonable adjustment between the two languages, the difference is very marked. The percentage of Welsh monolingualism at ages 5 to 8 was 20; in the groups aged 8 to 11 and 11 to 15 it was $2\frac{1}{2}$% and 0%, respectively (*Central Advisory Council (Wales)* 1953, Table II). Among English monolinguals the movement away from monolingualism was from 46% at age 8 to 14% at age 11 and 12% at age 15. Among Welsh-speaking pupils there was a regular, continuous, and rapid rise from one age group to the next not only in the number of bilingual pupils but also in the level of their ability in English. This was reflected by the fact that the percentage of pupils in Categories *B* and *C* declined in each successive age group and rose in Category *D*. In other words Welsh-speaking pupils tended as they grew older to shift quickly and uniformly from Categories *B* and *C* (low level ability in English) to Category *D* (high level ability in English). In Carmarthenshire as the children became older the amount of poor and indifferent English declined from 25% to 0% and the percentage of those with nearly native English moved from 28% at age 5 to 8 years to 85% at age 11 to 15.

Among the English-speaking children, however, after the initial step away from absolute monolingualism there was nothing like the same development towards effective bilingualism. For instance, in Caernarvon after the initial departure from monolingualism 25% of the group aged 5 to 8 remained in Category *B*, 12% of the group aged 5 to 8 remained in Category *C* and only 12% of group aged 5 to 8 are in Category *D*. By and large the bilingual development rate among English-speaking pupils was slow and tended to stop considerably short of effective bilingualism. For instance, the great majority of English children did not progress beyond Category *B* in Breconshire, Carmarthenshire, Flintshire, Montgomeryshire, and Cardiff. In the case of Anglesey it will be seen that there is a slight decline from the situation of 1951 when the percentages in Categories *C* and *D* were fairly even at 25 and 23: they now show a marked decline in Category *D* (22% to 12%) and an increase to the percentage in the lower Category *C* (33%).

The position of Welsh in Glamorgan should be noted because of the numerical importance of the area which produced nearly a third of the whole of the school population of Wales. As would be expected from the previous analysis the Welsh-speaking pupils in

1961 were bilingual at a very early age and 88% of them were thoroughly bilingual at 15. The position of the English-speaking pupils was very different: 78% were monolingual English and only 1% became thoroughly bilingual. The peak of bilingual attainment for the great majority of the English children who have some knowledge of Welsh at 15 years was no higher than Category *B* — 30% in 1951 but only 18% in 1961.

The results of the 1951 and 1961 surveys reinforce at all points the conclusions drawn from the analysis of the language characteristics of the total population. They do not offer much comfort to those who seek to maintain the Welsh language. These conclusions take on added significance because at all points they reinforce those we have been able to draw from an analysis of the total population of all ages. There is a very rapid rise in the number of Welsh-speaking children who achieve increasing competence in English to the extent that over two-thirds are thoroughly bilingual before they leave school. This would not be an unfavorable phenomenon were it not accompanied by two other tendencies. First, the progress in English of the Welsh-speaking children is nowhere even remotely matched by the English child's competence in Welsh. In 1961 only 2.3% of the English children knew Welsh thoroughly and only an additional 3.8% knew it moderately well; 69% never learned any Welsh at all. Furthermore, there is little evidence of an improvement between 1951 and 1961.

Second, the Welsh children not only became competent bilinguals but increasingly claimed English as their mother-tongue. Thus in 1951 only 17.7% claimed Welsh as their mother-tongue and this figure fell to 13.4% in 1961 — a decline of 25% in ten years. The evidence for this decline is most apparent in the areas of high-intensity Welsh. In Anglesey the decline was from 79% to 67%; Cardigan, 76—67%; Carmarthen, 62—53%; and Merioneth, 83—75%; because it is those areas which possess the highest potential for loss. But it is proportionately even more devastating in the industrial areas. For instance, in Glamorgan the decline was in the order of 50% — from 7.2% to 3.5%. It is noteworthy that no more than 1.3% of the school children of Merthyr, the focal point of early industrialization, claimed Welsh as their mother-tongue. These tendencies produce a situation in which increasing proportions of those who make any claim to speak Welsh have learned it as a second language. In 1951 the percentage who claimed to be able to speak Welsh was 21 of whom 3.3.% claimed English as their mother-tongue. In 1961 the overall percentage of speakers of Welsh fell by 25% to 13.4% but the percentage of those claiming to have learned Welsh as a second language rose by nearly 25% to 4.2%. This has a considerable influence on the polarization between the urban majority of speakers of Welsh and the rural minority. An increasing proportion of the former learn Welsh as their second language, while in spite of their fewness the rural minority acquire it as their mother-tongue. Their attachment to the traditional associations of the language differs widely.

3.2. The Sex Differential in the Composition of the Total Population and the Linguistic Consequences

From the beginning of the development of large-scale industry in Wales there was a preponderance of males among the industrial lifetime immigrants as well as among the temporary immigrants from the Welsh countryside. Consequently, the pattern of the distribution of the sexes in both urban and rural areas changed considerably during the last century. To take the case of greatest impact we find that in 1921, at the end of the period of maximum migration into Glamorgan, there were 2% more males than females in the total population, induced in part by the fact that among non-Welsh immigrants to Glamorgan the male advantage was over 7%. The national ratio favors women in the Welsh rural areas: 1,063 females per 1,000 males. In 1951 the ratio was even more favorable to the women: 1,131 per 1,000 males. The deficiency of young male adults is very pronounced in Merioneth: 17.2% compared with 19.6% in England and Wales. In Montgomeryshire too the disproportion of females was pronounced: 12.3% in the group aged 15 to 24 compared with 6.5% in England and Wales, with 12.3% in the group aged 25 to 44 also compared with 13.1% in England and Wales. This disproportion of women in the countryside was adjusted in counties such as Cardigan, Brecon, and Merioneth because of the combination of immigration of males to military establishments with the drawing powers of large construction projects.

   The main linguistic consequences of this imbalance have been felt among the monolingual Welsh. In each of the first age groups in the 1911 returns the men speaking Welsh only were proportionately more numerous than the women, but from 24 years of age upward the proportion of women increased. In 1911 the proportions of women was greater than the proportion of men in the category of bilinguals also, in each age group save the last. The proportion of males over females among the monolingual English population is greater in all age groups and increases generally with advancing age. Because of the assimilation of the monolingual English elements and their influence on the remainder of the community by mixed marriage and in other ways the differences between the two sexes in all linguistic categories are being softened. Thus in 1921 the proportions of monolingual Welsh males and females were identical at 3.9%: the differences between the bilinguals was males 33.2% and females 32.9%, and between the total Welsh-speaking population, monolingual and bilingual, males 37% to females 36.4%. In 1951 the differences between the two sexes was no greater than 0.1% in any of the categories. In 1964 the proportions of the two sexes who were *bilingual* in industrial South Wales was males 49.3% and females 50.3%. In rural North Wales the proportions were males 71.9% and females 71.0%. The differences are greater, however, when we consider the *monolingual* Welsh, the proportions in South Wales being 11.6% (males) and 13.3% (females), and in North Wales, where English immigration has not been so intense, 31% to 29%.

If we remind ourselves that it is the English male who is the immigrant and the Welsh male who is the emigrant we see that these disparities are directly related to the sex differential in the pattern of immigration and emigration. This analysis also illustrates the invariant pattern in such cases; following the initial migration phase there is a phase of settlement during which the sex differential eases. This is followed by a phase of integration when sex differential ceases altogether. What is true of total populations is equally true of linguistic subgroups of that population.

4. NON-DEMOGRAPHIC CONSEQUENCES OF THE CHANGES IN THE CHARACTERISTICS AND STRUCTURE OF THE POPULATION

4.1. *Introduction*

It was not until the beginning of the nineteenth century, in spite of the pressure of the English language and English administration, that the existence (as opposed to the quality and range of use) of the Welsh language within the boundaries established more than a thousand years earlier was really threatened. Thereafter, partly because of the continuous drain of emigration from the predominantly

304 Glyn Lewis

rural counties but mainly because of immigration into the industrialized areas of South Wales, the rapid decline of the language set in. The claim that population movements have been the main contributory factor to the decline of Welsh has been questioned. The most recently expressed view is that 'the Welsh in their search for industrial employment in the period of migration were not obliged to abandon their language' (John 1960:23). An economist supports this view and has claimed that 'the Welsh language was saved by the redistribution of a growing population brought about by industrialisation' (B. Thomas 1967:36). However, these two statements refer only to short-distance or internal migration. Even if we ignore the almost complete disappearance of Welsh monolingualism and a drop from 55% to 26% in the Welsh-speaking population between 1891 and 1961 the effect of the first phase redistribution of the population was simply to delay or to retard the predictable outcome. Furthermore if internal migration of Welsh speakers had a beneficial effect on the industrial areas it aggravated the difficulties of the Welsh language by starving the rural areas of their strength — the young adult males. It also disrupted the Welsh way of life, the foundation for the preservation of the language as anything but a patois. One is forced to conclude that industrialization inaugurated and long-distance migration enormously accelerated, the decline of Welsh. The urbanization of Wales, based on the influx of a large non-Welsh population which had never been assimilated, accentuated an already existing division. This is at the root of the various aspects of the linguistic and cultural polarization to which we have referred.

4.2. General Social Changes

4.2.1. Intermarriage and Family Background
It is to be expected that radical changes in the structure of the population will increase the number of marriages between members of the two linguistic groups. This is a universal characteristic of language contact. We have no official and precise estimates of the number of such marriages in Wales now or in the past. Furthermore what Welsh and English intermarriage does not necessarily involve is members of two distinct national groups. The spouses may be monolingual English men or women (who may be of English or Welsh nationality) and bilingual men or women (who may also belong to either national group). From the 1951 and 1961 surveys (Central Advisory Council (Wales) 1953 and Welsh Joint Education Com-

Table XIII.   Pupils Between 5 and 15 Years of Age in Maintained Primary and Secondary Schools Classified According to the Relation of Their First Language to the Language of Their Parents: 1951 and 1961 (Numbers in Thousands)[a]

	Pupils from homes where both parents speak Welsh						Pupils from homes where only the father speaks Welsh						Pupils from homes where only the mother speaks Welsh					
1	2		3		4		5		6		7		8		9		10	
Age group	Total number of pupils		Number of pupils whose first language is Welsh		3 as % of 2		Total number of pupils		Number of pupils whose first language is Welsh		6 as % of 5		Total number of pupils		Number of pupils whose first language is Welsh		9 as % of 8	
	1951	1961	1951	1961	1951	1961	1951	1961	1951	1961	1951	1961	1951	1961	1951	1961	1951	1961
5–6	6.3	4.7	4.7	3.8	75.5	81.2	2.3	1.9	0.18	170	7.9	8.6	1.9	1.6	0.28	248	14.8	14.7
6–7	7.0	4.7	5.2	3.7	73.9	78.5	2.5	2.1	0.15	151	6.0	7.1	2.1	1.7	0.29	233	13.9	13.4
7–8	7.1	5.1	5.1	3.7	72.4	72.3	2.7	2.4	0.15	190	5.7	7.6	2.3	2.0	0.24	240	10.6	11.9
8–9	6.5	5.3	4.6	3.8	71.5	71.3	2.5	2.5	0.12	181	4.9	7.2	2.1	2.1	0.23	241	10.9	11.3
9–10	6.2	5.1	4.3	3.7	68.8	71.9	2.3	2.5	0.14	151	6.0	5.8	2.0	2.3	0.17	222	8.3	9.6
10–11	6.4	5.2	4.3	3.7	67.7	72.3	2.3	2.6	0.10	174	4.4	6.6	2.1	2.2	0.18	248	8.6	11.0
11–12	7.3	5.5	5.0	3.8	65.6	69.3	2.7	3.1	0.15	177	5.8	5.7	2.4	2.7	0.22	269	9.0	9.8
12–13	6.7	5.7	4.5	4.0	66.7	71.5	2.6	2.9	0.19	230	7.3	7.6	2.2	2.7	0.23	343	10.1	12.5
13–14	6.5	5.9	4.4	4.2	67.0	71.8	2.4	3.2	0.17	229	7.2	7.0	2.2	2.7	0.23	334	10.5	12.1
14–15	5.8	6.0	3.9	4.2	62.9	70.3	2.0	3.1	0.12	196	6.4	6.2	1.7	2.9	0.14	352	8.7	11.6
Totals	66.2	53.7	46.4	39.1	70.0	72.8	24.8	26.8	1.5	1.8	6.1	6.9	21.5	25.3	2.26	2.73	10.5	11.7

[a] From *Central Advisory Council... Wales* 1953: 32, Table II, and *Welsh Joint Education Committee* 1961: 10, Table V.

mittee 1961), we can make certain inferences about the extent of such linguistically mixed marriages. See Table XIII.

The total number of pupils who come from homes where both parents speak Welsh had declined from 66,200 to 53,700, a difference of 19%. On the other hand there had been a rise from 1,500 to 1,800 (20%) in the number of homes where only the father speaks Welsh, and from 2,200 to 2,700 (20%) in the number where only the mother speaks Welsh. The total number of pupils between 5 and 15 years of age registered in the schools in 1951 was 329,400 and in 1961 it was 389,500. Thus in 1951 there were over 215,000 (65%) who came from homes where neither parent spoke Welsh and this had increased to 285,000 (73%) in 1961. It appears that the increase in the proportion of homes where neither parent speaks Welsh is roughly the same as the loss in the number where both parents speak the language; this combination of losses is disconcerting. Between 1951 and 1961 the loss, amounting to 13%, in the number of homes where both parents spoke the language is greater than the gain in the number of one-Welsh-parent homes. This loss is significant because the Welsh language is maintained far more effectively in homogeneous homes than in mixed language families. For instance, in 1961 81% of the children (75.5% in 1951) in the 'two-Welsh-parent' homes were considered to have Welsh as their mother-tongue on entering school as compared with 19% and 24.5% of the children in 'one-Welsh-parent' homes. Furthermore, the shift from Welsh to English, which occurs as the children grow older, is twice as much in the 'mother-Welsh' homes (21%) than in homes where both parents speak Welsh (10%) and nearly three times greater in the 'father-Welsh' homes (28%). There is a considerable difference between linguistically mixed families according to whether it is the father or the mother who speaks Welsh. In 1961 the age-determined shift towards English is 8% greater in 'father-only-Welsh' homes than in 'mother-only-Welsh' homes. If we take all age groups, the proportion of children who maintain Welsh as their preferred language from 'father-only-Welsh' homes was 6.1% and 6.9% in 1951 and 1961, respectively, while the percentages in 'mother-only-Welsh' homes were 10.5% and 11.7%.

The disparity between the linguistic consequences of different types of home language backgrounds becomes even more apparent when we compare the traditionally Welsh-speaking areas, for instance, Merionethshire and Caernarvonshire on the one hand and Glamorgan, an anglicized area, on the other. In the Welsh-speaking counties 96%

Table XIV. *Linguistic Consequences for Children of Mixed English-Welsh-Speaking Parentage: 4 to 7 Years Old and 11 to 14 Years Old*

Linguistic competence of the children	A Mother ME Father ME		B Mother ME Father BE		C Mother ME Father BW		D Mother BE Father ME		E Mother BE Father BE		F Mother BW Father ME		G Mother BW Father BW		Totals	
	4-7	11-14	4-7	11-14	4-7	11-14	4-7	11-14	4-7	11-14	4-7	11-14	4-7	11-14	4-7	11-14
1. Monolingual English	14	18	21	24	12	8	10	5	12	4	14	8	8	8	93	75
2. Monolingual Welsh	0	0	0	0	0	0	0	0	1*	0	0	0	1*	0	2	0
3. Bilingual Welsh	0	0	0	0	7	7	5	3	1	0	12	6	15	8	41	24
4. Bilingual English	7	10	5	8	4	12	18	11	4	8	10	12	5	11	53	72
Total number of children															189	171
Language dominance in the family																
Welsh dominant	0	0	0	0	8	7	5	3	2	0	12	6	16	8		67
English dominant	23	28	26	32	16	20	28	16	16	12	24	20	13	19		293

Explanations:

(a) ME = Monolingual English   BE = Bilingual English
    MW = Monolingual Welsh   BW = Bilingual Welsh
    Bilingual English means that English is the first language and bilingual Welsh means that Welsh is the first language.

(b) Nine linguistic combinations are possible but two of these were not represented in the sample, namely, mother bilingual English and father bilingual Welsh, and mother bilingual Welsh and father bilingual English.

(c) Estimate of dominant home language is obtained by combining linguistic categories 1 with 4 = English dominance. 2 + 3 = Welsh dominance.

(d) Children who are asterisked attend special Welsh kindergartens.

and 91% of the children from homes where both parents spoke Welsh maintained Welsh while only 42% of the children from Glamorgan did so. In the 'father-only-Welsh' homes 19% in Merioneth and 20% in Caernarvon maintained Welsh whereas only 4% did so in Glamorgan. In the 'mother-only-Welsh' homes the figures were 43% in Merioneth, 39% in Caernarvon, and only 7% in Glamorgan.

To continue this analysis of the effect of different types of homes on the maintenance of Welsh I have made a limited investigation in depth of a small random sample of 200 families in three fairly large and representative bilingual communities near Swansea. Table XIV indicates the position of the children in those families as far as language is concerned.

It must be emphasized that these families live in thoroughly bilingual areas though until forty years ago they were dominantly Welsh-speaking. At present the number of children from mixed language families where the English language is dominant is nearly four times the number from families where Welsh is dominant. This, however, does not convey the complete picture as given in this sample since the families in which English dominates have a higher ratio of children per family than the families in which Welsh dominates: 2.1. to 1.3. Consequently, the number of families in which Welsh dominates is 62 while the English families number 138, over twice as many. It is not surpising to find that English monolingualism, though it decreases slightly between the ages of 4 and 14, is the most probable result of mixed language families in the three communities. There is even a high degree of such monolingualism in families where mother and/or father claim Welsh as the first language. The second most likely linguistic outcome is bilingualism with English claimed as the preferred language and this increases with age – an effect of schooling and the general environment (all categories except D in Table XIV). On the other hand bilingualism in which the preferred language is Welsh declines with age (Categories C, D, E, F and G in Table XIV). When both parents are monolingual English the degree of bilingualism among the children is relatively small – half the number of the monolinguals in such families. When the mother is monolingual English or claims English as her first language the children tend to prefer English (Categories B and C). When the mother is bilingual with Welsh as a first language there is a greater tendency for the children to become bilingual than when the father is bilingual (Category C).

It is difficult to isolate the influence of the home and certainly unwise to exaggerate its importance in communities where there are equally and possibly more powerful influences outside the home acting contrary to or reinforcing the home tendencies. In fact increasing intermarriage is both a product of population movement in Wales as well as one of the most powerful reinforcements of the linguistic consequences of such movements. The linguistic consequences we have detailed are also not simply the outcome of actual contact between speakers of the two languages. English dominance is partly the result of the creation of different attitudes toward the two languages as well.

4.3. *Attitude Toward Welsh and English*

4.3.1. *Direction and Strength of Attitudes*
It would be strange if the history of the relationship between Welsh and English, as well as the extent and speed of recent social and industrial change in Wales, were not reflected in similar strains and stresses on individual and group attitudes to the two languages, whatever differences of age, locality, sex, or social status may distinguish them. Partly for this reason between 1967 and 1971 an extensive survey was conducted among school children and an independent series of investigations was conducted among adults, the latter more restricted in scale but aimed to probe more deeply into individual and group attitude as well as family linguistic affiliation.[4] In the school investigation a sample of fifty-seven junior primary schools, stratified according to size and according to three linguistic categories defined in terms of the intensity of Welsh in their localities, yielded 1750 10-year-olds. Twenty-seven secondary schools yielding 3650 students were also selected, twenty-one from the three linguistic areas referred to and six, irrespective of area, from among the total of schools which have been created in recent years to give Welsh a more prominent place in the curriculum and to use it more frequently and intensively to teach other subjects. Recruitment to the last group of schools was voluntary and highly selective, thus reflecting high motivation to maintain Welsh. The secondary school sample consisted of 2200 12-year-old and 1350 14-year-old students. Thurstone-type tests were taken by all the junior and secondary school students; a semantic differential scale was made for the secondary school students only.

The investigation brought out marked differences in the attitude patterns of those represented in the strata of the sample (Table XV).

Table XV. *Mean Scores for Attitudes Toward Welsh and English on Thurstone Tests According to Age and Linguistic Area*

Ages	A: 68–81% Welsh-speaking		B: 48–55% Welsh-speaking		C: 3–26% Welsh-speaking		D: Schools with Welsh as teaching medium	
	Welsh	English	Welsh	English	Welsh	English	Welsh	English
10+	3.97	5.87	4.22	5.66	5.39	5.06	3.21	6.75
12+	4.26	5.45	4.78	5.16	5.50	4.82	3.55	6.43
14+	4.86	4.81	5.16	4.92	5.92	4.58	3.70	5.76

The attitude toward Welsh becomes increasingly less favorable in all areas and types of schools as the students grow older and increasingly more favorable to English. In types of schools where English is generally favored (Category *C*) the disparity between Welsh and English attitudes increases. In schools where Welsh is generally favored (Categories *A*, *B*, and *D*) the disparity decreases to the extent that at the age of 14+ there is an attitudinal switch from Welsh to English except in Category *D* (Table XVI).

Table XVI. *Attitude toward Welsh and English Among Bilingual and Among Monolingual English Adults in Two Linguistically Different Areas According to Length of Residence*

	Bilinguals		Monolinguals	
	Area *B* only	Area *B*	Area *C*	
		Residence 2 years	Residence 10 years	Residence 2 years	Residence 10 years
Mean of attitude to Welsh and S.D.	6.2 (2.2)	7.4 (2.6)	6.8 (2.5)	7.1 (2.4)	6.9 (2.5)
Mean of attitude to English and S.D.	4.23 (2.1)	3.1 (1.8)	3.25 (1.7)	3.05 (2.0)	3.2 (1.9)
	1	2	3	4	5

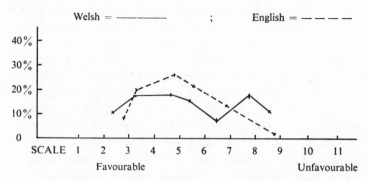

Figure 1. *Frequency Distribution of Attitude Scores*

In nearly half the sample population, and particularly in Categories *A, B,* and *D* schools, the distribution of 'attitude toward Welsh' responses is highly favorable. It is slightly unfavorable to the language in Category *C* schools. Figure 1 shows the curve in respect of the total population as having a peak covering the mean scores 3% to 4.5%, and a secondary peak covering the mean of 7.3%. The distribution of the English scores for all students is almost uni-modal, the percentages of the scores falling within the neutral zone being usually much higher than for Welsh.

4.3.2. *Study of Adults*

A Thurstone-type test was administered to two different adult samples each having 100 subjects between the ages of 20 and 30 years old (Table XVI). The first was drawn exclusively from Area *B* (48—55% Welsh) and consisted of competent bilinguals. The second, consisting of monoglot English speakers was drawn equally from Area *B* and Area *C* (3—26 Welsh). The distribution of the scores of the first (bilingual) sample showed first of all that the deterioration in attitudes toward Welsh among the school children continued among adults, the mean score of attitudes toward Welsh being 6.2% (S.D. [Standard Deviation] 2) which is considerably less favorable than that of the least favorable group of school students in the same area (5.16). A consistent progression is found in attitude toward English — mean 4.23% (S.D.2.1.) which is more favorable than the most favorable student attitude in the same area, 4.92%.

The second sample, which was evenly divided according to linguistic area, was further divided according to length of residence in Wales. Attitude is more favorable to Welsh and is less favorable to

English among bilinguals (column 1) than among monolingual English speakers in both areas irrespective of the length of residence. Among monolinguals the attitudes toward English and Welsh remain fairly constant irrespective of area of residence (compare columns 2 and 4, and 3 and 5); but increasing length of residence, independent of area, correlates with a more favorable attitude toward Welsh (columns 2 and 3, 4 and 5) and with a slightly less favorable attitude to English (columns 2 and 3, 4 and 5). Irrespective of differences in area or length of residence the attitude of monolinguals (English) toward English is very much more favorable than their attitude toward Welsh, and the disparity between the two attitudes among monolinguals is very much greater than is the disparity among bilinguals.

4.3.3. *Content of Attitudes: Children*
From an examination of the percentage response to each of the items in the tests administered it is possible to develop a content analysis of the attitudes toward the two languages and to offer a tentative categorization of those elements. First, it should be said that it becomes more evident than ever that the nature of the response from item to item in the questionnaires varies consistently with the area from which the subjects were drawn and that, because the Category *D* subjects were drawn from schools which by definition selected themselves as specifically committed to maintain Welsh, the responses of these subjects in respect to Welsh and to a lesser extent in respect to English, whether favorable or unfavorable, were almost unfailingly predictable. For instance, while the percentage responses of students in categories *A, B,* and *C* to item 3 of the English scale (English should be taught all over the world) ranged from 40% to 60%, varying according to age and area, the percentage response in Category *D* was half that, ranging 23% to 33% and varying according to age. Item 8 in the same list (English is a beautiful language) produced a range of 40–60% for all students except Category *D* where the figure was 21%. It is not unlikely that attitude toward the two languages and especially toward Welsh is a function of the linguistic character of the locality and that individual variance within localities is limited.

The attitude toward Welsh among children, as it can be interpreted from an examination of the Thurstone test results appears to have four major components. The first is a factor which we may term *General Approval* 'I would like to speak Welsh for the fun of it',

'Welsh is a language worth learning', 'I like speaking Welsh', etc., where the average response is favorable, 60—75%. The second factor is *Commitment to Practice*, represented by such statements as 'I want to maintain Welsh to enable Wales to develop' (50%); 'I should like to be able to read Welsh books' (45%); 'Likely to use Welsh' (40%); 'There are more useful languages than Welsh' (38%). While general approval was very favorable, response to items which might be taken to imply a decision actually to implement approval was relatively unfavorable. One indication of the apparent reluctance to take practical steps to promote Welsh is the fairly high percentage of responses in favor of individual choice in deciding to study Welsh: 'Welsh should not be forced upon non-Welsh-speaking pupils' (75%); 'The learning of Welsh should be left to individual choice' (78%).

The third factor in the attitude toward Welsh is *National Tradition*, represented by 'The need to keep up Welsh for the sake of tradition' (68%); 'We owe it to our forefathers to preserve Welsh' (78%); 'The Welsh language should be preserved because it is a sign of Welsh nationhood' (65%). This together with the first factor of general approval is the most important aspect of attitude to Welsh. The fourth factor, *Economic Importance*, plays a much less significant role. For instance, the percentage who considered that Welsh offered advantages in seeking good job opportunities was as low as 41% in the Welsh-speaking areas and in the English-speaking areas the percentage who thought that Welsh was important in Welsh economic life was below 50%. As far as Welsh is concerned, therefore, two factors, general approval and traditional nationalism, produce favorable responses and the two other factors, commitment to practice and economic importance, produce unfavorable responses on the whole. The components of each pair of factors appear to relate to similar or closely related aspects of the attitude toward Welsh so that we can speak of a favorable *emotional attachment* to Welsh which contrasts with a *realistic and unfavorable appraisal of the use of Welsh*, and these exert strong pulls in opposite directions.

The attitude toward English also has four major components, three of which correspond closely to components of the attitude toward Welsh — general approval, commitment to practice, and economic and educational importance — all of which receive very favorable responses. The fourth component of the attitude toward Welsh, traditional nationalism, has no place in the attitude toward English and is replaced by a factor which we may term

Necessary Bilingualism. This factor is expressed in favorable responses to such statements as 'I should not like English to take over from the Welsh language' (65%); 'The English language is killing the Welsh language' (80%); 'The Welsh should speak both languages' (72%); 'English should not be more important than Welsh in Wales' (68%). The existence of this fourth factor in the attitude toward English is in line with the nature of the curve of distribution of total responses to English (Table XVII), which is unimodal and to that extent is devoid of either extreme antipathy to Welsh or extreme commitment to English in Wales, but displays a degree of tolerance which is remarkable among relatively young children.

4.3.4. *Content of Attitudes: Adults*
The 100 bilinguals referred to in Table XVI submitted to a second test designed to ascertain their conceptualization of the significance of Welsh, their beliefs about the Welsh language, as well as the relative importance they attached to those beliefs. The initial preparation and pretesting of the instrument indicated the existence of five categories or groups of concepts about the Welsh language. In order of the importance attached to them these groups (with exemplifying statements) were: (1) *Familial and Local Considerations* (34%); the language is important to family life whether at home or in formal worship; it is vital to the integrity of small groups. (2) *Ethnic Considerations* (29%): the Welsh language is the symbol of Welsh life; the institutions of Wales are meant to preserve Welsh traditions. (3) *Personal Considerations* (21%): Welsh does not promote the kind of progressive outlook I approve of; it does not provide for an adequate range of aesthetic experience in literature, the theater, and the media. (4) Considerations of *Social Communication* (11%): Welsh promotes exclusiveness; it is of little use in making contact with the world outside Wales; it has few advantages in the search for career satisfaction or in higher education. (5) *Linguistic considerations* (5%): the Welsh language has not developed sufficiently to meet the demands of modern society, industry, and science; it is difficult to learn; the Welsh spoken on radio and television is remote from the Welsh spoken by the average Welshman. It will be seen that the beliefs which were most firmly approved had to do with intimate and ethnic-group affairs and affiliation. Pragmatic considerations or beliefs about the viability of the Welsh language, though tending to polarize as strongly approved/disapproved, nevertheless carried much less weight.

Another investigation involving adolescents and young adults attending clubs and recreational associations attached to chapels and churches, and youth organizations such as the Young Farmers Clubs in thoroughly Welsh-speaking areas (Category *A* and *B* areas) failed to elicit significant information about the 'belief content' of their attitudes toward Welsh, the responses clustering around the indeterminate or neutral. The enquiry failed to set up the kind of hierarchy of approval or disapproval which we identified among older adults. It may be that the Welsh sample of adolescents and young adults were unable or unwilling to articulate their beliefs or concepts of the language because of the rather extreme strength of their emotional reaction, whether favorable or unfavorable, which we have identified with the bimodal distribution of response frequency on the Thurstone test (Figure 1).

Because of this failure it was decided to attempt to elicit a 'rationale' for Welsh by investigating the reasons students gave for learning Welsh. Prior to the 1967–71 investigation the Welsh Department of the Ministry of Education conducted a survey of reading ability and reading interest in Welsh and English (1963) (Lewis and Peaker 1963). In connection with this investigation fifth form students (15+ years old) in secondary schools were asked to submit a list of possible reasons for studying the language and fifteen of the most frequently adduced reasons were used to formulate a questionnaire. The reasons suggested by the students fell into the following groups: (1) *Environmental*, 'there is so much Welsh in the area in which I live'; (2) *Institutional*, 'I need Welsh to be able to enjoy club or church group activities'; (3) *Familial*, 'my parents wish me to learn Welsh; I go on holidays to my Welsh grandparents'; (4) *Group Affiliation*, (a) *National*, 'I am a Welshman'; (b) *Aspirational Group*, 'I admire members of the Nationalist Party'; (c) *Economic Group*, I want a job in Wales'; (5) *Personal*, 'I like to master a language; I like the language; I like the Welsh people; it is easy to learn compared with other subjects; if I don't know Welsh I shall have no influence in Welsh life'. The pattern of approval of the statements did not indicate a precise order for the above categories but generally speaking it appeared that the most powerful motivation was *group affiliation*, the second *pleasure*, the third might be called *intellectual*, and the least important of the motives expressed by these groups were those which reflected the acceptance of Welsh as a means of satisfying a desire to exercise leadership, to influence Welsh life, *Ego Satisfaction*.

4.3.5. *The Dynamics of the Attitudes Toward Welsh and English:*
Internal Consistency of Attitudes

Insofar as the attitudes of children toward Welsh take the form of a
general emotional response, either to the aesthetic (musical and
'magical') attributes of the language or to its claims upon their
loyalty, those attitudes show a remarkable consistency both within
individuals (measured by the correlation of item scores) and between
different age and area strata (measured by the correlation of means).
Furthermore, the two areas of the emotional response to Welsh, the
'aesthetic' and the 'affiliative', whether that response is negative or
affirmative, reinforce each other in the sense that high or low scores
on items related to one aspect are supported by high or low scores on
items related to the other.

From one point of view the attitude to English is also generally
speaking internally consistent, though several more attributes of
English are identified as evoking an emotional response. Among
children selected from Welsh-speaking areas (*A* and *D* especially)
there are high scores favorable to the use of English, the appeal of
English reading material, its richness, its universality and prestige.
These characteristics of English, though they are given greater prominence among some age groups and in different language areas, appear
in the profiles of all such groups, the categories of items varying
consistently in respect to the strength of the favorable or unfavorable
response. This is also true of the attitude of adults toward Welsh. As
far as English is concerned, because of the far greater range of
attributes to which the adults respond, there is a tendency for the
scores to cluster around the mean as if the subject could not make up
his mind about the relative personal significance of the various
characteristics of the language.

However, a kind of inconsistency does characterize attitudes
toward both languages among children and adults alike. This derives
from the fact that the attitude toward either language reflects,
though in two very different ways, the attitude toward the other
language as well — there are two conflicting points of reference or
sources for both attitudes. Neither attitude is unequivocal and this is
true of subjects who are monolingual English or bilingual. As far as
attitude toward English is concerned the ambivalence is articulated
openly. For instance, the two statements in the English scale on
which there was greatest agreement are 'I should not like English to
take over from Welsh' and 'English will take you further than Welsh'.
We have noted earlier how the awareness of the value of both

languages, and not of English alone, emerges in the responses to the English test and the degree of tolerance which characterizes that awareness.

As far as attitude to Welsh is concerned the awareness of English expresses itself quite differently because it helps to exaggerate the potentially favorable or unfavorable response — to polarize the attitude and to produce a bimodal distribution with a limited area of neutrality. There is evidence of far greater conflict between attitudes toward Welsh and English in the Welsh-speaking categories of schools (*A* and *D*) than in the English areas. The conflict is least in Category *C* the most English-speaking. Where the awareness of the difference between the two languages is greatest we also find the least proportion of neutral responses. It appeared as if the impact which the awareness of the English language has on the Welsh child or adult creates an attitude conducive to an unequivocal choice between Welsh and English, while in the case of the English child's attitude toward Welsh the awareness of the two languages encourages an attempt to compromise.

This is only to be expected since English is nowhere felt to be threatened and attitudes of the majority can therefore afford to be moderately favorable. Welsh, especially in the category of Welsh-speaking schools, is seen to be — and in season and out of season is said to be — under threat so that the attitude to it becomes more explicitly favorable among the minority and more tolerant among the majority. In any case the analysis reveals a basic internal conflict resolved differently according to the language in question. This is probably characteristic of all bilingual situations where one language is seriously jeopardized. The vital factor in creating an attitude to either language in a bilingual country is the nature of the relationship of the two languages; that relationship is in turn determined in Wales by the pattern of social and demographic variables outlined at the beginning.

4.3.6. Discrepancy Between Verbal and Behavioral Response

One of the more interesting features of bilingualism in Wales is the difference between the verbal response to measures of attitude and the actual language behavior of the population, the degree to which they favor either language *in practice*. We have already noted the ambivalent attitude of parents who approve of Welsh in principle but are reluctant to act on their approval. Table XVII gives the results of a survey taken among eighty bilingual parents in three small com-

Table XVII. *Encouragement of Children by Parents to Use Welsh in Two Different Linguistic Areas (Percentage of Responses in Each Cell)*

Context of use of Welsh		I insist on Welsh always		I encourage Welsh		I don't mind		I tend to discourage Welsh		I am strongly opposed to Welsh	
		A	C	A	C	A	C	A	C	A	C
To grand-	M	38	40	40	45	18	14	3	1	1	0
parents	F	42	48	48	47	10	5	0	0	0	0
To either or	M	8	6	34	33	30	40	20	15	8	6
both parents	F	11	3	23	13	45	50	18	20	4	6
To brothers	M	5	4	15	12	45	46	30	31	5	7
and sisters	F	14	9	19	11	49	52	14	21	4	7
At play	M	8	3	11	5	54	60	19	23	8	9
	F	10	7	13	17	57	63	15	8	5	5
In school	M	13	8	20	13	37	41	24	28	6	10
	F	10	4	13	8	32	22	33	46	12	30
Listening to ra-	M	1	6	3	15	67	60	20	15	9	4
dio/television	F	1	8	7	18	54	42	25	21	13	11
Reading	M	0	0	16	12	50	42	29	35	5	11
	F	0	0	20	15	52	41	21	31	7	13

A = area with 68–81% Welsh   *M* = mother
C = area with 3–26% Welsh   *F* = father

munities in a thoroughly Welsh-speaking area and three in an English-speaking area. The parents were drawn from sixty families, twenty fathers and twenty mothers from separate families and both parents in twenty additional families equally divided between the two areas. The ages of the parents ranged between 28 and 42 years of age, the average being 34; age, however, did not emerge as a significant variable. Irrespective of area there is evidence of a disinclination among parents to encourage the use of Welsh by their children except in communicating with grandparents; in that context it is an expression of a 'familial piety' rather than a commitment to use the language as a matter of principle. In all other contexts of usage the characteristic is indifference. Only in the Welsh-speaking area — A — is there a tendency towards the encouragement of Welsh in any context. A greater tendency appears to discourage the use of Welsh in education, including listening to the radio and reading, more than in any other context. In effect where the use of Welsh is concerned, whatever their verbally expressed attitude parents make a practical distinction between those contexts which matter and those which do not. They do not encourage the use of Welsh in the former. Furthermore, there is an almost consistent difference in both linguistic areas and in respect to most contexts of usage between the fathers and mothers, the former being less encouraging. Where fathers and mothers in the same family were investigated they followed the same pattern as is found among separate parents.

The same discrepancy between verbal approval and a failure of overt behavioral support for Welsh emerged from analysis of the responses of the same group of parents to a second questionnaire. From a set of twenty-five statements two subsets were identified as eliciting the most positive and most negative responses. See Table XVIII.

The statements (B) which imply an acceptance of actual practical steps to give effect to a favorable attitude tend to receive negative responses and are very much in line with the responses of the same parents to the question relating to the encouragement of their children to use the language. It can be concluded that there is a

Table XVIII.

	% Response
A1. The Welsh language should be preserved because it is the traditional language of Wales.	58
2. It should be preserved because many people speak it.	52
3. It should be preserved because it is an advantage to be able to speak two languages.	64
4. It should be preserved because it adds color and variety to life in Wales.	54
B1. There should be greater use of Welsh in public administration.	31
2. It should be taught in all primary schools.	39
3. It should be taught in all secondary schools.	25
4. There should be more Welsh on radio and television.	36

marked discrepancy between entertaining the idea of approving or supporting the Welsh language in principle on the one hand and actually engaging in the use of Welsh or encouraging its use by members of the family on the other.

It is very easy to condemn this kind of inconsistency but if we continue to bear in mind the historical background of the use of Welsh and its current demographic and social status the inconsistency becomes almost inevitable. It arises from a conjunction of several factors. There is first of all the nature of the attitude toward Welsh which tends to derive its strength mainly from opposition to English. Belief in the affirmative value of Welsh appears to be severely limited even among the population of the Welsh-speaking areas. Attachment to the language is most positive in respect to the aspect which has the least practical significance, its historical 'authenticity'. The second factor in producing the discrepancy between theory and practice, belief and action is the nature of the alternative to Welsh. The English language has very strong claims upon all young people, inside Wales and elsewhere, and these claims are recognized even by the most ardent speakers of Welsh. To that extent the discrepancy arises from a conflict of different kinds of commitment — to one's ethnic group and to one's own personal requirements. The third factor is the situational restraint upon the translation of belief into practice, namely, the social environmental limitations upon the use of the Welsh language in important areas of communication and in intellectual life, limitations which reflect historical, social, and demographic processes. A fourth factor is the personal capacity of individuals to tolerate dissonance, a capacity which inevitably varies from person to person but to which generally speaking the majority, in a situation of conflict, learn to adapt with increasing success. On the other hand the minority who fail — or choose not — to exercise a capacity for tolerance respond by adopting extreme attitudes. These are all reflected in the situation we have analyzed.

4.4. *Correlations of Attitude with Other Variables*

4.4.1. *Linguistic Background*
There are four dimensions to area variation in the distribution of the Welsh language in Wales: vertical discontinuity between areas of Welsh and English speech; continuous area variation in the spread of Welsh and English so that the boundaries become blurred; complete co-occupation of the same territory by both languages; and finally,

interaction of individuals (bilinguals and monolinguals in either language) in areas of virtual separation. Investigation of the attitude among children and adults by selecting three types of linguistic area (3%–26% Welsh, 48%–55%, and 68%–81% Welsh-speaking) took into account, as far as possible, the first three dimensions of areal variation. The fourth, which is highly individualistic, is capable of being sampled only by very uneconomical procedures. In that event area variations were found to correlate closely at all ages with attitude to languages. Where Welsh is concerned it was to be expected that the sample of children in Category *D* should head the list of favorable areas since this category consists of schools which were created specifically to meet the demands of parents highly motivated towards Welsh. It was also not unexpected that the order of areal variation in respect to English should be the reverse of the order for Welsh. The effectiveness of the areal influence is emphasized by the fact that attitudes to Welsh among the monoglot English adults are much more favorable in Welsh-speaking areas than elsewhere. This areal polarization of attitude is entirely in line with the areal polarization in the demographic incidence of Welsh.

4.4.2. *Age*
Among children in all types of area and school the attitude toward English improves and the attitude toward Welsh becomes less favorable. This is continued into late adolescence and early adulthood. This could be either the consequence or one of the causes of the increasing decline of Welsh in successive age groups. However we look at it, the fact remains that the degree of convergence between the attitudes toward Welsh and English is negatively correlated with the intensity of Welsh in the area. The polarization of attitudes remains in spite of increasing age and it is reinforced by the linguistic background.

4.4.3. *Sex*
Sex is a significant factor in relation to attitudes of adults to both languages, the fathers being less favorable to Welsh and more favorable to English. Among school children the girls favor Welsh more than the boys but there is no significant difference in respect to English. Here too the sex differential in the incidence of Welsh correlates positively with sex differences in attitude. It is worth reminding ourselves that more women than men claim Welsh and that the intensity of Welsh in the rural areas is influenced by the

preponderance of women over men in the rural areas. The more favorable attitude of women compared with men probably has two interpretations: it may derive from the presence of superior numbers and it may in turn reinforce the numerical or demographic superiority.

4.4.4. *Length of Residence*

Length of residence favors the attitude toward Welsh among adults. Since none of the adults in the sample had spent more than twelve years in Wales it is more reliable as a criterion of the value of residence than in the case of the school children. Although residence was found to be second only to 'linguistic area' in significance, its effect in the school sample was confused by the fact that in that case no distinction was made between 'length of residence' and 'native-born'. This variable came to overlap with 'ethnicity' which was not tested for among the school children.

4.4.5. *Other Variables*

Of other variables *general ability* does not appear to correlate significantly with the attitude toward English or Welsh and *socioeconomic status* of parents (in respect to school children and to the samples of adults) appears to have a complex relationship with attitude. The lower the economic category the less favorable the attitudes toward Welsh and the more indifferent toward English. The higher socioeconomic group tends to polarize, among both pupils and adults, as highly favorable or highly unfavorable to both Welsh and English. A last variable, which was tested with school children in Lewis and Peaker (1963:28; supplementary individual interviews), is 'level of social aspiration' measured by a range of occupations which students of 15 years of age hoped to have in adult life. Aspiration to higher status occupations appears to correlate negatively with favorable attitude toward Welsh and positively with favorable attitude toward English.

4.5. *Attitude Polarization*

Attitudes towards Welsh and English among school children and adults reflect very clearly the strains and stresses produced by the historical relationship of the two languages and the manner in which English gained its present supremacy in Wales. Compared with recent immigration, industrialization, and urbanization, the conquest, centuries of political unification, and administrative uniformity did little to undermine the Welsh language. This is mainly because of the difference in the intensity and speed of the operations. However insidious its ultimate effect might be, the impact of political unification and domination was slow and selective. The Welsh had time to adapt to the general cultural change without losing their language. Industrial immigration and urbanization were concentrated within a period of less than seventy-five years and their effect was massive and immediate. There was little opportunity to effect a compromise or for the Welsh to escape from the linguistic consequences. Such has also been shown to be the case in the Soviet Union where, whenever the rate of industrialization in any area has exceeded the rate of native adaptation (e.g., the rate at which the indigenous population can be trained to run the industries), there is large-scale immigration (mainly by Russians) and a high rate of development of bilingualism and ultimately of language shift. Where the change is revolutionary, as it has been in Wales during the last century, attitudes also are apt to become extreme at both ends – an extreme revolutionary acceptance of the new language and an equally extreme reaction in favor of the native language.

This polarization of attitudes is promoted by another aspect of the same revolution. The traditional view has been that the rural areas are the main conservative agents of ethnic features, especially language. It is true that the proportion of native language communication contacts in the rural areas is likely to be greater than the proportion of second language contacts (the intensity factor favors the native language). But there are more native speakers of the language in the urban areas than elsewhere. This fact has to be taken in conjunction with another tendency. Urbanization does not simply change the statistical structure or the composition of the population. The greater social mobility of urban residents and the greater range and frequency of informational contacts make for greater social awareness in towns and cities. Furthermore, because they are a minority in the urban areas speakers of the native language have a more intense ethnic awareness. This is channeled into their feeling for the language because in the urban area more than elsewhere the language is their one distinctive characteristic. This tends to promote even greater polarization of the attitude toward the language.

Immigration has produced polarization of attitudes for other reasons. Because of its identification with industrialization and urbanization immigration has brought about a discontinuity in the geographic spread of Welsh and this in turn has initiated two further changes, a structural change in which ethnic and linguistic group boundaries are broken down and a substantive change in which the group norms themselves tend to be abandoned. Though group boundaries tend to be preserved in the rural areas because of the greater intensity of Welsh, the tendency is for substantive changes in the towns and cities to be attracted symbiotically into the surrounding areas. The towns are centers of higher education and administration and they spread their influence well beyond the radius of physical communication. The net result of these changes, whether confined to large urban centers or diffused more generally, is to polarize individual attitudes to the native language between group attachment on the one hand, a feeling of loyalty and a commitment to traditional cultural associations, and on the other hand a realistic-personal assessment of the immediate value of the language and a limited acceptance of its traditional associations. This division within the individual's attachment to language is exemplified by an analysis of the favored language in different domains of use.

5. CHANGES IN LINGUISTIC USAGE

5.1. *Institutional Usage*

Between 1960 and 1963 a survey was conducted into the institutional use made of the Welsh language in five major domains: administration, work, leisure, religion, and education (Council for Wales and Monmouth 1963). As far as the administration of local government is concerned the use of Welsh varies according to the degree of local and personal contact in which the administrative services are involved. There is considerable use of Welsh in the social services in the Welsh-speaking areas but hardly any in the English areas save in a few individual cases. A distinction must also be drawn between types of service. For instance, in matters which concern the military services or with the administration of trade and commerce Welsh has a very little part to play anywhere in Wales. Apart from the use of Welsh in contacts with citizens outside the administrative service itself, the customers and clients, there is the question of the use of the language in internal administration. Over 80% of even the most localized administrative bodies, the District Councils, were found to conduct all their activities in English, approximately 8% in both languages and only 12% in Welsh. Of the nearly 13,000 employees less than 24% were required to be able to use Welsh fluently and only 8% more were expected to have some proficiency in the language. This preponderance of English is reflected in the more general domain of occupation and work. The Welsh language tends to be employed in agriculture mainly because it is an industry which characterizes the Welsh-speaking areas. But even here there has been a decline during the last forty years. In the modern technological industries there is hardly any use of Welsh. In the retail trades the extent of the use of Welsh naturally varies with the locality and with the size of the store. English is replacing Welsh in the retail trade of thoroughly Welsh-speaking areas as large supermarkets replace small shops.

Broadcasting is perhaps the most important institution catering to the domain of leisure: though the broadcasting companies provide more time than the proportion of speakers of Welsh in the population would justify statistically, the number who listen habitually to Welsh programs is small. For instance, the number of children between the ages of 5 and 15 years registered in the schools of Wales in 1961 was 389,500. Of this number approximately only 35,000 (9%) listened to programs specially prepared for children and broadcast in Welsh. There is no daily Welsh language newspaper though fourteen periodicals have limited and specialized (usually denominational) circulation and English language newspapers may have occasional Welsh columns. In the last five years the number of new Welsh books published annually for adults had averaged around eighty-four and for children forty-seven. These publications are supported by central and local government grants but the number has declined nevertheless. Between 1957 and 1970 the annual sale of Welsh books of all kinds was 218,000; in the library in Glamorgan the number of Welsh books borrowed accounted for 1% of the total.

The use of Welsh in the domain of religion has declined at an accelerating pace during the last two decades, principally among the young. The relative status of the two languages in the Church in Wales (corresponding to the Established Church of England) and in the non-Conformist denominations is very different. Of the estimated 167,000 regular communicants of the former, approximately 12% attend wholly Welsh services, 85% wholly English, and 3% bilingual services. It is a feature of religious life that the same non-Conformist denomination may have two 'causes' or centers of worship in the same town, one conducting its services in English and the other in Welsh, membership of the latter becoming smaller and

more aged. The non-Conformist denominations claim 400,000 communicants of whom 66% attend services in Welsh and 6% attend
bilingual services. The use of Welsh in their sunday schools is becoming less acceptable to the young. Organizational matters are very
frequently discussed in English by the denominations even when the
services are conducted in Welsh. The Roman Catholic Church,
though a strong supporter of arguments for the maintenance of
Welsh, makes hardly any use of the language.

It would be impossible in this limited study to do justice to the
consequences of population change and bilingualism for the administration, organization, curriculum content, and attainment of pupils
in the system of education. For this reason only three related aspects
of the place of the languages in education will be referred to. First,
there is the problem of the proportion of children to whom Welsh
may be taught and within that group the different proportions who
may be taught it as a first and as a second language. In the whole of
Wales in 1961, of the 342,800 children over the age of 7 (the age
when a second language is normally introduced) 37,000 (11%) were
taught Welsh as a first language and nearly five times that number,
181,100, as a second language (53%). It is almost unique in a
developed country that a native minority language (whatever its
place in the tradition of that country) is taught in such disproportionate numbers as a second language.[5]

Not only is this a consequence of the type of situation which has
produced bilingualism in Wales, but its implications for the future of
the language in terms of ease, fluency, and conformity to the agreed
standards of use are causing serious concern among Welsh language
teachers and especially Welsh linguists. Irish linguists are similarly
concerned about their own problem.

A second aspect is the teaching and use of Welsh in higher
education. Of the seven constituent colleges and independent institutes of the University of Wales, which has a total student population
of over 25,000, in the last five years there was an average of 220
students studying Welsh at any one time. The percentage of the
annual college recruitment of students who are able to speak Welsh
was less than 25% during the same period and the proportion is
declining. It can therefore be appreciated that the degree to which
the Welsh language is or can be used with profit as a medium of
instruction in higher education is small though some provision is
made. In the eight colleges which exist exclusively for students
studying to become teachers, the Colleges of Education, the use of

Welsh is much greater. Finally, in a sample of 132 secondary schools representative of the whole of Wales, 32% made no use of Welsh as a teaching language; 17% used it for proportions of the school time varying from very little to a quarter; 20% used it for between a quarter and half the time; 19% used it from a half to three-quarters of the time; and 16% used it for over three-quarters of the time. Most schools using Welsh as a teaching language select particular areas of the curriculum for this purpose and in this respect the subjects most often taught in Welsh are religion and Welsh history. The sciences and mathematics are seldom included.

5.2. Personal Usage

So far discussion has been about the use of Welsh in formal or institutional domains. The use of the language is more prevalent in interpersonal, casual, and informal relationships. Slightly over 1,000 children aged 10+ years, a somewhat similar number of children aged 12+, and 900 14-year-olds, all of whom were recorded as fluent bilinguals, were asked to complete a questionnaire in which they indicated the extent of their use of Welsh (on a five-point scale) in eight domains or activities. In the thoroughly Welsh-speaking areas at age 10+ a great deal of Welsh was used in church and chapel and in talking to teachers in school. Less Welsh was used in running errands and in talking to people outside school though the bias was still towards Welsh. English was the dominant language in playing with friends, in private reading, and in listening to the radio and television. At age 12 the pattern did not change much though there was considerably more English in communicating with teachers. This shift was continued into the 14+ group and here too the use of English in private reading increased considerably. There were few significant differences between the four categories of linguistic background. Perhaps the most significant point is that the children attending the special schools created for the promotion of Welsh used English almost exclusively in running errands and used more English than Welsh in playing with friends, talking to adults outside school, and in reading. This is an indication of the overwhelming influence of population change, among other factors, in creating an environment where, whatever the intentions of the parents and the efforts of the schools, English is clearly dominant in nearly all domains of use.

The point is further exemplified in the case of adults from the ages

Glyn Lewis

Table XIX.   *Comparison of the Intensity of the Use of Welsh and*
             English by Two Adult Groups

Domain of use	Welsh nearly always		Welsh more often than English		Welsh and English about equal		Welsh less often than English		Welsh hardly ever	
	20–25	45–50	20–25	45–50	20–25	45–50	20–25	45–50	20–25	45–50
Religion	4.8	10.0	21.0	23.0	32.9	30.1	27.5	20.0	13.8	8.9
Family and children	6.5	15.0	14.1	33.3	18.3	22.4	37.5	20.8	23.6	8.5
Others	16.1	20.0	19.0	32.2	34.2	39.0	18.4	6.1	10.3	1.7
Friends	5.1	22.0	10.1	38.2	31.9	24.1	37.6	13.3	15.3	7.4
Work	0.2	7.5	14.2	15.7	19.1	22.5	42.4	47.5	24.2	6.8
Street	0.0	3.3	10.0	13.3	15.8	28.3	55.1	38.3	19.1	16.8
Clubs and societies	0.2	5.0	10.0	15.0	19.1	23.3	44.1	35.8	26.6	20.9
Correspondence	0.1	4.0	4.1	6.5	12.5	18.4	49.1	47.5	34.2	23.6

% of age group at each intensity level of use

of 20 to 25 and 45 to 50 years of age. One hundred twenty adults in
the younger age group and 125 in the older group were sampled and
interviewed personally. The sample included representatives of several
professions as well as manual workers, with a small number of students
in the younger group. The actual survey included mass media as one
domain but it was found that there were hardly any variances in the
use of English among the two age groups or between members within
either group. This is due no doubt to the fact that the media offer
very little opportunity to exercise personal choice — they are overwhelmingly English. In the case of mass media the responses of those
in the sample represented the amount of Welsh or English that was
available rather than the amount they *chose*. See Table XIX.

An analysis of Table XIX entitles us to draw the following conclusions. There is a well-marked tendency to use more English in all
seven domains. This is most apparent within the family: here too
there is a growing habit of using English even with the older members
of the family including wives, husbands, and grandparents. The
difference between the two age groups in the use of the two languages in talking to friends is also markedly in favor of English. The

amount of Welsh in the formal domain of correspondence and telephoning is very small among both groups and this is the case also in the domain of work. This is not unexpected because most of the individuals in the sample were engaged in highly mechanized industries or in related occupations. Few were involved in agriculture, for instance. The use of either language in the street is governed very largely by the fact that such situations are open and unpredictable. Consequently, the tendency is to play it safe and at least to inaugurate any communication in the one language which all the inhabitants can be assumed to know, namely, English. In closed situations like the home predictable encounters offer a greater incentive to habituate the use of one language to one person or group or activity and the other language to different groups or activities. The evidence we have of the extent and the nature of the use of Welsh bears out what was referred to earlier as the discrepancy between 'approval in principle' and actual implementation of the principle of favoring Welsh.

5.3. *Language Switching*

Another aspect of the use of the two languages is the frequency with which a speaker switches from one language to another, the occasions or factors which conduce to such a switch, and the relative importance or rank order of such factors. I investigated this in one bilingual community in the Swansea Valley, where I was born and bred and with which I am intimately acquainted. During a period of two months in 1970 this phenomenon was observed in a group of fifty-three bilingual men and women whose first language is Welsh. Their ages range from 15 to 65+. The recorded observations were made on occasions when all those who were present — in the home, on shopping journeys, in public meetings, including religious services, etc. — were able to speak both languages. There were some occasions in a discussion when the use of a particular language was obligatory, for instance, in quoting a speaker on the radio or a piece of writing from a periodical or book. When such quotations involved a switch they were not recorded as such. Nevertheless it should be noted that quotations in English were far more frequent than in Welsh and it was very apparent that when the conversation was in English speakers tended to translate rather than quote from Welsh.

Those who participated in the investigation were aware that I was gathering information about the use of Welsh in the community but they were not informed of the particular aspects I was studying. Conversations in closed situations, the home, or public meetings were taped. Other occasions were recorded in notes. During the two months I took accounts of 235 conversations or formal occasions of the use of Welsh, some lasting no longer than five minutes but some extending to over an hour and a half. Twelve thousand instances of switching occurred, over 80% of them from the main stream of Welsh usage to English. The length of the switch varied from a phrase of three or four words to a complete change in the dominant language of a conversation. The 'communication units' or 'speech occasions' were analyzed in order to ascertain the consideration which gave rise to a language switch. Any one switch quite obviously may be due to a combination of several factors and what follows are the results of a personal assessment of the main consideration. Since some of the middle- or low-ranking factors may operate subordinately more frequently than the high-ranking factors it should be accepted that the rank ordering may be erroneous. See Table XX.

These factors fall into four categories. First, there are those which arise from the nature of the topic of communication. The Welshness of a topic or its local significance tended to inhibit switching from Welsh to English and to encourage switching in the reverse direction, while subjects having to do with science and economics, or subjects in which there was considerable explanation as distinct from narrative appeared to facilitate switching from Welsh to English and to inhibit switching to Welsh. Controversial subjects were also correlated with frequency of switching from Welsh to English, and with inhibiting switching to Welsh.

The second category of factors has to do with the context of communication. Where the context was open and free and included a good deal of interruption, switching was frequent. Formality, whether in a discussion such as in a committee or in a straight monologue as in the chairman's account of a previous discussion, inhibited switching to Welsh but this factor did not operate to the same extent in influencing a switch to English. The size of the group was also found to be a factor, small groups of up to nine conducing to switching to Welsh. Larger groups of twenty-five and above tended to become formal and so inhibited switching to Welsh. As far as switching to English was concerned the size of the group appeared to become a significant factor only when it exceeded fifty, in which case it tended to be inhibitive but not to the same extent as in the case of switching to Welsh. The level of intimacy of acquaintance among

Table XX. *Factors or Considerations Affecting Language Switching in a Bilingual Community*

1 Factor	2 Direction of switch					
	Welsh to English			English to Welsh		
	a Rank order of frequency	b % of total frequency	c % of 2b	d Rank order of frequency	e % of total frequency	f % of 2e
Kind of participation	1	18		4	9	
(a) Size of group						
(i) 75+			9			2
(ii) 50–74			15			7
(iii) 25–49			29			11
(iv) 10–24			25			32
(v) 2–9			22			48
(b) Form of communication						
(i) discussion: formal			25			12
informal			37			39
(ii) monologue: formal, e.g., lecture			13			7
informal, e.g., account of sports event			25			42
Characteristics of topic:	2	15		3	14	
remoteness from normal experience			11			3
abstractness			45			5

Table XX. (continued)

Factor	2 Direction of switch					
	Welsh to English			English to Welsh		
	a Rank order of frequency	b % of total frequency	c % of 2b	d Rank order of frequency	e % of total frequency	f % of 2e
difficulty: explanations			36			12
narrative						
Welsh associations			8			80
Degree of personal involvement in context of communication:						
ego satisfaction of assertion of leadership	3	13	16	6	7	42
close participation in group			84			58
Level of competence in Welsh	4	12		8	5	
Intimacy of acquaintance within group:						
friends and family			84			85
strangers			10			5
prestigious persons			6			10
Emotional characteristics of situation:						
fatigue			20			30

Table XX. *(continued)*

1	2 Direction of switch					
	Welsh to English			English to Welsh		
Factor	a Rank order of frequency	b % of total frequency	c % of 2b	d Rank order of frequency	e % of total frequency	f % of 2e
controversy			70			6
authoritarian			4			9
ritual			6			55
Age of speaker:						
late adolescent			47			5
young adult			30			11
middle age			15			21
late age			8			63
Level of general education and socio-economic status:						
(i) higher education	8	7	40	9	4	
(iia) professional worker			60			42
(iib) manual worker						58
Personal attachment to Welsh culture and institutions, e.g. Welsh radio and periodicals	9	6		1	27	

participants was also important: the less well-acquainted the participants, the lower the level of switching; this was true of both directions of switching. This was equally true of the social status of the
participants. For instance, the presence of a minister of religion
seemed to inhibit switching to English but this may have been due to
the fact that he was regarded as ritualistically committed to Welsh as
the language of his local church.

The emotional characteristics of a situation influenced switching
to English more frequently than to Welsh. For instance, it was found
that late evening conversations after the day's work tended to reflect
fatigue and to incorporate relatively more switches than at other
times. Discussions in which a participant was clearly a partial or
biased protagonist induced emotional responses and excitement
which made it difficult for the speaker of Welsh to do himself justice
in Welsh alone. Controversy did not materially influence switching to
Welsh mainly because the controversial subjects which were recorded
related, generally speaking, to economic and political matters. Authoritarian situations such as preaching, and ritual situations such as
extemporary prayer at week night religious services, inhibited
switching because they impinged upon deep layers of sentiment. For
the same reason they promoted switching to Welsh. The fact that
ritual switching was less frequent to English than to Welsh may be
due to the fact that such utterances were largerly composed of
predictable linguistic formulae, hallowed by tradition and in any case
very well worn and memorized.

Personal attributes of participants constitute a third category of
factors. For instance, the participant's image of himself within the
group exercised a considerable influence on switching, but while it
inhibited switching to English it tended in comparison to promote
switching to Welsh, probably because of the Welsh traditional background of the community. A person who set himself up as a leader or
prospective leader tended to formalize his communications and thus
to avoid switching to English but to use Welsh as a means of group
identification. But where actual involvement in the group activities
which were directed outside the group were concerned there was a
tendency to respond more freely and switch with relative frequency
in both directions. An increase in age was correlated with frequency
and direction of switching according to the direction of the
switching, youth encouraging a switch to English and discouraging a
switch to Welsh. This may have been related to the level of acquaintance with Welsh, which was far less assured among the young who

would therefore be forced to have recourse to switching to English. The level of general education or the socioeconomic status of the participants played a relatively minor though interesting role, and in both directions of switching to almost the same extent. Those with higher education, which usually meant university, technical college, or college of education, were inhibited more than those who left school at the age of 15. But within the group with higher education there was a difference between those who followed science courses and the others. The scientists switched to English almost regularly but did not have frequent recourse to Welsh. The difference between the professional men and women, teachers, doctors, solicitors, and business managers on the one hand and manual workers — mainly steel workers and miners — on the other, was greater as far as switching to Welsh was concerned than to English. The professional workers were ambivalent. They were inhibited from switching to Welsh by status considerations but induced to switch by the nature of their professional training which was exclusively English. For the same reasons they had far less recourse to Welsh. On the other hand manual workers switched to Welsh far more frequently than they did to English but this was due very largely to the kind of discussions they were involved in — concerned with home, local, and sports activities. The fourth category, including factors relating to attitude toward language and to Welsh culture, had considerable influence in promoting a switch from English to Welsh and considerably less in the other direction. Whether this is the most influential factor depends on whether we consider its inhibiting or its promoting power.

5.4. *Linguistic Change*

5.4.1. *General*
Because the long-standing contact between Welsh and English, together with the dominant political and later the dominant if. not exclusive scientific and technological use of English in Wales, it is to be expected that the Welsh language, both 'langue' and 'parole', should be greatly influenced by English. Some of the very early importations represent forms which have been lost altogether to contemporary English or are found only rarely in dialectal use, for instance *barclod* from OE *bearnclath* 'apron', *costrel* from ME *costrel* 'flagon', and *llidiart* from OE *hlidgeat* 'gate'. These very early items have long been part and parcel of the Welsh language. This is so much

the case that one suspects the argument that more recent changes in the direction of English are not particularly significant. The fact is that the very long history of gradual English penetration and of Welsh approximation to aspects of English make it difficult to decide whether a new Welsh form is a recent importation or a derivative of a long-standing naturalized form. There are many instances of OE infinitive -*an* as in OE *cyssan* giving Welsh *cusan-u*; OE *styrian* giving Welsh *stwyrian*; OE *hangian* giving Welsh *hongian*. These continue to produce new Welsh verbs. The OE plural in -*es* appears in Welsh in a variety of derived forms, -*es*, -*ys*, -*ws*, -*os*, and -*as*, depending on the nature of the preceding vowel. For instance, we have ME *bagges* giving Welsh *bacas* 'stocking'; *cogges* giving Welsh *cocos* 'cogs of a wheel'. The final unstressed Middle English short vowel -*e* was obscure and appears in Welsh borrowings as -*a*, for instance, ME *bowe* gives Welsh *bwa* 'bow'; ME *tubbe* gives Welsh *twba* 'tub'. It is interesting to note that while recent and contemporary Welsh plural borrowings from English are invariably in -*s* there are many early instances of an English umlaut plural: for instance, -*mon* gives -*myn* as in *hwsmon* − *hwsmyn* 'houseman', *certmon* − *certmyn* 'cartman'. One result of the early and continuing contact may be the borrowing of an English form at an early stage which is now part of the Welsh language and a later form which is clearly identifiable as an importation, for instance, *board* > *bord* and later *bwrdd*; *fool* > *ffol* and *ffwl*; and *pund* > *punt* and *pound* (Parry Williams 1923; 1963).

5.4.2. Lexis
It is on the level of vocabulary that the English influence is most radical and extensive. In those domains where the Welsh language is infrequently employed English words have displaced the native vocabulary or made the development of new Welsh words unlikely. English, or international terminology borrowed through English, prevails in the sciences and in industry. This is the case not only in those areas of technological activity which are of recent growth such as electronics and precision engineering, for instance, but in the traditional industries and crafts of Wales such as agriculture and the country crafts. Whenever a craft dies out or an occupation disappears part of the language dies with it. The terminology of the industries characteristic of South Wales after the industrial revolution are almost exclusively English, for instance, in mining *hedin* 'heading', *ffas* 'face', *siafft* 'shaft', *lefel* 'level'; and in steelmaking *rowl twrner* 'roll turner', *ffwrnesman* 'furnace man'. The Welsh names of herbs

and the vocabulary of nature in general is rapidly disappearing in colloquial Welsh and is kept alive only by the efforts of the schools and the special programs broadcast by the BBC. The Welsh names are replaced by straightforward borrowings or translations. An instance of the latter is the name of the fungus Earth Star now only known by its recent label *seren ddaear,* a literal translation of the English. It is seldom that the Welsh names of plants, grasses, flowers, and animals are known or used by the children of South Wales. Very frequently the experts included in programs for radio listeners, when they deal with topics such as gardening, have to add the English names of plants, herbs, animals, and fruits. The same is true of place names, either foreign such as *Eidal* 'Italy', *Almaen* 'Germany', and *Efrog Newydd* 'New York'; or British such as *Cernyw* 'Cornwall', *Amwythig* 'Shrewsbury', or even the Welsh names of Welsh towns and localities such as *Casnewydd* 'Newport', or '*Yr Wyddfa*' 'Snowdon'.

Because of the disuse of Welsh in commerce and administration English loanwords proliferate in those domains particularly at the colloquial level. In ordinary conversation it is infrequently that one hears *heddlu* 'police', *treth incwm* 'income tax', *gweinyddes* 'nurse', *arolygwr* 'inspector', *llywodraeth* 'government'. In shops the prices are communicated in English even when the request for information is expressed in Welsh. For instance, *Faint yw hwn?* 'How much is this?' is given the answer 'Twenty pence' for *ugain ceiniog.* Bank manager, hire purchase, laundry, engineer, trunk-call, gas, petrol, typist, and battery — are words which are invariably used and I have never heard Welsh equivalents used in normal conversation. The same is true of foods though to a lesser extent — fish and chips, duck, green peas, lamb, beef, green vegetables, and meals such as breakfast and lunch. In domains represented by these examples and in many others the Welsh language appears to be losing the very capacity to augment its vocabulary from native resources or to renew itself except by wholesale borrowing.

It sometimes happens that a word borrowed from English assumes a form in Welsh which is only with difficulty distinguished from an existing native Welsh word of entirely different meaning. In these cases the importation which has come to be better known as well as more acceptable has ousted the native Welsh word from currency, or nearly so. For instance, the English word 'afford' has been assimilated as *fforddio* but there was already in Welsh the word *fforddio* 'to guide or lead'; in contemporary Welsh this early meaning of the word has been almost completely lost and the dominant meaning of *fforddio* is 'to afford'. There was also in Welsh the word *treio* 'to ebb'; the noun is still employed for ebb and flow *trai a llanw* but the English word 'try' was borrowed in the normal Welsh fashion as *treio* and the original meaning has been ousted from currency to a large extent. The same is true of the word 'to sign' in English which was borrowed in Welsh as *seinio*. An original Welsh word *seinio* 'to sound' is suffering the same fate as the others we have mentioned. This is also the case of the Welsh word *trwst* which produced the verb *trystio* 'to create a noise'. When the English word 'to trust' was borrowed as *trystio* it began to oust the original Welsh word from currency (Ffowkes 1940).

The proliferation of syntactic loan translations (calques) is an indication of the same tendency. This has been proceeding for a very long time so that hardly anyone, even the most consciously and militantly Welsh, appears to be aware of it. Some time ago a list of such 'calques' was culled from the writings of a Welshman who, in the process of promoting the case of 'pure Welsh', had attacked the influence of the English language. The list included the following *y stock wedu ei werthu allan* 'the stock having been sold out'; *y gwyr a gariodd ymlaen y gwaith* 'the men who carried on the work'; *y mae ugeiniau o Gymry wedi gweithio eu ffordd i fyny i swyddi pwysig* 'scores of Welshmen worked their way upwards to offices of importance', all of them almost precise literal translations retaining the English word order. The same is true of calques such as *gwneud eich meddwl lan* 'to make your mind up'; *chwarae'r peth lawr* 'play the thing down', etc., which are accepted as normal Welsh idioms and their English origins are never realized. This is due partly to the frequency of their occurrence and partly to the fact that many of them were introduced into Welsh as far back as the sixteenth and seventeenth centuries, some even earlier.

5.4.3. Morphology and Syntax

In spite of long contact with and the consequent importation of a large number of English words and loan translations the grammatical structure of the Welsh language has remained intact, though there are signs that it too is being modified. One of these signs is the removal of the preposition which normally precedes the pronoun or noun it governs to the end of the sentence so as to make it an independent unit. For instance, instead of Welsh *Am bwy mae e'n son?* we have *Pwy mae e'n son am?* 'Whom is he talking about?'; similarly, *Ble mae*

e'n dod o? 'Where does he come *from?*' and *Ble mae'n symud i?*
'Where is he going *to?*' The Welsh plural exemplifies significant
change. There are at least seventeen ways of forming plurals in Welsh,
fourteen of which involve the addition of a suffix such as *-au* or *-ion*.
The suffix *-s* or *-es* is not one of them. However, the most productive
plural suffix in contemporary Welsh is *-s* or *-ys*, borrowed from
English. For instance, *babi-s*, 'babies', *brws-ys* 'brushes', *ras-ys* 'races',
etc. Sometimes both the *-s* and *-ys* plural suffixes are used as in
rwm-s-ys 'rooms'. Furthermore, the intrusive *-s* or *-ys* is usurping the
place of a normal Welsh plural even in native words; for instance,
bradwr > *-wyr* is often now given as *bradwrs*, *llongwr* > *-wyr* gives
way to *llongwrs*, *pregethwr* > *-wyr* to *pregethwrs*. Another instance
of the same process is the use of the English plural in *-s* for zero
when the normal Welsh plural is formed by the omission of the
singular suffix as in *seren* 'star' > *ser* 'stars' which is now very often
given as *sers*.

Normally whatever is borrowed from English is assimilated into
the Welsh system and obeys the rules of the appropriate paradigm.
Most loan verbs acquired one of the several Welsh infinitive suffixes,
usually *-o* or *-io*. The verb is thereafter conjugated according to the
Welsh system. For instance, 'bath' gives *bathio*, and as first person
plural present indicative *bathiwn*; 'type' gives *teipio* and *teipiwn*;
'bat' gives *batio* and in the third person singular past tense *batiodd*.
The almost exclusive use of *-o* or *-io* is due to the fact that it is the
most productive of the Welsh conversion suffixes. Sometimes, however, an English suffix is borrowed and attached to a native root, the
most common among these borrowed suffixes being *-ance* as in
dihidio > *dihidans*, 'indifferent > indifference'. But generally
speaking the suffixes are of Welsh origin attached to English roots:
glas-aid 'glassful', *bocs-aid* 'boxful'. The influence of the native Welsh
system on English importations is seen when an English loan word
forms its plural in the Welsh fashion by mutating the internal vowel;
for instance, English 'fork' gives Welsh *forc* (singular) > *ffyrc*
(plural). Similarly an English word in the plural may form its singular
in Welsh by the addition of a Welsh singular suffix *-yn* (masculine),
-en (feminine) as, for instance, English 'rags' > *rhacs* (plural) and
rhecsyn (singular) and English 'wheels' > the Welsh singular *whilsen*.

One of the most important features of Welsh syntax is the mutation of initial consonants, and English loanwords conform to this
feature where it is appropriate to the mutation paradigm. For instance, in a deck of cards 'king' and 'queen', which are borrowed in

their English forms, are mutated quite normally though a native speaker finds it rather strange: *fy nghing* and *fy nghwin, dy ging* and *dy gwin, ei ching* and *ei chwin*. This mutational paradigm operates even in the case of phonemes which are imported from English and which approximate only slightly to the initial phoneme governed by the rules of mutation. For instance, *tsain* 'chain' undergoes soft mutation *dy jain*; *tshalk* 'chalk' gives *dy jalk* largely because the /t/ component of the initial consonant in 'chain' and 'chalk' has to be emphasized in the Welsh attempt to pronounce the English phoneme. The Welsh accentual system also operates very powerfully to modify the pronunciation of English loans. The Welsh system is to accentuate the penultimate syllable and this produces for the English *'gooseberries'* > *gwsbéris* 'víolet' > *vióled*. Both elements in a compound noun may be loanwords as in English 'wáll-paper' > Welsh *papur-wál,* 'mátch-boxes' > *bocs-mátsys* 'cár-lamp' > *lamp-cár.* The word order is reversed to conform to Welsh custom and the pattern of the accents is also Welsh.

One effect of the English contact is to modify Welsh syntax by simplification, particularly by eliminating elements of syntatic redundancy. This form of simplification is not entirely due to English influence but it has certainly been facilitated by it as is suggested by the fact that many instances of such simplification have proceeded farther and more rapidly in the anglicised areas than elsewhere. The elements which are eliminated earliest are those which are alien to the English language. Native speakers of English tend to ignore initial consonantal mutation because it is not characteristic of their language. In anglicised areas therefore it tends to be ignored even by speakers of Welsh as a first language. For instance, 'in Port Talbot' would normally be expressed in Welsh as *ym Mhort Talbot* and 'in Cardiff' as *yng Nghaerdydd.* But in colloquial Welsh one hears these forms less frequently; instead, the preposition is followed by the radical consonant *-yn Port Talbot* and *yn Caerdydd.* Nothing much is lost in comprehension since the nasal mutation in such cases is largely redundant, the meaning being conveyed fully by the preposition. This is not the case with the use of the singular masculine and feminine possessive adjectives both of which are pronounced *ei.* However, the masculine governs the soft mutation, e.g. *pen* 'head', *ei ben* 'his head', and the feminine *ei* governs the aspirate mutation, *ei phen* 'her head'. There is no way of distinguishing these except by the use of the appropriate mutation.

5.4.4. *Phonology*

Compared with the extent of English influence on the grammar and the vocabulary of the Welsh language, English phonological influence has been limited though there are many instances of changes induced by contact with English. Borrowed words are pronounced according to the Welsh phonemic pattern, and the necessary approximations are highly predictable (Pilch 1957—58:223—241). It is interesting to note that the way in which some borrowed words were modified during the process of assimilation reflects the historical development of Welsh sounds. For instance, the initial semivocalic Welsh /w/ derives from the mutated form /-gw/ and when English words beginning with /w/ are borrowed, e.g., English 'wardrobe' and 'widow', they acquire the lost Welsh initial /g/ — *gwardrob* and *gwidw*.

English has also introduced some new phonemes into Welsh, for instance, the vocalic phoneme /aw/ as in the borrowed words 'lawn' and 'brawn' (Pilch 238), the initial phonemes/dz/ as in 'jug' > *djwg*, /z/ as in Welsh *zoo*, /ts/ as in 'chair' and 'churn', Welsh *tsain* and *tswrn*, and /dj/ as in 'John'. /dj/ in medial position as in 'engine', Welsh *indjan*, is also an importation. Apart from quite novel phonemes some original features of the Welsh system have been brought into new positions and some which have not been in very common use are now found to enter increasingly into Welsh speech. The following consonant clusters are examples of this development: *rp, lt, rd, ld, ls, rc, ns,* and *ts,* particularly at the end of a syllable, as in the borrowings Welsh *siarp* 'sharp', *belt* as in English, Welsh *meild* 'mild', Welsh *gard* 'guard', *ffals* 'false', *marc* 'mark', *siawns* 'chance', and *bats* as in English. English influence must also be held to account for the development of Welsh /chw/ into a voiceless /w/, e.g., *chwerw* 'bitter' > *werw* (Sommerfelt 1962:84). The incidence of the latter is closely related to anglicised areas of South Wales and is now creeping into the more intensely Welsh areas of North Wales.

Finally, there is the question of length and vowel quality. Length is not an independent phonemic feature of English vowels since it is closely interrelated with other qualities of the vowel. The differences between the pairs 'beat' and 'bit', 'pull' and 'pool', 'hard' and 'had' are not due to the length of the vowel simply but to its conjunction with other qualities. The situation is becoming very much the same in some of the southern Welsh dialects where the short vowels are usually more open and central than the long vowels (Watkins 1967:25).

5.4.5. *Stylistic Influences*
The English influence is more pervasive than can be described by
itemizing borrowings, loan translations, morphological modifications,
and changes in the disposition of existing phonemes or the introduction of new ones. We have already referred to the proliferation of
syntactic loan translations which, apart from anything else, has
helped to change the 'feel' of the Welsh language. This is experienced
even by the non-Welsh-speaking students of Welsh literature and has
been identified as going back as far as the classics of the seventeenth
century and the much earlier classics of Welsh narrative, *Pedeir Cainc
y Mabinogi* (see Lewis, ed. 1932). Later still the dissemination of
English periodical and journalistic literature especially in the industrial areas encouraged a tendency towards inflated circumlocu-
tion, polysyllabism, and vague abstractions foreign to traditional
Welsh literature. It must be admitted however that the 'preacher's
Welsh' to which we shall refer in the next section contributed to the
development of this characteristic. The net result, it has been
claimed, is to produce a tempo and rhythm in Welsh speech and
writing which is approximating more and more nearly to English.

A native speaker of English . . . has the strange but familiar
sensation of "having been here before" while reading Welsh
passages that he knows he is reading for the first time . . . Welsh
has undergone not only the usual process of taking over loan words
and translating many idiomatic expressions but also the less
obvious process of modifying its prose style on the basis of
rhythmic considerations accompanied by factors of rime and
assonance. Entire sentences can be translated into Welsh with the
accentual distribution of the English original preserved intact
(Ffowkes 1943:247).

5.4.6. *Incipient Diglossia*
Perhaps one of the most significant results of the changes we have
discussed and illustrated is the development of a situation where two
different variants of Welsh, 'high' and 'low', can be distinguished as
having different contexts of use. The grammar of the literary language was standardized before the end of the fifteenth century
though the orthography was still in dispute until very recently. This
standard literary language became the basis for the translation of the
Bible in 1588. Since it was standardized according to the Welsh of
the bards of the late medieval period the standard was already

archaic when it received the imprimatur of the Bible translation. Archaic though it was, it is this Welsh which became the standard of formal oral Welsh, for instance, in preaching by the popular orators who travelled throughout Wales in the late eighteenth century. Consequently, there have been a written standard and a formal oral standard (pulpit Welsh), both archaic. Meanwhile Welsh dialects have diverged increasingly from these standards partly under the influence of English. For instance, the final *-t* of the verbal and pronominal plural *y maent* 'they are' and *hwynt* 'they' has been eliminated from colloquial Welsh *-ma* and *nw* though it is still preserved in written standard and in formal spoken standard, for instance, in news broadcasts. Colloquial Welsh also makes constant and increasing use of periphrastic conjugations, for instance *yr wyf fi yn mynd* 'I am going', while the standard written and spoken forms employ the simple contracted forms such as *af, ei, a, awn, ewch, ant* 'I, you, he goes, we, you, they go'.

The disparity between dialectal colloquial Welsh was largely promoted by the enormous prestige which attached to literacy as the means of salvation in the eighteenth century and the neglect of colloquialism under the incubus of the prestige of 'preacher's Welsh'. Writers and Welsh academics 'placed so much emphasis on correctness and so much effort has been put into the attempt to conform to a standard of "purity" in writing that those who have not followed higher academic courses in schools and colleges fear to use the language either in writing or speech' (Welsh Joint Education Committee 1965:6). Until very recently, therefore, the cultivation of a live oral standard has been ignored while at the same time the population movements we have described, bringing together men and women from different dialect areas, made it ever more necessary. One result of the failure to produce such a live standard was that when Welshmen speaking different dialects met they turned to their common if inadequate command of English. The decline in the prestige and influence of the preacher-orator as well as diminishing congregations made the archaic spoken standard less and less relevant. A third reason for the growing need for a live oral standard has been the fact that for more than half of those who are able to speak some Welsh the dialect differences are meaningless since they learn the language in school as their second tongue. Finally, the shift in emphasis towards an oral approach to language learning, whether as a first or second language, and the need (for economic and other reasons) to ensure that the materials used in the oral approach have a national currency, make it necessary to produce a live oral standard capable of being used by teachers brought up in one dialect area but teaching in a very different one. The aim of the new movement is 'not to undermine the local dialects but to suggest oral standards which will be acceptable everywhere in Wales . . . At the same time standard oral forms are related as closely as possible to literary standard Welsh provided the latter is contemporary and alive' (Welsh Joint Education Committee 1965:8). Such an insistence has been forced upon Welsh linguists and teachers because of their awareness of the gap between, on the one hand, the archaic literary and spoken standards used for formal and certainly for religious purposes and, on the other, the several increasingly anglicised dialects used on less formal, intimate, and workday occasions only. Those who could command and use only such dialects refused to attempt to communicate in the standard form simply because they were not conversant with its characteristic features.

Other measures which the urgent awareness of the disruptive effect of English has brought about are the adoption of a standard orthography and the expansion and enrichment of the vocabulary to meet the needs of contemporary society. When the grammar of the language was standardized its orthography was left in disarray, thus creating an area of considerable uncertainty. The efforts of those who wrote the dictionary during the seventeenth and eighteenth centuries and later were directed as much as anything at promoting their views concerning orthography (Morgan 1966:2–18). Some of these were not only personal but highly idiosyncratic. After many false starts some agreement was reached with the *Report of the Orthographic Committee of the Society for Utilizing the Welsh Language* in 1893 (edited by Morris-Jones). Though the suggestions of the *Report* were not implemented with any great enthusiasm by the majority of writers it did form the basis for all subsequent discussions within the University of Wales and at Oxford University, where the Celticist Sir John Rhys exercised considerable influence. In 1928 the University Board of Celtic Studies published its *Orgraff yr Iaith Gymraeg* [Orthography of the Welsh Language] (edited by H. Lewis). This, with some slight modifications, is the basis for the standard orthography for Welsh.

The dictionary writers were also concerned with extending the vocabulary and in this they were continuing the interest of Welsh linguists since the Renaissance. As early as the fourteenth century complaints were being made about the paucity of Welsh words 'for the purposes of the new philosophy and civilization. For this reason there must be a search for new words where Welsh is deficient' (Trefor 1544:45). At the same time other complaints were being made that English words and words from Latin were being used to excess (E. J. Jones 43). In the middle of the eighteenth century attempts were being made to extend the vocabulary in specialized areas without recourse to English. 'You must make your *cregyn* [shells] Welsh names if they have none . . . You must give them Welsh names. I'll send you a catalogue of the English names of some sales here . . . and it is an easy matter to invent new names, and I warrant they will be as well received as Latin or Greek names. Tell them they are old Celtic names, that is enough' (Morris 1755). The efforts of dictionary writers of later times have been supplemented in this century by the work of the University of Wales and the Welsh Department of the Ministry of Education in publishing lexicons for use in disciplines such as linguistics, phonetics, philosophy, music, chemistry, physics, and mathematics (*Termau Technegol* 1950).

6. CONCLUSIONS

This study has attempted to set out the relation of demographic factors and more especially aspects of migration changes in the status and the characteristics of Welsh. 'Demographic characteristics . . . are seldom treated as independent variables . . . and their effects in various combinations . . . have never been explored' (Hawley 1956:380). Though this is a somewhat sweeping statement it contains a large element of truth. For this reason an attempt has been made to identify some of the features of the process of migration in Wales from the middle of the last century to the present. Three aspects of migration as an independent variable have been described: the speed, the size, and the differences in origin of the migration flow. Several of the generalizations which have been made concerning migration have been illustrated, for instance, Zipf's (1949) that 'the rate of in-migration to a central point from each of several other points lying at a distance tends to vary inversely with the distance'. This generalization is particularly appropriate to Wales since it helps to explain the distinction between, on the one hand, the first, 'short-distance' and constructive phase of immigration from the Welsh-speaking areas into Glamorgan, and, on the other, the second, 'long-distance', destructive phase of emigration from England.

Though it has been desirable and necessary to examine in detail the characteristics of migration as an independent variable, there has been one main interest: investigation of the consequences of those characteristics. The composition of the population of Wales in both urban and rural areas has been modified especially with respect to the proportion of native- and nonnative-born, the proportion represented in different age groups, and to some extent in an imbalance between the sexes. But the major change in the composition of the population has had to do with language. Most important is that after about eight centuries of adverse English influence but only very gradual fall in the demographic status of Welsh, from the middle of the last century the language has declined precipitously. This decline has affected the numbers who claim to be able to speak Welsh, and the strength of the affiliation of those who do claim it, in the sense that among children of school age, those for whom it is the second language are nearly as numerous as those for whom it is the mother tongue. A third aspect of the decline is the continuous limitation of the range of its uses both institutionally and interpersonally.

The effect of the way in which migration, industrialization, and urbanization have affected the Welsh language is also found in several forms of 'polarization' between the Welsh- and non-Welsh-speaking groups. Primarily there is polarization of age groups, only the very young and the old in rural areas and only the old in urban areas tending to maintain the language. There is polarization between the predominantly agricultural counties with relatively high intensity but low proportionate representation of Welsh speech, and the industrial counties with very high proportions of the total of Welsh speakers but diffused very thinly among the mass of the population. This has led to a third form of polarization, namely, different concepts of what the Welsh language represents. In the populations of the high intensity and rural areas it is maintained not simply as a necessary means of communication but as a symbol of an ethnic, folk, and traditional culture. In the low-intensity industrial areas the Welsh language is maintained as part of an 'urban' consciousness and of a modern 'civic' culture which is little different in its essence from the broad sweep of Anglo-Saxon or even western consciousness. If it is to be maintained within this urban consciousness the Welsh language has to adjust itself to new demands. Contrary to the traditional folk culture still maintained in the area of high intensity of Welsh speech, the urban speaker of Welsh is brought up in a mixed and often in a highly mobile cosmopolitan community.

It is therefore not surprising that polarization of the conceptual bases of maintaining Welsh is accompanied by a polarization of the degree to which speakers are committed to its maintenance. The attitude toward either language is a reflection of attitude toward both — neither is unequivocal. As far as speakers of Welsh are concerned the effect of the awareness of the impact of English is to harden the attitude of resistance to a major threat, or conversely, to be disillusioned. There are few neutral or indifferent responses. As far as the English are concerned awareness of Welsh, since it implies no threat, induces an attitude of tolerance or at least of acquiescence. At the same time this tolerance is expressed in a theoretical acceptance of the need to maintain Welsh and seldom in a willingness to put the tolerance into effect. Even when practical use is made of the language, generally speaking this is not extended to areas which are regarded as central to economic life and social advancement. Because of this discrepancy between expressed attitude toward and actual use of the language, polarization between individuals and between groups is accompanied by inconsistency within the individuals themselves.

As the decline of the language continues the hardening of the attitude of the minority is aggravated and the distance between them and the theoretically acquiescent but actually indifferent majority is increased. This has led to increased frustration expressed in illegal activities, physical violence, and disruption of social life.

BIBLIOGRAPHY

Aellen, C., and W. E. Lambert
  1963 'Ethnic Identification and Personality Adjustments of Canadian Adolescents of Mixed English-French Parentage', mimeographed (McGill University).
Bowen, E. G., editor
  1957 *Wales: A Physical, Historical and Regional Geography* (London, Methuen).
  1801 - *Census of England and Wales,* Registrar General (London: H.M.S.O.).
  1971 [Reports on the census were issued decenially except in 1941. Reports on *The Language Spoken in Wales and Monmouthshire* were issued separately from 1881 onwards.]
Central Advisory Council for Education (Wales)
  1953 *The Place of Welsh and English in the Schools of Wales,* E. Glyn Lewis, editor (London, H.M.S.O.).

348   Glyn Lewis

Chadwick, N. K.
    1963 'The British or Celtic Part of the Population of England', in *Angles and Britons*, H. Lewis, editor (Cardiff, University of Wales Press).
Commission of Enquiry into the State of Education in Wales
    1847 *Commission of Enquiry into the State of Education in Wales, Report* (London, H.M.S.O.).
Commission on the State of the Mining Population
    1846- *Commission on the State of the Mining Population. Report* (London,
    1854   H.M.S.O.).
Commission of Enquiry into the State of Popular Education in England and Wales
    1858 *Commission of Enquiry into the State of Popular Education in England and Wales. Report* (London, H.M.S.O.). [Volume II was published in 1861.]
Commission (Royal) on Education in England and Wales
    1886- *Commission (Royal) on Education in England and Wales. Report* (Lon-
    1887   don, H.M.S.O.).
Commission of Enquiry into Industrial Unrest
    1817 *Commission of Enquiry into Industrial Unrest. Report* (London, H.M.S.O.).
Committee of the Privy Council on Education
    1840 *Committee of the Privy Council on Education, Report* (London, H.M.S.O.). [Reports were issued annually from 1840. The Committee was the forerunner of the Board of Education, which later became the Ministry.]
Council for Wales and Monmouthshire
    1963 *Report on the Welsh Language Today* (London, H.M.S.O.).
Davies, E. T.
    1957 *Monmouthshire Schools and Education to 1870* (Newport, Argus).
Davies, Rhys
    1945 *Selected Stories* (London, Heineman).
Edwards, J.
    1651 Introduction to Bishop Fisher, *The Marrow of Divinity* (London, no publisher).
Ffowkes, R. A.
    1940 'English Idiom in Welsh', *Word* 1.3.:239–248.
    1943 'Prosody in the Influence of English on Welsh', *Word* 4.1.:37–41.
Filip, J.
    1960 *Keltsa Civilisace a Jeji Dedictivi* [Celtic Civilization and its Heritage] (Prague, Czechoslovak Academy of Science).
Friedlander, D., and D. J. Roshier
    1966 'A Study of Internal Migration in England and Wales. Parts 1 and 2', *Population Studies* 19–20:239–80, 45–59.
Hauser, P. M., and Dudley Duncan, eds.
    1959 *The Study of Population* (Chicago, Chicago University Press).
Hawley, A. H.
    1959 'Population Composition', in *The Study of Population*, P. M. Hauser and D. Duncan, editors (University of Chicago Press) pp. 376–383.

Jackson, K.
1953 *Language and History in Early Britain* (Edinburgh, University of Edinburgh Press).
Jenkins, J.
1861 'Report on the State of Popular Education in the Welsh Districts of North Wales, Neath and Merthyr Tydfil in South Wales', in *Commission of Enquiry . . .* 1858, volume II, Appendix.
John, A. H.
1960 *The Industrial Development of South Wales, 1750—1850* (Cardiff, University of Wales Press).
Jones, E. J.
1956 'Lladin a'r Famiaith yng nghynod y Dadeni' [Latin and the Mother-Tongue in the Renaissance] *Llen Cymru* 9:40—45 (Cardiff).
Lewis, E. Glyn
1972 *Multilingualism in the Soviet Union* (The Hague, Mouton).
Lewis, E. Glyn, and G. F. Peaker
1963 'Reading Ability in English and Welsh', unpublished mimeograph (Cardiff, Ministry of Education and Science).
Lewis, H. editor
1928 *Orgraff yr Iaith Gymraeg* [The Orthography of Welsh] *Report of the Literature Committee of the Board of Celtic Studies of the University of Wales* (Cardiff, University of Wales Press).
1932 *Pedeir Ceinc y Mabinogi* (Cardiff, University of Wales Press).
Moore, W. E.
1959 'Sociology and Demography', in *The Study of Population*, P. M. Hauser and Dudley Duncan, editors (Chicago, University of Chicago Press).
Morgan, T. J.
1966 'Geiriadurwyr y Ddeunawfed Garnif' [Lexicologists of the Eighteenth Century] *Llen Cymru* 9:3—18 (Cardiff).
Morris, Lewis
1755 Quoted. in T. J. Morgan, 'Geiriadurwyr y Ddeunawfed Ganrif' [Lexicologists of the Eighteenth Century], *Llen Cymru* 9(1966):3—18 (Cardiff).
Morris-Jones, J.
1893 *Welsh Orthography: Report of the Orthographical Committee of the Society for Utilizing the Welsh Language* (Caernarvon, Welsh Press Co.).
Parry-Williams, T. H.
1923 *The English Element in Welsh* (= *Cymmrodorion Record Series* X) (London, The Honorable Society of the Cymmrodorion).
1963 'English and Welsh Loan Words', in *Angles and Britons*, H. Lewis, editor (Cardiff, University of Wales Press).
Phillips, Thomas
1849 *Wales: The Language, Social Condition, Moral Character and Religious Opinions of the People* (London, Evans).
Pilch, H.
1956 'Le Bilinguisme au Pays de Galles', in *Miscelenea homenage a Andre Martinet*, volume I (La Laguna de Tenerife, Canary Islands).

Pokshishevskiy, V. V.
1971 'Urbanization and Ethnographic Processes' [in Russian], in *Problemy Urbanisatsii* (Moscow, Moscow State University) pp. 53–62.

Ravenstein, E. G.
1879 'On the Celtic Languages in the British Isles', *Journal of the Royal Statistical Society* 42:579–636 (London).
1885 'The Laws of Migration', *Journal of the Royal Statistical Society*, New series 19:167–227 (London).

Roberts, G.
1969 *Aspects of Welsh History* (Cardiff, University of Wales Press).

Salesbury, W.
1547 *Oll Synnwyr Penn Kymbro* [The Wisdom of the Welsh] (London, no publisher).

Sharp, D., et al.
1973 *Some Aspects of Welsh and English: A Survey in the Schools of Wales* (London, Macmillan).

Sommerfelt, Alf
1962 *Diachronic and Synchronic Aspects of Language* (Oslo, Oslo University Press).
1950 *Termau Technegol* [Technical Terms] (Cardiff, University of Wales Press).

Thomas, B.
1930 'The Migration of Labour into the Glamorganshire Coalfield', *Economica* 10:275–292 (London).
1967 *The Welsh Economy: Studies in Expansion* (Cardiff, University of Wales Press).

Thomas, Dorothy S.
1938 *Research Memorandum on Migration Differentials* (New York, no publisher).

Tremenheere, S.
1840 'Report on the State of Elementary Education in the Mining Districts of South Wales', Appendix II of *Committee of the Privy Council on Education. Report* 1840 (London, H.M.S.O.).

Trefor, Bishop
1544 *Continuatio Eulogii.* Quoted in E. J. Jones, 'Lladin a'r Famiaith yng nghyfnod y Dadeni' [Latin and the Mother Tongue in the Renaissance], *Llen Cymru* 9(1966):40–45 (Cardiff).

Watkins, A.
1967 *Ieithyddiaeth* [Linguistics]. (Cardiff, University of Wales Press).

Welsh Joint Education Committee
1961 *Language Survey* (Cardiff, Welsh Joint Education Committee).
1965 *Cymraeg Byw* [Living Welsh] (Cardiff, University of Wales Press).

Williams, David
1950 *A History of Modern Wales* (London, Methuen).

Williams, D. T.
1934 'Gower: A Study in Linguistic Movements and Historical Geography', *Archeologica Cambrensis* 89:302–327 (London).
1935 'Linguistic Divides in South Wales', *Archeologica Cambrensis* 90:239–260 (London).

1936 'Linguistic Divides in North Wales', *Archeologica Cambrensis* 91:194–209 (London).
Williams, Glanmor
1967 *The Welsh Church from Conquest to Reformation* (Cardiff, University of Wales Press).
1970 'Language, Literacy and Nationality in Wales', *The Welsh History Review* 9:1–16 (Cardiff).
Williams, W. O.
1964 'The Survival of the Welsh Language After the Union of England and Wales: The First Phase', *The Welsh History Review* 2:67–93 (Cardiff).
Zipf, G. K.
1949 *Human Behaviour and the Principle of Least Effort* (Cambridge, Mass., Addison-Wesley).

NOTES

This article was researched and partly written while I was Co-Director, Languages Research Project, Department of Education, University of Wales, Swansea. Published for the first time in this volume.

1. The status of Monmouthshire has been ambiguous for many centuries. Geographically it has always been included within the borders of Wales. Administratively it has seemed to exist in a kind of legal limbo so that it was customary to speak of 'Wales and Monmouthshire'.
2. The process is to analyze and compare the numbers in each category of language competence (Welsh only, English and Welsh, etc.) at various ages in 1921 with the survivors of the corresponding category enumerated at ages ten years younger, in 1911, taking into account as far as possible the general bases for surviving (that is, as regards mortality and migration) experienced by the total population in the same age groups.
3. The number recorded as speaking Welsh only in the groups aged 5 to 10 and 10 to 15 in 1911 are 26,200 and 14,500, respectively, or nearly 41,000 in all (*Census of England and Wales* 1911, vol. XII, *Language Spoken in Wales and Monmouthshire* published in 1913).
4. The school investigation was designed by D. Sharp, E. Price and myself. The field work and the report on school children are the responsibility of Sharp and Price. Some of the conclusions stated here differ from theirs. The project was sponsored by the Schools Council. (Sharp, *et al.* 1973).
5. Although the Russian language is being taught to many millions of non-Russian Soviet children as a second language it will be a long time before there are fewer students acquiring it as their mother-tongue. Moreover, though the Russian language is taught as a second language in non-Russian Union Republics it is not native to any of those republics. The situation in the Republic of Ireland is comparable to Wales but the administration and the education experts insist that Irish should be taught as the first national language.

Issues and Trends in Frisian Bilingualism

INTRODUCTION

Friesland is one of the eleven provinces of the Netherlands and is situated in the northeastern part of the country. This region is populated by approximately 550,000 people or about 4% of the total population of the Netherlands. Although Friesland is known abroad primarily for its cheese, cows, and seed-potatoes, it has, particularly since World War II, lost its pronounced agricultural character; there has been considerable development in industry and services since that time. The largest city, and the capital of Friesland, is Leeuwarden (*Ljouwert* in Frisian), which has approximately 85,000 inhabitants.

Old Friesland covered a much larger area than the province discussed in this article. For two thousand years Frisians lived along parts of the North Sea coast, once — according to tradition — 'united' in the Seven Free Frisian Sealands. Historians remark that a notable trait of the old Frisians was a love of freedom, however that original freedom has been lost: in the northwestern part of the Netherlands, West Friesland (see Map I) has become more and more Dutch, and in Germany the North and especially the East Frisians have for the most part been absorbed by the Germans.

The Friesland discussed here became part of the Republic of the Netherlands in the sixteenth century. After the Napoleonic period Friesland lost its stadtholder house, its admiralty, its university, and its legislature. At that time Friesland became what it is today: a province of the Dutch state.

The Frisian language has been able to survive into modern times, but certainly not without some difficulty. Friesland became a Dutch province with Dutch as the main language of government, church, and education. But the Frisian language was able to withstand the pressure and Friesland is now a bilingual province: everyone understands and speaks Dutch but most of the population also understand and speak Frisian.

As in many bilingual areas the interaction between the two languages and cultures is not always harmonious. Large-scale conflicts are certainly not characteristic of the Frisian situation, although Frisian is continually a subject of dispute. Compared to Basque, French-Canadian, or Croatian standards these are only small skirmishes, but there are numerous examples of non-violent incidents concerning the Frisian language. Editorial remarks and letters-to-the-editor about the use of Frisian in education, about its use in giving street names, or about the status of Frisian in general appear almost weekly in the daily newspapers. Frisian is often the subject of discussion in the provincial and municipal legislatures. The Frisian Movement, the Frisian National Party, and the language-oriented magazines and demonstrations are but a few indications of concern and activity. Some years ago *Kneppelfreed* (rioters' Friday) took place: as a result of a trial in which the Frisian language was at stake, police and demonstrators were involved in a violent confrontation. Outside the provincial borders, i.e., in the rest of the Netherlands, one notices the Frisian problem much less, perhaps no more than the incidental discussions in the Dutch parliament and the commentaries on the radio and television or in the national newspapers about Frisian matters. All of this, however, is enough to help the Dutch realize that something is happening to the Frisians and their language. The Dutch ministers and parliament are beginning to reach some necessary conclusions as a result of recognizing Frisian as a second Dutch language and in various language matters government subsidies have been provided. This support is indispensable, for in an age such as ours, with its growth and expansion in practically every field, a small language area such as Frisian must be strong in order to survive, let alone grow.

This article deals mainly with the present language situation in bilingual Friesland and aims at discussing the following four subjects: (1) past and present in a nutshell; (2) the language situation in Friesland; (3) language ideology in Friesland; (4) from diglossia to ambilingualism.

1. PAST AND PRESENT IN A NUTSHELL

1.1. *Where Did Frisian Originate?*

It is thought that all the European languages except Basque, Finnish, Hungarian, and a few others have one proto-language in common, Indo-European. As we have no written sources for this language it must be considered a hypothetical language. According to the family tree theory, such language groups as Romance (e.g., French, Rumanian), Celtic (e.g., Gaelic, Breton), Greek, Sanskrit, and Teutonic (e.g., English, Danish, Dutch, Frisian and German) were derived from the Indo-European base language. During the first century A.D. Old German or Teutonic is thought to have been spoken in the northwestern part of Europe. The term Teutonic must be considered as general name for a group of languages which were at the time very closely related: they soon dissolved into an East Teutonic group (the only remains of which is a Biblical translation in Gothic), a North Teutonic group (Norwegian, Danish, Swedish, Icelandic) and a West Teutonic group. This last group includes German and Frankish on the one hand and Anglo-Saxon, Old-Saxon, and Frisian on the other. The latter group is termed North Sea Teutonic or Ingveonic; around 500 A.D. it was spoken along the North Sea coastline all the way from Dunkirk to the Danish coast.

After the invasion of Britain by the Angles and Saxons this language was also spoken in England. Thus Ingveons, also a hypothetical language, was spoken by Frisians, Anglo-Saxons, and Old Saxons (Saxons who had remained in Germany). Old Saxon as such has disappeared, old Frisian finally developed into modern Frisian, and English originated from Anglo-Saxon (together with the Norman contribution of French and Latin elements), thus explaining the close relationship between Frisian and English.

1.2. *Frisian Dialects*

As has already been mentioned, the Frisian region used to be much larger than it is now. Various place names remind us of this fact: in the northwest Netherlands we find a region called West Friesland and in Germany we find regions called North Friesland and East Friesland.

A number of Frisian dialects are still spoken in *North Friesland* (situated north of Hamburg and south of the Danish border), but, due to dialect differences, communication between the speakers of the various dialects is difficult. Moreover, these dialects are constantly being eroded by High and Low German. Frisian dialects are also found on the islands off the coast (Sylt and Föhr-Amrum), but Frisian is in a difficult situation there, as it is on Helgoland, the famous North Frisian tourist island.

East Friesland lies to the east of the Dutch border. The original Frisian language slowly died out there after the Middle Ages; during the twentieth century it died out on the islands off the coast of East Friesland. Two thousand speakers of East Frisian can be found in Saterland, south of the actual East Frisian area. Although there is an ample amount of linguistic literature concerning both North and East Frisian, little is written in the languages themselves nowadays (however there is a limited amount of nineteenth- and twentieth-century literature in North Frisian).

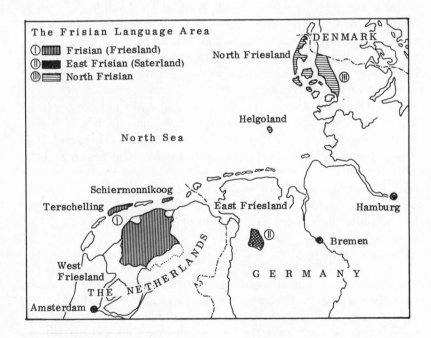

Map. I. *Frisian is Spoken in Some Areas of the Netherlands and Germany. This Article Deals with Area I (Friesland).*

Frisian has not been spoken in *West Friesland,* or for that matter in the entire part of the province of North Holland north of Amsterdam, for several centuries. It probably died out there as the main language at the end of the Middle Ages; there are no written sources for West Frisian at all. The same is true for Frisian in the province of Groningen, situated east of Friesland. The process in which Frisian was gradually exchanged for a Saxon dialect in Groningen began during the Middle Ages.

However, the Frisian language has been able to survive surprisingly well in the province of *Friesland.* The strengths and weaknesses of the position of the Frisian language there will be described as accurately as possible in section 2.

There are a number of dialect variants within the borders of the province of Friesland, for example, the island dialects of Schiermonnikoog (which shows a completely independent development from Old Frisian), of Terschelling, and of the town of Hindelopen, which has its own special dialect differing from standard Frisian not so much in vocabulary and syntax as in phonology. Language mixing (Frisian with Dutch) is found in a number of larger towns and in part of northwestern Friesland. So-called *Stadsfries* ('Town Frisian') is characterized by Frisian syntax and articulation and an ever-increasing Dutch vocabulary. Although everyone understands and speaks Dutch in Friesland, Frisian is almost always spoken in the rural areas, in the villages, and in smaller cities. In the larger cities the main language may be *Stadsfries,* Dutch, or Frisian.

1.3. *Other Languages in Friesland*

Until the sixteenth century Frisian was both the language of the people and of the government. However, even before 1500 Old Frisian ceased to be the only language in this region. From written sources it is apparent that Latin, for instance, was of great influence during the Middle Ages: it was the language of the church, of scholars, and of literature. The influence of Low German should also be mentioned here because it was the *lingua franca* for trade in northwestern Europe and reached its zenith in the heyday of the Hanseatic League, in the fifteenth century. In Friesland at that time, Dutch, Latin, and Frisian charters appeared side by side. After the Middle Ages French exercised some influence in Friesland as the language of the stadtholder's court and of nobility, but after the defeat of Napoleon and the incorporation of Friesland into the

Kingdom of the Netherlands, Friesland lost its stadtholder house and with it went the French influence for the most part.

Dutch has left an indelible mark on language usage in Friesland. In the course of the sixteenth century Dutch replaced Frisian as the language of the courts of law and of the government. The tradition of the Old Frisian charters and articles of law disappeared in the 1500s and shortly thereafter the use of Frisian in writing letters greatly decreased, which dealt a heavy blow to the tradition of writing in Frisian.

Dutch became the language of the churches as well, obtaining a permanent foothold during the Reformation and with the official translation of the Bible into Dutch in 1618. Dutch was virtually the only language used in the churches for three centuries thereafter.

It is a miracle that Frisian did not die out completely at that time, considering that Dutch was the main language of government, the courts, and the churches, not to mention education. Probably the seventeenth-century Frisian Renaissance poet Gysbert Japiks was partially responsible for the continuation of the Frisian language. His *Rymlerije,* published in 1668, used the literary genres of that time at an accomplished level and thus raised Frisian above the level of a dialect in the eyes of Frisians and Dutchmen alike.

The influence of Frisian again increased after 1800, partially due to the growth of Romanticism. This increased influence found its expression in literature and especially in campaigns and organizations which promoted all things Frisian. In the twentieth century this resulted in the recognition of Frisian as a second language in the Netherlands. Frisian has also recently been used on a large scale as the language of officialdom, but much more remains to be achieved.

1.4. *Goals of the Frisian Movement*

The organized Frisian Movement dates from the nineteenth century. In 1844 the 'Selskip foar Fryske Tael- en Skriftekennisse' was established, followed for seventy-five years thereafter by a multitude of organizations which, in some way or another, incorporated the battle for the maintenance and expansion of the Frisian language into their programs. The goals of the Frisian Movement as they are described by the 'Ried fan de Fryske Biweging' (the coordinative organization of many Frisian organizations) cover a larger area than only the language. Many political, economic, and social initiatives have been realized in Friesland in the course of the years with the 'Ried' leading the way, but maintenance of the Frisian language is still the main goal.

Many aims of the Frisian Movement have been achieved in the last decades: for instance, in 1915 the first church service in Frisian was conducted; in 1943 the Frisian translation of the Bible was completed, followed in 1955 by a Frisian Psalm and song book. A new ecumenical translation of the Bible, on which Protestants, Catholics, and others are working together, is now in the making and is expected to be ready for publication in 1976. It has undoubtedly been a great handicap for the development of the Frisian language that the Frisian Bible appeared so late (compared, for instance, to the Welsh Bible which was translated into Welsh in 1588) for as was already mentioned, Dutch was the main language of the Frisian churches for three centuries.

Of primary importance for the status of Frisian is not only the increasing use of the language in the provincial and municipal legislatures but also the subsidies received from the Frisian provincial government for the attainment of many Frisian language goals. The Dutch government is also, though hesitatingly, beginning to recognize its fiscal co-responsibility for Frisian.

In 1955 the Dutch parliament resolved to permit the oral use of Frisian in the courts of Friesland but the written use of Frisian in legal matters is still prohibited. Above all the establishment in 1938 of the Frisian Academy as a center for Frisian academic research has been of great importance for the stimulation of the language.

1.5. Education and Frisian

Dutch has been the main language in education in Friesland for the past centuries. During this century the Frisian Movement has been especially active in promoting the use of Frisian in education. In 1907 Frisian was allocated a position in education but the (optional) study of it had to take place outside the normal school curriculum. In the 1920s and 1930s Frisians fought zealously for acceptance of their language in schools in Friesland. Some progress was made in 1937 when a clause was included in the Dutch elementary school law which stated that lessons could be given optionally in elementary school in a 'regional language which was spoken alongside Dutch'. Frisian was not mentioned by name but an opportunity had been created for introducing it as a school subject.

In 1950 experiments began in nine elementary schools using

Frisian *as the language medium in the lower classes* with Dutch being taught as a subject. For pedagogical and psychological reasons it was assumed that it was a matter of primary importance for the child to receive his education in his native tongue. In 1955 these bilingual schools were fully recognized, and in 1959 the Office of Pedagogic Advice was set up to provide guidelines for bilingual schools. About seventy schools are now utilizing the clause in the 1955 law. The plans which have been made in the last few years for more flexible types of education for bilingual children certainly open new perspectives for education in Friesland.

The option provided in the 1937 law offering Frisian in the higher classes of the elementary schools (which usually amounted to one hour of Frisian a week in the fourth, fifth, and sixth grades) remained, because of its optional character, a temporary solution. Nonetheless more than half of the elementary schools now offer Frisian. The constant campaigns to make Frisian an obligatory subject at the elementary school level achieved their aim in 1972 when the Dutch government decided that, beginning probably in 1980, Frisian would become an obligatory subject in all Frisian schools.

At the secondary school level Frisian is still an optional subject. It only recently became possible to choose Frisian as an elective subject in the curriculi preparing students for the Dutch secondary school examinations (M.A.V.O., H.A.V.O., and V.W.O.).

Frisian is taught at several universities in the Netherlands: there are professorships in Frisian at the Free University in Amsterdam and at the State University in Groningen and special professorships (emanating from the Provincial Council of Education for Friesland) exist at Amsterdam Municipal University and at the State Universities in Leiden and in Utrecht.

Outside the Netherlands there is special interest in North Frisian in Kiel University and Copenhagen University and special attention is given to Old Frisian (Frisian up to about 1550) at several other foreign universities. Old Frisian has been of great importance for the study of Frisian at the university level, in fact, the study of Frisian was first approached via Old Frisian. Because the Old Frisian sources mainly consist of codes of law, jurists as well as linguists have been and continue to be highly interested in Old Frisian.

Lastly, we must add that many people have been introduced to Frisian language and culture in the last twenty years by special language courses (Frisian for non-Frisians and Frisian for speakers of the language) offered outside the schools and universities.

2. THE LANGUAGE SITUATION IN FRIESLAND

2.1. *Research*

There has been a great demand for precise data about the language situation in Friesland especially during the past ten years: how many people actually speak Frisian, can everyone understand this language, who reads Frisian books, and how many people can write Frisian? It had always been necessary to make do with estimates and that gave both the pro-Frisians and anti-Frisians ample scope to maintain their own suppositions about the language situation in Friesland. The provincial government as well as several Frisian organizations needed concrete data to assist them in policy-making and in spreading information about Friesland outside the province. Therefore in 1969 the Frisian Academy sponsored a report describing the reading and speech habits and attitudes of Frisians with regard to their language. In 1967 a representative sample was taken comprising 800 inhabitants of the province. The data were gathered by some twenty pollsters by means of an exhaustive questionnaire (the sampling method was two-stage: first eleven municipalities were chosen and then the persons to be questioned were selected by the systematic sampling method. The data were processed by the State University of Groningen Computer Center).

This section reviews some of the data of the report in order to clarify the role of Frisian (and Dutch) in Friesland. In the following discussion 'Frisians' refers to the inhabitants of Friesland (autochthons as well as allochthons). The data refer to 800 Frisians aged twelve years or older and, within the limits of sampling accuracy, are valid for the entire Frisian population aged twelve years or older (Pietersen 1969).

2.2. *Who Speaks Frisian and Where?*

A distinction must be made between the various situations in which Frisian is used as the spoken language because the language situation in the family, on the street, in the office, on official occasions, can be quite different: some Frisians speak mostly Frisian at home but seldom or never speak a word of Frisian at work, but among others Frisian is spoken outside the home and Dutch is spoken at home. Thus language usage is rather complicated and for the sake of clarity we will describe the situation in four domains: language spoken in the home, at the door (to tradesmen, etc.), in the shops, and to notables (i.e., the doctor, the minister, etc.). In this way we can immediately see in which domains Frisian is the strongest or whether the influence of Frisian differs from one domain to the next. If, together with Frisian, we include Dutch, Town Frisian, and the other dialects in this analysis, we can get a fairly good impression of Friesland's language constellation.

1. *Which language is spoken in the home.* Frisian is the language most often spoken in Frisian homes, as the following list illustrates.

Dutch	13%
Town Frisian	8%
Dialects	8%
Frisian	71%

Thus Frisian has a rather secure position as the main language at home. It is also clear that the century-long penetration of the national language (Dutch) through government, church, education, and communications media has resulted in only a rather marginal Dutch language influence in the home. It is perhaps interesting to examine home language usage among several more specific groups of Frisians. For the sake of convenience only the percentages for Dutch and Frisian will be given. First, the percentages for home language usage among the autochthons and allochthons:

	Autochthons	Allochthons
Dutch	6%	62%
Frisian	78%	16%

Certainly what is most striking in these figures is that 16% of the allochthons speak Frisian at home while only 6% of the authochtons speak Dutch at home.

What is the language usage pattern in the country compared with in the city (in this investigation a 'city' has at least 20,000 inhabitants).

	Country	City
Dutch	7%	25%
Frisian	81%	49%

Although Frisian is particularly strong in the country, it is also fairly strong in the cities: 49% of the inhabitants of cities speak Frisian at home. In the capital, Leeuwarden, Frisian assumes a less favorable position: 29% of the inhabitants speak Frisian at home. (It must be mentioned, however, that Town Frisian is spoken in most of the homes of Leeuwarden.)

Lastly a comparison of language usage in the home between people with little education and people with more education:

	Elementary school	Higher forms of education
Dutch	5%	56%
Frisian	75%	39%

The more education a person has had the less likely he is to use Frisian at home.

2. *Which language is spoken at the door.* What does one speak to tradesmen at the door? Is it correct to assume that the national language, Dutch, is spoken more often as soon as one is outside the family circle? The data indicate that this is the case.

	At the door	(In the home)
Dutch	22%	(13%)
Town Frisian + dialects	10%	(16%)
Frisian	68%	(71%)

The percentages for in-the-home language usage are included here for quick comparison of in-the-home and at-the-door language usage. Dutch usage increases from 13% to 22% while Frisian usage decreases slightly.

It should be mentioned that 8% of the people who *do not* speak Frisian at home *do* speak it at the door. This situation is not abnormal in areas where only Frisian is spoken.

3. *Which language is spoken in the shops.* The role of Dutch in the shops is even more important: the percentage of those who speak Frisian decreases again, as the data show.

	In the shops	(In the home)
Dutch	29%	(13%)
Town-Frisian + dialects	8%	(16%)
Frisian	62%	(71%)

Frisian, Town Frisian, and the dialects lose some of their prominence with consequent gains for the national language. Nonetheless the situation for Frisian is not unfavorable.

4. *Which language is spoken to notables?* As the data show, language usage changes again when Frisians come into contact with so-called notables (the doctor, the minister or pastor, the notary public, the director of a factory, etc.):

	To notables	(In the home)
Dutch	54%	(13%)
Town Frisian + dialects	4%	(16%)
Frisian	42%	(71%)

More than half of all Frisians use Dutch when communicating with people on a higher rung on the social ladder. Outside the home Frisian, Town Frisian, and the dialects lose ground rapidly. To show clearly how Frisian decreases and Dutch increases in importance outside the home, the data above are presented in Table I.

Table I. *Language Usage Among Frisians Aged Twelve Years or Older in Four Different Domains*

	Dutch	Town Frisian + dialects	Frisian
At home	13%	16%	71%
At the door	22%	10%	68%
In the shops	29%	8%	62%
To notables	54%	4%	42%

It is easy to draw several conclusions from Table I: Dutch does not assume a strong position in the home but outside the home it grows steadily in importance culminating in the situation of speaking to notables (growing from 13% to 54%, a 412% or fourfold increase in importance). Conversely, Frisian loses ground (from 71% in the home to 42% when speaking to notables).

This shift in language usage is of course not unusual. For hundreds of years Dutch has been the language of the powerful, the church, the newspapers, education, and science, as well as the official language of the land. Frisian was the language of family life and the village community. Frisian has 'broken through' as the language for science, the newspapers, literature, and officialdom for the first time in the past twenty to thirty years. It has always been traditional to switch over to Dutch outside of one's own milieu, and furthermore Dutch is a 'neutral' language in Friesland while Frisian is often a disputed language and the subject of sharp discussions between the advocates and opponents, both of whom accept Dutch. It is therefore often more prudent to choose the national tongue – a neutral language – to avoid controversy. There is another reason for using Dutch when visiting the doctor, the minister, etc.: many of the notables come to Friesland from outside the province and therefore often have only a limited knowledge of Frisian, and as a result many Frisian speakers have to use their second language, Dutch, when speaking with them. The position of a notable in itself also exercises a certain social pressure leading to the switch from Frisian to Dutch.

5. *Which language is used by the various prestige groups?* Which language is spoken by groups with high social prestige and which is spoken by those with low prestige ('prestige' being judged on the basis of occupations)? According to Van Tulder (1962) the data fall into six occupational groups: the leaders and well-to-do belong to social level 1 (the group with the highest social prestige); the employed middle classes belong to level 2; farmers to level 3; small shopkeepers to level 4; agricultural laborers to level 5; and the workers to the lowest prestige group, level 6. Table II describes language usage (for Dutch and Frisian only) in these prestige groups in two domains.

Table II.

Occupation group	Social level	Language at home		Language with notables	
		Dutch	Frisian	Dutch	Frisian
Leaders/well-to-do	1	64%	28%	81%	19%
Employed middle classes	2	27%	51%	74%	21%
Farmers	3	1%	96%	33%	66%
Small shopkeepers	4	7%	68%	52%	39%
Agricultural laborers	5	0%	84%	36%	56%
Workers	6	7%	77%	52%	44%

Dutch is the dominant language for the higher prestige groups while Frisian is strongest among the lower prestige groups. This is, needless to say, not a very happy fact for such a language as Frisian: language usage in higher prestige groups very often increasingly sets the tone for the lower groups.

6. *Speaking Frisian and the ability to speak Frisian.* There are a
number of people in the province of Friesland who have a *command*
of the Frisian language but almost never *use* it. Exactly how many
people do this? If we knew this we could immediately determine
how many people in Friesland have a command of Frisian. We do
know that 71% of Frisians speak Frisian at home but this figure does
not indicate how many people have a reasonable command of the
language. This section concludes with an overall description of language usage in Friesland.

Frisians (aged twelve or older):
Reasonable command of the language: 83%
Of this group,   85% speak Frisian at home;
                    10% sometimes speak Frisian;
                    5% never speak Frisian.

2.3. *Understanding, Reading, and Writing Frisian*

1. *Do you understand Frisian?* Not every inhabitant of Friesland
can understand Frisian. Frisian presents little difficulty when spoken
to people who have lived in Friesland for a long time, but for people
from outside the province and especially for those who settle in
Leeuwarden a bit of Frisian spoken rather quickly creates a great
language barrier. The number of inhabitants that do not understand
any Frisian at all is not tens of thousands: the language is used in so
many sectors of life (on the stage, cabaret, radio, at work, in the
street, in the shops, at meetings) that people from outside the
province are certainly confronted with it and, if they wish, are given
the opportunity to learn to understand the language.

Rather concrete data are available about the extent to which
Frisian is understood in the province of Friesland, as shown below.

Those who understand Frisian:

	Perfectly	Well	Fairly well	With difficulty or not at all
Frisians who understand Frisian	68%	21%	8%	3%

About 3% understand Frisian with difficulty or not at all; thus this
group is on the whole comparatively small. However, let us take a

closer look at the matter: what is the situation among the allochthons? For how many of them is Frisian an impassable barrier?

Those who understand Frisian:

	Perfectly	Well	Fairly well	With difficulty or not at all
Autochthons	74%	20%	4%	2%
Allochthons	28%	28%	29%	14%

Among the new inhabitants of Friesland there are still quite a few (14%) who have (too) much difficulty with Frisian. A negligible number of autochthons understand Frisian only with difficulty or not at all.

How do city inhabitants compare in their ability to understand Frisian with those who live in the country? One may assume that city inhabitants, because they have less contact with Frisian than country people, have more difficulties with the language.

Those who understand Frisian:

	Perfectly	Well	Fairly well	With difficulty or not at all
Country people	78%	17%	4%	1%
City people	30%	29%	14%	7%

Seven percent of the people living in cities have great difficulty understanding Frisian. In Leeuwarden, the Frisian capital, even more people have difficulty in understanding Frisian: 9% of the inhabitants have difficulty following someone speaking Frisian. This has consequences in language use: at meetings in the capital (and often elsewhere) it is often necessary to ask speakers to use the national language because otherwise a number of visitors cannot (or do not want to) understand what is being said. This constantly causes friction and hardly a week passes without the newspapers reporting another skirmish involving Frisian.

2. *Can you read Frisian?* The ability to read Frisian is a very important aspect of the maintenance of the language. A language whose literature is popular and of good quality has strong mainstays when its position is in danger. Literature will be discussed in section 2.5.; we shall concern ourselves here with the problems of how many people can read Frisian and who actually reads it. Because learning to read Frisian has nothing directly to do with schooling (as

Frisian is not a required language at school) we must not lose sight of
the non-compulsory character of learning the language when interpreting the following figures. Being able to read Frisian in Friesland
very often pre-supposes self-study of it.

Those who can read Frisian:

Perfectly	23%	With difficulty	24%
Well	22%	Not at all	7%
Fairly well	24%		

If we add up the first three figures we come to the conclusion that
two thirds (69%) of all Frisians aged 12 or older can read Frisian at
least fairly well. One-third finds it (too) difficult. Let us examine the
same data for certain specific population groups: first, the allochthons and the autochthons.

Those who can read Frisian:

	Perfectly	Well	Fairly well	With difficulty	Not at all
Autochthons	30%	24%	20%	22%	5%
Allochthons	10%	7%	24%	39%	19%

The above indicates that among the allochthons 58% find it difficult
to read a Frisian text and among the autochthons as many as 27%
have difficulty in reading Frisian.

Categorization by the amount of education may be of interest (it
is limited here to two extreme groups).

Those who can read Frisian:

	Perfectly	Well	Fairly well	With difficulty	Not at all
With elementary school education only	22%	21%	25%	23%	9%
With secondary education or more	41%	17%	24%	18%	0%

Eighty-two percent of the group with higher education are able to
read Frisian at least fairly well, while only 68% of those who received
elementary school education only are able to do so. This difference
cannot be explained by the amount of education *per se* because (as
mentioned earlier) Frisian is not a required subject at school.

3. Can you write Frisian? Frisian certainly does not have a great writing tradition. For hundreds of years people have certainly written in Frisian but, like reading, learning to write Frisian has mostly been done on a voluntary basis. Learning to understand and read Frisian is rather easy; learning to write it naturally requires great deal more effort. The written use of Frisian is one of the obstacles in acquiring proficiency in this language, as these figures show.

Those who can	Yes	11%
write Frisian:	A little	20%
	No	69%

Only 11% of all Frisians aged twelve or older can write Frisian with relative ease. More than two-thirds of the population is not able to express itself in Frisian in writing. And, as if this situation were not alarming enough, we must add that of the small number of people able to express themselves in Frisian on paper, more than half of them never make use of this ability.

2.4. Summary Table

The language situation in Friesland in terms of reading, understanding, writing, and speaking Frisian is shown in Table III.

Table III. *Frisians Aged Twelve or Older*

	Perfectly	Well	Fairly well	With difficulty	Not at all
1. Can you read Frisian?	23%	22%	24%	24%	7%
2. Can you understand Frisian?	68%	21%	8%	3%	0.4%
3. Can you write Frisian?		11%	20%		69%
4. Can you speak Frisian?					
a. Frisians who always, very often, or sometimes speak Frisian	73%	19%	6%	2%	0%
b. Frisians who rarely speak Frisian	5%	3%	15%	42%	35%

2.5. *Books in Frisian*

Besides education in Frisian, one of the mainstays of the language is considered to be books in Frisian. The sale of books in Frisian is dependent on both the number of people who are able to read Frisian and the number of these people who want to do so. How many Frisians occasionally read a book in Frisian? The general picture is as follows:

Reading habits among Frisians:

Non-readers		23%
Readers {	Frisian and Dutch books	41%
	Only Dutch books	36%

Let us take a separate look at the group which does read books.

Frisians who read books:

Frisian and Dutch books	53%
Only Dutch books	47%

A little more than half of those who do read are interested in books in Frisian. Do the allochthons ever read books in Frisian? Among the allochthon readers only 25% occasionally read Frisian, whereas among the autochthon readers 57% do. Among readers living in the cities 35% occasionally read books in Frisian and among the readers living in the country 63% do. Lastly, among the readers who speak Frisian at home 65% occasionally read books in Frisian, and among the readers who do not speak Frisian at home a surprising 27% read books in Frisian.

1. *Ownership of books in Frisian.* The percentage of the number of people who own books in Frisian are as follows.

Frisians who own books in Frisian:

Those who own no books		12%
Those who own books {	No Frisian books	45%
	Frisian books	43%

Looking at the owners of books separately, the percentages are as follows:

Those who own Dutch and Frisian books	49%
Those who own only Dutch books	51%

Almost half of the people who own books in Friesland own one or more books in Frisian. We must not expect too much of that Frisian library for the number of Frisian books owned is small. Only 14% of those who own books in Frisian have more than twenty-five of them. Conversely, 66% of all Frisians own more than twenty-five books (Dutch, etc.). Stated differently, less than 1% of the Frisian population owns 100 or more books in Frisian.

2. *Buying books in Frisian.* From the above it is easy to see that there is no run on books in Frisian, and this is indeed true: less than one-fourth of the Frisian inhabitants have ever bought books in Frisian for themselves or anyone else. The buying situation is as follows:

Book buying among Frisians:

Buy no books		32%
Do buy books {	Frisian and Dutch	23%
	Only Dutch	45%

In order to give a more reasonable picture of the buying situation we will limit ourselves to the buyers of books.

Those who buy: {	Only Dutch books	67%
	Dutch and Frisian books	33%

One-third of all those who buy books occasionally buy a book in Frisian.

3. *Reading Frisian.* We have already shown that about two-thirds of the Frisian population aged twelve or older is reasonably able to read a Frisian text. Therefore these are potential readers of Frisian, but a number of these people read no books at all and thus no Frisian either. Restricting ourselves to those who do read books, it appears that 73% of them are able to read Frisian. However, only 53% actually get around to reading a book in Frisian. In other words there is much undeveloped potential as far as reading Frisian is concerned.

4. *The Frisian book market.* Not too much should be expected of
the supply of new titles in Frisian. New titles do of course appear on
the book market each year but too few. Let us compare the Frisian
market with what annually appears in Dutch: at least 10,000 titles
and reprints appear yearly in the Netherlands, while in Friesland 60
to 80 titles appear yearly. It is true that the Dutch language area is
about thirty-five times as large as the Frisian area (i.e., the potential
market is much larger) but the costs per copy for the publishers of
both Frisian and Dutch books are about the same. The restricted
reading public and the even more restricted buying public inhibit
larger sales in Friesland. Two things must happen in Friesland: more
must be published and the number of copies per publication must
increase drastically.

Exactly how large is the turnover of Frisian books? To get an idea
of what the number of printings for Frisian books could be, we will
first give some figures for a number of bestsellers. The Bible and
parts of it are among the bestsellers in Frisian: over a period of
several decades more than 40,000 copies have been sold. The book
De Gouden Swipe has sold an estimated 23,000 copies but this also
took several decades. Recently 7,000 copies of *De Smearlappen* were
sold in about three or four years (an interesting comparison: the
Dutch translation of this book sold 30,000 copies in two years) and
almost the same number of copies of *Fabryk* were sold. The *Kristlik
Fryske Folks Bibleteek* (Christian Frisian People's Library) subscrip-
tion series must also be mentioned: more than 10,000 copies of a
single title are often printed.

However even the best Frisian books do not reach the average
number of copies of a Dutch novel (11,500 copies per book). Leaving
the Frisian bestsellers and looking at how the average book in Frisian
fares, it appears that an average of 1,500 copies are sold; for novels
and short stories the figure is 2,000 (if we include the *Bibleteek*
publications, about 2,700). This is an extremely small sale for books
that on the average are on sale for seven years, even considering that
Friesland has a population of only 550,000 while the Dutch language
area (the Netherlands and Flanders in Belgium) is 18,000,000 strong.

5. *Some other activities.* Books are, of course, not the only
medium by which written Frisian reaches us. Many Frisian periodicals and publications of Frisian organizations circulate in the province. A cultural magazine is published and the Frisian Academy
publishes an academic magazine. All this written material is intended
for (or read by) a rather small cultural group. Friesland's only weekly

Frysk en Fry was recently revived, after a short discontinuation, with the intention of reaching 10,000 readers within a year or two.

An interesting way of offering Frisian poems to the public was initiated in 1968 in the form of *Operaesje Fers* 'dial-a-poem'. Since that time hundreds of thousands of people with an 'appetite' for poetry have been satisfied in this way.

We must not forget to mention the daily half-hour radio program in Frisian: according to surveys at least 40% of the Frisian population occasionally listen to this Frisian program at times, while 6—10% can be counted as regular listeners.

Theater is a strong medium for spoken Frisian. Friesland has for a long time had a prosperous theater consisting of many very active amateur groups and in the past few years reinforced by a semi-professional group. Cabaret in Frisian is also popular though a number of talented Frisian cabaret players have switched from Frisian to Dutch in order to reach a larger public. Every small language area is a victim of its small potential public (because of the drain of creative talent): Frisian yields to Dutch and Dutch in turn yields to English and German.

The province of Friesland has never in its history had its own Frisian-language newspaper. Considering the language situation it would be difficult to maintain such a paper. Both provincial Dutch newspapers in Friesland (the *Leeuwarder Courant* with about 100,000 subscribers and the *Friesch Dagblad* with about 25,000) offer some Frisian in their columns and stimulate many Frisian language activities.

2.6. *Language Power and Status of Frisian*

1. *Language power.* The term 'language power' may be introduced here: it concerns the concrete position and practical usefulness of a language in a certain domain. Thus one aspect of the concept of language power is obviously the action radius of a given language (as compared with another) in a certain domain. Let us put this into concrete terms for such a province as Friesland as a whole.

a. Dutch has a larger range of usage, a larger reach as a communication medium, than Frisian in Friesland. Everyone in Friesland knows Dutch but not everyone knows Frisian well.

b. Moreover, Dutch covers domains such as religion, sports, art, science, etc., more easily and perhaps better for most people than Frisian. Frisian does not have as many words dealing with these subjects as Dutch does (at least most Frisians do not know these words).

We have already spoken at length about the causes of the dominance of Dutch in Friesland: education, the churches, the government, and the press are responsible for it; the fact is that people who speak Frisian at home easily switch over to Dutch once outside their own environment. Outside the home especially, the official national language (still) has unquestionably more language power in Friesland than does Frisian.

We can now take a closer look at the situation: at home the language power of Frisian is great; however, the range of usage diminishes outside of the home; only 59% of those who speak Frisian at home also do so when speaking to notables. Dutch, however, has become four times as strong (rising from 13% to 54%). For Frisian the loss is heavier in the cities than in the country. The percentage of those who speak Frisian in the largest city, Leeuwarden, is reduced from 29% at home to 7% when speaking to notables. But the percentage of Dutch rises from 28% at home to 90% (when speaking to notables).

Outside Leeuwarden the percentage of people who speak Frisian decreases from 80% at home to 40% when speaking to notables, and the percentage of Dutch speakers increases from 10% at home to 47% when speaking to notables.

All this factual information clearly indicates that everywhere in Friesland — whether in the cities or in the country — the language power of Frisian quickly diminishes when Frisians are outside their homes. If we add to this the fact that the churches, schools, government, public services, and industry use mostly Dutch, we easily arrive at the conclusion stated above: taking the province as a whole the language power of Dutch is greater than that of Frisian. In the last section (4. From Diglossia to Ambilingualism) we will analyze the process by which Frisian is gaining a firmer grasp in all of domains mentioned above.

2. *Another aspect of language power.* So far, in using the concept of 'language power' we have emphasized the range of usage of a given language, but this does not completely describe language power. If we emphasize the second part of this concept — i.e., power, not language — it becomes clear that language power also deals with the actual influence that one language exercises on the speakers of another language. By 'power' we mean the restriction (or expansion) of the behavioral alternatives of certain people or groups, thus in this

case a change in the language-behavioral alternatives of others. This can apply to simple matters such as refusing to understand a language at a meeting so that a whole group is forced to use another language for the sake of one person. It can also apply to more important matters such as not giving people the chance to be educated in their own language. It can apply as well to very crucial matters, e.g., breaking open the language borders violently and compulsorily imposing a language — the national language, for instance — on others.

The obligatory introduction of any language always carries a restriction (others would call it an expansion) of language alternatives with it; elements such as breaching norms, sanctions, exercise of power, and acceptance of power are at stake. The processes of power and social control may also be present under the surface, barely visible and not surrounded by all sorts of publicity media. Forms of power play a role everywhere, for instance, when a dialect is used alongside the national language. In most cases, however, the language power of the national language is simply accepted; at most the dialect is used in the family circle and in personal social contacts, but for the rest people dissociate themselves from it and use the national language. This language behavior on the part of the dialect speaker is viewed as being so natural that both conforming to and accepting the language power of the national language occur almost unconsciously. In such situations it is hardly explicit that concepts such as 'the exercise of language power' and 'possessors of language power' are at stake.

However, in Friesland people are much more conscious of these concepts: for many speakers of Frisian, for instance, there is the constant confrontation with the other language, with the larger language power. At the same time there is a constant appeal to the worth of one's own language — one's own ideological system. Moreover, the publicity media continually react to the Frisian language situation: Friesland has a language movement and a language struggle which has already been discussed at length.

3. *The status of a language.* Let us regard the 'status of a language' as the value or the prestige it has in the eyes of the people.

We may assume that the judgment of the respect a language has is very often not based on the language as a language *per se*: actually it is connected with factors that have nothing to do with the language itself. For example, the esthetic worth one gives to a certain language will often be coupled with the prestige of the population group speaking that language. Some languages are called beautiful and melodious, others crude and uncultivated; one wonders what factors these judgments are based on.

In our investigation of Frisian we asked the respondents to our questionnaire various questions about the prestige of a number of languages and dialects. They were asked to rate Frisian, Dutch, English, French, German, and two Dutch dialects, Limburgs and Gronings, from 'beautiful' to 'ugly'. Which language did they prefer to listen to, which language was the nicest? The results were as follows:

The nicest language:
1. Frisian
2. Dutch
3. English
4. German
5. Limburgs
6. Gronings
7. French

Frisian and Dutch are apparently the nicest languages to listen to. It is evident that these languages are understood best and this fact undoubtedly is of great influence in the evaluation. The economic usefulness of a language most certainly played a role too: Frisian and Dutch, as well as English, are languages of economic importance in the eyes of the respondents.

This usefulness factor is demonstrated even more strongly when the respondents are allowed to determine which of the seven languages they would prefer to retain and which might be discarded.

Which language should be retained:
1. Dutch
2. Frisian
3. English
4. German
5. French
6. Limburgs
7. Gronings

In other words Dutch, Frisian, and English are the languages most desirable to retain, while the two Dutch dialects, Limburgs and Gronings, can be most easily discarded. This order of preference is very similar to the 'beautiful' to 'ugly' order. A language that is understood or a language that is useful is seemingly valued and considered beautiful. This supposition proved to be right, as is shown by the response pattern which resulted from questions put to the respondents about the reasons certain languages have so much prestige.

Criteria for the prestige of a language:

Economic utility, you go far with it, world language	28%
You can follow, understand, comprehend it	27%
Lovely language	18%
Great literature and culture	6%
Congenial people, something else, or I don't know	21%

4. *The status of a population group.* Besides the prestige of a language we were also interested in the prestige of the population group which spoke that language or dialect. We obtained the following results.

Which population group is most prestigious:
1. Frisians
2. Hollanders
3. Limburgers
4. Groningers
5. English
6. Germans
7. French

The various native Dutch population groups had the highest prestige; all foreign populations had less prestige.

Lastly, it may be interesting to see whether the attitude one has about a language is connected with the attitude one has about that population group. Is there a clear relationship between the place a language has in the order of preference given above and the place of that population group? Indeed there is: the prestige of the language corresponds with the prestige of the people who speak it. In other words, someone who likes English and evaluates it as highly prestigious also evaluates the English people as highly prestigious (and *vice versa*). In fact, with one exception, in all the connections in the three orders of preference above evaluation of language agreed with evaluation of its speakers. We may assume that the opinion about a language very probably is a judgment about its speakers as well.

3. LANGUAGE IDEOLOGY IN FRIESLAND

3.1. *What is an Ideology?*

Ideology as a concept has had a long history: Marx and Mannheim, among others, discussed this concept at length. It is not necessary here to elucidate this concept through the works of the many philosophers, sociologists, theologists, and social critics who have written about ideological exegesis. I shall present my concept of ideology in order to describe what is meant by a language ideology.

First, an ideology is a system for the justification of the position, attitude, behavior, and values (of the members) of a certain group. 'It includes a reference to the central values of the group and infers norms, expectations and goals from this' (Van Doorn and Lammers 1959). The justification of one's own position takes a more definite form when the *status quo* of a society is attacked, when the legitimacy of the existing order is argued: this is true for both the supporters and the opponents of a certain social order. However, 'Das Faktum der Nichtübereinstimmung mit der herrschende Auffassung hat wichtige Konsequenzen; es erzeugt bei den Anhängern solcher Ideologiën ein intensives Bedürfnis das nicht-konforme Verhalten und Denken vor sich selbst und den andern zu rechtfertigen' (König 1958). Thus nonconforming groups are especially characterized by a strong ideological consciousness.

As a system of justification, ideology can function as an encouragement for certain activities and as a guideline for action especially in conflict situations. An especially strong emphasis on militant strategies can be included in an ideology and can lead, for instance, to radicalism which has thorough reform as its goal.

Ideology as an idea is mostly used in connection with political doctrine. In political ideology we find on the one hand the system of justification, the vision of social reality, and on the other — resulting from this — for both those who conform to the *status quo* and those who wish to change the existing order, the impact that people exercise on society. Ideologies of course are not restricted to political parties and groups only: many groups in society have their own system of justification which motivates their behavior and action. An ideology can also have the features of a myth: 'an inspiring, activating picture of the outside world. And this is all the stronger as value judgements refer to or are based on more central, affective group values' (Kroes 1964).

Ideologies explicitly and systematically formulate that which 'is vaguely and disconnectedly present in the minds and hearts of group members' (Van Doorn and Lammers 1959). It is apparent that nowhere near all members of a group know about these ideas (or accept them at face value) even though they are based on their feelings and attitudes: 'What the masses know of political doctrines in many cases boils down to some slogans, although these slogans do express rather accurately the unspoken opinions of the masses' (Van Doorn and Lammers 1959).

Another characteristic is that ideology as a system of justification is available and ready and is produced especially when the existing order is attacked (e.g., conflicts, wars) or under stress (at commemorations, on public holidays, etc.).

To summarize, in an *ideology* we find:

1. A *justification* of one's own group position; a reference to central group values.

2. This justification is invoked especially when an attack or stress on that position or those values occurs.

3. We also find *motivation* for action, for providing guidelines for behavior to exercise power, for the possible use of means of power, sometimes resulting in radicalism.

4. We also sometimes find mythical elements in the sense of an inspiring picture of reality, possibly nurtured by a glorification of the past.

3.2. What is a Language Ideology?

Ideologies are thus not limited to political groups or parties. Church groups, two different generations, occupational groups, even certain sports organizations or clubs, etc., can have their own ideology. Language groups can also build up such a system of justification. Thus it is apparent that we can join together the concepts language, language group, and ideology, resulting in the concept language ideology.

We can consider a language-ideological system as a system of views, norms, goals, expectations, etc., that contains an expressed justification of the position of the language group and that refers to central group values by which (followers and) members of a language group judge their own language attitudes and behavior as well as those of others. In such a language ideology we also find an encouragement and justification of action taken, for instance, to consolidate or strengthen the position of the language (group). The highest values defined by the ideology are represented here by, among others, the right to exist and the independence which any language has. A language ideology will tend to motivate action when this independence, this right to exist, is in danger or in a conflict situation.

Thus we may then assume that especially those language groups in which the language is repressed and threatened either from within or from the outside will have built up a language-ideological system. In this connection we might ask if there is a language ideology *vis-à-vis* Dutch in the Netherlands. The position of Dutch is certainly not being threatened in the Netherlands so there is no compelling reason to defend the ramparts of Dutch language there. However Dutch *is* being attacked in Belgium where Flemish has been (and still is) forced to defend itself against the French language. (Flemish is a variety of Dutch.) That the penetration of French in Flanders is experienced as a threat to the native language can be observed only very sporadically in the Netherlands: there are few Dutchmen who stand to arms for their native language in Belgium, so at first sight we have to assume that there is hardly a question in the Netherlands of a language ideology for Dutch. Further study would reveal the degree to which dormant ideological factors are present which for some reason or another do not reach the surface.

Of course the average Dutchman does have a certain opinion about the Flemish question just as he has a more or less well-founded opinion about the Frisians and their language. This Dutch attitude toward Frisian and toward the efforts of the Frisians to maintain their language can certainly not be called an ideology as far as the average Dutchman is concerned. Instead it is, to mention a number of possibilities, a prejudiced opinion or attitude, resentment, approval or disapproval, etc.

Again — for the sake of clarity — it is certainly not true that each language user by definition has an ideological tie to his own language. However, if he does have such a tie it may still require only a little effort for him to speak out for the rights of other language groups for language-ideological reasons: in this way a Frisian can speak out for Flemish or for a Dutch dialect, such as Limburgs, and also — as the case may be — for dialects in Friesland, such as Bildts and Stellingwerfs, at least if by doing so the native position of Frisian is not endangered.

A powerful native-language ideology can also have an unfavorable effect on other languages: the former French president de Gaulle was a warm advocate of French in the Canadian province of Quebec but this did not mean that he considered the claims of the Bretons in France to be justified.

Language will or language consciousness. A language ideology clearly is concerned with a particular language will, with a particular language consciousness aimed at retaining the native language and, if possible, the extension of that language. Of course some people will apply themselves much more consciously to their native language than others: some will feel much more emotionally bound to the language and its speakers than others. For many people the language they speak is nothing special — they hardly realize that they speak a certain language and that others speak another one: language use is something mechanical to them: they remain neutral toward it. Language speakers become more aware of their native language when it is in a situation of conflict, as so often is the case in bilingual areas. A language ideology *vis-à-vis* the native tongue tends to be developed in such areas. It is clear that the average user of the language can hardly be fully aware of the specific and systematic formulations of a language ideology such as those drafted and elaborated by an ideological vanguard (e.g., Frisian Movement in Friesland). Nevertheless these ideas often very clearly indicate the opinions of the average language user and often closely reflect his latent feelings and attitude.

3.3. *The Difference Between a National Ideology and a Language Ideology*

We should make a clear distinction between a language ideology and a national ideology. Naturally there are situations in which the goals of a language-ideological and a national-ideological movement are virtually the same: the implementing agency of both movements can, for instance, have as a goal the promotion of a certain language to the status of national and state language. But in general a national ideological movement has a more encompassing and differently directed objective than a language-ideological movement. Since we have already indicated what is meant by a language ideology, let us now very briefly describe the concept of a national ideology, discussing the idea of a nation first.

The various treatises which deal with the definition of the concept 'nation' are not at all unanimous in defining the characteristics which determine a 'nation', but there are enough similarities between the various definitions to make the following enumeration of characteristics acceptable: a supra-local group of people; an independent state or the pursuit of such a state; a native territory; a commonly shared past; a certain homogeneity of language, culture, descent; a feeling of unity and the desire to preserve this unity. We must not think that the absence of one factor — the language, for instance — is of vital importance: Switzerland has four languages but there is sufficient mutual communication, a commonly experienced past, personal connections, culture, and especially common institutions (the courts, education, laws, etc.) to experience national unity.

In a national ideology — as contrasted with a language ideology — we see a number of distinctive features, e.g., the pursuit of unity or the wish to protect that unity by means of an independent state in a native territory. The native identity, the authentification, and the integration culminate in *a political aspect:* the possession of or wish for an independent state. Inherent in this is the construction of an administrative apparatus which very often monopolizes power with respect to political, economic, administrative, educational, military, and police affairs. The system of justification in which the central values of the nation are contained, and thus the ideology of the supra-local group of people, are what we would call *nationalism.* It is perhaps useful to repeat that in nationalism not only is the aspect of political integration vital, but so are social and cultural integration.

National movements and language movements very often run parallel to each other but national movements are just as often not language movements. The movement for Irish independence is only remotely connected with the propagation of the native Irish language. It is also incorrect to see the separatist movements in Croatia or Scotland today — to mention a few examples — as significantly language movements. Conversely, there are the Frisian movement, the Welsh movement, and the Reto-Romance movement which are essentially language-ideological movements rather than national-ideological movements. Or, to mention several examples in which the territory of the speakers is irrelevant, the Yiddish movement before and after World War I in East Europe, the 'movements' concerning Latin in the Middle Ages and the Renaissance, and the movements on behalf of Esperanto and sometimes even Church Latin today.

Language movements, as history teaches us, can sometimes attract a larger field of activity and expand into national movements in order to create an independent and autonomous political, economic, and cultural integration in their own territory. Conversely, national movements can give up their far-reaching political aspirations and limit themselves to the preservation of the native language.

3.4. *Is There a Language Ideology in Friesland?*

In the previous sections we have referred to the existence of a language ideology in Friesland. Is it true that such a language ideology exists there? If so, how can one demonstrate this? It would be inadequate for an investigator merely to ask his respondents if according to them there was a language ideology in Friesland, since not all the respondents could be expected to know what this term means or feel free to respond validly. Thus it is not possible to measure such a concept as language ideology directly: it must be reinterpreted in research terms which make it possible to measure it, and to do this a number of indicators must be found which represent the concept. Questions and statements must be formulated, all of which seem to pertain to the concept of language ideology and which *are* directly presentable to respondents. Which topics should these questions and statements refer to? Surely something of the degree of attachment to the province and to the Frisian language must be demonstrated, as must the attitude about Frisian in the schools, churches, courts, etc. Questions and statements must be included which will reveal either a preference or dislike for the Frisian movement or a standpoint concerning state intervention in language issues. Information about actual language behavior such as listening to Frisian radio programs, reading and buying Frisian books, and speaking Frisian is also necessary. In many cases such actual *language behavior* will be causally interrelated with attitudes about Frisian. Thus we need to examine the degree of involvement in the entire value system pertaining to Frisian. The aim is to disclose those interrelated attitudes concerning Frisian which are hidden in the opinions, judgments, and views of the respondents. In other words, if it is true that there is a general attitude about Frisian, the pattern of answers to the separate questions and statements examined as a whole should demonstrate something about this attitude.

One of the techniques which can give a definite answer about whether there is a consistency, a coherency, in these statements and opinions is the calculation of the correlations between the answers and their composites by means of factor analysis. We are looking for an underlying factor which should be interpretable as a language ideology (a lasting system of group values which contains an expressed justification of the language and the language group).

This means that a clear connection must exist between the answers and that if there is a coherent language ideology, one clear factor will have to be designated by the factor analysis. Thus one condition for the acceptance of our hypothesis (that there is a language ideology in Friesland) is that the statements dealing with Frisian are one-dimensional and interpretable as a language-ideological factor.

3.5. *Proof by Factor Analysis*

Ten factors were extracted from an inter-correlation matrix of forty-nine items dealing with Frisian. The first factor taken as a whole easily revealed the highest loadings. The table of the ten factors unquestionably showed that there was one dominant factor running through all forty-nine indicators, a clear underlying factor: that is to say, all forty-nine questions and statements are concerned with one subject; one dominant dimension was present in all of them (for further details see Pietersen 1969). Analysis of the highly loaded indicators on this first factor revealed that it can be considered to be dealing with language; not only is the use of Frisian (speaking, reading, understanding) the issue, but the justification, maintenance, and possibly expansion of the Frisian language is also closely related.

3.6. *The Involvement of Various Population Groups with the Language Ideology*

How great is the language-ideological 'consciousness' of various population groups? Its strength is of course not evenly spread among the different population groups, e.g., farmers, allochthons, country people, and older people. We shall make use of the term 'involvement' to denote the degree of consciousness, the degree of participation in and sympathy for the language ideology. Thus the question is: to what extent is there a connection between this language-ideological involvement and such variables as age, occupation, education, etc. (In order to determine the connection between the above independent variables and the language-ideological system we first calculated the score for each person for the dominant first factor of the factor matrix. By means of these factor scores the involvement is 'ideally' represented.)

1. *Age*. It appears that older people are more involved with the language ideology than younger people. The percentages obtained for the degree of involvement made it possible to calculate that among the group under twenty-eight years old, 25% have *a rather strong involvement* with Frisian, while among the group older than forty years, this has increased to 40%. The people who possess *a strong involvement* are those who actively support Frisian, who read and buy Frisian books, who want Frisian to be taught regularly in the elementary schools, who listen to Frisian radio programs, who prefer to speak only Frisian, who defend Frisian, who feel strongly attached to the province, who give Frisian a high status, etc.

2. *Allochthons*. We may assume that the language-ideological system is primarily supported by the autochthonous inhabitants of Friesland. This supposition turns out to be correct: 6% of the allochthons have a rather strong involvement with the Frisian issue as compared to 38% of the autochthons.

3. *Country people*. Frisian has always been able to maintain itself best in the country. In the cities Frisian and Frisian culture are less strongly evidenced, and we may readily assume that the involvement in the country is greater than in the city. This hypothesis also turns out to be correct: 40% of the country people have a rather strong involvement with the language ideology as compared to 20% of the city people.

4. *Differences according to occupation*. We have examined how large the difference in involvement with the language ideology is for six occupational groups. The scores resulted in the following distinctions.

Those who scored rather high on the language-ideology factor:
1. 50% of the farmers
2. 43% of the agricultural laborers
3. 35% of the small shopkeepers
4. 33% of the workers
5. 24% of the employed middle classes
6. 17% of the leaders and the well-to-do.

It would be going too far to extensively examine the possible explanations of these differences. It is fairly evident that the most active Frisian cultural current should not be sought in the socially higher classes.

5. *Education.* The most active Frisian cultural current should not be sought in the socially higher classes. This also becomes apparent when we classify our respondents according to education: 42% of the group with only elementary education is involved rather strongly; 30% of the group with secondary education is strongly involved, and 18% of group with higher (university preparatory) education, according to attitude and behavior, is involved. Thus the higher the education the clearer and more regular the loss of involvement.

We may conclude, therefore, that the Frisian Movement does not find most of its supporters in the higher social levels or in groups with higher education; however, this of course does not necessarily imply that the ideological vanguard of the Movement — the makers and executers of programs — is not drawn from exactly that group (as indeed is the case!).

6. *Some more characteristics of those involved.* We have already shown the type of people that belong to the group with the greatest involvement. We can also demonstrate that those people who are most involved are also those who most enjoy living in Friesland and that they more often take part in the corporate life (i.e., fill more positions, attend more meetings) than those who are less or not at all involved.

Lastly, it is probably not especially surprising that those Frisians who are most involved support the Flemish in their language and emancipation struggle: the most involved Frisians consider the wishes of the Flemish more justified than those with little or no involvement.

4. FROM DIGLOSSIA TO AMBILINGUALISM

4.1. *Schematizing Bilingual Situations*

There are many possibilities for dividing countries into different language categories: these categories may be established on the basis of grammatical similarities and differences, internal linguistic homogeneity or heterogeneity, the language power of official languages both inside and outside the national borders, etc.

The linguistic and sociolinguistic literature contains many examples of attempts to order into a somewhat surveyable whole such difficult phenomena as monolingualism, bilingualism, multilingualism, languages with high or low status, national and regional languages, pidgin and creole languages, artificial and natural languages, varieties for intellectuals and for workers, approved languages and repressed languages, etc. Such ordering is of course necessary because fitting certain language phenomena into categories is the starting point for explanation and analysis. Even if one is not looking for highly abstract levels of explanation or complex theories about language phenomena, classification is nonetheless useful because by means of it, one language situation can at least be compared and contrasted with another.

Bilingual situations. To be more concrete about the above, the bilingual situations in Belgium and Friesland are not the same at all: we nonchalantly speak of the bilingualism of the Canadians, the Catalans, the Bretons, the Welsh, the Belgians, etc., but a little knowledge of the bilingual situation in these countries or regions shows us that completely different types of bilingualism are present in them. In Belgium, for instance, the problem is a bilingual country where in certain areas one language is dominant — Flemish in northern Belgium and French in the south — yet in the city or urban conglomeration of Brussels there is quite another variant of bilingualism with Dutch (Flemish) and French competing with each other. The same term ('bilingualism') is used for the Frisian situation in which a large group of people more or less actively use two languages: Dutch and Frisian.

Further analysis of the above-mentioned countries and regions thus yields two categories: the situation in Belgium and Switzerland where two or more languages are spoken but, where taken as a whole according to territory, they are monolingual; and the situation in Friesland, Wales, and Francophone Quebec where in general the inhabitants speak two languages.

When we introduce the criterion of *status* or *language power* it immediately becomes clear that the mutual relationships between the languages, their degree of legal status, their dominant or subservient roles, etc., are of relevant significance for the functioning of languages in bilingual situations. There are countries where both languages enjoy equal rights; there are more countries, however, where one language is clearly protected and stimulated while the other language is *de jure* and *de facto* kept subservient. This situation has resulted in many of history's well-known language conflicts. However, granting equal status and equal rights to both languages certainly does not imply an immediate solution to the tensions between two language groups.

From the above it is unquestionably clear that the concept of bilingualism covers completely different bilingual situations. For this reason bilingualism is such an imprecise term that the use of this concept for purposes of categorization is of little benefit. We must first further distinguish the various bilingual situations and give them names.

4.2. *A Scheme with Examples*

A scheme for differentiating bilingual situations is given below: a small group interested in Frisian bilingualism has worked with this scheme for the past few years and is of the opinion that it is a fairly handy instrument for interpreting bilingual situations into recognizable and existent categories, of course not forgetting that this division is not all there is to bilingualism. By posing the question 'how many languages function within a certain territory (a region, a country, a province, also a given social or political unit) and how?' we arrived at the categories indicated (see Table IV).

It is perhaps useful — though the descriptions in the schemes speak for themselves — to comment briefly on each of these categories.

1. *Monolingual.* It is becoming increasingly clear that a monolingual situation is a more exceptional situation than used to be assumed. Countries which really have only one language are few and statistics which indicate that 100% of the inhabitants of a country speak the native language must be regarded with some reserve. In Table IV (in which we find Portugal and Korea listed as monolingual) we have, for instance, not listed Norway as 100% monolingual since two languages are spoken there (both called Norwegian).

2. *Bilingual.* The term bilingual or multilingual only refers to the fact that in a territory more than one language is used. This says nothing about whether the languages have been officially recognized or not, about who speaks the various languages, etc., it simply refers to two or more languages used within a given social or political unity.

3. *Homogeneous bilingual.* When in a given territory the same people use two languages, a homogeneous bilingual situation may be said to exist and the people in such a social or political unity are therefore bilingual. Besides their first language they have had to learn a second one, very often because the society surrounding them demands this norm for complete participation in that society.

The positions of the two languages in a homogeneous bilingual situation can be completely different: for instance, one language may

Table IV. *Outline for Various Types of Bilingual Situations*

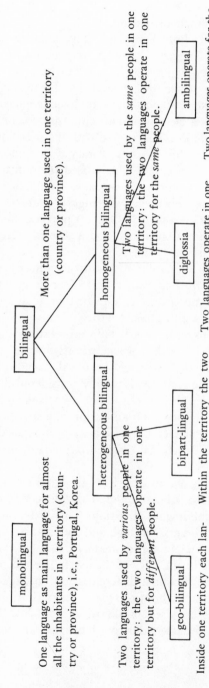

bilingual

More than one language used in one territory (country or province).

monolingual

One language as main language for almost all the inhabitants in a territory (country or province), i.e., Portugal, Korea.

heterogeneous bilingual

Two languages used by *various* people in one territory: the two languages operate in one territory but for *different* people.

geo-bilingual

Inside one territory each language has its own, separate geographical area; within that area monolingualism prevails; i.e., Belgium, Switzerland, Czechoslovakia.

bipart-lingual

Within the territory the two languages do not have their own separate geographical areas: two languages in one living area for different people. They live together but are divided by language; i.e., German and Czech before 1914 and after 1918 in parts of Czechoslovakia; European elites before World War I: mostly French, largest part of population another language; in Bagdad: Moslem, Christian, and Jewish Arabic.

homogeneous bilingual

Two languages used by the *same* people in one territory: the two languages operate in one territory for the *same* people.

diglossia

Two languages operate in one area for the same people but each language has its own domain: one is used for education, in the courts, administration, literature, at the official level; the other is used at home, in the street, at dialect level; a high and a low variety, thus, e.g., Paraguay: Spanish – Guarani; German-speaking cantons in Switzerland: High German – Schwytzerdütsch.

ambilingual

Two languages operate for the same people in one territory but both languages are used at the official as well as the dialect level; mastery of both languages is widespread for most purposes (e.g., Wales and *de jure* in Brussels).

be the official one while the other is used at the dialect level. It is also possible that both languages are equally important and therefore used at both the official and the dialect level. This leads to a further division within a homogeneous bilingual situation.

4. *Diglossia*. Diglossia is when both languages have their own separate functions. The official language is used for representative, formal situations, i.e., for education, church services, officialdom, etc. The other language is used more at the dialect level, i.e., for mutual communication at home, in the streets and shops, etc. Each language has its own domains and there is a clear differentiation functionally between the two languages. We are thus confronted within a social or political unity with a 'high' and a 'low' variety. Paraguay is a good example of a diglossia situation: Guarani is widely used for normal communication and Spanish is the official language. Paraguay is certainly not an exceptional case: wherever two languages are considered to be native languages but are used for different purposes and have their own domains — a situation which characterizes many bilingual areas — we have a diglossia situation.

Fairly extensive literature has been published about the concept of diglossia since it was introduced by Ferguson in 1959 (see Ferguson 1972). Gumperz and Fishman, among others, have further analyzed this concept and its applications (see Fishman 1970).

This had led to a certain consensus about its interpretation and application: in a diglossia situation each language has its own functionally exclusive domain; thus the languages involved have well described, separate functions. One language is usually considered the high variety and the other is the low variety. The two languages complement each other in the language communication of a social or political unity. Thus diglossia is characterized by a well-established, socially accepted, and protected functional differentiation (Fishman 1970).

5. *Ambilingual.* When two languages in a territory function for the same people and both can be used officially and at the dialect level we have what is called an ambilingual situation. The difference compared to diglossia is clear; there is no high and low status; the status of both languages is in principle approximately equal *vis-à-vis* formal status and *vis-à-vis* status in the eyes of the users. There is no socially accepted and protected functional differentiation but, again in principle, an area of application without too many restrictions for either language. Both languages are used in almost all domains. Of course in such an ambilingual situation the two languages are not

used together haphazardly: in practice there is probably a division of labor in which one language is used at home as the main language and not the other. But the point here is that both languages are *in principle* equal and therefore can be used in every domain.

In making this analytic scheme it was extremely difficult to find an appropriate term for bilingual situations such as these. Finally it was found in an article by Halliday, McIntosh and Strevens (1970) entitled 'The Users and Uses of Language' in which, however, this word was used to describe an individual trait: 'where a speaker has complete mastery of two languages and makes use of both in all uses to which he puts either; such a speaker is an ambilingual' (p. 141); and (more situational) 'there is no recognizable class of situations in which he could not use either of his languages' (p. 142). The content of this concept, used by Halliday *et al.* at the level of the individual, fits fairly well with the language situation we were considering so we took the liberty of expanding its area of application and using it to describe a bilingual situation for a group of individuals in a certain social or political unity. Clearly it is not easy to find examples of countries or provinces characterized by such an ambilingual situation. 'Complete mastery of two languages' and 'equal languages in general' are not language phenomena which occur daily. Section 4.4. discusses the extent to which Friesland belongs to this category.

6. *Heterogeneous bilingual.* When two languages function in one territory but for different people we speak of a heterogeneous bilingual situation. The difference compared to a homogeneous situation is that the homogeneous situation deals primarily with *bilingual people* while in the heterogeneous situation we are confronted by mostly *monolingual people*. Whether or not each language has its own territory makes a difference, and this brings us to our next division;

7. *Geo-bilingual.* The term 'geographic bilingual situation' is used when within one territory each language has its own separate geographical territory in which the people are monolingual. Well known examples are Belgium and Switzerland where different languages are spoken inside one political unity but also where each of these languages has a type of absolute power within a geographical part of that unity.

The languages in Switzerland are to a certain extent equal: the formal status given them by the central government is generally equal and each is absolute in its own region. After a struggle that lasted nearly 100 years the Belgians are working towards a similar equality:

Flemish is trying to free itself from the domination of French.

8. *Bipart-lingual.* There is no geographic bilingualism if within the given territory the two languages do not have separate geographic territories. In the case of a bilingual situation in which two languages are spoken in one living area by different people, we speak of a bipart-lingual situation. In such a complicated bilingual situation most people are monolingual even though they are living intermixed with (monolingual) speakers of other languages.

To find a name for this category we applied the word 'bipartite' (a unit in which two parts are distinguishable) to this special bilingual situation: a (social, political, religious, etc.) unit which is bipartite as far as language goes, in other words bipart-lingual.

Fishman (1970:92—93) gave as an example of this the use by the European elite before the World War I of a language which was different from that used by most of the population. The European elite spoke French, for example, while the population among which they lived spoke another language. There was little mutual contact and when it did occur it often took place by means of interpreters, distinctly indicating the monolingualism within the group. Despite national or political unity each class had its own language.

Fishman (1970) calls such a situation 'diglossia without bilingualism', a term which, considering our conception of diglossia, we clearly will not use here. In diglossia a speaker uses two languages for different purposes and that is certainly not the case here, for the speakers in this example are monolinguals; the languages in Fishman's example are also not complimentary variants and one of the main characteristics of diglossia — functional differentiation — is also not evident. There are no well described separate functions here and the function of one language is not different from that of the other, as is the case in diglossia. In this example there is one language for all purposes, one language at the 'official' level as well as for religion, literature, education, and the *same* language at the dialect level — at home and with friends. All this is clearly opposed to a diglossia situation. Here one language does not form the high variety and the other the low, but functions of both high and low belong to one language. Therefore the term 'diglossia without bilingualism' does not fit into our framework.

Of course there may be a difference in status between the two languages and one may boast of a more recognized literature or of a more refined jurisprudence and better balanced administrative codes in that language than in the other, etc., but that is not the point here.

4.3. The Long-Standing Diglossia Situation in Friesland

A country or a province of course does not necessarily have to remain typified by one and the same type of bilingualism forever. There are constant shifts in which one type eventually moves aside for another: stable bilingual situations which remain for hundreds of years are rare. A good example of a language situation in which various phases can easily be seen is that of Flanders in Belgium. According to Meeus (1971) the Flemish language situation can be plotted as follows (I shall make use of my own concepts for the various categories in which Meeus, following Fishman, discusses 'diglossia without bilingualism' — despite the fact that he elsewhere describes diglossia as a situation in which an actor uses various varieties for various domains — and 'bilingualism without diglossia' (1971:12).

1. *Flanders.*

Development of the language situation
Bipart-lingual	Diglossia	Ambilingual	Monolingual
1	2	3	4

The development can be outlined as follows: in the first phase the middle classes in the cities speak French while the bulk of the population speaks a Dutch dialect; in the second phase we find a bilingual population but French remains the language of preferment and respect; in the third phase both languages are made equal; in the fourth Flanders is 'de-Frenched' and the absolute power of Dutch is developed.

2. *Friesland.* The province of Friesland is neither typified by a geo-bilingual situation (in which Dutch and Frisian each have their own areas of application and two monolingualisms would rule in different parts of such an area) nor by a bipart-lingual situation (in which the inhabitants of Friesland live together, separated into a Dutch population and a Frisian population which could only barely understand each other). Of course in the course of Friesland's history both geo-bilingual and bipart-lingual situations have occurred in parts of Friesland; however, those were only sporadic. In general Friesland is characterized by a homogeneous bilingual situation, for the largest part of the population masters both languages — Dutch and Frisian.

How can we describe the Frisian situation further? Are we dealing with a diglossia situation or an ambilingual situation? The bilingual situation in Friesland has undoubtedly been characterized by diglossia for the most part. It was made abundantly clear in the first section of this article that Dutch had dominated for several hundred years. The national language was clearly predominant in governmental administration, education, the courts, and the churches: Dutch was the language for written and oral communication in all official business, however minor. Frisian, however was reserved for activities at the dialect level: for use at home, for the lower working classes, for in the street, for conversations with friends, for humorous situations, etc. In its language situation Friesland was characterized by a high variety — Dutch — and a low variety — Frisian. Both languages had functionally exclusive domains, both complemented each other in language communication in Friesland. There was undoubtedly a well-established, socially acknowledged and protected functional differentiation. Society had accustomed itself to this 'division of labor' between the two languages. We could almost say, following Fishman (1970), that while a group of behaviors, attitudes, and values was supported by and expressed in one language, another group of behaviors, attitudes, and values was supported by and expressed in the other language. As a result of the centuries of Dutch rule the people had grown accustomed to this state of affairs and conformed to it — at least the greatest part of the population did so, but Frisian history indicates that there have always been figures who have tried to break away from this imposed superior position of Dutch. These people tried to give Frisian a position alongside Dutch by interfering with the traditional language pattern of Friesland. One of their tactics was the elevation of Frisian literature and the organization of the pro-Frisian people in pressure groups.

4.4. *Transition Nowadays to an Ambilingual Situation*

The actual Frisian Movement got its start in the beginning of the nineteenth century and was more or less inspired by the Romantic Movement. The desires of the Frisian Movement were formulated in the activities of a number of movement organizations. Frisian literature also flourished in the nineteenth century, and especially the work of the Halbertsma brothers and Waling Dijkstra exerted great influence, particularly on the mass of the population who were brought into contact with the products of Frisian men of letters. More than ever before people were confronted with Frisian writing, theater, and songs, and the growing interest in this was to some

extent the result of the fact that many people began learning to read
at that time. The romantic climate — favorable for the respect of a
folk language and especially one such as Frisian, whose claimed
antiquity gave it extra appeal — formed fertile soil for the activities
of the Frisian Movement.

In the beginning of the nineteenth century Friesland began to free
itself of the diglossia situation. This kind of bilingualism lasted —
according to estimates, until about 1820 — which is not to say that
many characteristics of diglossia have not been applicable to the
Frisian situation in the last 150 years, for they certainly have; Dutch
language domination of official business, for example, has faded only
in the last decades. But there are many indications that especially
after 1820 Frisian was maneuvered out of its humble position by an
ever-increasing number of language-conscious Frisians. This continued with ups and downs during the entire nineteenth century and
on a larger scale in this century, and has resulted in a strengthened
position for the Frisian language in many social sectors. The Dutch
government has recognized Frisian as the second language in the
Netherlands and is cautiously recognizing the logical implications of
this recognition, for example, subsidizing language activities, permitting a Frisian oath in the courts, and the decision that in principle
probably beginning in 1980 Frisian will become a compulsory subject in Frisian elementary schools. The provincial Frisian government
understood its task as far as Frisian goes even before this time by
supporting all kinds of language activities on many fronts and currently makes use of Frisian during a large portion of the sessions of
the provincial legislature. This language usage is now the custom in
most of the town councils in Friesland, indicating the equality of
Dutch and Frisian in a number of sectors. Frisian literature has
shaken off its dialect stature and is gaining — despite insufficient
communication in Frisian because only a small part of the population can write the language — an ever-increasing number of writers
and readers. The introduction of Frisian into the churches is uncertain and a Frisian sermon is more often the exception than the rule.
The use of Frisian in academics has increased since the establishment
of the Frisian Academy, although in the main this is more the case
for the humanities than for the sciences.

The greatest part of the population tends to keep a slight distance
from these activities, and participation in the Frisian cause is undoubtedly still too small. However, the use of the Frisian language in
sectors in which it formerly was not admitted is being viewed more

and more as natural, and understanding for the native situation is being experienced more and more consciously. For example, in 1974 there was much opposition — especially in Friesland — to the national government's proposal to further limit the powers granted to the provincial governments. All the Frisian districts of all the national political parties were against this proposal. Indicative of this opposition was the fact that the Frisian National Party (which aims to protect all Frisian interests) won 7.4% of the votes in the 1974 provincial elections.

There is still no question of the existence of an ambilingual situation in Friesland. Both the formal status and the status in the eyes of the people, Dutch and Frisian, are still not equal: the two languages do not have the same value. There are too many restrictions for Frisian in the sectors of education, the churches, certainly in legal matters, and in governmental administration as well. Equality *in principle* and the possibility of application *in all sectors of life* — characteristic of an ambilingualism — has not yet been achieved by a long shot. The *complete mastery* of both languages — also characteristic of ambilingualism — is also nowhere near realization yet. Nonetheless, as this article clarified, Friesland is moving further and further away from diglossia and ever closer to ambilingual situation. The way in which the language situation has developed in the last decades enables us to state unconditionally that there is a cautious development toward full equality of rights for Frisian together with Dutch. The strong position of Dutch as the national language and therefore as the language for economic, judicial, business, scientific, governmental, and educational affairs, however, makes complete equality for practical purposes impossible — both now and in the future. Friesland is and will remain a Dutch province and this fact carries with it certain consequences for language attitude and behavior in Friesland.

What can be realized is the provision in general of equal rights to those sectors of social communication — the churches, the government, culture, and education — that do not pose a direct threat to the position of the Frisian inhabitants as Dutch citizens and especially as economically interested citizens. Thinking along these lines — for even the aims of the Frisian Movement do not go much farther — there is still considerable progress in prospect for Frisian. The realization of these goals is for the most part up to the Frisian population itself.

REFERENCES

Boelens, Krine
1973 'Het Fries', unpublished manuscript
Boelens, Boersma, Feitsma, Pietersen, Straatsma, Vledder, and Zondag
1971 *Twataligens* (Leeuwarden, A.F.U.K.).
Brouwer, Jelle, ed.
1958 *Encyclopedie van Friesland* (Amsterdam, Elsevier).
Doorn, J. A. A. Van, and C. J. Lammers
1959 *Moderne Sociologie* (Utrecht, Het Spectrum).
Ferguson, C. A.
1972 'Diglossia', in *Language and Social Context*, ed. by P. P. Giglioli (Middlesex, England, Penguin Books).
Fishman, Joshua A.
1970 *Taalsociologie* (Brussels, Labor).
Fishman, Joshua A., ed.
1970 *Readings in the Sociology of Language* (The Hague, Mouton).
Halliday, M. A. K., A. McIntosh, and P. Strevens
1970 'The Users and Uses of Language', in *Readings in the Sociology of Language*, ed. by Joshua A. Fishman (The Hague, Mouton).
König, René, ed.
1958 *Soziologie. Das Fischer Lexicon* (Frankfurt am Main, Fischer Bucherei).
Kroes, R.
1964 'Ideologie en Politiek in Nederland', *Sociologische Gids* (1964) (Meppel, Boom).
Meeus, B.
1971 'Taalwetgeving en Sociale Verandering in Belgie', unpublished manuscript.
Pietersen, Lieuwe
1969 *De Friezen en hun Taal* (Drachten, Laverman).
Tulder, J. J. M. van
1962 *De Beroepsmobiliteit in Nederland van 1919 tot 1954* (Leiden, Stenfert Kroese).

APPENDIX

Some Characteristic Features of Frisian

Syntax
Syntactically the difference between Dutch and Frisian is not very great. Some constructions which appear in spoken Dutch and in various dialects of the provinces of Holland belong to the Frisian norm but are not recognized as standard Dutch.

Word order in Frisian is much the same as word order in German, especially in the placement and order of the verbs in dependent clauses and infinitive constructions.

Dat hied er net dwaen moatten. 'He shouldn't have done that.'
Hwat soed er lulk west ha, as ik dat dien hie. 'How angry he would have
been if I had done that.'

Prepositional groups can be split so that the noun (-group) can be at the
beginning of the sentence as in English.

Dy stoel wol ik net op sitte. 'I don't want to sit on that chair.'

Like the *en* + infinitive construction in some Dutch and Low German dialects
there is an *en* + imperative construction (formerly *en* + infinitive construction) in
modern Frisian.

It slagge him en birik syn doel. 'He succeeded in achieving his goal.'
Hy soe him hwat mije moatte en wurkje net to hurd. 'He should be a little
careful and not work too hard.'

Morphology
There are two types of weak verbs in Frisian: one with an infinitive plus *-je* and
one with an infinitive plus *-e*; each has its own conjugation.

    miene 'mean'; *libje* 'live'.

Frisian has two types of infinitives: one that ends in *-e* and one that ends in *-en*;
the latter is used after the preposition *to*.

Hy wol ite. 'He wants to eat.'
Wy ite om to libjen. 'We eat in order to live.'

In inflectional and derived forms of nouns (and of adjectives and verbs, too) and
in the first part of compounds shortening or 'breaking' of the vowel often takes
place.

    amer-ammerke 'pail-small pail'; *raem-rammen* 'ram-rams',
    fier-fierder [fjɪder] 'far-farther',
    doar-doarren [dvaren] 'door-doors',
    tiid-tydskrift 'time-magazine'.

Phonology
The distinctive character of Frisian is shown most clearly in its phonology.
Frisian has a large number of vowels: nine short, nine long, six so-called falling
diphthongs with an *e*-ending and some with *i* and *u* as a second element.
    Vowels with an *e*-ending have 'breaking': *ea-je, ie-ji, oa-wa, oe-wo* (see
morphology).
In some positions the vowels are nasalized.

    winsk [weːⁿsk] 'wish'.

The palatal vowels appear comparatively frequently.

Frisian has initial consonant clusters with *j* and *w* which often give non-Frisians great difficulty in pronunciation.

> *strjitte* 'street' *stoarm* [stvarm] 'storm', *boartsje* [bvatšje] 'play'.

The initial clusters *ts-* and *tsj-* and the final diphtong *ai* are reminiscent of English.

> *tsiis* 'cheese' *'tsjerke* 'church', *wei* [waị] 'way' *mei* [maị] 'may'

As opposed to Dutch Frisian has no *sch* [sX] and no initial *ch* [X], [z] and (Dutch) *v* [v] ; instead Frisian has [sk] explosive [g], [s], and [f].

> *skoalle* 'school', *goed* 'good', *sé* 'sea', *fé* 'cattle'.

The *r* before dental consonants is silent.

> *swart* [svat] 'black', *feart* [flet] 'waterway'.

The above is certainly not an exhaustive description; it only calls attention to some salient points which non-Frisians usually notice immediately.

(Provided by Tony Feitsma, Free University of Amsterdam)

Doukhobor Russian Language Maintenance

Canada is officially a country with two languages — French and English — as specified in the British North America Act to retain the indefinite autonomy of the two ethnic groups which laid the historical foundations of the nation. The position of French as a protected second official language is in many ways an anomalous one. In the 1961 census only 19 percent of the Canadian population was unilingual in French while 67 percent was unilingual in English. Only 1 percent of the population, mainly recent urban immigrants, fails to speak one or the other of the official languages. French would, however, constitute a sizable minority if its speakers were evenly distributed throughout the nation. But of course the major concentration of French speakers is in the province of Quebec; in the western provinces less than 5 percent of the population is bilingual in the two official languages. In the three prairie provinces, Alberta, Saskatchewan, and Manitoba, approximately 50 percent of the population is of non-English or French ethnic origin. It has been inevitable in such a context that discussions of *bi*lingualism and *bi*culturalism turn persistently to ones of *multi*lingualism and *multi*culturalism, particularly in the West.

The political implications of linguistic diversity have been considerable, particularly in recent years. The four volumes of the reports of the Royal Commission on Bilingualism and Biculturalism which appeared between 1967 and 1970 made it clear that the Canadian public, especially outside Quebec, is unwilling to define Canadian linguistic problems as solely those of French and English. Indeed the fourth volume of the Commission reports dealt not with the official languages as outlined in its orginal mandate, but with the so-called 'other' languages actually spoken within the borders of the nation. Insistence on the multiethnic nature of the Canadian national identity, predictably enough, came primarily from the western provinces.

Political alienation of the west from the rest of Canada has become an increasing problem, highlighted by issues of the most recent national election. Efforts to resolve the perceived crisis on the part of westerners have included considerable attention to federal policies of 'multiculturalism' which would guarantee the right of each ethnic group to maintain its cultural and linguistic identity within a framework of Canadian nationalism. Recent government statements have avoided implications of official status for any language or languages other than English and French, speaking not of *multi*culturalism but *bi*lingualism. Benefits of the new programs are available to groups of all sizes, and the effort has been to increase a sense of common cause among members of diverse ethnic groups. The federal government is now hard at work preparing an extensive survey of Canadian language loyalties, seeking common sociological and therefore political factors among these groups.

Reaction among the various ethnic groups has been mixed. Many object strenuously to the special status given to French while simultaneously using the example of Quebec to argue for special status for their own groups. Protests are rampant that the government policies provide too little and too late for the meaningful maintenance of cultural and linguistic identity. 'Multiculturalism' is seen as a device of questionable ethical character to ensure the nationalistic loyalties of 'ethnic' Canadians. And, perhaps most seriously, members of the diverse ethnic groups feel that they have specific rights and needs based on their particular history and local conditions. A generalized policy of cultural and linguistic maintenance does not answer such needs; indeed revitalization of ethnic identity is often perceived as a personal and internal matter not appropriately within the concerns of government at any level.

A more realistic policy from the point of view of the minority groups themselves might have been the one proposed by J. B. Rudnyckyj as a minority report to the first volume of the reports of the Royal Commission on Bilingualism and Biculturalism. Rudnyckyj proposed special status for languages of important regional use. He noted that the Eskimo and American Indian languages in the Northwest Territories, German and Ukrainian on the prairies, Chinese on the west coast, and Italian in the urban centers of the east are major linguistic communities although their *national* importance is less obvious. Criteria were suggested for deciding what constituted an important regional language:

1. contiguous area,
2. functional use over a period of time,
3. oral and written traditions *in Canada,*
4. still used for multiple social functions.

The rest of this article will be devoted to examination of the language attitudes of one regionally important Canadian language — Russian as spoken in the Doukhobor communities of British Columbia and Saskatchewan. In the Kootenay area of British Columbia and parts of central and eastern Saskatchewan the Doukhobors constitute a majority of the population. In both areas members of this sect have survived as a cultural and linguistic entity in spite of some seventy years of pressure toward assimilation. Although they have lost their battle for communal land titles, Doukhobors are still living contiguously on lands which are now individually owned. The language has been an important means of maintaining Doukhobor identity and has served to separate members of the religious community from their non-Russian-speaking neighbors. Children are still learning Russian as a first language, and it is still extensively used in political and social life. A written tradition has developed through the publication of *ISKRA,* a Russian newspaper, and through the writings of numerous Doukhobors about their own history. Russian is still fully functional in Doukhobor communities.

It is clear that the Doukhobors meet Rudnyckyj's criteria for an important regional language and that they have, in the absence of outside encouragement, maintained much of their cultural and linguistic identity. However, the community has been faced with many problems and decisions in these matters. Assimilation is taking place, albeit slowly. Many Doukhobors are concerned that the old ways are being lost and look for new spiritual revelation to bring the youth back into the traditional community; for many the solution is to be found in the communalistic ideology of the Soviet Union. In any case there is considerable disenchantment with Canadian politics. Doukhobors tend to prefer withdrawal as a response to assimilative pressure, whether it be by means of the internal spiritual strength of the communities or by plans for a new migration in the direction of the homeland. Debate on these issues, often focused around the issue of language, is frequent in Doukhobor communities and continues due to variability of language skills and language attitudes.

We have been working in the Doukhobor community of Grand Forks, British Columbia, with brief stays in other Doukhobor com-

munities for the last three years.[1] What began as a survey of
Doukhobor dialect forms in Russian rapidly became a participation
in the language planning of Doukhobor communities for their children. The future of Doukhobor Russian clearly depends on continued initiative from within the Russian-speaking communities and
therefore on the attitudes held toward language maintenance by
present Doukhobors. These attitudes are of course continually
changing, with consequent effects on the continued viability of
Russian. The situation will be described in terms of generational
categories of speaking competence and of attitudes toward the bilingual situation in which Doukhobors now find themselves in Canada.

Although the concern to maintain Doukhobor language and culture is found throughout the entire generational framework of Grand
Forks and other Doukhobor communities, age groups vary in their
personal experiences of community living, religious conviction, and
linguistic competence. These changes reflect in large part the successive migrations of the Doukhobors from various parts of the Soviet
Union to Cyprus, to London, to Saskatchewan, and finally to British
Columbia. At all times in the history of the group, religious freedom,
especially in the realms of education and communal land ownership,
has been an issue. For many the process is not yet complete and the
promised land still lies ahead. At various times migrations have been
considered to the United States, South America, and most strongly
at the present time, back to the Soviet Union.

The oldest living generation of Doukhobors has lived through
much of this complex group history. These 'elders' of the present
communities were born in Russia and their speech retains much of
nineteenth-century Russian. The contrast to younger Canadian-born
Doukhobors is evident, with the speech of the elders being classified
as 'archaic' and highly valued as a reminder of the established
traditions of Doukhoborism. Most of these old Doukhobors are
monolingual, a fact which encourages their children and grandchildren to continue using the language to communicate with them.

The middle generation of adult speakers of Doukhobor Russian
were born in Saskatchewan and migrated to British Columbia as
children or young adults after a series of land allotments restricting
communal title in Saskatchewan in 1908—10. Many of these individuals are quite elderly in chronological terms, but they do not hold
the status of those who were born in Russia. Most are at least
partially bilingual. Moreover, even those who do not speak English at
all fluently speak Russian in a way which shows considerable influ-

ence from the English-speaking environment of the Canadian prairies. This generation does not for the most part value Muscovite Russian and does not attempt to imitate it as a standard language.

The younger generation of Doukhobor adults has been born in British Columbia since the most recent migration. These individuals are fluent in Russian but are divided among themselves as to the relative merits of Moscovite or Canadian Doukhobor Russian. In everyday life Russian is often used less frequently than English, although with few exceptions a serious effort is made to ensure that children will learn to speak Russian at home. It is in this generation that the declining emphasis on Russian language and culture causes greatest concern.

A fourth generation of Doukhobors is recognizable in the teen-agers who are involved in active efforts to revitalize the Russian language and Doukhobor culture. The community sponsors a youth choir which now sings folk music as well as hymns. Teenagers also provide the majority of the instructors for the 'Russian schools' which have been held after regular school hours in Grand Forks for nearly thirty years. These young people are concerned that the Russian they teach, based on textbooks printed in the Soviet Union, is not the Russian spoken in their community. They want to learn a Russian which will enable them to communicate with non-Doukhobor speakers of Russian and simultaneously be consistent with Doukhobor belief and Canadian environment. This group has a less conservative definition of what it means to be Doukhobor than their elders and tends to look toward the Soviet Union. The Union of Young Doukhobors based in Vancouver, British Columbia, has recently founded an English-language magazine *Mir* ('peace' or 'world') to encourage continued unity and identity among all Doukhobors. The ties of this group to conservative Doukhobor communities in British Columbia and Saskatchewan are strong.

The youngest Doukhobor generation, and perhaps the most important for the future of language maintenance, is the generation of children now growing up in Doukhobor communities. The community ideal is that parents will speak only Russian to their children until they begin school so that they will have a strong base in their traditional language. In practice, however, this is not often done, and parents are eager to shift some or all of the responsibility for language maintenance to community rather than family institutions. The older generations are concerned with the linguistic choices which will be made by this generation as they grow up, and the focus of all maintenance programs is on the children.

This generational framework is crucial to understanding the history of the Doukhobors in Canada. An initial study of semantic domains subject to cultural adaptation (Vanek and Darnell 1971a) indicated that the generations have indeed differed in their adjustment to the Canadian environment. The studies by Friedrich (1964, 1966, 1968) provide a baseline for the kin terms and politeness forms which would have been known to the Doukhobors who emigrated from Russia to Canada. Comparison to the usages now prevalent in Doukhobor communities permits isolation of sociocultural factors which modify social and semantic systems. The three adult generations of Canadian Doukhobors showed parallel changes in their use of kin terms, nicknames, and pronoun use (all forms of direct address) which reflected the increasingly Canadian character of their social environment. The traditional Russian system described by Friedrich was maintained virtually intact by the oldest generation. The middle generation modified and adapted the traditional speech patterns. The youngest adult generation retained the traditional Russian *forms* but lost the social criteria for their appropriate use in Russian.

The parallel direction of these changes validates the use of a generational framework reflecting intensity of contact with the Canadian way of life. The kinship terms which were appropriate to a large extended family are being slowly lost in response to the nuclear family organization more common in Canada; separate names for relatives who do not function in the new social contact may be expected to disappear. Nicknames formerly provided a way of expressing the social relationship between persons, reflecting relative age, degree of kinship, affection, approval or disapproval of conduct, etc. The flexibility of the old system has been lost, with many Canadian Doukhobors believing that the nicknames are themselves proper names or that a nickname is tied rigidly to a particular stage in the life cycle. The second person pronoun forms have also showed modification in relation to the Canadian environment. Younger Doukhobors do not know the complex Russian rules of status and personal intimacy (Brown and Gilman 1960) which govern choice of a formal or a familiar second person pronoun. For them, one uses the familiar form in the singular and the formal form in the plural. The absence of such a distinction in English makes this loss unsurprising.

Doukhobors of all generations are well aware of the increasing pressures toward assimilation which surround their communities.

Mass media, public education, wider economic dependencies, and geographical mobility are only a few of the factors which are likely to increase rather than decrease in years to come. Many Doukhobors see all change as cultural loss or degeneration and despair for the preservation of what is distinctively Doukhobor. Others realize that flexibility and adaptability to new situations show the vitality of the Doukhobor tradition and that the next generation will remain Doukhobor but in a new way. Conscious efforts to maintain Russian language and Doukhobor culture in a context appropriate to Canada and to the modern world increase the likelihood that young Doukhobors will continue to move through a normal life cycle of language use and social life in which speech roles and traditional culture become more available to them as they grow older. For some young people of course the emphasis is more on belief and cultural heritage, with English seen as an acceptable medium of Doukhobor communication.

One of the major bones of contention within the community of Grand Forks is the nature of the Russian spoken by Doukhobors. Canadian Doukhobor Russian differs from Standard Russian in a number of features, some of which are consciously recognized and evaluated by members of the group. Decisions have to be made regarding the relative prestige of these two dialects in order to run the Russian schools. The most salient marker of Doukhobor speech is the substitution of [h] for orthographic /g/ in Standard Russian (Vanek 1971). In Standard Russian orthographic /g/ is pronounced [v] in the genitive forms of adjectives, pronouns, numerals, particles, etc., and elsewhere as [g]. In Canadian Doukhobor Russian these exceptions to the rule have been lost; all /g/'s are pronounced [g] when attempting to imitate Standard Russian. Only a few speakers who have visited the Soviet Union are aware of the exceptions in Standard Russian. Use of the overgeneralized rule which changes Doukhobor [h] to [g] reflects, then, a conscious choice of desired identity as an educated Russian or as a Doukhobor. Greater communication with the Soviet Union in recent years and the emphasis of the educational system on Standard Russian have conspired to favor the Russian identity, particularly for younger Doukhobors. There is still, however, considerable feeling of pride in the forms of Russian maintained within the Doukhobor communities during their complex history. This is maintained in direct defiance of teachers and even members of the community who see the local forms of Russian as mere 'slang'. The Doukhobors have learned to apologize for the way they speak their native language. In some cases recent revitalization of cultural identity has caused positive value to be placed on the dialect forms, comparable perhaps to the movement away from a Parisian French standard in Quebec.

In the Saskatchewan Doukhobor communities an additional complication exists regarding the choice of [g] or [h]. Linguistic development has been different in these areas because of different cultural conditions. Dialect differences originating in Russia have been maintained to a greater degree than in British Columbia due to the greater proximity of speakers of other Slavic languages, primarily Ukrainian. Consequently there has been less standardization of Canadian forms of Doukhobor Russian. Efforts to preserve identity as Russian rather than Ukrainian have been an additional factor in choice of the Russian form [g] since Ukrainian, like Doukhobor Russian, has [h].

The remainder of the article will be devoted to a summary of the results of a language attitude questionnaire designed specifically for the community of Grand Forks, British Columbia, on the basis of the kind of information presented above. The areas of concern in the questionnaire are certainly broader in the study of Canadian linguistic groups than the Doukhobors, but the wording and organization is deliberately culture-specific on the grounds that only thus can it be comprehensible to members of an isolated community feeling little political or social consanguinity with other linguistic minorities. Results are not quantifiable because of the variety of rationales for various opinions. Interviews using the questionnaire as a general baseline were open-ended and often led into long discussions of politics, religion, and history. The questions themselves take for granted the situation in which the Doukhobors find themselves; this is the attitude taken by the community, whose members want solutions, not statements of the obvious. For example, the question 'Do you feel that it is difficult to maintain your linguistic and cultural identity?' would brand the interviewer as a fool.

Appendix I presents the Biographical Data Form used as a basic reference. It was not used formally but served as a checklist during and at the conclusion of interviews. The intention was to pinpoint the conservatism and place in the generational structure of the respondent. Place of birth of self and family were crucial because of the extensive Doukhobor migrations during this century. Education and occupation are effective indices of conservatism, particularly as reflections of social mobility from one generation to another. Religion is significant because of the degree of intermarriage with non-

Doukhobors and its influence on maintenance of conservative Doukhobor traditions. Information about other languages spoken or understood demonstrates the isolation or sophistication of the respondent about linguistic diversity generally. Not surprisingly, the trend on all of these indices is for younger Doukhobors to be less conservative and better informed about the outside world.

Appendix II presents the Language Attitude Questionnaire. It begins with the only two questions included in the last Canadian census which are relevant to the study of multilingualism. These deal with 'mother tongue which is still spoken' and 'ethnic origin'. For every individual answering the questionnaire the answer to both questions would be 'Russian'. Yet it will be obvious that the complexity of Russian-English bilingualism in Doukhobor communities exists but is entirely evaded by the census questions.

'Mother tongue still spoken' can be quickly broken down on the basis of usual function. One wants to know which language is spoken at home; if both are used, what criteria define their relative domains? Not surprisingly, the tendency was for older people to use Russian most frequently or even exclusively at home. Households including a grandparent were more likely to use Russian at home.

Old people felt that English was a very hard language to learn; many had never really done so (and were interviewed in Russian). Adult Doukhobors who entered the Canadian school system speaking only Russian also felt that English was harder to learn. Almost all of this group wanted to spare their children the agony of learning English for the first time in school. They wanted Russian to be taught to the children but as a second language. The young people, for many of whom English is the effective mother tongue, tended to feel that Russian was much harder to learn than English. In all cases the reasons given were contrasts between English and Russian which would cause interference for the language learner. Without exception respondents believed that Russian is easier to learn if you are a Doukhobor (understood in this sense to mean 'of Russian descent'). Most people seemed to feel that this was biological rather than cultural in cause. This belief was of course crucial to the belief that language maintenance was an internal problem of the community and that outsiders had no reason to learn Russian (and no business learning Russian).

Most Doukhobors in Grand Forks have had very little contact with Doukhobors or other Russian speakers from the Soviet Union. Most people felt that Soviet Russian was more 'correct' or 'proper' than their own. Few could cite differences other than Doukhobor [h] for /g/. Opinions did not seem to depend on whether the individual knew any Soviet Russian speakers. Understanding of other varieties of Russian seemed to depend more on perceived identity than on actual dialect features; for example, an individual visitor would be understood whereas a militaristic speech on the radio would not.

Most people thought that Saskatchewan Doukhobors spoke the same way they did. The reason was given they were the same people only sixty years ago. No one spontaneously mentioned Ukrainian influence on the Russian in Saskatchewan. Respondents also felt that everyone in Grand Forks spoke Russian the same way. A few people were felt to 'put on airs' by trying to speak like they were from Moscow but this was not thought to affect the basic pattern of Doukhobor speech. A small number of individuals volunteered criticisms of the local form of Russian in answer to this question, stating that there was too little variation in Grand Forks Russian and that it was all bad Russian.

Everyone agreed that old people spoke Russian better than most others. Most felt that very few young people spoke Russian as well as their parents. This situation was lamented as probably irretrievable cultural loss by members of all generations. There was general recognition that many Doukhobors could not speak the language although almost everyone was thought to understand it passively. Again this was felt to be lamentable. Most people thought that many Doukhobors were monolingual in Russian but qualified this that they were all old people. Everyone realized that a large number of Doukhobors were now monolingual in English.

When asked to identify individuals who spoke Russian very well, most people chose active political figures of the middle adult generation. It seemed to be assumed that old people spoke the language well but that they were removed from the everyday affairs of the community. It was more admirable when a younger individual had taken the trouble to learn to speak Russian very well. It was also rare that an individual mentioned as a good speaker a member of his immediate family. The question was interpreted to mean 'who is a good speaker in the eyes of the community'. The question of who spoke English well was apparently meaningless. People speak English, but skill in doing so is not evaluated.

Individuals identified as knowing Russian stories and proverbs were almost always grandparents in family units. These were never the same individuals identified as being good speakers in general.

There is very little interest in traditional Russian folklore among the Doukhobors, this apparently being felt to be frivolous in light of the sect's religious convictions. Philosophical or religious homilies and history are felt to be more appropriate subjects for teaching even by old people entertaining children. There did not seem to be much in the way of oral literature especially for children. People said that their grandparents told them stories but were not able or willing to present examples. Most likely this was felt to be part of the intimate private life of a family and was simply not susceptible to analysis by questionnaire or interview.

Opinion was general that few Doukhobor children now learn exclusively Russian at home. Linguistic maintenance was felt to be successful if the children are at least bilingual when they come to school. Most respondents probably overestimated the amount of assimilation to English only which has actually occurred. Certainly, however, they are correct that this is the trend. Older and middle-aged Doukhobors said they learned Russian from their parents and secondarily from their grandparents. Many teenagers also cited their grandparents as primary teachers within the informal context of the family. A number of young people, however, said they learned Russian in Russian school. In a few cases this meant that formal teaching was in the extra-curricular classes but in many instances the young people actually had not gained any real fluency in Russian at home.

There was great division of opinion about whether people would like to speak Russian differently. Old people in general were satisfied with their Russian. Many younger adults said they wished they knew more Russian and that English had encroached too much on their everyday life. Young people often felt that their fluency in Russian was insufficient for normal social interaction. Many people answered the question in terms of the dichotomy between Soviet and Doukhobor Russian, expressing either desire for more 'correct' speech or loyalty to the local speech forms; a number of individuals outlined the two sides of the argument and clearly believed both, depending on the context.

Most people felt that Doukhobor speech had not changed during seventy plus years in Canada. Nor did they feel certain that Doukhobors in the Soviet Union would speak differently; they were after all Doukhobors. On the other hand a number of respondents obviously felt that anyone who lived in the Soviet Union spoke Standard Russian. There was no understanding of local dialect variations in any language spoken over a wide area.

Very few people were willing to grant Canadian Doukhobor Russian an autonomous status. They conceived it more as a dialect or substandard language. Consistently, then, few recognized a written form of the Canadian Doukhobor Russian. Writings by Canadian Doukhobors were felt to be in Standard Russian and to represent great learning. In linguistic fact, however, many features of the Canadian Russian are preserved in the writings of Canadian Doukhobors, and this is a major source of information about the dialect.

Doukhobor publications in Russian, particularly the newspaper *ISKRA,* were felt to be very important in maintaining the use of Russian language. Doukhobor publications in English were valued as a means to maintenance of cultural and religious identity; many older Doukhobors regretted the use of English but realized that it was the only practical means to communicate with many of the young people. A number of secondary effects of the publications were mentioned: Doukhobors felt pride in their newspaper as a product of community effort. People worked together to put out the papers and this made them closer in spirit to original Doukhobor teachings.

In many cases the people cited as good speakers of Russian were prominent leaders in the Doukhobor organization, the Union of Spiritual Communities of Christ. This organization helps to maintain contact among Doukhobors in different areas, and its officials seem to have become symbols of group identity and unity.

Everyone felt that it was much harder for Doukhobors to continue speaking Russian if they did not live in a Doukhobor community. They realized that Doukhobors living in cities often tried to speak Russian but were not optimistic about their success. There seemed to be no feeling that members of the different Doukhobor sects would speak Russian any differently.

The question 'how can parents encourage their children to speak Russian?' was vacuous to most respondents. Parents *should* encourage their children to speak Russian. This seemed to mean they should only speak Russian to the children; apparently it was all right to punish children for not wanting to speak Russian.

Public media had very little relation to the Doukhobor conception of language maintenance. Few people were enthusiastic about television and radio programs in Russian with Doukhobor content. In contrast Russian news broadcasts or the recording of a Doukhobor choir concert on television sparked great enthusiasm. Language, however, was not something people saw in a public function. Only Doukhobors would be interested, and they could talk to each other anyway. Ethnic radio and television programming is of course one of the key planks of the government's program toward multiculturalism. Even when told that the government might pay for such programs little interest was generated.

Most people thought that Russian should be taught in British Columbia high schools. They did not see why French should be taught and did not want their children to learn it. The unsaid implication was that forcing Doukhobor children to learn *English* was quite enough imput from the Canadian public school system. School courses should be in Standard Russian because it was more 'correct' and schools are supposed to teach things that are 'correct'. In spite of this attitude, however, people were concerned that children of Doukhobor ancestry should not be ridiculed for speaking the way they learned at home.

Russian should be taught because the community was Russian in its historical background, not because Russian *per se* was a language that everyone should learn. Most people thought that Doukhobor parents in Grand Forks would like their children to learn Russian but that no one else would care. Parents tended to assume their children would want to learn Russian if given an opportunity. Their reaction to the possibility of protest was puzzled, followed by willingness to assert parental authority if necessary. In fact, two classes of high school Russian were taught in the Grand Forks school during the 1972—73 year with large enrollment and reasonable success. One assumed spoken knowledge of the language and the other did not. The teacher, normally a social science teacher, is a member of the Doukhobor community. The same individual is chairman of the Russian school committee of the U.S.C.C. which plans classes for grade school children after school hours. This class used to continue through high school level but for some years now there has been no one to teach it. Most of the present Russian school teachers had this high school training from a teacher who has now retired.

Doukhobor history was seen as irrelevant to the community in general and inappropriate to the public school system even for Doukhobors. It might be included in local history social studies units but these were also seen as peripheral to the business of education. Schools were supposed to teach things that children could not learn at home. This does not mean, however, that Doukhobors are not interested in Doukhobor history. Sunday school classes are con-

A. L. Vanek and Regna Darnell

ducted which deal with this subject for children of the community; Sunday school is carefully differentiated in function from Russian school and from public school. Efforts have been made by the community to preserve their own pioneer history, particularly through the opening of a Doukhobor museum and the restoration of several communal buildings. The town museum gives little attention to the Doukhobor background of Grand Forks, and this does not seem to upset the Doukhobor community. Doukhobor history should be preserved primarily for Doukhobors.

No one felt that the Russian schools should be abolished. Almost everyone, however, thought that changes were necessary. The man who had run the program for years had retired and no one had appeared to take his place. More and more of the Russian school students did not speak Russian when they entered the classes, which made it almost impossible to teach reading and writing of Russian in the limited time available. There was a conflict among the teachers, partly generational in its basis, between local dialect forms of Russian and standard Russian forms. High school students did not really have sufficient training to teach younger children and the community did not have the internal resources to train them further. Teachers were paid small salaries to teach in their spare time and lacked sufficient time to prepare complex lessons. Children in the classes did not really learn as much as they were supposed to; many did not learn to speak fluently and the curriculum stressed writing, leaving little time for conversation. Textbooks were Soviet and stressed some ideology, particularly military, which was in direct conflict with Doukhobor beliefs. There was nothing in the textbooks about the Canadian environment in which students actually lived. Most adults realized that the children were frequently bored in Russian school and were willing to consider innovations in the program if interest could be increased thereby.

In the last several years some steps have been taken to modify the Russian school program so that it will more nearly fulfil the needs of the community. The school teachers have met with the Russian school committee at length to discuss teaching methods and materials. Plans are being made for revision of existing manuscripts and preparation of new Canadian-oriented materials. In the summers of 1972 and 1973 the teachers spent a week at Simon Fraser University practicing Russian and learning about language teaching methods. Parents of the teachers support the program and have encouraged their teenagers to attend these workshops and to apply what they learn to the Russian school classes. A number of these teachers hope to go on to university to study Slavic languages and are eager to learn how to make the transition from the Russian heritage of their home community to the Russian recognized as standard by the larger society.

Most members of the community felt that written Russian should continue to be taught in Russian school. In part, however, this stress on writing seemed related to lack of information about oral language teaching methods. None of the adult Doukhobors had ever formally studied a language to obtain speaking knowledge. The French courses required of British Columbia high school students could hardly provide a model for the kind of oral program which would be appropriate for the Russian school. Parents do realize that many children no longer speak Russian fluently and that it is difficult for such children to complete a rigid curriculum stressing reading and writing. In fact, the major complaint of the teachers seems to be that the textbooks provide far more material for each grade than can be covered during a single year of Russian school classes. They omit portions which are ideologically displeasing (which causes student confusion over grammar and other logically related material). Each fall the teachers begin a new textbook regardless of whether the students have completed the previous one. Under such circumstances, of course, the students are forced to memorize rather than understand the language, especially if they are not already fluent speakers of Russian. Understanding that such problems exist, however, does not automatically lead to a solution. Parents and teachers alike feel that if the curriculum is diluted to meet the abilities of the students, then the Russian school has failed. Sentiment is common that because Doukhobor children are of Russian ancestry they should be able to learn the language even under adverse conditions. From their own education many adult Doukhobors seem to have absorbed the notion that education must be boring and difficult in order to be successful. Some of the teachers have indeed been criticized for innovative methods which are felt to be disruptive of the true purpose of the Russian schools.

Children enrolled in the Russian school seem to regard it rather like death and taxes — always with them but not much fun. Parents seem to take it for granted that their children will attend. There are over 300 children enrolled in the program in Grand Forks and attendance is reasonable. Teachers complain that some of the children do not take their Russian classes seriously and forget between one class and the next. The children do not appear to feel that they can have any effect on the curriculum and passively accept whatever materials they are given. Few of the grade school children have absorbed the conviction of their high school age teachers that they have a responsibility to maintain Russian language and culture.

Very few Doukhobors thought that anyone not of Doukhobor ancestry would want his children to study Russian in public school. The only people who learned Russian without being Doukhobors were those who married into the Doukhobor community, but they did so privately and informally. Doukhobors of all generations objected to the notion of the Russian schools being incorporated into the regular public school curriculum. That way the Doukhobor community would lose control over the course; Russian school functioned to maintain Doukhobor unity at all age levels as well as to teach Russian to the children.

Few people objected in principle to the notion that other languages besides Russian might be introduced into the public school curriculum. Nor did they show any particular interest in having their children learn other languages. The effort to maintain a viable bilingualism in Russian and English seemed to take all available linguistic energy. If other ethnic groups wanted their languages to be taught they should teach them — again the public school system was not seen as the appropriate or obvious medium for such instruction. These attitudes are, however, quite explicable in light of the long history of Doukhobor disputes with educational authorities. The Doukhobors have learned from their experience that their opinions on public school curriculum are not welcome and that whatever they want to teach their children, they will have to teach themselves. It is not surprising that recent trends toward liberalization of ethnic language policies have failed to modify these entrenched responses.

Very few of the Doukhobors in Grand Forks speak or understand any languages other than English and Russian. In the Saskatchewan communities, however, many Doukhobors have learned Ukrainian or other immigrant languages through social interaction with speakers of them. No Doukhobors appear to have formally studied other languages (except English and French when forced to do so), and the sect has been quite definitely opposed to education, particularly advanced, until quite recently. Doukhobors in Grand Forks are not aware of other language groups living near them, and indeed most of their contact with non-Doukhobors involves native speakers of English. Interaction in such cases is linguistically one-way — the

Doukhobors learn English but the English-speaking Canadians do not learn Russian.

Few Doukhobors are strongly motivated to seek ties with other Canadian immigrant groups. For example, until quite recently the editorial policy of *ISKRA* has been to avoid comparisons to similar religious groups as not relevant to the Doukhobor experience. At the present time, however, the trend appears to be toward greater communication with other groups and opinions, breaking down the former isolation of the Doukhobor communities. Changes in attitudes are likely to result among the younger generation, but whether these young Doukhobors will remain within the traditional communities is still uncertain.

Almost all Doukhobors feel that it is harder to be Canadian if you are also Doukhobor. Again, the sect has been subject to considerable conflict over ideological issues with the Canadian government and alienation is not surprising. Most Doukhobors do not seem to feel any particular kinship with speakers of other Slavic languages. In British Columbia few claim to understand other Slavic languages although in Saskatchewan greater contact has produced a quite different situation. British Columbia Doukhobors are not aware that their fellow Doukhobors in the Soviet Union or in Saskatchewan learn other languages. Russian is the easiest language for them to learn because they are Russian. The concept of learning a third language does not seem to be present. At a very superficial level people state that it is good to learn languages because it makes you a better human being, but they show no great interest in becoming better human beings by such means. Overall the Doukhobors have maintained a remarkably isolated worldview; they are preoccupied with the problems of linguistic and cultural maintenance for their own group and do not feel compelled to extend their way of dealing with the outside world to include sympathy for the position of anyone else.

In summary, then, it is clear that Doukhobor attitudes toward language maintenance are inseparable from the peculiar historical position of the group in Canada. The Doukhobors emigrated in the expectation of a promised land where their views on communal ownership and pacifism would be respected. During the seventy years of their Canadian residence they have been disillusioned many times and have reacted by withdrawal from the mainstream of Canadian society whenever feasible. Community boundaries have been maintained by a religiously motivated separatism; the result has been fairly effective maintenance of cultural and linguistic identity. Particular testimonies of the Doukhobor religion have also encouraged tendencies toward separatism and isolationism. Political action, including voting, is considered antithetical to the search for religious truth; young people are changing this position especially with regard to pacifism as a political philosophy. Emphasis on hereditary leadership and prophecy have also encouraged members of the communities to look inward. Lack of emphasis on formal education has had similar effects.

The Canadian government has been of little help to the Doukhobors in maintaining a dual identity as Russian and Canadian. The failure of the government to recognize religious groups as having special kinds of problems within the larger society has forced further withdrawal by Doukhobor communities. Indeed the new multicultural policies are explicitly worded to discourage applications from religious groups. Yet it is a simple sociological fact that many subgroups of ethnic origin within the mosaic of Canadian society *are* religiously bounded. This should not disqualify them from political concern for their ability to maintain their language and ethnic identity. The Doukhobor communities cannot wait for the Canadian government to develop another new policy which will meet their needs. They are faced with a crucial double bind in which help from outside is not enough to ensure cultural continuity, and the outside world is rationally perceived as threatening to Doukhobor unity. At the same time the internal resources of the communities may not be sufficient to meet their needs either. Practical support in cultural and linguistic maintenance has recently come from the Soviet Union and this provides hope for many; yet there are also problems with simply ceasing to be Canadian and many aspects of Soviet society are recognized as incompatible with Doukhobor belief. In the past history of the Doukhobors such conflicts have been resolved by migration and splintering of existing groups; yet the Doukhobors are a small group and many fear that unity is the only route to maintenance of an independent identity. The solution still lies in the future.

REFERENCES

1967-   *Report of the Royal Commission on Bilingualism and Biculturalism*
1970   4 vol. (Ottawa, Queen's Printer).
Brown, Roger, and Albert Gilman
1960   'The Pronouns of Power and Solidarity', in Thomas Sebeok, ed., *Style in Language* (Cambridge, M.I.T. Press).

Friedrich, Paul
  1964 'Semantic Structure and Social Structure: An Instance from Russian',
      in Ward Goodenough, ed., *Explorations in Cultural Anthropology* (New
      York, McGraw-Hill).
  1966 'The Linguistic Reflexion of Social Change: From Tsarist to Soviet
      Russian Kinship', *Sociological Inquiry* 36.
  1968 'Structural Implications of Russian Pronominal Usage', in William
      Bright, ed., *Sociolinguistics* (The Hague, Mouton).
Vanek, Anthony
  1971 'The Psychological Reality of g/h and its Implications for the Theory of
      Grammar', *Papers in Linguistics* 4 (2).
Vanek, Anthony, and Regna Darnell
  1971a 'Canadian Doukhobor Russian in Grand Forks, B.C.: Some Social As-
      pects', in Regna Darnell, ed., *Linguistic Diversity in Canadian Society*
      (Edmonton-Champaign, Linguistic Research Inc.).
  1971b *A Doukhobor Russian Lexical and Dialectological Questionnaire*
      (Edmonton-Champaign, Linguistic Research Inc.).

APPENDIX I

Biographical Data Form

Name: Father's place of birth:
Address: Mother's place of birth:
Date of birth: Spouse's place of birth:
Place of birth: Other members of household:
Education: Religion of mother:
Education of father: Religion of spouse:
Education of mother: Religion of children:
Education of spouse: Other places lived:
Education of children: Time spent outside Doukhobor communities:
Occupation: Languages spoken (besides English and Russian):
Occupation of father: Languages understood (besides English and Russia
Occupation of mother: Languages spoken by father:
Occupation of children: Languages spoken by mother:
Occupation of spouse: Languages spoken by spouse:
Religion of father: Languages spoken by children:

APPENDIX II

Language Attitude Questionnaire

1. What is your mother tongue?
2. What is your ethnic origin?
3. What language(s) do you speak at home?
4. If more than one, which is used most frequently?
5. On what occasions is it used?
6. Which language is hardest to learn? Why?
7. Is it easier to learn Russian if you are of Doukhobor ancestry?
8. Is Doukhobor Russian the same as the Russian spoken in the Soviet Union? How does it differ?
9. Do you know any Russian speakers from the U.S.S.R.?
10. Can you understand them easily?
11. Do Doukhobors in Saskatchewan speak the same way as those in British Columbia? How is their speech different?
12. Does everyone in your community speak Russian the same way? What differences are there?
13. Do old people speak Russian better than others in your community?
14. Do young people speak Russian as well as their parents?
15. Do some people understand Russian who do not speak it?
16. Are there many Doukhobors who speak only Russian?
17. Are there many Doukhobors who speak only English?
18. Which individuals in your community speak Russian very well?
19. Which individuals in your community speak English very well?
20. Which individuals know Russian stories and proverbs?
21. Are there special stories or other forms in Russian which are especially for children?
22. Do many Doukhobor children learn ONLY Russian at home?
23. Are many pre-school children bilingual?
24. From what individual did you learn most about speaking Russian?
25. Would you like to be able to speak Russian differently? In what ways?
26. Do Doukhobors still speak the same way they did when they came to Canada? What differences are there?
27. Do Doukhobors in Canada speak the same way now as Doukhobors who remained in the Soviet Union? How does their speech differ?
28. Is there a 'Canadian' form of Doukhobor Russian?
29. Is Canadian Doukhobor Russian a written language?
30. What is the role of Doukhobor publications in maintaining use of Russian?
31. Are people who are the best speakers of Russian members of the Doukhobor organization?
32. Do Doukhobors who live in Vancouver, Los Angeles, or other large cities continue to speak Russian? Does their Russian differ from that spoken in Doukhobor communities?
33. Do members of the different Doukhobor sects speak differently? How does their speech differ?

34. How can parents encourage their children to speak Russian?
35. Would you like to see television and radio programs in Russian? What should be their content?
36. Should Russian be one of the languages taught in British Columbia high schools?
37. Should school courses teach Doukhobor or Soviet Russian?
38. Would most parents in your community like their children to learn Russian?
39. Would most students in your community like to learn Russian?
40. Should Doukhobor history be taught in the schools?
41. Should Doukhobor history be taught to all students, not just those of Doukhobor ancestry?
42. Do you think French should be taught in the schools?
43. Do you want your children to learn French?
44. Do the Russian schools as now taught in Grand Forks fulfil a community need?
45. Should the Russian schools stress Russian as spoken in the community or Soviet Russian?
46. Who should teach the Russian school classes?
47. Do the children in Russian school learn to speak Russian WELL?
48. What sort of textbooks should be used in the Russian schools?
49. What topics should be studied?
50. Should spoken or written Russian be stressed?
51. Would non-Doukhobors in the community be willing to have their children learn Russian in public schools?
52. Should other additional languages (besides Russian) be added to the public school curriculum? Which ones?
53. Do you speak any languages besides English and Russian? Which ones?
54. Do you understand any languages besides English and Russian? Which ones?
55. How did you learn these languages?
56. What other languages are spoken around your community?
57. Have many non-Doukhobors in your community learned Russian?
58. Do you feel common language problems with other Canadian immigrant groups?
59. Do you feel particularly close to speakers of other Slavic languages?
60. Is it harder to be Canadian because you are of Doukhobor ancestry? Why?
61. Can you talk to speakers of other Slavic languages, for example, Czech, Ukrainian, Polish?
62. Is Doukhobor Russian more closely related to one of these other Slavic languages?
63. Do Doukhobors in Russia learn Ukrainian or any other Slavic language in addition to Russian?
64. Have many Canadian Doukhobors, especially in Saskatchewan, learned Ukrainian or any other Slavic language?
65. Which language is easiest to learn?
66. Is it easier to learn a third language than a second?

A. L. Vanek and Regna Darnell

NOTE

This research has been sponsored by the General Research Fund of the University of Alberta and by the Citizen's Culture Division of the Secretary of State Department, Ottawa. The results apply primarily to the community of Grand Forks, British Columbia, except where stated otherwise. We would like to thank the Russian School Committee, the Russian School teachers, and also the following individuals: Alex Harshenin, Jim Kolesnikoff, John and Mary Kolesnikoff, Peter Legebokoff, Steve Maloff, Eli Popoff, and J. J. Vereigen.

The Assimilation and Non-Assimilation of European Linguistic Minorities
A Sociological Retrospection

1. INTRODUCTION

This article has a mainly analytical character. I will endeavor to use some sociological concepts such as social class, social mobility, ideology, identification, and institutionalization in order to analyze — naturally within a rather speculative framework of hypotheses — the assimilation processes among European linguistic minorities during the past hundred years. I also intend to describe these assimilation — and emancipation — processes. For various reasons (of which surveyability is the most important) I will as much as possible concentrate on a few linguistic groups: South Tyroleans, Sudeten Germans, Swedish Finns, Magyars, Baltic Germans, Czechs, and Flemings. Of course the analysis of each of these cases could have been extended but I hope that even these few cases will contribute to a more general theory of the phenomenon of differential linguistic assimilation.

2. EUROPEAN LINGUISTIC MINORITIES

In this article I am specifically concerned only with the assimilation of linguistic minorities in Europe. As a result I will of necessity ignore certain assimilation patterns typical of 'European' linguistic minorities in America, e.g., the intergenerational conflict, which is unknown in a European context. The most important differences between linguistic minorities in European and in immigrant American settings are determined by their historical background, ecological character, ethnic character, national aspirations, and above all by their social composition and status. American linguistic minorities are very young and do not owe their relations to each other or to the dominant Anglo-American population to a long and common history

of living together in the same society. In America linguistic assimilation does not coincide with established linguistic-geographic boundaries but rather occurs as a consequence of a recent confrontation
between the dominant Anglo-American culture and the relatively
small and socially weak groups of immigrants living more or less
concentrated in parts of the countryside or in specific urban areas.
One of the most impressive differences between linguistic minorities
in a European versus an immigrant American context is found in the
more purely linguistic character of the former. In America, language
is just one of the differentials, among which social class, social values
(culture), religion, and possible racial differences are much more
decisive for the total processes of assimilation. In Europe linguistic
minorities often differ only in their speech from dominant linguistic
groups. Even religious boundaries very seldom fall together with
linguistic or with other ethnic (in Europe folkloristic) peculiarities.[1]

With the exception of the very specific position of the Yiddish
minorities and some German minorities in eastern Europe (Galicia,
Rumania, and the Ukrainian-Ruthenian area) one has to remember
that ethnic boundaries in Europe usually exist(ed) at a folk-societal
level and in consequence are not as sharp or as relevant to social
interaction as they are in America. In spite of the incongruence
between language and other ethnic markers in Europe, language has
proved to be an astonishingly dominant symbol of group identity for
more than one-and-a-half centuries. I am referring here to the most
important difference between European and American minorities:
those in America may be called 'integrationist' because of their
willingness to integrate into the Anglo-American society, while in
Europe much older common national identities have split up precisely alongside linguistic boundaries. Language and group identity
are closely connected in Europe; even when largely unilingual nations
fell apart — the Irish from the English; the Norwegians from the
Danes — they looked for a language of their own as a national
symbol. Thus, while assimilation in Europe is not only 'linguistic',
linguistic assimilation is, indeed, an indication of the choice of another
(national) identity.

3. ASSIMILATION OF LINGUISTIC MINORITIES

Assimilation is a well-known concept in the language sciences. From
a purely linguistic point of view assimilation indicates a process by

which two units (usually sounds) become realized in one articulatory structure. In sociolinguistics assimilation at times indicates a process by which two or more languages become involved in a linguistic melting-pot resulting in the birth of a new so-called creolized language. Such a new language begins to serve as a *lingua franca* between the respective linguistic groups participating in an ethnically mixed society. The *lingua franca* or 'pidgin' itself may be considered as an interpretation of the language of the socially dominant group (e.g., the colonisers by the members of the dependent groups (e.g., the autochthons or slaves accompanying the dominant group). In most cases the original minority languages die out and the new pidgin becomes a mother-tongue, a 'creole'. Such pidgins and creoles can be found in the Antillean area, on the African coasts, in the Pacific and in Southeast Asia, in societies with a more or less colonial background, and in commercial centers (Hymes 1968:14,15). Some languages have a basically creolized character although they never were pidgins: here I am thinking of languages of larger groups of European immigrants in America and of the Boers in South Africa. Because of the lack of contact between those groups and their mother countries their languages often underwent a particular development influenced by other languages and by bilinguality and resulting in creolized features too (Kloss 1952:120–123).

So far I have described the linguistic effects of contacts between culturally and racially different groups in a more or less colonial situation. We may expect a more steady development in a European context: in Europe pidgins never played an important role and consequently creolized languages were rare and their lives have been short. However, we have to recognize two important languages as creolizations: English and Yiddish. Perhaps we may interpret the mainly lexical character of these creolizations and the absence of syntactic and lexical simplification as typical of a 'European' situation. To be precise: in recent times creolizations developed in Europe only in processes where intense contact between different linguistic groups existed over a long time and where literacy was not at a high level. Among the socially lowest strata of the Brussels population a Netherlandic-French mixture can still be heard although it is quickly dying out, while in the Bernese Jura a French-German mixture is spoken in some isolated bilingual villages (Van Haegendoren 1962:193).

A more typical assimilation reaction in Europe is that of group fusion between two different linguistic groups or between one linguistic group and part of another. In such cases a new group does not develop but one of the groups becomes involved in a process of absorption within the identity of the other. The shaping of new linguistic entities can hardly be found in Europe: perhaps the English entity may be considered as the product of the assimilation of one (Anglo-Saxon) linguistic group with a part of another (Norman-French) resulting in a new (English) linguistic identity. Within the past hundred years it has happened that parts of linguistic groups reacted to the fact of the standard language with which their colloquial language (dialect) was cognated becoming the national symbol and communicative medium of a nation in which they did not want to participate. In these cases groups became bilingual with their chosen national language as a standard medium and their original vernacular as a colloquial; new linguistic identities developed with a regional character subordinated to the national identity. Examples are the Alsatians, a part of the Slovenes ('Wends') in Carinthia, a part of the Poles ('Shlonsakians') in Silesia, of the Cashubs and Mazurians (Polish dialect groups) in former West and East Prussia, and of some Flemings during one particular period.

The decision to elect for another linguistic identity — whether or not inspired by national feelings — is usually taken by groups which are already bilingual. This decision is followed by a process of assimilation in which the bilingual stage is evolving towards a new stage of unilinguality. Temporarily the two decisions — the national option and the choice for the corresponding national language as the only one — do not run parallel. We meet both reaction patterns in the cases of Brussels and Budapest. Originally Budapest was inhabited by a numerical and social majority of Germans. Until 1860 the majority of the citizens spoke this language as standard and a number of them used a West Yiddish variety of it as colloquial. The same situation existed in other important capitals of the non-German-speaking provinces of the Hapsburg Monarchy: Prague, Brünn/Brno, Pressburg/Poszony/Bratislava, Lemberg/Lwów/L'viv, Laibach/Ljubljana, Czernowitz/Černovi/Cernăuţi, and others. In these cities the mainly Jewish citizenship was strongly influenced by German culture and used German as a more or less supernational medium of understanding between the various peoples of the Hapsburg *Vielvölkerstaat*: German national feeling was not involved in this. Until the 1860s the German linguistic group in the Hungarian capital dominated cultural and economic life. Afterwards the internal affairs of Hungary were organized within the framework of the

Table I. *Linguistic Groups in Budapest*

	German linguistic group		Magyar linguistic group	
	Total	Of which bilingual	Total	Of which bilingual
1857	60,441 56.0%		38,440 36.0%	
1880	119,902 33.2%	48,621 40.6%	198,742 55.1%	131,908 71.7%
1890	118,018 24.0%	58,658 49.7%	345,283 71.6%	199,137 57.7%
1900	104,520 14.3%	73,952 70.7%	578,458 79.0%	307,348 53.1%
1910	78,882 9.0%		756,070 85.9%	
1920	60,425 6.5%		837,858 90.2%	

Magyarization of the country, which was especially directed at the assimilation of all non-Magyar-speaking elements (55% of the population) (Hutterer 1965:142).

The census figures for Budapest (Table I) reflect the official policy of the leading class against the linguistic minorities who were exposed to a set of measures systematically aimed at assimilation of language, of national feeling, and even of superficialities as geographical indications and surnames. This Magyarization was reflected in the unequal division of votes, in restrictions on the freedom of the non-Magyar press, in restrictions concerning the non-Magyar schools, in the selection of public servants, and finally in the census: in 1850 41.6% and in 1910 54.5% of all Hungarians spoke Magyar as 'mother-tongue'!

The Hungarian Germans numbering 14% of the population, and particularly the Jews among them, had always been prototypes of the nonlinguistic national identity typical of loyal subjects of the Hapsburg Monarchy. The important, culturally well developed and wealthy but small group of the Transylvanian Saxons (*Siebenbürger Sachsen*) may be taken as being the only German group in Hungary with national self-consciousness.

These figures (from G. Thirring 1907 and *Magyar statisztikai Közlemények,* 1880, 1890, 1900, 1910, 1920) show a strong diminution of the German group between 1880 and 1910 while, during the same period, the number of bilinguals increased. We may thus assume that this bilingual group formed a stage of transition between the two national identities or between an older linguistic identity and a new national identity which did not any longer imply one another.

Another example is Brussels (Table II), which was originally inhabited by a unilingual population speaking Netherlandic.[2] Since

Table II. *Linguistic Groups in Brussels*

	Unilingual Netherlandic (a)	Bilingual (b)	Bilingual with a Netherlandic preference (c)	Total Netherlandic (a + c)
1788				94.5%
1846				66.7%
1880				55.0%
1890		51.3%		
1900		47.8%		
1910	23.9%	48.2%	46.5%	46.3%
1920	16.4%	53.7%	39.9%	37.8%
1930	13.3%	47.8%	40.6%	33.7%
1947	7.2%	58.3%	25.7%	24.2%

Brussels became the capital of bilingual states — first as capital of the
medieval Duchy of Brabant where Netherlandic was dominant — the
city has fulfilled a bilingual Netherlandic-French function. In those
medieval times court and chancellery were bilingual while the life of
the 'burghers' was accompanied by Netherlandic language and culture. When Brussels became the capital of the Burgundic realm in the
fifteenth century the influence of French was growing: the upper
class (nobility) underwent a strong orientation towards France. In
the sixteenth century the Netherlands were unified by the emperor
of the Holy Roman Empire, and this caused the stabilization of
French language and culture in the circles of the court and the
nobility, where it nevertheless became more and more dominating.
So the higher bourgeoisie did not follow the example of the nobility
until the eighteenth century — in the meantime the Netherlands were
separated into a northern and a southern (bilingual) state — when
French became at least the second language of all European elites.
During the French Revolution and the annexation of Belgium (the
southern Netherlands) by France, public administration, schools,
theater, newspapers, and the church were ordered to use French,
while at the same time old social, clerical, and economic structures,
traditional strongholds of the Netherlandic culture, were destroyed
(Hemmerechts 1966). Since that time French culture and language
has occupied a dominant and lasting position in Brussels life, so
much so that Brussels became the second capital of the French
cultural world and a refuge for French political and intellectual
émigrés of the Restoration period. Within a few decades the middle

classes of Brussels bourgeoisie Frenchified at least to a stage of bilinguality; immigration from France and Wallonia (the French-speaking southern part of Belgium) and assimilation caused a steady development of a unilingual French group from 5% in 1795 to 40% in 1947. Notwithstanding a far larger immigration from Flanders the unilingual Netherlandic group disappeared: 85% in 1795 to barely 10% in 1947. This unilingual Netherlandic group may thus be considered as a supplier of the bilingual group, growing to an absolute majority within one century and keeping that position at Flemish costs in spite of a constant loss to the French group (figures from *Volkstelling van het Koninkrijk België*, 1910, 1920, 1930, 1947).

4. NATIONAL IDENTITY AND LINGUISTIC IDENTITY

I stated earlier that I would examine the relation between two methods of group identification, one based on national community and the other on linguistic community.[3] Orginally the two concepts were by no means identical. For as long as people have been aware of the fact that they lived in a community with a particular language — naturally implying the community of other cultural characteristics as well — feelings of identification must have been in existence among the members of such a community. Those feelings hardly conditioned the origin of early medieval states as they did in modern times; their function may have been an initiating one among other factors. The state itself, originally a framework of rights and obligations, norms and values, political, economic, and juridical power, proved to be fertile soil for the development of another feeling of community: national identification. So nationalism may be described as a complex of values, norms, and aspirations operating within a social collectivity and based on togetherness originating from sharing a common history: it is a complex which evolved historically and internalized in a way which the individual members of a nation accepted and which they decided to continue in a formal and legal framework: the state. It appears to be a contradiction: states which evolved in early medieval times are seldom an expression of the feelings described; it is often just the opposite: national feelings seem to have arisen — even when more than one linguistic, religious, or cultural group participated in that state — only after a long period of living together and sharing the same vissicitudes. The original concept of nationality is clearly reflected in the division of medieval student populations in international university cities such as Paris, Prague, Padua, etc.: the students were officially divided into, say, a Bohemian, a Silesian, a Polish, a Hungarian 'nation'; all these 'nations' consisted of more than one linguistic group and all comprised members of one and the same linguistic group, in this case the German one.

We do, however, see some evidence of the relevance of linguistic identities to politics in some medieval states. For instance, territorial expansions of the French kingdom were sometimes motivated by the linguistic character of the occupied countries. One of the linguistically most complex nationalities must have been the population of the *Heilige Römische Reich* ('Holy Roman Empire') comprising parts of the German, Low German, Netherlandic, Frisian, French, Italian, Czech, Polish, Sorbian, Slovenian, Italian, and Romansh linguistic groups. However, some linguistically homogeneous states also came into being in early times: the Scandinavian, Polish, Portugese, and English nations had exclusive linguistic identities at the time they established a state. As a consequence of territorial expansion most of these states lost their linguistic homogeneity before the end of the Middle Ages. The still very weak relation between linguistic identities and national identities was complicated during the period of cultural Renaissance and religious Reformation. Once the religious unity of Europe had been broken, religious affiliations could become another breeding-ground for the development of collective (national) identities and consequently for the development of new states just as in an earlier stage, religion had been the main factor in the rise of a Ruthenian-Ukrainian nation within the Polish Kingdom, in the separation between Croats and Serbs, and in the national uprising of the Czechs (Hussites). In the sixteenth and seventeenth centuries some national identities were even split up, notwithstanding their linguistic community, as a consequence of such different religious affiliations: the Netherlandic nation fell apart into a northern Netherlandic (commonly called Dutch) and a southern Netherlandic (Belgian) nation, Englishmen and English-speaking Irishmen grew apart, and in the Holy Roman Empire a polarization between the northern Protestant and the southern Roman Catholic countries took place in which Prussia became the champion of the one and Austria of the other party. This antithesis persisted till the end of the last century.

Religion has even been an important factor in awakening linguistic identities. National and cultural emancipation of most European

peoples was subject to strong impulses from sixteenth-century re-
formist and occasionally counter-reformist movements. Protestantism, in particular, was related to the development of new standard
languages among the peoples of eastern and central Europe. The
connection between Protestant belief and language is a profound
one; in Protestantism language, the sacral medium of the Biblical
word and truth, has taken over the function of older Catholic
ritualism and mysticism in many respects.

Other factors determining the development of European nations
have been geographical distance, specific economic interests, and a
more or less cultural and social isolation. Factors such as these were
important to the birth of the Irish,[4] American, Norwegian, and
Finnish[5] nations, originally participants within a political and linguistic unity with the English, Danish, and Swedish.

A very recent factor is difference in social order: the German
Democratic Republic is growing into nationhood as a result of deep
differences in societal structure and political administration. Dynastic affiliation may be observed, e.g., among the Frisians living on the
island of Fehr Föhr, when they opted in favor of Denmark in 1920
while the other Frisians expressed an unanimous wish to belong to
Germany. We meet this factor again with the 'Baltic Barons' and the
cysarskimi.

All the factors mentioned so far played a role from the beginning
of the early Middle Ages, with some being of more importance than
others at different times. Language seems to be one of the most
recent factors to play a role, but in just this quality it had a great
impact upon the shaping of modern Europe.

So far we have distinguished several factors in the birth of a nation
and noted that their prevalences to one another changed from time
to time and from country to country. Language as a criterion and
symbol of a national identity became pertinent in the past century
when linguistic and national identity were standardized as one and
the same concept. This process is considered to be a product of
Romantic thought. Some scholars look upon German Lutheranism as
the soil for the growth of such ideas; early nineteenth-century
nationalism in the German countries was evidently a secularized form
of Lutheranism in which the German linguistic group and the German nation merged (Wittram 1954b gives a very interesting survey; I
refer here to pp. 76–94).

During the nineteenth century nationalism became more important than it ever had been before, a development related to the rise

of a middle class looking for an identity of its own and an ideological base for its participation in the democratically reorganized European society. Language in particular was looked upon as an old distinguishing symbol of originality in a culturally more and more leveling world. Romantic attitudes to national identity were adopted initially by European 'democrats' during the first half of the last century. Between 1840 and 1920 the new ideas also became acceptable — even very useful — to the authorities of the established states of Europe. It can be said that in the years 1860—80 European national identities were generally reformulated on the basis of linguistic group feeling. Consequently a desire for a huge and violent reorganization of the framework of states developed culminating in World War I. With the proverbial exception of Switzerland even states with an essentially bilingual national identity — Belgium, Finland, Ireland, Scotland — were subject to a process of disintegration following linguistic divisions or towards a stage of unilinguality. On the other hand new nations and states — Norway, for example — felt obliged to develop their own linguistic identity by constructing a new national language (Landsmål), still in competition with the older standard language (Riksmål) which was considered to be simply a Norwegian version of Danish. Luxembourg tried to promote its (German) dialect to a new standard; similar attempts in Switzerland failed. Landsmål, Letzebürgesch, and Schwyzerdütsch did not assume a dominant position!

The new national 'linguistic' Romanticism fragmented several older national identities with a multilingual character: the Prussian ('Borussian') identity comprising German-, Polish-, Lithuanian-, Sorbian-, Danish-, Frisian-, Czech-, and Walloon-(French)-speaking subjects; the Hungarian identity comprising Hungarian-(Magyar)-, Slovakian-, German-, Rumanian-, Ruthenian-, Slovenian-, and Serbo-Croatian-speaking subjects; and the Austrian identity comprising German-, Czech-, Polish-, Ruthenian-, Italian-, Romansh-, and Slovenian-speaking subjects. The Prussian national concept was not formally abandoned until the war of 1870 which resulted in the unification of Germany under Prussian leadership. The Austrian national concept — more than others based upon dynastic traditions — was alive among parts of the German Austrians and among some groups of other linguistic identities such as the Ruthenian *cysarskimi* (Kaiser's people) until the end of the World War I (Nahirny and Fishman 1966:345).

In the 1840s the Hungarian national identity evolved from a

traditional and feudalistic multilingual identity to a new linguistic (Magyar) identity. It manifested itself by the democratic movement in the first half of the century aimed at the authoritarian and centralistic Austrian administration of Vienna. To give a clear picture of the development of a linguistic national identity I will discuss this particular case more thoroughly.

Hungary was ruled by parliament, administration, and court in Latin — a characteristic symbol of a multilingual nation — until 1844. The Hungarian bourgeoisie in almost all Hungarian towns spoke German, as did the gentry, while the true nobility (the 'Magnates') used French and German as daily vernacular. Hungarian as spoken by the peasantry was not fit to serve as literary language. As such Hungarian was no more significant to the Hungarian nation than was German in the towns (and several parts of the countryside), Slovakian in the north, Rumanian in the east or Serbo-Croatian in the south. After 1840 a national revival led to a revolutionary outburst in 1848. It was followed by a period of repression from Vienna which nevertheless culminated in the formation of an autonomous Hungarian kingdom within the Hapsburg Monarchy in 1866. In this short period modern Magyar, the newly developed Hungarian language, became the symbol of the reborn Hungarian nation. The urban population and the gentry were swiftly mobilized for the new ideas, became linguistically assimilated and participated in the new state as an elite core, and firmly decided to assimilate all non-Magyar-speaking elements (Graf zu Brandis 1926:138).

A more recent illustration of the evolution of a straightforward linguistic identity into a national identity is the former Austrian province of Galicia. In Galicia religious affiliation and linguistic group feeling were identical for some centuries: Jews were Germans, Roman Catholics were Poles, and Greek Catholics were Ruthenians. In

Table III. *Religion and National Identity in Eastern Galicia*

	Roman Catholics	Poles	Greek Catholics	Ruthenians
1890	5,561	6,573	10,847	11,248
1900	7,532	28,395	12,825	12,213

	Jews	Germans
1890	21,677	22,198
1900	22,399	932

434   P. H. van der Plank

Table IV.   Numerical Evolution of Absolutely Declining European
            Linguistic Minorities

Germany	1890	1900	1910	1925
Frisian-speaking	52,469	20,775	17,668	7,311
Danish-speaking[a]	140,664	142,058	10,275	5,709
Sorbian-speaking	115,481	107,583	102,801	72,626
Mazurian-speaking	327,696	276,801	268,628	81,098
Polish-speaking[a]	2,922,475	3,305,749	803,244	783,880
Lithuanian-speaking[a]	125,053	107,876	24,811	5,241

Austria (boundaries 1919)	1880	1910	1939	1961
Slovenian-speaking	102,252	82,212	± 45,000	25,498
Croatian-speaking	41,063	43,633	± 40,000	26,149

Hungary	1880	1890		1910	
Croatian- and Serbian-speaking (boundaries before 1919)	4.6%	678,747	4.5%	656,324	3.6%
German-speaking	13.6%	1,988,589	13.1%	1,903,357	10.4%
Slovak-speaking	13.5%	2,002,165 (1900)	11.9%	1,946,357	10.7%
(boundaries 1919)		1880		1930	
German-speaking		607,131		478,630	

Italy (boundaries before 1919)	1860		1921	
French-speaking	120,067		90,700	

Great Britain and Ireland	1851	1881	1911	1931	1961
Irish Gaelic-speaking	1,524,286	949,932	582,446		
Welsh-speaking				909,261	656,002
Scottish Gaelic-speaking		231,594	202,398	136,135	80,978

(Censuses concerning linguistic minorities were never made in France and Spain so estimates must suffice for these countries.)

France	1928	1960
Breton-speaking	1,400,000	1,000,000
Flemish-speaking[b]	250,000	100,000

Spain	1936	1954
Basque-speaking	700,000	525,000

[a] Linguistic groups marked [a] were living in border areas with a national frontier more or less revised according to the linguistic boundaries in the treaties and plebiscites after the World War I. The figures for 1910 and 1925 concern those parts of these groups which remained German citizens after the war.
[b] Only autochthonic Flemings; the numerous Belgian immigrants in the French speaking mining area of Lille are not included.

the final decades of the last century the Polish elite of citizens and gentry tried to Polonize the country. The effect of their campaigns is shown in Table III. In 1890 the numerical difference between the religious and national groups was no more than 5% but ten years later 95% of the bilingual Polish-Yiddish Jews manifested their national and not just their traditional linguistic option in a new national linguistic affiliation[6] (figures from *Die Ergebnisse, 1890 und 1900*).

The new linguistically defined national identity was often used as a motive for territorial expansion toward the boundaries of a particular linguistic area — French aspirations toward Belgium, German aspirations toward Alsace-Lorraine, Sudetenland, and Schleswig-Holstein, while Italy was interested in Trentino and Istria — or as an excuse for the forced assimilation of deviant linguistic groups. So it often happened that quite loyal members of a nation not speaking the 'national' language felt obliged to assimilate in order not to constitute a threat to their state. Parts of linguistic groups found themselves in the unfortunate position of living just on the other side of the frontiers of that very state in which their language was used not only as a colloquial vernacular but as an official medium and a national symbol as well. Some of these groups accepted their fate, accepted the reformulated national identity together with the language, while others revised their national choice. Some became bilingual and accepted the new national language as a national symbol and literary language without abandoning the original vernacular as their daily speech (the Alsatians). Others even resisted linguistic assimilation, thus amounting to a constant threat of disloyalty and a focus for territorial claims from neighboring states. All were the subject of legal measures directed toward assimilation. The fate of these minorities is shown in Table IV by the census data of the most important European states from the middle of the last century to the present day. Most of these minorities did not survive the period.

5. LINGUISTIC MINORITIES AND SOCIAL MINORITIES

In a bilingual society an important function of language is the so-called identification function. By speaking a particular language one allows oneself to be identified socially with a particular linguistic group. The collective stereotype, the social image of a linguistic group, is in that way transferred to the individual member. For example, speaking Flemish in the city of Brussels, or at one time speaking German in Prague and Budapest, or Finnish in Helsingfors, was a sign of lower social prestige leading to a weaker position in social contacts and consequently in the process of social mobility.

All individuals who wish to rise socially are confronted with external (group) criteria influencing their chances: for instance, signs of racial, political, social, religious, geographical, or linguistic group identity. In a European bilingual society one of the most important criteria is found in the linguistic identity. The groups occupying a power position in the structure of these societies will, through their control over the assignment of individual positions, ensure their collective position by applying the language of their linguistic group as one of the criteria for upward mobility. In this way an assimilation process is started in which the dominating linguistic group absorbs socially rising elements of the subordinated linguistic group(s).

The motives of these elites have to be sought in a striving for exclusivity, feelings of cultural superiority, linguistic solidarity, nationalistic feelings, the need of political support by the members of their linguistic group. Even if such a linguistic group forms a numerical minority we call it a linguistic majority because it shows all the

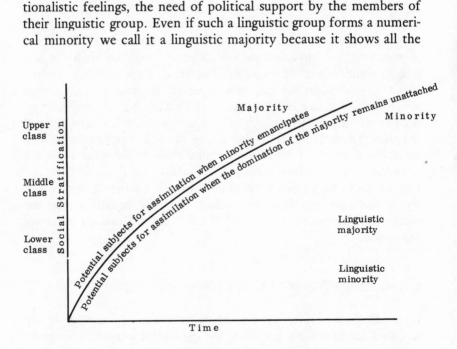

Figure 1. *The Role of Class Divisions in Assimilation Processes.*

characteristics of a group in a socially superior position. The graph in Figure 1 endeavors to clarify the role of class divisions in assimilation processes.

An example is the French-(Walloon)-speaking population of Belgium which never constituted more than 40—45% of the entire population. Nevertheless, from the foundation of the Belgian state up to the present day French-speaking Belgians have formed a linguistic majority, as is shown in the fact that Netherlandic-(Flemish)-speaking subjects are still affected by assimilation while the reverse is not and never has been the case. In Bohemia and Moravia the German part of the population, amounting to one-third,[7] was a linguistic majority during the Austrian period. After 250 years of German linguistic hegemony the major role of the German linguistic group was taken over by the Czechs in a fierce political and economic struggle ending in the expulsion of the Germans in 1945. The extent and character of the assimilation processes accompanying these social changes is approximately quantifiable, e.g., if we take surnames as being valid indications of original linguistic group identity. Among the so-called Sudeten Germans approximately 15% had Czech names while in 23 Czech-speaking country boroughs in the vicinity of Prague 10—35% of the population, according to their names, proved to be of more or less recent German background. That, in the first place, socially elevated elements had been German for some time is perhaps indicated by the fact that more than one-third of the upper class in these towns had a German name as against more than a quarter in the middle class and one-seventh in the lower class (Müller 1950:266—269). The same figures can be found in other linguistic boundary areas such as the former German province of Posen/Poznań. There a large proportion of the German majority bore Polish surnames but even 8% of the Poles had a German name. The latter were exclusively Roman Catholic and this is an indication of the influence of religion upon assimilation (Broesike 1912:385). I will discuss this connection below.

Without doubt the Baltic Germans must be considered a classic example of a linguistic majority in the position of a numerical minority. The Baltic Germans descended from mainly Low German, but also from Scandinavian, and of course from assimilated autochthonic noblemen, civil servants, merchants, artisans, and soldiers in the so-called Baltic countries: the countries of the Esthonians, Livonians, and the Latvian tribes. Shortly after 1200 this area was occupied by German crusaders motivated by commercial interests, lust for adventure, and missionary passion. After one-and-a-half centuries of establishing their power over the autochthons and against the competing Russians and Lithuanians, the Germans consolidated their position, the absolute control of the whole political, spiritual, cultural, and economic life of the so-called *Baltikum*. The Baltikum, finally organized into three counties (Estonia, Livonia, and Courland, the latter two constituting the Latvian Republic in 1919), maintained their external independence until the middle of the sixteenth century. Since then they have belonged to different realms such as Poland, Sweden, and finally Russia — but each time they were able to regain internal autonomy. The German group consisted of some hundreds of noble families — the 'Baltic Barons' — from which the clerical, political, and military authorities of the counties were drawn. Sons of these families played important roles — depending on the changing situation as regards political dependence — in the civil service and above all in the higher ranks of the armies of Poland, Prussia, Sweden, and Russia and in the Stockholm and Petersburg ministries. Five to ten percent of the German group belonged to this noble caste, which represented almost the whole of Baltic landlordism (80—95% until the land reforms in the beginning of the present century). The Baltic urban dwellers[8] and the urban magistrates were also German although important numerical minorities in (and around!) the towns were of Scandinavian, Russian, Polish, and autochthonic origin. During the latter half of the last century the majority of the urban dwellers already spoke languages other than German, but it was not until the first decade of this century that the urban magistracy lost its German character. More than three-quarters of the urban upper class — the *haute bourgeoisie* or *Ehrenbürger* — belonged to the German group, as did more than half of the civil servants, even during the period of intensive Russification between 1880 and 1905. The rural population was almost exclusively autochthonic except for the nobility and the country notables: clergymen, civil servants, foresters, notaries, teachers, medical men, millers, and some artisans. As late as 1881 the German elite consisted of only 160,000 subjects living among two million Estonians and Latvians: 9.7% in Livonia, 8,7% in Courland, and 5.8% in Estonia.

It is evident that German culture exerted a great influence upon the Esthonians and Latvians. One possible indication of this is that more than a half of all the books printed in Esthonian or Latvian were of German origin in the period preceding World War I. This influence has to be considered in connection with the Lutheran faith and rural parish work — 85% of all ministers were of German stock — and with the primary school system, widespread throughout the country and excellently organized by the Baltic knighthood (*Ritterschaft*) and the church.

But social interaction between the German elite and the autochthons had always been limited and restricted to rigid, traditional roles of master and servant. Mobility was very low between the different castes, which were granted specific privileges with specific administrative laws and even with specific jurisdiction. Only the towns offered a road to a better social status but not before German culture and language were accepted. The separation between Germans and Estonians and Latvians was deliberately aspired to by the German elite and Germanization exercised, as it was in Germany, upon linguistic minorities failed to occur. On the contrary, barriers were placed in the way of learning German and it was even forbidden to farmers on baronial property, while clergy and teachers used the autochthonic languages as the exclusive means for communicating with the people.[9] Some estimates put the number of Germanized autochthons at not more than 50,000: one-third of the whole German group but no more than 2% of the original population.

Since 1870—80 the autonomy of the Baltic caste society was reduced by a Czarist policy directed at the administrative unification of Russia and the Russification of all non-Russian elements. At the same time mobility perspectives were created by industrialization and urbanization, processes by which the towns lost their German character. Although German dominance was replaced after 1880 by Russification the caste-structured society remained untouched. The Baltic elite did not resist Russification of public life and of the autochthons as long as its own priviliged way of life allowed it to protect its culture and language in its private social sphere. The continued blocking of mobility opportunities, even the difficulty of rising socially by assimilation, contributed to a revolutionary outburst among the Estonians and Latvians in 1905. After that date, and definitely after 1919 when Estonia and Latvia became independent democratic republics, the role of the German elite gradually declined. Diminishing numerically for a long time due to a low birthrate, the German group became subject to a strong emigration to Germany and its number dropped to 75,000 in 1939, the year in which the Germans were expelled. The German urban middle class in particular had come to occupy a very weak position, while the nobility lost most of its property in land reforms. However, even in 1939 20% of the entire national property of Esthonia was in the hands of the Germans, at that time constituting no more than 1.2% of the population (Wittram 1954a).

I will conclude my consideration of the concept 'linguistic minority' with a more topical example: the Swedish-speaking Finns. Finland was occupied by Sweden around 1250. This occupation was accompanied by Swedish colonization of the sparsely inhabited coastal areas in the south (Nyland) and the northwest (Österbotten) and the foundation of some towns, combining the function of fortress with that of political and commercial center. From the beginning the Swedish Finns constituted an upper class of merchants, large landowners, gentry, clergy, military and medical men, politicians and civil servants, and later industrialists and bankers. Nevertheless the numerical majority of the Swedish Finns consisted of small farmers and fishermen, just like the Finnish-speaking part of the population.

From the thirteenth until the nineteenth century Finland may be considered as an integral part of the Swedish Kingdom. During the nineteenth century this situation was continued, from a sociocultural point of view, under Russian supervision.[10] Swedish was at that time the only language of cultural, commercial, political, and public life, while Finnish played a purely literary role in the churches of the 'hinterland'. In the second and third decades of the last century Finnish language and folklore became subject to the national sentiments of some scholars and students, members of the Swedish elite. Their enthusiasm did not have immediate consequences for the position of the Finns and their language. However, these initiatives bound 'Swedish' Finns and 'Finnish' Finns together in one nationality for the future although later a certain amount of antagonism was to arise between the two linguistic groups. It was only in the 1860s that the Finns were able to make a start with their emancipation. Between 1863 and 1883 Finnish was granted a place as the second internal language, first in a passive and later in an active role. Swedish, however, retained its position as the exclusive medium of the external civil service. Secondary education in Finnish started in 1870 with three schools, as opposed to seventy-four Swedish institutions. Only twenty years later the number of Finnish and Swedish institutions was equal — approximately fifty of both. But in 1920 29% of all pupils in secondary education still belonged to the Swedish linguistic group constituting 11% of the population at the time. The universities remained under Swedish domination until the

1920s. But a basis for constitutional emancipation was created in 1906 when universal suffrage was introduced and when the Finns could put their overwhelming numbers (85% of the population) into political power. In Finland emancipation and democratization were linked to industrialization and urbanization, as is shown by the fact that in 1880 more than half the town inhabitants were Swedish compared to 25% in 1910 and 8.7% in 1960.

Even after half a century the majority character of the Swedish linguistic group has not been fully wiped out. Their number fell from 14% in 1880 to 7.5% in 1960 and from 354,000 in 1940 to 330,500 in 1960; of the generations living at present 2% per year may be considered to leave the Swedish group for the Finnish. These are typical signs of a declining linguistic minority. But 17% of all large-scale farms (exceeding fifty hectares) and 25% of Finland's entire industrial production[11] is in Swedish hands, while the Swedes exceed their national proportion with more than one-third in the occupational sector of trade and commerce and among university students (Meinander 1965).

Evidently the Swedish elite is no longer willing to use its language publicly as a criterion for upward social mobility in the occupational spheres under its control. The elite fears damaging its own economic position, aware of the power of an overwhelming Finnish majority in legislative bodies and the force of public opinion. After 1880 some German-speaking industrialists and large landowners in Bohemia and Moravia demonstrated the same situation of an elite detaching itself from its original linguistic group. However detaching does not at all simply mean assimilation in the case of elites alone. The public and political role of the old French-speaking elite of Flanders is definitely over but recent investigation still discloses its position at the top of the occupational stratification: 0% of the laborers, 20% of the clerks, 30% of the lower and 60% of the higher executives, and 85% of the members of the board of directors in industrial concerns in the province of East Flanders spoke French at home or at least within their own group (Deleeck 1959).

6. LINGUISTIC MINORITIES, SOCIAL MOBILITY, AND INDUSTRIALIZATION

My concept of a linguistic majority/minority based upon socio-economic power and the role of a social elite over the assignment of positions in a bilingual society becomes manifest when such a society is mobilized. Social mobility — the process of moving up or down the social ladder — has to be considered as a consequence of industrialization and is closely connected with urbanization. When dealing with the concept of the linguistic minority I have indicated that control over the assignment of positions by the linguistic majority forces socially rising elements to assimilate. Indeed, we see an acceleration of linguistic assimilation in urban areas, evidently related to the highly mobilized stage of development of the urban bilingual society. In another article (van der Plank 1972) I gave some illustrations bearing out this hypothesis which deserve repetition in summary form. The towns of South Styria, a former Austrian province now a part of the Yugoslavian republic of Slovenia, were originally medieval German settlements.[12] Although situated in an area which was altogether Slovenian (97%) these towns maintained their German character until modern times. At the end of the last century the majority of the urban dwellers originated from the Slovenian countryside but in 1880 65% and in 1910 as many as 78.5% of them wished to be considered as belonging to the German linguistic group. A second illustration is Upper Silesia, the second largest industrial center of the former German Empire. This province tripled its population between 1870 and 1910 mainly by emigration from the Polish-speaking surrounding areas. Nevertheless the proportion of Germans rose from 30% to 60% in the urban part of the province while it stayed approximately the same in the countryside (± 10—20%).

To these a third example should be added. Between 1880 and 1910 the linguistic minorities of Hungary, although maintaining the relative proportion of their urban members, saw their position in the towns undermined very rapidly (Table V) (*Magyar statisztikai Közlemények, Új folyam 1, Új sorozat 27 and 64*).

Table V. *Linguistic Minorities in the Hungarian Kingdom*

As % of the urban population	1880	1910	As % of their own group	1880	1910
Slovaks	7.3	4.3	Urban Slovaks	8.6	8.2
Germans	18.4	9.7	Urban Germans	21.1	19.2
Serbs and			Urban Serbs and		
Croats	5.2	2.8	Croats	17.5	19.2
Magyars	63.2	76.6	Urban Magyars	21.2	28.6

The relative proportion of Magyars in the municipalities, according to their size, increased from 34.3% in the category < 1,000 inhabitants to 44.7% in the category 1,000–5,000 and 63.8% in the category 5,000–10,000, and to 76.7% in the category > 10,000 inhabitants. These figures coincide in the occupational structure. The Slavo-Rumanian minorities of Hungary amounted to 33% of the population but to only 7% of the middle bourgeoisie, to 20% of the lower bourgeoisie, and to 42% of the agrarians. Nevertheless these agrarians owned not more than only 20% of Hungary's soil (*Les négotiations de la paix hongroise,* Tome III/A [Budapest, 1920]: 27–30: see *Magyar statisztikai, Új sorozat 56*).

As a last example let us take Moravia, the former Austrian province east of Bohemia. With the exception of those living in the parts bordering in the north on Germany (Silesia) and in the south on (Lower) Austria the Moravians spoke Czech: 67% of the population in 1880 and 72.5% in 1910.[13] But also in the Czech-speaking area, towns had a German character consolidated in the last decades of the Austrian period: figures for the most important towns are given in Table VI.

Urbanization and industrialization had a similar effect in Moravia, of which the industrial area of Mährisch Ostrau/Moravské Ostrava is a good example. This area, entirely Czech-speaking in 1880, was Germanized in an astonishingly rapid way after a period of industrialization (Zèmmrich 1912:164; *Österreichische Statistik*).

South Tyrol, admittedly, is an exception. Recent industrialization dominated by the Italian linguistic majority had no effect upon the German minority: assimilation did not occur. However, South Tyrol does show, in a specific and very clear way, the same connection between socioeconomic power and assimilation. Normally bilingual societies have integrated socioeconomic structures of which an inte-

Table VI. *German-Speaking Towns*
         of Moravia

German-speaking (%)	1880	1910
Brünn/Brno	60	66
Olmütz/Olomouc	64	65
Iglau/Jihlava	84	80
Troppau/Opava	84	92
Teschen/Těšín	50	63

grated occupational system is the most important part, the outcome of a long common history of linguistic majority and minority together. In that case industrialization, implying acceleration of mobility, causes assimilation and urban areas become centers of such processes. South Tyrol is more than simply an example: it is a unique situation for testing my hypothesis about the connection between social mobility, urbanization, and assimilation.

South Tyrol is a recently urbanized and industrialized society and although these processes have always been dominated by the Italian-speaking majority of the population, assimilation is a rare phenomenon among the German-speaking minority. An explanation can partly be found in the fact that the Germans are sharply divided from the Italians in their own more or less autonomous mobility system of a predominantly agrarian and traditional character. Here there is no question of an integration between the different linguistic groups in the same occupational stratification. After the annexation of Austrian South Tyrol as 'Alto-Adige' by Italy in 1919 the new authorities tried to Italianize the province by outnumbering the original population. In a relatively short time, mainly between 1938 and 1947, tens of thousands of laborers and public servants moved in from Italy. However, the German-speaking town inhabitants of South Tyrol were forced to leave their country under an agreement made between Italy and Nazi Germany. Since World War II the towns and industrial areas have been largely controlled and inhabited by Italians while the rural population has retained its almost exclusively German-speaking character. At present 34% of the population of Alto-Adige speaks Italian; in the eight most important towns this figure is 73% and in the countryside 11%. The dividing line between the occupational systems of Italians and Germans is based upon the urban/rural opposition; the recruitment of industrial laborers and public servants is not taking place in the countryside but in Italy and in the South Tyrolean towns (Table VII).

In 1961 agriculture (97%), commerce (67%), and handicraft (72%) belonged mainly to the German-dominated occupational system, while industry (65%) and public services (88%) were operated by Italians. The boundaries between agriculture, commerce, handicraft, industry, and public service are not fading away. On the contrary, the Germans are moving ahead in the commercial area but hardly at all in industry,[14] while the Italians are displaying more and more activity in public service and industry. This development is confirmed by the pattern of secondary school education. Secondary

Table VII. *Occupational-Lingual Divisions in South Tyrol.*

	1939		1961	
	German	Italian	German	Italian
Agriculture	61	6	45	4
Commerce	12	22	29	23
Handicraft	15	24	10 ⎫ 21	9 ⎫ 39
Industry			11 ⎭	30 ⎭
Public services	2	8	4	20

school education is apparently not a prerequisite in a mainly agrar-ian-handicraft-oriented occupational system while it is for industry or public service. In 1968—69 75% of all primary school pupils spoke German while 39% of all secondary school pupils belonged to the German group; 12% of the Germans had graduated from secondary schools as compared to 30% of the Italians! (van der Plank 1972; Pan 1971:102—109).

7. INSTITUTIONALIZATION AS A FORM OF SELF-DEFENSE AGAINST ASSIMILATION

Institutionalizing a linguistic minority is the process of structuring the members of a linguistic group in associational patterns: an educational system, a religious system, a political system, and as a final consequence an occupational system. The example of South Tyrol shows an occupationally divided structure: two different and autonomous occupational systems. Although in South Tyrol this situation is more or less coincidental, its attainment can be the conscious policy of the minority. Institutionalization indicates the structural aspects of the emancipation of a minority; it also includes and initiates processes of culture formation with which institution-alization in the strict sense is in interaction. This means that new cultural and social values, norms, and ideals arise within the associa-tional systems mentioned; these cultural elements may give birth to the development of new systems, or at least associations, and so on. In the first place, before institutionalization (emancipation) can even be an aspiration of members of a minority one precondition must be fulfilled. The members of that minority have to become aware of a common urgent problem: social discrimination of the whole group. It need not be argued that this problem was actually made manifest in the creation of mobility perspectives, the possibility of rising socially combined with restrictions for the members of the minority. In other words industrialization has proved to be the beginning of the emancipatory struggle of linguistic minorities. Their emancipation was often connected with political radicalism. Parallels between the emancipation of linguistic minorities and the emancipation of the working class are obvious.

In a more or less autonomous occupational system a minority is able to withdraw from the influence of the elites controlling the assignment of positions in a bilingual society in favor of the majority. The most common way of achieving a more or less autonomous circuit of positions within the occupational structure of a bilingual society is by cooperative. This cooperative was one of the first methods used by the socialist movements in their struggle for emancipation of the working class! Such an occupational autonomy may be achieved simply by linking the consumptive demand of a minority to its supply of goods. Economic autonomy means economic and political pressure which is important in the achievement of formal rights as well. Of course such a radical reformation of societal structures remained an ideal but the cooperation, e.g., of banks, consumers, and producers (farmers), expressing the solidarity of the members of a linguistic minority, exerted a profound influence upon the relations between the German majority and the Czech and Polish minorities in the former provinces of Bohemia and Posen/ Poznań, these being the most militant parts of the Slavic-speaking area in Austria and Germany before World War I (Münch 1949:288; Hoetsch 1913:616; Szembek [n.d.]).

I have already argued that the relevance of precisely this type of institutionalization is preconditioned by a more or less mobilized and industrialized stage of the social structure of bilingual society. This stage may be considered as a critical one in the life of linguistic minorities; if attempts to institutionalize fail, a rapid and inevitable assimilation threatens in urbanized and industrialized areas, the Slovenes, Moravians, Silesian Poles, and most Hungarian minorities being cases in point. In most cases assimilation and emancipation occur at the same time and their respective effects can be measured only after a long period.

In order to be able to work up to leadership elite and to fulfil higher positions created in more or less occupational autonomy a minority educational system is essential. I have already mentioned the growth of Finnish secondary schools, one example among many. In Bohemia, for example, 53% of the secondary school establishments were German in 1883. This number declined to 44% in 1914 after a period of Czech emancipation (Schamelhout 1929:147, 182).

Institutionalization of political organizations is very important when the bilingual society in question is run in a democratic way and when the numerical weight of the minority becomes a significant power in the play of democracy.

We have seen that democratization accompanies the introduction of industrial ways of life, dismantling the position of linguistic majorities which are numerically too small by detachment of their core: the elite of the bilingual society. When, in a bilingual society, at least a more or less numerical equilibrium exists between majority and minority, detachment will not be necessary for an elite group to maintain its position. Then assimilation of socially rising elements not belonging to the linguistic majority becomes likely. In reality the political relations and the balance of power are much more complicated. There may be political antagonism between (a part of) the elite and the rest of the linguistic majority. In that case the elite may use a coalition with the minority to ensure its interests. The support given by some groups of German landowners and industrialists in more or less feudal Austrian Bohemia was of importance to Czech emancipation during the final decades of the last century (Münch 1949:85, 267–275). Solidarity between the working classes of majority and minority is a rare phenomenon; it is often precisely the reverse. Emancipation of a (working-class) minority is opposed by the working class of the majority in view of the competition in their respective opportunities for rising socially. Again Bohemia provides an example with the German laborers opposed to their fellow Czech 'class members'. In Brussels (and Wallonia) we can still see the same situation between French- and Netherlandic-speaking laborers and political organizations (van der Plank 1971:114).

The Czechs showed an extreme form of political institutionalization. Even the mainly internationalistic socialist party had to split up into a German and Czech section after 1893. The Flemings – numbering nearly two-thirds of the population just like the Czechs – failed to create specific political parties to put their number into power. It was only during the past decade that some Flemish (and Walloon) parties arose while the largest party, the Christian Democrats, was split into two autonomous sections. Before 1960 it was customary for the Flemish representatives in legislative bodies to introduce their suggestions for improvements in the position of their linguistic group and of the Netherlandic language in a weakened form because of the solidarity requested by their French-speaking fellow party-members, It is significant that the Czechs needed half a century (1860—1910) to achieve at least a formal position of equality, while the Flemish had to wait nearly a whole century to see their discriminated position (the last bastion being the army) formally withdrawn (1860—1940) (van der Plank 1971:121).

Religious community serves as a framework for institutionalization. It was the church which possessed an educational organization (theological seminaries) in which the study of the culture and language of the minority was given a place, this language being considered as pastoral equipment necessary for priests working among the minority. In the seminaries the development of the first minority leaders could take place, although they were not necessarily members of the minority themselves. In addition, one should remember that theological seminaries represented one of the very few opportunities for members of a minority to rise socially in a premobilized society (van der Plank 1971:125). In Europe, both church and school were based on the clergy in the last century and there was often a personal union between the functions of priest and schoolteacher. In the struggle between the clergy and the state as to whether or not education had to be given in the language of the minority or in the national language, clerical schools and religious lessons became a stronghold for the emancipation of the minority and sometimes the starting point for constructing an independent educational system.

The influence of religion and of clerical structures upon the development of political parties, mass media, public opinion, trade unions, cooperatives, education, in short the whole framework for connubium, convivium, and occupation, is obvious in Europe. In America, on the other hand, we sometimes see the reverse in religious associations which have arisen within and are dependent upon the secular social structure of minority. Religion sometimes had an important impact on nationalism: 'loss of language meant loss of faith, loss of faith meant loss of eternity', Ducharme (1943:92) said about the French-Canadians. In such cases fusion between ethnic and religious values results in a strong collective and emotional, centrifugally directed power among the minority (Walker 1961:16). The Poles and their nationalism form a European illustration of these statements. The impossibility of identifying national with religious beliefs forced one-quarter of the Bohemian Czechs to leave the Roman Catholic church — because of its internationalistic standpoint sneeringly called the Austro-Catholic church — at the beginning of this century (Winter 1938:377; Gause 1952:252).

In a bilingual society the 'majority culture' is often considered by the pastoral leaders of the minority as the personification of 'culture' and wordly life, science, and urbanity. It was not unusual for country priests in nineteenth-century Flanders and Alsace-Lorraine — even those who did speak French as their mother tongue — to obstruct the teaching of French and the reading of French books. They tried to prevent their parishioners from becoming able to participate in the 'perverted' French culture (Lévy 1932, chapter 13; Wolfram 1934:55). In Flanders some clericals wished to see a similar isolation from the 'heretic' (Protestant) North Netherlandic culture which was made accessible by the 'Dutch' standard language.[15] We can trace the same religious motives in the use of a Slovak standard. In Slovakia the Lutherans used Czech as a standard language for some centuries before a national need arose for a Slovakian standard. This Czech was looked upon as a 'heretic' (Hussite) medium by the Catholics. At the same time Lutherans and Catholics decided to construct a Slovakian literary language. The former took Central Slovakian and the latter took West Slovakian dialects as their models for the new standard. It was not until some generations later that both religious groups came together and adopted one variety: Central Slovakian (Locher 1931:64, 98, 170). The same religious opportunism contributed to the choice of the English language instead of the old symbol of Irish Christianity, Gaelic, by the authorities of the Roman Catholic Church in Ireland. The emigration of millions of Irish to England, Scotland, the United States, Canada, Australia, and New Zealand established the position of the Irish clergy as the Roman Catholic primates of the entire English-speaking world, including the colonies as subjects to missionary. Even in America the Irish priesthood is considered to be the most important opponent of so-called ethnic parishes and non-Roman rites (Nahirny and Fishman 1966:333–337; 364). This position could only be confirmed by the acceptance of the English language in Ireland as well, which contributed to the disappearance of Gaelic (Müller-Ross 1931:49). It seems an astonishing fact that Gaelic was not taught until 1893 at Irish seminaries (Aucamp 1926:55).

In any event religion and clerical organization proves to be the
core and the starting point of emancipation of a large number of
European minorities. However, it was specifically the lower clergy
which was able to combine religious values and interests with the
linguistic existence of minorities, often by becoming the initiator and
leader of emancipatory movements; higher clerical authorities always
identified themselves with the culture and language of the majority
as can be seen in the case of the Roman Catholic church in Belgium,
Bohemia, Ireland, and even among some leaders of the Lutheran
churches of Hungary and Poland, traditional strongholds of the
Slovakian and German minorities in those countries. One exception
should be mentioned: the Polish minority in the former German province of Posen and the Roman Catholic clergy could be identified,
up to and including the highest clerical authorities, with each other
even when the German majority was partly Catholic.

Generally speaking, when majority and minority belong to the
same denomination, clerical institutionalization will be dominated by
the majority, leading to assimilation of the linguistic minority. On
the contrary, when majority and minority are divided not only by
language but also by religion, religious and linguistic identity tend to
become identical and in a process of institutionalization the
minority finds a successful defense against assimilation. Since such
religious/linguistic cross situations hardly occur in Europe we have to
put this hypothesis to the test in situations where minority and
majority belong in part to the same religion. In my thesis I have
made a systematic and extensive comparison of the course of linguistic assimilation within all those western and central European
minority/majority confrontations in which the linguistic groups are
separated into various religious groups. In each case one part of the
linguistic minority shared the religious conviction of the linguistic
majority while the other part adhered to another religion which was
non-existent among the majority (van der Plank 1971, Chapter IV).[16]

The comparisons show that within assimilation processes, polarization arises on the base of religious conviction: those parts of the
linguistic minorities belonging to the same religion as the majority
assimilate while the other religiously exclusive parts do not or do so
to a lesser degree. The role of institutionalization is evident in these
remarkable differences.

8. CONCLUSION

Summarizing and interpreting my description of the European linguistic minorities in a general way, I note three distinct stages.

In the period 1820–70 a reformulation and revaluation of national identity caused a development in which linguistic identities evolved to become national identities.

Between 1870 and 1920 the framework of European states was reorganized and based on this national concept. Each nationality had to become a national identity, each state a national state. In consequence internal policies had to be directed towards the assimilation of minorities. Measures concerning assimilation were taken or suggested in France and former Hungary around 1850, in Germany in the 1860s and in Russia in the years after 1870. It must be said that former Austria was the most positive exception during all that time!

Finally, large multilinguistic states split up into several new 'national states': e.g., Austria, Hungary, Russia. At an earlier stage Germany and Italy arose as fusions of different states because of similar ideas concerning national identity and language. These developments did not result in nationally homogeneous states since linguistic and new political boundaries did not coincide. Indeed, large minorities such as the Poles and Czechs disappeared as a result of constituting national states after World War I but the number of minorities increased and with them the latent conflict situations: 50,000,000 Europeans, more than one-tenth of the total population, belonged to a linguistic minority. Latent minority problems became crises and contributed to bring about the World War II. The period 1920–40 may be interpreted as a culmination of minority problems. Assimilation failed as a solution for national homogeneity and so expulsion of large numbers of Europeans from their homelands was common in the years 1939–47. Even so, 20,000,000 Europeans are still in a minority situation. Their problems and even their very existence are often denied by states and public officials but this attitude is not sufficient as a solution, nor does it contribute to their final assimilation. From time to time new protests erupt and we may expect such eruptions to continue as long as a breeding ground for their problems, the assertion of social and cultural inequality, remains a characteristic reaction of the national society in which they try to live.

The problem of European linguistic minorities is not an ideological problem — as is often assumed and as was partly the case in the past — but it is and will remain a social problem.

REFERENCES

Aucamp, J.
1926 Bilingual Education and Nationalism (Pretoria).
Broesike, M.
1912 'Deutsche und Polen der Provinz Posen im Lichte der Statistik', Zeit-
       schrift des Königlichen Preussischen Statistischen Landesamts 41.
Deleeck, H.
1959 De Taaltoestanden in het Vlaamse Bedrijfsleven (Brussel).
Deneckere, M.
1951 Het Vooruitschrijden van het Frans in Vlaanderen (Gent).
1890- Die Ergebnisse der Volkszählung in den im Reichsrate getretenen König-
1900 reichen und Ländern, 1890 und 1900. I. Heft (Büro der Kaiserlichen-
       Königlichen Statistischen Zentralkommission).
Doebner, T.
1903 'Der Einfluss der deutschen Kultur auf die Letten', Deutsche Erde
       2:13—17 (Gotha).
Ducharme, J.
1943 The Shadows of the Trees (New York).
Gadolin, A. von
1968 'Die Schwedische Volksgruppe in Finnland', Europa Ethnica 25:7, 9
       (Vienna).
Gause, F.
1952 Deutsch-slavische Schicksalsgemeinschaft (Kitzingen).
Graf zu Brandis, C.
1926 Die Ungarische Seele (Zurich).
Haegendoren, M. van
1962 De Vlaamse Beweging II, Nu en Morgen (Hasselt).
Hehn, J. von
1951 Die baltischen Lände (Kitzingen).
Hemmerechts, K.
1966 'Brussel of het Triëst van het Noorden', Ons Erfdeel 9:3/4 (Rekkem,
       Belgium).
Hoetsch, O.
1913 'Nationalitätenkampf und Nationalitätenpolitik in der Ostmark', in Die
       Deutsche Ostmark (Lissa).
Hutterer, C.
1965 'The Phonology of Budapest Yiddish', in U. Weinreich, ed., The Field
       of Yiddish. Studies in Language, Folklore and Literature, Vol. II (The
       Hague).
Hymes, D.
1968 'Pidginization and Creolization of Languages: Their Social Contexts', in
       Social Science Council Items, Vol. 22, nr. 2 (New York).
Kloss, H.
1952 Die Entwicklung neuer germanischer Kultursprachen von 1800 bis
       1950 (Munich).

Lévy, P.
1932   *L'histoire linguistique de l'Alsace et de Lorraine: II* (Nancy, Paris).
Locher, T.
1931   *Die Nationale Differenzierung und Integrierung der Slowaken und Tschechen in ihrem geschichtlichen Verlauf bis 1848* (Haarlem). *Magyar statisztikai közlemények.*
Meinander, R.
1965   'The Status of the Linguistic Minorities in Finland', *Europa Ethnica* 22:2—8 (Vienna).
Müller, K.
1950   'Volksbiologische Beziehungen zwischen Tschechen und Deutsche', in H. Preidel, ed., *Die Deutschen in Böhmen und Mähren* (Gräfeling).
Müller-Ross, F.
1931   *Die irische Grenzfrage: Ulster, Irland und Gross-Britannien* (Ohlau in Schlesien).
Münch, H.
1949   *Böhmische Tragödie* (Brunswick, Berlin, Hamburg).
Nahirny, V., and J. Fishman
1966   'Ukrainian Language Maintenance Efforts', in J. Fishman, ed., *Language Loyalty in the United States* (The Hague).
Pan, C.
1971   *Südtirol als völkliches Problem* (Vienna and Stuttgart).
(n.d.)   *Österreichische Statistik, Neue Folge I.* Heft I. (Vienna). [This information is more easily available in: H. Gans 'Zur Entwicklung der Sprachgrenze westwärts der Oderpforte im Laufe eines Jahrhunderts', in *Deutschmährisch-schlesische Heimat* 23:258 (1937).]
Piccard, L.
(n.d.)   *De Vlaamse Beweging* (Antwerp and Amsterdam).
Plank, P. van der
1971   *Taalassimilatie van Europese Taalminderheden* (Rotterdam).
1972   L'assimilation linguistique dans les sociétés urbaines' Recherches *sociologiques* 3 [Louvain] [Translated from an unpublished speech read at the IIIrd International Congress of Applied Linguistics, 1972.)
Renner, K.
1918   *Das Selbstbestimmungsrecht der Nationen I. Teil: Nation und Staat* (Leipzig and Vienna).
Riemann, E.
1937   *Ostpreussisches Volkstum um die Ermländische Nordostgrenze* (Königsberg).
Schamelhout, G.
1929   *De Volkeren van Europa en de Strijd der Nationaliteiten* vol. II (Amsterdam).
Steinbach, F.
1962   *Studien zur westdeutschen Stammes- und Volksgeschichte* (Darmstadt).
Szembek, A.
(n.d.)   'Les associations économiques des paysans polonais sous la domination prussienne' (no place of publication).

Thirring, G.
1907 Budapest szekesföváros statisztikai évkönyve (Budapest).
Volkstelling van het Koninkrijk België/Recensement général. Statistiques du
      Royaume de la Belgique. Bevolking: Talen/Population: Langues,
      1910, 1920, 1930, 1947, edited by Ministerie van Binnenlandse Zaken/
      Ministère de l'Intérieur (Brussels).
Walker, D.
1961 Politics and Ethnocentrism: The Case of the Franco-American (Bruns-
      wick, Maine).
Weiss, B.
1951 'Sprach- und Konfessionsgrenzen als Kongruenzen', Laos. Études com-
      parées de folklore ou d'ethnologie régionale, S. Erixon, ed. (Stockholm)
      pp. 96–110.
Weiss, A. von
1959 Hauptprobleme der Zweisprachigkeit, eine Untersuchung auf Grund
      deutsch/estnischen Materials (Heidelberg).
Winter, E.
1938 Tausend Jahre Geisteskampf im Sudetenraum (Salzburg and Leipzig).
Wittram, R.
1954a Baltische Geschichte (Munich).
1954b Das Nationale als europäisches Problem (Göttingen).
Wolfram, G.
1934 'Die Bibliotheken', in Das Reichsland Elsass-Lothringen 1871–1918:
      Wissenschaft, Kunst und Literatur (Frankfurt).
Zemmrich, J.
1912 'Die Ergebnisse der Volkszählung vom 31 Dez. 1910 in den öster-
      reichischen Sudentenländern, (insbes) Schlesien', Deutsche Erde 11
      (Gotha).

NOTES

1. A characteristic 'European' situation exists in Switzerland. There religious
   and folkloristic divisions run diagonally through the German-speaking area,
   approximately 50 kilometers east of the main linguistic boundary, in this
   case between the German and French languages (Weiss 1951). The same
   situation existed in the former German province of East Prussia where the
   boundaries between Low and Central German and Mazurian (a Polish
   dialect) did not coincide with religious or folkloristic divisions (Riemann
   1937).
2. Netherlandic dialects spoken in North Belgium are usually indicated by the
   term 'Flemish'. This, in fact, is simply a sociopolitical indication since this
   'Flemish' comprises three different (southwestern, central southern, and
   southeastern Netherlandic) dialects all of which are also spoken in the
   adjoining part of the present-day Kingdom of the Netherlands (popularly
   called 'Holland'). These dialects form a part, with northeastern and central
   Netherlandic dialects, of one Netherlandic linguistic and cultural area which
   has been unified since the Middle Ages by one and the same standard

language, Netherlandic', popularly but incorrectly called 'Dutch'.

3. Terminology on this subject is most confusing. Renner formulated some clear and operational definitions which we will use in place of the more formal-juridical interpretation usual in English (Renner 1918). 'People' (*Volk*): a group, not fully conscious of the existence of a common cultural heritage (often bordered on and symbolized in a common language) and not aware of its national implications such as a common destiny and solidarity. 'Nation': a people conscious of the aforementioned community and its implications and consequently trying to realize the establishment of autonomy or of an independent state. When we use terms like ethnic or linguistic group identity we are using them in the first sense; national identity refers to nation and nationalism. Nationality will be applied as an indication of formal citizenship.

4. Here I have in mind the eighteenth-century nonreligious nationalism of the so-called United Irishmen which was initiated by Protestant dissenters.

5. The separation of Finland from Sweden was initiated by the Swedish-speaking upper class of Finland.

6. The figures relate to the towns of Przemyslany, Niemirów, Uhnow, Clust Miasto, Mosty Wielki, Żurawno, Kalusz, and Boryslaw (Polish spelling); since World War II these towns are incorporated in the Ukrainian Soviet Socialist Republic).

7. Declining from 35% in 1860 to 28% in 1940.

8. The Baltic counties numbered thirty boroughs of military and regional-administrative and cultural importance and two important international *stapletowns*, Riga and Reval Tallinn.

9. The exclusive and elitist character of the Baltic Germans is illustrated by their university in Dorpat/Tartu. This important establishment was connected with the activities of a large number of scholars in Dorpat itself and at universities in Germany and Russia. The Baltic Germans supplied one professor per 3,000 members of their group! In many respects − literary, scientific, religious, cultural − the *Baltikum* was an integrated part of the German world of the eighteenth and nineteenth centuries (as it was of Russia in political and military respects!).

10. Finland was occupied by Russia in 1808; autonomy in the form of a grand duchy was granted and so Finland was not touched by linguistic Russification. In 1917 Finland became an independent republic.

11. Even 75% of big industry and two of the three most important banking institutions are still controlled by Swedish Finns.

12. Marburg − Maribor, Cilli − Celje, Pettau − Ptuj, Friedau − Ormož, Gonobitz − Konjice, Rann − Brežice, Windisch Feistritz − Slovenj Bistrica, Weitenstein − Straže and Windischgraz − Slovenj Gradec.

13. By Moravia I mean more correctly the former Austrian province of Moravia combined with the province of Austrian Silesia where the population spoke partly German, Polish, and Czech. These Poles are included with the Czechs in the figures given.

14. Large industries are exclusively Italian; Germans are mostly found in smaller industrial establishments of a more traditional character. The iron and steel

industry is largely controlled by Germans; construction is in Italian hands.
So even within the industrial sphere structural differences exist.

15. The use and acceptance of the terms 'Netherlandic', 'Dutch' and 'Flemish' is
most confusing, since to some extent they are synonyms. The Netherlandic
standard language of the sixteenth and seventeenth centuries (based on
southern dialects!) has been subject to a slightly different development in
the largely Protestant northern Netherlands (since the sixteenth century an
independent republic, transformed into the Kingdom of the Netherlands in
the past century, or popularly 'Holland') than it has in the Roman Catholic
southern Netherlands (remaining part of the Holy Roman Empire as a
Hapsburgian province, since the past century the Kingdom of Belgium, of
which Flanders is the Netherlandic-speaking part). Although the northern
variety (popularly 'Dutch') has also been used as standard by the southerners
(the Flemish) since the middle of the past century, some clericals in the south
tried to maintain a southern variety or even to construct a new standard based
on the dialect of West Flanders (Piccard [n.d.] : II, 50—55; III:10), Deneckere
1951:17).

16. (1) the German minority as opposed to the Roman Catholic French majority in Fribourg (West Switzerland), (2) the French minority as opposed to
the Protestant German minority in the Lake district (Seebezirk, Berne
Canton, Switzerland), (3) the Rhaeto-Romanic minority as opposed to the
Protestant German majority in the canton of Graubünden (East Switzerland), (4) the German minority as opposed to the Roman Catholic Magyar
majority in western Hungary, (5) the Polish minority in the (former) German provinces of East Prussia, Posen, and Silesia, (6) the Sorbian minority
as opposed to the Protestant German majority in Lusatia (Lausitz, Saxony).
The time span applying to these comparisons varies from 1860 to 1960 in
Switzerland, from 1880 to 1920 in Hungary, and from 1890 to 1910 in
Germany.

The Spread of Languages of Wider Communication

ROBERT L. COOPER   **10**

The Spread of Amharic in Ethiopia

The spread of Amharic in Ethiopia is a clear example of the expansion of an indigenous national language in a highly multilingual country as a principal factor in national integration. This article examines that phenomenon and describes the mechanisms underlying it.

GEOGRAPHIC AND DEMOGRAPHIC PRELIMINARIES

Ethiopia forms a rough triangle with its apex in the north. It is bounded by the Sudan in the west; by the Red Sea, the French Territory of the Afars and the Issas, and Somalia in the east; and by Somalia and Kenya in the south. In area it is roughly six times the size of New England and more than four times the size of Great Britain and Northern Ireland. It has a population which was estimated at about 24,000,000 in 1967 (Central Statistical Office 1968).

Many factors make Ethiopia unique among African nations: its exceptionally mountainous terrain which makes transportation and the construction of roads exceedingly difficult; its ancient tradition of Christianity which was adopted by the Aksumite Emperor Ezana in the middle of the fourth century; its long isolation, not only from the West but also from its Muslim neighbors, during which time it was able to develop its own forms of art, music, and poetry; and, except for the brief Italian occupation in the 1930s and the longer Italian colonization of Eritrea, its ability to prevent European imperialism.

Like many African countries, however, Ethiopia is extremely diverse linguistically, with seventy to eighty indigenous languages (Bender *et al.,* 1976). Of these, the ones spoken by the largest number of people are Amharic, Galla, and Tigrinya. The best estimates of the proportion of the population speaking each as a mother tongue are Amharic, 31%; Galla, 27%; and Tigrinya, 14% (Bender *et al.*). Amharic is the language of the Amharas, the ethnic group to which the Emperor belongs. Although it is a minority language, it is spoken by more Ethiopians than any other, not only as a first but also as a second language, and it is enshrined in the nation's constitution as the empire's official language (Bender *et al.*) Amharic and Tigrinya are Semitic languages and Galla is a Cushitic language. Most native speakers of Tigrinya live in the northern apex of the Ethiopian triangle; most native speakers of Amharic live in the western and central portions of the northern half of the country; and most of the people who speak Galla natively live in the north-west, north and southern portions of the southern half of the country, although a corridor of Galla speakers also exists in the northern half of the country to the east of the Amharic-speaking heartland.

Primarily agricultural, the country has one of the lowest per capita incomes and one of the lowest literacy rates in Africa. Its economic development is hindered by, among other factors, transportation difficulties. Both difficulty in transport and economic undevelopment can be seen from the fact that more than half the area of the country lies beyond thirty kilometers from a road (Meflin 1972:61).

HISTORICAL PRELIMINARIES

Sometime between the ninth and twelfth centuries other languages replaced Giiz, the imperial language of Aksum, as vernaculars on the Abyssinian plateau.[1] With the 'restoration' of the Solomonic dynasty in 1270 the locus of Abyssinian power had moved southward to the Amhara region and for most of the time since then the Amharas have been the politically dominant force in Ethiopia. Their language became known as the language of the king (Amharic: *yenigus qwanqwa*).

Although Giiz was extinct as a mother tongue by the time of the Solomonic restoration it continued to be Ethiopia's literary language almost to the present day and it is still the liturgical language of the Ethiopian Orthodox Church. 'Frozen' as a literary medium sometime in the ninth or tenth centuries, its great literary flowering occurred between the thirteenth and seventeenth centuries, several centuries after it had ceased to be spoken as a mother tongue. During the period of its literary efflorescence it probably existed together with Amharic in a relationship of *diglossia*, i.e., a situation in which the functions allocated to two languages in a speech community are separate, one language being used for one set of functions and the other language being used for another (Ferguson 1959). In this case, Giiz was reserved for literary, ecclesiastical, and ceremonial functions and Amharic was used in the ordinary interactions of day-to-day life. The observation by the seventeenth-century European scholar Ludolph that his very learned Ethiopian informant Gregory could not speak Giiz without mixing it with Amharic words indicates that in the Ethiopia of that day (and probably for hundreds of years before that), Giiz was not used for ordinary spoken purposes. On the other hand Gregory found it even more difficult to write Amharic (Ullendorff 1965:17) since that language was typically not used for written purposes.

Although some imperial songs were written in Amharic in the fourteenth century, the literary monopoly of Giiz was not broken until the late sixteenth and early seventeenth centuries when the Portuguese Jesuits employed Amharic for religious pamphleteering. After the Jesuits were expelled, however, little was written in Amharic until the reign of Tewodros II, in the middle of the nineteenth century. Tewodros was the first Ethiopian monarch to have the Ethiopian royal chronicles written in Amharic. The chronicles, written at the command of most Ethiopian rulers since the thirteenth century, had been written in Giiz until Tewodros' time. His promotion of Amharic literature was part of his campaign to reunify Abyssinia. With the exception of his successor, Yohannis IV, a Tigrean emperor and Tigrinya speaker, the use of Amharic as an instrument of national unification has continued as imperial policy (Ullendorff 1965:155).

By the beginning of the twentieth century Minilik II had enlarged his empire to include territories not traditionally or continuously ruled by Ethiopian monarchs. During his reign the areas south and west of Shewa Province were annexed and the Gallas and Somalis to the east were brought under control. Except for Eritrea, which had been an integral part of the Aksumite empire, traditional Abyssinia had been reunited by Minilik and the limits of its territory greatly expanded. Shewa Province, which had been the southernmost part of the empire, became the empire's center. Just as Amharic by the seventeenth century had spread from its home base, east and north of Lake Tana, through much of central Ethiopia, it is to be expected

that the language of the king will spread once again within the
boundaries of an expanded empire.

SOME EXAMPLES OF LANGUAGE SPREAD

There are at least three ways in which the substantial use of a
language can spread. One way is as a *lingua franca,* when the language
becomes commonly used for purposes of between-group communication, i.e., between persons who have different mother tongues. A
second way is as a mother tongue, when people adopt the language as
the language of their home. A third way is as a superposed variety,
i.e., the language spreads for purposes of within-group communication but not as a mother tongue.

There have been examples of the spread of *lingua francas* in Africa
(Greenberg 1965). Some of these have been indigenous languages
such as Hausa and Malinke in western Africa and Swahili in eastern
Africa. Others have arisen as pidginized forms of African languages
in the European contact situation such as Sango and Lingala in
central Africa. Still others have been European languages, particularly English and French, in the former colonial areas. (For an
extensive treatment of African *lingua francas* see Heine 1970).

When a language spreads as a *lingua franca* it spreads as a second
language. The people who learn it continue to speak their mother
tongue for purposes of within-group communication. When a language spreads not as a *lingua franca* but as a mother tongue, people
gradually abandon their mother tongue and adopt the new language
for purposes of within-group communication. The latter type of
language spread, mother-tongue displacement, may occur when
migrant peoples adopt the dominant language of the area to which
they have come, as in the case of most American immigrant groups.
Mother-tongue displacement may also occur when the political and
economic pressures exerted by a dominant minority induce a subor-
dinate majority to abandon their mother tongue. There have been
many times in which the territorial expansion of an empire has
created wholesale mother-tongue displacement among its subject
populations, as in the case of Latin.

The spread of a language as a superposed variety resembles both
the spread of a *lingua franca* and mother-tongue displacement. It
resembles the spread of a *lingua franca* because the new language is
learned and maintained as a second language. It resembles mother-

tongue displacement because the new language is used for purposes of within-group communication. When a language spreads as a superposed variety it displaces the original language in certain functions only, while the original language holds fast to other functions.[2] In such circumstances the displacing language and the language it partially displaces come to coexist in a diglossic relationship. An example of such partial displacement can be found in Paraguay, where Spanish has replaced the indigenous Guarani for some purposes or contexts (e.g., in nonrural, formal, nonintimate contexts) but where Guarani is maintained for others (Rubin 1968). With respect to Amharic it is likely that it is spreading in all three of the ways outlined: as *lingua franca*, as mother tongue, and as superposed variety.

MECHANISMS UNDERLYING THE SPREAD OF AMHARIC

What are the forces which have promoted the spread of Amharic and which continue to promote its spread throughout Ethiopia? Some of these forces are general or well-known agents of language spread, having operated in many different places and times. Others, if not peculiar to the Ethiopian setting, are less common.

Brosnahan (1963) has pointed out several 'general features' which were common to the spread of Arabic, Greek, and Latin. First, these languages spread with military conquest, becoming the language of administration in the annexed territories. Second, the military authority which had imposed these languages lasted for at least several centuries. Long political stability gave these languages the time in which to make a lasting impression in the conquered areas. Brosnahan pointed out that the language of Attila, for example, although widely dispersed in Europe by force of arms, was not maintained by military authority and thus disappeared there. Third, these languages spread in areas which were multilingual. A common administration made it both possible and necessary for people with different mother tongues to communicate with one another and the language of the administration could serve as *lingua franca*. Finally, the spread of Arabic, Greek, and Latin were all marked by the fact that knowledge of the imposed language, if not an absolute requirement for entrance to education, government employment, or commercial activity, greatly enhanced the speaker's opportunities in these fields.

While it is difficult to reconstruct the spread of Giiz, we can assume that it was marked by most if not all of the general features which characterized the spread of Arabic, Greek, and Latin. Giiz spread with the expansion of the Aksumite empire whose power and cohesiveness endured for centuries, long enough for Giiz to make a lasting impression on the Abyssinian plateau. Although we do not know what degree of linguistic diversity existed on the plateau among the peoples conquered by the Aksumite emperors, it is not unlikely that Giiz spread among peoples speaking several different Cushitic languages and that Giiz served as a *lingua franca*. Finally, knowledge of the imperial language must have been a material advantage.

It would appear that the general features which characterized the spread of Arabic, Greek, Latin, and probably Giiz as well, are also characteristic of the spread of Amharic. The feature of military conquest is of course unequivocal. Amharic has spread as a consequence of Amhara military conquests and political supremacy. Amharic is not only the language of the imperial administration; it is also an instrument of government policy as part of the government's attempt to unify the country.

With respect to the duration of military authority Amharic has been the language of administration in the areas annexed by Minilik for over seventy years. In many of these regions, however, the government's presence was not strongly felt until there was an improvement in communications and transport, made possible by the airplane and the building of roads, and until the founding of towns. Thus in some regions the government's influence has been felt relatively recently. It seems clear that continued political stability under a government committed to Amharic as an agent of national integration will be necessary for Amharic to make permanent inroads in many if not most of the non-Amhara parts of the empire. If several hundred years are required for a language to make a lasting impact, then not enough time has passed. However, a substantial beginning has been made.

With respect to linguistic diversity Ethiopia like many African countries is multilingual: dozens of indigenous languages are spoken there, including several spoken by at least a half million people. Interactions among linguistically diverse peoples, promoted by their incorporation within the same political entity and their interactions with the central government, help to make a *lingua franca* necessary. Amharic has long been a *lingua franca* in Ethiopia. As early as 1620 Manoel de Almeida, a Portuguese Jesuit traveller, noted that Amharic served as *lingua franca* among the linguistically diverse peoples of Ethiopia (Levine 1971:15). The emergence of Amharic as Ethiopia's principal *lingua franca* would be reasonable not only in view of its position as the language of the politically dominant group but also in view of its position as the language of the numerically largest group. Thus the smallest number of people would have to learn a second language if Amharic were the nation's principal *lingua franca*. At the present time it is apparent that Amharic is widely used as a *lingua franca* although it seems to be used as such primarily in the towns. Although there are other *lingua francas* in Ethiopia, Amharic is clearly the most important both in the number of its speakers and in the range of its uses. The most important *lingua francas* other than Amharic are regional ones: Tigrinya in the north and Galla in the south. Neither of these has Amharic's advantage as the official language and neither is as widely dispersed through the towns. Much less important as *lingua francas* are Arabic, Italian, and English.

With respect to the material advantages associated with knowledge of Amharic, they are undeniably great. Knowledge of Amharic is a prerequisite for educational and political advancement. However, the benefits of a knowledge of Amharic are still confined principally to the urban population and to that part of the rural population with relatively easy access to towns.

In addition to military conquest, the duration of imperial administration, linguistic diversity, and the acquisition of material advantages facilitated by knowledge of the language, there appear to be other characteristics of the spread of Amharic which have been common to the spread of other languages in other places. These are urbanization, public education, industrialization, mass communication, and nationalism. Although these characteristics, like the general features noted by Brosnahan (1963), are neither parallel (some are processes, others are products) nor discrete (they are overlapping and mutually reinforcing), it may be helpful to consider them separately.

Ethiopia's urban population is increasing at a faster rate than its rural population (Davis 1969), a characteristic pattern in Africa, where people migrate to towns in search of employment, health benefits, or education. Half of Ethiopia's urban population were not born in the town in which they presently reside. The linguistic diversity created in towns by the presence of migrants from different language areas promotes Amharic as an urban *lingua franca* because Amharic is Ethiopia's leading urban language. In urban sample surveys carried out by the Central Statistical Office (1968) Amharic was claimed as mother tongue by the largest number of respondents. Even in traditionally non-Amhara areas there are urban centers in which substantial proportions of Amharic mother-tongue speakers are found. If the towns of Aggaro, Jimma, and Asela are typical of towns with large numbers of Amharic mother-tongue speakers in non-Amhara areas, then most non-Amharas in such towns learn Amharic (Bender *et al.*, 1976). The presence of sizable numbers of Amharic speakers in almost all the towns of the empire serves as an agent for the diffusion of Amharic into the surrounding countryside. Amharic, moreover, is the dominant language of Addis Ababa, the capital and principal city. This is important with respect to the spread of Amharic because Addis Ababa, like most capitals in developing countries, is a center for the diffusion of cultural innovations. The relationship between urbanization and the spread of Amharic is presented in detail in Bender *et al.*

Public education is promoting the spread of Amharic because Amharic is the medium of instruction in all government schools throughout the primary grades. (It can be noted that only under the Italians was an attempt made to use local vernaculars in education, a tactic intended to divide the country.) If non-Amharas want an education at public expense they must learn Amharic. At present, government schools, which are found primarily in towns, are not within the reach of the Ethiopian masses. Only 12 per cent of the elementary school-aged population were enrolled in school in 1966–67. Thus public education has not been able to reach the bulk of the population directly. It was found in surveys conducted in Kefa and Arusi provinces, for example, that more than half of the Gāllas who knew Amharic had not been to an Amharic-medium school and that the proportion of Gallas who knew Amharic was related primarily to the proportion of Amharic mother-tongue speakers who lived nearby (Bender *et al.*). As more Ethiopians go to school, however, governmental insistence on Amharic as the sole medium of primary school instruction will create large numbers of Amharic-speaking people.

Industrialization is likely to promote the spread of Amharic because the personnel requirements of large factories encourage migration, resulting in linguistic diversity among the industrial work force and the consequent need for a *lingua franca*. Large numbers of Gurages and Kembatas, for example, are found in the factories of the Wonji-Shoa Sugar Estates, located in a largely Galla-speaking area. In five factories surveyed in Shewa Province almost the entire work force knew Amharic, although in three factories there were more Galla mother-tongue speakers than Amharic mother-tongue speakers, and in a fourth the two groups were about equal in number (Bender 1976). Another way in which industrialization may promote the spread of Amharic is through its increasing demand for skilled workers who are more likely to be literate than non-skilled workers. Literacy in turn is likely to be associated with knowledge of Amharic because of Amharic's monopoly as the medium of instruction in primary schools and in literacy campaigns. Increasing industrialization will also create more funds for education, which in turn will make it possible for more people to learn Amharic.

The effect of mass media on the spread of Amharic is potentially great because of the dominance of Amharic in these media. Regular publication is carried out in only one other Ethiopian language, Tigrinya. In part this is due to official discouragement of publication in other languages and in part it is due to the fact that most other Ethiopian languages do not have a tradition of writing. Because the literacy rate is low and because most Ethiopian literates can read Amharic or Tigrinya, the market for publications in other Ethiopian languages is too small and too poor for an economically viable non-Amharic or -Tigrinya press. In radio broadcasting the preponderance of Amharic programming should eventually make the language familiar in non-Amhara areas and should help speakers who are learning Amharic as a second language to improve their facility in the language. Radio's effectiveness for these purposes, however, is limited at present by the lack of electrification in the countryside and by the great expense which a transistor radio represents to rural Ethiopians.

Rising nationalism, common in the developing countries, is also found in Ethiopia although its force is presently limited primarily to urbanized and educated Ethiopians. Amharic as the language of government is a symbol of Ethiopian nationhood and national distinctiveness. Although some Ethiopians may resent the imposition of Amharic by fiat, many non-Amharas would probably vote for Amharic as official language if a vote were to be taken. Its status as the language of the largest ethnic group and its literary tradition would probably impel many non-Amharas to view it as a rational choice. Its use for over seven hundred years as the language of the Abyssinian court, moreover, gives it the additional claim of a glorious tradition. Amharic is also a distinctively Ethiopian language, being spoken in no other country. Its present constitutional status has enhanced its position as a national symbol which will strengthen and be strengthened by those forces which are creating a common consciousness of national identity.

The characteristics of language spread which have been cited thus far operate not only in Ethiopia but in other countries as well. Ethiopia's language situation is by no means unique. It may be described as one in which there are many indigenous languages but only a single dominant one, the latter having a literary tradition, and in which there is also a dominant foreign language which serves as a language of communication with foreigners and which plays a role in education. Examples of other countries with this language situation are Iran, where Persian and English are the dominant indigenous and foreign languages, and Burma, where these languages are Burmese and English. The Iranian example has another parallel to the Ethiopian situation inasmuch as English replaced French as the dominant foreign language in both countries. There seems to be no other country in Africa with an exactly comparable situation. A more common situation in Africa is one in which the dominant indigenous language does not have a literary tradition, as in Senegal, for example, where Wolof is the dominant indigenous language and French the language of wider communication.

Although Ethiopia's language situation is not unique, there still are some features which, if not peculiar to Ethiopia, are at least not as widespread as the features of language diffusion cited earlier. These less common features are the role of foreign missionaries, lack of significant dialect variation, and the existence of a common writing system which is distinctive and traditional.

The activities of foreign missionaries have promoted an Ethiopian language during three different periods of Ethiopian history. Christian monks from Syria and Anatolia facilitated the spread of Giiz during the period of the Aksumite empire by using it as the language of instruction and worship. These men, glorified in Ethiopian tradition as the Nine Saints, introduced improved agricultural practices and handcrafts along with the Gospel, thus providing both religious and economic incentives to learn Giiz. At the end of the sixteenth century and at the beginning of the seventeenth, Portuguese Jesuits, as noted above, promoted the use of written Amharic by producing tracts in that language. Although their missionizing activities ultimately ended in failure, their pamphleteering broke the literary monopoly which Giiz had enjoyed. Today Christian missionaries from Europe and America are helping to promote the spread of spoken and written Amharic. The present regime has insisted that missionaries work in 'open' areas, i.e., areas in which the people are not Ethiopian Orthodox Christians. Since most of these areas are places in which Amharic is not spoken natively and, since missionaries are required by statute to learn Amharic and teach via Amharic, missionaries have become agents of Amharicization. The missions have become places where Amharic is spoken and taught and they act as sources for the diffusion of Amharic into the countryside surrounding them.

Amharic is notable for its relative uniformity, i.e., lack of major dialect variation, so that the problems of choosing a standard among competing varieties is not critical. Decisions need not be made as to which variety of Amharic should be used in radio broadcasting, in the press, in textbooks, and in the classroom. Further, when non-Amharas in various parts of the country learn Amharic through contact with Amhara migrants, the language they learn will be much the same. This can be contrasted with the position of Akan in Ghana. Akan, like Amharic, is spoken by the most populous group and is the language of the elite. Akan, however, not only has substantial dialect differentiation but also is written in different orthographies (Dickens 1953).

Ethiopia is like many African countries in that several writing systems are in use within the country. Both Roman and Arabic script are employed in Ethiopia, as in many other African countries, but Ethiopia is unlike most African countries in also having an indigenous, distinctive, and traditional script, the ancient Giiz syllabary which is used for writing modern Ethiopian languages. There are other indigenous African scripts, particularly in West Africa, but these were created relatively recently and for the most part have not been widely used. Ethiopia is also unlike most African countries in that Arabic and Roman scripts are, with few exceptions, used only to write foreign, not indigenous languages. (Exceptions are Harari, which is written in Arabic characters, and Kunama, which is written in Roman script.) Whereas Hausa and Swahili, for example, are each written both in Arabic and Roman script, almost all Ethiopian languages are written only in the Ethiopian syllabary. Even when publications are clandestine (missionary tracts in Galla, for example) the Ethiopian script is used. There is little resistance to the use of this syllabary. The existence of a common script for Amharic in particular and for Ethiopian languages in general removes one barrier to the spread of Amharic.

FACTORS INHIBITING THE SPREAD OF AMHARIC

Whereas there appear to be many interrelated mechanisms underlying the spread of Amharic, there are also some factors that are inhibiting it. First of all Amharic does not seem to serve as a *lingua franca* for trade, at least at the retail level in markets (Cooper and Carpenter 1969). Thus a common mechanism for the spread of a language, its use as a market *lingua franca*, does not seem to be operating for Amharic. Second, many of the mechanisms which are promoting the spread of Amharic are primarily urban phenomena and the urban population is still a small proportion of the total population, only about eight per cent. Although the spread of a language through the towns and along the roads that connect the towns often precedes the dispersion of that language into the surrounding countryside, it is not likely that Amharic will be learned by the majority of rural non-Amhara Ethiopians until their access to towns is improved and until more schools are built in the countryside. At present most rural Ethiopians live in areas which are relatively homogeneous linguistically and which are very far (in terms of the time required for travel) from a town. Although many rural Ethiopians may be favorably disposed toward learning Amharic, as were respondents in Kefa and Arusi provinces (Bender *et al.*, 1976), they cannot do so without the immediate opportunity to learn, nor will they do so if the need is not clear and present. Schools and roads will provide both need and the opportunity to learn. However at least another generation will probably have to pass before there are enough schools and roads to make Amharic accessible to most non-Amhara Ethiopians.

Although other African *lingua francas* spread across national boundaries, it is not likely that Amharic will do so. Of Ethiopia's four neighbors, one of them, the Somali Republic, is linguistically homogeneous (almost all of its citizens speak Somali as their mother tongue) and thus needs no *lingua franca*. Two of Ethiopia's other neighbors, the Sudan and Kenya, are linguistically diverse but these already have *lingua francas*, Arabic in the Sudan and Swahili in Kenya. As for the fourth neighbor, the French Territory of the Afars and the Issas, Amharic is unlikely to make much headway there at the present time in competition with Afar, Somali, and French. In the event that the French leave the Territory, Ethiopia may be given control of the port of Djibouti (Hess 1970:205) and the influence of Amharic may grow. However, the spread of Amharic as *lingua franca* is likely to be confined within Ethiopia's national boundaries.

THE POSSIBILITY OF MOTHER-TONGUE DISPLACEMENT

To what extent is mother-tongue displacement, as distinct from the spread of a *lingua franca*, taking place? An analysis of urban language data suggests that some urban non-Amhara have adopted Amharic as mother tongue (Bender *et al.*, 1976). These data were also consistent with the hypothesis that the educational and occupational mobility of some non-Amhara groups was associated with their adoption of Amharic as mother tongue. It is not likely, however, that all urban non-Amharas respond to the pressure of Amharic in the same way. One factor that serves to promote or retard mother-tongue displacement is the relative prestige of the groups whose languages are in contact. Groups whose prestige is high are less likely to abandon that symbol of group identity, the mother tongue, than groups whose prestige is low. Thus, for example, educational and occupational mobility is not likely to cause Tigrinya mother-tongue speakers, living outside of towns in which Tigrinya is the majority language, to abandon Tigrinya. The cultural kinship shared by Amharas and Tigrinya speakers and their participation in a common tradition have given a greater prestige to the latter, *vis-à-vis* the Amharas, than to other groups. While the prestige of a language in general is inseparable from the prestige of those who speak it, Tigrinya also has a source of prestige which is independent of its group, namely the fact that it is the only Ethiopian language besides Amharic in which publication is regularly carried out. It was in fact the language in which the first Ethiopian daily newspaper appeared. Current publication yields prestige to the language and provides an additional incentive for those who speak it natively to retain it. For example, in a study of Ethiopian university students it was noted that the Tigrinya speakers appeared more loyal to Tigrinya than did the Gallas and Gurages to their mother tongues (Bender *et al.*). The position of Tigrinya in Ethiopia may perhaps be compared to that of Catalan in Spain. Both languages are employed in a continuing literature and both languages embody a long-standing tradition and are spoken by substantial numbers of people, yet neither is employed as a medium of instruction or has official status.

Relative prestige is only one variable related to mother-tongue displacement. Among other factors which can accelerate or retard such displacement is the size of the mother-tongue group in question. The larger the mother-tongue group the more useful its language as a vehicle of communication, and thus the more reluctant are mother-

tongue speakers to abandon that language. Furthermore, the larger
the mother-tongue group the easier it is for members to form
colonies or groups which can be insulated from contact with the
displacing language. Thus, while considerations of relative prestige
may promote the shift to Amharic among some Galla mother-tongue
speakers, the very large size of the Galla mother-tongue group may
impede mother-tongue displacement.

Whereas we may predict with some confidence the gradual spread
of Amharic as *lingua franca* within the country's national boundaries,
given continued political stability and a continuation of the government's present language policy, the prediction as to which groups if
any will adopt Amharic as mother tongue is at best hazardous, given
the state of our current knowledge. Probably the best guess is that
the spread of Amharic will be accompanied by maintenance of most
mother tongues and that eventually a situation of relatively stable
bilingualism will emerge for non-Amhara groups, a situation which is
common in African countries (Greenberg 1965). Amharic, in other
words, will spread as a superposed variety. The mother tongue will be
the language of traditional customs and local identity and Amharic
will be the language of education, supra-regional communication,
government, modernization, and national consciousness.

THE SPREAD OF ENGLISH

Although Amharic may spread within the empire so that it becomes
the common vehicle of communication among Ethiopians who have
different mother tongues, Amharic cannot be used as a language of
wider communication, i.e., a language which can be widely used
outside of Ethiopia's national boundaries or between Ethiopians and
non-Ethiopians. Other languages must be used for this purpose (see
Center for Applied Linguistics 1961). During the height of the
Aksumite empire it is likely that Greek served this function. During
the isolation which followed the decline of the Aksumite empire,
what little need there was for wider communication was probably
met by Coptic and later by Arabic. When greater communication
with the outside world began in the nineteenth century Italian and
French were the principal languages of wider communication. Today
the chief language of wider communication in Ethiopia is English.

Although only a small minority of the country can speak English
the language has great prestige because of its use as the government's

principal foreign language and because of its use as the medium of instruction in government secondary schools and in the university. The prestige of English can be seen in the great number of people naming it as a language they would like to know, as observed in household sample surveys and in factory sample surveys (Bender *et al.*, 1976). Illiterate peasants several kilometers from the road as well as literate urban dwellers named it although the opportunities for them to use it in day-to-day transactions must be quite small. The factory workers had a greater use for English, however, since it is a language of higher technology and since it is a language which some of their supervisors use at work. Knowledge of English, then, should spread with the growth of industrialization although industrialization will not provide as great an impetus to the spread of English as it will to the spread of Amharic.

It might be argued that knowledge of English will also rise with an increase in secondary education. However, greater numbers of secondary school graduates will make available more teachers able to teach via Amharic and will thus create pressure for raising the grade level at which Amharic is used as the medium of instruction. While increased production of secondary school graduates may cause more people to study English, it may also result in a smaller percentage knowing it well if the number of years in which it serves as medium is reduced. (This should not be construed as an argument for the preservation of English as medium of instruction. The choice among competing mediums is a complex matter. Clearly the use of a foreign language as medium entails disadvantages as well as advantages.) As long as English remains a quasi-official language, however, and as long as it retains its dominance in higher education and its marked advantage over Amharic as the more common medium for the publication of scientific and technical information, English is likely to retain its position as the most important nonindigenous language in Ethiopia.

CONCLUSIONS

Amharic, the national language of Ethiopia, although a minority language, is spoken as a mother tongue by more people than any other, is more frequently learned as a second language than any other and it is the language of the culturally and politically dominant group, the predominant language of the principal city, and the

indigenous modern language with the most impressive body of literature. Just as Giiz, the classical language of Ethiopia, spread as a
national language in the ancient Aksumite empire, modern Amharic
is steadily expanding as a *lingua franca* and as a mother tongue. The
spread of Amharic is accompanied by the increasing use of English as
an international language of wider communication, with important
educational and technical uses within the country. Although English
may lose ground to Amharic as a medium of instruction, it is likely
to maintain its position as Ethiopia's most important nonindigenous
language.

Amharic is spreading steadily but it is likely that at least another
generation of continued political stability, continued government
promotion of the language, increasing educational opportunities,
rising industrialization, and increasing improvement in transport will
be required before Amharic is spoken by most non-Amhara Ethiopians throughout the empire. Moreover there is likely to be a
differentiated response to the impact of Amharic on the part of
different mother-tongue groups. Some may shift to Amharic as
mother tongue. Others may ultimately be characterized by stable
bilingualism, with Amharic used for public institutional settings and
the mother tongue reserved for use at home and in informal contexts
with those who speak it natively. The study of the spread of
Amharic, including different Ethiopian groups' responses to the
impact of Amharic, should not only contribute to our understanding
of the general processes of language shift and of the spread of *lingua
francas*, but it should also enable us to describe more adequately the
processes of national integration in Ethiopia and in other multilingual countries.

REFERENCES

Bender, M. Lionel, J. Donald Bowen, Robert L. Cooper, Charles A. Ferguson, *et
    al.*
1976   *Language in Ethiopia* (London, Oxford University Press).
Brosnahan, L. F.
    1963 'Some Historical Cases of Language Imposition', in John Spencer, ed.,
          Language in Africa (Cambridge, Cambridge University Press).
Center for Applied Linguistics
    1961 *Second Language Learning as a Factor in Development in Asia, Africa,
          and Latin America: Summary Statement and Recommendations of the
          International Meeting of Specialists Held in London, December 1960* (=

Language Information Series I) (Washington, D.C., Center for Applied Linguistics).

Central Statistical Office
1968 *Survey of Major Towns in Ethiopia* (Addis Ababa, Central Statistical Office).

Cooper, Robert L., and Susan Carpenter
1969 'Linguistic Diversity in the Ethiopian Market', *Journal of African Languages* 8 (Part 3):160—168.

Davis, Kingsley
1969 *World Urbanization 1950—1970*, Volume 1, *Basic Data for Cities, Countries, and Regions* (Berkeley, University of California Press).

Dickens, K. J.
1953 'Unification: The Akan Dialects of the Gold Coast', in Unesco, *The Use of the Vernacular Languages in Education* (Paris).

Ferguson, Charles A.
1959 'Diglossia', *Word* 15:325—350.

Greenberg, Joseph H.
1965 'Urbanism, Migration, and Language', in Hilda Kuper, ed., *Urbanization and Migration in West Africa* (Berkeley, University of California Press).

Heine, Bernd
1970 *Status and Use of African Lingua Francas* (Munich, Weltforum Verlag).

Hess, Robert L.
1970 *Ethiopia, the Modernization of Autocracy* (Ithaca and London, Cornell University Press).

Levine, Donald L.
1971 'The Roots of Ethiopia's Nationhood', *African Report* 16(5):12—15.

Meflin Wolde, Mariam
1972 *An Introductory Geography of Ethiopia* (Addis Ababa).

Rubin, Joan
1968 *National Biligualism in Paraguay* (The Hague, Mouton).

Ullendorff, Edward
1955 *The Semitic Languages of Ethiopia, A Comparative Phonology* (London, Taylor's Foreign Press).
1965 *The Ethiopians: An Introduction to Country and People*, revised edition (London, Oxford University Press).

NOTES

The field work on which this article is based was carried out under the auspices of the Language Survey of Ethiopia, which was part of the five-nation Survey of Language Use and Language Teaching in Eastern Africa, supported by the Ford Foundation. The article was written when I held a Social Science Research Council Postdoctoral research training fellowship. Grateful acknowledgement is made to both foundations. I also wish to thank Charles A. Ferguson for the many observations and suggestions he offered during various stages in the writing of this article and M. Lionel Bender, J. Donald Bowen, and Joshua A. Fishman

for their comments on an earlier draft. Another version of this paper appears in
Bender *et al.* (1976). This paper was written in 1972.

1. The historical preliminaries recounted here rely primarily upon Ullendorff
   (1955: 1965). No position is taken here with respect to the genealogy of
   Amharic: whether it is a direct descendent of Giiz or whether it is descended
   from an unknown sister language of Giiz, or from other language.
   By Abyssinia is meant traditional Christian Ethiopia, the territory
   within the north and north center of modern Ethiopia and encompassed by
   major portions of today's provinces of Eritrea, Tigre, Begemdir, Wello,
   Gojjam, and Shewa.
2. I am indebted to Joshua A. Fishman for pointing out that a language can
   spread by a process of partial (rather than complete) functional displacement.

English in South Asia

1. INTRODUCTION

In recent years there has been a distinct change in attitude, both of South Asian and western scholars, toward the *varieties*[1] of English which have developed primarily as second languages (hereafter abbreviated L_2) in South Asia or other parts of the world. This is essentially a post-World War II development which grew out of the new attitude of 'linguistic tolerance' after the rapid growth of the linguistic sciences in the West during that period. It was then that the demands of 'hands off Pidgin' (see Hall 1955) or 'status for the colonial Englishes' were heard on both sides of the Atlantic and interest was shown in the *new Englishes*, namely West African English, Filipino English, South Asian English, etc. This tolerance became more marked when South Asian countries achieved freedom from direct political domination by Britain and the new independent governments in these areas decided to preserve English as a *link* language for national and international communication. There was a renewed enthusiasm for continuing English in three major countries in South Asia, i.e., Ceylon, India, and Pakistan. Thus for the first time English had patronage from the local governments. Before 1947 English had a precarious position in South Asia. On the one hand it was considered a symbol of British power and, what is worse, a politically superimposed language. On the other hand by the English themselves the regional varieties of English were considered 'substandard' and were often characterized as *Babu English* or *Cheechee English*,[2] or simply labeled *Indian* or *Ceylon* English in a derogatory sense.[3] The thirties and forties were times of acute pessimism about the South Asian varieties of English. It was during that period that J. R. Firth, who knew the Indian subcontinent so well, wrote in typical Firthian manner that 'Most Indian English is badly overdrawn. *But it is kept going by the Government*, and though it has therefore a certain local currency, *it has no gold backing*' (my italics) (Firth 1930, 1964 ed., p. 176). This was true in the thirties, and it took two more decades and the independence of the region from the British to create that 'gold backing' for English. The fact is that the British went to South Asia with the English language and, in due course, the natives took the language and the Englishmen took over the land. It was later realized that English had much deeper roots in South Asia than the *Raj* had. The *Raj* crumbled and became a part of history; but the English language has been *South Asianized* and has become a part of the culture of that vast area.

The process of *South Asianization* of the English language manifests itself in three aspects. First, it supplies rich data for language contact study in a cross-cultural and multilinguistic context, thus being of interest from a sociolinguistic point of view. Second, it raises many typologically interesting theoretical and methodological problems about the descriptions of the *New Englishes* which have developed from the L_1 varieties of English (say, for example, American English, Australian English, British English, Canadian English) as *second* or *foreign languages*. Third, there is a large body of *South Asian English* (hereafter abbreviated SAE) writing in different forms (e.g., poetry, prose, fiction) which is interesting from a stylistic point of view. This rapidly increasing body of writing is now being recognized in the English-speaking world as a significant development of the English language in a subcontinent where English is spoken only by a small minority out of the total literate population.

I shall first briefly review the literature which gives a historical introduction to the spread of bilingualism in English in South Asia. This, I think, is directly connected with the three linguistically relevant aspects which will be discussed later.

2. THE SPREAD OF BILINGUALISM IN ENGLISH IN SOUTH ASIA

2.1. *The Beginnings of Bilingualism*

There is no detailed work on the early stages of bilingualism in English in South Asia. Whatever is published is found in the official reports, or books, which deal mainly with the history of education, history, political science, and histories of missionary work in the area. The following summary presents a review of the available literature on the sociopolitical and historical studies which deal with the development of bilingualism in English in South Asia.

The growth of bilingualism in English in this region is closely connected with the beginnings of colonization of the area by the British. The early serious efforts of contact with South Asia started in the sixteenth century and by the eighteenth and nineteenth centuries the area was under the political domination of the British. As the British were deepening their roots in the colonies, the English language also was getting roots (earlier, perhaps, unconsciously); and eventually a large number of English L_2 speakers grew whose competence in English varied considerably (see section 3.1.).

It is customary to trace the roots of English on the Indian subcontinent to December 31, 1600, when Queen Elizabeth granted a Charter to a few merchants of the City of London giving them a monopoly of trade with India and the East.[4]

2.2. Three Early Phases

There are a large number of surveys which discuss the reasons given by three distinct groups for introducing bilingualism in English on the Indian subcontinent and Ceylon. The efforts of these three groups began as three independent phases and, eventually, all three forces joined together. The first phase comprises the efforts of the missionaries who went to South Asia essentially for proselytizing purposes. The second includes the efforts of a small group of Ceylonese and Indians who were fascinated by the progress of the West and desired to use the English language as a vehicle for scientific and material progress. The third was a political phase which firmly established the English language in South Asia.

2.2.1. First Phase: The Missionaries

A detailed account of the impact of the missionaries is found in the publications of Richter (1908), Sherring (1884), Law (1915), and Duff (1837). The efforts started in 1614 and became more and more effective once the missionaries were allowed to use the ships of the East India Company after 1659. In 1698 when the Charter of the Company was renewed a 'missionary clause' was added to it (see Sharp, ed. 1920:3). This policy, however, changed again in 1765 when encouragement of missionaries was stopped. This created great resentment in missionary circles in England and the Clapham sect started an agitation demanding freedom for missionary work in India. The efforts of Charles Grant have been specially mentioned in this context.[5] Grant summarizes the main reasons for trouble on the Indian subcontinent in the following statement:

'The true curse of darkness is the introduction of light. The Hindoos (sic) err, because they are ignorant and their errors have never fairly been laid before them. The communication of our light and knowledge to them, would prove the best remedy for their disorders. (Grant 1831–32:60–61).'

In 1813, with the efforts of Charles Grant, William Wilberforce, the Foreign Secretary, and Lord Castlereagh, the House of Commons in its 13th Resolution:

'Resolved that it is the opinion of this Committee that it is the duty of this Country to promote the interests and happiness of the native inhabitants of the British dominions in India, and that measures ought to be introduced as may tend to the introduction among them of useful knowledge, and of religious and moral improvement. That in furtherance of the above objects sufficient facilities shall be afforded by law to persons desirous of going to, or remaining in, India.[6]'

This helped the missionary work in India and thus the proselytizing and educational activities of the missionaries — which were very restricted and unplanned from 1600 to 1765 — were revitalized. A brief account of the missionary activities in the three states of Bombay, Bengal, and Madras is given in Kanungo with useful bibliographical references. (Kanungo 1962:11–14).

In Ceylon the Rev. James Cordiner went as chaplain to the garrison in Colombo in 1799 and took over as the principal of all the schools in the settlement. There again the efforts in teaching English were first made by the missionaries and it was not until 1831 that the government started imparting English education. By the time the government took over there were already 235 Protestant mission schools out of which only ninety were under the direct control of the government.

The foundation of the 'Christian Institution' was laid in Ceylon in 1827 by Sir Edward Barnes, 'to give a superior education to a number of young persons who from their ability, piety, and good conduct were likely to prove fit persons in communicating a knowledge of Christianity to their countrymen.' (Barnes 1932:43; see also Ruberu 1962).

The Education Report of the Special Committee of Education in Ceylon makes it clear that in Ceylon up to 1886 a large number of schools were Christian schools (Report of the Special committee 1943). It should be noted that during the earlier period the method-ology of teaching and the language background of the teachers had great influence on SAE.

2.2.2. Second Phase: The Demand from the South Asian Public

A study of Adam's Report (Basu, ed. 1941) shows that before Raja Rammohun Roy's plea for introducing English in India there was already a small group of Indians, especially in Bengal, who wanted to study English in addition to Persian and Bengali. Perhaps this was one way for Hindus to show their concern about the domination of Persian or Arabic; or perhaps this was done essentially for socio-economic and educational reasons. It is well known that in aiding the passing of the crucial Minute of 1835, Macaulay's hand was con-siderably strengthened by a small group of Indians led by Raja Rammohun Roy who preferred English to Indian languages for academic, scientific, and other international reasons. Roy's often-quoted letter to Lord Amherst, dated December 11, 1823, is an important document which contributed to the introduction of bilin-gualism in English on the Indian subcontinent.[7]

2.2.3. Third Phase: the Government Policy

There is a considerable amount of literature on this phase of English in South Asia but the main aim of the writers of these studies is not to present a systematic history of the English language in South Asia. These works are written either by political scientists or historians.

It was after 1765 that the East India Company became a political power in India and its attention was, naturally, attracted by wider problems. The education of Anglo-Indian children became second-ary, whereas it had earlier been one of the main objects of the schools. In 1787 the Court of the Directors of the East India Com-pany appreciated the efforts of the Rev. Swartz to establish two schools in Tanjore and Marwar for the children of soldiers by encouraging him with a grant of 250 'pagodas' per year per school. It was an initial but crucial stage for it might have left no mark had the later discussions not gone in favor of English. The highly contro-versial and very significant Minute of 1835 was passed on February 2 of that year.

The Minute, however, was not passed without debate and contro-versy. At that time there were clearly two views about educating the people of South Asia in English. (This controversy, in different forms, has continued up to the present time.) One group which favored English was led by Charles Grant, Lord Moira, and T. B. Macaulay. The other group, not very strong, was led by the Hon. H. T. Princep, who was against the use of English as a compulsory language and termed the Minute 'hasty and indiscreet'.[8] In his dissenting Minute he wrote: 'The next step will be to transfer the professors' allowance to teachers of English, and then will follow in due course the voting of Arabic and Persian to be dead and damned.'[9]

On the side of English there was Macaulay, a powerful person with very strong views, who looked at the problem differently and, as he says, aimed at forming 'a class who may be interpreters between us and the millions whom we govern — a class of persons, Indians in blood and colour, but English in taste, in opinion, in morals and in intellect'.[10] Referring to Sanskrit and Arabic he says: 'I have no knowledge of either Sanskrit or Arabic. But I have done what I could to form a correct estimate of their value . . . I am quite ready to take the oriental learning at the valuation of the orientalists themselves. I have never found one amongst them who could deny that a single shelf of a good European library was worth the whole native literature of India and Arabia.'[11]

The Minute got the Seal of approval from Lord William Bentinck, and on March 7, 1835 an official resolution endorsing Macaulay's policy was passed. This established firmly the beginnings of the process of producing English-knowing bilinguals in India. In Ceylon, however, the firm roots of English were established much later. It was not until 1827 that merchants and planters settled in that part of South Asia.

2.3. The Diffusion of Bilingualism in English

After the initial stage the bilingualism in English spread wider on the Indian subcontinent and developed deeper roots in the educational system. On July 9, 1854 Sir Charles Wood sent the Courts of Directors the Despatch — which came later to Lord Dalhousie, the Governor-General of India. It was due to this Despatch that in 1857 three Universities were established in India, viz. Bombay, Calcutta, and Madras.[12] By the end of the nineteenth century, the Punjab (Lahore) and Allahabad Universities were established. With the spread of colleges and the increase of Universities, the importance of English was rising, and in the early twentieth century English was formally established as the official and academic language of India. English thus became the 'prestige' language, completely replacing Persian and Indian languages (or what were then called the *vernaculars*). In the second decade of the twentieth century, as the nationalist movement gained strength, an anti-English feeling emerged but strangely enough the medium of the movement itself was English. By 1928 a reasonably influential English press and a taste for English publications had been created. After World War I (1914—18), there was a significant increase in educational institutions and schools and colleges spread in the interior of India. This naturally helped in spreading bilingualism in English further among the middle and lower classes of Indian society.

The comparative statement (cf. Edwards n.d.: 1) in Table I of the publications in Indian English and Indian languages during this period should make it clearer that bilingualism in English was being rooted among the educated classes of India in the early decades of this century:

Table I. *Statistics of Publications for 1928*[13]

Language	Number of Publications
English	240
French	1
Gujarati	506
Hindi	79
Kanarese	85
Marathi	677
Sindhi	346
Urdu	83
Classical languages	101
Other dialects	25

3. THE LINGUISTIC ASPECTS OF SOUTH ASIAN ENGLISH

In section 2 the desire for bilingualism in South Asia was not viewed merely as a trend toward acquiring a new dominant language. There were sociopolitical pressure groups which were clearly divided; one favored the spread of English and another considered it dangerous for the indigenous languages and religions. Whatever the controversies, one thing was certain: slowly but definitely a South Asian variety of English was growing.

This variety is *transparently* South Asian in the sense that the educated or 'standard' speakers of the area share a large number of features at different *formal* levels.[14] Thus it is possible to present an *overall* analysis (cf. Gleason 1961:324; 443; see also Hockett 1958:334 ff.; 339 ff.) of SAE roughly on the same principles as have been followed to describe 'educated' British English or 'standard' American English.[15] It is also possible to use the available research in this area to work out such an analysis.

3.1. *Standard South Asian English*

The use of a cover term SAE does not mean that I ignore the language diversity in the use of English in South Asia. The diversity in SAE is mainly of two types. The geographical diversity can be related to the differences in the languages of the area, and to some extent to the cultural differences. The second diversity is of class or ethnic groups, and it is claimed that it cuts across the language boundaries. Spencer's (1966) analysis of Anglo-Indian[16] speech is perhaps the first attempt to describe the English of ethnic groups in South Asia. There are other groups, too, on which work may be done. Spencer, however, starts his statement with an erroneous presupposition that the Anglo-Indians are one 'distinct group of Indian citizens whose *native tongue* is English'. It is, still true that its members have 'a characteristic way of pronouncing English, such that it has been possible in India to talk of an Anglo-Indian (or earlier Eurasian) accent'. (1957:66).

It may be said that a *standard* variety of SAE has evolved which has its regional subvarieties. The standard form has been termed an *educated* or *modified*[17] form of SAE. The literature shows that this identical educated standard has partly been achieved by the five main South Asian countries, i.e., Bangladesh (50,840,000; *The Statesman's Yearbook*, 1974:220), Ceylon (Sri Lanka) (12,747,755; *The Statesman's Yearbook*, 1974:480), India (546,955,945)[18], Nepal (195,260)[19], Pakistan (61,960,000)[20]. There are mainly two language families in this area, namely Dravidian and Indo-Aryan. The speakers of other languages comprise a small proportion of the total population of the whole area.[21] (Cf. Table II).

The features of an overall analysis of standard SAE would include those phonological features which cut across the political and/or geographical boundaries of the area. It is crucial to emphasize the notion 'standard' or 'educated' because the competence of the

Table II. *The Main Languages of South Asia*[22]

Ceylon		India		Pakistan		Nepal	
Dravi-dian	Indo-Aryan	Dravi-dian	Indo-Aryan	Dravi-dian	Indo-Aryan or Iranian	Indo-Aryan	Tibeto-Burmese
Tamil	Sinhalese	Tamil Telugu Malaya-lam Kannada	Assamese Bengali Gujarati Hindi Kashmiri Marathi Punjabi Urdu	Brahui	Balochi Bengali Gujarati Pashto Punjabi Sindhi	Nepali	Newari

speakers of English varies so much that one is prone to find a kind of confusion. It has been suggested that the English-knowing bilinguals of this area should be ranked on a *scale* — even an arbitrary one — so that one can separate them on the basis of their competence in different modes of English. In some studies of Indian English the term *Cline of Bilingualism* has been used (cf. Kachru 1966; 1965:3). The cline comprises three 'measuring points', i.e., the *zero point*, the *central point*, and the *ambilingual point*. These three points present a gradation towards an educated form of SAE. The zero point is the bottom point on the axis, but it is not the end point at the bottom. In South Asia it is very common to come across users of English who have acquired some control of restricted items of English but cannot use the language in any serious sense. Some such varieties have been labeled *Babu English, Butler English, Bearer English, Kitchen English* (Yule and Burnell 1903).

There are already some collections of South Asian writing in English from different points on the cline of bilingualism. Hunt, Gokak,[23] and others have published some such examples from Indian English as written by bilinguals who rank around the zero point. The following observation of Kindersley is interesting.

'In that well-known example of Indian English *Onoocool Chunder Mookerjee: A Memoir* (1873), such sentences as the following occur: *The house became a second Babel, or a pretty kettle of fish. His elevation created a catholic ravishment throughout the domain under the benign and fostering sceptre of great Albian.*

This adventurous kind of English is still used, especially by professional petition-writers and in the writing of young Indians who have lately left school or college. The extent of its use has, however, in the opinion of the writer and of the above observers consulted by him, been much over-estimated. (Kindersley 1938).'

Referring to 'educated' Indian English he continues:

'The English commonly spoken and written by professional men and clerks in most provinces is a more cautious and restricted type of language. Great use is made of a limited number of clichés, such as "do the needful in the matter" and "better imagined than described". More metaphorical expressions are used on occasion; but they come from a very limited and stereotype repertory. Pleonastic clichés such as "each and every" are substituted for simple forms. In general, the language has little variety or range; but the caution observed in its selection does not secure the complete exclusion of malapropisms (Kindersley 1938:26).'

The educated variety of SAE is mainly used by those bilinguals who rank around the central point. This includes the large number of civil servants or educationists in Bangladesh, Ceylon, India, Nepal, and Pakistan who make use of typically South Asian *registers*[24] of English in their respective areas of operation.

3.2. *The South Asianness at Different Levels*

3.2.1. *Phonetics and Phonology*
There have been more studies on phonetics/phonology of SAE than on any other area. There may be two reasons for this. First, during approximately the last fifteen years South Asia has been exposed to the structuralist linguists and their undue emphasis on phonetics/phonology manifests itself in the research. Second, pedagogically this level has always been treated as a primary level and since these studies were done essentially from a pedagogical point of view, the pedagogical presentation naturally attracted more attention.

These studies are mainly about the *regional* varieties of SAE treating the L_1 of the speaker as a demarcation point, or in some cases, about the larger areas such as *Dravidian English, North Indian English,* or *Ceylon English*. It seems that so far not much research has been done on the four major varieties of Dravidian English (i.e.

Telugu, Tamil, Malayalam, Kannada). Gopalkrishnan (1960) presented a very sketchy analysis of the South Indian pronunciation of English. The following studies refer to the general phonetic characteristics of SAE speakers of a large area cutting across the language boundaries: Barron (1961), Lahiri (1956), Pandit (1964), Passé (1947), Rao (1961), Varma (1957).

3.2.2.
The phonetic/phonological deviations in SAE are essentially determined by the phonetic/phonological structures of the L_1.[25] These deviations are of two types, (a) those of segmental phonemes, and (b) those of non-segmental phonemes. In most analyses of SAE it is mainly the segmental differences which have been worked out (except in DeLanerolle (1953), Passé (1947), and Hai and Ball (1961). The discussions on the nonsegmental features are either very sketchy or have been completely ignored.

3.2.3. *The Segmental Phonemes*
On the basis of available analyses (both contrastive and noncontrastive), it is possible to present certain generalizations about SAE. The basis of such generalizations can be the underlying typology of the languages of the region. These generalizations are of two types, i.e., *structural* and *systemic.*

3.2.4.
By structural and systemic differences, in the case of SAE, I mean the following. The term structure is used in a syntagmatic sense, and the term system in a paradigmatic sense. Thus in many cases the structure of L_1 may be absent in L_2 (in this case English) or the structure may be 'identical', yet there may be systemic differences. Consider, for example, the following three languages of South Asia: Hindi-Urdu, Kashmiri, and Sinhalese. We find that in these three languages (as in English) CVC morpheme structure is possible. Thus in this restricted sense these languages may be considered 'identical' with English at the phonetic level. Note, however, that these vary in the *elements* which operate (cf. Barron 1961) in the systems. For example, /f, θ, ð/ do not occur in the above languages as members of any system. This results in *transfer* or *substitution* of L_2 elements by L_1 elements. In phonetic terms this transfer is of two types. First, it may be a substitution of one or more phonetic elements in a full series of sounds, e.g., the fricative series, which is not absent in South

Asian languages (hereafter abbreviated SAL [s]) but shows gaps when compared with the same series in English. Second, there may be complete transfer of a series, e.g., the whole alveolar series is substituted by a retroflex series in SAE. The degree of retroflexion in SAE varies from the South of India to the North of India. Note also that systemic differences may be in terms of *distribution*. A SAL and English may have 'identical' phonetic elements but these *shared* sounds may operate in different systems. For example, both in Hindi and English the following clusters are present: *sk, st, sp*. The differences, however, are distributional, i.e., structurally these elements are shared but systemically they differ. In many varieties of Hindi *sk, st, sp*, do not occur in word initial position. The result is that in Indian English (as spoken in the so-called Hindi region) we get the following forms:

'station'   [iste:šen]   'speak'   [ispi:k]
'school'   [isku:l]   'stall'   [ista:l]

What happens, (usually unconsciously) is that the most approximate sound is substituted from the phonological inventory of L_1 wherever there is a 'gap' in the system. It is this substitution and 'overhauling' of the phonological systems (both segmental and non-segmental) which results in the deviations and, ultimately, in the phonological characteristics termed *South Asianness*.

A detailed typological analysis of the systems should give us the *subvarieties* of SAE. These subvarieties, as discussed earlier, apply to the regional varieties, and also to the ethnic varieties of SAE. We may then start with the broad classification of *Dravidian English* and *Indo-Aryan English*[26] and work towards the subsystems of these on the basis of individual languages, for instance, Tamil, Malayalam, Hindi, Sinhalese. The features of Dravidian English or Indo-Aryan English may thus be abstracted on the basis of the typological features of these languages.

An overall analysis of SAE is an abstraction of the same nature as *Standard American* or *Educated British*. There has not been any attempt to work out an analysis of this type for SAE. The aim of aforementioned analyses has been essentially pedagogical and the result is contrastive descriptions of a very superficial type. It is important that an overall analysis be ultimately related to the phonetic level where deviations may be shown in terms of the phonetic substance in different language regions of South Asia.

In a general typological statement of SAE two things are to be taken into consideration: first, the subsystem of the loan phonology of different SAL's; second, the subsystems of *nonshared* items in different South Asian languages. A good example of the first is provided by Hindi-Urdu, Punjabi, Kashmiri, and Sinhalese. In the spoken English of the L_1 speakers of the above languages the /ph, f/ distinction is maintained by a large number of people who are exposed to the loan phonology (say acquired from Arabic, Persian, or other languages) in their respective L_1's. Note that /ph, f/ distinction is not found in the nonloan phonology of these languages.[27] In Sinhalese /š/ is found only in Sanskrit loanwords. A number of such examples may be added from other languages, too. Thus it is on the basis of two phonological systems, the main system and the subsystems, that the analysis of SAE is to be worked out. By nonshared items in SAL's I mean, e.g., the implosive in Sindhi or lateral flap in Marathi, which are not shared by all the South Asian languages.

It is possible to abstract from the aforementioned analyses[28] the influence of (a) nonshared items, (b) ethnic-group differences (J. W. Spencer 1957), (c) caste dialects,[29] and (d) religious dialects[30] of the SAL's on SAE. In many North Indian or Pakistani varieties of English we find that certain distinctions found in one language merge into one distinction in another language. Consider, for example, phonemes /s/ and /š/. In Bengali, English *same to you* becomes *shame to you*. On the other hand on the borders of Bengal and Orissa the situation is quite the opposite; there /š/ changes to /s/, thus *she* and *see* are not homophonous.

There has been a controversy in current literature to decide what are the underlying reasons for 'readjustments' in the consonant system of English in SAE (cf. K. S. N. Rao 1961; and Pandit 1964), especially the initial /p, t, k/. Rao does not consider that the L_1 s and the process of transfer can be the main reason. 'The *real* explanation lies elsewhere. It is in the way that English is taught in India, and in the way English is spelt.' (K. S. N. Rao 1961).

Pandit suggests that 'the non-realization of aspirated voiceless allophones of the phonemes /p, t, k/ by Indian speakers should be interpreted in the larger framework of the consonant systems of English and Indian languages. Most of the Indian languages (except Assamese and perhaps Tamil-Malayalam) have a five-way position contrast from bilabial to velar and a four-way manner contrast of voiceless vs. voiced, and unaspirated vs. aspirated in the stop consonant series.' (Pandit 1964).

We might then say that certain features such as series substitution (e.g., retroflex series for alveolar series) are typically South Asian and other features may depend both on the *competence* of a speaker in English and his L_1 background.

3.3. *Nonsegmental Phonemes*

The main phonological features of SAE which separate it from the L_1 varieties of English are not necessarily the deviations in the segmental phonemes but the deviations in stress, rhythm, intonation, etc. It is obvious that the intelligibility between an L_1 speaker of English and an SAE speaker suffers much because of the second type of deviation. There are no serious and intensive studies of this extremely interesting feature of SAE. Passé (1947), DeLanerolle (1953), Gopalkrishnan (1960), and Hai and Ball (1961), have discussed certain nonsegmental features of some varieties of SAE. Usmani (1965) has given an analysis of Urdu and English. The main points of Passé are:

1. All stressing in Ceylon English is comparatively weak as 'stress (or force accent) is comparatively weak in Sinhalese and Tamil'.
2. There is no vowel reduction.
3. There is no distinction between strong and weak forms.
4. The English words are 'incorrectly' stressed (Passé 1947).

The observations of Usmani on the role of stress in Urdu and English are naive and misleading. He gives the following rules for the stress pattern of Urdu:

1. Single-syllable words with short vowels are slightly less loud than those with long vowels,

    /mil/'mix'   /mi:l/'mile'

2. Polysyllable words have an 'even scale of stress' if all syllables have short vowels,

    /|bʌr|tʌn/'pot'

3. Polysyllable words have louder stress on the long vowels if they have short and long vowels,

    /zəl'ma:na/'period'

Usmani concludes '. . . Urdu stress depends in some cases upon the length of the vowels. In general the stress pattern is very simple and kept to an even scale of loudness.' His analysis of intonation of Urdu is equally superficial and misleading (e.g., 'A comparative study . . . shows that Urdu and English follow the same pitch patterns.')[31]

Gopalkrishnan's observations on the English spoken by South Indians also apply to the Tamil speaking Ceylonese.[32] His main points are summarized below:

1. A general unawareness of the patterns of primary as well as secondary stress, e.g.,
   /'maekbeθ / for /mek' beθ /;/'tju:ʃen/ for /tju(:)'iʃen/

2. A tendency to ignore differentiating the stress patterns of nouns and adjectives on the one hand and verbs on the other hand.

3. An unawareness of the shift in stress found in different parts of speech derived from the 'same Latin or Greek root'.

Taylor's study on 'The Indian English Stress System' is based on a widely spoken North Indian language (i.e., Hindi). The North Indian English stress features, however, are not different from what Gopalkrishnan has written about Dravidian English. Taylor's tentative conclusion, subject to the findings of much wider speech samplings, may be summed up as follows:

'The Hindi L_1 speakers of English tend to give generally stronger and more nearly equal stress to the unstressed and weak syllables of English. Their stress distribution and points of juncture tend to be unpredictable. Within the overall framework of relatively stronger stress for unstressed and weak forms, the observed speech samples indicate the following deviations:

(1) A tendency in some instances to place stress on the suffix itself and in other instances randomly rather than where predictable on the penultimate syllable.

(2) A tendency to accord weak-strong stress to nouns as well as verbs in the group of two-syllable words showing grammatical contrast through stress.

(3) A general lack of recognition of the primary/tertiary pattern of stress for compound nouns as opposed to the secondary/primary pattern used with free noun/noun combinations; a tendency to use the secondary/primary pattern for both.

(4) A *strong* tendency to give full value to auxiliary verb forms written as contractions, and to accord them a relatively strong stress as well.

(5) A strong tendency to break up grammatical units arbitrarily within sentences, thus violating the confines of 'sense groups' and placing a strong stress on words other than those normally found to have 'sense stress'.'[33]

It may be mentioned here that the underlying reasons for the deviations in stress are the following: all the main SAL's are syllable-timed languages, as opposed to English which is a stress-timed language. This results in a distinct South Asian rhythm in SAE which is based on arranging long and short syllables, and not stressed and unstressed syllables. This may be the main reason for labeling SAE as a 'sing-song' English, and for stating that it hampers intelligibility with the L_1 speakers of English.[34]

The above fragmentary studies on the three major areas of SAE speakers (i.e., Ceylon, South India, and North India) show that on the whole the characteristics of this phonological feature are shared by all. It may then be said that these typical features of South Asian stress (if a system can eventually be worked out) and rhythm rather than the segmental phonemes mark a typical SAE speaker.

3.4. *Grammar*

3.4.1.

The grammatical characteristics of SAE should prove a very interesting area of investigation. In order to get clearer clues about the role of L_1's in standard SAE grammar, detailed contrastive analyses may provide a helpful background. In recent years the grammatical aspect has attracted the attention of some scholars.[35]

There have also been studies on restricted topics concerned with certain grammatical points. A very obvious characteristic of SAE's is the *absence* of a *parallel* category of the article in their deictic system as opposed to that of English. The manifestation of this feature has been worked out in detail by Dustoor (see Dustoor 1954; 1955) using Indian English writing as the basis. Dustoor's analysis, however, is of restricted value for two reasons. First, there is no mention of the specific sources which were used for his analysis. Second, he does not provide any clues as to the competence of his writers in English. This naturally makes it difficult to rank them on the cline of bilingualism.

There is also a comparative grammatical statement of 'identical' restricted languages in British English and Indian English.[36] Its aim is to present a comparative statement about:

1. The deviations in structures and systems in the verbal groups and nominal groups.
2. The frequency of grammatical patterns in the two varieties, with their statistical significance.

This attempt has failed to show any revealing differences. The reasons for this failure are both methodological and theoretical. It is, however, interesting to note that the two registers of Indian English under discussion do not show statistically very significant deviations from British English which was treated as the norm.

The following are the results of the study. In the verbal group, at the primary degree of *delicacy,* the differences are not very significant. Perhaps that is understandable since a conscious attempt was made to choose the Indian text from the upper point on the cline of bilingualism. There are, however, marked differences in the elements which operate in the structures.

1. The differences in the use of finite verbs and non-finite verbs do not show a marked deviation. The Indian English text has a high percentage (1.96%) of finite verb forms. The British English text has 1.96% more nonfinite verb forms than the Indian English text.
2. In extension of finite verbs Indian English has the highest frequency (i.e., 1.35%). The difference between the two texts is 1.49%.

The X^2-test (Chi-squared test) shows that in the following three categories the differences are significant, i.e., *interrogative, negative,* and *modalized* verbs. In the case of *passive, preterite, continuous* and *perfect* the differences are not significant.

In the nominal group again the texts under discussion do not show any marked differences at the primary degree of delicacy. The differences become marked only in the elements which function in the nominal group. Consider, for example, the following:

1. In relation to total words the nominal group shows a higher percentage of 1.49% in Indian English texts.
2. In the two texts the grading of nominal modifiers shows that the

maximum number of items has been modified by one item. The
modifiers are used on a 'descending' scale up to the maximum of
five. Note the differences shown in Table III.

Table III.

Grading of Modifiers	Indian English	British English
One modifier		+ 2.36
Two modifiers		+ 0.09
Three modifiers	+ 2.29	
Four modifiers		+ 0.02
Five modifiers	+ 0.04	(no occurrence)

The analysis was based on a very restricted corpus and the results
cannot be generalized.

Note also that in a comparative study of this type another distinction was needed between (1) those deviations which are *contextually*
significant, and (2) those deviations which are *stylistically* significant.
In the verbal group, for example, the frequency differences in *nega-
tion, interrogation,* and *person* are included in (1), and *aspect, mood,*
and the *time* categories are included in (2).

3.4.2.
An earlier paper written by Kindersley in 1938 has some interesting
observations. These observations, he makes clear,

'are concerned not with the broken sort of English spoken by
servants or other Indians of little or no "English" education, but
with the English of those who have learnt the language in schools.
They apply, generally speaking, to the English of clerks and of the
less well educated among the professional Indians who use English
daily, such as pleaders and magistrates. That is, they apply to a form
of speech intermediate between the almost completely normal
English of many Indian writers on the one hand, and the dog English
of the schoolboy on the other. Many of the usages herein contained,
however, occur only from time to time in the English of the highly-
educated. Of this fact ample evidence could be produced in the shape
of notes taken from books and speeches by well-known Indians.
(Kindersley 1938:25).'

Kindersley comments on the following grammatical features of Indian English and tries to give reasons for them.[37]
1. In the reflexive verbs (e.g., *enjoy, exert*) the reflexive pronoun is omitted. 'This is usually due to inaccurate observation in the first instance, followed by the spreading and stereotyping of the mistake.'
2. In place of transitive verbs, intransitive verbs are used (e.g., *reach, waive*), or the other way round (e.g., *preside, dissent*).
3. In constructions such as verb + particle (e.g., *dispose of*), the particle is added to such verbs as normally do not take the particle, (e.g., *tear off, eat off*). The reasons, says Kindersley, are that 'These are derived to some extent by extension of English usage. But a strong influence has been the extremely common use of auxiliary verbs, both in Indo-Aryan and Dravidian, as Hindustani *mar-gayā*, Tamil *irandu-vittar*.' His observations on 'the syntax of the verb' are useful and open up an area of potential research. He has also attempted to give the underlying reasons for these deviations. The complete list of deviations mentioned by Kindersley is given below.

'A number of Indicisms is found in the syntax of the verb. In detailing the principal of these, the verb *to do* (transitive) or *to run* or *come* (intransitive), will be used as examples.
(1) *I am doing* for *I (constantly) do*. P, B, D similarly *I was doing* for *I (constantly) did*. P, B, D.
(2) *I am doing it* (for *I have been doing it*) *since six months*. Similarly with the past tense. P, B, D. Dr. as well as IA usage.
(3) *I did* for *I have (just or hitherto) done*. P, B, D.
(4) *I had run* for *I ran*, following the use of the IA pluperfect form, H *maî daurā thā*, which carries the implication that something of greater interest, or some change has occurred since, but not the reference back from one point of time to an anterior point which is borne by the European pluperfect. P, B, D.
(5) *It is done* for *It has been done;* and *It was done* for *It had been done*. P, D.
(6) *If I did*, for *If I do*.
(7) *When I will come* and *If I will come* for *When I come* and *If I come*. P, B, D.
(8) *You will do* for *I beg you will do* or *Will you please do?* P, B, D. Dr. as well as IA usage.
(9) *Would* to express a vague future or indefinite present. P, B, D. Dr. as well as IA usage.

(10) *May* in jussive or optative sense, cf. *You may kindly come,* I *may* (for *let me*) *go.*

(11) Favoring of the passive voice rather than the active, P, B, D. Due partly to the passive form, with the agential case, of the IA preterite. But also found in other tenses of the verb, especially in the jussive form of the present. Cf. *This may be done* for *Please do this.* B, D.

(12) *For doing* for *to do,* expressing purpose or object. Cf. *Award imprisonment for improving his character.*

(13) Idiomatic use of the perfect participle active: *I did this after taking thought* for *I took thought after doing this,* or *I did not do this without taking due thought beforehand.* (Kindersley 1938:28).'

Kindersley gives the following reasons for these deviations.

'In the IA area the above are all due to vernacular usage, except for 11, which has no foundation in Bengali so far as the preterite is concerned. 11 may be inferred to have spread from neighboring IA regions into Bengal. Similarly a number of the above originating in purely IA usage, may be inferred to have spread from the IA into the Dr. area. (Kindersley 1938:29).'

In his 'A Transformational Treatment of Indian English Syntax' Unpublished Ph.D. thesis (University of Illinois, 1968) Robert P. Fox 'attempts to show that language learners who have passed the beginning stages of language learning make errors only on the transformational level of grammar'. Fox's analysis is based on the written papers of Hindi L_1 speakers who are at least graduates of Indian universities. The study is divided into the following sections:

'Chapter I is devoted to a discussion of the role of the English language in India from its introduction up to the present time, and to the method and corpus used for the study.
Chapter II is the main chapter of the dissertation. It is the analysis of selected, syntactically deviant sentences from the corpus to illustrate the level on which the deviancy occurs. The system of analysis is that presented by Noam Chomsky in his *Aspects of the Theory of Syntax.* The analysis concentrates on nominalization, pronominalization, adjectivalization and various aspects of the verb phrase. The comparative, passive, questions, expletive "there", adverbs and deletions are also discussed.

In Chapter III, questions, relatives, nominal modifiers, subject-verb agreement, the comparative and passive in Hindi and English are contrasted. The contrastive analysis is included in an attempt to show that despite differences in the base component, it will be the transformational component that will be the source of difficulty for the language learner.'

3.5. *Lexis*

In lexis I shall include two characteristic types of SAE vocabulary. The first is concerned with that part of lexis which is, by and large, *nonshared* with those varieties of English which are used as the L_1. The other comprises those items which are transferred from the SAL's to the L_1 variety of English and have become part of the borrowed lexicon of English.

It was mainly the first aspect of SAE vocabulary that captured the attention of earlier scholars. The reasons for this attention were mainly pragmatic; most of the lexical items in this category are *register-restricted* and *culture-bound*.[38] The administrators of the *Raj*, who worked in the interior of South Asia, needed them for communication with the natives. This type then is represented by those South Asian lexical items which are used, for example, in the registers of administration, agriculture, law, etc. Such studies are no contribution to lexicography in any serious sense.

Note the following observation of Yule and Burnell (1903:XV):

'Of modern Glossaries, such as have been the result of serious labor, all, or nearly all, have been of a kind purely technical, intended to facilitate the comprehension of official documents by the explanation of terms used in the Revenue department, or in other branches of Indian administration. The most notable examples are (of brief and occasional character), the Glossary appended to the famous *Fifth Report* of the Select Committee of 1812, which was compiled by Sir Charles Wilkins; and (of a far more vast and comprehensive sort), the late Professor Horace Hayman Wilson's *Glossary of Judicial and Revenue Terms* (40, 1855) which leaves far behind every other attempt in that kind?

A collection of such items for Ceylon was published in 1869 under the title *Ceylonese Vocabulary*.

It is the second type of lexical work which is of interest to us.

It was in 1886 that Yule and Burnell published a glossary of what they termed 'Anglo-Indian Words' with a hybridized title *Hobson-Jobson*.[39] This soon became a classic for its wealth of information and its style. The main title was chosen 'to have an alternative title at least a little more characteristic.' The preface says that

'If the reader will turn to *Hobson-Jobson* in the Glossary itself, he will find that phrase, though now rare and moribund, to be a typical and delightful example of that class of Anglo-Indian *argot* which consists of Oriental words highly assimilated, perhaps by vulgar lips, to the English vernacular; whilst it is the more fitted to our book, conveying, as it may, a veiled intimation of dual authorship. (Yule and Burnell 1903:IX)?

The second edition edited by William Crook was published in 1903.

During this period English had already started borrowing (and often assimilating) words of South Asian origin. In 1892 Fennell listed the following numbers of South Asian words.

Hindoo (sic) 336; Sanskrit 32; Dravidian 31 (Fennell 1892:XI). It should be noted that

'Words of Indian origin have been insinuating themselves into English ever since the end of the reign of Elizabeth and the beginning of that of James, when such terms as *calico, chintz,* and *gingham* had already effected a lodgment in English warehouses and shops, and were lying in wait for entrance into English literature. Such outlandish guests grew more frequent 120 years ago, when, soon after the middle of the last century, the numbers of Englishmen in the Indian services, civil and military, expanded with the great acquisition of dominion then made by the Company; and we meet them in vastly greater abundance now. (Yule and Burnell 1903:XV).'

Before the publication of *Hobson-Jobson*, Wilson (1855) and Whitworth (1885) had published their works, and Yule and Burnell drew intensively upon their materials.

It was much later that many specialized studies on the South Asian elements in English appeared. Lexicographers and linguists had been conscious of the South Asian element in English earlier. Serjeantson gave a short and useful account of loanwords from 'Indian dialects' and the Dravidian languages in her book, *A History of Foreign Words in English*. In 1954 G. S. Rao's study entitled *Indian Words in English* appeared posthumously.

'It brings together the history of the British in India and the result of this in enriching their own language during a period of three centuries and a half. It gives in detail the extent to which the words thus made familiar have played their part in English literature from the seventeenth century down to the present time. (see Craigie 1954).'

3.5.1.

There is another aspect of SAE which may be discussed in the section on lexis, i.e., *Collocational Deviation*.[40] There are references to it in Goffin (1934) and Passé[41] and in two recent papers (Kachru 1965; 1966) this aspect of Indian English has been discussed. It is argued there that collocational deviation is one crucial feature that marks what may be termed the *South Asianness* of SAE.

It is claimed (Kachru 1965; 1966) that the collocational deviations may be of three types. First, there may be grammatical deviations from the varieties of English which are used as the first language. This would account for a large number of examples of Ceylon English listed under 'ignorant-English' by Passé (1947), or some examples of Indian English given by Pearse-Smith.[42] Second, there may be *loanshifts* or *lexis-bound translations* from SAL's; thus in English these naturally appear deviant (Kachru, 1965, 1966 and 1975a). Consider the following examples from Ceylon English (Passé (1947),

to break rest; bull work; to give a person bellyfull

These examples show the transfer of *fixed collocations* of Sinhalese into English. The following are 'literal translations' of Sinhalese expressions: *to buy and give; to jump and run; to run and come* (home); *to take and come*. Third, the deviation may be contextual and not formal. This involves a *semantic shift* of English lexical items (see section 4.0.).

Examples of such deviations may be given from Standard Indian English writing. The following possibilities of deviation from L_1 varieties of English have been shown.

1. The members of a collocation may be usual in the sense that in L_2 varieties of English that collocation is possible, but the contextual use of the collocation may be typically Indian (e.g., *flower-bed* [*MM*[43] 105]).

2. The lexical items of a collocation may be collocated in non-native collocations. Thus we get lexically and contextually Indian collocations (e.g., *sister-sleeper* [*V of G* 130] *dining-leaf* [*WM*, 84]).

3. The contextual use of a collocation may present no difficulties to L₁ users of English, only the collocability of an item with the *node* of a collocation may be unusual. This, then, may be explained as violation of a selectional rule of the language.

3.5.2.
Another interesting lexical feature of SAE is the use of *Hybridization.* A hybrid (or *Mixed* formation) is described as one which comprises two or more elements and in which at least one element is from a SAL and one from English. (E.g., *kumkummark [Kanth,* 159], *tiffin-carrier [DD,* 78]). It is possible to make a further distinction between (a) *Open-set* hybrid items (e.g., *lathi-charge [HS.* 15-6-59], and (b) *Closed-System* hybrid items (e.g., *police-wala* [*SMH,* 61]) (cf. Kachru 1965; 1966 and 1975a).

This aspect of SAE should provide fascinating materials for socio-linguistic studies of different areas of South Asia.[44]

3.6. Style-Features and 'Tone'

By *style-features* and *tone*[45] I mean those formal features which are attributed to the different varieties of SAE. These may overlap with some of the features discussed earlier under grammar (see section 3.4.) and lexis (see section 3.5.). They may be summed up as follows:

1. *Latinity:* There is a tendency toward a kind of Latinity in SAE. An Indian, says Goffin (1934), would prefer *demise* to *death,* or *pain in one's bosom* to *pain in one's chest.*

2. *Polite Diction:* An excess of polite forms (Goffin 1934) is immediately discovered by native speakers of English when they visit South Asia. The main reason for this is that originally the registers of English introduced in India were of Administration and Law; both these registers are full of polite forms and these became part of South Asian conversational English.

3. *Phrase-mongering:* A tendency toward phrase-mongering (Goffin 1934:31, see also section 3.5.1.), as mentioned earlier, is determined by the structure of L₁ and also by various types of collocational deviations. The underlying reasons for it have not been given. Goffin gives the following examples of what he terms 'phrase-mongering':

Himalayan-blunder; nation-building; change of heart, dumb-millions (Goffin 1934).

4. *Initialisms:* In this area SAE seems to surpass the offical registers of American English. Note the following:

'H.E.'s P.A. has written D.O. to the A.S.P. about the question of T.A.'s. The D.C. himself will visit the S.D.O.P.W.D. today at 10. A.M.S.T.' This letter should read as follows:

'His Excellency's Personal Assistant has written a demi-official letter to the Assistant Superintendent of Police about the question of Travelling-Allowances. The Deputy Commissioner himself will visit the Sub-Divisional Officer of the Public Works Department today at 10 a.m. Standard Time.' (Goffin 1934).

5. *Moralistic tone:* Goffin makes a specific reference to the English of the Indian subcontinent and considers it moralistic in the sense that the Indians cannot keep God out of it (Goffin 1934).

6. *Clichés:* Kindersley gives the following examples to illustrate the excessive use of clichés in Indian English: *better imagined than described* (easily imagined); *do the needful; each and every* (pleonastic for 'each'); *leave severely alone* (for 'leave alone') (Kindersley 1938:26).

7. *Deletion:* In a large number of South Asianisms in English (e.g., Indianisms, Ceylonisms) a syntactic unit belonging to a higher rank in the L_1 variety of English is reduced to a lower rank in SAE. In certain cases where an L_1 speaker of English tends to use a group or a clause, an SAE user might use a unit of a lower rank. In SAE many nominal formations of modifier + head + qualifier (MHQ) structure are reduced to MH structure (Kachru 1965).

A large number of Indianisms are thus produced by *Rank Reduction*, i.e., they involve first the process of deletion and then permutation of the lexical items. Consider, for example, the following nominal groups of English: (1) *an address of welcome*, (2) *a bunch of keys*, and (3) *love of God*. In Indian English these are reduced to (1) *welcome address* (IE, 14.8.59), (2) *key bunch* (*AD*, 178), and (3) *God-love* (*Un*, 205). It is argued

'that the tendency towards deletion in IE [Indian English] results in many such Indianisms which vary not necessarily grammatically, but only in the "acceptability" by a native speaker of English; the reasons for "non-acceptability" are varied ... The acceptability of IE collocations forms a scale, and the native speaker's reaction toward such Indianisms may be *acceptable, unacceptable,* or *more-or-less acceptable.* (Kachru 1965:405).'

The rank reduced formations have been labeled by Whitworth 'wrong compounds' and Goffin finds in these formations a tendency toward 'phrase-mongering'. Whitworth thinks that Indians are following the process of analogy of Sanskrit *tatpurusha* compounds, like *deva-putra* 'a son of God', and transfer such formations into Indian English (e.g., *deva-putra* as 'God-son').

8. *Yes-no 'confusion':* Goffin also makes observations about the spoken form of the Indian variety of English. The first observation is with regard to the 'curious over-use of the opening "well . . ." ', and the second deals with the use of 'no' where an Englishman would say 'yes'. Goffin holds the English textbook readers responsible for the first point where the 'dialogue' is amply treated and he also thinks it may be a device used to gain time in replying. Perhaps the use of 'well' as a hesitation marker in SAE needs further investigation. The second point seems to be the result of wide confusion not only in Goffin but also in other scholars. The explanation for the *'yes-no'* confusion (if this is confusion) is purely formal. What happens is that in many languages (e.g., Russian, Japanese, South Asian languages) the choice of *yes* or *no* in a question depends on (a) the form of the question and (b) the facts of the situation. If the above (a) and (b) have the same polarity (both positive or both negative) the answer is positive. If on the other hand the polarity is not the same (say, the question is in the positive and the situation is negative or the converse) the answer is negative. The selection of *yes* or *no* in English mainly depends on the facts of the situation. If the situation is positive the answer is *yes*, if it is negative the answer is *no*. Kindersley also mentions this point. (Cf. ' "Yes" is answer to a negative question, for English "no", i.e., *You have no objection? Yes, I have no objection* [following IA and Dr. usage]': Kindersley, 1938; see also French 1949:6).

9. *Reduplication:* The high frequency of reduplication of items (often in the spoken medium) is usually noticed as an SAE marker by the L₁ speaker of English. The reason for the reduplication of the verbs and nouns (and other items, too) is again the underlying structure of the SAL's. This is a typological feature which all SAL's share. Passé gives the following examples from Ceylonese English showing the transfer from Sinhalese: *punci punci keeli* '(to cut into) small, small pieces'; *unu unu* '(to eat something) hot, hot'; *hemin hemin* '(to proceed) slowly, slowly'; *andaa andaa yanavaa* 'to go crying crying'; *monava monava* 'What and what (did he say)?'; *kavuda kavuda* 'Who and who (came to the party)?' (Passé

1947:384–385). It is not rare to find, for example, that Hindi, Telugu, or Kashmiri speakers transfer this feature into their English.
10. *Bookishness:* There are two possible reasons for what is referred to as bookishness of SAE users. The first is that both in spoken and written mediums SAE users tend to use certain lexical items, and grammatical constructions, which have either been dropped or are less frequent in modern English. Mathai, commenting on this aspect of Indian English, writes:

'Although there were "English" teachers of English in many of the Schools and Colleges of India, inevitably the Indian learned a great part of his English from books. Indian English was therefore always inclined to be bookish, and not adequately in touch with the living English of the day; and when we remember that the books which we re-read as models of good English were the works of Shakespeare and Milton and the other great English poets and dramatists and prose-writers, it is not surprising that the more eloquent utterances of Indians (whether spoken or written) were often freely garnished with phrases and turns of expression taken from the great writers. Sometimes these phrases were used without proper recognition of their archaic or obsolescent or purely poetic character. (Mathai 1951:97–98.)'

The second reason in a way stems from the first. Spoken SAE does not sound *conversational,* as the spoken medium has been seldom taught as an academic discipline in the South Asian educational system. Thus the SAE speakers are not made conscious of the characteristics of spoken English as, for example, the contracted forms.

4. LINGUISTIC ASPECTS OF SOUTH ASIAN ENGLISH LITERATURES

In the last three decades a considerable body of creative writing in English has grown in South Asia.[46] It is not only South Asian in a geographical sense but also in content and form. The largest contribution has been made by the Indian writers. The Indian part of South Asian writing is generally termed *Indian English* writing, though for a long time there has been a controversy regarding a proper label for it. The discussion in this section will be mainly concerned with the Indian part of SAE writing and especially with the linguistic aspects of it.

In Indian English writing a distinction is made between the following types of writing: 1. Anglo-Indian; 2. Indo-Anglian; 3. Indo-Anglican; 4. Indo-English; 5. Indian English.

The term *Anglo-Indian* writing has been restricted to that body of creative writing which treats the Indian subcontinent as the central theme. But the main point to note is that Anglo-Indian writers are those non-Indian writers of English who use English as their L_1. These writers have two points of linguistic interest for those working on SAE. First, they create many formations for the Indian contexts; second, they borrow profusely from the SAL's. These include, for example, Rudyard Kipling, E. M. Forster, John Masters. A detailed treatment of these authors is given in Oaten (1908; 1907—27) and Singh B., (1934), to name two.

Indo-Anglian writing essentially includes the work of those Indians who use English as an L_2 and write mainly about India. The confusing term *Indo-Anglican* gained currency for a short time during the World War II and now has rightly been withdrawn (Iyengar 1945; 1962). *Indo-English* seems to have been alternately used with Indo-Anglian until recently when Gokak attempted to redefine it in the following terms: 'What I would call 'Indo-English' literature consists of translations by Indians from Indian literature into English' (see Gokak 1964). I am not sure if such a separate category is needed at all or what it accomplishes. The term *Indian English* sounds perhaps less elegant but is linguistically significant and contextually self-explanatory. This term is gaining more currency and replacing other terms, certainly in linguistic literature. The first group of Indian scholars who used this term were Anand, Bhushan, Dustoor, and Jha.[47]

Since the World War II serious work has been done in the writing and critical evaluation of the Indian part of SAE writing. In the 1930s this new development was viewed with considerable pessimism which slowly disappeared after World War II. Consider the following statements. Bhupal Singh, discussing 'some Indian writers of Indian fiction' in a 'note' as an Appendix to his study in 1930 commented:

'An interesting feature of twentieth century Anglo-Indian fiction is the emergence of Indians as writers of fiction in English. This is a natural result of the spread of education in India and the increasing familiarity of Indians with English literature. (1934:306).'

Concluding, he says:

'Indian writers and story-tellers, on the whole, do not compare favorably with Anglo-Indian writers. That they write in a foreign tongue is a serious handicap in itself. Then few of them possess any knowledge of the art of fiction; they do not seem to realize that prose fiction, in spite of its freedom, is subject to definite laws. In plot construction they are weak, and in characterization weaker still. (1934:309–310).'

Gokak, himself a noted Indian English writer, presents a recent attitude toward Indian English writing:

'Indo-Anglian writing is direct and spontaneous, − like creative writing in any other language. It is conditioned in many ways by the peculiar circumstances of its birth and growth ... Gordon Bottomley is said to have described typical Indo-Anglian poetry as "Matthew Arnold in a *sari*". He should rather have referred to it as Shakuntala in skirts. (1964:162).'

In South Asia now, SAE writing is being considered a part of the literary heritage of the area in the same sense in which the regional literatures are part of the culture of South Asia. Iyengar's following statement is significant. He asks: 'How shall we describe Indian creative writing in English?' and answers: 'Of course, it is Indian literature, even as the works of Thoreau or Hemingway are American literature. But Indian literature comprises several literatures ... and Indian writing in English is but one of the voices in which India speaks. It is a new voice, no doubt, but it is as much Indian as others (1962:3).'

Rao has succinctly summarized the position of a South Asian writer in English.

'The telling has not been easy. One has to convey in a language that is not one's own the spirit that is one's own. One has to convey the various shades and omissions of a certain thought − movement that looks maltreated in an alien language. I use the word "alien", yet English is not really an alien language to us. It is the language of our intellectual make-up − like Sanskrit or Persian was before − but not of our emotional make-up. We are all instinctively bilingual, many of us writing in our own language and in English. *We cannot write like the English. We should not.* We cannot write only as Indians. We have grown to look at the large world as part of us. *Our method of expression therefore has to be a dialect which will some day prove to be as distinctive and colourful as the Irish or the American.* Time alone will justify it. [My italics.] (see R. Rao 1938, 1963 ed. p. VII.)'

Referring to the Indian 'style' of English, he continues:

'After language the next problem is that of style. The tempo of Indian life must be infused into our English expression, even as the tempo of American or Irish life has gone into the making of theirs. We, in India, think quickly, we talk quickly, and when we move we move quickly. There must be something in the sun of India that makes us rush and tumble and run on. (Rao 1938, 1963 ed., p. VII).'

The question now is: Why is SAE writing of interest to a linguist? A partial answer has been given in the Introduction (see 1); that is, this body of writing is of stylistic and sociolinguistic interest. This aspect of SAE has not so far attracted the attention which it deserves from linguists or literary critics. The two available analyses are rather fragmentary and concentrate only on a few sociolinguistically significant points (Kachru 1965; 1966 and 1976a).

The linguistic study of the following features of SAE has proved useful not only in understanding the formal features of the texts, but also in relating these to typically Indian contexts:

1. Register variation
2. Style variation
3. Collocational deviation
4. Semantic shifts
5. Lexical range

There is no detailed work on any of these features. I will attempt to elaborate upon what I mean by these terms.

  1. *Register Variation.* The term *register* is used here in the British sense, meaning a restricted language which is contextually delimited on the basis of formal features. Thus in South Asia, non-British or non-American registers of the caste system, newspaper writing, social roles, etc. have developed and deserve to be studied. The notion of register and its interplay in culture is perhaps specially relevant in

understanding creative writing in English. It is said that a register is South Asian in the sense that both contextually and formally it has certain features which are absent in L_1 varieties of English (Kachru 1966:268 ff.). A large number of *register-determined* formal terms can be found in the newspapers published in English in South Asia or in other SAE writing.

2. *Style Variation.* I have used the term *style* broadly in the sense in which it is used now in linguistic literature. It refers to those formal features of a text which enable us to distinguish not only the participants but also the *situationally determined choices* which are made by a writer out of the total closed-system or open-set choices possible in a language.

By *style variation* is meant the variation in formal exponents in SAE writing for the participant relationships in typically South Asian contexts. These contexts may either be nonexisting in the cultures of L_1 speakers of English, or one may have to redefine a context in a South Asian situation. The following examples will illustrate what is meant by these two types of variation:

1. *'Welcome! My eyes have gone blind looking at the way along which you were to come to grace my house.'* (C, 202).
2. ' *"Since you have blessed my hovel with the good dust of your feet, will you not sit down a moment and drink the cold water of a coconut?" Girish hurried to fetch a floor mat.'* (SMH, 55).
3. *'Why did you sit down on my foot step? . . . You have defiled my religion . . . now I will have to sprinkle holy water all over this house.'* (Un).
4. *'He caught the jelebis which the confectioner threw at him like a cricket ball, placed four nickle coins on the shoe-board for the confectioner's assistant who stood ready to splash some water on them.'* (Un).

The above 1 and 2 are *speech functions* used in 'greetings' and are determined by the relationship of the participants; 3 and 4 cannot be appreciated unless the register of the caste system and the *contextual units* (Kachru 1966:259–260; 268 ff.) are first understood in the typically Indian sense. Note that in the register of the caste system certain formal items acquire a distinct meaning in terms of the participants and if this distinct characteristic of the register is ignored the formal deviations are obscured. Thus the intelligibility of such items (for English L_1 speakers) is essentially contextual. Those items which operate in specific contextual units have been termed *contextual items* (cf. Kachru 1965). A contextual item has been defined as an item of any grammatical rank which has normal collocation, but at the contextual level the item needs specific semantic markers. A good example of extremely Indianized use of style variation may be found in Raja Rao's *Kanthapura,* both in the character types and the *style range* which is given to the characters. This work may provide an interesting study for stylistic analysis. Consider, for example, the following nominal groups (modifier + head structure) labeled *identificational* and formally deviant from the L_1 varieties of English: *cardamon-field Ramachandra* (p. 19); *corner-house Moorthy* (p. 5); *four-beamed house Chandrasekharayya* (p. 22); *front-house Akkamma* (p. 4); *gap-tooth Siddayya* (p. 10); *iron-shop Imam Khan* (p. 133); *that-house people* (p. 21).

3. *Collocational Deviation.* The collocational deviations have already been defined in section 3.5.1. On the basis of comparative stylistic analyses at the collocational level one might find that stylistically this is a crucial clue for marking the South Asian features of SAE.

4. *Semantic shifts.* There is no detailed investigation of *semantic shifts* of English lexical items in SAE. The following three types of shifts may be mentioned. First, an item of English may be assigned additional semantic markers in SAE which are not necessarily assigned to it in the L_1 varieties of English. This may also lead to *register shift* (or *extension*) and thus, for an L_1 speaker of English it results in what is termed *register-confusion.* Consider, for example, the use of *flower-bed* (*MM,* 90) in the sense of *nuptial bed* or the term *government* (*TP,* 40) or *master* (*V of G,* 19) as *modes of address.* Second, an item of English may be assigned an extra feature in SAE literature. In English *brother, sister,* or *brother-in-law* all belong to the lexical set of kinship terms. In SAE (in this case Indian English) extra semantic features are to be assigned and their range of function in other lexical sets widened, e.g.,

[+ affection]
[+ regard]
[+ abuse]
[+ mode of address]

Kindersley (1938:30) also mentions the item *co-son-in-law* used for wife's sister's husband (cf. Tamil *cagalam*). A list of other items with such semantic shifts in Indian English is given by Kindersley.[48] Note, among others, the following: *bawl, beat, charm, respectable, senseless, thrice,* etc.

The result of these shifts is that ambiguities are caused which can be resolved only when the texts are understood in terms of South Asian semantic features. Thus these lexical items are to be *redefined* in terms of South Asian contextual units.

5. *Lexical Range.* The question of lexical range (or lexical 'openness') of SAE has been discussed in section 3.5. This aspect becomes very obvious not only in SAE creative writing but also in SAE journalism. A large-scale borrowing from a large number of SAL's is thus responsible for widening the distance between SAE and other varieties of English. Lexical borrowing manifests itself in two ways. First, it is a simple transfer of lexical items and second, it results in hybridized formations (see section 3.5.2.; also see Kachru 1975a and 1975c).

Table IV. *South Asian Languages in Hybridization*

Language		Percentage
Bengali		3.8
Dravidian	(Other than Tamil)	4.1
Gujarati		0.4
Hindustani		38.6
(High) Hindi		38.6
Marathi		0.8
Punjabi		0.8
Tamil		2.0
(High) Urdu		8.9
Doubtful Language-source		2.0

Note that in Table IV the distinction between Hindi, Hindustani, and Urdu is not very clear. By doubtful items I mean the lexical items such as *tiffin-carrier.*

5. SOCIOLINGUISTICS AND SOUTH ASIAN ENGLISH

In South Asia the fact that the English language has become part of the sociocultural setting has significant formal implications. The interrelation of formal and contextual categories from a sociolinguistic standpoint has not been discussed in any single work in detail. Sociolinguistically relevant questions have, however, been raised in 'Indian English: A Study in Contextualization' (Kachru 1966).

It is argued there that 'The categories have been set within the framework of linguistic science, the aim being 'to make statements of meaning so that we can see how we *use* language to *live*' [my italics]. This approach has contributed towards bringing out the *Indianness* of the Indian idiom of English as opposed to the *Englishness* of British English and the *Americanness* of American English' (Kachru 1966:255; also see Kachru 1976a).

The collocational deviations have been discussed in relation to the contextual units of South Asia. It is suggested that collocational deviations have the possibilities shown in Table V.

Table V.

Item		Collocation of items	Contextualization of items	Deviation
(i)	usual	usual	unusual	contextual
(ii)	usual	unusual	unusual	formal/contextual
(iii)	at least one item unusual	unusual	unusual	formal/contextual

'The contextually deviant formations are those formations which function in IE [Indian English] contextual units, and would perhaps be unintelligible to a native speaker of English only because he is not acquainted with Indian contexts of culture. (Kachru 1966:267).'

Though in this study the illustrative material has been drawn from Indian English, the process is not typically Indian and applies to the whole of South Asia.

It has also been suggested that a sociolinguistically relevant distinction is needed between a *formally determined collocation* and a *contextually determined* (or *culturebound*) *collocation* (Kachru 1965). It is then argued that *America-returned* (*F of F*, 105) is formally deviant, while *bangled-widow* (*Kanth.* 233), *forehead-marking* (*MrS*, 206), and *carfestival* (*OR*, 15.7.59) are contextually deviant.

5.1.

Sociolinguistically significant aspects of SAE are the following:
1. South Asian registers of English.
2. South Asian speech functions.
The term register has already been discussed (see section 4); under it I shall also include *Social Roles*. The social roles are, however, to be separated from what have been termed *Speech Functions*. In demarcating language according to social roles one has first to find the relevant contextual units and then to establish parallel exponents at one or more formal levels (Kachru 1966).

The formal exponents may or may not deviate from the L_1 varieties of English. The dividing points for the contextual units referring to the social roles are arbitrary since the *roles* overlap and clear demarcation lines may not be established.

In order to illustrate this important aspect of SAE I shall consider the registers of *ceremonies, rituals,* and *politics* essentially at the lexical level in Indian English.

Notice the following items which are used in Indian English writing for individual or social ceremonies or rituals:
1. *Individual: hair cutting ceremony (Kanth.* 56); *hair ceremony (Kanth.* 28); *invitation-rice (Kanth.* 173); *naming ceremony (NS.* 160); *rice-eating ceremony (Kanth.* 171); *rice-invitation ceremony (SMH.* 30); *seventh-month ceremony (Kanth.* 37); *turmeric-ceremony (MM.* 70).
2. *Social: aširvad ceremony (MM.* 115); *bath-milk (He Who.* 130); *brother-anointing ceremony (He Who.* 160); *ploughing ceremony (F of F.* 88).

In the South Asian political register the problem is not one of 'redefining' items in this particular register (such as the use of *democracy* or *dictatorship* in the U.S.A. and the U.S.S.R.) but of finding typically South Asian meanings of lexical items. Consider, for example, the lexical items used in the political writing of the Indian subcontinent. (A linguistically interesting study of this register of SAE can be made from the speeches delivered at the Indian National Congress Sessions and the political writings of the Indian leaders.) The three lexical items *ahimsa, satyagraha,* and *khadi* or *khaddar,* used in Gandhian context, illustrate the point. These are now included in most of the lexicons of English. These, then, give us the following *Lexical Sets: ahimsa camp: -leader; -soldier (WM.* 78); *ashram disciple (MM.* 82); *-sweeper (Un.* 218); *khadiboard (SL.*

8.6.59); *-camp* (*WM.* 82); *-competition* (*WM.* 97); *clad* (*SL.* 6.6.59);
-coat (*Kanth.* 148); *-shop* (*Kanth.* 135); *khaddarclad* (*1000 Nights*,
14); *-jibba* (*WM.* 44); *-sari* (*WM.* 48); *satyagraha campaign* (*BJ.*
7.6.59); *field satyagraha* (*Kanth.* 240). Note also *salt-march* (*RH.*
36); *salt-laws* (*H in A.* 55); *salt-making* (*H in A.* 35) which are related
to Gandhi's campaign for removing the salt-tax in India. *Swadeshi-
movement, swadeshi-cloth* are used with Gandhi's campaign for
khaddar.

The above examples illustrate a very restricted aspect of the
political register. An earlier study[49] examines a large number of
lexical items which function in the context of inter-religious conflicts.

5.2.

The acculturation of SAE has crucial linguistic implications; the
more *culture-bound* it becomes the more *distance* is created between
SAE and the L_1 varieties of English. An interesting example of this
has been presented earlier in the extended semantic domain of
kinship terms of English in one variety of SAE (see section 4).

6. THE IMPACT OF ENGLISH ON SOUTH ASIAN LANGUAGES

In previous sections I have reviewed those studies which discuss
essentially the process of transfer from SAL's to SAE. This accounts
for only a part of the linguistic situation and gives one side of the
picture. There is another linguistically and stylistically interesting
aspect to it, i.e., the influence of the English language on SAL's. This
influence has been of two types. First, there has been the impact of
English on SAL's at all the formal levels. Second, it has introduced
new literary genres in many SAL's.

The vocabulary of practically all SAL's shows transfer from
English. Rao claims, for example, that spoken Telugu contains 'at
least 3000 English words' (G. S. Rao 1954:2). Mishra has shown how
different literary forms of Hindi have been influenced by English
(1963).

A limited number of studies on this aspect of English in South
Asia are already available. But they include very meagre information
on the formal impact of English on SAL's.

I will refer here only to some of the more important studies. Latif

(1920) has discussed the influence of English on Urdu. Sen (1932), Das Gupta (1935), and Bhattacharyya (1964) have taken three separate aspects of Bengali. Mishra's work mentioned above shows deeper insights than Chandola's (1963) sketchy paper on Hindi. Walatara, discussing the impact of English on Sinhalese, writes:

'In Ceylon the contact with English has revitalized Sinhalese literature. New genres have appeared in Sinhalese — the novel and the short story . . . not only have Sinhalese writers imitated these foreign models, but they have even absorbed their influence and produced something on their own . . . Sinhalese drama has thriven on English and Western models. (1960).'

And Gokak observes, 'It is no exaggeration to say that it was in the English classroom that the Indian literary renaissance was born.' (Gokak 1964:3). I will discuss some aspects of the formal transfer from English into Hindi to illustrate the influence of English on SAL's.[50] The process has been roughly identical in other SAL's though the extent of influence and its manifestation in each language varies.

Bhatia (1967) and Dhar (1963) have shown the scope of lexical borrowing of English into Hindi and have also shown how the borrowed items have been assimilated into the phonological system of the language. It should be noted that in all the languages the borrowing has been *register-determined*. Mishra (1963:163) has given short lexical lists showing the 'translation equivalence' of English and Hindi lexical items in a large variety of registers. In addition to lexical borrowing, there has also been borrowing of *idioms* and *sayings*. A large number of adverbial phrases have been transferred into Hindi. Note, for example, *after sometime* — 'kālāntar'; *according (to orders)* — 'ājñā anukūl'; *according to rule* — 'niyamānusār'; *on the other hand* — 'dūsrī or'.

It is claimed that the grammatical influence of English on SAL's has been of two types. First, the categories of grammatical description were directly borrowed from the grammatical theories of English, which were based on Latin and Greek. Second, some syntactic features of English have been transferred to SAL's (Mishra 1963:177).

In support of the first assumption some evidence is available, but in support of the second we have only superficial fragmentary analyses. Consider, for example, the following features which Mishra

presents as evidence of the influence of English syntax on Hindi
(Mishra 1963:171 ff.).

1. *Change in word order.* Hindi sentences have subject, object,
verb construction and in certain texts this order is changed. Instead
we find object, subject, verb or subject, verb, object construction.

2. *Use of parenthetical clause.* Kamta Prasad Guru claims that this
structure was not found in Hindi before the influence of English. It
was first found in Lalluji Lal (1763–1835).

3. *Use of amorphous sentences.*[51] This evidently is a very superficial analysis, and ignores the fact that the above syntactic deviations may have been used as stylistic a device and such permutation does not always need a foreign influence. In fact there are
scholars who doubt that the parenthetical clause is owing to the
influence of English. It is claimed that this stylistic device was used
in early Brajbhāshā prose also.

The other syntactic feature of Hindi that shows English influence
is the impersonal construction (e.g., *kahā jātā hai, dekhā gayā hai,
sunā gayā hai*) which may be traced back to English structures such
as *it is said, it has been seen, it has been learnt.* In Hindi the active
forms (e.g., *kahte hai, dekhte hai, sunte hai*) would normally be used.
This feature is essentially lexical. It has been termed by Chandola
Anglicized Hindi (Chandola 1963:12–13). This, however, applies to
other SAL's too (e.g., Punjabi, Kashmiri). (For further discussion see
Kachru, 1975c and 1976c).

7. THE PLACE OF ENGLISH IN CURRENT LANGUAGE PLANNING IN
   SOUTH ASIA

In recent publications on language problems and *language planning* in
South Asia, the reaction toward English shows five distinct attitudes
of five groups. The motivations for these attitudes — or the change of
attitudes — is not always determined by educational or administrative factors. Instead the sociopolitical pressure groups play a very
distinct role. Thus the present attitudes toward English are determined on the one hand by *language loyalty* and on the other hand by
pragmatic consideration. These two considerations are not always in
conflict.

In language planning the South Asian countries face two types of
questions. First, what should be the place of English *vis-à-vis* the
regional languages of the area? Second, which is linguistically more

pertinent, what L_1 variety of English should be accepted as the 'model' for the teaching of English in South Asia?[52] Or should 'educated' SAE be treated as the model? The first question has been debated in recent literature and official reports. The second question, though crucial, has not been discussed in any serious sense.

A brief discussion of publications showing the attitudes of the following groups toward English may not be out of place here. The groups are: (1) South Asian governments, (2) South Asian English writers, (3) South Asian anti-English groups, (4) South Asian pro-English groups.

Perhaps a fifth, the non-South Asian group, should be included here, i.e., those scholars who belong to that part of the English-speaking world which uses English as L_1. Their attitude towards SAE has shown marked changes.

The attitude of this group may be marked in two ways: first, how they react to SAE creative writing[53] and second, what future they visualize for SAE. This group, however, does not directly affect the language planning in the area, although by many indirect means it has been in a position to influence the decisions of educators or politicians in South Asia.

7.1.

The current trend of attitudes of South Asian government toward English has had three phases: the first before independence; the second, immediately after independence; and the third, after the period of reassurance which resulted once the post-independence nationalistic upsurge had subsided. In a way in the three main South Asian countries (i.e., Ceylon, India, and Pakistan) the process has been identical, though the magnitude of language problems and reactions toward English have been varied. It is difficult to sum up the current policy of the South Asian governments towards English.[54] On the whole English continues as an important *link* language for national and international purposes. And one or more of the regional languages is given the status of a national language. In Ceylon, Sinhalese and Tamil have that status. The Constitution of India (Articles 343—351) says that 'Hindi in Devanagari script' is the 'official language of the Union'. In addition to Hindi the Indian Constitution also recognizes sixteen other languages including English and Sanskrit. In Pakistan, Bengali and Urdu have been recognized as national languages.

In language planning, there are religious and political considerations which determine policies.[55] Consider, for example, the following statement of Hamid Ahmad Khan, Vice Chancellor, University of Punjab:

'It is difficult to express yourself in a language in which you do not think, and it is therefore desirable to develop Urdu so that it becomes rooted in West Pakistan. *Urdu, like Bengali, is an India-based language. Ultimately, we do not want in this country to have India-based languages.* [My italics] (Khan 1964:279).'

The new role assigned to the SAL's has created new problems in *language planning*. Peitrzyk (1964; see also Kachru 1971) has discussed these problems in relation to Hindi in India. In South Asia the new role of English is to be viewed essentially as a *link* or *complementary* language.[56] The recent position is presented in Kachru (1971 and 1976b).

The *three language formula* has been proposed by the present central government. It involves learning three languages, namely the regional language, Hindi, and English. The so-called Hindi-speaking area, according to this formula, is expected to encourage the study of a Dravidian language from the south of the country. This formula has not been accepted by all the states of India. In the same paper Kachru sums up the present position of English in India as follows:

'In India English is the widely taught second language at practically all levels of education. All the Indian universities, graduate colleges, and junior colleges have separate departments for the teaching of English. But unfortunately in these departments a majority of students get no serious exposure to English as a living language. Their appreciation of the classics of English — often taught to a dazed class — is very superficial. The teachers are not trained at all in the basic methodology of teaching languages or in teaching the structure of English. This has created a serious pedagogical and educational problem.
The English departments and professors of English continue to believe that teaching literature is "prestigious". The result is that there is a large number of teachers of literature with no enthusiasm for language teaching. The textbooks and teaching techniques are outdated and often not relevant to the Indian context or appropriate to the future needs of a student.

A small group of scholars and educationists has realized the problem. After serious deliberation a Central Institute of English was set up in Hyderabad in 1958 (see Kachru 1975b). The announcement of the Institute reads as follows:

"Whereas, considering the falling standards of English in India, especially at the secondary stage of education, it is deemed necessary to take steps to improve the teaching of English, both through organization of research in the teaching of this subject and the training of teachers in the most suitable techniques . . ."

Some of the education ministries of different States of India have also started regional institutes of English which function in close cooperation with the Central Institute of English.

The approach to the teaching of English is becoming increasingly more realistic and the professors of English and academic administrators are slowly realizing that there is a pressing need: (1) to develop "register-oriented" teaching materials in English suitable to the Indian educational system; (2) to train teachers of English at all levels in contemporary methods of language teaching and in the different branches of the linguistic sciences; (3) to reorganize graduate and undergraduate programs in English both in literature and language (it is often claimed − and not wrongly − that for the Indian departments of English literature, English literature ends with the 19th century!); (4) to reduce the dichotomy between literature-oriented and language-oriented faculties; (5) to develop a realistic attitude toward teaching English "literature" in India; and above all, (6) to initiate debate and cooperation among literary scholars and language specialists in Indian universities so the Indian scholars themselves can give some theoretical foundations to the teaching of English and also make it goal-oriented and significant to Indian linguistic, cultural, and educational settings.

The new Indian approach to the teaching of English has to be relevant to the needs of the students at different levels in the Indian educational system (see Mohan, mimeographed).

It is also being realized that the training centers for the teaching of English as a foreign (or second) language in the English-speaking countries (America or Britain) are unable and ill-equipped to understand the problems of the non-English speaking areas of Asia. Their current programs, therefore, have no serious relevance to these countries. There is also cynicism about the academic content and theoretical foundations of such western programs.' (Kachru 1971:5−6)

7.2.

The term *South Asian English writers* does not include only creative writers but also SAE journalists. The importance of the SAE press can be seen from the part English newspapers play in the over-all daily papers in South Asia (see Tables VI—VII).

Table VI. *Number of Newspapers and Periodicals Published in India According to Language and Periodicity*

Language					Dailies	Weeklies	Others	Total
English	..	..	..	..	82	2,75	1,890	2,247
Hindi	..	..	..	..	2,13	1,168	1,313	2,694
Assamese	..	..	..	..	3	10	25	38
Bengali	..	..	..	..	17	1,62	5,28	7,07
Gujarati	..	..	..	..	50	1,33	3,94	5,77
Kannada	..	..	..	..	38	76	1,33	2,47
Malayalam	..	..	..	..	53	72	3,07	4,32
Marathi	..	..	..	..	73	2,48	3,59	6,80
Oriya	..	..	..	..	5	20	78	1,03
Punjabi	..	..	..	..	14	98	1,24	2,36
Sanskrit	..	..	..	..	1	2	24	27
Sindhi	..	..	..	..	4	31	37	72
Tamil	..	..	..	..	47	78	3,96	5,21
Telugu	..	..	..	..	15	1,00	2,46	3,61
Urdu	..	..	..	..	1,00	3,99	3,99	8,98
Bilingual	..	..	..	..	26	2,25	6,12	8,63
Multilingual	..	..	..	..	2	43	1,54	1,99
Others	..	..	..	..	12	22	1,00	1,34
Total					755	3,162	7,119	11,036

Table VII. *Daily Newspapers in Different Languages in Ceylon, Nepal and Pakistan*

	Bengali	English	Gujarati	Nepali	Newari	Sindhi	Sinhalese	Tamil	Urdu	Bilingual	Total
Ceylon		4					3	2			9
Nepal		4		4	1						9
Pakistan	6	13	3			5			50	7	84

The statistics for book production in South Asia demonstrate that the role of English in the bilingual linguistic situation is impressive. Consider, for example, the following figures for Ceylon and India. (See *Unesco Statistical Yearbook*, Belgium, 1972, pp. 700–701.)

Table VIII. *Book Production in Ceylon, 1970*

Total books published: 1566

Language	Number of books published	% of Total (Approx.)
English	360	23%
Sinhala	744	47.3%
Tamil	264	17%
Other Languages	6	.4%
Books in two or more languages	192	12.3%

Table IX. *Book Production in India, 1970*

Language	Number of books published	% of Total (approx.)
English	4,666	33
Hindi	2,641	18.6
Marathi	1,134	8.1
Bengali	1,048	7.4
Tamil	953	6.7
Gujarati	740	5.2
Telugu	739	5.2
Kannada	554	4.0
Malayalam	515	3.7
Punjabi	419	2.9
Urdu	260	1.8
Oriya	205	1.5
Assamese	192	1.4
Sanskrit	60	.4
Other Languages	19	.1

The figures in Table X demonstrate the high percentage of English publications in the Indian publishing industry for 1957 and 1964 (see Ray 1969:121).

Table X. *Relative Shares of Books Published in 1957 and 1964.*

Year	English	Hindi	Marathi	Gujarati	Tamil	Bengali	Total
1957	40.8	17.5	5.4	4.9	6.7	7.2	100
1964	51.2	12.8	8.6	5.6	3.3	5.8	100
Increase in percent of relative shares:							
	+25	−37	+59	+14	−51	−26	

The story of the SAE creative writer is different. At home he is still
suspect and, on the whole, in the wider international context he does
not, even now, feel very secure. He is suspect in the sense that the
writers of regional languages suspect his loyalties and motivations as
a writer.[57] He is insecure because he really does not know what his
position is in the vast world of the English-using creative writers. He
looks at English as the medium which raises his creative capabilities
before the international reading public. This is both an advantage and
a challenge. Iyengar has discussed the creative writer's problem in
detail (1962:17). Gokak sums up the attitude of SAE writers as
follows:

'The English language has linked India with the world. It has conducted sparks of inspiration from the world outside to India and
from India to the world. We are blessed with the two-way traffic that
English has afforded us. We have paid a heavy price in the past for
this privilege. But in our indignation over the price that has been
paid, let us not throw away the privilege that is already ours. We may
then have to condemn ourselves like Othello:
   "Of one whose hand,
   Like the base Indian, threw a pearl away,
   Richer than all his tribe."
English is certainly not richer than our tribe. But it is a pearl all the
same, and it would be foolish to throw it away. (Gokak 1964:178−
179).'

In this section I have very briefly shown the conflicting attitudes in
South Asia toward English and the influence of these attitudes on
language planning. The situation is not finally settled. In the present
context, it is difficult to visualize what the role of the English
language will be in South Asia after two decades.[58] The following

remarks written by J. R. Firth in 1930 are very meaningful: they were meant for India (then undivided) but they apply to the whole of South Asia.

'Of all the civilized peoples of the world, the Indians are faced with the most difficult cultural and linguistic problems. It is becoming increasingly clear that the "higher" but psittacistic, alien culture will have to be sacrificed to popular enlightenment in the popular languages. And the great chemists and physicists of India will soon be able to do their work in Urdu or Bengali or Tamil quite as well as in English. The superficiality characteristic of Indian education is an inheritance from the superficial Lord Macaulay. And so long as the English language is the instrument of power in the land, it will be difficult to get fathers ambitious for their sons to take their own languages seriously. But if India is to take any sort of equal place in our Commonwealth they will have to be taken seriously, and the sooner the better. It has often been said that Indian education was organized to turn out clerks. But by far the greater number of Indians "literate" in English are not even good clerks. The few brilliant men succeed in spite of the system. The increasing Indianization of the Services will make the abandonment of English as the official language of the more or less autonomous provinces easier of accomplishment. The few Englishmen who go to provincial services can do their work in the official language of the province. English will still be necessary at Imperial Headquarters and perhaps in the central Assemblies for many years, though the mutually intelligible Hindi-Urdu-Hindustani might eventually be more satisfactory, as they are spoken by over ninety million people. That English, even in an Indian form, can ever be more than a second language to the future educated classes of India, it is quite impossible to believe. (1930:210–211).'

In 1930 it took a Firth to say this. To a large extent these words of Firth's have been prophetic and are still true.

8. SUMMARY AND CONCLUSION

In this review SAE has been seen in a wider context by including the process of bilingualism in English in this region, and also by including attitudes toward English. The discussion on the spread of bilingualism was considered essential in order to put the development of SAE in the right perspective. I have throughout emphasized the formal aspects of the South Asian variety of English, but, at the same time, the formal and non-formal aspects have been viewed in the whole linguistic and cultural setting of South Asia. One might say with justification that a South Asian variety of 'educated' English has developed, both in the spoken and written modes. The large body of South Asian writing in English (e.g., fiction, poetry, prose) has by now established itself as an important part of the Commonwealth literatures in English.

It has also been argued that the English language has not only been *South Asianized* by the South Asian linguistic and sociological complexes, but, what is more important, on its part the English language has left a definite mark on the major SAL's and literatures. Thus the process of influence has been two-way.

It is difficult to assess the future of the English language in South Asia. One can, however, definitely say that both from linguistic and literary points of view, the English language has contributed substantially to the languages of the area and has also been influenced by the sociolinguistic setting of the area. This impact has added a new dimension to both the English language and literature and the languages and literatures of South Asia. In many respects this is a unique example of the growth of an international language with different varieties (and sub-varieties) on different continents.

List of abbreviations used for South Asian English sources

The abbreviated forms used for the SAE (South Asian English) texts are given in parentheses. The place of publication is London unless otherwise indicated.

1. BOOKS
   Abbas, K. A., *One Thousand Nights on a Bed of Stone* (*1000 Nights*); Anand, M. R., *Untouchable*, 1935 (*Un*); *Coolie*, 1936 (*C*); Bhattacharya, B., *So Many Hungers*, 1959 (*SMH*); *Music for Mohini*, 1959 (*MM*); *He Who Rides a Tiger*, 1960 (*He Who*); Ghosh, S. N., *The Flame of the Forest*, 1955 (*F of F*); Lall, A., *The House in Adampur: A Study of Modern India*, 1959 (*H in A*); Markandaya, K., *Nectar in a Sieve* 1954 (*NS*); Narayan, R. K., *The Astrologer's Day, and Other Stories*, 1947 (*AD*); *Mr. Sampath*, 1952 (*MrS*); *Waiting for the Mahatma*, 1955 (*WM*); Rajan, B., *The Dark Dancer*, 1958 (*DD*); Rao, Raja, *Kanthapura*, 1938 (*Kanth*); Singh, K., *Train to Pakistan*, 1956 (*TP*); *The Voice of God*, Bombay, n.d. (*V of G*); Rau, S. R., *Remember the House*, 1956 (*RH*).

2. NEWSPAPERS
Bharat Jyoti (BJ), Bombay; *The Hindustan Standard (HS)*, Calcutta; *Indian Express (IE)*, Delhi; *Leader (L)*, Allahabad; *The Search Light (SL)*, Patna.

3. PERIODICALS
Orissa Review (OR), Bhubaneshwar.

SELECTED BIBLIOGRAPHY ON SOUTH ASIAN ENGLISH

Ahmad, M.
1963- 'A Contrastive Phonological Study of English and Urdu with Special
1964   Reference to Some Major Problems of Pronunciation', unpublished
        study (Bangor, Department of Linguistics, University of North Wales).
Anand, M. R.
1948   *The King Emperor's English: or the Role of the English Language in
        Free India* (Bombay, Hind Kitabs).
1968   'A Plea for English for Higher Education (An Open Letter to the Union
        Minister for Education)', *Quest* 30—39 (April).
Ashraf, S. A.
1964   'The Study of English Literature in Pakistan', in J. Press, ed., *Common-
        wealth Literature: Unity and Diversity in a Common Culture* (London,
        Heinemann Educational Books Ltd.).
Asrani, U. A.
1964   *What Shall We Do About English?* (Ahmedabad, Navajivan Publishing
        House).
Bandaranaike, Yasmine Dias
1961   *'The Literature of Ceylon'*, in A. L. McLeod, ed., *The Commonwealth
        Pen: An Introduction to the Literature of the British Commonwealth*
        (New York, Cornell University Press).
Bansal, R. K.
1962   'A Study of the Vowel System of Indian English as Spoken by Edu-
        cated Hindi Speakers of Delhi, East Punjab, and U.P.', *Bulletin of the
        Central Institute of English* 2:27—32 (Hyderabad).
1966   'The Intelligibility of Indian English: Measurements of the Intelligibility
        of Connected Speech and Sentence and Word Material Presented to
        Listeners of Different Nationalities', Ph. D. thesis (University of Lon-
        don).
1969   *The Intelligibility of Indian English (Monograph 4, Central Institute of
        English)* (Hyderabad).
Barron, A. W. J.
1961a   'The English Dental Fricatives in India', *Bulletin of the Central Institute
        of English* 1:84—86 (Hyderabad).
1961b   'English Vowels for Indian Learners', *Bulletin of the Central Institute
        of English* 1:77—83 (Hyderabad).
Belliappa, N. Meena
1967   'East-West Encounter: Indian Women Writers of Fiction in English', in
        C. D. Narasimhaiah, ed., *Fiction and the Reading Public in India*
        (Mysore, University of Mysore), pp. 18—27.

Bhattácharyya, D. C.
1964 'The Impact of English Borrowings on the Bengali Language', *Calcutta Review* 172:49—56 (July).

Bhargava, P. S.
1968 'Linguistic Interference from Hindi, Urdu and Punjabi and Internal Analogy in the Grammar of Indian English'. Unpublished Ph.D. dissertation (Cornell University).

Bhatia, K. C.
1967 *Hindī mẽ angrezī ke āgat śabdõ ka bhāsha tātvik adhyayan,* (Allahabad, Hindustani Academy).

Bhushan, V. N., ed.
1945a *The Moving Finger* (Bombay).
1945b *The Peacock Lute* (Bombay).

Bibliography of Indian English, (Hyderabad, Central Institute of English and Foreign Languages, 1972).

Brosnahan, L. F.
1963 *The English Language in the World* (Wellington, New Zealand).

Brown, C. P.
1852 *The 'Zillah' Dictionary in the Roman Character, Explaining the Various Words Used in Business in India* (Madras).

Burton, J. G.
1957 'The Teaching of English as a Foreign Language', *Shiksha: The Journal of the Education Department, U.P.* (April) 56—60.
1961a 'English with a Purpose', *English Language Teaching* 15:2. 56—63 (Oxford University Press).
1961b 'Report of the Central Institute of English PUC Materials and the Experimental Course', *Bulletin of the Central Institute of English* 1:60—76 (Hyderabad).
1961c 'Some Modern Misconceptions about the English Language and about Language Teaching Current in India', *Bulletin of the Central Institute of English.* 1:16—20 (Hyderabad).

Butter, P.
1960 *English in India* (The Queen's University of Belfast).
1963 'Some Indian Periodicals', *A Review of English Literature* 4:2.35—44 (April).

Captain, R. M.
1949 'The Place and Teaching of the English Language and English Literature in University Education in India', unpublished report for Associateship (Institute of Education, University of London).

Carnegy, Patrick
1877 *Kachahri Technicalities. A Glossary of Terms, Rural, Official and General in Daily Use in the Courts of Law and in Illustration of the Tenures, Customs, Arts and Manufactures of Hindustan* (Allahabad).

Ceylonese Vocabulary. List of Native Words Commonly Occurring in Official Correspondence and Other Documents (Colombo, 1869).

Chagla, M. C.
1967 *On Language and Unity* (Bombay, Popular Prakashan).

Chatterjee, B.
1965 'The Teaching of English in India with Special Reference to the Needs of University Students of Science and Technology', unpublished dissertation (Institute of Education, University of London).
Chavarria-Aguilar, O. L.
1966 'English and Hindi in India', paper presented at a Conference on Language Problems of the Developing Nations, at Airlie House, Warrenton, Virginia, November 1—3.
Chenchiah, P.
1954 *Problems of Linguistic States in India* (Calcutta, YMCA Publishing House).
'Conference on University Training and Research, Held in London, 1960', in *English Teaching Abroad and the British Universities* (London).
Das Gupta, H. M.
1935 *Studies in Western Influence on Nineteenth Century Bengali Poetry* (Calcutta, Chukervertty, Chatterji).
Dakin, J.
1963 'A Survey, with Bibliographical Notes, of the Discussion of the Medium of Instruction in India Since 1947', unpublished dissertation (University of Leeds).
Datta, J.
1960 'Indo-English Creative Writers', *Quest* (Winter).
Deb, S. C.
1965 *Presidential Address Delivered to the XVIth Conference of the Indian Association for English Studies* (Allahabad).
De Lanerolle, K.
1961 'The Decline and Fall of English', *Journal of the National Education Society of Ceylon* 10:1.26—33.
1963 'The Intonation of Sinhalese Speech and its Relevance in the Initial Stages of the Teaching of English as a Second Language to Sinhalese Children', unpublished dissertation (Institute of Education, University of London).
DeMules, Donald H.
1962 'Some Thoughts on Method and Content in Teaching English in Pakistan', *The Jamia Educational Quarterly*, 3:3.58—61 (July) (Karachi).
Derrett, M. E.
1966 *The Modern Indian Novel in English: A Comparative Approach* (Editions de l'Institut de Sociologie de l'Université Libre de Bruxelles, Belgique).
Desai, M. P.
1956 *Our Language Problem* (Ahmedabad, Navajivan Publishing House).
1964 *The Problem of English* (Ahmedabad, Navajivan Publishing House).
DeSilva, C. R.
1956 'The Contribution of English to the Development of Law and Politics in Ceylon', *Journal of the National Education Society of Ceylon* 5:4.8—12.
Dhar, K. L.
1963 'English Loanwords in Hindi', unpublished paper (University of Leeds).

1966 'Some Semantic features of English Loan-Words in Hindi', *Teaching English* IX. 1 (April). (Bombay).

Dhall, G. B.
1955 'Observation of Some Common Peculiarities in the English Speech of the People of Orissa', *Indian Linguistics* (*Chatterji Jubilee Volume*) 16:276–282. (Poona).

Dil, A. S.
1966a 'The Position and Teaching of English in Pakistan', in *Shahidullah Presentation Volume* (= *Pakistani Linguistics* special issue) pp. 185– 242.
1966b 'The Teaching of English in Pakistan: A Study of Some Problems', paper presented at the Third Annual Conference on Teaching English to Speakers of Other Languages, New York (March).

Dupree, L.
1965 'A Pakistani Novel', *American Universities Field Staff Reports. South Asian Series* 10:6 (Pakistan).

Dustoor, P. E.
1946 'An Introduction to the Study of English Usage in India', *Longman's Miscellany* 4 (Calcutta).
1950 *The English Language in India Today* (= *Agra University Extension Lectures 1–11*) (Agra University).
1954 'Missing and Intrusive Articles in Indian English', *Allahabad University Studies* 31:1–70.
1955a *The Problem of Pronunciation* (= *Agra University Extension Lectures 16–27*) (Agra University).
1955b 'Wrong, Usurping and Dispossessed Articles in Indian English', *Allahabad University Studies* 32:1–17.
1957 'Presidential Address Delivered at the Seventh Session of the All India Teachers' Conference, Dharwar (December, 1956)', *Shiksha: The Journal of the Education Department, U.P.* (April) 61–71.
1968 *The World of Words* (Bombay). (Chapters on 'Indian English', 'The problem of pronunciation', 'English in Independent India'.) (Bombay, Asia Publishing House).

Ekambaram, E. J.
1967 'Some Aspects of Indian Response to Fiction in English', in C. D. Narasimhaiah, ed., *Fiction and the Reading Public in India*, Vol. 1 (Mysore, University of Mysore) pp. 16–27.

Eliezer, C. J.
1956 'Science and the English Language', *Journal of the National Education Society of Ceylon* 4:4.23–26 (November).

Elliott, H. M.
1945 *Supplement to the Glossary of Indian Terms* (Agra, Bengal Civil Service). (See also Wilson 1855).

Fernando, E. N. M. B.
1958 'An Investigation into the Written English of Ceylonese Candidates for the General Certificate of Education', unpublished M.A. dissertation (Institute of Education, University of London).

Fishman, Joshua A., *et al.*
1968 *Language Problems of Developing Nations* (New York, Wiley).
Fox, Robert P.
1968 'A Transformational Treatment of Indian English Syntax', unpublished Ph.D. thesis (Urbana, Illinois, University of Illinois).
Gaind, D. N., and R. P. Sharma
1963 *Talks to Teachers of English in India* (Agra, Ram Prasad & Sons).
Gandhi, M. K.
1965 *Our Language Problem*, A. T. Hingorani, ed. (Bombay, Bharatiya Vidya Bhavan).
Glossary of Indian Terms Containing Many of the Most Important and Useful Indian Words Designed for the Use of Offices of Revenue and Judicial Practitioners and Students (Madras, 1877).
Goffin, R. C.
1934 'Some Notes on Indian English', *S.P.E. Tract No. 41* (Oxford).
Gokak, V. K.
1961 *English in India (A National Perspective)*, Presidential Address, All India English Teachers' Conference, December 1960 (Hyderabad).
1964 *English in India: Its Present and Future* (Bombay, Asia Publishing House).
Gooneratne, Y.
1968 *English Literature in Ceylon 1850–1878* (Colombo).
Gopal, Ram
1966 *Linguistic Affairs of India* (Bombay, Asia Publishing House).
Gopalkrishnan, G. S.
1960 'Some Observations on the South Indian Pronunciation of English', *Teaching English* 6:2.62–67 (April), (Bombay).
Gowda, A.
1975a 'Mulk Raj Anand', *Literary Half-Yearly* 5.1 (January) (Mysore).
1975b 'R. K. Narayan', *Literary Half-Yearly* 5.1 (January) (Mysore).
Gujarat, Government of, Education Department
1961 *Report of the Committee Appointed by the Government to Re-Examine the Present Syllabus in English for Standards VIII, IX and X* (Ahmedabad).
Gunawardhana, Bandula Sri
1967 *New Aims of Learning English in Independent Ceylon* (Colombo).
Hai, M. A., and W. J. Ball
1961 The Sound Structures of English and Bengali (East Pakistan, University of Dacca).
Hamza, Al.
1960 'English in Pakistan', *The Pakistan Times*, April 19–20 (Lahore).
Haq, S. A.
1959 *The Teaching of English in Pakistan* (Lahore).
Harry, P.
1962 'A Study of Spoken Gujarati in its Relation to the Teaching of English to Gujarati Learners', unpublished paper (School of Applied Linguistics, University of Edinburgh).

528 *Braj B. Kachru*

Hashmi, A.
1963 'A Comparative Study of Some Phonological Features of Urdu and English', unpublished paper (School of Applied Linguistics, University of Edinburgh).
Helversen, J.
1965 'The English short story in Ceylon', *United States Educational Foundation Ceylon Newsletter* (December) (Colombo).
Hill, L. A.
1961 'English in the Commonwealth: 1 — Teaching of English in India', *English Language Teaching* 15:2.49—56 (Oxford University Press).
1959- 'A Comparison Between Initial Clusters in English and Hindi', *Transac-
1960 tions of the Linguistic Circle of Delhi, Dr. Siddheshwar Varma Volume* 37—40.
1966 'The Teaching of English in India', *The Journal of English Language* 2:2.64—68 (August).
Hota, M. M.
1962 'India in English Novels', *Caravan* (June).
Hughes, M. N.
1959 'Some Generalized Comparisons with Textbooks for the Teaching of English as L$_2$ Based on Approved Syllabuses Compiled for Indonesia and East Pakistan, from the Point of View of General Principles, Grading of Materials and Methodology', unpublished paper (School of Applied Linguistics, University of Edinburgh).
Hunt, C.
1931 *Honoured Sir — from Babujee* (London, Allan P.).
1935 *Babujee Writes Home:* being a new ed. of *Honoured Sir* (London, Allan, P.).
Husain, S. Sajjad
1961 'The Literature of Pakistan', in A. L. McLeod, ed., *The Commonwealth Pen: An Introduction to the Literature of the British Commonwealth* New York (Cornell University Press).
Hussain, S. S.
1958 'The position of English in Pakistan', *The Pakistan Review* (July) (Lahore).
India
1957 *Official Language Commission. Report, 1956* (New Delhi).
Indian Vocabulary, to Which is Prefixed the Forms of Impeachment (Stockdale, 1788).
'India's Search for Self-Expression', in *A language in Common*, Part of a special number of the Times Literary Supplement, originally published August 10, 1962 (London).
Iyengar, K. R., Srinivasa
1943 *Indo-Anglian Literature* (Bombay, International Book House).
1945 *The Indian Contribution to English Literature* (Bombay).
1959 'Indian Writing in English', *Contemporary Indian Literature: A Symposium* second edition, revised and enlarged (New Delhi, Sahitya Akademi).
1961 'The Literature of India', in A. L. McLeod ed. *The Commonwealth Pen: An Introduction to the Literature of the British Commonwealth* (New York, Cornell University Press).

1962   *Indian Writing in English* (New York, Asia Publishing House).

Jalil, M. A.

1963   'Major Difficulties Experienced by Bengali Learners of English with Regard to Grammar and Sentence Structure', unpublished paper (University of Leeds).

Jamil, M.

'English in Pakistan', *Pakistan Quarterly* 11:3.38–42 (Karachi).

Jayasekera, U. D.

1956   'A Study of Methods of Reading Instruction in English Schools Together with a View to Their Adaptation to Schools in Ceylon', unpublished paper (Institute of Education, University of London).

Jha, A. N.

1940   *Address at Conference of English Professors, Playwright and Critics* (Lucknow).

John, K. K.

no date *The Only Solution to India's Language Problem* (Madras, K. K. John).

Jyoti, D. D.

1955   'The Study and Teaching of English Language and Literature at the Secondary and University Levels: English as a Mother-Tongue in England, as a Foreign Language in India', unpublished report submitted for Associateship (Institute of Education, University of London).

Kachru, Braj B.

1959   'An Instrumental Phonetic Analysis of Some Prosodic Features of Indian English and Received Pronunciation', unpublished paper (School of Applied Linguistics, University of Edinburgh).

1962   'An Analysis of Some Features of Indian English: A Study in Linguistic Method', unpublished Ph.D. thesis (University of Edinburgh).

1964   'A Note on Indian Writing in English' (Comments), *Harvard Educational Review* (Winter).

1965   'The Indianness in Indian English', *Word* 21.3 (New York).

1966   'Indian English: A Study in Contextualization', *In Memory of J. R. Firth*, C. E. Bazell *et al*, eds. (London, Longmans).

1970   'Some Style Features of South Asian English', *National Identity*, K. Goodwin, ed. (London: Heinemann).

1971   'English in India – a Pan-Indian and International Link', *English Around the World*, May 4.

1973   'Toward a Lexicon of Indian English', *Issues in Linguistics: Papers in Honor of Henry and Renée Kahane*, Braj B. Kachru *et al*, eds. (Urbana, Illinois, University of Illinois Press).

1975a   'Lexical Innovations in South Asian English', *International Journal of the Sociology of Language*, No. 4, January.

1975b   'A retrospective study of the Central Institute of English and Foreign Languages and its relation to Indian Universities', In Melvin Fox ed. *Language and Development: a Retrospective Survey of Ford Foundation Language Projects 1952–1974*. (New York, The Ford Foundation.)

1975c   'Toward structuring the form and function of code-mixing: An Indian perspective', *Studies in the Linguistic Sciences*, Vol. 5, No. 1, Spring.

1976a   'Models of English for the Third World: White Man's Linguistic Burden or Language Pragmatics?' *TESOL Quarterly*, Vol. 10, No. 2.

1976b 'Indian English: a Sociolinguistic Profile of a Transplanted Language', *Studies in Language Learning*, Vol. 1, No. 2, Spring.

do What it Does in the Indian Sociolinguistic Context', paper presented to the IX Annual TESOL Convention, Los Angeles, March 4—9, 1975.

1975c 'The Englishization of Hindi: Notes on Language Rivalry and Language Change', *Linguistic Method: Papers in Honor of Herbert Penzl*, I. Rauch *et al*, eds. (to appear).

Kamath, V. B.

1966 *Linguistic Vivisection of India — Why Not Stop it?*,(Bombay, Bharatiya Vidya Bhavan).

Kanaday, V. R.

1965 'A Comparative Study of English and Marathi Tenses', unpublished paper (University of Manchester).

Karanth, K. S.

1967 'How Deep is Western Influence on Indian Writers of Fiction?' in C. D. Narasimhaiah, ed., *Fiction and the Reading Public in India* (Mysore, University of Mysore). pp. 126—133.

Kelkar, Ashok R.

1957 'Marathi English: A Study in Foreign Accent', *Word* 13:2.266—82 (New York).

Kindersley, A. F.

1938 'Notes on the Indian Idiom of English: Style, Syntax, and Vocabulary', *Transactions of the Philological Society* (1938):25—34 (Oxford).

Khan, Razia

1960 'The Problems of Teaching English Literature in an Eastern Country Such as India', *Teaching English* 6:2.34—43 (April) (Bombay).

Kumaramangalam, S. M.

1965 India's Language Crisis: an Introductory Study (Madras, New Century Book House).

Lahiri, K. C.

1956 'Peculiarities in Spoken English of Indians and the Question of a Standard for Them', *The Research Bulletin (Arts) of the University of the Punjab* 19:3.

Lal, P.

1960 'A Reply to Mr. Datta' (see J. Datta) *Quest* (Winter). 'English and English Writing in India', *Conspectus* 2:2 (New Delhi).

1964 'Indian Writing in English', *Harvard Educational Review* (Spring. 316—319).

Language and Society in India: Transactions of the Indian Institute of Advanced Study, vol. 8 (Simla, Indian Institute of Advanced Study 1969).

Latif, S. A.

1920 'The Influence of English Literature on Urdu Literature', Ph.D. thesis (University of London).

Le Page, R. B.

1964 *The National Language Question: Linguistic Problems of Newly Independent States* (New York, Oxford University Press).

Limaye, Mohan R.
1965 ' "H" for a Marathi speaker of English', *English Language Teaching* 20:1.72—6 (October) (Oxford University Press).
Majumdar, A. K.
1965 *The Problem of Hindi — A Study* (Bombay Bharatiya Vidya Bhawan).
Masica, Colin et al.
1972 *The Sound System of Indian English*, (Hyderabad, Central Institute of English).
Mathai, S.
1951 'The Position of English in India', in E. Partridge and J. W. Clark, eds., *British and American English Since 1900*, 96—101 (New York, Philosophical Library) pp. 96—101.
McCutchion, David
1969 *Indian Writing in English: Critical Essays* (Calcutta, Writers Workshop).
McLeod, A. L. ed.
1961 *The Commonwealth Pen: An Introduction to the Literature of the British Commonwealth* (New York, Cornell University Press).
Menon, T. K. N., and Patel, M. S.
1957 *The Teaching of English as a Foreign Language* (Baroda, Acarya Book Depot).
Mishra, Vishvanath
1963 *Hindī bhāshā aur sāhitya par angrezī prabhāv (1870—1920)* (Dehradun, Sāhitya Sadan).
Mohan, K.
1965 'A Report on Some Problems of Teaching English as a Foreign Language in India at the University Level, and a Few Suggestions for Solving Them', unpublished report submitted for Associateship (Institute of Education, University of London).
1966a 'A Note on "a", "an", "the", and "to" in R.P. and Spoken Indian English', *Teaching English* IX. 1 (April) (Bombay).
1966b 'A Note on "r", "h", "t", and "l" in R.P. and Spoken Indian English', *Teaching English* IX, 2 (April) (Bombay).
Mohan, Ramesh
1969 'The Teaching of English at the University Level in India', mimeographed paper.
Mohiyuddin, M.
1963 'English for East Pakistanis: What Kind?', *The Teachers' World, Journal of the Institute of Education and Research, University of Dacca* 2:2.11—13.
Morgan, D. Y.
1964a 'English Textbooks for Pakistan', in Anwar S. Dil, ed., *Pakistani Linguistics* (1963):97—103 (Lahore).
1964b 'Suggestions for the Improvement of English Teaching in West Pakistan', in Anwar S. Dil and Afia Dil, eds., *New Trends in Education: Miscellany Three* (Lahore) pp. 24—28.
Moss, W. R.
1964 'English in the Commonwealth: 7 — Pakistan', *English Language Teaching* 18:2.63—69 (January) (Oxford University Press).

Mukherjee, Meenakshi
1971   The Twice Born Fiction: Themes and Techniques of the Indian Novel
       in English (New Delhi, Heinemann).
Nadkarni, M. V.
1964   'Teaching Spoken English in Colleges', *Bulletin of the Central Institute
       of English* 4:5.
Nagarajan, K.
1949   'The Development of the Novel in India', *Art and Letters* 23.1.
Nagarajan, S.
1964   'The Study of English Literature in India', in J. Press., ed., *Common-
       wealth Literature: Unity and Diversity in a Common Culture* (London,
       Heinemann Educational Books, Ltd.).
Naik, M. K. et al., eds.
1968   *Critical Essays on Indian Writing in English* (Dharwar, Karnatak Uni-
       versity).
Narasimhaiah, C. D.
1964   'The English Language in India', *Hemisphere* 8:26–30 (April).
Narayan, R. K.
1964   'English in India', in J. Press, ed., *Commonwealth Literature: Unity and
       Diversity in a Common Culture* (London, Heinemann Educational
       Books Ltd.).
Nayaguam, Xavier S. Thani
1956   'Language Rights in Ceylon', *Tamil Culture* 5:3 (July).
Neteland, E., and Lee H. Stoner
1962   'Teacher Education in Pakistan', *Bulletin of the School of Education*
       38:3 (May).
National Council of Educational Research and Training
1963   *Report on the Conference on the Teaching of English in Schools*, Delhi,
       April 15–20.
National Education Commission: Interim Report, 1961, Ceylon, Government
       Publication Bureau, Sessional Paper I (Colombo, 1962).
Oaten, E. F.
1908   *A Sketch of Anglo-Indian Literature* (London, K. Paul, Trench, Trübner
       & Co.). (The Le Bas prize essay for 1907).
1907- 'Anglo-Indian Literature', *The Cambridge History of English Literature*
1927   XIV (Cambridge University Press).
Pande, N. R. W.
1964   'English in India', *Triveni* 33:68–75 (October).
Pandit, P. B.
1964   'Indian Readjustments in the English Consonant System', *Indian Lin-
       guistics* 25:202–205 (Poona).
Passé, H. A.
n.d.   'Education and the English Syllabus for University Entrance and Higher
       School Certificate', *University of Ceylon Review* 5:2.
1943   'The English Language in Ceylon', *University of Ceylon Review* (Novem-
       ber).
1947   'The English Language in Ceylon', unpublished Ph.D. thesis (University
       of London).

1955 *The Use and Abuse of English Common Errors in Ceylon English* (Madras).

1967 'The Problems of English Language Teaching in Ceylon Today', *English For Our Schools* 1:1.1—3 (July).

Patel, M. S.

1962 'The Structural Syllabus at Work in India', *English Language Teaching* 16:3.145—151 (Oxford University Press).

1958 'Teaching English in India', *English Language Teaching* 12:3.79—86 (Oxford University Press).

Position of English Teaching in the States of India, The Directorate of Extension Programmes for Secondary Education (New Delhi, Government of India, Ministry of Education, 1960).

Position and Teaching of English in India. Outline Report, The (Washington D. C., Center for Applied Linguistics, August, 1966).

Prabhakar Babu, B. A.

1970- 'Prosodic Features in Indian English: Stress, Rhythm and Intonation',
1971 *Bulletin of the Central Institute of English* 8:33—39 (Hyderabad).

Pradhan, Yubaraj, S.

1970- 'The Teaching of English as a Foreign Language in Nepal'. Report
1971 submitted for Associateship of the Institute of Education, University of London.

Prakasha, Veda

n.d. *The Future of the Three Language Formula* (New Delhi, Government of India, Ministry of Education).

Press, J. ed.

1963 *Conference on the Teaching of English Literature Overseas 1962 at Cambridge* (London).

Project Report on the Improvement of the Teaching of English at Secondary and Intermediate Levels (Lahore, Government of West Pakistan Education Department, 1962).

Quirk, Randolph

1963 'A Report on English Teaching in India', Mimeographed paper (London, University College).

Rahman, F.

1953 *New Education in the Making in Pakistan: its Ideology and Basic Problems* (London, Cassell).

Rajagopal, M. V.

1967 'The Study of English in India, an Educational Appraisal', *Triveni* 36:3.59—66 (October).

Rajagopalachari(ar), C.

1956 'The Place of English in Indian Education', *Tamil Culture* 5:1 (Jan.).

1962 *The Question of English* (Madras).

Rajan, Balchandra

1963 'Contemporary Indian Writing in English', *The Illustrated Weekly of India* 84:21.44—45 (May 26).

1964 'Identity and Nationality', in J. Press, ed., *Commonwealth Literature: Unity and Diversity in a Common Culture* (London, Heinemann Educational Books Ltd.)

1965 'The Indian Virtue', *The Journal of Commonwealth Literature* 1:79–86 (September).

Rao, Subba
1954 *Indian Words in English: A Study in Indo-British Cultural and Linguistic Relations* (London, Oxford University Press).

Rao, K. S. N.
1961 'A Footnote to the Indian Pronunciation of the Initial /k t p/ and /v/ and /w/ in English', *Indian Linguistics* 22:160 (Poona).

Rau, M. C.
1963 'The Indo-Anglians', *The Illustrated Weekly of India* 84:21.45 (May 26).

Ray, Punya Sloka
1969 'The Economics for and Against English in India', in *Language and Society in India, Transactions of the Indian Institute of Advanced Study*, vol. 8 (Simla, Indian Institute of Advanced Study) pp. 118–121.

Reid, C.
1959 'An Analysis and Comparison of Two Syllabuses Used as a Basis for Textbooks for the Teaching of English in India', unpublished paper (Edinburgh, School of Applied Linguistics, University of Edinburgh).

Reid, John T.
1965 *Indian Influences in American Literature and Thought* (Delhi, Indian Council for Cultural Relations).

Report of the Official Languages Committe, Government of Gujarat (Baroda, 1960).

Report of the Special Committee on Education (Ceylon), *Sessional Papers XXIV* (1943).

Roberts, T. T.
1800 *An Indian Glossary*, consisting of some thousand words and forms commonly used in the East Indies (London, Printed for Murray and Highley, Fleet Street).

Roy, Mira
1969 'Some Problems of English Consonants for Bengali Speakers', *English Language Teaching* 23:3 (Bombay).

Ruberu, Ranjit
1962 *Education in Colonial Ceylon: (Being a Research Study on the History of Education in Ceylon for the Period 1796 to 1834)* (Kandy, Ceylon).

Ryburn, W. M.
1961 *The Teaching of English* (= *Teaching in India Series* II) (London).

Sahaya, S.
1953 'The Methods of Teaching English as a Foreign Language in India', unpublished paper (Dublin, Trinity College, University of Dublin).

Sen, Priyaranjan
1932 *Western Influence in Bengali Literature* (Calcutta, University of Calcutta).

Senthamilan, A.
1955 'The Problem of a "National" or "Official" Language in India', *Tamil Culture* 4:2 (April).

Serjeantson, M. S.
1961 *A History of Foreign Words in English* (New York, Barnes & Noble).

Seshadri, T. K.
1965 *The Language Question (An Historical Analysis)* (Bangalore).
Shah, A. B.
1968 *The Great Debate: Language Controversy and Higher Education* (Bombay, Lalvani Publishers).
Sidhanta, N. K.
1961 'English Studies Today', *Bulletin of the Central Institute of English* 1:3—6 (Hyderabad).
Sinhalese and Tamil as Official Languages. Report of a Select Committee of the State Council, Sessional Paper XXII (1946).
Singh, Bhupal
1934 'A Note on Some Indian Writers of English Fiction', in *A Survey of Anglo-Indian Fiction* (London) pp. 306—310.
Soysa, Jagathadeva
1967 'Sinhala and English — as Complementary Techniques for Promoting Language Discipline', *English for Our Schools* 1:1.18—22 (July).
Speight, E. E.
1934 Indian Masters of English (Longmans, London).
Spencer, D. M.
1960a 'Introductory Essay on Indian Society, Culture and Fiction', in *Indian Fiction in English: An Annotated Bibliography* (Philadelphia, University of Pennsylvania).
1960b *Indian Fiction in English: An Annotated Bibliography* (Philadelphia, University of Pennsylvania).
Spencer, J. W.
1957 'Notes on the Pronunciation Problem', *Shiksha: The Journal of the Education Department, U.P.* (April) 91—97.
Spencer, J.
1966 'The Anglo-Indians and Their Speech: A Socio-Linguistic Essay', *Lingua* 16:57—70 (Amsterdam).
Sreekantaiya, T. N.
1940 'English as the Kannadiga Speaks it', *The Bulletin of Phonetic Studies* 1 (October) (Mysore, The University Phonetic Association).
Subramanian, A.
1966 'Tamilian English: A Phonological Study', M. A. Thesis (Department of Linguistics, Annamalai University).
Subrahmanian, K.
1960 'A Study of the Teaching of English as a Foreign Language and Possible Application to Schools in India', unpublished paper (London, Institute of Education, University of London).
Taylor, S.
forthcoming 'A Preliminary Study of the Stress System in Indian English'.
The teaching of English in India, Report of the Conference on the Teaching of English in Schools, National Council of Educational Research and Teaching, New Delhi, April 15—20, 1963 (New Delhi, 1963).
Theivananthampillai, K.
1970 'A Comparative Study of the English and Tamil Auxiliary Verb Systems and Prediction of Learning Problems for Tamil Students of English',

International Review of Applied Linguistics in Language Teaching
8.1:21–47 (Heidelberg).

Tickoo, M. L.
   1963 'English Pronunciation in India: The Choice of a Model', *Language
         Learning* 13.3:171–175 (Ann Arbor; Michigan).

Tyrner, A. G.
   1966 'Indo-Anglian Literature and the Indian Elite', *The Cornell Journal of
         Social Relations* 1:1.25-32 (Spring).

Ure, J. M.
   1963 'Modern Approaches to English Teaching in India', in *Proceedings of a
         Symposium Held by the Linguistic Circle of Delhi in April, 1963,
         Transactions of the Linguistic Circle of Delhi* (Delhi) pp. 6–12.
   1959- 'The Teaching of English in India', in *Transactions of the Linguistic
   1960 Circle of Delhi, Dr. Siddheshwar Varma Volume* (Delhi) pp. 79–84.

Usmani, Mufti, A. H.
   1965 'A Study of the Teaching of English as a Foreign Language in the
         Secondary Schools of the Peshawar Region, West Pakistan', unpub-
         lished Ph. D. dissertation (Texas Technological College).

Varma, Manindra K.
   1966 'A Synchronic Comparative Study of the Structure of the Noun Phrase
         in English and Hindi', unpublished Ph.D. dissertation (Ann Arbor,
         University of Michigan).

Varma, S.
   1957 'The Pronunciation of English in North-Western India', *Indian Lin-
         guistics, Bagchi Memorial Volume* 18:86–88 (Poona).

Verghese, C. Paul
   1970 'Indian English', *Indian Literature* 13:1. (New Delhi, Sahitya Academy)

Verma, S. K.
   1962 'A Study of Errors in English Made by Hindi-Speaking Students in
         Bihar', unpublished paper (Edinburgh, School of Applied Linguistics,
         University of Edinburgh).
   1964 'A Study in Systemic Description of Hindi Grammar and a Comparison
         of Hindi and English Verbal Group', unpublished Ph.D. thesis (Univer-
         sity of Edinburgh).

Viswanath, L.
   1963- 'Kanadese and English, a Comparison of Their Phonologies', unpub-
   1964 lished paper (Bangor, Department of Linguistics, University College of
         North Wales).

Wadia, A. R.
   1954 *The Future of English in India* (Bombay, Asia Publishing House).

Walatara, D.
   1960 'The Scope and Limitations of Bilingualism with a Second Language
         with Specific Reference to the Case of Ceylon', *Teaching English*
         6:3.3–9 (Bombay).
   1964 *The Teaching of English as a Complementary Language in Ceylon*
         (Colombo, Lake House Investments).

Walsh, W.
   1964 *A Human Idiom* (London, Chatto and Windus).

Wasti, S. M. J.
1962 'The Teaching of English in Higher Classes', *The Jamia Education Quarterly* 3:3.51–57 (July) (Karachi).
Whitworth, G. C.
1885 *An Anglo-Indian Dictionary* (London, Kegan Paul & Co).
1907 *Indian English: An Examination of Errors of Idiom Made by Indians in Writing in English* (Herts, Garden City Press).
Wilson, H. H.
1855 *A Glossary of Judicial and Revenue Terms and of Useful Words Occurring in Official Documents Relating to the Administration of the Government of British India* (London).
1842 'Glossary of Indian Terms' (A preliminary unpublished edition).
Yadav, R. K.
1960 'A Comparative Study of the Language Problem at the University Level in India', unpublished M.S. thesis (Institute of Education, University of London).
1969 *The Indian Language Problem: A Comparative Study* (Delhi, National Publishing House).

REFERENCES

Abercrombie, D.
1964 'A Phonetician's View of Verse Structure', *Linguistics* 6 (June) (The Hague).
Ahmad, M.
1964 'A Contrastive Phonological Study of English and Urdu with Special Reference to Some Major Problems of Pronunciation', unpublished study (Bangor, University of North Wales).
Anand, M. R.
1948 *The King-Emperor's English: Or the Role of the English Language in Free India* (Bombay).
Asrani, V. A.
1964 *What Shall We Do about English?* (Ahmedabad).
Bansal, R. K.
'A Study of the Vowel System of Indian English as Spoken by Educated Hindi Speakers of Delhi, East Punjab and U.P.', *Bulletin of the Central Institute of English* 2:169–165 (Hyderabad).
Barnes, Sir Edward
1932 *The History of Royal College* (Colombo). [It was earlier called Colombo Academy].
Barron, A. W. J.
1961 'The English Dental Fricatives in India', *Bulletin of the Central Institute of English* 1:84–86 (Hyderabad).
Basu, A. N., ed.
1941 *Adam Reports (1835–38)* (Calcutta).

Bhatia, K. C.
1967 *'Hindi mẽ angrezi ke āgat śabdõ kā bhaśa tātvik adhyayan,* (Allahabad, Hindustani Academy).
Bhattacharyya, D. C.
1964 'The Impact of English Borrowings on the Bengali Language', *Calcutta Review* 172:49—56 (July).
Bhushan, V. N.
1945a *The Moving Finger.* (Bombay, Padma Publications).
1945b *The Peacock Lute.* (Bombay, Padma Publications).
Bright, William,
1960 'A Study of Caste and Dialect in Mysore', *Indian Linguistics* 21 (Poona).
1961 'Linguistic Changes in Some Indian Caste Dialects', in *Linguistic Diversity in South Asia,* C. A. Ferguson et al, ed. (= *International Journal of American Linguistics Supplement* (July) (Bloomington, Indiana).
Brown, W. N., ed.
1960 *India, Pakistan, Ceylon* (Philadelphia).
Catford, J. C.
1959 'The Teaching of English as a Foreign Language', *Studies in Communication* 3:137—138 (London).
Chandola, A. C.
1963 'Some Linguistic Influences of English on Hindi', *Anthropological Linguistics* 5:2.9—13 (Bloomington, Indiana).
Census of India, 1961 (Delhi, 1964).
Ceylonese Vocabulary: List of Native Words Commonly Occurring in Official Correspondence and Other Documents (Colombo, 1869).
Craigie, W. A.
1954 'Introductory Note', in G. S. Rao 1954.
Das Gupta, H. M.
1935 *Studies on Western Influence on Nineteenth Century Bengali Poetry* (Calcutta).
Deb, S. C.
1965 *Presidential Address Delivered at the XVIth Conference of the Indian Association for English Studies, Jadavpur* (Allahabad).
DeLanerolle, K.
1953 'The Intonation of Sinhalese and its Relevance in the Initial Stages of the Teaching of English as a Second Language to Sinhalese Children', unpublished paper (London, Institute of Education).
Dhall, G. B.
1965 'Observations on Some Common Peculiarities in the English Speech of the People of Orissa', *Indian Linguistics* 16:276—282 (Poona).
Dhar, K. L.
1963 'English Loanwords in Hindi', unpublished study (University of Leeds).
Dil, A. S.
1966 'The Position of English in Pakistan', in *Shahidullah Presentation Volume* (= *Pakistani Linguistics* special issue) pp. 185—242.
Duff, Alexander
1837 *New Era of the English Language and English Literature in India* (Edinburgh).

Dustoor, P. E.
1954 'Missing and Intrusive Articles in Indian English', *Allahabad University Studies* 31:1—70.
1955 'Wrong, Usurping, and Dispossessed Articles in Indian English', *Allahabad University Studies* 32:1—17.
Edwards, Sir Parker
n.d. *Statement Showing the Statistics of the Publications for the Year 1928* (Bombay).
Fennell, C. A. M.
1892 'Preface', *The Stanford Dictionary of Anglicised Words and Phrases* (Cambridge, England).
Firth, J. R.
1930 *Speech* (London). (Reprinted, Oxford University Press, London, 1964).
Fox, Robert P.
1968 'A Transformational Treatment of Indian English Syntax', unpublished Ph. D. thesis (University of Illinois).
French, F. Q.
1949 *Common Errors in English* (London).
Gleason, H. A., jr.
1961 *An Introduction to Descriptive Linguistics* (New York, Holt Rinehart & Winston).
Goffin, R. C.
1934 'Some Notes on Indian English', *S.P.E. Tract No. 41* (Oxford).
Gokak, V. K.
1964a *English in India: Its Present and Future* (Bombay, Asia Publishing House).
1964b 'English and the Indian Renaissance', in *English in India: Its Present and Future* (Bombay).
Gopalkrishnan, G. S.
1960 'Some Observations on the South Indian Pronunciation of English', *Teaching English* 6:2.62—67 (April) (Bombay).
Grant, Charles
1831- 'Observations on the State of Society among the Asiatic Subjects of
1832 Great Britain, Particularly with Respect to Morals, and the Means of Improving It', in *General Appendix to Parliamentary Papers* 1831—32 (London).
Hai, M. A., and W. J. Ball
1961 *The Sound Structures of English and Bengali* (University of Dacca).
Hall, Robert, A.
1955 *Hands Off Pidgin English!* (Sydney, N.S.W.).
Halliday, M. A.K.
1961 'Categories of the Theory of Grammar', *Word* 17 (New York).
Halliday, M. A. K., *et al.*
1964 *The Linguistic Sciences and Language Teaching* (London, Longmans).
Harry, P.
1962 'A Study of Spoken Gujarati in its Relation to the Teaching of English to Gujarati Learners', unpublished paper (Edinburgh, School of Applied Linguistics).

Hill, L. A.
1959 'The Pronunciation Difficulties of Hindi Speakers Learning English', *Teaching English* 6:1 (August) (Bombay).
Hockett, C. F.
1958 *A Course in Modern Linguistics* (New York, Macmillan).
Hunt, Cecil
1931 *Honoured Sir from Babujee* (London).
1935 *Babujee Writes Home* (London).
Iyengar, K. R. S.
1945 *The Indian Contribution. to English Literature* (Dharwar, Karnatak University).
1962 *Indian Writing in English* (Bombay).
Jespersen, O.
1964 *Essentials of English Grammar* (Alabama, University of Alabama Press, reprint of 1933 edition).
Jha, A. N.
1940 *Address at Conference of English Professors, Playwrights and Critics* (Lucknow).
Kachru, Braj B.
1959 'An Instrumental Phonetic Analysis of Some Prosodic Features of Indian English and Received Pronunciation', unpublished paper (Edinburgh, School of Applied Linguistics).
1962 'An Analysis of Some Features of Indian English: A Study in Linguistic Method', Ph.D. thesis (Edinburgh).
1965 'The Indianness of Indian English', *Word* 21.3 (New York).
1966 'Indian English: A Study in Contextualization', in *In Memory of J. R. Firth* (London).
1969 *A Reference Grammar of Kashmiri* (University of Illinois, Department of Linguistics).
1971 'English in India: A Pan-Indian and International Link', *English Around the World* (May):1–7.
1973 *Introduction to Spoken Kashmiri* (Urbana, Illinois).
1975a 'Lexical Innovations in South Asian English', *International Journal of the Sociology of Language* no. 4, 55–74.
1975b 'A retrospective study of the Central Institute of English and Foreign Languages and its relation to Indian Universities', In Melvin Fox ed. *Language and Development: a Retrospective Survey of Ford Foundation Language Projects 1952–1974.* (New York, The Ford Foundation.)
1975c 'Toward structuring the form and function of code-mixing: An Indian perspective', *Studies in the Linguistic Sciences*, Vol. 5, No. 1, Spring.
1976a 'Models of English for the Third World: White Man's Linguistic Burden or Language Pragmatics?' *TESOL Quarterly*, Vol. 10, No. 2.
1976b 'Indian English: a Sociolinguistic Profile of a Transplanted Language', *Studies in Language Learning*, Vol. 1, No. 2, Spring.
1976c 'The Englishization of Hindi: Notes on Language Rivalry and Language Change', *Linguistic Method* = Papers *in Honor of Herbert Penzl*, I. Rauch et al, eds., (to appear)

Kanungo, Gostha Behari
 1962 *The Language Controversy in Indian Education: An Historical Study*
       (Chicago).
Kelkar, A. R.
       'Marathi English: A Study in Foreign Accent', *Word* 13:2.268–282
       (New York).
Khan, Hamid Ahmad
 1964 *Pakistani Linguistics (1963)* (Lahore).
Kindersley, A. F.
 1938 'Notes on the Indian Idiom of English: Style, Syntax, and Vocabulary',
       Transactions of the Philological Society (1938): 25–34 (London).
Lahiri, K. C.
 1956 'Peculiarities in Spoken English of Indians and the Question of a
       Standard for Them', *The Research Bulletin (Arts) of the University of
       the Punjab* 19:3.
Latif, Sayad Abdul
 1920 'The Influence of English Literature on Urdu Literature', Ph.D. thesis
       (London).
Law, N. N.
 1915 *Promotion of Learning in India by Early European Settlers* (London).
LePage, R. B.
 1964 *The National Language Question* (London).
Limaye, M. R.
 1965 ' "H" for Marathi Speakers of English", *English Language Teaching*
       20:1.72–76 (Poona).
Mathai, Samuel
 1951 'The Position of English in India', in *British and American English since
       1900*, E. Partridge and John W. Clark, eds. (New York).
Mishra, V. N.
 1963 *Hindī bhāshā aur sāhitya par angrezi prabhāv (1870–1920)* (Dehra-
       dun).
Morris, Henry
 1904 *The Life of Charles Grant* (London).
Narasimhaiah, C. D.
 1964 'The English Language in India', *Hemisphere* 8:26–30 (April).
Nurullah, S., and Naik, J. P.
 1951 *A History of Education in India (During the British Period)* (Bombay).
Oaten, F. F.
 1908 *A Sketch of Anglo-Indian Literature* (London).
 1907- 'Anglo Indian Literature', in *The Cambridge History of English Litera-
 1927 ture,* Vol. 14 (Cambridge).
Pande, N. R. W.
 1964 'English in India', *Triveni* 33:68–75 (October).
Pandit, P. B.
 1964 'Indian Readjustments in the English Consonant System', *Indian Lin-
       guistics* 25:202–205 (Poona).
Parliament Debate, 1813

Passé, H. A.
  1947 'The English Language in Ceylon', unpublished Ph.D. thesis (London).
Pearse-Smith, T. L. N.
  1934 *English Errors in Indian Schools* (Bombay).
Perren, G. E., and F. M. Holloway
  1965 *Language and Communication in the Commonwealth* (London).
Pietrzyk, A.
  1964 'Problems in Language Planning: The Case of Hindi', in *Contemporary India*, B. N. Varma, ed. (Bombay) pp. 249–270.
Rajagopalachari, C.
  1962 *The Question of English* (Madras).
Rajan, Balchandra
  1965 'The Indian Virtue', *Journal of Commonwealth Literature* 1:80–81 (September).
Rao, K. S. N.
  1961 'A Footnote to the Indian Pronunciation of the Initial /k t p/ and /v/ and /w/ in English', *Indian Linguistics* 22:160 (Poona).
Rao, Raja
  1938 *Kanthapura* (London). (Later edition, New York, 1963).
Rao, Subba
  1954 *Indian Words in English: A Study in Indo-British Cultural and Linguistic Relations* (London, Oxford University Press).
Ray, Punya Sloka
  1969 The Economics for and Against English in India', in *Language and Society in India, Transactions of the Indian Institute of Advanced Study*, Vol. 8 (Simla) pp. 118–121.
Report of the Official Language Commission, 1956 (New Delhi, 1957).
Richter, Julius
  1908 *A History of Missions in India*, Sydney Ḥ. Moore, trans. (New York, Chicago).
Roy, Raja Rammohun
  1823 Letter to Lord Amherst, December 11, 1823, *in Selections from Educational Records, Part I (1781–1838)* pp. 99–101.
Ruberu, Ranjit
  1962 *Education in Colonial Ceylon* (Kandy).
Sen, Priyaranjan
  1932 *Western Influence in Bengali Literature* (University of Calcutta).
Serjeantson, M. S.
  1961 *A History of Foreign Words in English* (New York).
Shah, A. B., ed.
  1968 *The Great Debate: Language Controversy and Higher Education* (Bombay).
Sharp, H., ed.
  1920 *Selections from Education Records, Part I, 1781–1879* (Calcutta).
Sherring, Matthew A.
  1884 *The History of Protestant Missions in India from their Commencement in 1706 to 1871* (London).

Singh, Bhupal
1934 *A Survey of Anglo-Indian Fiction* (London).
Singh, Rajendra Pal
1964 'The Language Issue and Macauley's In-famous Minutes', *Program of Education* 3952—55 (September).
(Report of the) Special Committee of Education, Ceylon, Sessional Paper 24 (1943).
Spencer, J. W.
1957 'Notes on the Pronunciation Problem', *Shiksha: The Journal of the Education Department, U.P.* (1957): 91—97 (April).
Spencer, John
1966 'The Anglo-Indians and Their Speech: A Socio-Linguistic Essay', *Lingua* 16:57—70 (Amsterdam).
Sreekantaiya, T. N.
1940 'English as the Kannadiga Speaks It', *The Bulletin of Phonetic Studies* 1 (October) (University Phonetic Association, Mysore).
The Statesman's Yearbook (New York, 1974).
Taylor, Susan
to appear 'Preliminary Study of the Stress System in Indian English'.
Tickoo, M. L.
1963 'English Pronunciation in India: The Choice of a Model', *Indian Linguistics* 13:3—4. 171—175 (Poona).
Unesco Statistical Yearbook (Brussels, 1972).
Usmani, Mufti A. H.
1965 'A Study of the Teaching of English as a Foreign Language in the Secondary Schools of the Peshawar Region', unpublished Ph.D. thesis (Texas Technological College).
Varma, Manindra
1966 'A Synchronic Comparative Study of the Structure of the Noun Phrase in English and Hindi', Ph.D. thesis (University of Michigan).
Varma, Siddheswar
1957 'The Pronunciation of English in North-Western India', *Indian Linguistics* 18:86—88 (Poona).
Verma, Shivendra K.
1964 'A Study in Systematic Description of Hindi Grammar and Comparison of the Hindi and English Verbal Group', Ph.D. thesis (Edinburgh). (Published under the title *The Structure of the Noun Phrase in English and Hindi* (Delhi, 1971).
Viswanath, L.
1964 'Kanarese and English, A Comparison of Their Phonologies', unpublished study (Bangor, Department of Linguistics, University College of North Wales).
Wadia, A. R.
1954 *The Future of English in India* (Bombay).
Walatara, D.
1960 'The Scope and Limitations of Bilingualism and Second Language with Specific Reference to the Case of Ceylon', *Teaching English* 4.3:3—9 (Bombay).

544 Braj B. Kachru

Whitworth, G. C.
  1885   *An Anglo-Indian Dictionary* (London).
  1932   *Indian English* (Lahore). [An earlier edition was published in England,
         Letchworth, Herts, 1907.]
Wilson, H. H.
  1855   *A Glossary of Judicial and Revenue Terms and of Useful Words Oc-
         curring in Official Documents Relating to the Administration of the
         Government of British India* (London).
  1940   *A Glossary of Judicial and Revenue Terms of British India* (Calcutta).
Yule, N., and A. C. Burnell
  1903   *Hobson-Jobson: A Glossary of Colloquial Anglo-Indian Words and
         Phrases, and of Kindred Terms, Etymological, Historical, Geographical
         and Discursive* (London).

NOTES

This chapter is a revised and updated version of an article published in *Current
Trends in Linguistics*. Thomas A. Sebeok, ed., Volume 5, *Linguistics in South
Asia* (The Hague, Mouton, 1969).
This study was completed in India during my tenure as a Faculty Research
Fellow (1967—68) of the American Institute of Indian Studies, Philadelphia,
Pennsylvania. I am grateful to the Institute for their support. I am also thankful
to the Center for International Comparative Studies, University of Illinois, for
their grant which enabled me to go for research to other parts of South Asia
during my stay in India.

1. I shall use the term *variety* to mean two or more varieties of a language
   'developed' in different *contextual* settings. These may either be those
   varieties which are used as *first* or *primary* languages (e.g., American English,
   British English, Canadian English), or those varieties which are used as
   second or *foreign* languages, (e.g., Indian English, Filipino English, West
   African English). Note also that following J. C. Catford's convention I shall
   use the abbreviations 'L₁' for a *first* or *primary* language, and 'L₂' for a
   second or *foreign* language. See Catford 1959.
2. In Yule and Burnell 1903, there is the following note: 'A disparaging term
   applied to half-castes or *Eurasians* (q.v.) (corresponding to the Lip-Lap of
   the Dutch in Java) and also to their manner of speech. The word is said to
   be taken from *chi* (Fie!), a common native (S. Indian) interjection of
   remonstrance or reproof, supposed to be much used by the class in question . . .' p. 186. See also p. 133 for *butler-English:* 'The broken English
   spoken by native servants in the Madras Presidency; which is not very much
   better than *Pigeon-English* (sic) of China. It is a singular dialect; the present
   participle (e.g.) being used for the future indicative, and the preterite
   indicative being formed by "done"; thus *I telling* = "I will tell"; *I done tell:*
   = "I have told"; *done come* = "actually arrived." Peculiar meanings are also
   attached to words; thus *family* = "wife". The oddest characteristic about

this jargon is (or was) that masters used it in speaking to their servants as well as servants to their masters.'

3. Cf., e.g., the use of the term in Whitworth 1932. An earlier edition was published in England (Letchworth, Herts in 1907). See also Passé, 1947. Cf. also Mathai 1951:96–100. 'Indian English has sometimes been the subject of amusement and has been made fun of under names like "Babu English". It is true that some Indian users of English made amusing mistakes ... in unwarranted coinages and "portmanteau" expressions. As examples of un-English expressions that may be met with in the speech and writing of even well-educated Indians we may cite "to marry with", "to make friendship with", "make one's both ends meet", "England-returned", "A pindrop silence", "A failed B. A.", "A welcome address" ... Expressions such as these are recognized as wrong or clumsy by the more careful writers and speakers in India, but certain neologisms of Indian origin are frequently used even by the most careful.' (p. 98–99).

4. For a brief discussion and excellent bibliography on the historical aspects of Indian education and the role of English in it, see Nurullah and Naik 1951.

5. See Morris 1904, see also 'Observations on the State of Society among the Asiatic-Subjects of Great Britain, particularly with respect to morals, and the means of improving it', by Charles Grant (1831–32:8.734).

6. *Parliament Debate*, 26:562–563 (1813).

7. The following excerpts from his letter are illuminating:
'Humbly reluctant as the natives of India are to obtrude upon the notice of Government the sentiments they entertain on any public measure, there are circumstances when silence would be carrying this respectful feeling to culpable excess. The present Rulers of India, coming from a distance of many thousand miles to govern a people whose language, literature, manners, customs, and ideas are almost entirely new and strange to them, cannot easily become so intimately acquainted with their real circumstances as the natives of the country are themselves. We should therefore be guilty of ourselves, and afford our Rulers just ground of complaint at our apathy, did we omit on occasions of importance like the present to supply them with such accurate information as might enable them to devise and adopt measures calculated to be beneficial to the country, and thus second by our local knowledge and experience, their declared benevolent intentions for its improvement.'
'... When this Seminary of learning (Sanskrit School in Calcutta) was proposed, we understand that the Government in England had ordered a considerable sum of money to be annually devoted to the instruction of its Indian subjects. We were filled with sanguine hopes that this sum would be laid out in employing European gentlemen of talents and education to instruct the natives of India in mathematics, natural philosophy, chemistry, anatomy, and other useful sciences, which the natives of Europe have carried to a degree of perfection that has raised them above the inhabitants of other parts of the world ...'
'... We now find that the Government are establishing a Sanskrit school under Hindoo Pundits to impart such knowledge as is clearly current in India ...'

Roy then gives some arguments against spending money on Sanskrit studies and continues:
'If it had been intended to keep the British nation in ignorance of real knowledge the Baconian philosophy would not have been allowed to displace the system of the schoolmen, which was the best calculated to keep the country in darkness, if such had been the policy of the British legislature . . .' Cf. Roy 1823:99—101. See also Wadia 1954:1—13. Note also the following remarks of Deb 1965:8:
'It has been a mis-fortune that no discussion of the beginnings of English studies in India has brought to the fore the socio-cultural as opposed to the political facts. I have heard not merely polemists and hot-headed revivalists but sincere educationists telling me that English was forced on the Indian public by the English conquerors of India. The facts are very much otherwise. English was not taught because the English desired it; in the beginning they were actively opposed to such a measure, but because Indians wanted it for their advancement. Specially the Hindo (*sic.*) majority and the growing urban Hindo middle class whether in Calcutta or in Madras anxiously demanded it, not merely to get out of the hands of the narrow-minded and corrupt Mughal Government of the day, but also to find a way to the light of the clear and unsullied world of western science and thought, away from the close and oppressive air of the Sanskritic learning of the day.' (p. 6). '. . . it would be a prejudiced version of the history of India which said that English was forced upon the Indian, it was welcomed by the Indian, specially between 1815 and 1890, if not as late as 1905. No more distinguished thinkers could be chosen from among the eminent men of the years 1800—1850 than Raja Ram Mohan Roy and Dwarka Nath Tagore. Both were opposed to the teaching of Sanskrit, if it was to continue in the old pattern; they felt that the mind of India's youth was being shut off from the light of the modern world. The leaders who followed these two great men were equally anxious to keep up the study of English. They felt that, in spite of the humiliation of political subjugation, so complete after 1857, India and England should not be opposed to one another in the field of education and intellectual enquiry.' (p. 8).
Also cf. R. P. Singh 1964.

8. Cf. *Selections from Educational Records* 1781—1839:103—105 (see Sharp, ed.)
9. *Selections from Educational Records* 1781—1839:103—105.
10. *Selections from Educational Records* 1781—1839:116.
11. *Selections from Educational Records* 1781—1839:109.
12. Historically this Despatch is significant in two ways: First, it emphasizes the use of *vernaculars* instead of Sanskrit and Arabic. Second, it says, 'The English language should be taught where there is a demand for it.' See *Selections from Educational Records*, 1800—1900:367—368.
13. This statement does not include Bengali, Tamil, Telugu, etc.
14. Cf. Halliday 1961:3. Most of the technical terms in this paper have been used roughly in the Hallidayan sense.
15. The term 'educated' is used here in the sense in which J. R. Firth uses 'educated English', in Firth 1930:198—199: 'Educated English, then, shows

a wide range of permissible variation in pronunciation and usage. It is controlled partly by a literary norm and partly by social sanctions, though the half educated often abandon good local speech for something which is difficult to refer to a norm . . . On account of the wide range of permissible variation, educated English is difficult to describe. Many speakers of educated English have an accent, traceable to familiar or local speech habits. They are apt to use words which among the "best" people would sound "bookish". They do not exactly talk like books, but they sometimes give common social currency to words and phrases which in other circles are meant to be seen and not heard.'

16. Yule and Burnell, 1903:344. The term *Anglo-Indian* was originally used for persons of mixed European and Indian blood. Also see Spencer.

17. See, for example, Passé 1947:34. He suggested 'modified English' as a possible standard for Ceylon. 'For practical and other reasons the almost certain course will be the teaching of the Ceylonese variety of "Modified Standard" English'.

18. *Statesman's Yearbook* 1974:334. These figures include Sikkim and exclude the Pakistan-occupied areas of Jammu and Kashmir.

19. *Statesman's Yearbook* 1974:1160.

20. *Statesman's Yearbook* 1974:1206. Note that in this paper the term Indian subcontinent refers to the two political entities i.e., India and Pakistan.

21. For a detailed discussion on the languages of South Asia see: *Census of India, 1961,* 1964:1:2c(ii). CLIX-CCXXVI. Language Tables; Brown, ed. 1960; Dil, 1966a.

22. Cf. Perren and Holloway, 1965. See also *Census of India, 1961, op. cit.* Note that this is not an exhaustive list and includes only the major languages. The Tibeto-Burmese group and the tribal languages have not been included here.

23. See Hunt 1931; 1935. See also Gokak 1964:6. He has given a large number of examples to illustrate that 'There seem to be as many kinds of English as there are candidates appearing for an examination'. This helps in showing how SAE writers greatly vary in their competence in the language. See especially pp. 6–9.

24. This is used as a technical term. Cf. Kachru 1966:26 ff; also cf. Halliday et al. 1964:87–98.

25. The language-wise distribution of the studies which consider L_1 transfer into L_2 is as follows:
    1. Dravidian:
       Kannada: Sreekantaiya 1940; Viswanath 1964.
    2. Indo-Aryan:
    (a) *Bengali* Hai and Ball 1961.
    (b) *Gujarati:* Harry 1962.
    (c) *Hindi:* Bansal 1962; Hill 1959; Kachru 1959; J. W. Spencer 1957.
    (d) *Marathi:* Kelkar 1957; Limaye 1965.
    (e) *Oriya:* Dhall 1965.
    (f) *Sinhalese:* Passé 1947; DeLanerolle 1953.
    (g) *Urdu:* Ahmad 1964; Usmani 1965.

26. For the phonetic analysis of these two varieties see Gopalkrishnan 1960;

Varma 1957; Passé 1947.

27. This does not necessarily apply to Sinhalese.

28. Cf. studies listed in footnote 25.

29. Since some of the caste dialects vary in their phonological systems, this naturally reflects on the speakers' L_2. See e.g. Bright 1960; 1961.

30. For a discussion of religious dialects with special reference to Kashmiri see Kachru 1969; 1973.

31. Usmani, 1965:120. Note also that his phonemicization of Urdu vowels is as misleading as his statements on the stress system and intonation in Urdu.

32. Gopalkrishnan 1960. The transcription of the segmental phonemes in the examples is the same as given by the author. I doubt that differences are only of stress.

33. Cf. Taylor, to appear. Also note the following observations of J. W. Spencer 1957:66—67, about the stress pattern of the Anglo-Indian speakers of English in India. 'It is, however, in certain prosodic features that the most distinctive deviation from R.P. [Received Pronunciation] is to be observed; in particular the relationship between stress, pitch and syllable length. The tendency in Anglo-Indian is for stressed syllables to be accompanied by a fall in pitch; indeed for a fall or low-rise to replace stress, since Anglo-Indian pronunciation does not show such marked variations in syllable intensity as R. P. The fall in pitch on the "stressed" syllable is normally followed by a rise on the succeeding syllable, even on final unstressed syllables in state- ments. The tonic "accent" is accompanied by a lengthening of the syllable in question; but this lengthening usually takes the form of a doubling of the final consonant(s) before the transition to the following "unstressed" syllable.'

34. See Abercrombie 1964 for a discussion on stress-timed languages and syllable-timed languages. Note also that in the South Asian languages, by and large, there is no distinction between contracted forms and noncon- tracted forms in verbs; that may be one of the reasons why SAE sounds more *bookish* than *conversational*. (Cf. Section 3.6 Style Features and 'Tone').

35. E.g., Shivendra K. Verma, using the scale and category model of Halliday, has worked out a comparative description of Hindi and English verbal groups (see Verma 1964); see also M. Varma 1966.

36. Kachru 1962. The two restricted texts were taken from the debates on 'fisheries', i.e., (i) *Lok Sabha Debates* 4:5, April 7, 1953 and (ii) *Parliament Debates* (Commons), July 25, 1955.

37. Kindersley 1938:25, Note the following abbreviations which Kindersley uses: B, Bengal; Bo, Bombay and Sind; D, Dravidian linguistic area of South India; Dr., Modern Dravidian languages of South India; E, English; Guj., Gujarati; H, Hindustani; IA, Modern Indo-Aryan languages of India; Ind E, Indian English; P, Punjab; Tam., Tamil; Tel., Telegu (*sic*). He adds: 'The initials P, B, and D signify, unless the word "only" is affixed, that, in addition to being common in the Bombay Presidency and Sind, the usage in question is found in common use in the province or area indicated' (foot- note, p. 25).

38. Wilson 1940. '*Ryot* and *Ryotwar*, for instance, suggest more precise and

positive notions in connection with the subject of the land revenue in the South of India, than would be conveyed by cultivator, or peasant, or agriculturalist, or by an agreement for rent or revenue with the individual members of the agricultural classes.' p.i. (Cf. also K.S.,N. Rao 1961:3, footnote 1).

39. Yule and Burnell 1903. An Indian edition (Reprint) of it has been published by Munshiram Manoharlal, Delhi-6 in 1968.

40. For a detailed discussion of the term 'collocation' see Halliday 1961; Kachru 1966:265 ff.

41. Passé 1947. footnote 4. Note that Goffin 1934 has termed such deviations 'phrase-mongering' and Passé (1947) 'errors of expression that have become more or less fixed in Ceylon English and which the user would be startled and shocked to hear stigmatized as "un-English" '. It is obvious that Passé has taken a stand from a pedagogical point of view and ignores the underlying linguistic reasons.

42. Pearse-Smith 1934. Note that this is essentially a pedagogical manual for the guidance of school teachers.

43. For the meaning of this and the following abbreviations see the List of Abbreviations on pp. 522—523.

44. A detailed treatment of this aspect is given in Braj B. Kachru 1975a. Also cf. Kachru 1965.

45. The term 'tone' is used in a non-technical sense, as used by Goffin 1934.

46. For a detailed account of it see Iyengar 1945; 1962 and Mukherjee 1971.

47. Cf. Anand 1948 and Bhushan 1945a and 1945b. Bhushan uses the term *Indo-English*. These two works of Bhushan are representative anthologies of Indian English poetry and Indian English prose. See also Dustoor 1954; 1955; Jha 1940.

48. Also Passé 1947 has given a large number of such items from Ceylon English, for example, consider the following: *place, junction, fronthouse.*

49. Kachru 1966:278—280. Notice also the use of such items as *fissiparous tendencies* (*Leader* 23.11.65).

50 There is a large number of published and unpublished works on this aspect of South Asian languages. In this study I shall restrict it to some selected features of Hindi. Note also the following remarks of Priyaranjan Sen (1932:382—383). 'We have found that the literature has been affected by its contact with an alien culture, a foreign literature, and that the changes extend both to the thoughts which constitute the matter or contents, and also to the forms of expression both in prose and verse. The language itself shows signs of the new influences; there has been remarkable contribution to the vocabulary; the prose style has been formed and the poetic improved in quality . . . Bengali drama has been practically a new form; such has been the case with Bengali novels; and the epic has grown into something new, quite distinct from the *Mangal gans* that had been the vogue in the centuries that had preceded. The lyric also shows abundant signs of the richness of the new influence, and its technique at the present day, the prosody and the phrasing owes much to the model of English literature. The greatest change, however, is noticeable in Bengali prose. Whether the essay or the periodical literature, the prose biography or history through prose, theological disserta-

tions or philosophical discourse, – everything is a departure from the established ways of the previous centuries. If this is so with regard to the mere form, how much remains to be said as regards the spirit of the literature, its new moods and tendencies, its matter and contents!'

51. Mishra 1963:179. Mishra uses Jespersen's definition of an amorphous sentence. See O. Jespersen 1964:105: 'While the sentences of complete predicational nexuses are (often, at any rate) intellectual and formed so as to satisfy the strict requirement of logicians, amorphous sentences are more suitable for the emotional side of human nature. When anyone wants to give vent to strong feeling, he does not stop to consider the logical analysis of his ideas, but language furnishes him with a great many adequate means of bringing the state of his mind to the consciousness of his hearer or hearers.'

52. See Tickoo 1963. Note also the following interesting observation of Passé 1947:33. 'It is worth noting, too, that Ceylonese who speak "standard English" are generally unpopular. There are several reasons for this: those who now speak standard English either belong to a favoured social class, with long purses which can take them to the English public schools and universities, and so are disliked too much to be imitated, or have rather painfully acquired this kind of speech for social reasons and so are regarded as the apes of their betters; they are singular in speaking English as the majority of their countrymen cannot or will not speak it . . . standard English has thus rather unpleasant associations when it is spoken by Ceylonese.' See also Kachru 1976a.

53. The reaction of L₁ speakers of English has varied during the last two decades. Earlier it was more patronizing than critical. Only recently SAE writing has been critically evaluated. Note also Balchandra Rajan's following observation on Indian English writers in Rajan 1965. 'The difficulties are compounded for the writer in English. There is a sense in which English has never had it so good. The obituary notices for the language, written and postponed over the last seventeen years, have now been reluctantly withdrawn. English is described in officialese as a "link language" which means that an instrument of imperialist exploitation has now been ironically transformed into an important force in bringing about national unity . . . The *bonafides* of the writer in English are continually being impugned. Using what is allegedly a foreign language, he is said to be incapable of expressing the inwardness of Indianness. He is accused of selling his artistic conscience for financial rewards, though one glance at his royalty statements will usually show that he earns considerably less than the writer in Bengali or Malayalam. His mixed sensibility is not only cosmopolitan but rootless. He has no nationality and therefore no identity. The critical assumptions behind these attacks (which, characteristically, are usually made in English) do not deserve serious scrutiny . . . A further rite of extenuation is the pursuit of chimeras such as Indian English. This is not to deny the possibility of an English specific to India, rooted in both the contemporary, and the metaphysical landscape. Such an English, however, can only emerge as the creative product of writers determined to be writers. It cannot spring from gestures of cultural appeasement; and it must at all times be clear that if a man writes in English which enables his vision to

proclaim its deeper life, it cannot be held against him that his language is not "Indian". Nationality is only a blue print unless authenticity makes it a creative act.'

54. For a detailed treatment of the language question in India see *Report of the Official Language Commission, 1956* (1957); Asrani 1964; Narasimhaiah 1964; Pande 1964; Shah, ed. 1968.

55. A summary of these problems about South Asia is given in the following titles: Perren and Holloway 1965; Le Page 1964; Dil, 1966.

56. Cf. Mathai 1951:101, 'When we remember that after nearly a century of English Education only something like 3 per cent of the population know English, it seems obvious that English cannot be the language in which the millions of India will be educated. In 1900 the urban population of India received English as the language of the future, a knowledge of which was essential for their advancement. To-day, though English is still the only language that serves as a *lingua franca*, and a knowledge of it is still necessary for participation in national and international affairs, it seems certain that the future in India does not lie with English. What will actually happen in the future it is difficult to say, but it seems clear that for many years to come it will be in India's interest to retain English at least as an important second language and thus keep open her only door to the knowledge and culture of the larger world.'

57. Iyengar 1962:17, discussing the position of Indian English creative writers in India, says: '. . . the interest in Indo-Anglian literature is pitifully fitful, and the impression still is that the Indo-Anglians are India's literary cranks if not worse, that their work lacks both vitality and any intrinsic worth, and that it is best to leave them alone'. Cf. also B. Rajan 1965.

58. The arguments of the anti- and pro-English groups have been discussed, among others, in the following works: Kanungo 1962; Rajagopalachari 1962; Wadia 1954.

Distribution of Contact Languages in India

A Study of the 1961 Bilingualism Returns

India is regarded as one of the 'sociolinguistic giants', representing languages and cultures of diverse linguistic and ethnic groups. It presents a vivid example of linguistic heterogeneity with a picturesque mosaic of about 200 classified languages spread throughout the country.[1]

The federal organization of the country comprises twelve principal language areas, each dominated by a different language enjoying full or partial recognition in the spheres of public communication within that area. Much of the confusion in interpreting India's language scene comes from the tendency to deal with the subcontinent either as a whole or as a series of small linguistically isolated units. A better understanding of trends can be achieved by grouping these language areas together into four major linguistic regions: these show many parallels in their overall communication environments in spite of a widespread linguistic heterogeneity within each region:

1. the South, dominated by *four* Dravidian languages (Telugu, Tamil, Kannada, and Malayalam), with a population of 110,600,000, i.e., 25.2% of the total population.

2. the East, dominated by *three* East Indo-Aryan languages (Bengali, Oriya, and Assamese), with a population of 67,000,000, i.e., 15.2% of the total population.

3. the West, dominated by *two* Indo-Aryan languages (Marathi and Gujarati), with a population of 60,900,000, i.e., 13.9% of the total population.

4. the North-Center dominated by *two* Central Indo-Aryan (the Hindi-Urdu amalgam[2] and Panjabi) languages and *one* Dardic language (Kashmiri), covering 200,700,000, i.e., 45.7% of the total population.

Of the sixteen linguistic states, Hindi is the official language of five states (Uttar Pradesh, Bihar, Madhya Pradesh, Rajasthan, and Haryana) and also of two union territories (Delhi and Himachal Pradesh). The remaining eleven states recognize each of the eleven major languages for state purposes. Urdu continues to enjoy the status of an official language in Jammu and Kashmir, though gradually Kashmiri and Dogri (Panjabi) are taking place of Urdu in certain fields of public communication. Most of the union territories represent multilingual pockets within different linguistic regions. Two union territories, Manipur in the East and Goa in the West, recognize their local languages, *viz.* Manipuri, a Tibeto-Chinese language, and Konkani, an Indo-Aryan language, for official purposes. Some multilingual territories, such as Nagaland and the Andaman and Nicobar Islands, retain English as their administrative language.

1. OVERALL PICTURE

The 1961 Indian bilingualism returns recorded 42,500,000 people (9.7% of the entire population) who claim subsidiary languages. It is evident from the introductory statement prefacing these returns that no serious attention has been paid to the problems in eliciting or tabulating the data on bilingualism. The question on bilingualism in the 1961 Census was:

'7 (b) Any other language(s).
After recording the mother tongue enquire whether the person knows any other language(s), Indian or foreign, and write the language(s) returned by him against this question. In case he does not know any other language, put "X".
The number of languages recorded against this question should not be more than two. These languages should be other than his mother tongue which he speaks and understands *best* and *can use with felicity* in communicating with others. *Such* language or languages will exclude *dialects* of the same mother tongue.
Although, in the case of respondents who spoke and understood more than one language in addition to their mother tongue, *two* languages were recorded by the Census enumerator, the tabulation was based *only* on the language recorded *first* by him.' [my italics] (Mitra 1964:437).

One notices in these remarks that the enumerator is not provided with any guidelines for determining a particular speech claimed in response to question 7(b) as 'a dialect of the same mother tongue' (MT) or altogether 'a different language', and also for deciding on the *quality* of the speech reported as subsidiary language by the claimant. Both of these factors are highly relevant in getting the correct estimate of bilingualism in the Indian sociolinguistic context, as we shall discuss below. The tabulation further impairs the quality of the information by processing only the language recorded *first* by the claimant, though the enumerator might have recorded *two* languages without any prescribed order.

Hence it will be rather misleading to treat these returns as a factual record of bilingualism in the absolute sense. These returns at best can be described as the expression of speakers' attitudes toward the languages around them, and also to some extent as the expression of the enumerators' implicit (or explicit) bias.

Further, the *ad hoc* treatment of returns by the census authorities makes it more difficult to correlate the first subsidiary language claims with other significant characteristics (such as age, mobility, urbanity, education, religion, etc.).[3] Details of bilingualism claims of only 114 prominent MT groups out of 1652 MTs have been given with the breakdown in each state and union territory. An account of the overall claims of each subsidiary language has been provided for only fourteen of the languages specified in the Constitution (at the time of the 1961 Census). These include Sanskrit, an Indian classical language, and Hindi and Urdu which are recognized as two separate literary languages in the Constitution. The other eleven are the state languages of eleven non-Hindi States.

The term 'first subsidiary language' or 'language subsidiary to the MT' of the 1961 Census is referred to in this article as 'primary contact language' (CL), and claimants of a particular subsidiary language are called 'contact speakers' of that language, distinguishing them from the native-speaking population.

The constitutionally privileged languages cover 72% of the total CL claims. A major CL outside the VIII Schedule is English, claimed by 26% of the total bilingual population.[4] Details of the native and contact speakers of the fifteen major languages (including English) are given in the Appendix (Table A, p. 573).

Shares of different CL claims among bilinguals, and their ratios to the total nonnative population, are shown in Table I.

Table I.   Ratio of a CL is obtained on the basis of the proportion of
the nonnative population of a particular language claiming
that language as a CL

$$R = \frac{\text{contact speakers of language A}}{\text{total population} - \text{native speakers of language A}} \times 1000$$

	% to total bilingual population	R/1000 to nonnative population
English	25.7	25
Hindi	22.1	30
Tamil	8.7	9
Kannada	8.5	9
Telugu	7.8	8
Marathi	6.5	7
Urdu	4.7	5
Bengali	4.6	5
Assamese	3.9	4
Oriya	2.6	3
Gujarati	1.3	1
Panjabi	1.1	1
Malayalam	0.5	a
Sanskrit	0.5	a
Kashmiri	0.1	a

[a] less than one per 1000

Hindi and Urdu, though recognized as separate languages at the
literary and political levels, actually form one unified language amalgam from the communication point of view.[5] Hence, in this article,
the claims of Hindi and Urdu will be combined under the label
Hindi-Urdu (H-U), at the cost of some duplication.[6]

We notice that H-U and E together cover more than half of the
entire bilingual population (52.2%). Eleven major languages other
than H-U share over 45% of the bilingual population, 25.5% claiming
four southern languages, 11.1% claiming three eastern languages, and
7.8% claiming two western languages. Two northern languages other
than H-U, Panjabi and Kashmiri, are claimed by only 1.2%. The
communicative load of the classical language Sanskrit is not numerically significant in comparison to the foreign language English.

2. DISTRIBUTION

Most of the CLs are concentrated in their home states (Appendix, Table B). On the basis of their spread in home and neighboring regions we get *four* types of CLs:

1. CLs largely confined to their home states:
   More than 80% of contact speakers for these languages are reported from their home states, i.e., where the language is the native speech of the predominant population. Their use for intergroup communication outside their home states would be rather restricted. There are *six* such languages, listed in descending order of confinement to their home states:
   A, Ksh, Tm, Or, Kn, Mr

2. CLs spilling over into neighboring states within the linguistic region:
   In this case the home states account for less than 80% of claims of its predominant speech as a CL, but nevertheless its claims within the linguistic region exceed 80%. Hence its impact outside its own linguistic region could be restricted. There are *five* such languages, listed in descending order of confinement to their home states:
   G, P, Tg, Ml, B

3. CLs spread beyond their home region:
   H-U
   Unlike other state languages the H-U amalgam is not confined to one or two states. But it dominates the entire North-Central region, comprising five states and two union territories. Apart from this, practically half of the H CL claims and one-third of the U CL claims are reported outside the home region.

4. CLs not belonging to any region:
   E, Sk
   The strength of both languages is mainly based on their CL claims spread throughout the country. Contact speakers of these languages by far exceed native speakers. E and Sk contact speakers are approximately fifty and sixty times more than their respective native populations in the country. Numerically they do not hold a dominant position in any area.

For intergroup communication purposes H, U, E and Sk can be regarded as pan-Indian languages. The North-Central region, the largest of the four, claims a significant share of these CLs, see Table II.

Table II.

	North-Central %	Remaining three regions %
Sk	84.0	16.0
U	65.2	34.8
H	52.5	47.5
E	40.0	60.0

The scope of the eleven regional languages for intergroup communication can be stated on the interregional scale as shown below:

CL claims outside the region (in descending order):
(i)	above 10%	B, Mr
(ii)	between 5—10%	Or, Kn, G, Tg
(iii)	between 1—5%	Ml, P
(iv)	below 1%	Tm, Ksh, A

CL claims of the following languages exceed 100,000 in outside regions:

B   in the North-Center
Mr   in the South
Kn   in the West
Tg   is split in the East and the West regions.

3. INTENSITY OF BILINGUALISM

CL claims of fifteen states (at the time of the 1961 Census) and Delhi Union territory have been processed in the Tables C, D, E, and F (in the Appendix). Union territories other than Delhi have not been included in the study as, in the broad sense, their CL patterns resemble those of neighboring states.

The intensity of bilingualism varies from one state to another, ranging between 2.5 and 24.1%, the lowest ratio being claimed by Rajasthan and the highest by Delhi (Table C). Minority language populations testify to the degree of heterogeneity in each state, ranging between 5.0 and 55.7%, the least heterogeneous being Kerala and the most heterogeneous being Bihar.

One would presume that heterogeneous communication environments would promote bilingualism. But surprisingly the North-Central region, which is linguistically the most heterogeneous (minority populations between 15.0 and 55.7%), claims the lowest proportion of bilinguals: only 5.9% of the total population. The all-India bilingualism average is 9.7%. Three other regions claim significantly higher ratios of bilingualism, ranging between 10.9 and 13.5%.

State-wise one finds some rough correlation between the degree of heterogeneity in native population and the intensity of bilingualism in the regions other than the North-Center. In the North-Central states one does not find a match between the two.

Outside the North-Central region, (1) two homogeneous states (with minority populations of less than 10%), Kerala and Gujarat, have bilingualism ratios of less than 7%, i.e., below average; (2) three partially homogeneous states (minority populations between 14 and 18%), AP, WB, and Orissa, claim bilingualism ratios which are very close to the all-India average (between 8.5 and 11.0%); (3) three nonhomogeneous states (minority populations between 22 and 43%), Maharashtra, Mysore, and Assam, show significantly higher intensity of bilingualism, ratios ranging between 15 and 22%. Tamilnadu is an exception which, though being a partially homogeneous state, claims a relatively higher ratio of bilingualism (15.6%).

In the North-Central region all states except UP claim linguistically heterogeneous populations. But it is only Delhi which claims the highest bilingualism ratio (24.1%), being the federal capital and also being largely urban. Two bilingual states, JK and Panjab, claim bilingualism ratios close to the all-India average (10%). The remaining three nonhomogeneous states, MP, Bihar, and Rajasthan, and a homogeneous state, UP, claim fairly low bilingualism ratios ranging between 2.5 and 8.2%.

4. CONTACT PATTERNS

Considering the significant CLs in each state we notice a general pattern of three major languages occurring prominently in every state: the state language, Hindi-Urdu, and English (Table C).

In the North-Central region bilinguals have a rather restricted choice, as most speakers in the region claim pan-Indian H-U as their mother tongue. This factor to some extent accounts for the low claims of bilingualism in the region and also for the preference registered for E among literate bilinguals.

Bilinguals in other regions have a wider choice. The West shows a preference for H-U whereas the East and the South register highest preference for state languages, next comes FE, and H-U is the least favored choice.

Preferences of the different states claiming a given language as a predominant CL are given below.

1. H-U is the predominant CL in *six* states: Three Hindi states, MP, Bihar, and Panjab, and three non-Hindi states, JK, Gujarat, and Maharashtra, make claims ranging between 43 and 83% of the bilingual population in each state. These states contain a population which is approximately one-third of the entire population of the country (163,000,000).

2. E is the predominant CL in *five* states: Three Hindi states, Delhi, UP, and Rajasthan, and two non-Hindi states, Kerala and WB, make claims ranging between 49 and 71% of the total bilinguals. These states have a population of approximately 148,000,000.

3. Five state languages, Tm, A, Or, Kn, and Tg, are predominant languages (in that order) in their respective home states, with claims ranging between 51 and 65% of the total bilinguals in each state. These states have a population of approximately 123,000,000.

4. Other state languages which do *not* claim predominant share in their home states as CLs are: Mr, G, B, with modest claims ranging between 32 and 39% of the total bilinguals; P, Ml, Ksh, with very low claims ranging between 7 and 17% of the total bilinguals in each state.

One remarkable feature of states preferring E (other than Delhi) is that the bilingualism ratio per total population of these states is below average, ranging between 2.5 and 8.5%. Circumstances leading to the exceptional claims of Delhi are discussed in an earlier section. References for H-U or for the state language do not show any correlation with the intensity of bilingualism.

On the basis of CL predominance a large part of the country can be segmented in *four* contact belts:

1. H-U (basically Urdu) Belt: JK and Panjab
2. E Belt: UP, Delhi, and Rajasthan
3. H-U (basically Hindi) Belt: Gujarat, Maharashtra, MP, and Bihar
4. State languages Belt: Orissa, AP, Tamilnadu, and Mysore

Extreme corner states such as WB and Kerala form isolated E camps; Assam is also an isolated state language camp.

Apart from the three prominent CLs, other sporadic CLs claimed by sizeable populations in some neighboring states are given below (in descending order of the total claims):

CL		in neighboring states
Tg	—	Mysore, Tamilnadu, Orissa
B	—	Assam, Bihar, Orissa
Mr	—	Mysore, AP
Kn	—	Maharashtra, AP, Kerala
Tm	—	Mysore, AP, Kerala
P	—	Delhi
Sk (has no region)	Up	

5. CONTACT PRESSURES

Patterns of intragroup and intergroup communication and the education system encouraging the 'three-language formula' show that many parts of the country are congenial to operating in more than one CL.

A majority of the people belonging to various minority speech groups, and those living outside their home regions (which comprise over 22% of the country's population), are *potentially* exposed to three CLs: E, H-U, and a state language (when it is different from H). A large majority of the non-H-U speech groups residing in their home states (over 46% of the population) are exposed to two CLs: E and H-U (in some situations possibly to a neighboring state language as well). H and U native speakers residing in their home region (about 32% of the population) are generally exposed to only one prominent CL: E. Several MT groups show significant contrast in CL claims depending on many ecological and socioeconomic factors which determine the incidence of bilingualism in a community, e.g., size and status of the MT group, attitude of speakers, contact environments (heterogeneity, urbanity, etc.), schooling opportunities, economic strata of individuals, occupational conditions (Weinreich 1957; Khubchandani 1973).

In heterogeneous environments many speech groups in different states show a tendency to acquire more than one CL. Tabulation of *only first* subsidiary language claims of bilingual speakers by the Indian census makes us look into these declarations more critically. These claims, by and large, reveal the extent of pressures developed among different speech groups for intragroup and intergroup communication.[7] It is not difficult to find that in many cases the degree of proficiency or intensity of use of the declared CL does not exactly correlate with an individual's claims, which are made under the pressure of social identification to associate with a particular group equivalent to his educational and economic standing, or due to his affiliations in the language controversy in the transient post-colonial period of shift in language functions and privileges.

Different factors contribute to the claims of state language, H-U, and E as CLs in a state. State languages vary a great deal in their strength as CLs in their home regions. Spread of H-U and E also shows varying degrees of intensity in different regions (as was discussed earlier). In order to measure the relative strength of these CLs in each state, I suggest the compilation of CL pressure indices by correlating one of the significant variables with the claims of a particular CL in the state.

1. *State Language Pressure Index:*
State language claims largely depend on the demands made by the dominant speech group on the rest of the population in the state. A 'State Language Pressure Index' is obtained on the basis of the proportion of minority speech groups claiming the dominant state language as CL (Table D):

$$\frac{\text{state CL claims}}{\text{linguistic minorities population (in the state)}} \times 100$$

E.g., in Tamilnadu, six out of ten non-Tamilians claim Tm as their CL, but in Rajasthan, only one out of 100 non-Hindis claim H as CL.

2. *Hindi-Urdu Pressure Index:*
The spread of H-U as a CL throughout the country can be assigned to two major factors, (i) H-U native speakers proliferate in almost all neighboring and nonneighboring states outside the five Hindi states. Six out of ten non-H states have contiguous borders with the H region; 9,500,000 U native speakers (42%) and 4,500,000 H native speakers (3%) are reported from outside their home region. (ii) H-U amalgam, by virtue of being the most dominant language of the largest region, exercises a good deal of influence in intergroup communication throughout the country (of course with varying degrees of intensity in different regions). It had virtually acquired the position of a *lingua franca* for trade, entertainment, and informal communication in heterogeneous situations (mainly urban, industrial, and military settlements) throughout the country, *well before the hectic involvement of official and semiofficial agencies in the promotion of H.*

The 'H-U Pressure Index' outside H states is worked out on the basis of the first major factor, i.e., the proportion of H-U CL claimants to the number of H-U native population settled in these states (Table E):

$$\frac{\text{H-U CL claimants}}{\text{H-U native speakers}} \times 100$$

E.g., in Gujarat, we have seventy-five H-U contact speakers per 100 H-U native speakers, whereas in Tamilnadu there are only ten H-U contact speakers per 100 H-U native speakers.

3. *English Pressure Index:*
Even after independence E continues to be an important part of the communication matrix of urban India. As already mentioned, E contact speakers are approximately fifty times more numerous than E native speakers spread throughout the country. The spread of E in different states primarily represents the schooling opportunities and the degree of occupational specialization demanding a certain minimum proficiency in E. In situations of multiple choice the prestige attached to an international language also seems to be one of the vital factors in claiming E as the primary CL. One finds a remarkable correlation between the ratio of literate population (*Gazetteer of India*, 1965) and E claimants in different states; that

correlation is used here as the basis for obtaining the 'E Pressure Index' (Table F):

E claimants
——————————— × 100
literate population

E.g., in the Panjab 16% of literates know E, whereas in JK only 4.5% of literates claim E.

6. STATE PROFILES

These pressure indices, by and large, signify the degree of disposition of the bilingual population of a state toward a particular CL. The relative position of sixteen states (including Delhi) on the respective index scales is given below (in descending order):

1. State Language Index of ten non-H states: range 1.5—60 (Appendix, Table D). Tamilnadu, AP, Mysore, Assam, Orissa, Maharashtra, Gujarat, WB, Kerala, JK.

2. State Language Index of six H States: range 1.3—23 (Table D). MP, Delhi, Bihar, UP, Panjab (H and P), Rajasthan.

3. H-U Index of eight non-H states (excluding JK and Kerala): range 10—75 (Table E). Gujarat, Maharashtra, Assam, Orissa, AP, Mysore, WB, Tamilnadu.

In JK and Kerala the number of H-U contact speakers by far exceeds those of H-U native population and the Index in these states shoots up to 874 (JK) and 223 (Kerala), directly revealing the significance of the second major factor contributing to the spread of H-U as CL throughout the country.

4. E Index of fifteen states (excluding Delhi): range 4.5—15 (Table F). Panjab, WB, UP, Tamilnadu, AP, Kerala, Assam, Bihar, Maharashtra, Rajasthan, MP, Mysore, Orissa, Gujarat, JK.

The relative rise in the Index for Delhi (30) can be attributed to its being the federal capital and consisting of having a largely urban population (89%).

The State Language Index in H states needs further clarification. H and U speech groups in these states seem to be more sensitive to their distinct identities. One notices that many literates among H and U native speakers tend to identify U (written in Arabic script) and H (in Devanagari script), respectively, as their CL. Hence, for obtaining the State Language Index in these states only H natives have been counted as the predominant group, and U native speakers along with the rest of the non-H-speaking population have been considered as a minority population.

On a statistical basis, in Bihar and Rajasthan the number of speakers claiming H as their MT comprises only 44% and 33% of the total population. But many speakers claiming Bihari and Rajasthani vernaculars as their MT in the respective states regard themselves as part of the H 'tradition' and treat their MTs as substandard varieties of H (Khubchandani 1969b:15—17 ff). Many other speech groups in the North-Central region, such as Pahari, Chhatisgarhi, Awadhi (even some Panjabi and Lahnda speakers), accept the position similar to Bihari and Rajasthani speakers. Though many of them would know H-U as a CL, they mostly declare themselves as monolinguals in the census. Hence the bilingualism claims in the North-Central region are to a great extent under-represented. This explains why the State Language Index in the entire region is miserably low compared with the corresponding Index for the states in other regions.

In order to clarify the broad contours of pressure patterns in each state, each index scale is divided into two grades: a scale above the group mean representing relatively strong influence (Grade I), and a scale below the group mean representing relatively weaker influence (Grade II) of a CL in the state. Grade II is further divided, somewhat arbitrarily, into average (IIa) and weak (IIb) grades; see Table III.

Table III.

Grades	State Index (Non-Hindi)	State Index (Hindi)	H-U Index	E Index
Scale	1.5 – 60	1.3 – 23	10 – 75	4.5 – 15
Group mean	28	9	36	10
Strong (I)	28 – 60	9 – 23	36 – 75	10 – 15
Average (IIa)	18 – 28	5 – 9	23 – 36	6 – 10
Weak (IIb)	1.5 – 18	1.3 – 5	10 – 23	4.5 – 6

Table IV represents the grades of the three prominent CLs in each state.

Table IV. *Pressure Grades*

State	State language	H–U	E
Wider choice states:			
AP	I	IIa	I
Tamilnadu	I	IIb	I
Mysore	I	IIb	IIa
Kerala	IIb	I*	IIa
WB	IIb	IIb	I
Orissa	I	IIa	IIa
Assam	I	I	IIa
Maharashtra	IIa	I	IIa
Gujarat	IIa	I	IIb
JK	IIb	I	IIb
Restricted choice states:	*State language (Hindi)*		*E*
UP		IIa	I
Bihar		IIa	IIa
MP		I	IIa
Panjab	H	IIa	I
	P	IIb	
Rajasthan		IIb	IIa
Delhi		I	I

* The number of H–U CL claimants in Kerala is not very large. The 'strong' pressure grade in this case merely reveals that bilinguals in the state are favorably disposed to H–U.

We notice that every state presents a distinct profile. By highlighting the dichotomy between grades I and II we notice a pattern according to which, in the wider choice states, two CLs claim similar grades and the third one holds the position opposite to the two. Three pairs of such CLs claiming similar grades emerge: (1) state language and H-U, (2) state language and E, and (3) H-U and E. Whatever grade is claimed by the pairing CLs, the one left out holds the opposite position (grade I or II as the case may be): e.g., Assam comes under the first pair where both A and H-U claim strong positions, and E holds the opposite. In Maharashtra, the second pair, Mr and E claim the relatively weaker positions, whereas H-U claims the stronger. See Table V.

Table V.

Grade	State langauge and H–U	State language and E	H–U and E
I Strong	Assam (E II)	AP, Tamilnadu (H–U II)	x
II Not strong	WB (E I)	Maharashtra, Gujarat Kerala, JK (H–U I)	Orissa, Mysore (state language I)

In the states with restricted choice both CLs (state language, i.e., H, and E) can either claim similar grades or one CL holds the grade opposite to the other, as shown in Table VI.

Table VI.

Grade	State language and E	Only state language
I Strong	Delhi	MP (E II)
II Not strong	Bihar, Rajasthan	UP, Panjab (E I)

These profiles conclusively reject the much debated assumption among various pressure groups in India, and also among many political scientists abroad, that there is a significant breach between the southern states (comprising Dravidian languages) and the rest (states mainly comprising Indo-Aryan languages) as far as the language attitudes of bilinguals are concerned.

568   Lachman M. Khubchandani

7. COMMUNICATION ENVIRONMENTS

By combining native and contact speakers of each prominent language in a state we get a general idea of the communication environments prevailing in each state (Table G). Every state, apart from the state language, has from one to six outside or minority languages which are spoken by more than twenty persons per 1000 of the population. A brief account of the prominent languages in each state is shown in Table VII (the languages are given in descending order of their populations).

Table VII.

State	State language(s)	Other prominent languages
1. UP	H–U	E
2. Panjab	H–U, P	E
Delhi	H–U	E, P
AP	Tg	H–U, E
Gujarat	G	H–U, Sindhi
Kerala	Ml	E, Tm
3. Rajasthan	Raj, H–U	Bhili, P
WB	B	H–U, E, Sant
4. JK	Ksh	P, H–U, Pahari, Raj
Maharashtra	Mr	H–U, G, E, Kn
Tamilnadu	Tm	Tg, E, Kn, H–U
Orissa	Or	H–U, Kui, Tg, Sant
5. Bihar	H–U	Bhoj. Maith, Mag, Sant, B
MP	H–U	Chh, Raj, Mr, Gondi, Bhili
6. Mysore	Kn	Tg, H–U, Mr, Tm, Tulu, Konk
Assam	A	B, H–U, Khasi, Bodo, Garo, E
Total	13	16 additional languages

Population-wise the relative strength of the state languages in different states ranges between 556–965 per 1000. States in the descending order of the homogeneity scale are as follows:

State language speakers   States
per 1000 total population

(i)	over 900	UP, Kerala, Gujarat, Tamilnadu, AP
(ii)	between 800–900	Orissa, WB, Delhi, Maharashtra
(iii)	between 700–800	Mysore, MP, Assam
(iv)	between 500–700	Panjab, Bihar, Rajasthan, JK.

The H-U amalgam occupies a significant position in the communication environments in almost all states with the exception of Kerala. Apart from six home states in the North-Central region the amalgam has:

> second position in five states: Maharashtra 160/1000, AP 91, WB 90, Gujarat 66, Orissa 33
> third position in three states: Mysore 103, JK 93, Assam 68
> fifth position in one state: Tamilnadu 21.

E as a significant CL among urban elites occurs prominently in only nine states, having:

> second position in Delhi 158/1000, Kerala 41, UP 25
> third position in WB 43, Tamilnadu 37, Panjab 36, AP 25
> fourth position in Maharashtra 26
> seventh position in Assam 24.

Apart from this pan-Indian pattern, there are eight sporadic languages which hold significant positions in the communication environments of their neighboring states:

1. P in JK 276/1000, Delhi 127, Rajasthan 21
2. Raj. in JK 59, MP 50
3. G in Maharashtra 30
4. Mr in Mysore 43, MP 41
5. B in Assam 207, Bihar 25
6. Tg in Mysore 116, Tamilnadu 112, Orissa 22
7. Kn in Tamilnadu 30, Maharashtra 21
8. Tm in Mysore 42, Kerala 33.

There are six prominent minority languages which occupy second or third positions in their home states: Bhojpuri (Bihar) 171/1000,

Maithili (Bihar) 107, Chhatisgarhi (MP) 91, Bhili (Rajasthan) 41, Kui (Orissa) 29, Sindhi (Gujarat) 24. Santali is spread in a region covering three states: Bihar 36/1000, WB 33, Orissa 21. (The languages of union territories other than Delhi will not be discussed in this article).

8. CONCLUDING REMARKS

Bilingualism serves as a communication bridge between different speech groups. On the basis of the fact that only 9.7% of the total population of the country claims to be bilingual, which means that virtually 90% of the population claims to be monolingual according to the figures provided in the 1961 census, one is led to the conclusion that the degree of interaction among over 200 speech groups must be fairly low, and the diversity of languages must be putting up strong communication barriers in the growth of a nation. But critical study of the 1961 bilingualism returns brings to light several sociopsychological characteristics of different speech groups which have great bearing on the individual's claims to one or more CLs.

1. The concept of 'language' is to a speaker not the same as it is to a linguist. In many multilingual societies, and also where speech conventions are relatively less stabilized, 'language' has to a speaker more symbolic significance, of identifying oneself with a group, than it has purely formal characteristics. In this regard we notice a remarkable difference in the MT returns of the North-Central region and other regions. The North-Central region is regarded as the 'Fluid Zone' where areas of predominant languages are not clearly marked and declarations keep fluctuating in every census, representing constant shifts in their MT allegiance. In contrast, areas of predominant languages in other regions are clearly marked and their MT returns show an increase parallel to the normal growth in the total population (variation restricted to ±3%) (Khubchandani 1969b).

In the North-Central region one finds that there is a super-homogeneity in communication patterns based on different linguistic hierarchies. Hence the entire region has been treated as a composite communication region and labelled 'Broad Hindustani region' or 'Hindi-Urdu-Panjabi (HUP) region' (Khubchandani 1969a:178—180). It represents a unique case where identificational considerations of communication (covering such a vast region) override the linguistic characteristics. Many prominent languages in the region, such as Rajasthani, Bhojpuri, Maithili, Pahari, Chhatisgarhi, and Awadhi, are functionally as well as psychologically accepted by their speakers as 'dialect-like tools for informal and oral communication' (Kloss 1967), and many communities live under 'stable diglossia' conditions.[8]

2. Claims of a subsidiary language under these circumstances depend very much on the *psychological distinction* which one consciously feels between one's native speech and the formal standard speech. For many speakers in the region H-U could be almost an associate native speech[9] depending on the degree of mobility and urbanization, and for them switching of linguistic codes from native speech to H or U is similar to the switching of styles in a monolingual situation (Gumperz and Naim 1960:100). Most of them are quite unaware of their bilingual or multilingual behavior and consider themselves to belong to H or U 'tradition'. This seems to be one of the primary reasons that the North-Central region, though relatively more heterogeneous, claims very low returns of bilingualism.

This phenomenon becomes crystal clear when we compare the ratio of H-U contact speakers to the non-H-U native population in H states (Table D) with certain states outside the H region (Table E). It is rather amazing to note that Rajasthan's claims of H-U contact speakers (12/1000) are even lower than those of certain southern states such as AP and Mysore (17 and 14/1000, respectively). JK claims a higher ratio of H-U contact speakers (86) than Panjab (74). Bihar claims only 68/1000 H-U contact speakers which is virtually equal to Maharashtra's claim (66/1000). The highest claims of Delhi (291), MP (231), and UP (137) fall very much short of the State Language Index in most of the non-Hindi states: Tamilnadu 601/1000, AP 397, Mysore 373, Assam 320, Orissa 310, Maharashtra 249, Gujarat 219 (Table D).

3. Linguistic composition of all the 330 districts, distributed in twenty-six states and union territories (at the time of the 1961 Census) reveals the prevalence of linguistically pluralistic societies in many parts of the country. The population of nearly half of the total number of districts (152, i.e., 46%) is exposed to heterogeneous surroundings where minority speech groups exceed 20% of the total population (District Profile in the Appendix, Table H, p. 580). Such a widespread heterogeneity can potentially be considered as a significant factor promoting bilingual interaction among different speech groups. But the low returns on bilingualism do not testify to the intensity of such interaction.

Another major factor contributing to low claims seems to be the conviction among many speech groups that knowledge of a CL is to be associated with the ability to write that language in its prevalent script. Overlapping claims of U (identified by Arabic script) and H (Devanagari script) made by nearly 2,000,000 H and U natives is sound evidence in support of this tendency (Table E). To what extent this conviction can blur the bilingualism picture is evident from the claims of Sindhi immigrants as reported in the 1951 Census: 2,000 Sindhi bilinguals from Bombay Province (3.4% of the total of bilinguals), predominantly women, were shown as claiming Panjabi to be their primary CL. Sindhi is usually written in Arabic script. Some Sindhi Hindus, particularly women, read and write Sindhi in Gurumukhi script as well, and this knowledge is regarded as acquiring another language, namely *Gurumukhi*. Panjabi is also written in Gurumukhi script. Hence it is very likely that Sindhi speakers' claims of knowing 'Gurumukhi' have been interpreted as knowing the Panjabi language, which is far from the case (Khubchandani 1963:36).

Many such legendary convictions distort the objective account of bilingualism among the Indian population. The extent to which many CLs are spoken or merely understood cannot be fully dealt with by census returns. Hence we will have to accept these returns as a rather conservative account of bilingualism. At the same time these returns present a valuable picture of the attitudes of speakers and their trend of social identification at a particular juncture of time. Despite these limitations one cannot underestimate the importance of the data made available through these returns.

APPENDIX: CENSUS OF INDIA - 1961

Abbreviations

A	Assamese
AP	Andhra Pradesh
Aw	Awadhi
B	Bengali
Bal	Balti
Bhoj	Bhojpuri
Chh	Chhatisgarhi
CL	contact language
E	English
G	Gujarati
Garh	Garhwali
H	Hindi
HUP	Hindi-Urdu-Panjabi (region)
H-U	Hindi-Urdu amalgam
JK	Jammu & Kashmir
Khan	Khandeshi
Konk	Konkani
Kn	Kannada
Ksh	Kashmiri
Kum	Kumauni
Lad	Ladakhi
Mag	Magahi
Mahara	Maharashtra
Maith (Mth)	Maithili

Manp	Manipuri
MP	Madhya Pradesh
Mr	Marathi
Ml	Malayalam
MT	mother tongue
Mth (Maith)	Maithili
Nep	Nepali
Nic	Nicobarese
N-C	North-Central (region)
Or	Oriya
P	Panjabi
Pah	Pahari
R	ratio per 1000
Raj	Rajasthani
Sant	Santali
Sd	Sindhi
Sk	Sanskrit
TC	Tibeto-Chinese
Tg	Telugu
Tm	Tamil
U	Urdu
UP	Uttar Pradesh
UT	union territory
WB	West Bengal

Table A. *Major Languages Profile*

Major languages		Native speakers (in millions)	Native ratio/1000 to total population	Contact speakers (in. thousands)	Contact ratio/1000 among nonnative population	Native + contact ratio/1000 (3 + 5)
(1)		(2)	(3)	(4)	(5)	(6)
INDIA		439.2		42,536	97	–
Hindi[a]	H	129.2	294	9,363	30	324
Telugu	Tg	37.7	86	3,279	8	94
Bengali	B	33.9	77	1,907	5	82
Marathi	Mr	33.3	76	2,724	7	83
Tamil	Tm	30.6	70	3,659	9	79
Urdu[a]	U	23.4	53	2,006	5	58
Gujarati	G	20.3	46	558	1̂	47
Kannada	Kn	17.4	40	3,551	9	49
Malayalam	Ml	17.0	39	218	0.5	39
Oriya	Or	15.7	35	1,075	3	38
Panjabi[b]	P	11.0	25	465	1	26
Assamese	A	6.8	16	1,649	4	20
Kashmiri	Ksh	2.0	5	25	0.1	5
Sanskrit	Sk	(2,500)	. . .[c]	149	0.5	–
English	E	(224,000)	. . .	10,915	25	25
Others (over 180)			138		2	–

[a] Hindi and Urdu figures differ slightly from those given in the Census Report. Hindi figures do not include the Awadhi and Chhatisgarhi speakers as these are treated as separate languages. Urdu figures include those of Hindustani, which is treated as an alternate label for Urdu. The Census authorities classify Hindustani as a separate language distinct from Hindi and Urdu (Khubchandani 1969c).

[b] Panjabi figures also include Dogri speakers; Dogri has since been granted the status of a separate language.

[c] In all the tables, . . . indicates very small numbers

Table B. *Distribution of Contact Languages*

Major contact languages	Home state	Percentages of contact speakers						
		within the region		outside the region				
		in home state	outside the home state	Total	South	East	West	North-Central
(1)	(2)	(3)	(4)	(5)	(6)	(7)	(8)	(9)
South								
Tm	Tamilnadu Pondicherry	93.3	6.3	0.4	–	...	0.3	0.1
Kn	Mysore	86.3	7.8	5.9	–	...	5.9	...
Tg	AP	61.1	33.4	5.5	–	2.9	2.2	0.3
Ml	Kerala Laccadive Islands	61.0	36.7	2.3	–	...	1.8	0.4
East								
B	WB, Tripura	57.3	23.0	19.7	...	–	...	19.4
A	Assam	98.9	1.0	0.1	...	–	...	...
Or	Orissa	89.4	1.7	8.9	2.5	–	...	6.4
West								
Mr	Maharashtra	84.7	0.7	14.6	11.3	...	–	3.2
G	Gujarat	77.1	17.3	5.6	0.7	...	–	4.8
North-Central								
H	entire region	52.5		47.5	6.2	9.7	31.6	–
U	entire region	65.2		34.8	23.4	3.9	7.4	–
P	Panjab, JK	76.7	22.0	1.3	0.2	...	0.9	–
Ksh	JK	98.3	1.5	0.2	...	...	0.2	–
Without region								
E		–	–	100.0	29.8	18.7	11.4	40.0
Sk		–	–	100.0	9.3	2.0	4.6	84.0

Table C. *Bilingualism in States*

State	State language(s)	Total population (in millions)	Bilingual population (in thousands)	%	State language	H–U	E	Other prominent CLs
(1)	(2)	(3)	(4)	(5)	(6)	(7)	(8)	(9)
INDIA		439.2	42,536	9.7	45	27	26	
South		110.6		13.5	69	7	22	
AP	Tg	36.0	3,938	10.9	51	8 + 8 = 16	22	Kn, Tm
Tamilnadu	Tm	33.7	5,259	15.6	65	1.25	23	Tg
Mysore	Kn	23.6	5,194	22.0	59	4 + 2 = 6	9	Tg, Mr, Tm
Kerala	Ml	16.9	959	5.7	14	4 + .. = 4	71	Kn, Tm
East		67.0		10.9	57	14	28	
WB	B	34.9	2,984	8.5	32	15 + 3 = 18	49	–
Orissa	Or	17.5	1,528	8.7	63	9 + .. = 9	15	Tg, B
Assam	A	11.9	2,531	21.3	64	11 + .. = 11	11	B
West		60.9		12.4	36	42	17	
Maharashtra	Mr	39.6	5,971	15.1	39	41 + 2 = 43	16	Kn
Gujarat	G	20.6	1,326	6.4	32	40 + 4 = 44	21	–
North-Central		200.7		5.9	(H 41, U 11, P 4)		37	
UP	H	73.7	3,258	4.4	–	19 + 12 = 31	55	Sk
Bihar	H	46.5	3,397	7.3	–	50 + 2 = 52	22	B
MP	H	32.4	2,639	8.2	–	61 + 2 = 63	15	Mr
Panjab[a]	H, P	20.3	2,036	10.0	–, 17	23 + 22 = 45	36	–
Rajasthan	H	20.2	509	2.5	–	33 + 9 = 42	49	–
JK	U, Ksh	3.6	367	10.3	–, 7	17 + 66 = 83	5	P
Delhi (UT)	H	2.7	641	24.1	–	19 + 9 = 28	65	P

[a] Since 1966 the bilingual Panjab has been divided into separate Panjabi and Hindi states, namely, Panjab and Haryana.

Table D. *State Languages*

(numbers in thousands)

State	State language population	Linguistic minorities		State language		State language native and contact speakers (2) + (5)
		population	% to total population	contact speakers	% to minority population (Index)	
(1)	(2)	(3)	(4)	(5)	(6)	(7)
AP	30,935	5,048	14.0	2,006	39.7	32,941
Tamilnadu	28,016	5,671	16.8	3,405	60.1	31,421
Mysore	15,372	8,215	34.8	3,063	37.3	18,435
Kerala	16,066	838	5.0	133	15.9	16,199
WB	29,436	5,490	15.7	945	17.2	30,381
Orissa	14,444	3,105	17.7	961	31.0	15.405
Assam	6,784	5,089	42.9	1,631	32.0	8,415
Maharashtra	30,279	9,275	23.4	2,308	24.9	32,587
Gujarat	18,673	1,960	9.5	430	21.9	19,103
JK Ksh	1,938	1,623	45.6	25	1.5	1,963
				group mean	28	

H. States:

UP	62,975	10,771	15.0	631	5.9	63,606
Bihar	20,581	25,875	55.7	1,713	6.6	22,294
MP	25,272	7,100	31.9	1,607	22.6	26,879
Rajasthan·	6,715	13,441	66.7	169	1.3	6,884
Delhi (UT)	2,057	602	22.6	122	20.3	2,179
Panjab H	11,299	non-H 9,008	44.4	472	5.2	11,771
Panjab P	8,343	non-P 11,964	58.9	352	2.9	8,695
				group mean	9	

Table E. *Hindi-Urdu*

			(numbers in thousands)					
State	Native speakers	Contact speakers			Index	Non-H–U popu-lation	CL ratio to non-H–U popu-lation per 1000	Native + contact speakers (2) + (5)
		claimants	over-lapping claims	net	$\frac{5}{2} \times 100$			
(1)	(2)	(3)	(4)	(5)	(6)	(7)	(8)	(9)
AP	2,693	634	39	595	22	35,290	17	3,288
Tamilnadu	656	66	1	65	10	33,031	2	721
Mysore	2,117	318	12	306	15	21,470	14	2,423
Kerala	16	37	...	37	(223)	16,888	2	53
WB	2,731	511	118	393	14	32,195	12	3,124
Orissa	433	139	7	132	32	17,116	8	565
Assam	535	275	3	272	51	11,338	24	807
Maharashtra	3,956	2,526	161	2,365	60	35,598	66	6,321
Gujarat	787	585	12	573	75	19,846	29	1,360
JK	35	306	2	304	(874)	3,526	86	339
				group mean[a]	36			
H States:								
UP	70,867	1,014	618	396	–	2,879	137	71,263
Bihar	24,730	1,784	300	1,484	–	21,726	68	26,214
MP	26,012	1,658	187	1,471	–	6,360	231	27,483
Panjab	11,557	916	269	647	–	8,750	74	12,204
Rajasthan	7,225	215	64	151	–	12,913	12	7,376
Delhi (UT)	2,210	183	52	131	–	449	291	2,341

[a] Excluding Kerala and JK.

Table F. *English*

State	Literates per 1000[a]	Contact speakers	Native speakers	Total	Ratio per 1000 to total population	Index $\frac{6}{2} \times 100$
			(in thousands)			
(1)	(2)	(3)	(4)	(5)	(6)	(7)
AP	212	882	14	896	25	11.8
Tamilnadu	314	1,215	34	1,249	37	11.8
Mysore	254	390	18	408	17	6.7
Kerala	468	678	7	685	41	8.8
WB	293	1,460	39	1,499	43	14.7
Orissa	217	235	0.7	236	14	6.5
Assam	274	288	2	290	24	8.8
Maharashtra	298	963	60	1,023	26	8.7
Gujarat	305	285	2	287	14	4.6
JK	110	17	0.2	17	5	4.5
UP	176	1,802	23	1,825	25	14.2
Bihar	184	754	8	762	16	8.7
MP	171	390	6	396	12	7.0
Panjab	242	733	1.4	734	36	14.9
Rajasthan	152	248	1.3	249	12	7.9
Delhi (UT)	527	415	4	419	158	30.0
					group mean	10

[a] *The Gazetteer of India*, Vol. I.

Table G. *Communication Environments*

	Native and contact speakers ratio per 1000			
State	State language	H–U	E	Other prominent languages (over 20/1000)
(1)	(2)	(3)	(4)	(5)
SOUTH	[Tg 357, Tm 306, Kn 182, Ml 154]	[59]	[29]	
AP	915	91	25	–
Tamilnadu	932	21	37	Tg 112, Kn 30
Mysore	781	103	17	Tg 116, Mr 43, Tm 42, Tulu 36, Konk 21
Kerala	959	3	41	Tm 33
EAST	[B 508, Or 236, A 126]	[70]	[31]	
WB	871	90	43	Sant 33
Orissa	880	33	14	Kui 29, Tg 22, Sant 21
Assam	707	68	24	B 207, Khasi 31, Bodo 30, Garo 25
WEST	[Mr 540, G 334]	[129]	[22]	
Maharashtra	823	160	26	G 30, Kn 21
Gujarat	939	66	14	Sindhi 24
NORTH-CENTRAL	[H 660, U 76, P 57, Ksh 10]	–	[22]	
JK	Ksh 545	93	5	P 276, Pahari 69, Raj 59
Panjab	P 428	601	36	–
Rajasthan	Raj 556	365	12	Bhili 41, P 21
Bihar	–	564	16	Bhoj 171, Maith 107, Mag 61, Sant 36, B 25
MP	–	748	12	Chhat 91, Raj 50, Mr 41, Gondi 32, Bhili 21
UP	–	965	25	–
Delhi (UT)	–	867	158	P 127

Table H. District Profile: 1961 Census. Composition of Districts According to Languages (from Khubchandani 1969c)

State	Languages at district level	Districts number	Communication environments							
			Homogeneous		Partially homogeneous		Non-homogeneous		Multilingual	
			Language	Number	Language	Number	Language	Number	Languages	Number
1.	2.	3.	4.	5.	6.	7.	8.	9.	10.	11.
1. Jammu and Kashmir	Kashmiri, Panjabi, Pahari, Ladakhi, Balti	9	Ksh	1	Ksh / P	2 / 2	P	1	Ksh, etc. / Pah, etc. / Lad-Bal	1 / 1 / 1
2. Panjab	Hindi, Panjabi, Pahari	18	H	2	H / P	3 / 1	H / P	2 / 6	H–P / H–Pah	3 / 1
3. Uttar Pradesh	Hindi, Kumauni, Garhwali, Urdu	54	H / Kum	7 / 1	H / Kum / Garh	29 / 1 / 1	H / Garh	10 / 2	H–U / H–Kum / H–Garh	1 / 1 / 1
4. Bihar	Hindi, Bhojpuri, Maithili, Magahi, Urdu, Tribal (Santali, etc.)	17	—	—	H / Bhoj	1 / 1	H / Bhoj / Mth	5 / 2 / 2	H–U / H–Mag / H–Sant / Tribal	1 / 1 / 1 / 3
5. Madhya Pradesh	Hindi, Chhatisgarhi, Awadhi, Rajasthani, Marathi, Bhili, Gondi	43	H	14	H / Chh	9 / 1	H	8	H–Chh / H–Aw / H–Raj / H–Mr / Bhili–H / Gondi, etc. / H, etc. / Bhili–Raj	1 / 1 / 2 / 2 / 2 / 1 / 1
6. Rajasthan	Rajasthani, Hindi, Bhili, Panjabi	26	Raj / Bhili	1 / 1	Raj / H	8 / 3	Raj / H / Bhili	7 / 1 / 1	Raj–H / Raj–P	3 / 1
7. Gujarat	Gujarati, Sindhi (Kachhi), Bhili, Khandeshi	17	G	8	G	7	—	—	G–Sd / Bhili–Khan	1 / 1

Table H. (*continued*)

State	Languages at district level	Districts number	Communication environments							
			Homogeneous		Partially homogeneous		Non-homogeneous		Multilingual	
			Language	Number	Language	Number	Language	Number	Languages	Number
1.	2.	3.	4.	5.	6.	7.	8.	9.	10.	11.
8. Maharashtra	Marathi, Khandeshi	26	—	—	Mr	14	Mr	10	Mr, etc. / Khan–Mr	1 / 1
9. Orissa	Oriya, Kui, Tribal (Santali, etc.)	13	Or	3	Or	4	Or	4	Or–Kui / Or–Tribal	1 / 1
10. West Bengal	Bengali, Nepali Santali	16	B	3	B	9	B / Nep	2 / 1	B–Sant	1
11. Assam	Assamese, Bengali, Khasi, TC (Tibeto–Chinese) languages	11	—	—	A	2	A / B	4 / 1	TC languages (Bodo, Garo, Mikir, Lushai) / Khasi	3 / 1
12. Andhra Pradesh	Telugu	20	Tg	3	Tg	10	Tg	7	—	—
13. Mysore	Kannada, Telugu, Tulu, Coorgi	19	—	—	Kn	4	Kn	9	Kn, etc. / Tg–Kn / Tulu–Kn / Coorgi–Kn	3 / 1 / 1 / 1
14. Tamilnadu (Madras)	Tamil, Kannada	13	Tm	1	Tm	7	Tm	4	Tm–Kn	1
15. Kerala	Malayalam	9	Ml	6	Ml	3	—	—	—	—
Union Territories										
1. Delhi	Hindi	1	—	—	—	—	H	1	—	—
2. Himachal Pradesh	Pahari, Mandeali, Chameali, Sirmauri, Hindi	5	—	—	—	—	Pah	1	Pah–H / Mandeali–Pah / Sirmauri–H / Chameali, etc.	1 / 1 / 1 / 1

Table H. (*continued*)

State	Languages at district level	Districts number	Communication environments							
			Homogeneous		Partially homogeneous		Non-homogeneous		Multilingual	
			Language	Number	Language	Number	Language	Number	Languages	Number
1.	2.	3.	4.	5.	6.	7.	8.	9.	10.	11.
3. Manipur	Manipuri	1	—	—	—	—	Manp	1	—	—
4. Tripura	Bengali	1	—	—	—	—	B	1	—	—
5. Nagaland	Konyak, Ao, Angami Sema	3	—	—	—	—	—	—	Konyak Ao–Sema Angami	1 1 1
6. NEFA	Tibeto–Chinese languages	1	—	—	—	—	—	—	TC languages	1
7. Goa, Daman & Diu	Konkani	3	—	—	Konk	3	—	—	—	—
8. Dadra & Nagar Haveli	Marathi (Varli)	1	—	—	—	—	—	—	Marathi (Varli)	1
9. Pondicherry	Tamil	1	—	—	Tm	1	—	—	—	—
10. Laccadive Islands	Malayalam	1	—	—	MI	1	—	—	—	—
11. Andaman & Nicobar Islands	Nicobarese, Bengali, Malayalam	1	—	—	—	—	—	—	Nic–B–MI	1
TOTAL		330		51 (15.5%)		127 (38.5%)		93 (28.1%)		59 (17.9%)

Notes: *Homogeneous*

Totally homogeneous   A district having minority language(s) speakers in less than 5% of the total population.
Partially homogeneous   A district having minority language(s) speakers in between 5 and 20% of the total population.

Heterogeneous

Non-homogeneous: A district having minority language(s) speakers in between 20 and 40% of the total population.
Multilingual: A district with no language predominant, or minority languages in more than 40% of the total population.

REFERENCES

Bose, Ashish
1969 'Some Aspects of Linguistic Demography of India', in *The Proceedings of the Seminar on Language and Society of India*, 1967 (Simla, Indian Institute of Advanced Study) pp. 37—51.
Das Gupta, J., and J. A. Fishman
1970 'Intra-State Migration and Subsidiary Language Claiming: An Analysis of Selected Indian Census Data', *International Migration Review* 1970, 5: 227—249.
Davidson, T. T. L.
1969 'Indian Bilingualism and the Evidence of the Census of 1961', *Lingua* 22. 2—3:176—96 (Amsterdam).
Ferguson, Charles A.
1966 'National Sociolinguistic Profile Formulas', in W. Bright, ed., *Sociolinguistics* (The Hague, Mouton).
The Gazetteer of India, Vol. 1 (Delhi, Government of India).
Gumperz, John J., and C. M. Naim
1960 'Formal and Informal Standards in the Hindi Regional Language Area', in C. A. Ferguson and J. J. Gumperz, eds., 'Linguistic Diversity in South Asia', *International Journal of American Linguistics* 26.3 (Baltimore).
Kelkar, Ashok R.
1968 *Studies in Hindi-Urdu*, Part I (Poona).
Kelley, Gerald
1966 'The Status of Hindi as a Lingua Franca', in W. Bright, ed., *Sociolinguistics* (The Hague, Mouton).
Khubchandani, Lachman M.
1963 'The Acculturation of Indian Sindhi to Hindi: A Study of Language in Contact', Ph.D. thesis (University of Pennsylvania, microfilm).
1968 'Hindi-Urdu-Hindustani: A Sociolinguistic Study', *Zagreb Linguistic Circle* (1968).
1969a 'Functional Importance of Hindi and English', in *The Proceedings of the Seminar on Language and Society of India*, 1967 (Simla, Indian Institute of Advanced Study) pp. 178—89.
1969b 'Mother Tongue in Multilingual Societies: An Interpretation of Indian Census Returns', paper presented at the IInd International Congress of Applied Linguistics, Cambridge, England. [Also in Economic and Socio-Cultural Dimensions of Regionalisation: An Indo-U.S.S.R. Collaborative Study (= Census Centenary Monograph 7, Census of India) (New Delhi, India, Office of the Registrar General, 1972) pp. 427—50.]
1969c 'Linguistic Composition of India: A Demographic Study of Communication Environments', mimeographed.
1970 'Language Situation of India', *Indian and Foreign Review* (June) (New Delhi).
1973 'Indian Bilingualism and English: An Analysis of the 1961 Census Data', *Demography-India* 2.1 (Delhi).
Kloss, Heinz
1967 'Bilingualism and Nationalism', *Journal of Social Sciences* 23.2:40—47.

Lieberson, Stanley
1966 'Language Question in Censuses', *Sociological Enquiry* 36.2:262—79.
Mitra, Asok
1964 *Census of India — 1961*, Vol. I, India, Part II—C (ii), Language Tables (Delhi, Government of India).
Weinreich, U.
1957 'Functional Aspects of Indian Bilingualism', *Word* 13.2:103—23 (New York).

NOTES

This was presented at the Indian Census Centenary Seminar organized by the Registrar General of India at New Delhi, October 1972.

Abbreviations used in this article are listed on p. 585.

All figures, unless specified otherwise, are from Mitra 1964.

1. Profiles of classified languages are discussed in Khubchandani 1969c.
2. Hindi and Urdu are two standardized forms of the same dialect, Khariboli, and sharply divided in their scripts (Devanagari and Perso-Arabic) and literary trends (Khubchandani 1968).
3. Surprisingly, no grand totals of language claims are given at any stage in the all-India Report. All calculations in the Appendix to this article (pp. 573—582) have been worked out by manual operations, rounding off small figures in certain cases.
4. The totals of English CL claims are taken from Davidson 1969.
5. A detailed discussion of the Hindi-Urdu amalgam is found in Khubchandani 1969b.
6. Over 1,000,000 Urdu native speakers claim Hindi as CL and about 800,000 Hindi native speakers claim Urdu as CL.
7. Salient features of three types of bilingualism, namely, intragroup, intergroup territorial, and intergroup migrant bilingualism, are discussed in Khubchandani 1973.
8. 123,000,000 people give Hindi (proper) as their MT in the 1961 Census though many of them speak markedly different varieties or altogether different languages for primary communication (Khubchandani 1969b).
9. Kelkar (1968:5—6) calls such groups 'adherent speakers', distinguishing them from 'native' and 'foreign' speakers.

A Survey of English Use in Jordan

In March 1972 a team of specialists visited Jordan at the request of the Ministry of Education and the University of Jordan to examine the English language teaching situation. In their report (Campbell *et al.* 1972) they proposed an English language policy survey which was actually carried out between June and December 1972. The survey, as embodied in the final report (see Harrison, Prator and Tucker 1975), consisted of two parts. The first part contained four chapters: Chapter I, a description of the stated and implicit aims of English instruction; Chapter II, a description of the dimensions of English instruction in the country; Chapter III, a description of curricula and instructional materials; and Chapter IV, a description of teacher training activities.

In the second major part we described and presented data from a field study (Chapters V and VI) that we conducted with a large number of Jordanians of varied educational attainment from a representative sample of occupations.

In Chapter VII we presented a critical analysis of the present English teaching program in relation to the data collected during the Field Study, and in Chapter VIII we summarized the recommendations that we made throughout the report. The purpose of this article is to describe the field study in detail.

Rationale for the Study

The Field Study was conducted to collect information from a large group of Jordanians about their patterns of language use. Specifically we wanted to obtain a detailed description of the extent to which they use English in a wide variety of situations, for both business and nonbusiness matters; and then we wanted to assess the relationship between their actual use of English and factors such as educational attainment, occupation, location of business, age, sex, and salary. Furthermore we wanted to collect reasonably complete information about their educational history, their language training, and their reported English proficiency.

In this way we hoped to be able to provide a body of facts and documented opinions for Jordanian educators concerning the extent to which English is actually *used* by various groups of Jordanians and the extent to which the formal program of English language teaching in the schools meets the respondents' needs.

One factor in this rather intensive investigation of English language policy which has helped to make our task easier has been the relative simplicity of the language situation in Jordan. Arabic is the mother-tongue of a vast majority of the population and the language most widely used by the people to communicate with other Jordanians or Arabs from neighboring countries. Arabic is the exclusive medium of instruction in government schools through the secondary level, and even private schools offer a core curriculum (e.g., the nature of the Arab homeland, the history of the Arabs, the geography of the Arab states) via Arabic at the secondary level. In addition to this homo-geneity of mother tongue, English is, for all practical purposes, the only foreign language taught in the schools. Therefore the educa-tional system comprises a large number of students who speak the same language at home, who receive the bulk of their instruction via the same language, Arabic, and who study the same foreign language, English, following nationally prescribed curricula. Thus we have been able to make observations or recommendations which have general relevance for the entire public educational system of Jordan rather than just for one small segment of the system.

We view the present investigation of the more traditional or formal aspects of a country's foreign language teaching program within the framework of a specially conducted, broadly based sociolinguistic survey as a unique contribution to the rapidly growing body of data collected by language and educational planners (see for example Fishman, Ferguson, and Das Gupta 1968; Rubin and Jernudd 1971; Whiteley 1971).

To our knowledge, previous investigators have not used this dual approach. They have typically assessed the success of language teaching programs by administering some standardized test to groups of students or by visiting a series of classes and by evaluating the performance of the teachers using a checklist specifically prepared to represent one theoretical bias or another (see for example Brownell 1967; Jacobs, ed. 1966; Ladefoged, Glick, and Criper 1971).

We believe that it is meaningless to assess the success of a language teaching program by administering a standardized test of dubious validity. The knowledge that Jordanian secondary school graduates score better or worse than their Egyptian or Lebanese counterparts becomes meaningful only to the extent that we possess detailed information about the relative importance or necessity for English in each of these countries, the types of English programs which exist, the background of the students, etc. Likewise, to evaluate a program by relying solely upon classroom visitation could easily produce an incomplete or biased view.

We believe that our data will be of interest and value not only to Jordanian educators as they examine their English language program within the framework of their general educational philosophy but also to educational planners in other countries who contemplate the systematic evaluation of their language programs. We believe that both the data *and* the methodology of the present study will interest researchers.

Methodology

At the request of the Ministry of Education the field study was formally conducted by the Jordanian Department of Statistics. Staff from the Department, collaborating closely with Harrison, Prator, and myself and with a liaison committee from the Ministry of Education, assumed responsibility for selecting the sample of respondents, hiring and training the enumerators, printing the questionnaires, and collecting, coding, punching, and analyzing the data.[1] This work was expertly conducted under the direct guidance of Mr. Wasef Azar.

The Sample
The respondents were chosen to represent a sample of the Jordanian work force stratified by level of educational attainment. We drew representatives from five levels: 13% had completed less than preparatory education; 15% had completed preparatory but not secondary schooling; 30% had completed secondary schooling; 13% had completed post-secondary institute training; and 29% had completed university training (Bachelor of Arts or beyond). At each of the five levels we selected a sample of respondents randomly with respect to

occupation. Respondents were chosen from both the public and the private sector. The size of the sample was 4804.

We wish to state clearly that our sample does *not* reflect the present distribution of the Jordanian work force by level of educational attainment. We have over-represented in our sample the percentage of highly educated respondents. We have done this intentionally. By doing so we believe that we can provide the Ministry of Education with a more meaningful and useful set of data upon which to base their educational decisions for the next decade. The Ministry, for example, anticipates an increased enrollment of 300% at the secondary level over the next eight years, and it is clear that the percentage of Jordanians proceeding to higher education will increase drastically in the near future. Furthermore it has been our experience with previous language surveys that the reliability of the information has increased with the respondents' level of educational attainment.

The Questionnaire
A forty-seven item, three-part questionnaire was designed in collaboration with the liaison committee from the Ministry of Education. This questionnaire is reproduced in English in the Appendix (pp. 624–632). We collected basic demographic information (questions 1 to 9 and 19 to 22), sociolinguistic information concerning the respondents' use of the various English skills with a variety of interlocutors in diverse situations (questions 10 to 18), and information about topics such as their subjective impressions of their English language proficiency and their satisfaction with various aspects of their formal English language training at school (questions 23 to 47).

The original questionnaire was prepared in English and then translated into Arabic by specialists at the Department of Statistics. The liaison committee from the Ministry of Education verified the accuracy and appropriateness of the final form of the questionnaire.

A systems analyst, Mr. Abdulla Sammour, working with us, developed a coding format to be incorporated into the questionnaire to facilitate data processing. The final, pre-coded questionnaires were then printed in Arabic by the Department of Statistics.

The Enumerators
Enumerators were hired and trained thoroughly by the Department of Statistics personnel. Their training included an introduction to survey techniques and an intensive familiarization with the questionnaire. They also conducted a series of supervised 'practice' inter-

views. After the one-week training program and a written examination, thirty-four university graduates were selected as enumerators for the field study. A member of the liaison committee from the Ministry of Education attended all training sessions and acted as one of four supervisors during the field study. All interviewing was conducted in Arabic.

Duration of Study

The formal interviewing began on July 8, and all field work was completed by August 7.

Method of Analysis

As the questionnaire was being developed we worked closely with systems analyst Mr. Abdulla Sammour to make certain that questions and response alternatives were stated in a manner amenable to rapid, unambiguous coding, punching, and processing. This meant that a majority of the questions had a series of forced-choice response alternatives (i.e., they were not open-ended).

Specification of Output

As the final form of the questionnaire was being prepared we developed simultaneously the complete set of 93 'dummy' tables to specify explicitly the anticipated form of the data. The analyses in general take the form of tables summarizing the frequency and proportion of respondents choosing each alternative for each question as well as a series of bivariate or multivariate distributions examining the relationship among response patterns and demographic characteristics such as educational attainment, occupation, or sex.

By specifying completely the desired form of the output *before* the data were collected, we accomplished two purposes: first, we were able to eliminate redundant or meaningless questions from our questionnaire; second, the programming necessary to analyze the data was completed while the interviewing was in progress.

Coding and Punching of Data

The questionnaires were precoded, and data were punched directly from the documents. This was done by regular employees of the Department of Statistics.

Processing of the Data
The data processing began on August 17 and was completed on September 9. The data took the form of three copies of the ninety-three specified tables.

Availability of Data
The raw data are available on tape at the Department of Statistics. They may be used for further analyses with the permission of the Ministry of Education and the Department of Statistics.

Cost of Field Study
The cost of the Field Study exluding senior consultants' salaries was approximately US $12,000.

RESULTS AND DISCUSSION

Demographic Characteristics of the Sample

The 4804 respondents were selected to represent a random sample of public and private sector employees at each of five levels of educational attainment. All were Jordanian citizens. The sample comprised 88% males and 12% females; 80% of the respondents were employed in Amman; 16% in various towns with a population greater than 5000; and 4% in villages with a population less than 5000. An overwhelming majority (98%) reported Arabic to be their mother tongue. Likewise, the majority (80%) were Moslems although a sizeable minority claimed to be Christian (20%). Apparently the actual percentage of Christians in Jordan is somewhat less than 20%. By our deliberate selection of many highly educated respondents we may have over-represented in our sample groups of individuals who tend to be Christian such as teachers in private schools.

The mean age of the respondents was 29.8 years (standard deviation = 8.2). They had received formal schooling for an average of 12.6 years (standard deviation = 3.3).

Thirty-eight percent had received their entire education in government schools; 11% had attended only private schools (either foreign or national); 2% had attended only schools located outside Jordan; 49% of the respondents had attended a combination of schools for varying portions of their training (16% government and private schools; 20% government and schools outside Jordan; 5% private and schools outside Jordan; 8% government, foreign, and schools outside Jordan). In summary, then, 82% of the respondents had received at least some part of their education in Jordanian government schools, 40% had received some portion of their education in Jordanian private schools, and 35% of the respondents received some of their education in schools outside Jordan.

Table I. *Distribution of Respondents by Level of Educational Attainment and by Occupation*

	Educational attainment[a]									
	Less than preparatory		Preparatory		Secondary		Institute		B.A.		Total	
Occupation[b]	F	%	F	%	F	%	F	%	F	%	F	%
0–1	37	6.1	113	15.4	435	30.3	268	41.2	797	58.0	1650	34.3
2	13	2.1	64	8.7	126	8.8	91	14.0	270	19.7	564	11.7
3	107	17.6	251	34.1	653	45.4	245	37.7	246	17.9	1502	31.3
4	28	4.6	105	14.3	121	8.4	21	3.2	50	3.6	325	6.8
5	119	19.6	61	8.3	23	1.6	3	0.5	4	0.3	210	4.4
6	0	0	0	0	6	0.4	4	0.6	3	0.2	13	0.3
7–8–9	303	49.9	142	19.3	74	5.1	18	2.8	3	0.2	540	11.2
Total	607	100.0	736	100.0	1438	100.0	650	100.0	1373	100.0	4804	100.0

[a] Abbreviated titles have been used to refer to the five levels of educational attainment specified in question 6 (see Appendix).
[b] The code numbers refer to the following general occupational classifications. We have followed the practice of the Department of Statistics by combining categories 0 and 1 and 7, 8 and 9.

0–1 Professional, technical and related workers
2 Administrative and managerial workers
3 Clerical and related workers
4 Sales workers
5 Service workers
6 Agricultural, animal husbandry, and forestry workers
7–8–9 Production and related workers, and transport equipment operators and laborers.

As mentioned, respondents were selected to represent a random sample of public and private sector employees. Table I summarizes the distribution of respondents by level of educational attainment and by occupation. It is apparent that the jobs in categories 0–1, 2, and 3 tend to be held predominantly by highly educated respondents while those in categories 7–8–9 are held by poorly educated respondents.

Furthermore respondents who have completed the most formal schooling earn the highest average salaries per month (B.A. = JD 71.2; institute = JD 39.7; secondary = 37.0; preparatory = 35.8;

less than preparatory = 26.0). Respondents with a B.A. or beyond, employed as administrative and managerial workers (category 2), reported the highest average salaries ($\bar{x}$ = JD 84.4) while those with less than preparatory completion, employed as service workers (category 5), reported the lowest ($\bar{x}$ = JD 19.7). We were very surprised to learn that the average salaries earned per month by respondents who had completed preparatory, secondary, or institute training differed so little. In addition, the salaries reported by respondents from the villages ($\bar{x}$ = JD 31.1) were substantially lower than those reported by people from Amman ($\bar{x}$ = JD 46.2) or the various towns ($\bar{x}$ = 45.4).

We believe that our respondents do in fact represent one important sample of the Jordanian population. They represent a diverse group of citizens whose viewpoints and experiences will surely become increasingly important and sought after as the country continues to move rapidly to expand its educational facilities and to broaden and strengthen its base of economic growth. Although we have over-represented highly educated respondents in our sample, it should be remembered that we did select subjects randomly at each of the five educational levels.

It is also important to note that our sample does *not* include any representatives from the armed forces, other security personnel, or self-employed farmers. These groups of people do comprise a substantial segment of the Jordanian citizenry and of its work force. Although we can speculate that farmers, as a group, have relatively little need for formal English training, we do feel that the needs of military and other security personnel should be considered by the government when reviewing its various programs of English language instruction and the role of English instruction in the total curriculum.

Results of the Field Study

In this section we present the results from our field study. For each question we summarize the general responses and then, when appropriate, examine the answers to a particular item as a function of the respondents' level of educational attainment, occupation, location of work, or sex. Copies of the tables are on permanent file at the Ministry of Education and at the Department of Statistics in Amman.

1. *Language Use at Work*

In answer to the question 'What languages (including Arabic) do you use in your work' (see Appendix A, question 10), Arabic was listed as the language most frequently used by 93% of the respondents (7% listed English) while English was listed as the language used second most frequently. Sixty-three per cent of all respondents (3023 of 4804) indicated that they use English at work. Conversely, 37% of all respondents (1781 of 4804) reported that they do *not* use English at work. Of those who do use English, 10% reported it to be their most frequently used language while 89% reported it to be the language which they used second most frequently. Other languages such as French and German were reported by fewer than 1% of the respondents.

What factors characterize the 3023 respondents who report using English at work? In Table II we have summarized the distribution of respondents who report using English at work by occupation and education. Respondents employed in administrative or managerial jobs, including government administrators, report the highest use of English at work (85%), followed by sales people (74%), professional or technical workers, including teachers (70%), and clerical and related employees (62%). Far fewer respondents in other occupations report using English at work — service workers (36%), production and related employees (27%) and agricultural and forestry workers (23%). As might be expected, a relatively small proportion of those with little education report using English (e.g., 26% of the respondents with less than preparatory completion) while 80% of the respondents with a B.A. report using English.

Table II. *Proportion of Respondents Who Report Using English at Work by Occupation and Education*

	Educational attainment					
Occupation[a]	Less than preparatory	Preparatory	Secondary	Institute	B.A.	Total
0–1	20/37 = 54[b]	78/113 = 69	256/435 = 59	166/268 = 62	630/797 = 79	1150/1650 = 70
2	8/13 = 61	43/64 = 67	114/126 = 90	76/91 = 84	236/270 = 87	477/564 = 85
3	48/107 = 45	140/251 = 56	399/653 = 61	162/245 = 66	183/247 = 74	932/1502 = 62
4	12/28 = 43	75/105 = 71	101/121 = 83	12/21 = 57	41/50 = 82	241/325 = 74
5	29/119 = 24	27/61 = 44	14/23 = 61	3/3 = 100	2/4 = 50	75/210 = 36
6	0/0 = 0	0/0 = 0	1/6 = 17	1/4 = 25	1/3 = 33	3/13 = 23
7–8–9	41/303 = 14	56/142 = 39	38/74 = 51	9/18 = 50	1/3 = 33	145/540 = 27
Total	158/607 = 26	419/736 = 57	923/1438 = 64	429/650 = 66	1094/1373 = 80	3023/4804 = 63

[a] See footnote b, Table I for an explanation of this entry.
[b] This indicates that twenty out of the thirty-seven (or 54%) respondents from occupational category 0–1 who had less than preparatory completion reported using English at work.

There appears to be relatively little variation in English usage among respondents who completed preparatory education (57%), secondary education (64%), or institute training (66%). Overall the respondents who report using English most are administrative or managerial personnel with university degrees (87%), while those who report using English least are production or related employees with less than preparatory completion (14%).[2]

Additional information was obtained about the usefulness and necessity for English from question 31, 'Is a knowledge of English necessary for success in your job?' Fifty-four per cent of *all* respondents replied 'Yes, definitely', 24% answered 'It helps; but it's not necessary'; 22% replied 'No'. Thus 78% of the respondents regard English as being either helpful or necessary for job success. By comparing this figure with the 63% who actually report using English at work we can draw the tentative conclusion that an additional 15% of our respondents might be able to utilize English profitably in their jobs. On the other hand only 54% of the respondents did indicate that a knowledge of English was definitely necessary for job success.

Which respondents report a definite necessity for English? Those employed in administrative or managerial positions report the greatest need for English (73%), followed by professional or technical employees (65%), sales people (64%), clerical or related workers (48%), agricultural or forestry workers (38%), service personnel (27%), and finally, production or related workers (25%). Thus a high proportion of the 'white collar' workers (occupations 0–1, 2, 3, 4) do seem to require a knowledge of English for job success. We find it extremely interesting, however, that even among the other occupations which traditionally require less formal education as a precondition to employment (categories 5, 6, 7–8–9), at least 25% of the respondents report a need for English. Likewise, there exists a positive relationship between level of educational attainment and the need for English for job success (B.A. graduates = 73%; institute = 55%; secondary completion = 54%; preparatory completion = 48%; less than preparatory completion = 23%). Presumably these data reflect in part the fact that those occupations which require the type of special training that may be acquired by advanced education also require a knowledge of English.

In general it seems as though respondents at the lower levels of education who use English at work hold relatively *better* jobs than their counterparts with similar educational backgrounds who do not report using English (see Table III). However, the nature of this

Table III. *Relationship Between Distribution of Respondents by Education and Occupation and Distribution of Respondents Who Use English at Work by Education and Occupations*

| | Less than preparatory | | | | Preparatory | | | |
| | Total | | Use English at work | | Total | | Use English at work | |
Occupation	F	%	F	%	F	%	F	%
0–1	37	6.1	20	12.7	113	15.4	78	18.6
2	13	2.1	8	5.1	64	8.7	43	10.8
3	107	17.6	48	30.4	251	34.1	140	33.4
4	28	4.6	12	7.6	105	14.3	75	17.9
5	119	19.6	29	18.4	61	8.3	27	6.4
6	0	0.0	0	0.0	0	0	0	0.0
7–8–9	303	49.9	41	25.9	142	19.3	56	13.4
Total	607	100.0	158	100.0	736	100.0	419	100.0

| | Secondary | | | | Institute | | | |
| | Total | | Use English at work | | Total | | Use English at work | |
Occupation	F	%	F	%	F	%	F	%
0–1	435	30.3	256	27.7	268	41.2	166	38.7
2	126	8.8	114	12.4	91	14.0	76	17.7
3	653	45.4	399	43.2	245	37.7	162	37.8
4	121	8.4	101	10.9	21	3.2	12	2.8
5	23	1.6	14	1.5	3	0.5	3	0.7
6	6	0.4	1	0.1	4	0.6	1	0.2
7–8–9	74	5.1	38	4.1	18	2.8	9	2.1
Total	1438	100.0	923	100.0	650	100.0	429	100.0

| | B.A. | | | |
| | Total | | Use English at work | |
Occupation	F	%	F	%
0–1	797	58.0	630	57.6
2	270	19.7	236	21.6
3	246	17.9	183	16.7
4	50	3.6	41	3.7
5	4	0.3	2	0.2
6	3	0.2	1	0.1
7–8–9	3	0.2	1	0.1
Total	1373	100.0	1094	100.0

relationship remains open to further investigation.

In addition we found that female respondents reported a greater need of English for job success (61%) than did males (54%). This apparent discrepancy may be a statistical artifact resulting from our relatively small and perhaps atypical sample of females or may simply reflect the fact that females more often choose occupations which require a knowledge of English. Lastly, a knowledge of English seems to be a much more important criterion for job success in Amman (56%) and in the towns (52%) than in the villages (38%).

2. Use of English at Work for Specific Purposes

Questions 11, 12, and 13 probed the frequency with which respondents use English for a variety of specific purposes at work with diverse interlocutors. We wanted to find out what percentage of the respondents who had reported that they use English at work (63% of our sample) actually do so on a *daily* basis. Grouping together the responses of those who indicated that they use English many times daily and those who reported that they use English at least once every day, we found that 41% (of the 3023 respondents identified above) use English to discuss business or technical matters at least once every day with their colleagues: 32% with their superiors; 26% with clients; and 21% with subordinates. We then examined in detail the relationship between the respondents' use of English with colleagues and their level of educational attainment and occupation. Daily use of English is associated with both a high level of educational attainment (B.A. = 50%; institute completion = 44%; secondary completion = 36%; preparatory completion = 31%; less than preparatory completion = 27%)[3] and a relatively high status job (e.g., professional and technical workers = 57% but service personnel = 20%). These data are summarized in Table IV.

The relative frequency of using English on a daily basis did not vary between Amman (41%), and the towns (43%); but only 28% of the villagers report using English daily. It appears, then, that relatively few villagers use English at work, and furthermore that they do so less frequently than their urban counterparts.

The responses to questions 11 and 12 permit us to compare the percentage of respondents who report using English at work for business versus nonbusiness purposes. These data may be examined by comparing the entries in Tables V and VI. The data indicate that the respondents do *not*, for the most part, use English at work for informal communication. Except for a relatively small number of

Table IV. Respondents Using English at Work Every Day to Discuss Business with Colleagues by Level of Educational Attainment and Occupation.

Occupation	Educational attainment																	
	Less than preparatory			Preparatory			Secondary			Institute			B.A.			Total		
	F	N[a]	%	F	N	%	F	N	%	F	N	%	F	N	%	F	N	%
0–1	10	20	50.0	36	78	46.1	103	256	40.2	79	166	47.6	360	630	57.1	588	1150	51.1
2	0	8	0.0	14	43	32.5	54	114	47.3	35	76	46.1	102	236	43.2	205	477	43.0
3	11	48	22.9	47	140	33.6	137	399	34.4	63	162	38.9	70	183	38.2	328	932	35.2
4	2	12	16.7	10	75	13.4	24	101	23.8	3	12	25.0	13	41	31.7	52	241	21.6
5	6	29	20.7	2	27	7.3	3	14	21.4	3	3	100.0	1	2	50.0	15	70	21.4
6	0	0	0.0	0	0	0.0	0	1	0.0	0	1	0.0	1	1	100.0	1	13	7.7
7–8–9	13	41	31.7	22	56	39.3	13	38	34.2	5	9	55.6	1	1	100.0	54	145	37.5
Total	42	158	26.6	131	419	31.2	334	923	36.1	188	429	43.8	548	1094	50.1	1243	3023	41

a This entry refers to the number of respondents in each category who had previously reported that they use English at work. It does *not* refer to the total number of respondents in each category. The marginal percentages for the number of respondents, out of the total possible in each category, who report using English daily are as follows: Occupation 0–1 = 36%; 2 = 36%; 3 = 22%; 4 = 16%; 5 = 7%; 6 = 8%; 7–8–9 = 10%; Total = 26%; education less than preparatory = 7%; preparatory = 18%; secondary = 23%; institute = 29%; B.A. = 40%.

Table V. *English Use at Work to Discuss Business Matters*

	Colleagues		Superiors		Subordinates		Customers	
Frequency	F	%	F	%	F	%	F	%
Never	1040	34.4	1232	40.8	1476	58.9	1007	34.2
Very rarely	498	16.5	519	17.2	383	15.3	766	26.0
At least once per week	242	8.0	290	9.6	122	4.9	407	13.8
At least once per day	390	12.9	366	12.1	213	8.5	314	10.7
Many times daily	853	28.2	616	20.4	313	12.5	449	15.3
Total	3023	100.0	3023	100.0	2507	100.0	2943	100.0
(Not applicable)[a]	(1781)	–	(1781)	–	(2297)	–	(1861)	–

a The category 'Not applicable' was used to identify people who intentionally skipped over a question or portion of a question because they did not use English for one of the purposes specified.

Table VI. *English Use at Work to Discuss Nonbusiness Matters*

	Colleagues		Superiors		Subordinates		Customers	
Frequency	F	%	F	%	F	%	F	%
Never	1559	51.6	1939	64.1	1881	74.3	1708	58.0
Very rarely	616	20.4	508	16.8	371	14.7	654	22.2
At least once per week	285	9.4	205	6.8	104	4.1	248	8.4
At least once per day	314	10.4	203	6.7	84	3.3	159	5.4
Many times daily	249	8.2	168	5.6	92	3.6	177	6.0
Total	3023	100.0	3023	100.0	2532	100.0	2946	100.0
(Not applicable)[a]	(1781)	–	(1781)	–	(2272)	–	(1858)	–

a The category 'Not applicable' was used to identify people who intentionally skipped over a question or a portion of a question because they did not use English for one of the purposes specified.

respondents, English is used at work for *business* purposes.

With question 13 we attempted to examine, in more detail, how Jordanians actually use English at work. The data, summarized in Table VII, indicate that they use English most frequently to read for professional advancement (39% of those who use English do this on a daily basis) or to read instructions or directions (32% daily). We presume that people who read for professional advancement have relatively higher status jobs, but we did not specifically investigate this relationship. We found it interesting that 29% of the respondents report filling out forms in English on a daily basis while 20% write daily English business letters. The responses to questions 11 and 13 reveal that a substantial number of Jordanians do use English regularly for business purposes, particularly to communicate orally with their colleagues (26% of *all* respondents) or their superiors (20%),

Table VII. English Use at Work for Diverse Tasks.

Frequency	Listen to instructions		Give instructions		Read directions		Read journals		Complete forms		Write letters	
	F	%	F	%	F	%	F	%	F	%	F	%
Never	1426	47.2	2088	69.1	990	32.7	825	27.3	1035	34.2	1521	50.3
Very rarely	447	14.8	307	10.2	550	18.2	436	14.4	702	23.2	526	17.4
At least once per week	377	12.5	154	5.1	514	17.0	570	18.9	405	13.4	358	11.8
At least once per day	321	10.6	197	6.5	376	12.4	567	18.8	306	10.1	238	7.9
Many times daily	452	15.0	277	9.2	593	19.6	625	20.7	575	19.0	380	12.6
Total	3023	100.0	3023	100.0	3023	100.0	3023	100.0	3023	100.0	3023	100.0
(Not applicable)a	(1781)	–	(1781)	–	(1781)	–	(1781)	–	(1781)	–	(1781)	–

a The category 'Not applicable' was used to identify people who intentionally skipped over a question or a portion of a question because they did not use English for one of the purposes specified.

and to read for professional advancement (25%), to read instructions, directions or orders (20%), or to fill out forms (18%).

Thus we wish to draw the tentative conclusion that there does exist, at the levels of Jordanian society which we have sampled, a demonstrated need for English.

3. English Use Outside Work

Four questions, 14–17, were included to probe the respondents' use of English outside work. Arabic was reported to be the language used most frequently outside work by 98% of all respondents. The language used next most widely was English, which was listed by 51% of all respondents (2466 out of 4804). Of these, 2% report that they use it most frequently while 94% report it to be the language used second most frequently. French, German, and 'other' were each claimed by fewer than 5% of the respondents.

In question 16 we examined the respondents' use of English outside work to discuss matters *not* related to work with certain interlocutors. That is, we examined their use of English for informal communication. The data, summarized in Table VIII, reveal that more respondents regularly use English outside their work for informal communication with certain people than use it for informal purposes at work (compare Tables VI and VIII). For example, 15% of *all* respondents use English outside work at least once every day to communicate with their family (14% with their friends) compared with 12% who use English with colleagues at work for informal communication. However, only 8% of the respondents regularly use English with their colleagues outside work for informal purposes compared with 12% at work.

When we examine the respondents' use of English outside work for other purposes, a slightly different pattern emerges. Thirty-nine per cent of *all* respondents report that they use English once or more *every day* for listening to the radio, the movies, television, etc. This figure represents 72% of those respondents who reported using English for informal purposes. The informants' responses to question 17 are summarized in Table IX.

Unfortunately we have no more specific information about how these respondents actually use English. For example, do they listen to radio programs from the BBC? If so, what type of programs – news, popular music, etc. – do they prefer? Do they frequently attend English language movies? If so, how many of them listen to the dialogue and how many merely read the Arabic subtitles?

We were also interested to note that 21% of *all* respondents use English daily to read for professional advancement (this represents 38% of those reporting the use of English outside business). Although we did not examine the pattern of responses to question 17 as a function of education or occupation, we can speculate that the bulk of these 992 respondents have university degrees and hold relatively high-status jobs. If such a large proportion of the respondents do find it necessary or desirable to read English materials outside work on a daily basis, this suggests that the majority of Jordanians who hope to obtain employment in occupational categories 0–1, 2, or 3 could profit by very extensive training in English, and particularly that they need to be exposed formally and systematically to a much broader quantity and range of reading materials than is now the case.

Respondents were asked in question 15 to what extent they used English *outside* work to discuss business matters with a variety of individuals. Their answers, which have not been summarized in tabular form, indicated that a majority of the respondents do *not* use English for this purpose. (With family, 85% of all respondents *never* use English to discuss business matters; with friends, 70%; with fellow workers, 73%; with professional people, 72%; with government employees, 84%; and with strangers, 78%.) The responses to this question must also reflect, at least partly, the fact that the respondents spend relatively little time discussing their business concerns outside of working hours in any language with these categories of people.

In the final question dealing with their use of English (question 18) the respondents were asked to indicate what percentage of their total use of English occurs at work and what percentage occurs outside of work. They reported that 57% of their English use is work related and 43% not work related. The data, summarized in Table X, indicate a disproportionately high use of English *at work* by respondents with preparatory completion or less (63%). These data reinforce the notion that there exists a real need for English at work on the part of a sizeable segment of Jordanians who have completed only the compulsory cycle of education or less. These data do not of course provide us with any direct information about *how much* English is used at work or outside work in any absolute terms.

Next we shall examine the respondents' reported proficiency in English and the manner in which they acquired this skill.

Table VIII. *English Use Outside Work to Discuss Nonbusiness Matters*

Frequency	Family		Friends		Colleagues		Professional people		Government employees		Strangers	
	F	%	F	%	F	%	F	%	F	%	F	%
Never	1046	39.9	509	19.4	1111	42.4	1300	49.6	1628	62.1	1208	46.1
Very rarely	487	18.6	867	33.1	742	28.3	659	25.1	654	24.9	797	30.4
At least once per week	361	13.8	580	22.1	335	12.8	298	11.4	206	7.9	297	11.3
At least once per day	435	16.6	394	15.0	266	10.1	189	7.2	83	3.2	160	6.1
Many times daily	294	11.2	273	10.4	169	6.4	177	6.7	52	2.0	161	6.1
Total	2623	100.0	2623	100.0	2623	100.0	2623	100.0	2623	100.0	2623	100.0
(No answers)	(2181)	–	(2181)	–	(2181)	–	(2181)	–	(2181)	–	(2181)	–

Table IX. *English Use Outside Work for Diverse Purposes*

Frequency	Read for pleasure		Read serious literature		Read professional journals		Listen to mass media		Write personal letters	
	F	%	F	%	F	%	F	%	F	%
Never	401	15.3	944	36.0	637	24.3	111	4.2	999	38.1
Very rarely	626	23.9	726	27.7	350	13.3	216	8.2	991	37.8
At least once per week	885	33.7	532	20.3	644	24.6	399	15.2	496	18.9
At least once per day	428	16.3	256	9.8	595	22.7	1113	42.4	67	2.6
Many times daily	283	10.8	165	6.3	397	15.1	784	29.9	70	2.7
Total	2623	100.0	2623	100.0	2623	100.0	2623	100.0	2623	100.0
(No answers)	(2181)	–	(2181)	–	(2181)	–	(2181)	–	(2181)	–

Table X. *Average Percentage of English Used at Work by Level of Educational Attainment and by Occupation*

Occupation	Educational attainment: Less than preparatory	Preparatory	Secondary	Institute	B.A.	Total
0–1	74.7	64.8	51.5	50.7	57.0	55.5
2	83.8	66.5	65.4	62.6	58.8	62.1
3	68.5	60.5	52.9	53.6	50.0	54.4
4	83.5	73.9	67.2	61.3	55.8	67.7
5	56.5	53.8	61.5	56.7	82.5	56.9
6	—	—	36.7	75.0	30.0	43.0
7–8–9	50.1	58.2	51.7	48.8	50.0	53.3
Total	62.8	63.1	55.3	54.0	56.1	56.9

4. *Subjective Proficiency in English*

Since the self-rating scale has been shown by Macnamara (1969) to be a reasonably reliable indicator of relative foreign language skill, we asked all respondents to estimate their listening comprehension, speaking, reading, and writing skills in English using a series of subjective rating scales (questions 23–26). Their responses are sum-

Table XI. *Subjective Proficiency in English*[a]

	Skill							
	Understanding		Speaking		Reading		Writing	
Degree	F	%	F	%	F	%	F	%
Not at all	73	1.5	105	2.2	102	2.1	110	2.3
Only a few words	502	10.4	452	9.4	500	10.4	437	9.1
Basic	1353	28.2	1943	40.4	1157	24.1	1352	28.1
Most	1120	23.3	1727	35.9	2529	52.6	2553	53.1
Everything by Jordanians[b]	920	19.2	–	–	–	–	–	–
Everything	836	17.4	577	12.0	516	10.7	352	7.3
Total	4804	100.0	4804	100.0	4804	100.0	4804	100.0

a The reader should refer to the Appendix, questions 23–26, for the exact wording of the items and the response alternatives.

b This response alternative was included only for question 23.

marized in Table XI. The number of respondents reporting a very high level of proficiency (i.e., those who chose the response alternatives 'most' or 'everything') was striking: understanding = 60% of all respondents; speaking = 48%; reading = 63%; writing = 60%. This high level of reported proficiency may reflect an over-estimate by the respondents of the efficacy of their lengthy English study (i.e., 72% of the sample had completed secondary schooling), or the fact that many respondents have had the opportunity to use English regularly at work since they completed their formal schooling. Although the respondents may have over-estimated their subjective proficiency, it is nevertheless important that they rated their perceived level of achievement in speaking substantially lower than their level of achievement for reading, writing, or understanding.

5. Reasons for Studying English
Respondents were asked to consider, in question 35, five possible reasons for studying English and to rank them in order of personal relevance from most important to least. The consensus of the respondents was that the *most* important reason for studying English is because a person who masters English has a much better chance of studying abroad or of obtaining a job abroad ($\bar{x}$ = 2.08).[4] This was followed by the statement that a person who masters English has a much better chance of obtaining a job in Jordan ($\bar{x}$ = 2.79). Both of these statements characterize reasons that have been referred to by previous researchers as instrumental. The finding that respondents perceive a thorough mastery of English as important for instrumental reasons appears consistent with their responses to other items on the questionnaire where they reported a positive relationship between knowledge of English and job success. The other reasons for considering the study of English to be important were as follows: a person who masters English can keep himself better informed about developments outside the Arab world ($\bar{x}$ = 2.90); a person who masters English can become more sensitive to the values and traditions of people from various parts of the world ($\bar{x}$ = 3.51); and, least important, a person who masters English has better access to world literature ($\bar{x}$ = 3.71). These data suggest strongly that our respondents view English as a vehicle for educational and occupational mobility.

The inference is supported by the data reported in Table XII which indicate a positive relationship between a perceived high level of ability to understand, speak, read, and write English and holding a

Table XII. *Distribution of Respondents Who Report Superior Proficiency in English by Occupation*[a]

Occupation	Understanding F	%	Speaking F	%	Reading F	%	Writing F	%	Total F
0–1	1200	72.7	962	58.3	1289	78.1	1222	74.0	1650
2	487	84.7	426	75.5	483	85.6	468	83.0	564
3	844	56.1	640	42.7	929	61.9	881	58.7	1502
4	188	57.9	159	48.9	182	56.0	180	55.3	325
5	40	19.1	28	13.4	38	18.1	43	20.5	210
6	7	53.9	4	30.8	7	53.8	6	46.2	13
7–8–9	119	22.0	85	15.8	125	21.6	105	19.4	540
Total	2876	59.9	2304	47.9	3045	63.3	2905	60.4	4804

a The entries refer to the number of respondents in each occupation who report, for example, understanding *most* or *everything* of what they read. The percentage in each case is based on the total number of respondents for that occupational category.

good job (e.g., 85% of the respondents with category 2 jobs report superior proficiency in understanding spoken English in contrast to only 19% of those having category 5 jobs). There also exists a positive relationship between superior ability in English and average monthly salary. Eighty per cent of the respondents who earn JD 50 or more per month report being able to communicate *most* or *everything* that they wish to say in English versus only 27% of those who earn less than JD 35 per month. The same relationship applied to understanding (85% vs. 40%), reading (86% vs. 45%), and writing (83% vs. 43%).

We attempted to focus more directly on the relationship between occupational mobility and English knowledge with question 32, 'Has your knowledge of English made it possible for you to earn more money or to advance professionally?'. Forty-four per cent of all respondents replied that they 'have a better job because of [their] knowledge of English'. This response was given by 14% of those with less than preparatory completion, and the percentage increased with level of educational attainment (preparatory completion = 37%; secondary completion = 42%; institute completion = 44%; B.A. = 62%). Once again there was a noticeable relationship between occupational classification and perceived utility of English. Respondents employed as administrative or managerial workers (66%), sales personnel (56%), and professional or technical employees (52%) answered most positively followed by clerical or related workers (37%), agriculture or forestry workers (23%), production or related workers (18%), and service personnel (17%). Knowledge of English was more related to job advancement for the workers from Amman (46%) than for those from the towns (36%) or the villages (29%).

The data which have been presented thus far indicate that the mastery of English is extremely important for a reasonably large segment of the Jordan population. How do Jordanians acquire their knowledge of English? Do they feel that the current school programs of English language instruction train them adequately to meet their personal needs?

6. *Respondents' Impressions of their Formal School English Training*
As we mentioned previously, 82% of all respondents completed at least some portion of their education in government schools. With their diverse backgrounds, they would seem to constitute a group well qualified to comment upon the scope and adequacy of English training in Jordan. Respondents were asked to indicate in question 27 the extent to which each of six factors helped them personally to learn English. The distribution of responses to this question is summarized in Table XIII. The single most important factor (of those which we surveyed) appears to be school study: 52% of all respondents reported that their school study aided them 'very much'. The perceived importance of this factor is particularly meaningful since *all* Jordanians do have an opportunity to study English formally at school. They are at least partially satisfied by their school program. Traveling and studying in English-speaking countries was an important factor (48%) for those respondents (29% of the total) who

Table XIII. *Aids to Learning English*

| Factors | Degree of importance | | | | | | | | |
| | Not at all | | Somewhat | | Very much | | Total | | No answer |
	F	%	F	%	F	%	F	%	F
School study	193	4.0	2092	43.7	2499	52.2	4784	100.0	20
Private study	293	15.9	706	38.2	849	45.9	1848	100.0	2956
Home usage	1093	51.8	842	39.9	175	8.3	2110	100.0	2694
Work usage	692	21.1	1415	43.2	1169	35.7	3276	100.0	1528
Informal usage	711	26.5	1508	56.1	469	17.4	2688	100.0	2116
Travel and study	493	35.9	228	16.6	654	47.6	1375	100.0	3429

Table XIV. *Relationship Between Importance of School Study as an Aid to Learning English and Level of Educational Attainment*

Education	Not at all		Somewhat		Very much		Total	
	F	%	F	%	F	%	F	%
Less than preparatory	91	15.2	330	55.2	177	29.6	598	100.0
Preparatory	27	3.7	310	42.2	397	54.1	734	100.0
Secondary	27	1.9	608	42.5	796	55.6	1431	100.0
Institute	12	1.8	276	42.5	362	55.7	650	100.0
B.A.	36	2.6	568	41.4	767	55.9	1371	100.0
Total	193	4.0	2092	43.7	2499	52.2	4784	100.0

(Degree of importance)

answered that portion of the question. Speaking English with family members (8% 'very much') or with friends outside of work (17% 'very much') did not constitute major aids to learning English; but private study was important (46% 'very much') for a select group of respondents. We shall return to the issue of private study. Lastly, 36% of the respondents who use English at work reported that this experience has helped them to learn or presumably to improve their English.

These data suggest first that formal schooling may provide a large number of individuals with a set of basic skills to which they may later add depending upon their individual needs and, more importantly, that the respondents' school experiences *per se* do not suffice to meet their English needs.

The responses to two parts of this question (27) have been summarized in Tables XIV and XV. Only 30% of the respondents who have completed less than preparatory schooling report that their school study aided them 'very much' while at least 52% of each of the other groups report a similar degree of aid (see Table XIV). This represents a discrepancy of 22% or more. By contrast, 29% of the respondents who have completed less than preparatory schooling report that using English at work aided them 'very much', while the consensus of the other four groups approximates 35% — a discrepancy of only 6% (see Table XV). Work experience, therefore, may

Table XV. *Relationship Between Importance of Speaking English at Work as an Aid to Learning English and Level of Educational Attainment*

| | Degree of importance | | | | | | | |
| | Not at all | | Somewhat | | Very much | | Total | |
Education	F	%	F	%	F	%	F	%
Less than preparatory	59	31.1	76	40.0	55	28.9	190	100.0
Preparatory	85	18.8	209	46.2	158	35.0	452	100.0
Secondary	235	23.0	429	42.1	356	34.9	1020	100.0
Institute	84	18.3	209	45.5	166	36.2	459	100.0
B.A.	229	19.8	492	42.6	434	37.6	1155	100.0
Total	692	21.1	1415	43.2	1169	35.7	3276	100.0

represent a relatively more important factor in English mastery for the less-educated respondents.

Reports by the respondents concerning their subjective proficiency in English complement the data reported in Table XIV. The data, presented in Table XVI, indicate a positive relationship between a perceived high level of ability to understand, speak, read, and write English and level of educational attainment (e.g., 91% of those respondents with a B.A. report superior proficiency in reading English, but only 10% of those who have completed less than

Table XVI. *Distribution of Respondents Who Report Superior Proficiency in English by Level of Educational Attainment*[a]

| | Understanding | | Speaking | | Reading | | Writing | | Total |
Education	F	%	F	%	F	%	F	%	F
Less than preparatory	57	9.4	40	6.6	63	10.4	56	9.2	607
Preparatory	290	39.4	209	28.4	278	37.7	265	36.0	736
Secondary	870	60.5	662	46.0	945	65.7	909	63.2	1438
Institute -	469	72.2	350	53.9	507	78.0	478	73.5	650
B.A.	1190	86.6	1043	76.0	1252	91.2	1197	87.2	1373
Total	2876	59.9	2304	47.9	3045	63.3	2905	60.4	4804

[a] The entries refer to the number of respondents at each educational level who report, for example, understanding *most* or *everything* of what they read. The percentage in each case is based on the total number of respondents for that educational level.

Table XVII.   *Distribution of Respondents Who Report Superior Proficiency in English by Total Years Study of English*[a]

Years of study	Understanding		Speaking		Reading		Writing		Total
	F	%	F	%	F	%	F	%	F
5 or less	75	10.1	41	5.5	79	10.6	68	9.1	744
6	67	33.6	52	26.1	71	35.7	68	34.4	199
7	122	43.6	90	32.1	115	41.1	109	38.9	280
8	493	49.9	337	34.0	569	57.1	526	53.2	989
9	213	66.9	165	51.9	231	72.6	215	67.6	318
10	294	73.7	218	54.6	310	77.7	298	74.7	399
11	284	79.8	220	61.8	287	80.6	270	75.8	356
12	631	79.8	538	68.1	690	87.3	661	83.7	790
More than 12	697	95.6	643	88.2	693	95.1	690	94.7	729
Total	2876	59.9	2304	42.9	3045	63.3	2905	60.4	4804

[a] The entries refer to the number of respondents who have studied English for the years specified who reported, for example, that they understand *most* or *everything* of what they read. The percentage in each case is based on the total number of respondents for each of the years of study.

preparatory schooling). It is important to note that there are regular increments in perceived ability associated with *each* increase in level of educational attainment although the difference is greatest in every case between those who have not completed preparatory schooling and those who have completed their preparatory education. These data are complemented by those summarized in Table XVII which indicate a similar positive relationship between a perceived high level of ability to understand, speak, read, and write English and the number of years of English study. The discrepancies in perceived ability between those who have studied for five years or less versus six years, eight years versus nine years, and twelve years versus more than twelve years are particularly noteworthy. These correspond, respectively, with the completion of preparatory schooling and the beginning of secondary study, the completion of secondary schooling and the beginning of advanced study, and with the completion of university study. One inference to be drawn is that the level of perceived ability in English by respondents with less than preparatory completion is *very* low.

To gain additional information about the impact of school study on English mastery, we asked a series of direct questions about the respondents' views of their school experiences. In response to question 36, 55% of *all* respondents reported that they believe that their children will *not* learn to communicate effectively in English by following the present government school curriculum. An additional

32% reported that they believe that their children will learn to communicate effectively following the government school curriculum if it is *supplemented* by outside help. Only 7% of the respondents indicated that school study alone would be sufficient. The respondents' impressions, if accurate, are quite disturbing. They suggest that neither the explicit or implicit instructional aims of the Ministry for the teaching of English are being met. The present data also suggest that secondary school graduates who attend the science faculty at the University of Jordan and are now expected to study *via* English might not be well enough prepared for this undertaking.

These relatively pessimistic views were somewhat tempered by the report (question 28) that 63% of all respondents considered their teachers of English to have been either 'excellent' or 'moderately good'. Only 11% remembered their teachers as being 'poor'.

The responses to question 29 ('do you wish your teachers of English had given more emphasis to any of the following' [nine activities or skills]) are summarized in Table XVIII. The data appear to suggest that relatively more emphasis should have been given to active skills such as free conversation, pronunciation, writing and composition, and translation. Presumably these beliefs reflect the respondents' occupational needs. We were surprised, however, that so few respondents indicated a desire to have read more material chosen from specific fields such as science, commerce, or agriculture.

Table XVIII. *Desire for Increased Emphasis Within English Program*

| | Answer | | | | | | |
| | Yes | | No | | Total | | No response |
Activity	F	%	F	%	F	%	N
Grammar rules	3814	80.8	905	19.2	4719	100.0	85
Free conversation	4431	93.6	301	6.4	4732	100.0	72
Serious literature	2064	44.0	2627	56.0	4691	100.0	113
Specific literature	3170	67.2	1548	32.8	4718	100.0	86
Writing mechanics	3427	72.3	1313	27.7	4740	100.0	64
Pronunciation	4111	86.8	623	13.2	4734	100.0	70
Rapid reading	3061	65.4	1616	34.6	4677	100.0	127
Composition	4187	88.4	549	11.6	4736	100.0	68
Translation	4059	85.8	670	14.2	4729	100.0	75

Table XIX.　Relationship Between Most Important English Skill and Occupation

Activity	Occupation															
	0–1		2		3		4		5		6		7–8–9		Total	
	F	%	F	%	F	%	F	%	F	%	F	%	F	%	F	%
Grammar rules	395	24.0	126	22.6	412	27.5	90	28.8	69	34.5	3	23.1	140	27.9	1235	26.1
Free conversation	859	52.2	278	49.9	677	45.3	149	47.6	63	31.5	6	46.2	167	33.3	2199	46.5
Serious literature	28	1.7	18	3.2	28	1.9	5	1.6	3	1.5	0	0.0	11	2.2	93	2.0
Specific literature	55	3.3	20	3.6	34	2.3	16	5.1	7	3.5	1	7.7	21	4.2	154	3.3
Writing mechanics	8	0.5	2	0.4	7	0.5	1	0.3	4	2.0	0	0.0	11	2.2	33	0.7
Pronunciation	51	3.1	20	3.6	39	2.6	6	1.9	10	5.0	2	15.4	26	5.2	154	3.3
Rapid reading	15	0.9	13	2.3	15	1.0	10	3.2	4	2.0	0	0.0	10	2.0	67	1.4
Composition	159	9.1	43	7.7	167	11.2	19	6.1	23	11.5	1	7.7	51	10.2	453	9.6
Translation	86	5.2	37	6.6	117	7.8	17	5.4	17	8.5	0	0.0	65	12.9	339	7.2
Total	1646	100.0	557	100.0	1496	100.0	313	100.0	210	100.0	13	100.0	502	100.0	4727	100.0
(No answers)	(4)		(7)		(6)		(12)		(10)		(0)		(38)		(77)	

Question 30 was intended to complement and extend question 29. Respondents were asked to identify the one skill which they considered to be *most important*. Their responses are summarized by occupation in Table XIX. Remember that they were asked to identify the one most important skill, not the one skill which most needed to receive additional attention.

Free conversation was selected by the largest number of respondents from each occupation except category 5, service workers, as the *most important* skill. This was followed by rules of English grammar, writing and composition, and translation. Except for the minor discrepancy in category 5, the pattern of choices did not differ by occupation but rather represented accurately the consensus of all respondents. Presumably respondents need to be able to communicate effectively via English both orally and in writing, and they perceive that mastery of the rules of English grammar will help them to achieve these goals. We infer, however, that they view the mastery of English grammar rules as a means to accomplishing a specific purpose since fewer respondents indicated a desire for more emphasis on this activity (question 29) than on conversation, composition, or translation. This finding presumably also reflects the possibility that a great deal more of the respondents' class time had been directed toward teaching them grammar than encouraging spontaneous conversation.

As a corollary to this question, we asked (question 37) whether the Secondary Certificate Examination in English actually emphasizes the skills that respondents need in their work. Only 6% of all respondents replied that the examination system emphasizes the needed skills; 42% replied 'not at all'; and 20% answered 'only partially'. This finding supports our earlier observations about the lack of correspondence between the examination system and the explicit goals mentioned in the curriculum guide and presumably also reflects the need which many respondents have for oral proficiency.

In summary, the respondents' answers to questions 27, 29, 36, and 37 reveal their relatively firm belief that school programs alone do not adequately prepare them in English and their feeling that these programs are not likely to prepare their children adequately either.

Some Jordanians who believe that they have not been adequately prepared in English by their formal school training continue to study English privately.

616   G. Richard Tucker

7. Private Study of English

In an attempt to explore the strength of our respondents' commitment to improving their facility in English, we asked whether they had *ever* studied English privately (question 22) and whether they were *now* studying English privately (question 33). Both questions were designed for respondents who were following *formal* programs of English language instruction (e.g., attending courses at the Modern Language Center). Twenty-six per cent of all respondents reported that they had, at some time, studied English privately. This means that 26% of our sample felt, for one reason or another, the necessity to supplement the English instruction which they had received at school by additional formal study. Furthermore it is likely that the majority did so at their own personal expense. This finding further strengthens the argument that there exists a relationship between English mastery and occupational mobility, that respondents perceive the importance and magnitude of this relationship, and that the typical school program of English language instruction does *not* adequately prepare them to meet this need.

The data summarized in Table XX support this inference. These data indicate that the respondents with the *lowest* level of perceived superior ability in English skills are those who began their study of English from 1960 to the present. Interestingly, these are the respondents who because of their age are *least* likely to have had additional English language training beyond that offered in school.

Eighteen per cent of all respondents reported that they are *now* attempting to improve their English by formal study. We found, to

Table XX. *Distribution of Respondents Who Report Superior Proficiency in English by Date of Beginning Study*[a]

Date study began	Understanding		Speaking		Reading		Writing		Total
	F	%	F	%	F	%	F	%	N
Before 1920	10	83.4	9	75.0	8	66.7	9	75.0	12
1920–29	73	83.9	67	77.0	70	80.5	72	82.7	87
1930–39	246	70.7	231	66.3	247	71.0	230	66.1	348
1940–49	637	68.0	541	57.7	841	68.4	599	63.9	938
1950–59	1652	73.4	1281	49.2	1762	67.7	1690	64.9	2605
1960–present	258	31.7	175	21.5	317	39.0	305	37.5	814
Total	2876	59.9	2304	47.9	3045	63.3	2905	60.4	4804

[a] The entries refer to the number of respondents who began to study English in the years specified who reported, for example, that they understand *most* or *everything* of what they read. The percentage in each case is based on the total number of respondents for each of the dates of beginning study.

our suprise, that a sizeable percentage of respondents from each
occupation was *currently* studying English: professional workers =
18%; administrative and managerial workers = 20%; clerical workers =
23%; sales workers = 15%; service workers = 9%; agricultural workers =
23%; and production workers = 9%. We do *not* have any details about
their courses of study, the duration of their study, etc.; but we can
speculate that private study results in a higher level of proficiency
which in turn must afford greater occupational mobility.

In fact when we examine the relationship between 'reported
proficiency' and private study, we find that relatively more individuals (from 14% to 19%) who have studied privately report being
able to understand, speak, read, or write *most* or *everything* in
English than their counterparts who have not studied privately. Thus
private study appears to be associated with increased proficiency in
English.

Paradoxically the percentage of respondents studying privately
was related to level of educational attainment with relatively more
better-educated respondents currently studying English privately;
B.A. = 23%; institute = 19%; secondary = 19%; preparatory = 15%;
and less than preparatory = 7%. Thus it appears that those who have
already studied the greatest amount of English at school are most
likely to continue to study privately. This must reflect, in part, the
requirements for the types of occupations toward which well-
educated respondents realistically aspire. Men who work in villages
are least likely to study privately (8%), while women working in
Amman are most likely to do so (22%).

Apparently the English program in its present form does not
provide the training necessary to meet completely the needs of all
respondents. Do they feel that a mastery of English is important for
their children? How would they modify existing English language
programs to better train their children?

8. *Respondents' Views Concerning English Language Instruction for Children*

When asked in question 34, 'How important is it for you that your
children learn to communicate effectively via English?', 93% of the
respondents who answered the question (3528 of 4804, or 73%, did
reply) chose the alternative 'very important' and another 6% chose
'relatively important'. Respondents with families, then, are almost
unanimous in wanting their children to be able to communicate
effectively in English. Since they apparently believe the government

school program of English instruction will not adequately prepare their children (see question 36), what viable alternatives do they have available?

In question 38 we asked 'if you went to a private school (at any time from grade 1—12) or if you have sent a child or intend to send one to private school, what was your main reason for that?' This question was answered by an astonishingly high 83% of all respondents. (The most liberal estimate possible from our data indicates that 62% of the respondents may have attended a private school for some portion of their schooling.)

Fifty-six per cent of those who answered reported that they did (would do) so because private schools put more emphasis on English instruction than government schools. A sizeable minority (28%) believed that the general level of education is better in private schools than in government schools while an even smaller segment (4%) appreciate the religious instruction offered by some private schools (this reason was chosen with equal relative frequency by Christians and by Moslems). Clearly one alternative considered by a sizeable sample of our respondents, then, is a private school education for their children.

Do pupils who attend private school actually attain a higher level of English proficiency than their peers who attend government schools? The distribution of respondents who reported a superior level of English proficiency by their type of schooling is presented in Table XXI.

It is readily apparent from Table XXI that relatively few respondents who have attended *only* government schools (this includes various institutes as well as the University of Jordan) report superior proficiency in contrast to respondents from any other source or combination of sources of training. Unfortunately we did not distinguish between foreign and national private schools in our questionnaire. These data cannot be interpreted unambiguously, of course, but they are suggestive.

Do respondents believe that alternative approaches to English language instruction should be tried within the government system?

In answer to question 40, 61% of all respondents reported that they favored *more*, rather than fewer, hours of English instruction each week. They were not asked to distinguish between English instruction in the compulsory and the secondary cycle. In a related question (39) respondents were asked when they thought that government schools should begin to teach English; 87% of *all* respon-

Table XXI. *Distribution of Respondents Who Report Superior Proficiency in English by Type of Schooling*[a]

Type of schooling	Understanding		Speaking		Reading		Writing		Total
	F	%	F	%	F	%	F	%	F
Government only	735	40.6	510	28.2	837	46.3	772	42.6	1806
Private only	272	52.8	245	47.6	273	53.0	255	49.5	515
Government and private	471	60.0	337	43.0	473	60.3	451	57.5	784
Government and foreign[b]	748	78.7	624	65.7	807	84.9	782	82.3	950
Private and foreign	235	97.1	227	93.9	232	95.8	234	96.7	242
Government, private and foreign	351	88.4	306	77.1	358	90.2	351	88.4	397
Foreign only	64	59.9	55	51.4	65	60.7	60	56.1	107
Total	2876	59.9	2304	47.9	3045	63.3	2905	60.4	4804

[a] The entries refer to the number of respondents who attended each type of school or combination of types who reported, for example, understanding *most* or *everything* of what they read. The percentage in each case is based on the total number of respondents for that type of schooling.
[b] The term 'foreign' is here used to refer to schools located *outside* of Jordan.

dents favored introducing English *before* grade 5, the present level. The consensus of these respondents was that such teaching should commence at the grade 2 level ($\bar{x}$ = 1.73, standard deviation = 1.09)! We did not ask how they would staff such an expanded school program. Although we did not examine specifically the relationship between advocacy of such an expanded program and the respondents' level of occupation or education, it is clear that the overwhelming endorsement for the earlier introduction of English must cut across the various levels of our sample.

In question 41 respondents were asked whether government schools should begin to teach content subjects via English instead of continuing to teach them exclusively via Arabic; 64% of *all* respondents supported such a change. Furthermore 92% of the respondents who favored the change indicated that they would teach science via English, while 82% would teach mathematics. However, only 28% would teach social studies in English. This probably indicates a recognition of the necessity to better prepare students who will proceed to the University, where science instruction is conducted exclusively through the medium of English. The discrepancy between respondents' preferences for teaching science and mathematics but not social studies in English probably also reflects their awareness of the importance of presenting very personal information about their own values and traditions in their mother tongue together with some uncertainty about the possibility or desirability of translating these materials into English. The fact that people, although generally favorable to the idea of teaching content subjects via English, nevertheless reacted differentially in relation to different subjects prompts us to interpret these responses as carefully considered expressions of their firmly held beliefs about the necessity to broaden the base of English language instruction in Jordan.

The main focus of this field study centered on examining the relationship between the respondents' need for and use of English and their training in English. However, we also asked two questions about the teaching of foreign languages other than English.

9. Desirability of Teaching Other Foreign Languages

At the present time, with the minor exceptions noted earlier, English is the only foreign language taught in Jordanian government schools. The answers to two questions (43, 44) indicate the existence of popular support for teaching other foreign languages. Twenty-eight per cent of the respondents reported that they had studied a foreign language other than English. More than half of these people (16%) reported that they had studied this foreign language in Jordan. The two most widely studied foreign languages were French (51 individuals) and German (294 individuals). In contrast to the relatively small percentage of respondents who had studied an additional foreign language, 80% reported that they believed that government schools should offer instruction in a foreign language besides English. The respondents' own experiences appear to have affected their preferences, with 86% endorsing French at the most desirable language, and only 8% favoring German. These findings do seem consistent with the popular notion that French was considered to be the language of the 'educated' people in Jordan, at least during the 1940s.

CONCLUSIONS

The presentation of data from the field study necessarily involved a great deal of interpretive comment. In this brief concluding section, therefore, let me merely summarize the findings.

We have tabulated and examined the responses by 4804 randomly selected Jordanians to a forty-seven item, three-part questionnaire which probed their educational background (particularly their study of English), their use of and perceived need for English, and their views concerning the program of English language instruction in government schools.

We found that a large segment (63%) of the respondents reported that they use English at work. In fact 26% of *all* respondents indicated that they use English at work at least once *every day*. They use English primarily to communicate orally about business matters with their colleagues or their superiors and to read such materials as professional journals or printed directions.

Positive relationships were found between their level of proficiency in the various English skills and their type of occupation as well as their monthly salary. Even among respondents with relatively little formal education, the ones who reported a high degree of facility in English hold better jobs than those who lack this skill. Fifty-four per cent of all respondents reported that knowledge of English was necessary for success in their jobs (the average percentages, by occupation, ranged from 25% to 73%). Superior proficiency in English appears to be a virtual prerequisite for obtaining employment in many of the 'higher-status' occupations.

We should of course consider an alternative interpretation: that the widespread use of English at diverse levels of Jordanian society may not represent a real 'need' for communication via English; rather it may represent an artifact of the long and widespread training which provides such a large segment of the Jordanian population with systematic instruction in English. We cannot investigate the 'validity' of this apparent widespread need for English using the present data. We can only observe that mastery of English *is* associated in actual fact with occupational mobility and that the majority of respondents perceive this relationship.

The development of proficiency in English, then, represents an important goal for Jordanian citizens. Ninety-three percent of *all* respondents considered their children's development of effective communication skills in English to be 'very important'. The Ministry of Education takes very seriously its responsibility to train students in a foreign language. It attempts to fulfill this responsibility by offering a substantial program of English language instruction to all pupils beginning at grade 5.

Only 7% of the respondents felt that their children will learn to communicate effectively in English by following the present government school curriculum. This impression was substantiated, in part, by data which revealed that relatively few respondents who had attended only government schools reported a superior level of proficiency in English when compared with those who had attended any

622   G. Richard Tucker

other type or combination of types of schools. Furthermore 18% of
all respondents are currently studying English privately, and private
study seems to be related to increased proficiency.

Fifty-two per cent of the respondents reported that their school
study had helped them to learn English 'very much'. This observation,
plus the existence of a positive relationship between level of educational attainment (or years of school English study) and English proficiency suggests that students who have completed at least the preparatory cycle acquire a set of basic skills upon which to base and to
extend their later study of English. We infer, however, that some
later (presumably out-of-school) supplement to their school experience is necessary since the respondents who reported the lowest
relative level of superior proficiency had begun their study of English
most recently. Furthermore, the implementation of the school
English language program seems to be closely tied to the secondary
certificate examination and may not accurately reflect the actual
needs of the pupils. Respondents must communicate orally at work
and be able to read a variety of technical materials. They view 'free
conversation' as the single most important classroom activity and
wish that it had been emphasized more in their own training.

A majority of the respondents endorsed a series of relatively
'radical' suggestions for curricular reform: 87% supported the introduction of English earlier than the present grade 5 level; 64% supported the teaching of selected content subjects such as science and
mathematics via English; and 61% felt that more periods should be
devoted to English instruction each week. We believe that these
suggestions reflect the respondents' firmly held beliefs about the
necessity to broaden the base of English language instruction in
Jordan. Let me emphasize again that we have collected a large body
of facts and documented opinions from certain, *but not all,* segments
of the Jordanian population. Educational planners will, no doubt,
wish to consult representatives from some of the segments that we
did not sample, and they will certainly wish to reconsider and to
reinterpret the data which we have collected in light of subsequent
discussions and newly formulated questions.

REFERENCES

Brownell, John A.
1967 *Japan's Second Language* (= *Kappa Delta Pi International Education*

Monograph) (Champaign, Illinois, National Council of Teachers of English).
Campbell, Russell, Yehia El-Ezaby, and William Harrison
  1972 'English Language Teaching in Jordan: A Preliminary Study', mimeographed (Cairo, Ford Foundation).
Fishman, Joshua A., Charles A. Ferguson, and Jyotirindra Das Gupta, eds.
  1968 *Language Problems of Developing Nations* (New York, John Wiley).
Harrison, William W., Clifford H. Prator, and G. Richard Tucker
  1975 *English-Language Policy Survey of Jordan*, (Arlington, Va., Center for Applied Linguistics).
Jacobs, Robert, ed.
  1966 'English Language Teaching in Nigeria', mimeographed (Lagos, Ford Foundation).
Ladefoged, Peter, Ruth Glick, and Clive Criper
  1971 *Language in Uganda* (Nairobi, Oxford University Press).
Macnamara, John
  1969 'How can one measure the extent of a person's bilingual proficiency?', in L. G. Kelly, ed., *Description and Measurement of Bilingualism* (Toronto University Press) pp. 80–97.
Rubin, Joan and Bjorn Jernudd, eds.
  1971 *Can Language Be Planned?* (Honolulu, University of Hawaii Press).
Whiteley, Wilfred H., ed.
  1971 *Language Use and Social Change* (London, Oxford University Press).

NOTES

This article is a *revised version* of Chapters 5 and 6 from the *English Language Policy Survey of Jordan* by Harrison, Prator, and Tucker (1975). The research was supported by a grant from the Ford Foundation to the Jordanian Ministry of Education.
The research was completed and this article was written while I was a Project Specialist with the Ford Foundation. Although the Foundation made my services available, the views expressed in this report are my own.

1. This liaison committee consisted of Miss Salma Jayy'usi, Mr. Ahmad Tawil and Mr. Ibrahim Arna' out.
2. We realize that 100% of the individuals in one category did report using English, but there were only three respondents in that group.
3. I.e., 50% of the people with a B.A. who report that they use English at work with colleagues do so on a daily basis.
4. The value 1 was assigned to that reason chosen as most important, 2 for the second most important, etc. The arithmetic mean was then computed over all respondents for each of the five possible reasons. Hence, the lowest average identifies the most important reason; the highest average, the least important.

APPENDIX

Field Study Questionnaire: English Version
Background Data and Sociolinguistic Data
(Data punched on first IBM card)

1. Sex   Male 1
                                            Female 2

2. Age at last birthday   . . . .
   (in years)

3. Religion   Moslem 1
                                            Christian 2
                                            Other, specify 3

4. Present place of work   Amman 1
                                            Towns (pop. > 5000) . . . . . .
                                            2
                                            Villages (pop. < 5000) . . . . . .
                                            3

5. Years of schooling   . . . .
   (school or university)

6. Highest schooling standard
   (a) less than preparatory   1
   (b) Preparatory completed but less than
       junior general certification examination   2
   (c) Junior general certification examina-
       tion passed but less than B.A.   3
   (d) Institutes completed but less than B.A. 4
   (e) B.A. and beyond B.A. (M.D., Ph.D.,
       etc.)   5

7. Occupation   . . . .
   (actual work)

8. Monthly income from occupation   . . . .

9. Mother tongue   Arabic 1
                                            Other, specify 2

10. What languages, including Arabic, do you
    use in your work? (List by use frequency.)   1. . . . .
                                            2. . . . .
                                            3. . . . .
                                            4. . . . .

    Note: If English hasn't been listed go to
           Question 14.

11. Do you use English at work to discuss business or technical matters? How frequently?

With:	Never	Very rarely	At least once a week	At least once a day	Many times daily
(a) Fellow workers					
(b) Superiors					
(c) Subordinates					
(d) Customers (clients)					

12. Do you use English at work to discuss nonbusiness or nontechnical topics (weather, sports, current events, etc.) and how frequently?

With:	Never	Very rarely	At least once a week	At least once a day	Many times daily
(a) Fellow workers					
(b) Superiors					
(c) Subordinates					
(d) Customers (clients)					

13. Do you use English in:

	Never	Very rarely	At least once a week	At least once a day	Many times daily
(a) Listening to instructions presented orally					
(b) Giving instructions and directions orally					
(c) Reading instructions or directions or orders					
(d) Reading for professional advancement					
(e) Filling out forms					
(f) Writing business letters					

14. What languages, including Arabic, do you
    use outside of your work? (List by fre-
    quency of use).   1. ....
                                                   2. ....
                                                   3. ....
                                                   4. ....
    Note: If you don't use English outside
          your work, go directly to Question
          18.

15. Do you use English outside of your work (at home, recreation, etc.) to discuss
    matters related to work?

With:	Never	Very rarely	At least once a week	At least once a day	Many times daily
(a) Family members					
(b) Friends					
(c) Fellow workers					
(d) Professional people					
(e) Government employees					
(f) Strangers					

16. Do you use English outside of your work (at home, etc.) to discuss matters
    not related to work (current events, sports, etc.)?

With:	Never	Very rarely	At least once a week	At least once a day	Many times daily
(a) Family members					
(b) Friends					
(c) Fellow workers					
(d) Professional people					
(e) Government employees					
(f) Strangers					

17. Do you use English outside your work to:

	Never	Very rarely	At least once a week	At least once a day	Many times daily
(a) Read popular material (books, newspapers, etc.) for your own pleasure?					
(b) Read serious literature (novels, plays, etc.)? (c) Read for professional advancement?					
(d) Listen to the radio, watch TV, go to the movies, etc.?					
(e) Write personal letters?					

18. Considering your use of English at work and outside as 100%, what proportion is:
a) used at work? .... %
b) used outside work? .... %

English Language Proficiency, Study, and Attitudes
(Data punched on second IBM card)

19. In what year did you begin to study English? ....

20. For how many years did you study English (either as a subject or as a medium of instruction)?

(a) Total years of studying English ....
(b) Years in government schools (including University of Jordan) ....
(c) Years in private schools ....
(d) Years in schools outside of Jordan (including universities) ....

21. Did you study English in:

(a) Government schools only (including institutes and University of Jordan) 1
(b) Jordanian private schools only 2
(c) Government schools and Jordanian private schools (including institutes and University of Jordan) 3

(d) Government schools and schools outside Jordan (including institutes and
universities)   4
(e) Private schools and schools outside
Jordan (including institutes and univer-
sities)   5
(f) Government and private schools and
schools outside Jordan (including
institutes and universities)   6

22. Have you ever studied English privately
(formal study)?   Yes 1
                                                   No 2

23. How well can you understand spoken English?

(a) Not at all.   1
(b) Only a few words.   2
(c) Enough to satisfy my basic needs (e.g.,
locate food, transportation).   3
(d) Enough to understand most (but not
all) of what is said.   4
(e) I understand everything that is said by
Jordanians but not everything said by
native speakers.   5
(f) I understand everything that is said by
Jordanians as well as by native speakers.   6

24. How well can you speak English?

(a) Not at all.   1
(b) Only a few words.   2
(c) Well enough to communicate simple
ideas, requests.   3
(d) Well enough to communicate most
ideas.   4
(e) I can speak fluently.   5

25. How well can you read English?

(a) Not at all.   1
(b) I can understand only a few words when
I read.   2
(c) I can understand about half of what I
read (with a dictionary).   3
(d) I can understand most of what I read
(with a dictionary).   4
(e) I understand everything I read.   5

26. How well can you write English?
    (a) Not at all. 1
    (b) Few words with difficulty. 2
    (c) Well enough to communicate simple ideas, requests with many errors. 3
    (d) Well enough to communicate most ideas with few errors. 4
    (e) I can write with native-like control. 5

27. Which of the following helped you personally to learn English?

	Not at all	Somewhat	Very much
(a) My school study			
(b) Private study			
(c) Speaking English with family members			
(d) Speaking English at work			
(e) Speaking English outside of work with friends			
(f) Traveling and studying in English-speaking countries			

28. Do you think that the teachers of English you had in school were (on the average):
    Excellent 1
    Moderately good 2
    Adequate 3
    Poor 4

29. Do you wish your teachers of English had given more emphasis to any of the following:

	Yes	No
(a) Rules of English grammar	...	...
(b) Free conversation	...	...
(c) Serious literature	...	...
(d) Literature specifically chosen from various fields (science, etc.)	...	...
(e) Mechanics of writing (handwriting, punctuation, etc.)	...	...
(f) Pronunciation	...	...
(g) Rapid silent reading	...	...
(h) Writing and composition (sentences, letters, correct spelling, etc.)	...	...
(i) Translation (Arabic to English or the opposite)	...	...

30. Which of the previous do you consider to be
    the *one most important* skill?   . . . .

31. Is a knowledge of English necessary for
    success in your job?
    (a) No.   1
    (b) It helps but it's not necessary.   2
    (c) Yes, definitely.   3

32. Has your knowledge of English made it possible for you to earn more
    money or to advance professionally?
    (a) No, English is not necessary in my
         work.   1
    (b) No, I don't know enough English to
         help me.   2
    (c) Yes, I have a better job because of my
         knowledge of English.   3
    (d) Has not helped.   4

33. Are you presently attempting to improve your English by formal study (by
    studying in a school or an institute, etc.)?
                                            Yes. 1
                                            No 2

34. How important is it for you that your children learn to communicate effec-
    tively in English?
    (a) Very important   1
    (b) Relatively important   2
    (c) Unimportant   3

35. Why do you consider the study of English to be important? (Rank the five
    choices from most important (one), to least important (five), 1 to 5.)

    A person who masters English:
    (a) has a much better chance of obtaining a good job here in Jordan.
    (b) has a much better chance of studying abroad or of obtaining a job
         abroad.
    (c) can keep himself better informed about developments outside the Arab
         world.
    (d) can become more sensitive to the values and traditions of people from
         various parts of the world.
    (e) has better access to world literature.

36. Will your children (if you have any now or plan to in the future) learn to
    communicate effectively in English by following the present government
    school curriculum?

    (a) No, the present . curriculum is not
         adequate.   1

(b) Yes, definitely, with no outside work. 2
(c) Possibly, but with outside help.   3

37. Does the secondary certificate examination in English emphasize the skills that you actually need in your work?
     (a) Not at all.   1
     (b) Only partially.   2
     (c) Very accurately.   3
     (d) No opinion.   4

38. If you went to a private school (at any time from grades 1–12), or if you have sent a child or intend to send a child to private school, what was your main reason for that?
     (a) The general level of education is better than that of the government schools.   1
     (b) English was emphasized more than in the government schools.   2
     (c) To obtain religious instruction.   3
     (d) Other (specify).   4

39. When do you think government schools should begin to teach English?
     (a) Grade 5 (the present level)   1
     (b) Earlier than grade 5   2
     (c) Later than grade 5   3
     Note: If the answer was not grade 5, specify
            which grade.   . . . .

40. Should the government schools offer more hours of English instruction each week? (At present 6 periods per week are offered in the compulsory cycle and 6–8 periods per week in the secondary cycle).
                           No 1
                           Yes. 2

41. Should the government schools begin to teach content subjects via English instead of teaching them via Arabic?
                           Yes. 1
                           No 2
     Note: If the answer is 'no' go to Question 43.

42. What subjects do you think should be taught via English?

	Yes	No
(a) Science	. . .	. . .
(b) Mathematics	. . .	. . .
(c) Social studies	. . .	. . .
(d) Other, specify	. . .	. . . .

43. Do you think that government schools should offer instruction in a foreign language besides English?

    (a) No, it's not necessary   1
    (b) Yes, I prefer:

        (1) German   ....
        (2) French   ....
        (3) Spanish   ....
        (4) Italian   ....
        (5) Turkish   ....
        (6) Russian   ....
        (7) Other, specify   ....

44. Have you studied any foreign language besides English?

    (a) No, not at all.   1
    (b) Yes, in Jordan.   2
    (c) Yes, abroad.   3
    (d) Yes, both in Jordan and abroad.   4

45. If yes, what languages did you study and where?

Languages	Never studied it	Inside Jordan	Abroad	Inside Jordan and abroad
German				
French				
Spanish				
Italian				
Turkish				
Russian				
Other, specify				

46. Name one book in English you have read in the last month.

....
....

47. Name one newspaper or magazine in English you have read in the last month.

....
....

PART FOUR

The Re-Establishment of Functional Allocation

Trends in the Study of Athapaskan Language Maintenance and Bilingualism

INTRODUCTION

While the United States has long been, as Haugen (1938) pointed out, an ideal place for the study of bilingualism and language contact, the field has had little attention until recently. This is even more true in the case of American Indian communities, for although they have provided the main riches of American linguistics, it has been their language rather than their use of it that has interested the scholar. With a few distinguished exceptions, the student of an Amerindian language has paid little attention to the sociolinguistic situation of his informants except to remark how few speakers there are or how poorly they remember the language. From their studies one can learn incidentally about a language's loss and destruction, but seldom are there indications of the process itself, of what other languages are adopted, or of the nature of bilingualism. Only very recently, with the impetus of interest on the one hand in the ethnography of speech and on the other in bilingual education, has there been a smattering of studies focusing on Amerindian bilingualism.

We have chosen to concentrate in this article on Athapaskan languages in order to provide some reasonable limit to our work. The Athapaskan language family is especially suitable because it permits us a wide territorial coverage — from New Mexico to Alaska — and because it includes the widest range of language maintenance situations, from a flourishing Navájo spoken by 120,000 people to a full selection of dying or extinct languages. The restriction unfortunately forces us to leave out what is probably the best study of Amerindian bilingualism (Dozier's [1967a] description of the Hopi-Tewa bilingualism of Hano) but in the main it gives, we believe, a not unreasonable picture of the wider field.

In this article we first give a sketch of the kind of incidental references to language maintenance that can be found in the literature. On the basis of published and unpublished studies and personal communications we then present an outline of the present status of Athapaskan languages. In the next part of the article we summarize specific studies of language maintenance and bilingualism. From this it will become clear that while the Athapaskan language family provides rich resources for sociolinguistic studies, these resources have as yet been largely untapped. Only now, when most of the languages are extinct or obsolescent, have a revival of ethnic identity and a growth of Indian nationalism promised that this might be corrected.

1. THE NATURE OF THE DATA

Most published references to the strength of American Indian languages have been in the form of pleas addressed to linguists and anthropologists calling on them to carry out salvage work with languages about to become extinct.[1] There have been few if any general studies or statements on language maintenance. But if one examines carefully the reports of ethnographic and linguistic research a good deal of relevant data can be gathered. From Sapir's account of his field work with Hupa, for instance, we can infer a great deal about the sociolinguistic status of the language.

'We soon discovered that first class informants were by no means difficult to secure. The old Indian culture has largely disappeared, it is true, and what remains of it cannot resist the inroads of civilization much longer, but there are many men and women who still remember the old life and the language is still spoken in its purity by many even of the younger people.' (Sapir 1927:10).

When the documentation on a people is particularly sketchy and when they appear to speak an aberrant language, anecdotes on last surviving speakers assume a special importance. Such a language group is the Tsetsaut. Boas gathered the existing corpus on the Tsetsaut language in Kincolith, British Columbia, in 1894. The Tsetsauts had suffered at the hands of the Tlingit and Tsimshian, and Boas reported that there were twelve of them left alive, only two of whom could speak their language correctly. Two of Boas' three informants, aged fourteen and twenty-one, spoke Nishka better than Tsetsaut, and his older informant aged fifty-five, spoke Tsetsaut well but was exceedingly difficult to work with. Boas had to work with him in Chinook jargon through a Nass interpreter. Nevertheless the Tsetsaut corpus reveals a highly significant labial series, which has continued to intrigue Athapaskan scholars (Boas and Goddard 1924:1; Rohner 1969:155—169; Tharp 1972; Krauss 1973). It was presumed that Tsetsaut became extinct about the beginning of this century. In 1907 Emmons (1911:21—3) discovered seven Tsetsaut living in poverty on the Portland Canal. But the language survived as late as 1927 when Barbeau learned of a woman informant, 'Ala'óó (Krauss 1973); presumably, therefore, there were other younger speakers at the time Boas did his field work. There are rumors that there are still Tsetsaut speakers alive but a visit to Kincolith by Rigsby (1967) and correspondence with the descendants of Boas' informants by Krauss (personal communication) have failed to find any. Tsetsauts may still have lived in the Kincolity-Alice Arm area into the 1930s but there seems to be no one alive who has even heard the language. The language probably died with Boas' two young informants, Noah and Timothy Dangeli, and 'Ala'óó.

Occasionally ethnographic studies contain fairly specific information on language maintenance. In the preface to his biography of Jim Whitewolf, Brant remarks on the decline of Kiowa Apache in 1949—50:

'Most of the present day Kiowa Apache know English. Among those under forty years of age English is rapidly becoming the major language of everyday affairs. The old people have a lesser command of English and tend to use the native language among themselves. Individuals of the younger generations can understand Kiowa Apache but tend to speak it haltingly and very imperfectly, employing English words freely when they cannot recall native words. Children know only English, and it seems to be merely a matter of time — perhaps another generation or two — before the native language will entirely be replaced by English.' (Brant 1969:18—19).

Jim Whitewolf's memory of his first days in school when he knew practically no English underscores the decline in Kiowa Apache that has taken place in his lifetime (Brant 1969:81).

From incidental references such as these it is possible to build a picture of the speed of language loss, and occasionally to find hints on the development of bilingualism. The data are sketchy but altogether they give an understandable picture. In the following section we survey the language status of the various Athapaskan languages; as we do so it will become clear how the data have been gathered from accounts of the kind we have just illustrated.

2. THE PRESENT STATUS OF ATHAPASKAN LANGUAGES

We treat the languages geographically with an ordering from least to most vitality. Therefore, we group the extinct Kwalhioqua-Tlatskanai language of Oregon and Washington with the Pacific Coast languages despite the fact that it is considered to be the southernmost offshoot of Canadian Athapaskan. For each of Pacific Coast Athapaskan, Canadian Athapaskan, Alaskan Athapaskan, and Apachean (Southern Athapaskan) we discuss first the general historical situation, then we give notes on languages for which we have been able to gather information; finally, we summarize the present language situation in tabular form. We also include the three Na-Dene languages: Eyak, Tlingit, and Haida.

The dialect relationships between the Athapaskan languages, particularly for Canadian Athapaskan, are still not understood. The language groupings employed in this survey generally correspond to the subdivisions traditionally employed by Athapaskanists (Hoijer 1963). However, it should be pointed out that these subdivisions are based on the Stammbaum model of language classification employed by Hoijer and do not properly reflect the dialect chains that exist throughout Athapaskan speaking areas.

Tables I–IV give language names, a maintenance classification, an estimate of the number of present speakers and their ages, and a brief comment. For the classification we use a modified form of Miller's (1972) system as follows:

I. Full maintenance (Miller's I, 'flourishing'). Speakers of all ages; a proportion of monolingual speakers (including children); evidence of numerical increase in the number of speakers; language modernization; some literacy; relatively large population. Examples are Chipewyan and Navajo.

II. Bilingual maintenance (included in Miller's I). A few monolinguals; speakers of all ages; regular use in some domains; small populations. Examples are Mescalero Apache and Upper Kuskokwim.

III. Bilingual loss (Miller's II, 'obsolescing'). Children bilingual or English dominant; generational differences in language use; domains becoming mixed. Examples are Tlingit, Kaska, and Jicarilla Apache.

IV. Relic (Miller's III, 'Obsolete'). Last few speakers. Examples are Hupa, Eyak, Sarcee, Kiowa Apache.

V. Extinct. (Miller's IV, 'extinct'). No known living speakers. Examples are Bear River and Nicola.

2.1. *Pacific Coast Athapaskan*

All of the Athapaskan languages of Washington, Oregon, and California are either extinct or are spoken only by persons over 60.[2] In every case, Pacific Coast Athapaskan languages were spoken by small tribal groups none of which had an aboriginal population much more than 1000. They were localized communities situated usually in the valleys of the coastal range. There is far more internal linguistic diversity in Pacific Coast Athapaskan than in Apachean, but it was probably never an undifferentiated linguistic community. Krauss has proposed that the area be viewed as a dialect complex in terms of patterns of isoglosses. He summarizes these relationships as follows:

'Hupa is rather aberrant (and relatively conservative) from the rest of the California group, which then shades through perhaps two or three stages of mutual unintelligibility or low intelligibility from Mattole (and Bear River) through Lassik, Nongatl, Sinkyone to Wailaki and then Kato. In Oregon Umpqua is the most aberrant, and most of the rest are perhaps mutually intelligible to a rather high degree, shading from Tolowa through Chetco into the Tututni (sub-) dialects (of which Euchre Creek is one), and eastward through Chasta Costa to Coquille, with Galice-Applegate as an isolated (but still not distant) extreme. The only major point that is somewhat unexpected from the geography is that Umpqua shares a number of traits in common with the California group.' (Krauss 1973).

All of the groups suffered severely from the sudden influx of white settlers and miners on the West Coast after 1850. At a very early date the native communities were disrupted, dispersed, relocated, or annihilated. In Oregon most of the Athapaskan speakers were herded onto the Siletz and Grande Ronde reservations in 1856. At Grande Ronde Chinook Jargon became the *lingua franca* and had replaced Athapaskan by an early date. Athapaskan was retained for a somewhat longer time at Siletz (Pierce and Ryherd 1964:142).

2.1.1. Chasta Costa
The man with whom Sapir worked on Chasta Costa in 1906 was still alive in 1942 when Harrington gathered a fair amount of material from him (Krauss 1973).

2.1.2. Hupa-Chilula-Whilkut
The Hoopa Reservation was established in northern California in 1865. Hupa is today the strongest Pacific Coast Athapaskan language for a number of reasons. (1) Despite the importation of other tribal and linguistic groups to their reservation the Hupa were always numerically superior to the other groups present. For example, in 1910 over 450 of the 600 reservation residents were Hupas. (2) The Hoopa Reservation includes most of the aboriginal territory of the tribe. (3) There was no gold found on that particular stretch of the Trinity River.

Hupa is now spoken by about ten to twenty elderly persons. It is also possible that a few persons who speak the closely related *Chilula* and *Whilkut* dialects are still alive. In 1968 a Hupa language evening course began in Hoopa. At that time the course focused on gathering materials. In 1971 two Hupas were given teaching certification under a 'distinguished persons' provision in the California certification code, and they began teaching the language full-time in all levels of the elementary and high school. In addition an evening language course is offered for adults.

2.1.3. Mattole-Bear River
Mattole was a relic language in 1927 when Li did his field work with an elderly informant. Mary Haas did some additional work on Mattole in the 1950s. Apparently the last reference to the closely related Bear River dialect was made by Li in 1927. 'I have obtained a number of words from a Bear River woman, who, being married to a Wiyot Indian, speaks Wiyot now but has a vague memory of her native speech which she calls "Bear River talk" ' (1930:2).

2.1.4.
There is a possibility that a very few persons with some remembrance of *Kato, Wailaki,* and *Lassik* are still alive (Victor Golla, personal communication).

2.1.5. Tolowa
There are six remaining Tolowa speakers, none younger than sixty, and there are younger persons who have partial knowledge of the

language. A class in Tolowa is being taught at Smith River High School (R. J. Parr, personal communication to Krauss).

2.2. *Alaskan Athapaskan*

Recent estimates by Krauss reveal that the Athapaskan languages of Alaska are in almost every case declining rapidly.[3] In fact the pattern of language loss that has already taken place in Oregon and California Athapaskan seems to be repeating itself throughout Alaska at an accelerated pace. Krauss describes the situation as follows:

'Alaskan Athapaskan languages are either dying fast, with only the older generations speaking them, or if children are still speaking them, the community is on the verge of capitulating to English under pressure from the school. In most places the youngest generation speaks only English, depending on the place, from 20 on down to even 40 on down. In many places the communities are beginning

Table I. *Pacific Coast Athapaskan*

Language group	Rank	Population	Comments on language strength
Chasta Costa	V		extinct in 1940s.
Chetco	IV	3	last recorded in 1935.
Coquille-Flores Creek	V		extinct by mid-1960s.
Galice-Applegate	V		extinct in 1963.
Hupa-Chilula-Whilkut	IV	10–20	all speakers over fifty years of age
Kato	V(?)		1925:50.
Kwalhioqua-Tlatskanai	V		8 in 1857: extinct before 1940.
Lassik	V(?)		last fluent speaker died in 1969.
Mattole-Bear River	V		extinct in 1950s.
Nongatl	V		1910:6.
Sinkyone	V		24–36 (including half-breeds) in 1925.
Tolowa	IV	6	over 60
Tututni-Euchre Creek	IV	6	over 70
Umpqua	V		extinct in 1940s.
Wailaki	V(?)		1910: 200 (mostly half-breeds).

now to lament the loss of the languages, and are getting increasingly interested in practical grammars of their own languages and programs for teaching them as a second language to their own children, but often with the parents capable of speaking Athapaskan and yet speaking only English to the kids, and now wanting the school to teach Athapaskan!' (Krauss, personal communication).

The Alaskan speech communities like the Pacific Coast communities were generally quite small and localized aboriginally. The date of initial contact with European society and the intensity of contact varies widely in Alaska. Language loss has proceeded rapidly in this century in the bush communities even though most of these villages are still predominantly native in population. English was firmly established as the *lingua franca* and prestige language by the 1930s.

The seven communities where Athapaskan is being spoken (such as Nikolai and Tetlin) are in most cases quite isolated and lack a large white population; but physical isolation has not been sufficient to maintain languages in many parts of Alaska. For example, Lime Village, population thirty to forty, is the most isolated village in Alaska and has never had a school. Nevertheless no children there now speak Tanaina. Where the Pacific Coast showed the effects of a rapid extermination of languages by settlers, Alaska demonstrates rather the rapidity with which modern technology leads to the loss of their native language by small groups.

2.2.1. *Ahtena*
Most of the Ahtena villages are populated only by older people. The largest Ahtena settlement is Copper Center where some children can understand the native tongue but cannot speak it fluently.

2.2.2. *Kutchin*
Kutchin is the strongest Athapaskan language in Alaska. In the communities of Arctic Village, Birch Creek, and Venetie, Kutchin is learned as a first language while in the larger settlement of Fort Yukon most children know Kutchin and English when they come to school. The Alaska State-Operated Schools run bilingual programs now in Fort Yukon and Arctic Village under the direction of Richard Mueller, but the Bureau of Indian Affairs school in Venetie has not yet introduced the language into the school.

Apparently the Kutchin language in Alaska is stronger than it is in Canada. In the Canadian Kutchin-speaking communities of Old Crow and Fort McPherson children are no longer learning Kutchin. This is an exception to the general pattern that Canadian Athapaskan languages tend to be maintained better than those in Alaska.

2.2.3. *Tanaina*
In all Tanaina communities (including the relatively isolated Tyonek) there are few if any speakers under forty years of age. The only exceptions to this are Nondalton and Lime Village where there may be younger speakers. In Kenai there are only ten speakers, the youngest of whom is fifty-two. The forty-year-old generation can understand a great deal of the language but cannot speak it. Recently interest in native ways has increased in Kenai and a number of the younger tribal leaders talk of reviving and passing on the language.

2.2.4. *Upper Kuskokwim*
The village of Nikolai is an extremely isolated, all-native community. The children are bilingual in Upper Kuskokwim and English and the parents are tending to speak more English than Athapaskan to their children now. Nikolai is also the site of a bilingual program sponsored by Alaska State-Operated Schools and directed by Ray Collins.

2.2.5. *Upper Tanana*
The Upper Tanana language is quite strong in Tetlin and Northway. This is true despite the fact that Northway is just off the Alaska Highway and has a large airport. The Alaska State-Operated Schools sponsors a bilingual program in Northway directed by Paul Milanowski, but the Bureau of Indian Affairs school in Tetlin has so far refused to allow one to be established there.

2.2.7. *Tlingit*
Krauss summarized the situation:

'The future of the language seems very doubtful. Though there are over 1000 persons still speaking Tlingit, almost none of these are children. The proportion of those under twenty-five years of age competent in Tlingit is low everywhere, and almost none are under twenty except in Angoon where many as young as ten understand a lot. There are at least two eighteen-year-olds and one twelve-year-old there who speak Tlingit. At the same time as the Tlingit language continues to be thus abandoned, probably beyond the point of no return as a normally living language, a native cultural renaissance, as

Table II. *Alaskan Athapaskan*

Language group	Rank	Population	Comments on language strength
Ahtena	III-IV	250	all speakers over twenty years of age.
Han	IV	30	over 20.
Holikachuk	IV	30	over 20.
Ingalik	IV	100	over 30.
Koyukon	IV	600	over 30.
Kutchin	II-IV	900 (in Alaska)	all ages in some communities.
Tanaina	IV	300	over 20.
Tanana			
Central	IV	200	over 30.
Transitional	III-IV	110	some children at Tanacross.
Upper Kuskokwim	II-IV	100	all children at Nikolai.
Upper Tanana	II-IV	300	most children at Tetlin and Northway.
Eyak	IV	3	over 70.
Tlingit	III	1000 (some in Canada)	over 20.

part of the general movement of social upheaval concerning minority groups or cultures in the United States and Canada has definitely invaded the Tlingit. These two powerful opposing forces for assimilation have converged now on the Tlingit people, who are caught in powerful cross-currents. Classes in Tlingit are becoming common in Tlingit schools, but there is a lack of trained teachers and of materials, and the movement lacks organization. With these problems remedied, however, it would be difficult to predict to what extent and in what sense or function the Tlingit language may yet survive.' (Krauss 1973:936).

Since 1971 several Tlingit language workshops have been held under the direction of Krauss to train teachers in the Tlingit orthography and to produce Tlingit materials.

2.3.0. *Canadian Athapaskan*
The data on Canadian language maintenance are rather vague and inaccurate.[4] Chafe's (1962) estimates are the only figures in many cases. One additional source of information, the band population

figures published by the Department of Indian Affairs and Northern Development (1970), is of little use as a gauge of language strength. Some tribal affiliations given in that work, e.g., Nahani for Kaska or Kutchin for Tutchone, do not correspond to what we know about the dialect groupings. Krauss (1973) has reinterpreted these data and we now have a fair idea of the Canadian language situation.

In Table III Chipewyan is presented as a monolithic language spoken by over 5,000 speakers of all ages, while the actual fact is that the strength of Chipewyan differs from community to community.

Anthropologists and linguists have long noted the quite arbitrary bases that underlie the traditional Canadian tribal classifications. Teit noted in his field work with the Kaska and Tahltan in 1915:

'The Indians seem to consider all within their ken as bands or scattered groups of the family speaking the same kind of language differed only in slight degree in certain localities. They seem to take no cognizance, for instance, of the linguistic groups of the Nahani, Sekani, and Slave.' (1956:104).

Some of the troublesome aspects of Canadian Athapaskan language classification are touched on by Richmond who is gathering data on ethnic identity and language differences for the Southern Arctic Drainage Athapaskans:

'Athapaskan speakers will often not attempt to speak another Athapaskan language or dialect but *will* be able to understand it. Visitors usually speak in their own dialect if they assume the people present know enough to understand what is being said. This practice has undoubtedly preserved many local speech variations and has encouraged the sense of being one group of related people over an extended area. Of course it is not the case that all Southern Arctic Drainage Dene can understand each other. It is simply that there are no sharp language boundaries and probably not even focal centers. When full data for speech communities is available, I predict that they will show only gradients of change.' (1970:143–144).

In contrast to the situation in Alaska, the Athapaskan languages of Canada are relatively strong. There are many conservative, isolated bush speech communities (such as Nahani Butte Slavey described below) where there is still a large percentage of monolinguals.

Generally speaking the maintenance of Canadian Athapaskan reflects provincialism and a less accelerated technological development. Nevertheless linguistic replacement is taking place rapidly in a number of the Canadian communities. This is most evident along the Alaska Highway where since the highway's construction in the 1940s, Sekani, Kaska, Fort Nelson Slave, and Tutchone have undergone rapid language loss and disruption of their communities.

2.3.1. Carrier
Robert Young (personal communication) reports that Carrier was spoken by speakers of all ages in 1939. Carrier and Chilcotin in Central British Columbia are by no means isolated language groups, but, apparently, both languages are maintaining well.

2.3.2. Kaska
The community of Lower Post has undergone rapid linguistic acculturation since 1941 when the Alaska Highway was constructed. In 1944–45 there were 200 Kaska at Lower Post plus numerous construction workers and service men (Honigman 1965:201). Today it seems that no children speak Kaska there.

2.3.3. Sarcee
Robert Young (personal communication) reports that in 1939 Sarcee was still a viable language with speakers of all ages. Apparently the language has declined rapidly since then to the point that Cook reports there is only a handful of elderly speakers (Krauss 1973). The Sarcee Reserve is now practically within the city limits of Calgary, and apparently there has been considerable intermarriage.

2.3.4. Nicola
Very little is known about Nicola. In 1895 they were visited by James Teit in the Upper Nicola Valley of British Columbia. At that time there were only a few elderly Nicolas. They had intermarried with Okanagan and Thompson Salish and their language was replaced by Salish. Apparently Harrington was unable to locate a Nicola speaker in 1942 (Haruo and Rigsby, to appear).

2.3.5. Slavey
The ethnological field data of Holly Reckord gathered in the Slavey community of Nahani Butte, Northwest Territories, offers very interesting insight into the dynamics of language contact. Nahani Butte

is an isolated all-Indian community that can be approached only by boat or by air. It has a population of sixty-four. About 50% of the community is monolingual in Slavey. The oldest English speakers are in their late twenties. These English speakers were the first members of the community to attend school. School was instituted in the community in 1958. Since that time there has been increasing English usage amongst the younger generation. Most of the children are essentially monolingual in Slavey until they arrive in school. In some larger families preschool children learn some English from their older siblings. Generally the children use Slavey amongst themselves (with a degree of English loanwords), and English is confined to the school and to occasional meetings with outsiders. Generally the level of English in Nahani Butte is described as quite limited. The best speakers are those who have attended twelve years of school and have worked outside in larger communities.

It is of interest that a few of the elders are literate in Slavey, the result of literacy efforts by Oblate missionaries earlier this century. There is a newspaper in Fort Simpson that publishes a page in the Slavey syllabary that is read by the elders. Also there is some letter writing in the Slavey syllabary. For the past year or so the local school has been making some effort to use Slavey but this is treated as a separate language lesson and has very limited technical support. It cannot be considered bilingual education.

The degree of language maintenance in the northern bush areas apparently varies from community to community and is clearly correlated with the onset of schooling and the relative isolation of the community.

2.3.6. *Tagish*
The Tagish were 'Tlingitized' during the latter part of the nineteenth century. At present there are fewer than five Tagish speakers in the Carcross area, all of whom are over the age of seventy and all of whom know Tlingit. It is uncertain if any of these Tagish can consistently sort out their Tagish from their Tlingit.

2.3.7. *Tutchone*
A loosely defined dialect area in the Southern Youkon. In most Tutchone communities children are no longer learning the language (Milanowski and Henry 1969). For example, in Burwash and Champagne, Indian communities on the Alaska Highway, most persons under twenty-five years cannot speak the language. Even in an

extremely isolated community, such as Aishihik, children are reported to be rather weak in Tutchone (Holly Reckord, personal communication).

2.3.8. *Haida*

The Northern Haida dialect spoken in Hydaberg, Alaska, has about 100 speakers, older than fifty, but there are some forty-year-old speakers. One person aged twenty-eight is reportedly a good speaker. Reports on the number of speakers of the other Northern Haida dialect Masset vary. Some children may speak it, and they may number 75 to 100 in Alaska (with some in Seattle) and 100 to 300 in Masset. The Southern Haida dialect, Skidegate, is only intelligible with Northern Haida. Total population is 250 and fluent speakers are over fifty. The total number of speakers may be twenty-five to fifty. The first Haida language workshop was held in 1972 under the direction of Krauss, and the revitalization movement is now very strong in Hydaberg and Ketchikan.

Table III. *Canadian Athapaskan*[5]

Language group	Rank	Population	Comments on language strength
Beaver	I	300 [789]	all ages.
Carrier	I	1000-3000 [5155]	all ages.
Chilcotin	I	1400	all ages.
Chipewyan	I	3400-5600 [5612]	all ages.
Dogrib	I	800 [1202]	all ages.
Hare	I	600 [715]	all ages.
Kaska	III	200-500 [533]	few children.
Kutchin	I	1200 (including Alaskan)	mostly adults in Canada.
Nicola	V		extinct in early part of century.
Sarcee	IV	10	over 50.
Sekani	III	350	no children.
Slavey	I	1000-2000 [3334]	all ages.
Tagish	IV	5 or less	over 70.
Tahltan	I	[702]	all ages.
Tsetsaut	V		extinct in 1930s.
Tutchone	III	1000	few children.
Haida	IV	300-550	over 50, some children in Masset.

2.4. *Apachean (Southwest Athapaskan)*

Of all areas, it has the fullest range of language maintenance situations, with an example of each level.[6] It has also been the area in which the languages have been most successful in surviving modern contact.

2.4.1. *Navajo*
Most striking is the case of Navajo, which with over 120,000 speakers seems to have the strongest prospects for survival. In the 1940s descriptions of the Navajo language situation referred to almost complete monolingualism, to 'a definite disinclination to learn and speak the languages of other people' (Reed 1944). In the thirty years since then there has been a marked change, for while there has been absolute increase in the number of speakers of Navajo there has been an even greater increase in the use of English by Navajos.

There have been a number of recent studies of Navajo language maintenance. As a preliminary to a study of the feasibility and effect of teaching Navajo children to read in their own language first (Spolsky and Holm 1971), a survey was carried out of the language use of six-year-old Navajo children entering school. In 1969 and again in 1970, teachers in a hundred or more schools on or near the Reservation were asked to rate, on a simple five-point scale, the language capability of their six-year-old pupils. In the 1969 survey (Spolsky 1970) data were thus obtained on a total of 2893 children; in the 1970 survey (Spolsky 1971a), the survey included 3653 children, which was 84% of the six-year-old Navajo children in school. The validity of the procedure was checked by teams of bilingual judges using a specially developed interview (Spolsky, Murphy, Holm, and Ferrel 1972). The surveys showed that 30% of the children were judged on entering school to be monolingual in Navajo, compared to 5% monolingual in English. Another 40% were reported as dominant in Navajo, knowing a little English but not enough to do first-grade work in it; and another 20% to be equally at home in either language. On this basis one could guess that 70% of the children came from homes where Navajo was the only language used, 20% from homes where both languages were used, and 10% from homes where English is now used. The data also revealed a clear distinction between Bureau of Indian Affairs schools, where the normal situation is for a child to come from a Navajo-speaking home, and Public Schools, where about 20% of the children seem to come from English-speaking homes and another 30% from bilingual ones. Analysis suggests that this reflects the relative accessibility of the school and the nearest town as factors in the spread of English (Spolsky 1971b). On the basis of these surveys it is possible to make some general guesses about the speed of language loss. Assuming, conservatively, 1949 as the last year when almost all Navajo children would have come to school monolingual in Navajo, by 1969 we find that 30% have some serious exposure to English before coming to school. With near universal education, the proportion knowing English will continue to increase rapidly. Given present trends, one would very soon expect to find three clear divisions among Navajos: English speakers living away from the Reservation whose children know no Navajo; bilinguals in the more urbanized parts of the Reservation whose children speak English but hear Navajo from their grandparents; and a continually decreasing group of Navajo speakers in rural areas whose children will start learning English at school. There are factors which could change this, such as the growing nationalist movement with its related move to Navajo-controlled education, or speed it up, such as a flurry of road building. But of all Athapaskan languages Navajo seems to have the best prospects for survival (Spolsky, in press).

2.4.2. Western Apache

There are about 11,000 Western Apaches living on the two Arizona reservations. About 7,500 live on the Fort Apache Reservation and about 4,500 on the San Carlos Reservation. The Apache language at Fort Apache appears to be very strong. There are still a few monolingual Apache speakers, most of whom are women over the age of sixty-five. Almost all children know Apache but there are few, if any, who are monolingual in Apache when they reach school. There is a clear split in the use of Apache by the children, English being the language of school and the outside world and Apache the language of intimacy. About eight years ago there was some anti-Apache sentiment expressed by tribal leaders, but in recent years the Tribal Council has given strong support to the use and maintenance of Apache. Although from the external point of view the language at Fort Apache appears to be thriving, elders within the tribe perceive changes in the language of the children. They claim that the youngsters do not speak well. They note that elaborate verbal constructions are being regularized. Interest in bilingual education is growing but as yet there is no formal effort to use Apache in the school.

The language situation at San Carlos is not as well known, but there are signs that there is an increase in English use by children there.

2.4.3. *Mescalero*

Although there are no precise figures it is estimated that about 1200 of the 1500 Indian residents at Mescalero are Mescalero speakers (the total population on the reservation is 1740). Most of the population is concentrated in the town of Mescalero. Mescalero has always been the dominant and preferred language on the reservation. It is likely that all younger persons speak Mescalero rather than Chiricahua. There are still a few elderly people who are monolingual Mescalero speakers but the formal function of interpreting on the reservation ceased in the late 1940s or early 1950s. By the early 1960s tribal council meetings were predominantly in English with spot translations to clarify issues for the benefit of the elders, and for private conferences. In 1958 Scott (1960) tested 53 Mescalero high-school students in English. From his results it is possible to assume that for most of them Mescalero was still the dominant language. The five Mescaleros that Scott found speaking English as a first language each had one parent who did not speak Mescalero.

Today few if any persons under the age of sixty are monolingual in Apache. There is relatively little outside marriage, and Apache is the predominant home language. Most children know some English before they come to school, and there are signs that English usage among younger children has increased in the last four or five years. Children over ten years almost always play in Apache while five- and six-year-olds use noticeably more English. Still fewer than 10% of the Apache children know only English. In recent years there has been growing loyalty to the Apache language. Parents remark on the change in the speech of their children. The tribal chairman often urges parents to use Apache with the children in order to carry on the language. At present Apache is not being used in the school, but apparently there is some interest in bilingual education.

2.4.4. *Chiricahua*

The Chiricahua Apache were moved to Mescalero in several stages from southeastern Arizona and southwestern New Mexico in the latter part of the nineteenth century. It is not certain how many persons can still speak Chiricahua, but it is likely they are all of the oldest generation. Chiricahua is very close to Mescalero, a mutually intelligible dialect. Today there is an awareness of Chiricahuaisms in the language now spoken at Mescalero, but evidently all younger Apaches speak a single Mescalero Apache dialect.

2.4.5. Lipan

The Lipan were moved to the Mescalero Reservation in small groups between 1879 and 1905 from southwestern Texas and northern Sonora. When Opler and Hoijer did field work in Mescalero in the 1930s there were about seven families that were all or predominantly Lipan and another nine families that were part Lipan. Opler notes that even in the 1930s the Lipan speakers had a hard time separating their language from Mescalero or Chiricahua. There are reputed to be a few elderly Lipans at Mescalero, all over seventy years old, and it is not certain if they can speak Lipan. One elderly Lipan woman is reportedly bilingual in Spanish.

2.4.6. Jicarilla

There are signs that the Jicarilla language has been slipping rapidly in recent years. Most of the 1800 Jicarilla tribal members are in or near the town of Dulce (but the population is less concentrated than at Mescalero). A fairly large percentage of the marriages of Jicarilla tribal members are to non-Jicarillas. Generally parents use English with their children while grandparents talk to them in Apache. Only a minority of the children entering school speak Jicarilla well and children's play is predominantly in English. On the other hand many 17- or 18-year-old Jicarillas can speak Apache. Recent efforts by two teachers to use Jicarilla in the Head Start program have focused primarily on vocabulary identification. No written language is being used. In the past parents have generally expressed a concern that their children learn English rather than Apache. Adults over sixty years old are clearly dominant in Apache but most know English. English is the language of administration. Tribal council meetings are mostly in English while Apache is used in private conferences. A tribal leader in recent years made one of his campaign issues the fact that he was a better speaker of Jicarilla than his opponent. There is a fair amount of trilingualism among persons over forty in Spanish-English-Apache. The twenty-year-olds, however, tend to know just English and Apache. There is some consciousness of language loss in Dulce particularly amongst the high school students.

2.4.7. *Kiowa Apache*
The Kiowa Apache aboriginally were a small group that lived with the Kiowas in the Plains area. Although we know of no reference to the aboriginal sociolinguistic situation of the Kiowa-Apache, they did maintain their language strongly until this century. In 1891 Mooney reports that there were 325 Kiowa Apache living in Oklahoma. They suffered from a severe flu epidemic in 1892 and in 1905 their numbers were reduced to 155 (Mooney 1910:703). As mentioned above, Brant observed that only older persons knew Kiowa-Apache in the late 1940s. Today there are 10 to 20 persons over the age of 50 who know the language.

To fill out the range of possibilities in the Southwest, there is evidence that before 1700 there were other groups in the area which are sometimes classified as Athapaskan. These include the Janos, Jumanos, Jocomes, Sumas, Cholomes, Mansos, Pelones, and Sibolos (Forbes 1959). All these groups were extinguished or assimilated with other Apaches at an early date.

Table IV. *Apachean (Southwest Athapaskan)*

Language group	Rank	Population	Comments on language strength
Chiricahua	IV	100(?)	all speakers over 50 years of age
Jicarilla	III	1000	over 10
Kiowa-Apache	IV	10-20	over 50
Lipan	IV	-5	over 70
Mescalero	II	1200	all ages
Navajo	I	120,000	all ages
Western Apache		10-11,000	
Ft. Apache	I	7,500	all ages
San Carlos	II	4,500	all ages

3. STUDIES OF ATHAPASKAN BILINGUALISM AND OTHER SOCIOLINGUISTIC TOPICS

3.1. *Language Maintenance Studies*

Considering the importance and the complexity of the topic, it is surprising that there are so few hard data or detailed studies dealing with sociolinguistic aspects of American Indian languages. For the general area of language maintenance this is equally true. Fishman (1966) does not deal with the subject, except for a reference to Chafe (1962) with his estimate that only 40% of the 300 American Indian languages or dialects still extant had more than 100 speakers, and that more than half of these had speakers of very advanced ages only. The Congressional hearings on bilingual programs in 1967 had before them estimates of the United States Indian population, but the only figures on language were the unofficial estimates made by William Gage (1967) in 1960 for Navajo (65,000), North Eskimo (10,000), Ojibwa (12,000), and South Alaskan Eskimo (14,000). Kinkade (1970) gives data on the languages spoken by Indian students at Haskell Institute in 1969, repeating an earlier study at the same school by Stuart (1962). But, as Kinkade points out, the data are not strictly comparable, nor do they provide a basis for studies of language loss or maintenance because the sample is very biased. Recent studies such as those referred to above for Navajo and others for Alaska have been motivated by the relevance of the data to language education policy.

One notable exception are the extensive references to Athapaskan languages in Voegelin, Voegelin, and Schutz (1967). In this work they summarize (unfortunately without precise references) a number of studies of Apachean, suggesting the place of the languages studied within the Arizona language situation. They quote various estimates of numbers of speakers and gather a number of sociolinguistic observations. They conclude that, while the Navajo remained mono-lingual during the acculturational periods, they will soon become bilingual.

3.2. Studies of Bilingualism

Other than the recent research on Navajo language maintenance described above, there are only passing references in the published literature to the incidence and degree of Athapaskan bilingualism. For example, Krauss (1973) mentions that speakers of Kuskokwim Ingalik are bilingual in Eskimo. Brant (1969:19) notes that

'in their contacts with other tribes, the Kiowa Apache usually employ English. In the event of intertribal contacts with old people who know no English, the tendency is to use Comanche, which has become a sort of Indian *lingua franca* because it has the reputation of being very easy to learn.'

For Navajo, as well as the implications of the maintenance studies, there have been comments on the relative use of English and Navajo (Spolsky 1972). Of all domains the one most closely related to English is the school. With the exception of the still few bilingual programs and of the practice within dormitories, school is the one institution that demands spoken English. Traders make an effort to use Navajo (see below); Public Health and other officials use interpreters. Tribal Council and chapter meetings use Navajo and tribal courts also permit the giving of evidence in Navajo. A large number of radio stations on or near the Reservation broadcast for many hours a day in Navajo. Thus all institutions except school permit spoken Navajo. But almost all writing (and reading) is in English. Signs in trading posts and stores are in English; Tribal Council minutes and court records are kept in English; the announcers speaking in Navajo work from English scripts. And the official Tribal newspaper is in English.[7] The situation is clearly exemplified by a tribal councillor addressing, in fluent Navajo, a conference on bilingual education: his speech was in Navajo but the typed text in front of him was in English. Only with the recent revival of literacy associated with Navajo bilingual education has written Navajo slowly shown signs of gaining ground. Further evidence on the nature of Navajo bilingualism is to be found in the loanword study referred to below (Holm, Holm, and Spolsky 1971) where the two major groupings were objects associated with the domain of school and non-Navajo foods.

A start on a study of the nature of adolescent bilingualism is the work by Dubin (1971) who reports a number of tests of language proficiency and attitudes in a group of Navajo high school students.

3.3. *Studies of Linguistic Acculturation*

Alongside these somewhat sketchy studies of Athapaskan bilingualism one may place studies of another aspect of language contact — linguistic acculturation.

In 1921 Sapir remarked:

'The Athapaskan languages of America are spoken by peoples that have had astonishingly varied cultural contacts, yet nowhere do we find an Athapaskan dialect that has borrowed freely [one might say, 'has borrowed at all', E.S.] from a neighboring language. These languages have always found it easier to create new words by com-

pounding afresh elements ready to hand. They have for this reason
been highly resistant to receiving the linguistic impress of the
external cultural experiences of their speakers.' (1921:196).

Documentation on Athapaskan linguistic acculturation is still spotty,
and the deep implications of Sapir's statement — that Athapaskan
languages structurally resist loanwords — i.e., that lack of loans is not
just a product of social isolation, has not received direct attention.

   In their survey of American Indian dictionaries for signs of linguistic acculturation, Voegelin and Hymes note that Li's (1933)
1500 item Chipewyan stem list shows no loanwords. They raise the
question that loans may have been purposely excluded by the
author: 'The effect of linguistic acculturation appears almost entirely
in the extension of old Chipewyan forms' (1953:638). Based on
Chipewyan field work done in 1967, Haas (1968:170) notes
numerous extension of native materials but she also gives a few
French loanwords. Hoijer's (1939) study of Chiricahua yielded only
nineteen loanwords from Spanish including two interesting verb
loans. Krauss (1965) notes 103 loans in Eyak, the largest number of
which are from neighboring and genetically related Tlingit. The
recently published Western Apache dictionary lists twenty-two loanwords from Spanish (Perry 1972:122).

   The literature on Navajo contains few loanwords. Sapir and Hoijer
(1967) and Reichard (1951) list fewer than forty loanwords. Haile
(1941:1) writes, 'Pueblo contact has not influenced Navaho to a
noticeable degree, while Spanish elements are comparatively few, and
English elements practically none'.

   Based on published evidence of Athapaskan loanwords it would
appear that Sapir's hypothesis has been corroborated. Yet there is
evidence that in the Navajo of today, loanwords are being used more
freely. A computer count of loanwords in the speech of Navajo
six-year-olds revealed that 9% of the words used by the children were
loans; these were 3.6% of the total words used (Holm, Holm, and
Spolsky 1971). This marked increase in loanwords in Navajo in the
past thirty or fifty years corresponds with the changing language
situation on the Reservation, supporting Dozier (1967b) in his in-
tuition that sociocultural rather than structural factors explain
whether a language will be ready to accept loanwords.

   Today we can no longer identify a core of loans, e.g., *bááh, béeso,*
only from Spanish. Rather there is, at least among younger persons, a
looser use of English terms (and consequent replacement of some

older vocabulary) which reflects the increase in competence in English. An early sign of the effects of bilingualism on Navajo is Young's excellent analysis of a slang loan verb *jaan* that was used for a time in the 1940s (Young 1945).

The other aspect of Athapaskan linguistic acculturation, the languages' propensity for 'compounding afresh from elements ready to hand', has received little concentrated study although there exists a number of sources for pursuing such research. Sapir's study of Sarcee personal names (1924), Young and Morgan's list of Navajo personal names (1951:428–445), and the various studies of Navajo place names (Van Valkenburg 1941; Young and Morgan 1947) amply document the tendency for Athapaskan to coin elaborate descriptive terms. Examples of semantic extension are illustrated in the classic analysis of the etymology of four Navajo words by Sapir (1936) and the study of Western Apache car terminology by Basso (1967) in which he shows the car terms to be based entirely on extension of body part terms (e.g., liver = battery).

3.4. *Ethnographies of Speaking*

Thus far there have been few detailed 'ethnographies of speaking' studies of Athapaskan speech communities. Most notable is the study of silence in Western Apache culture by Basso (1970). In a study based entirely on secondary sources, Darnell (1970) reconstructs in considerable detail Kaska speech behavior. She characterizes the Kaska speech community by its informality and its lack of formal speech roles.

A most significant contribution to Navajo and Athapaskan ethnography of speaking research and to linguistics in general is the study by Werner (1963) of the Navajo being spoken by four anglo traders. Trader Navajo is a prepidginized language that is used by the traders in their intercourse with Navajos. The Navajos respond almost entirely in regular, nonsimplified Navajo. Trader Navajo is not a language to the extent that no two people ever communicate with one another in it. Though each of the four traders studied varies in proficiency and has learned his version of Trader Navajo independently, there are some remarkable similarities in their phonemic inventories and verb morphology. Silverstein (1972) has demonstrated that these similarities in Trader Navajo can be explained by marking conventions, where the traders most naturally seek the least marked member of the paradigm. Another interesting fact revealed by Werner's study is the difficulty with which all four traders handle verb morphology. In fact Werner observed that the two better speakers had more incorrect verbs than the two worst speakers.

3.5. Dialect Studies

Due to their extreme morphological complexity the Athapaskan languages are of particular interest for studying dialect diversity and linguistic change. To date there have been only five such studies. Hill (1963) has noted some of the dialect differences between San Carlos and White Mountain Apache. She focused mainly on phonetic differences.

The best known studies of Navajo dialect diversity are by Reichard (1948; 1951:369–382). Recently Saville-Troike (1973) and Kari (1973) have presented some new dialect material. These Navajo studies cover a wide range of speech variation, lexical, phonetic, and morphophonemic.

The study of morphophonemic variation has particular relevance for future sociolinguistic research. There are numerous indications that the complex Navajo verb paradigms are undergoing various kinds of change and reanalysis. For example, a very restricted, morphologically marked rule that truncates the *oh-* second person dual pronoun to *o-* in perfective verbs ϕ- or χ- classifier is being used optionally by many speakers. At the same time this highly marked rule is being *extended* to a new environment that involves the presence of an absolutely neutralized *d-* classifier. In fact, the over-generalization of this rule seems more predominant than its suppression. Such a marker as the *oh-* truncation rule could be neatly incorporated into a sociolinguistic investigation of generational speech differences. It appears that morphophonemic variation in Navajo will show both regional, i.e., dialect, diffusion and generational i.e., rule, simplification differences. Thus there is evidence that Navajo and other Athapaskan languages will be most productive media for the study of linguistic change (Kari 1973).

4. CONCLUSIONS

This review, sketchy though it has been, will hopefully have made clear both the potential richness and the actual poverty of studies of sociolinguistic aspects of the Athapaskan languages. Two trends must be mentioned that will supply correctives to this situation. The first is of course the greater interest among linguists in studies of language in use: studies of context, of diversity, and of the sociological aspects of language which are no longer considered uninteresting. The second is concerned with the fact that whereas those working with Amerindian languages were usually motivated by a concern for the language itself, there is evidence of an increasing sense of responsibility towards the speakers of the language. This is manifested in two ways. First is the fact that so many scholars are now working in association with bilingual education programs. Thus, whatever their primary interest, they are necessarily involved in a form of educational sociolinguistics. The second is the increasing emphasis on training native speakers as linguists. Thus, where once an Athapaskan linguist meant a scholar studying Athapaskan, it will soon also mean an Athapaskan speaker studying linguistics.[8] As this becomes more true, we may expect rapid advances in the study of Athapaskan language maintenance and bilingualism.

REFERENCES

Aoki, Haruo, and Bruce Rigsby
in press. 'The Non-Salishan Languages of the Plateau', in *The New Handbook of American Indians*, the Plateau Volume (Washington, D.C., Smithsonian Institution).
Basso, Keith
1967 'Semantic Aspects of Linguistic Acculturation', *American Anthropologist* 69:471–477 (Washington, D.C.).
1970 ' "To Give Up on Words". Silence in Western Apache Culture', *Southwestern Journal of Anthropology* 26:213–230 (Albuquerque, New Mexico).
Boas, Franz, and Pliny Goddard
1924 'Ts'ets'aut, an Athapaskan Language from Portland Canal, British Columbia', *International Journal of American Linguistics* 3:1–35 (Bloomington, Indiana).
Brant, Charles S.
1969 *Jim Whitewolf: The Life of a Kiowa-Apache Indian* (New York, Dover Publications).
Chafe, Wallace L.
1962 'Estimates Regarding the Present Speakers of North American Indian Languages', *International Journal of American Linguistics* 28:162–171 (Bloomington, Indiana).
1965 'Corrected Estimates Regarding Speakers of Indian Languages', *International Journal of American Linguistics* 31:345–346 (Bloomington, Indiana).

Darnell, Regna
1970 'The Kaska Aesthetic of Speech Use', *Western Canadian Journal of Anthropology* 2:130—140 (Edmonton, Alberta).
Department of Indian Affairs and Northern Development
1970 *Linguistic and Cultural Affiliations of Canadian Indian Bands* (Ottawa).
Dozier, Edward P.
1967a *Hano* (New York, Holt, Rinehart, and Winston).
1967b 'Linguistic Acculturation Studies in the Southwest', in *Studies in Southwestern Ethnolinguistics*, Dell Hymes and William Bittle, eds. (The Hague, Mouton) pp. 389—403.
Dubin, Fraida
1971 'Language and Attitudes Among Navajo Adolescents', unpublished Ph.D. dissertation (University of California at Los Angeles).
Emmons, G. T.
1911 *The Tahltan Indians* (Philadelphia).
Fishman, Joshua A.
1966 *Language Loyalty in the United States* (The Hague, Mouton).
Forbes, Jack
1959 'Unknown Athapaskans: The Identification of the Jano, Jocome, Jumano, Manso, Suma, and Other Indian Tribes of the Southwest', *Ethnohistory* 6:97—159 (Bloomington, Indiana).
Gage, William
1967 'Speakers of Various Languages in 1960', in *Bilingual Education Programs: Hearings before the General Subcommittee on Education of the Committee on Education and Labor, House of Representatives, Nineteenth Congress* (Washington, D.C., Government Printing Office) pp. 414—415.
Haas, Mary
1968 'Notes on a Chipewyan Dialect', *International Journal of American Linguistics* 35:167—176 (Bloomington, Indiana).
Haile, Fr. Bernard, O. F. M.
1941 *Learning Navaho*, Vol 1 (St. Michael's, Arizona).
Haugen, Einar
1938 'Language and Immigration', *Norwegian-American Studies and Records* 10:1—43 (Northfield, Minnesota).
Hill, Faith
1963 'Some Comparisons between the San Carlos and White Mountain Dialect of Western Apache', *University of California Publications in Linguistics* 29:149—54 (Berkeley).
Hoijer, Harry
1939 'Chiricahua Loan-Words from Spanish', *Language* 15:110—115 (Baltimore).
1963 'The Athapaskan Languages', in *Studies in the Athapaskan Languages* (= *University of California Publications in Linguistics* 29) (Berkeley) pp. 1—29.
Holm, Agnes, Wayne Holm, and Bernard Spolsky
1971 *English Loanwords in the Speech of Six-Year-Old Navajo Children* (= *Navajo Reading Study Progress Report* 16) (Albuquerque, The University of New Mexico).

Honigman, J. J.
1965 'Social Disintegration in Five Northern Canadian Communities', *Canadian Review of Sociology and Anthropology* 2:199–215 (Calgary).
Kari, James
1973 'Navajo Verb Prefix Phonology', unpublished Ph.D. dissertation (Albuquerque, The University of New Mexico).
Kinkade, M. Dale
1970 'Indian Languages at Haskell Institute', *International Journal of American Linguistics* 36:46–52 (Bloomington, Indiana).
Krauss, Michael
1965 'Eyak: A Preliminary Report', *Canadian Journal of Linguistics* 10:167–187 (Toronto).
1973 'Na-Dene', in *Current Trends in Linguistics,* Thomas A. Sebeok, ed. Volume X, *Linguistics in North America* (The Hague, Mouton).
Kroeber, A. L.
1925 *Handbook of the Indians of California.* (= *Bulletin of the Bureau of American Ethnology* 78) (Washington, D.C., G.P.O.).
Li, Fang-Kuei
1930 *Mattole, an Athapaskan Language* (Chicago, University of Chicago Press).
1933 'A List of Chipewyan Stems', *International Journal of American Linguistics* 7:122–151 (Bloomington, Indiana).
Milanowski, Paul, and David Henry
1969 'Tutchone Survey', unpublished manuscript.
Miller, Wick R.
1972 'Obsolescing Languages: The Case of the Shoshoni Language', *American Indian Education* (Winter):1–15 (Tempe, Arizona).
Mooney, James
1910 'Kiowa-Apache', in *Handbook of American Indians North of Mexico* (= *Bulletin of Bureau of American Ethnology* 30:701–703) (Washington, D.C.).
Perry, Edgar
1972 *Western Apache Dictionary* (White Mountain Apache Tribe, Ft. Apache, Arizona).
Pierce, Joe E., and James M. Ryherd
1964 'The Status of Athapaskan Research in Oregon', *International Journal of American Linguistics* 30:137–144 (Bloomington, Indiana).
Reed, Erik
1944 'Navajo Monolingualism', *American Anthropologist* 46:147–149 (Washington, D.C.).
Reichard, G.
1945 'Linguistic Diversity among the Navajo Indians', *International Journal of American Linguistics* 11:156–169 (Bloomington, Indiana).
1951 *Navaho grammar* (New York, J. Augustin).
Richmond, Sara
1970 'Cognitive and Structural Bases for Group Identity: The Case of the Southern Arctic Drainage Dene', *Western Canadian Journal of Anthropology* 2(1):140–150 (Edmonton, Alberta).

Rigsby, Bruce
  1967   'Nass River Field Notes', unpublished manuscript.
Rohner, Ronald P.
  1969   *The Ethnography of Franz Boas: Letters and Diaries of Franz Boas
          written on the Northwest Coast from 1886 to 1931* (Chicago, University
          of Chicago Press).
Sapir, Edward
  1921   *Language* (New York, Harcourt, Brace).
  1924   'Personal Names among the Sarcee Indians', *American Anthropologist*
          26:108—119 (Bloomington, Indiana).
  1927   An Expedition to Ancient America: A Professor and a Chinese Student
          Rescue the Vanishing Language and Culture of the Hupas of Northern
          California', *The University of Chicago Magazine* 20:10—12 (Chicago).
  1936   'Internal Linguistic Evidence Suggestive of the Northern Origin of the
          Navaho', *American Anthropologist* 38:224—235 (Washington, D.C.)
          (Reprinted in *Selected Writings in Language, Culture and Personality*,
          Mandelbaum, David G., ed. (Berkeley, University of California Press,
          1949, pp. 213—225).
Sapir, Edward, and Harry Hoijer
  1967   'The Phonology and Morphology of the Navaho Language', *University
          of California Publications in Linguistics* 50 (Berkeley).
Saville-Troike, Muriel
  1973   *Variation and Change in Navajo: Some Preliminary Notes* (= *Language
          and Linguistics Working Papers* 7) (Washington, D.C., Georgetown
          University).
Scott, Richard B.
  1960   'English Language Skills of the Mescalero Apache Indians', *America
          Indigena* 20:173—181 (Mexico, D.F., Mexico).
Silverstein, Michael
  1972   'Goodbye Columbus: Language and Speech-community in Indian-
          European Contact situations', unpublished manuscript (The University
          of Chicago, Department of Anthropology).
Spolsky, Bernard
  1970   'Navajo Language Maintenance: Six-Year-Olds in 1969', *Language
          Sciences* 13:19—24 (Bloomington, Indiana).
  1971a 'Navajo Language Maintenance II; Six-Year-Olds in 1970', *Navajo
          Reading Study Progress Report* 13 (Albuquerque, The University of
          New Mexico).
  1971b 'Navajo Language Maintenance III: Accessibility of School and Town as
          a Factor in Language Shift', *Navajo Reading Study Progress Report* 14
          (Albuquerque, The University of New Mexico).
  1972   'Advances in Navajo Bilingual Education 1967—72', *Bureau of Indian
          Affairs Curriculum Bulletin* 13 (Washington, D.C.).
  in press 'Prospects for the Survival of the Navajo Language', to appear in a
          volume in honor of C. F. Voegelin.
Spolsky, Bernard, Penny Murphy, Wayne Holm, and Allen Ferrel
  1972   'Three Functional Tests of Oral Proficiency', *TESOL Quarterly*
          6:221—235 (Washington, D.C.).

Spolsky, Bernard, and Wayne Holm
  1971 'Bilingualism in the Six-Year-Old Navajo Child', *Preprints of the Confer-
        ence on Child Language* (Quebec, Laval University Press) pp. 225–239.
Stuart, C. I. J. M.
  1962 'American Indian Languages at Haskell Institute', *International Journal
        of American Linguistics* 28:151 (Bloomington, Indiana).
Teit, James
  1956 'Field Notes on the Tahltan and Kaska Indians', *Anthropologica*
        3:39–171 (University of Ottawa).
Tharp, George
  1972 'The Position of the Tsetsaut among the Northern Athapaskans', *Inter-
        national Journal of American Linguistics* 38:11–25 (Bloomington,
        Indiana).
Van Valkenburgh, R.
  1941 'Dine Bikeyah', mimeographed (Window Rock, United States Depart-
        ment of the Interior).
Voegelin, C. F.
  1941 'North American Indian Languages Still Spoken and Their Genetic
        Relationships', in *Language, Culture, and Personality*, L. Spier,
        A. Hallowell and S. Newman, eds. (Menasha, Wisconsin, Sapir Memorial
        Publication Fund) pp. 15–40.
Voegelin, C. F., and Dell Hymes
  1953 'A Sample of North American Indian Dictionairies with Reference to
        Acculturation', *Publications of the American Philosophical Society*
        97:633–644 (Philadelphia).
Voegelin, C. F. and F. M., and Noel Schutz, Jr.
  1967 'The Language Situation in Arizona as a Part of the Southwest Culture
        Area', in *Studies in Southwestern Ethnolinguistics,* Dell Hymes and
        William Bittle, eds. (The Hague, Mouton) pp. 403–452.
Werner, Oswald
  1963 'A Typological Comparison of Four Trader Navaho Speakers', un-
        published Ph.D. dissertation (Bloomington, Indiana University).
Young, Robert W.
  1948 'What's in a Name?', *El Palacio* 55:86–89 (Santa Fe, New Mexico).
  1972 'Written Navajo: A Brief History', *Navajo Reading Study Progress
        Report* 19 (Albuquerque, The University of New Mexico).
Young, Robert W., and William Morgan
  1947 'Navajo Place Names in Gallup, New Mexico', *El Palacio* 54:283–85
        (Santa Fe, New Mexico).
  1951 *A Vocabulary of Colloquial Navajo* (Phoenix, United States Indian
        Service).

NOTES

The preparation and writing of this article was partly supported by a grant from the Ford Foundation for the Navajo Reading Study of the University of New Mexico. We gratefully acknowledge the help of a number of researchers in preparing it; we thank Michael Krauss, Robert Young, Holly Reckord, Keith

Basso, Faith Hill, Bruce Rigsby, Harry Basehart, Elaine Clark, Karen Cantrell, and Morris Opler for providing unpublished information without which this article would have been even more sketchy. In particular we thank Michael Krauss who read an earlier version of this article and contributed many valuable suggestions and much recent information.

1. Cf. e.g., Voegelin 1941; Chafe 1962; and Pierce and Ryherd 1964.
2. Unless stated otherwise, information on the status of California Athapaskan groups in the early part of this century is from Kroeber 1925. Information on Oregon Athapaskan is from Pierce and Ryherd 1964. Information on Hupa is from Kari (fieldwork). Information on Chetco and Tolowa is from R. J. Parr (personal communication to Victor Golla). For spelling of language names throughout we generally follow Krauss (1973).
3. Information on the population and status of Alaskan Athapaskan is from Krauss (1973) and from numerous personal communications. Information on Ahtena is from Holly Reckord (personal communication) and on Kenai Tanaina from Kari (fieldwork).
4. The source of information for Slavey is Holly Reckord (personal communication); for Nicola, Bruce Rigsby (personal communication); and for Kaska, Tagish, and Tutchone, Kari (fieldwork).
5. Population figures in brackets are from the Department of Indian Affairs and Northern Development (1970). Those not in brackets are from Chafe 1962 or are more recent estimates quoted in Krauss 1973.
6. Data on the Western Apache are from Keith Basso and Faith Hill, on Mescalero and Chiricahua are from Harry Basehart, Elaine Clark, and Robert Young; on Lipan, from Morris Opler and Elaine Clark; on Jicarilla, from Karen Cantrell, Robert Young (all from personal communications) and Kari (fieldwork).
7. From 1943 to 1957 there was a newspaper published in Navajo. For an account of this and of the history of written Navajo see Young (1972).
8. Doyen of such Athapaskan-speaking linguists is William Morgan, Sr., whose work with Robert Young in the 1940s led to the dictionary and grammar; Young and Morgan are now collaborating on a revision of the dictionary. Among Navajos studying with Hale at the Massachusetts Institute of Technology is Paul Platero, who has played a major part in the development of an annual Navajo Linguistics Workshop. Also an experienced Navajo bilingual teacher, Laura Wallace, will be studying Northern Athapaskan with Krauss at the University of Alaska.

Values, Language, and Politics in Canada

INTRODUCTION

Languages as a Link to Values

There is a widespread tendency to dichotomize the populations of bilingual societies into sharply differentiated linguistic groups.[1] The practice conceals the fact that some citizens occupy a linguistic space between the two major language groups, so to speak, or more precisely a dimension overlapping both. Canada, for instance, which has provided the empirical data for this study,[2] is invariably thought of as being populated by anglophones and francophones, but a recent post-election survey shows that at least 14 percent of the electorate cannot be so classified without ambiguity. We shall examine this group of 'linguistic misfits' below, as well as the more conventional language types after we have given our reasons for utilizing language as the characteristic identifying a major social cleavage which might, some would say, be equally aptly expressed in ethnic or origin terms. We are concerned with cultural differences which can be identified with language use but which are usually measured in terms of origin or ethnicity.

Ethnicity is a notoriously elusive concept if one wishes to pin its meaning down or to operationalize it as an explanatory variable. Being a composite notion usually comprising origin, language, and religious background, it tends to subsume a cluster of characteristics which need to be isolated, particularly in many of the instances in which the idea of ethnic background is related to political perceptions and behavior.

Origin, one of the components of ethnicity, is slightly less catholic but it also poses serious problems of definition. In many societies, particularly those exhibiting high rates of geographic and social mobility, significant numbers of citizens can boast ancestors collectively belonging to two or more national groups. It is difficult to know, in such cases, which is dominant or relevant. In some societies there are in fact large numbers of the population who simply do not know their origins. It is not uncommon in Canada, for example, to encounter a paleface possessed of an unmistakably Irish name, speaking only French, who insists that his ancestors came from Canada.[3] The difficulties of defining origin precisely, and other problems associated with 'origin' do not of course rob the concept of all its uses, but they do suggest that alternate ways of defining subpopulations in heterogeneous societies might fruitfully be explored.

Language use, while not without its own problems, as we shall see, as an indicator of social cleavage and cultural differences is one of the variables which can usefully be invoked to supplement, or in some cases to replace, concepts such as ethnicity or origin in explaining social and political behavior.

All of the above is so obvious that to mention it is almost in poor taste, even when it is done in as cursory a fashion as here. It would in fact be totally out of place were it not that the points sketched above are ignored by so much of the literature on social and political cleavage and political alignments, as well as by many important general comparative studies.[4]

Two major problems confront the attempt to approach ethnic cleavage through the means of identifying the groups concerned according to the language they speak. One of these arises from the point made at the outset of this article: the question of how linguistic groups and subgroups are to be defined. The other relates to the nature and meaning of linguistic differences: what is it that is really represented by language use?

The second problem will detain us only briefly, not because it is unimportant but because it is much too vast to be considered here. We shall have to be satisfied with simply noting that language is a vessel which does affect its cargo. Ideas and modes of thought reflect the language in which they are formed and expressed, and vice versa. In the present context this aspect will simply be taken for granted without its nuances being explored.[5]

Language is viewed in this article as an indicator of the degree to which various groups of Canadians are linked to the two cultures or societies comprising the country. I am using these terms in the manner defined by the Royal Commission on Bilingualism and Biculturalism, which understood by culture 'a way of being, thinking, and feeling . . . a driving force animating a significant group of individuals united by a common tongue, and sharing the same customs, habits, and experiences'. The Commission saw 'the two dominant cultures in Canada . . . embodied in distinct societies', designating by society 'the types of organization and the institutions that a rather large population, inspired by a common culture, has created for itself or has received, and which it freely manages over quite a vast territory, where it lives as a homogeneous group according to common standards and rules of conduct'.[6]

Despite the fact that Canada, unlike the United States, has never espoused an aggressive 'melting pot' policy with respect to its ethnic minorities, the presence of the two official languages has meant that a large proportion of the country's citizens whose origin is neither French nor English has become part of one or the other of the linguistic societies. As a result about one quarter of those whose mother tongue is English are 'immigrants' to that language in the sense that they or their ancestors switched to it from another tongue. This applies even to those whose origin is French, since only about nine out of every ten Canadians of French origin claim French as his mother tongue. The drift *to* French is much less pronounced than to English.

The use of language as the indicator of social cleavage therefore obviously conceals the origin of many of the citizens. It is nevertheless useful since language use tells us a good deal about the individual's day-to-day exposure to one or the other of the cultures and to its values. It is thus assumed here that the English-speaking Canadian will reflect the values of the dominant, i.e., English, society and that the francophone will hold values of the minority society.[7]

But how to measure the degree of language exposure, given the fact that, as was suggested above, significant numbers of Canadians are not clear-cut French or English speakers?

Mother tongue is usually considered a reliable indicator of the linguistic character of populations, but it has severe limitations because it 'freezes' language use in one moment of time and in relation to only one sphere of activity. In highly mobile societies in which political perceptions may vary considerably with the age of citizens this criterion thus leaves much to be desired: it neither takes into account the distance between the individual's original and actual languages, nor does it reflect the possibility that a person may regularly speak more than one language and thus maintain active links with two or more cultural groups.

A more revealing means of identifying the linguistic characteristics of subpopulations in heterogeneous societies is to discriminate between the areas of activity with which certain languages are associated and/or to take into account also the statuses of the individuals communicating with one another in one of several possible tongues.[8]

The Language Scale

In this study each respondent in the national survey was placed on a five-point language scale depending on the number of levels on which he spoke English, French, or another language. Each of the 2767 persons interviewed was asked what language he or she spoke at home, at work, and among friends.[9] Those who spoke French or English at all *three* levels were classed as 'pure' English or French speakers; respondents speaking either of the major languages at any *two* of the three levels were identified as 'partial' anglophones or francophones, and those who spoke French and/or English at only *one* or *no* level were placed in the middle as the linguistically 'mixed' members of our sample. The following language continuum was, therefore, established: pure English – partial English – mixed – partial French – pure French.

Table I summarizes some of the more relevant attributes of each of the five linguistic groups.

The reader interested in a complete and thorough profile of our five language groups could profitably spend a good deal of time tracing the similarities and differences among them, as encapsuled in the table. I shall merely draw attention to some of the most important or potentially misleading aspects.

In dealing with the section on origin we see that two-thirds of the pure anglophones, or their forefathers, come from the British Isles. The remaining third is drawn in relatively small numbers from a variety of countries, virtually all of them in western and eastern Europe. The partial English and mixed groups are a veritable Noah's Ark, if one imagines that ship to be populated by European specimens of homo sapiens rather than animals originating throughout the world. The relatively low (70 percent) proportion of people whose origin is French, among the pure francophones, is misleading since, in addition, virtually all of the 19 percent in this group who indicated that their ancestors came from Canada are of French origin. I estimate that only about 6 or 7 percent of the pure French are non-French in origin. Our partially francophone group is also almost completely French. This section of Table I reveals an important feature of Canada's linguistic pattern — one, by the way, which greatly alarms those concerned with the survival of the French language — namely, the inexorable mobility of an overwhelming proportion of all immigrants to the English language and through it into the anglophone society.

Only one of the 566 full francophones for whom we know his religion was not a Catholic! More surprisingly, even among the partial French speakers, only two (2 percent) of the respondents declared their religion as being something other than Catholic. This sheds a suggestive light on the degree to which Protestants fail to become integrated, even partially, into Canada's francophone society. At any rate the concentration of Catholics on the French side of the language continuum must be borne in mind when interpreting our data: it will be necessary to guard against ascribing to factors associated with language use, attitudes possibly related more to the religious background of the groups concerned.

Another possible misreading of our data might follow from the failure to realize that there are significant differences in the educational experiences of our five language groups. The relevant part of Table I indicates a striking disparity in the proportion of those with only eight years or less of schooling between the pure anglophones on the one hand and the francophones and mixed group on the other. The difference between the partial French and English speakers is also great. The pure French speakers and the mixed group have had the fewest number of years in school; they are followed by the two linguistically partial groups and finally by the pure anglophones whose educational opportunities were considerably better than anyone else's.

The two francophone groups are somewhat younger than the pure and partial English speakers, but it is the mixed group which stands out in the age portion of the table. They are the oldest group by far, comprising only 8 percent under thirty years of age and over 40 percent of members who have passed a half century of life.

Little need be said about the occupational background of our five groups — it essentially reflects what we have observed about their educational history, except that the occupational table suggests that in terms of jobs, at least, the inequality between French and English has been softened somewhat, although not eradicated.

A distinct disproportion between men and women exists among

Table I. *Characteristics of Five Language Groups (In Percentages - N In Brackets)*

	Pure English	Partial English	Mixed	Partial French	Pure French	
	A	B	C	D	E	Total
Total Sample	(1799)	(135)	(143)	(118)	(572)	(2767)
	65	5	5	4	21	100
Origin						
British	66	18	4	4	5	(1206)
French	4	13	4	63	70	(511)
German, Austrian	7	11	9	2	1	(160)
Italian	1	4	16	2	–	(50)
Other West European	7	15	13	6	2	(182)
Russian, Ukrainian	4	15	19	1	–	(124)
Other East European	4	15	16	1	–	(106)
Canadian, U.S.A.	2	2	3	20	19	(148)
British and French	1	2	4	–	1	(38)
British plus any other	3	2	–	–	–	(62)
French plus any other	–	–	–	2	1	(16)
Other	1	4	4	–	–	(22)
	100	101	101	101	99	
Total	(1755)	(130)	(141)	(106)	(493)	(2625)
Religion						
Roman Catholic	19	46	62	98	100	(1153)
Other	81	54	38	2	–	(1518)
	100	100	100	100	100	
Total	(1723)	(128)	(136)	(118)	(566)	(2671)
Education						
Up to 8 years	26	34	56	43	57	(960)
9 to 13 years	60	55	33	38	32	(1406)
14 years or more	15	11	12	19	11	(374)
	101	100	101	100	100	
Total	(1791)	(131)	(138)	(116)	(564)	(2740)
Age						
21–30	22	19	8	29	29	(639)
31–50	44	42	50	44	38	(1183)
51 and over	34	39	42	27	34	(945)
	100	100	100	100	101	
Total	(1799)	(135)	(148)	(108)	(572)	(2767)
Sex						
Male	50	64	52	59	45	(1388)
Female	50	36	48	41	55	(1379)
	100	100	100	100	100	
Total	(1799)	(135)	(143)	(108)	(572)	(2767)

Table I. *Continued*

	Pure English	Partial English	Mixed	Partial French	Pure French	
	A	B	C	D	E	Total
Occupation of head of household						
Professional, owner, manager	21	21	13	21	18	(467)
Sales and clerical	18 •	9	15	20	14	(390)
Skilled labour	37	42	44	40	39	(899)
Unskilled labour	14	16	23	13	20	(369)
Farmers	11	12	6	7	9	(231)
	101	100	100	101	100	
Total	(1549)	(118)	(120)	(102)	(467)	(2356)
Language spoken at home						
English	100	70	8	3	–	(1907)
French	–	9	13	96	100	(716)
Other	–	22	79	2	–	(144)
	100	101	100	101	100	
Total	(1799)	(135)	(143)	(118)	(572)	(2767)
Language spoken at work						
English	83	82	38	41	–	(1696)
French	–	6	9	32	73	(479)
Other	–	–	24	7	–	(42)
No answer[a]	18	13	30	20	27	(550)
	101	101	101	100	100	
Total	(1799)	(135)	(143)	(118)	(572)	(2767)
Language spoken with friends						
English	100	36	8	25	–	(1890)
French	–	12	1	52	100	(650)
Other	–	52	90	23	–	(227)
	100	100	99	100	100	
Total	(1799)	(135)	(143)	(118)	(572)	(2767)
Length of domicile in Canada						
Born in Canada	82	53	34	96	99	(2264)
Arrived in 1945 or before	10	22	20	3	1	(236)
Arrived in 1946 or after	9	25	47	2	1	(263)
	101	100	101	101	101	
Total	(1797)	(135)	(143)	(118)	(570)	(2763)

[a] This group consists largely of housewives but it also includes some retired people. The language of work was recoded, for the purposes of this article, so as to correspond to the language spoken at home.

our two partial groups, largely, I suspect, because of the device, mentioned elsewhere in this paper, of recording the language at work of housewives to correspond in all instances to their language spoken at home. This may incorrectly have taken some partial French- and English-speaking women into the 'pure' columns. This was thought to have been a necessary but the least distorting step, since it left the partial groups uncontaminated and, given the large numbers to be found in the 'pure' groups, was unlikely to distort the reporting of their answers.

It is this group of housewives (which also includes widows and unemployed spinsters) which is identified in the 'Language Spoken at Work' section of the table as 550 individuals giving no answer. They were originally coded as such but, as indicated, the 'language at work' item was recoded for purposes of creating our language scale.

From the final section of the table we learn that the two francophone groups are by far the most indigenous Canadians and that only about a third of the mixed group was born in Canada. Almost half of these least English and/or French users immigrated since the end of the Second World War. A quarter of the partially English-speaking group found their way to Canada in this period, and a little over one-fifth did so before 1945.

Having described the five language groups, we can at last explore the relationships we expect to find between position on the language continuum on the one hand and political perceptions and alignments on the other.

Hypotheses: Language-use and Areas of Perception

If language use is a link to the values of cultural groups, we will expect the pure French- and the pure English-users to come closest to embodying 'in the purest form' the values respectively of the majority and minority cultures in Canada. It is well known, for example, that the Liberal party has in recent years received considerably more support from French Canadians and that Conservative allegiance was more strongly rooted among voters of British origin. We therefore expect Liberal support to be substantially greater among our pure French than among the pure English speakers. This, as we shall see, is in fact the case and it will suprise no one.

But to understand the anatomy of political alignments it is necessary to look beyond mere partisanship and to examine a wide range of perceptions and evaluations of the electorate. Social cleavages find expression in differential responses to phenomena which range from the most private, moral sphere to the large political issues confronting society. It is therefore assumed in this article that differences between the pure English- and French-speaking respondents will not be spread uniformly but that the two cultural groups will be fairly close to one another in some areas and that in others the distance between them will be considerable. Specifically, it is anticipated that we shall find the gap widest in areas which are the subject of controversy between them (the status of Quebec in Canada, attitudes to the Monarchy, liking of General de Gaulle); that a narrower but nevertheless clear-cut margin will be found in fields where the religious and moral values of the electors come into play (religiosity, attitudes to homosexuality, divorce, etc.); and that there will be relatively little or no difference with respect to reactions towards general public policy issues and concerns such as foreign policy questions, American influences on Canada, or the liking of L. B. Pearson.

What of the partial users of Canada's official languages? The predominantly English-speaking group can safely be hypothesized as approximating the perceptions and affects of the pure English, although I expect them in some instances to be somewhat closer to our linguistically 'mixed' group, occupying the middle of the language scale. The partial English users are, as Table I shows, individuals of diverse origins who, while generally speaking English, have retained a vestigial language which links them to the values of one of Canada's many ethnic minorities. Their political perceptions and values are therefore likely to be very close to the political culture of the English-speaking majority except that in some areas — those in which the interests of their own ethnic group may be particularly affected, for example — they may find themselves closer to our midpoint, linguistically (and therefore ethnically) least British or French category. A small proportion of them is of course of French descent.

The partial French group in some ways constitutes our most interesting case. Forty per cent speak English at work, and we are here confronting members of a large ethnic minority who are earning their living in the language of the country's dominant culture. While some of them may like this, it is a reasonable assumption that they have little choice in the matter and that many of them are simply responding as effectively as they can to the economic realities of Canada. In any event, this group, while French, maintains a continuous and probably highly meaningful link with the dominant cultural group and its values. It is possible to make two completely contradictory assumptions about the consequences of this exposure to the English-speaking world. (1) Partial submersion in the anglophone community exercises a powerful socializing effect, and the politically relevant perceptions of our partial French group will therefore approximate those of the pure English; they will at least be closer to them than to those of the pure French. (2) Constant exposure of the partially French-speakers to the dominant anglophone culture acts as an irritant by emphasizing the minority and generally less privileged position of people of French Canada in many sectors of Canadian life. This situation thus induces in the partially French group a resentment of the dominant culture and a consequent strongly national posture towards the issues and themes of Canadian politics. The partial French will consequently be placed at least as far from the pure English as the pure French, and possibly even farther away.

It is possible to resolve, or at least blunt, the paradox posed by these two hypotheses by recalling one of our earlier expectations: the distance between linguistic groups is likely to vary depending on the area of life and politics concerned. We will thus expect the partially French to differ most from the pure and partial English users in their perceptions of, and affects towards, items closely related to the tensions between French and English Canada but to approximate the positions of the English-speaking groups closely in, matters in which the general Canadian or even American political cultures are likely to exercise a strong 'ethnically neutral' influence on the individuals exposed to them.

At the risk both of dwelling on the obvious and of adding further to the complexity of our story, we must note that differential perceptions are inevitably to be observed among linguistic groups not only in relation to different phenomena but also *within* the membership of any given cluster of language users. In the present context, for example, I expect that among the partially French speakers, the best educated and also the youngest members are most likely to be the most nationalist, and that on questions closely relevant to the ethnic concerns of French Canada they will therefore be found at a greater distance from the anglophones than the less well educated and the older members of their linguistic group. The same should hold for the pure French speakers but a little less so.

Mixed language users — the group whose members speak English and/or French at only one or none of the three levels we have used in constructing our scale — are presumably less closely identified with either the French or English speakers than the partial groups, and their political perceptions are therefore likely to differ from either. It is to be expected, however, that this linguistically least anglicized and/or frenchified group is nevertheless likely to be socialized most by the numerically and economically dominant group in Canada — the English speakers. Since the partial English group is very similar in the heterogeneity of its ethnic composition to the mixed group, I expect the responses of the latter to be closer to the partial than to the pure English. In spheres where the particular cultural traditions of members of the mixed group might evoke a unique response, however — respect for political leaders, for example — I expect the response of our middle group to deviate widely from the norm set by the English users and also from those of the francophones.

A rather crude diagram (Diagram 1) can be constructed summarizing the above hypotheses concerning the relationships we expect to find between the language use of various groups and their political perceptions. I have arbitrarily chosen to represent the position of the culturally dominant pure English speakers as the norm against which the position of the other groups is measured. In so doing I have not tried to suggest that this position should in any way be considered as a basic norm — it would have served our purposes equally well to have chosen the pure French as our baseline, except of course that we expect most of the other groups to approximate them less than they do the pure anglophones.

In Diagram I the expected distance between the language groups is roughed in by means of five circles or circular lines which move from 'Private' to 'General Public' and to 'Ethnically Relevant Public' areas in which the language groups perceive, and react towards, phenomena which have some relevance to their political alignments. The pure (A) and partial (B) English speakers are represented by concentric circles in close propinquity and the middle, mixed group (C) is also nearby, somewhat less regular because of the expected influences of special 'ethnic' factors. Our pure francophones (E) are most distant from the A group on political questions affecting French-English relations in Canada; they approach the anglophones somewhat in matters of private morality and come even closer to them in their perceptions and evaluations of questions of general public policy. Finally, the partial French (D) are shown as being the most distant group from the English users in areas affecting French-English relations but they are closer to the dominant cultural group in the

676   *John Meisel*

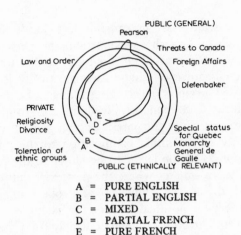

A = PURE ENGLISH
B = PARTIAL ENGLISH
C = MIXED
D = PARTIAL FRENCH
E = PURE FRENCH

Diagram I. *Language Use and Perceptions of Phenomena Relevant to Political Alignments*

private values sector and also in that of general public policy.

In testing our hypotheses we shall examine each of the three areas in turn, beginning with Private Values defined quite narrowly.[10] We shall then cast a glance at some Private Values which, however, are more closely related to the General Public Policy and finally we shall consider Private Values touching on problems of Ethnic Relations in Canada. Then we shall look at the General Public Sector and finally at the Ethnically Relevant Public Sector. Throughout we shall draw freely on various questions from the 1968 post-election Canadian survey. Since this is very much an exploratory exercise we shall select those questions or indices which are particularly useful in testing our hypotheses focusing on examples which either strongly support or question the expectations we described above. This loose method provides an admirable means of roaming freely among the available data and of seeking illuminating examples of the points raised and of finding instances confirming or challenging our expectations. It does not, however, lead to the immediate drafting of a formal theory permitting sure predictions about the relation between social structure (or its linguistic and cultural aspects) and political alignments. This may come later; this article is, at best, a small and halting step towards such a formalization. Its more general use will be touched upon in the conclusion.

PRIVATE VALUES

Religiosity

Our first 'test' concerns the religiosity of the members of the five language groups. 'Religiosity' is here conceived as being related both to the individual's exercise of religious practices and to the more social and societal aspects of religion.[11] As the Chart I shows, the mean scores obtained by the five language groups rise in an orderly fashion from a low of 5.3 for the pure English users to a high of 8.8 attained by the pure francophones. The difference between the two extreme poles is substantial. Both groups of partial users display mean scores which are less extreme than their 'purer' neighbors. The distance is particularly noticeable between the partial and pure French. The linguistically mixed respondents' score places them between the anglophones and the francophones, somewhat closer to the former than to the latter.

Education, as the row of figures at the bottom of Chart I shows, has some influence on the religiosity scores within some of the language groups, particularly among the two partial users and the pure French: in each of these three cases the least educated displayed the highest degree of religiosity and the best educated the lowest. Educational background had little effect on the religiosity scores of groups A and C. But the chart makes it clear that language use washes out the educational influence: the scores of the subgroups corresponding to educational experience rises as we move from language group A to language group E.

The age of our respondents has had less effect even than education in offsetting the influences represented by language use. The oldest cohort, as indicated by the top row in the chart, registered a marginally higher religiosity score than its language group's overall mean in all cases but that of the pure English users and of the partial French but that is about the only relation of age to religiosity worth noting, except of course that language use is an incomparably more relevant variable. In view of some observations to be made later about the middle-aged group among the partial French speakers, we should, however, note this cohort's relatively low religiosity score among the two francophone groups.

Studies of the attitudes of Protestants and Catholics towards various aspects of religion lead us to expect 'Catholic' religiosity scores to be consistently higher than those of the others.[12] As the insets in the five circles in Chart I show, this was in fact the case. The mean score of the pure anglophone Catholics (left inset) was 6.3, that of the non-Catholics (right inset) 5.3. The comparable figures for the partially English are 6.3 and 5.2; for the mixed group 6.5 and 6.0. There are not enough non-Catholics among the francophones to provide comparable data but the scores for the Catholics in groups D and E are significantly higher than those of the English-speaking Catholics. We see, therefore, that even when religion is held constant, the francophone members of our sample displayed a substantially higher degree of religiosity than the anglophones and than the mixed group.

Chart I. *Religiosity*

In this and the following charts, each of the balls shows the means as follows:

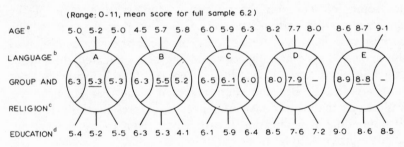

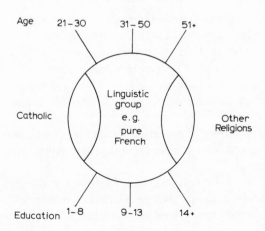

Moral Values

Very similar results obtain when we examine the reactions of our five language groups to homosexuality and divorce.[13] In both instances the two anglophone groups are more liberal (indicated by a higher score in Chart II [a] and a lower mean in Chart II [b]) and the distances separating the English from the French groups are substantial. The partial francophones are slightly closer to the position of the anglophones than the pure French speakers; the partial English have the same mean score as the pure English with respect to the treatment of homosexuals and are slightly closer to the francophones than the A group in their attitude towards divorce.

With only minor exceptions (notably the D group's assessment of divorce laws) education is positively correlated with a liberal stand but position on the language use continuum exerts an even stronger influence than education in enabling us to predict the attitude of our respondents to homosexuality and divorce. With respect to divorce the mean scores of those with the lowest number of years of schooling are very close to one another in all but the pure French-speaking group. The pure English and partial French, for example, share a reading of 2.6. The differences between the language groups on the moral values dimension are generally greater among the best educated than among the other two educational categories.

No significant relationships between age and moral values are revealed in Chart II. We should, however, again note that among the partial francophones, the middle-aged group appears to be slightly

---

Notes to Chart I.

a *Age* The three categories for each of the language groups correspond to those in Table I. The score of the 21 to 30 year group is on the left, that of the 31 to 50 cohort in the middle and of the 51 and over group on the right.

b *Language Group* Pure English A; Partial English B; Mixed C; Partial French D; Pure French E. The score is underlined.

c *Religion* The score of the Catholics is in the left inset, that of all others in the right inset. The sample was divided into only two groups: Catholics and all others. The mean score of each of the language groups does not always correspond to that computed for the whole sample because 96 cases, whose religious affiliation is not known, had to be excluded. This explains the differences in the mean scores of Catholics and of the whole language group in D and E.

d *Education* The scores of those who have had up to eight years of schooling are at the left, those with nine to thirteen years of schooling in the middle, and of those with fourteen years or more on the right.

Chart II. *Moral Values*

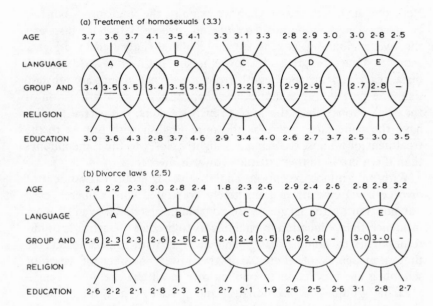

(a) Treatment of homosexuals (3.3)

AGE   3·7   3·6   3·7   4·1   3·5   4·1   3·3   3·1   3·3   2·8   2·9   3·0   3·0   2·8   2·5

LANGUAGE GROUP AND RELIGION

A: 3·4 | 3·5 | 3·5   B: 3·4 | 3·5 | 3·5   C: 3·1 | 3·2 | 3·3   D: 2·9 | 2·9 | –   E: 2·7 | 2·8 | –

EDUCATION   3·0   3·6   4·3   2·8   3·7   4·6   2·9   3·4   4·0   2·6   2·7   3·7   2·5   3·0   3·5

(b) Divorce laws (2.5)

AGE   2·4   2·2   2·3   2·0   2·8   2·4   1·8   2·3   2·6   2·9   2·4   2·6   2·8   2·8   3·2

LANGUAGE GROUP AND RELIGION

A: 2·6 | 2·3 | 2·3   B: 2·6 | 2·5 | 2·5   C: 2·4 | 2·4 | 2·5   D: 2·6 | 2·8 | –   E: 3·0 | 3·0 | –

EDUCATION   2·6   2·2   2·1   2·8   2·3   2·1   2·7   2·1   1·9   2·6   2·5   2·6   3·1   2·8   2·7

more liberal than the youngest group; this pattern is not found among the pure French, however.

The difference between Catholics and non-Catholics in our total sample is greater with respect to their attitudes to homosexuals than to divorce. In the former case the mean scores are 2.9 for the Catholics as compared with 3.5 for the others. The comparable mean scores of their attitudes to changes in the divorce laws are 2.8 and 2.3. The difference in attitudes to homosexuals must, as section (a) of Chart II shows, be ascribed almost entirely to the presence in our universe of French-speaking Catholics, since the scores for their English-speaking and linguistically mixed coreligionists diverge only very little from those of the other religious groups, when these are lumped into one category. There is a slightly greater Catholic–non-Catholic split with respect to divorce but even here it is small, and among the non-French groups, confined to the pure anglophones. The scores for the partial French and English Catholics are, interestingly, the same.

A comparable examination of attitudes toward the abolition of the death penalty (chart omitted) indicated that while there clearly is a difference between the five language groups, it is smaller than in the two instances discussed above. The partial French-speaking group is marginally the most liberal and the middle-aged members of the two francophone groups are, again, more liberal than the youngest group.

Our hypotheses with respect to Private Values are confirmed when these are related rather narrowly to religiosity and attitudes on societal reactions to divorce, homosexuality, and capital punishment; a substantial difference is to be observed between pure anglophones and pure francophones; members of the partial groups differ slightly from their linguistically 'purer' brethren by placing themselves closer to the other language pole. The mean scores of the mixed, centrally located linguistic subpopulation generally fall between the franco-phones and the anglophones, in somewhat greater proximity to the latter. We shall now try to discover whether we can make the same observations about moral valuations which are more directly related to questions of public policy.

Law and Order

We have selected the issue of law and order as one of our test cases and shall take two sets of snapshots, so to speak, of it: on the one hand we shall see how the language groups reacted to a number of questions in which the breaking of laws under certain stated con-ditions can be condemned or condoned. Some of these refer to areas of life closely relevant to the interests of the language groups. On the other hand we have obtained assessments from our respondents of the importance of, and their liking for, a number of offices and agencies concerned with maintaining law and order.

Anglophones are revealed by our index to have a distinctly higher regard for law and order than francophones.[14] The scores are as follows:

Group A	Group B	Group C	Group D	Group E
6.9	6.7	6.4	6.1	5.4

Once again the partial users of each of the two main languages are placed close to the pure users but in this instance the partial franco-phones are quite a long way towards the anglophone pole and are, in fact, closer to the partial English users than to the pure French. The mixed group continues to stand between the English and French users, somewhat closer to the former than to the latter. It is surprising, in view of the ethnically highly relevant component of the index (the second question listed in footnote 14), that the difference between the pure language groups is not greater.

A less direct means of exploring attitudes towards law and order yields more muted results. Our respondents were asked to indicate how much they *liked* certain groups and how *important* they thought certain public offices to be. The police and the military were included among both the groups and the offices; judges and the Supreme Court were added to the latter category.[15] While this is a clumsy and perilous way of going about our business it was judged a useful exercise for the purposes at hand.

Chart III tells us that the differences between the language groups are so small as to be meaningless. The results are in fact pointing in opposite directions: the police are rated more highly by the anglophones than by the francophones, whereas the military receive a slightly higher score from the pure French than from the pure English. This suggests that the items used are not valid indicators of attitudes to law and order but, as we shall see, they display acceptable consistency when used to assess the *importance* our respondents attach to offices concerned with maintaining law and order.

Chart III. *Liking of Policemen and the Military*

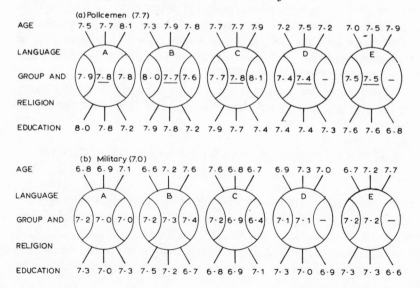

The data summarized in Chart III do nevertheless reveal some interesting differences between our language groups. The most highly educated among the pure and partial French rate both the police and the military least favorably. With respect to age we find that in all cases except the scores of the mixed group and, interestingly, the partial French-speakers' rating of the policemen, the youngest cohort like the agents of law and order less than their seniors.

No pattern emerges when the relationship is examined between religion and language use in the assessment of policemen; Catholics in all but one language group rate the military at 7.2. This might suggest that religion is more related to feelings towards the military than linguistic ties but the margins between the groups are so small (except in C), and the direction of the differences so inconsistent as to preclude our making any generalizations in this respect. Although we have avoided reporting on occupational differences (they were found to be generally uninteresting) it should be noted as a curiosity that whereas all other occupational groups among the pure French users scored the police at 7.4 or 7.5, pure francophone farmers were able to muster only a mere 6.9.

It is reasonable to assume that one's attitude to law and order is related to the importance one assigns the institutions society has established to maintain them. Before turning to Chart IV, which tabulates the data, it is useful to note that francophones and anglophones ranked the agents of law and order differently, relative to the other offices about which they were questioned. All our groups thought the police to be the most important among the four law enforcement agencies but whereas both the anglophone and the mixed groups assigned them second place, immediately after that of the prime minister, the two francophone groups placed them fourth, below the provincial premiers and the federal members of Parliament. This pattern is reinforced by each of the four sections in the chart which also show that a real, although not pronounced, difference between our language groups exists in the importance they attach to the law enforcing offices and that the scores are higher among the anglophones.

The partial anglophones rate the four offices slightly more highly than the other groups; they are followed by the pure anglophones, the mixed, the partial French and finally by the pure French users. The difference between the 'neighboring' language groups are small but consistent.

As previously, the most educated subgroups among the franco-

Chart IV. *Importance Attached to Law and Order Agencies*

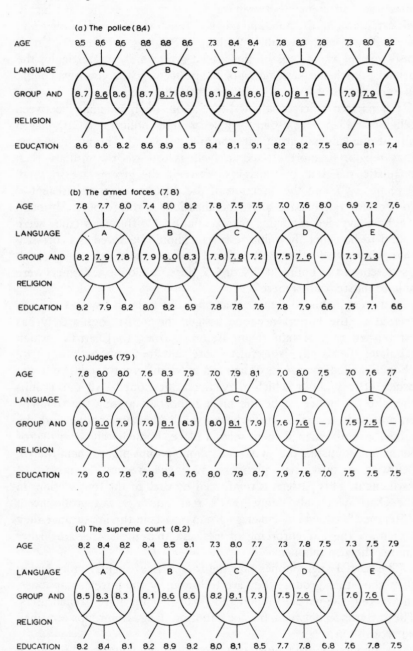

(a) The police (8.4)

AGE	8.5	8.6	8.6	8.8	8.8	8.6	7.3	8.4	8.4	7.8	8.3	7.8	7.3	8.0	8.2
LANGUAGE	A			B			C			D			E		
GROUP AND	8.7	8.6	8.6	8.7	8.7	8.9	8.1	8.4	8.6	8.0	8.1	—	7.9	7.9	—
RELIGION															
EDUCATION	8.6	8.6	8.2	8.6	8.9	8.5	8.4	8.1	9.1	8.2	8.2	7.5	8.0	8.1	7.4

(b) The armed forces (7.8)

AGE	7.8	7.7	8.0	7.4	8.0	8.2	7.8	7.5	7.5	7.0	7.6	8.0	6.9	7.2	7.6
LANGUAGE	A			B			C			D			E		
GROUP AND	8.2	7.9	7.8	7.9	8.0	8.3	7.8	7.8	7.2	7.5	7.6	—	7.3	7.3	—
RELIGION															
EDUCATION	8.2	7.9	8.2	8.0	8.2	6.9	7.8	7.8	7.6	7.8	7.9	6.6	7.5	7.1	6.6

(c) Judges (7.9)

AGE	7.8	8.0	8.0	7.6	8.3	7.9	7.0	7.9	8.1	7.0	8.0	7.5	7.0	7.6	7.7
LANGUAGE	A			B			C			D			E		
GROUP AND	8.0	8.0	7.9	7.9	8.1	8.3	8.0	8.1	7.9	7.6	7.6	—	7.5	7.5	—
RELIGION															
EDUCATION	7.9	8.0	7.8	7.8	8.4	7.6	8.0	7.9	8.7	7.9	7.6	7.0	7.5	7.5	7.5

(d) The supreme court (8.2)

AGE	8.2	8.4	8.2	8.4	8.5	8.1	7.3	8.0	7.7	7.3	7.8	7.5	7.3	7.5	7.9
LANGUAGE	A			B			C			D			E		
GROUP AND	8.5	8.3	8.3	8.1	8.6	8.6	8.2	8.1	7.3	7.5	7.6	—	7.6	7.6	—
RELIGION															
EDUCATION	8.2	8.4	8.1	8.2	8.9	8.2	8.0	8.1	8.5	7.7	7.8	6.8	7.6	7.8	7.5

phones rate the law enforcers lowest with two interesting exceptions: the educational background had no visible effect on the scores received by the judges and the Supreme Court from the pure French users. Language use is generally related to the scores more closely than education except in one instance in which the rating obtained by the armed forces from the most highly educated among the partial English users was uncharacteristically low.[16]

The youngest cohort tends generally to rate the four offices lower than the older groups and with respect to judges and the Court, respectively, displayed complete constancy in the case of both French-speaking and the mixed groups. In these cases the differences in mean scores between the language groups must be ascribed to the older generations.

Catholics among the pure anglophones and the mixed group have a slightly higher opinion of the importance of the four offices than non-Catholics, but the situation is reversed among the partial English users. The scores of the Catholics generally drop as they move from the pure English to the French poles of the continuum but this is not so in the case of the other religious groups. The higher regard for law and order among the partially English-speaking population than among the pure anglophones is in fact attributable to the higher scores received by the four offices from the non-Catholic members of the sample.

If the public's reaction to law and order, as identified above, is viewed as an extension of its private values towards some more general community values, then we can conclude tentatively that some of our hypotheses stated earlier are confirmed, while others appear less acceptable. Taking the various readings of attitudes together we find that the anglophones place law and order more highly in the scheme of things than francophones but that the difference between the linguistic groups in this area is smaller than was the case when we were considering Private Values in a narrower sense. The position occupied on the law and order index by the partial French users — closer to the partial anglophones than to the pure French — suggests, however, that our expectation may have to be revised, that in matters touching on ethnic interests the partial French would differ from the anglophone majority *more* than the pure francophones. This is a matter to which we shall return later.

The two English-speaking groups are again close together but the partial anglophones are by no means always nearer to the center of our language continuum, as expected. The mixed group occupies its customary place between the two extremes, somewhat closer to the English pole.

The response to our probing into the degree to which law and order agents are liked casts doubt on our hypothesis that the best educated partial francophones are likely to resemble the anglophones even less than the pure francophones. We saw that the best educated among the last group scored the police and military much lower than the less well educated but that this was not the case among the partial French users. The data also indicate that while generally the youngest group displayed the least affection for the officers of law and order, the mixed group and, more surprisingly, the partial francophones, failed to conform to this pattern.

We saw no reason, when formulating our hypotheses, to expect the partial anglophones to adopt 'extreme' positions in the sense of being more distant from the francophones than even the pure English speakers. It was therefore surprising to find that they did attach more importance than their pure colinguists to all four of our law and order offices. On the other hand the expected behavior of the best educated francophones and of the youngest cohort was encountered in the answers to our question about the importance of the four law and order offices, except with respect to the failure of the best educated pure French to rate the judges and Supreme Court lower than the less well educated members of their group.

Ethnic and Religious Toleration

One area in which the Private Values of individuals impinge on ethnically relevant issues in a heterogeneous society concerns how they affect their attitudes to other groups. We shall concentrate on how those belonging to our five language categories like a number of groups of different origins and religions. We shall then probe generally into the degree to which each would like to see Canada display ethnic and religious heterogeneity.[17]

Table II indicates that there are some interesting similarities, as well as differences, between the five language groups. The scores received by Americans and Negroes, for example, do not vary noticeably insofar as the francophones and anglophones are concerned but, in the case of the Americans, show a perceptible difference between pure and partial language users. Differences between language groups are greater with respect to 'known' or 'near' groups than with the more 'remote' ones such as Negroes or Americans. For members of

Table II. *Liking of Selected Groups*[a]

Selected groups	Language group				
	A	B	C	D	E
English Canadians	7.5	7.6	7.3	7.6	6.8
French Canadians	6.2	6.6	7.0	8.6	8.9
'Other' Canadians	6.8	7.2	7.4	6.4	6.0
Americans	6.8	7.1	6.9	7.2	6.6
Negroes	6.6	6.6	6.4	6.9	6.8
Jews	6.3	6.4	6.0	6.1	5.5
Protestants	7.5	7.2	6.6	6.9	5.9
Catholics	6.9	7.5	7.4	8.0	8.4

[a] For an explanation of the scores see footnote 15. Pure anglophones A; Partial anglophones B; Mixed C; Partial francophones D; Pure francophones E.

the 'other' ethnic groups and Jews, the pure francophones report lower scores than the pure English, and the margin, while not very wide, does reveal a meaningful difference in affect. It is likely that the French-English difference in the rating of some groups and not of others is related to the proximity of the respective groups and, in some measure, to the degree to which they may be viewed as potential competitors. Americans and Negroes are more remote and therefore appear less of a threat to the francophones who are likely to be particularly sensitive to the competition in the Canadian economy provided by minority groups of whose presence in Canada they are aware.

As in virtually all other cases we have examined, the partial French users usually respond more like the English users than the pure French and in most cases by a fairly considerable margin. Surprisingly, among the English-speaking groups the partial anglophones tend to record the higher scores.

When English- and French-speaking Canadians indicate how much they like one another, we find that the latter group is somewhat more generous: our pure anglophones give the French Canadians a score of 6.2 but the pure francophones rate English Canadians at 6.8. The partial French users surprisingly join the partial anglophones in assigning the highest score to English Canadians. Both francophone groups like English Canadians better than compatriots who are neither English nor French, but the anglophones scored the latter group higher than they did French Canadians.

Although the anglophones may be less tolerant of French Canadians than vice versa, they seem to offer a somewhat more generous score than the francophones on the religious dimension (table omitted). We have already noted their higher score for Jews; when religion is held constant we find that English-speaking protestants rate Catholics at 6.6 whereas the pure French group, which is entirely Catholic, assign the protestants a mere 5.9, as Table II shows.

While the above glimpse of the way in which the language users like or dislike various groups confirms our general hypothesis that exposure to the values of the other culture through the use of language narrows the gap between Canada's two value systems, it also presents a somewhat confused picture of the differences in their tolerance of minorities between French- and English-speaking Canadians, assuming of course that liking or disliking of a group can be equated with tolerance.

A clearer picture emerges when one examines the response to two statements suggesting that Canada would be a better place if it were homogeneous ethnically and religiously.[18] Chart V shows that a substantial gap separates the occupants of the two poles on our language continuum, particularly on the ethnic dimension and that the usual progression is again evident with only one exception (Groups C and D in Chart V [b]). Francophones prefer a more homogeneous Canada; anglophones are more receptive to heterogeneity. There is a faint suggestion in the chart that English-speaking Canadians find heterogeneity along ethnic lines slightly more acceptable than in the religious sphere and that the francophones display an opposite reaction: a religiously mixed Canada is a little less off-putting to them than an ethnically varied one. But the difference is very slight. The partial and pure anglophones are very close to one another here; the gap between the pure and partial francophones is more significant.

Partial French speakers with post-secondary education are more tolerant than their pure francophone educational peers, but the gap is at least as great between some of the less educated subgroups. That education is a powerful factor is nevertheless clear: the distance in each linguistic category between the educational subgroups is considerably greater than the distance between the language groups themselves. The younger cohorts are generally more tolerant than the older ones among the anglophones and the mixed group but this pattern is not evident among the francophones. Catholics appear to

Chart V. *Ethnic and Religious Toleration*

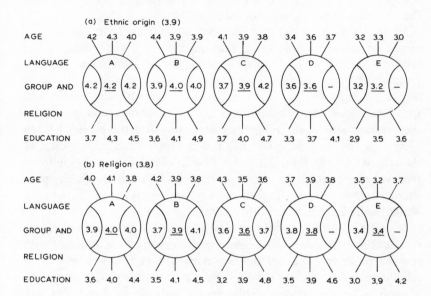

be very slightly more intolerant than the other groups but the evidence here is slender indeed.

According to our expectations, the gap between the English- and French-speaking groups should be particularly wide when their private values are linked to issues touching on the relations between ethnic groups. With reference to toleration, therefore, we expected the distance between the two anglophone groups, on the one hand, and the two French-speaking ones, on the other, to be wider than in any other area discussed so far. We also anticipated that the best educated and youngest among the partial francophones would reveal responses substantially different from the anglophones and from less educated and older members of their own language group.

Some of these predictions were confirmed but by no means all of them. No difference between the language groups was observed in relation to the liking expressed for Americans and Negroes — groups which were deemed ˙to be largely unrelated to Canada's ethnic tensions. Considerable differences were, however, manifest when attitudes to Jews, Canadians of non-French or non-British origin, were considered and particularly, and not surprisingly, when ratings were compared of French and English Canadians.

Contrary to what we anticipated, the partial French users revealed a strong liking for the English Canadians and anglophones indicated that on the whole they did not like the French very much.

In indicating a preference between an ethnically and religiously mixed or uniform Canada, our respondents did display some of the attitudes we expected: the gap between the two dominant language groups was wider than that separating them on questions relating to divorce, homosexuality, and the dealth penalty. We also found that the distance between anglophones and francophones was greater on the ethnic than on the religious dimensions. But the partial French users appeared anything but the rather rabid, nationalist group we thought we might find. They were much closer to the anglophones than we expected, occupying a position midpoint between the pure French and the partial English users in one instance, and being even closer to the English pole in the other.

Some of our expectations clearly need to be examined more closely since they are challenged by the evidence we adduced with respect to Private Values defined narrowly at first, as related to religiosity and some moral issues, then more broadly with respect to a question in the general public area — that of law and order and, finally, in an area of some ethnic sensitivity — toleration of ethnic and religious minorities.

GENERAL CANADIAN ISSUES (PUBLIC POLICY)

Having exemplified our method of proceeding in examining differences between five classes of Canada's language users with respect to Private Values, we can now move with greater dispatch while considering some general national issues more related to Public Policy. Again, areas of concern will be selected quite arbitrarily because they serve our current purposes, and no attempt will be made to produce a microcosm of the main current Canadian preoccupations. Our attention is directed towards three areas: liking for certain leaders, perceptions of what threatens Canada, and some foreign policy questions.

Liking of Johnson, Pearson, and Diefenbaker

Our respondents were asked to tell us how much they liked or disliked a number of political leaders by giving them a score on the

Table III. *Liking for Johnson, Pearson, and Diefenbaker*[a]

Political figure	Group A	Group B	Group C	Group D	Group E
Lyndon B. Johnson	6.2	6.1	6.0	6.1	5.7
L. B. Pearson	6.8	7.1	7.4	6.9	6.7
J. G. Diefenbaker	6.5	6.1	6.0	5.5	5.1

[a]For an explanation of the scores see note 15.

thermometer-type question to which reference has already been made above. The three individuals scored in Table III were chosen here because one — the former President Johnson — is likely to be 'ethnically' noncontroversial, whereas the other two represent national leaders who had adopted quite different approaches to French-English relations. Lester Pearson was well known for his sympathetic attitude to French Canada; John Diefenbaker had failed to establish bonds of confidence with Quebec.

With respect to President Johnson there is no significant difference among all the groups except the pure francophones who clearly thought less of him than the others. Mr. Pearson is liked equally well by both pure language users and is viewed with particular favor by the mixed group. The former prime minister, Mr. Diefenbaker, is liked better than President Johnson only by the pure English, and his popularity declines quite steeply as we move towards the French end of the continuum.

Table IV. *Perceptions of Threats to Canada*

Threat	Pure English	Partial English	Mixed	Partial French	Pure French	Total
	A	B	C	D	E	(N)
Internal disunity	24	26	25	24	22	(608)
Communism	14	14	17	18	14	(368)
Atomic war	36	42	43	41	42	(984)
Resource depletion	6	4	3	5	4	(138)
U.S. domination	20	14	13	13	18	(487)
	100	100	100	100	100	
Total (N)	(1692)	(122)	(120)	(111)	(540)	(2585)

These scores suggest that the differences between French and English users can disappear when a noncontroversial national personage like Mr. Pearson is evaluated, but that quite a pronounced difference occurs when an 'ethnically' relevant issue is presented. This is hardly surprising but what is rather unexpected is that the differences between the partial and pure French speakers do not vary much as we move from an ethnically 'neutral' to an ethnically 'sensitive' person. It is also surprising that the pure francophones should judge President Johnson less favorably than the other language users. Table IV, to which we turn next, suggests that this low score is not likely to be the result of greater pure francophone fear of American influences on Canada.

Perceptions of Threats to Canada

In responding to the question 'Which of the following is the most dangerous to the survival of Canada?' the respondents were to choose from among the following:

(a)   Internal disunity resulting from English-French conflict
(b)   External danger of communism
(c)   An atomic war
(d)   The using up of natural resources
(e)   American economic and social domination

With the exception of fears of an atomic war there were only minor differences between the two pure language groups. Not even the threat of Canada being disunited because of the French-English conflict elicited a highly differentiated response. In the case concerning the war threat the pure francophones reacted in a manner very similar to that of all the other groups except the pure anglophones who were more sanguine than everyone else about this menace.

The partial and mixed groups react somewhat differently from the pure ones to both communism and American domination. It is the partial francophones who are most concerned about communism, followed closely by the mixed group. The differences are small but, in the case of the partial French particularly, nevertheless puzzling. One-third of the mixed group has east European origins and can therefore be expected to have a somewhat stronger reaction to communism, but the same cannot be said of the members of our D category. They also share with the mixed group the lowest percentage of individuals fearing American economic and social domination. Here both the pure groups showed noticeably greater concern, the anglophones a shade more so.

Foreign Policy

General questions of foreign policy, when unrelated to the *Francophonie* or to Quebec's international presence, might be expected to evoke a rather similar response from anglophones and francophones in Canada and were therefore considered useful items for the testing of our hypotheses with respect to the distance likely to separate our linguistic groups in areas of General Public Policy.

There is, however, little point in trying to seek opinions on policy questions from individuals who have little or no interest in or knowledge of them. Our respondents were accordingly led through a gateway which allowed the more interested to be retained for further questioning and the less interested to get on to other things. A fairly wide gap separated the francophones from all others on the screen question, which sought to discover whether our respondents were extremely, fairly, or not too interested in foreign affairs:[19]

Group A	Group B	Group C	Group D	Group E
3.0	3.0	3.0	3.3	3.6

The response of the partial francophones seems somewhat contaminated by their contact with the English-speaking world. Differences between our language groups assume a much finer texture, however, when we continue questioning the 1476 individuals (53 percent of the total) who passed through our gateway by stating that they were at least fairly interested in foreign policy questions.

On balance, there is more agreement than disagreement among the language groups on this battery of eight questions. Table V shows that there was a fairly impressive English-French difference over the idea that Canada should become more involved in Latin America and also between the pure francophones on the one hand and all the rest on the other with respect to Canada not needing its existing level of military forces. A modest margin separated the two pure language groups' positions on foreign aid and on Canada providing the United States with air space and bases, but the difference on all other issues is so small as to be insignificant. There is, thus, something ap-

Table V. *Attitudes to Foreign Policy Issues*[a] *(N = 1475)*

	Language Groups				
	A	B	C	D	E
(a) Greater involvement in Latin America	3.2	3.1	3.0	2.7	2.3
(b) No need for present level of forces	3.5	3.5	3.3	3.4	2.7
(c) Closer relations with China	3.0	3.1	3.3	3.6	3.2
(d) Reduce foreign aid	3.6	3.3	3.3	3.1	3.2
(e) Help U.S.A. in Vietnam	4.3	4.4	4.0	4.3	4.2
(f) Give U.S.A. Canadian bases	2.2	2.4	2.5	2.3	2.6
(g) Greater independence from U.S.A.	2.1	2.1	2.1	2.4	1.9
(h) Increase immigration from Asia and Africa	3.6	3.4	3.3	3.9	3.5

[a] The exact wording of the question was: 'Here are some of the suggestions that have been made about what Canada should do in world affairs. For each, please tell me whether you agree strongly, agree mildly, disagree mildly or disagree strongly. If you have no opinions, please say so. (a) Canada should become more involved in Latin America; (b) Canada does not need to maintain its present level of military forces; (c) Canada should establish closer relations with Communist China; (d) Canada should *reduce* its foreign aid; (e) Canada should send military forces to help the United States in Vietnam; (f) Canada should continue to give the United States the use of Canadian bases and air space; (g) Canada's foreign policy should be more independent of the United States; (h) Canada should encourage an increase in the number of immigrants from Asia and Africa.' The mean scores were arrived at by adopting our usual coding scheme for this type of question: Agree strongly 1; Agree mildly 2; No opinion 3; Disagree mildly 4; Disagree strongly 5.

proaching agreement on all issues which are not ethnically relevant: Latin America has, for obvious reasons, been of greater interest to francophones than to anglophones, and the pure francophones' posture on statement (b) may reflect French Canada's long history of opposing military involvement in Europe.[20]

The mixed group displays a curious inconsistency in adopting the most hawkish position of the five with respect to Canada's getting involved in Vietnam and at the same time indicating the second strongest opposition to Canada offering the United States bases and air space. Another arresting pattern is provided by the partial French speakers who record the strongest disagreement with establishing closer ties with China, with Canada adopting a foreign policy more independent of the United States, and with increasing immigration from Asia and Africa. These postures were perhaps foreshadowed in some of the threat perceptions (communism and American domination) but they do not seem congruent with those adopted by the same group in other areas.

Our excursion into a number of General Public Issues has confirmed our expectations about this area in at least one important respect: the distance between the language groups, particularly the pure anglophones and francophones, is narrower here than in the area of Private Values, and frequently disappears altogether. But the gap between them tends to widen (as Mr. Diefenbaker's scores and the attitudes to closer ties with Latin America indicate) as soon as the general sphere assumes some special significance, even fairly remote, to ethnic relations in Canada.

When dealing with Private Values we observed a general tendency for the partial, and to some extent also the mixed, groups to fall into a neat progression endowing most of the series or our continuum with what appears like a highly scaleable quality. This pattern is much less evident in the examples of responses to Public Issues we consulted above. The partial groups in many instances seem, so to speak, to stake out a position for themselves somewhat independent of the pure language users. The pattern observed here, however, does not confirm one of our hypotheses, namely, that the partial francophones might become more extreme, nationalist, and radical than their French-speaking neighbours, when they confront ethnically sensitive questions and problems. We will be able to shed more light on this aspect of our analysis when we focus fully on some issues which are of unmistakable ethnic relevance — a task to which we turn next.

ETHNICALLY RELEVANT PUBLIC ISSUES

From the plethora of examples available to us we shall select some related to the place of the monarchy, constitutional change, to some issues specifically related to current political controversies between French- and English-speaking Canadians, and to the liking of three controversial politicians.

The Monarchy and Constitutional Change

Charts VI and VII yield insights into perceptions of the monarchy by
summarizing some data on how important the Queen and the
Governor General were judged to be, and by recording reactions to
the proposal that the monarchy be abolished in Canada.[21] In addition
to the latter, Chart VII also indicates what was thought of making
changes in the constitution and of enabling provincial governments
to participate in international educational conferences (both currently hot issues in French-English relations).[22]

Chart VI. *Importance Attached to Queen and Governor General*

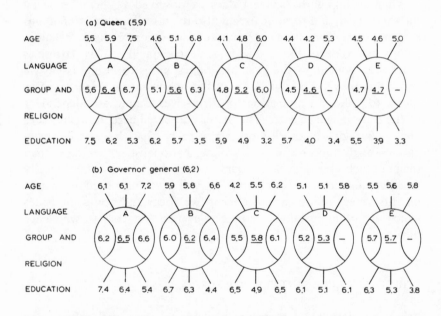

Distances are great between the francophones and the anglophones, particularly among the pure language users. It is indeed in
this cluster of responses that we find the greatest gaps occurring
between Canada's language groups — a result that is hardly surprising.
The mixed group generally continues to place itself in the middle.
But our interest focuses specially on the partial users. Here we see a
rather wide margin separating the partial from the pure anglophones,
with the exception only of one dimension — (c) in Chart VII,

Chart VII. *Attitudes to Some Ethnically Relevant Issues*

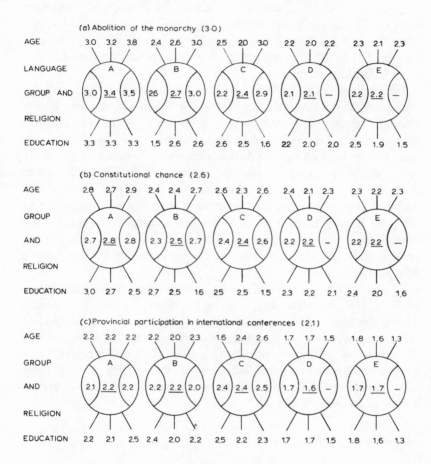

Group A is clearly more royalist and in the present context more conservative. It should, however, be noted that although the pure anglophones may appear to be considerably more devoted to the Queen and the Governor General than our other groups, they still consider them to be far less important than any of the other offices cited.

If the partial anglophones exhibit a somewhat atypical relationship with their pure co-linguists, the attitudes of the partial French users are even more interesting. On all but one of the positions reported upon in Charts VI and VII the partial French take a more French-Canadian nationalist position than the pure French speakers. The distance is small, but it will be recalled that in virtually all previously examined cases they were *between* the pure French- and the English-speaking groups. Partial language use (or, more precisely, what is represented by it) thus appears to be conducive to the adoption of a more nationalist stance.

Educational levels achieved by the francophone respondents are not related to a more nationalist position quite in the way I anticipated. Among the pure French users there is an unmistakable pattern of the best educated being the most nationalist, but we did not find, as we had expected, that this was even more pronounced, and consistent, among the partial French speakers. The contrary was the case. We cannot leave a discussion of the effects of education without noting that the post-secondary group in all categories but the pure English made a similar, very low assessment of the Queen's importance; only among the pure anglophones was this pattern broken and even here the best educated groups assigned the Queen a relatively low score.

The youngest members of the francophone groups were not found to be the more nationalist. Although differences between cohorts within the francophone groups are small, such as do appear tend to reveal the middle-aged group as most radical in this sense. Roman Catholics are distinctly more anti-royalist than the other religious groups combined but English-speaking Catholics less so than those who speak French. On the constitutional dimension Catholics appear a little more conservative.

Attitudes to Quebec

Some of the highly suggestive patterns, particularly in the responses of the partial francophones are not, alas, confirmed when we zero in on questions dealing specifically with the French-English crisis. One of the bones of contention here has been the status of the province of Quebec in the Canadian federation: should it occupy a special position or should no difference be made between it and the other provinces? The response to this question is a good indicator of where an individual stands with respect to the French-English controversy. About 90 percent of our anglophone respondents wished Quebec to be treated like the other provinces but the response of the francophones was rather less clear-cut.[23]

	Group A	Group B	Group C	Group D	Group E
Treated like others	88%	90%	78%	70%	56%
Special status	6%	7%	12%	25%	35%

Despite containing a very much larger proportion of individuals who prefer Quebec to enjoy special status, more than half of the pure francophones (Group E) support the idea that Quebec should be treated like the other provinces. The partial French speakers, who had heretofore been so much more nationalist, show themselves to be quite considerably less so on this question. For the best-educated partial francophones the corresponding percentages are even more startling (73% for equal treatment, 14% for special status, N = 9) but there are too few cases to make anything of this. Among the pure francophones, the post-secondary group (N = 60) divides itself equally between the two options.

Differences among the language groups with respect to the possible separation of Quebec from Canada mirror those just discussed, and they make it quite obvious that even the francophones were opposed, in impressive numbers, to the establishment of a state of Quebec.[24]

Group A	Group B	Group C	Group D	Group E
4.4	4.6	4.5	4.2	4.1

The distance between the two groups at the extremes of our scale is noticeable but not very wide. The partial anglophones are most opposed to separation, followed by the mixed group. Group D, the partial francophones, instead of being more separatist than Group E as we predicted, turn out to be slightly less so and quite close to the pure anglophones in this regard. Among the mixed and the two anglophone groups, the opposition to separation grows uniformly with years of schooling (the figures are not given). The post-secondary group among the pure French speakers are most favorably disposed towards Quebec independence (3.9), but among the partial francophone group it is the least educated who are most nationalist and the difference between the secondary and post-secondary groups is insignificant.[25]

Liking for De Gaulle, Lévesque, and D. Johnson

Since we have run into inconsistent and contradictory responses

700   *John Meisel*

from the partial francophones, the group which interests us most
here, we need at least one more look at them; we can do this best,
for our present purposes, by situating them on some ethnically
specially provocative terrain. We shall accordingly examine responses
to three personalities who, in various degrees, have become the
subjects of controversy between French and English Canadians.
General de Gaulle, addressing a large crowd during a visit to Quebec,
used the separatist slogan, 'Vive le Québec Libre!'; René Lévesque, a
former leading member of the Provincial government, became the
most illustrious separatist leader; Daniel Johnson, Quebec's premier
until his death, was a tough and able protagonist of Quebec in its
negotiations with the federal government. The distance between the
two pure language categories is, as expected, quite enormous, but
what of the margins separating the pure from the partial categories,
particularly on the French side?

Table VI. *Liking for De Gaulle, Lévesque, and Daniel Johnson*[a]

Political Figure	Group A	Group B	Group C	Group D	Group E
General de Gaulle	3.4	3.5	4.7	5.2	5.9
René Lévesque	4.4	4.2	5.0	5.4	5.6
Daniel Johnson	5.2	5.3	5.9	6.8	7.2

[a]For explanation of the scores see note 15.

We see in Table VI that the scores in the D column are consistently lower than in column E and that the margin, at least with respect
to General de Gaulle and former Premier Daniel Johnson, is not
insignificant. Among the partial francophones, the best educated
liked de Gaulle least! In any event we must conclude that in this
example the partial francophones did not appear to be more nationalist and that their attitudes to the monarchy and to constitutional
change cannot be taken as representative of all their postures. Little
need be said about the mixed group which, as almost always,
occupies the center of our continuum not only logically but also in
terms of its liking of de Gaulle, Lévesque, and Daniel Johnson. The
position of the partial English is, to all intents and purposes,
identical to that of the pure anglophones.

On questions which have some relevance to the relations between French and English Canadians, the distance between our two pure language groups was of course extremely great. This, the most obvious of our hypotheses, was confirmed. But we also predicted that the partial francophones might be more distant from the anglophone 'norm' than the pure French users, and this expectation was confirmed only partially and was in fact contradicted by two sets of responses. We found that the best educated on the whole adopted the most nationalist positions among the pure francophones but did not do so among the partial French speakers. The middle-aged members of this language group also tended to be more nationalist than the youngest cohort. There was little difference between the two anglophone groups, although a tendency is apparent among the partial English users of taking a position slightly farther from the French pole than the pure anglophones. The mixed group seems not to wish to budge from its central location.

POLITICAL ALIGNMENTS

Before reviewing our effort to see how perceptions and evaluations of the five groups of language users vary, in relation to the area in which they occur (Private Values, General Policy, Ethnically Relevant Spheres), we shall look at political alignments. To compare the partisan positions of our five language groups is in some measure to retrace our steps, since these alignments are obviously related to all three of the areas we have identified as influencing the distance between their views. The foregoing testing of our hypotheses will thus be supplemented by seeing to what extent the patterns observed so far are repeated with respect to the various aspects of the political alignments of the five language groups.

Even more than previously we shall present a good many data in rapid succession without attempting to exploit anything like their full meaning, except with reference to the most striking differences between the five language groups.

TOTALS

Table VII shows that both in terms of Party Identification and the 1968 vote, the distance between the different language users is quite

Table VII. *Party Identification and 1968 Vote (In Percentages)*

Party		Language group				
		A	B	C	D	E
LIBERAL	Vote	50	66	84	69	64
	Identification		61	81	73	68
CONSERVATIVE	Vote	33	15	12	14	20
	Identification	33	18	9	12	20
NDP	Vote	14	20	3	9	5
	Identification	14	19	6	7	4
CREDITISTE	Vote	–	–	–	8	9
	Identification	–	–	–	7	8
SOCIAL CREDIT	Vote	2	–	2	1	1
	Identification	4	2	4	1	1
	Vote	99	101	101	101	99
TOTALS	Identification	99	100	100	100	101

immense.[26] Over 80 per cent of the mixed group are Liberal, whereas
the pure anglophones do not quite manage to place more than half
their number in the Liberal camp. The range between the groups is
much narrower with respect to the other parties of course, but the
proportion of Conservative pure anglophones is in all but one case
twice as great as that of the mixed or partial groups. Only the pure
anglophones display anything other than a colossal margin between
the proportion of their number supporting the Liberals and that
identifying with, or voting for, the Conservative or any other party.
The very wide margin separating the pure Liberal anglophones from
the group containing the next largest proportion of Liberals might
suggest that there is a deep political cleavage in Canada and that the
degree of polarization is extremely high. That this is not quite the
case is attested to by even the 'low' pure anglophones delivering half
their members into the Liberal camp. From the viewpoint of this
article it is most interesting that the rather orderly sequence of scores
moving in stately propriety from one end of our continuum to the
other, which we observed in so many previous series, is totally absent
here. The order of the language groups is quite atypical. Taking
Liberal support as our basic dimension we can rank the groups in
descending order as follows:

Vote:	C	D	B	E	A
Identification:	C	D	E	B	A

Instead of speculating at this point about the reason for, and significance of, the partisan pattern, we shall examine some related data.

Our respondents were asked to state how much difference they
saw between the federal parties and also how much difference it
makes which party is in office in Ottawa and in their provincial
capital.[27] The francophones, as Table VIII shows, are somewhat less
impressed by the difference between the parties, and by the degree
of difference it makes which is in office at either level of government. The gap is not great, however, and the partial groups seem on
the whole to place themselves on these questions in the positions we
saw them occupy in most cases previously. There is no difference
between the pure and partial types of either language in one case,
and in another (the difference at the provincial level), the partial
anglophones and francophones have the same mean score. The mixed
group sees the least difference between the parties. One of the most
interesting features of the table is its message with respect to the
similarity in the response of French- and English-speaking respondents to the importance of parties at the two levels of government.
The francophones might have been expected to think that it made a
greater difference which party was in power at the provincial level
but the responses of the language groups here are quite similar.

After the dramatic difference displayed by the language groups in
their party alignment it is curious to see such a bland response to the
items covered by Table VIII. The contrast becomes even more
astounding when we glance at another of our findings. After

Table VIII. *Difference Between Parties*[a]

Area of difference	Language group				
	A	B	C	D	E
Degree of difference between parties (2.3)	2.2	2.2	2.7	2.4	2.4
Importance of which party in power (federal) (2.0)	1.9	2.0	2.1	2.1	2.3
Importance of which party in power (provincial) (1.9)	1.8	2.0	2.1	2.0	2.2

[a] The lower the score, the greater the difference or importance.

704   *John Meisel*

inquiring about the respondent's financial state we asked 'Do you think that the way the election turned out will make any difference in how well off you are?' and received the following response:

	Group A	Group B	Group C	Group D	Group E
Yes	21%	20%	20%	11%	10%
No	66%	59%	59%	76%	79%

Although a great many of the francophones gave the Liberals electoral support, a large proportion of them did not think that the outcome of the election would affect them financially.

Very little difference was evident between the pure anglophones and francophones with respect to their numbers who found the leader or the candidate most important in their voting decision. Indeed, among all language groups, about 40 per cent, as Table IX tells us, thought the leader the most important factor. The francophone groups claimed to have been influenced more than the others by the work of the parties' MPs but attached less weight to the party as a whole.

Table IX. *Factors in the Voting Decision*[a] *(In Percentages)*

Factors	Language group					
	A	B	C	D	E	TOTAL
Leader	39	40	39	39	38	(1069)
Work of MP's	7	7	5	12	14	(229)
Candidate	16	7	10	15	16	(421)
Party as a whole	35	38	33	29	27	(906)
Do not know	3	7	14	5	6	(122)
	100	99	101	100	101	
Total	(1783)	(135)	(141)	(116)	(572)	(2747)

[a] The question read: 'In deciding what you would do in this recent election, which was most important to you: the leaders, the work of the MP's, your local candidates, or the parties, taken as a whole?'

While the partial English-speaking members of our sample took the leader and the party as a whole slightly more seriously than their pure brethren, the partial francophones stood, if anything, a hair closer to the English pole of the continuum than the full French-speaking group. But the differences are so small with respect to the partial groups that the only thing that one can really say is that they did not behave in as idiosyncratic a manner as in their party identification and vote.

Since the leader and the party as a whole were declared the most important factors in the respondents' decision it will be well to see what the reactions were to the individual leaders and to the way in which the parties approached the major election issues. The mean scores received by the leaders of the three main parties on a thermometer-type question were as follows:[28]

	Group A	Group B	Group C	Group D	Group E
Trudeau (Liberal)	5.7	6.3	6.8	6.5	6.0
Stanfield (P.C.)	4.9	4.4	4.4	4.3	4.5
Douglas (NDP)	5.0	4.7	4.4	3.8	3.4

While the distance between the language groups is not nearly as impressive as that separating them on the vote, it is interesting that the sequence in which they ranked Mr. Trudeau is the same as that which we observed with respect to their 1968 Liberal vote: C D B E A. The sequence for Mr. Stanfield is more congruent with our earlier results (although the partial French rate him slightly lower than the pure) and that for Mr. Douglas demonstrates an even, graceful descent from the English to the French poles.

The intriguing ranking of the groups, according to their rating of Mr. Trudeau, parallel to that of the Liberal party, raises the question of what, if any, causal connection there is between these results. At this preliminary stage of our inquiry we can do little more than note the problem. We should, however, recall that Mr. Pearson, the former Liberal leader, was scored quite differently in terms both of magnitude and sequence (C B D A E), but that there is some similarity in the distance between D and E in each case and in the two pure groups scoring lowest, although they are not in the same order.

Our respondents were asked two sets of questions tapping their attitudes to current issues. One sought to elicit unprompted responses and simply asked what the most important problems were which the new government should tackle and then asked further that they be ranked. The second mentioned a number of election issues and asked whether each was extremely, very, fairly, or not too important to the respondent. We were therefore able to construct an ordinal scale and compute mean scores indicating something of the intensity of feeling aroused by the issues.

For present purposes the most important conclusions to be drawn from these data are that a variety of economic issues were of great importance – unemployment and the cost of living being the chief among them; that the questions of whether Canada would have a majority government loomed extremely large (minority ministries had been in office since 1962); and that the constitutional position of Quebec was worrying a lot of people. The mean scores on the prompted questions dealing with these areas were:[29]

	Group A	Group B	Group C	Group D	Group E
Majority government (2.2)	2.2	2.1	2.4	2.2	2.3
Economic issues (2.4)	2.3	2.4	2.5	2.4	2.6
Quebec in Canada (2.7)	2.7	2.8	3.0	2.5	2.7

In response to the question of which party comes closest to the respondent's views on each of the listed issues we discovered that the Liberal party occupied a very special position in the eyes of the Canadian electorate and that on almost all issues the other parties lagged far behind. In the field of welfare the NDP and the Conservatives did appeal to some significant sections of the electorate but in all other areas the Liberals drew almost half the number of responses, even among the pure anglophones – the group least prone to support them.

Table X tells the story and contains the dramatic exception to the general pattern – an exception which is of critical importance to the understanding of party alignments in Canada. Leaving aside the totally deviant case of the issue of Quebec, we note that in all instances the two English-speaking groups found the Liberals most remote, the pure anglophones a good deal more so than the partial ones. On the social policy questions – medicare and welfare – there is a perfect progression from the French to the English side, but this pattern is not maintained with respect to the economic sphere where the pure francophones are replaced, as the group finding the Liberals most to its liking, by the mixed and partial French groups. The pure French-speaking group (unlike the others) tends to find the Liberals most congenial precisely on those issues which they find most important.

Turning now to the Quebec issue we find a total reversal of the

Table X. *Percentage of Respondents Finding Liberal Party Closest on Selected Issues*

Issues	Language group					
	A	B	C	D	E	Numbers[a]
Medicare	39	49	55	65	76	(347/676)
Welfare	46	44	59	59	68	(387/746)
Housing	47	57	75	73	68	(399/750)
Unemployment	48	56	66	84	70	(419/764)
Cost of living	47	58	74	74	70	(541/1002)
Regional inequality	49	61	68	71	73	(280/499)
Quebec	67	83	82	72	65	(674/987)

[a] The first number represents the respondents who said that the Liberal party was closest on the issue; the second gives the number of respondents who were asked the question. It was put only to those who said they were extremely or very interested in an issue.

previous pattern: the pure anglophones place themselves into closer proximity to the Liberals than the pure French and the partial English speakers display quite unusual exuberance *vis-à-vis* that party. The mixed and partial groups are as a whole more pro-Liberal here than the pure ones, but the partial French somewhat less so. The most significant feature of Table X is that it shows that on the question of Quebec the two language groups come much closer than on any other, in finding the Liberal party most congenial. Although the gap is much wider, the second issue on which the language groups are least remote from one another (when their support for the Liberal position is taken as the yardstick) is the general question of the economy, the only other issue on which more than half the pure anglophones found the Liberals most congenial.

Two of the three key issues are thus ones in which the Liberals can draw on the most 'balanced' support from the main language groups, the francophones being more Liberal on the economic side and the anglophones on the Quebec problem. What of the third — majority government? This was a question which was of greater importance to anglophones than to the other groups. We have no survey data on how the parties were perceived in this context but there never was the slightest question, at the time of the 1968 election, that only the Liberals as led by Pierre Trudeau had a chance of winning a majority. The widely shared desire of the anglophones for a majority government almost certainly contributed to their support of the Liberal party which, on these and more so on other grounds, made a strong appeal to the francophone members of the electorate.

The alignment of such large proportions of the pure French- and English-speaking voters with the Liberal party, while not of course fully explained by the above discussion, is at least perfectly plausible within it. What of the mixed and partial groups who, as we saw above, rallied to the Trudeau party in even larger proportions? Again, we cannot brave anything like a complete account explaining their pattern of behavior but our analysis does permit us to make a contribution towards such an explanation. We saw above that the mixed group on the whole adopts positions *between* those of the two major language groups — in a sense they find themselves at the convergence of three value systems: their own traditional one and those of the anglophones and the francophones. They are consequently in a somewhat unstable position which, under their generally less favored socioeconomic conditions, is surmised to predispose them to seek stable, reassuring political options. The Liberal party in this sense offered by far the most attractive choice.

Essentially the same argument, although with less force, also applies to the partial groups. They have one foot, so to speak, in each linguistic camp, and as this article shows, while usually near 'their' majority culture, they appeared in a great number of cases somewhat closer to the center of our continuum than their pure co-linguists. They too are, therefore, under cross pressure and exposed to both personal and political instability under contemporary Canadian conditions. No wonder then that the party they each prefer is one which appears most likely to establish majority government and to be able to cope with the two sets of issues they think most important: national unity (the place of Quebec in Canada) and economic problems, particularly unemployment and inflation. The value systems, to which they are linked through their linguistically dual life, and their socioeconomic status thus seem to combine to predispose them towards the Liberals.

In examining the Party Identification and vote of our five language groups, and then the differences between the parties and how important it was thought which of them was in office, we discovered a rather inconsistent pattern. There was a staggering distance between the language groups in their partisan support, but the intensity of feeling about which party was in office was neither great nor was there much difference between the language groups. The most surprising finding, however, concerned the placing of the groups *vis-à-vis* one another. Diagram II shows what would happen if we magnified the portion of Diagram I (page 676) to show the position of the circular lines representing the Liberal vote of the language groups.

Diagram II. *Distance between Language Groups with Respect to Liberal Votes*[a]

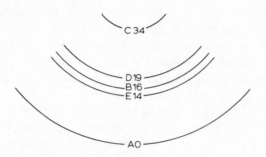

[a]The numbers represent the percentage points separating the language groups from the anglophones. For the actual percentages see Table VII.

This is a far cry from any part of Diagram I which, however, as an ideal model, served most of our other analyses tolerably well. We saw that there was relatively little difference between the language groups in the degree to which their voting decision was influenced by the two most often-cited factors – the leader and the party taken as a whole – and, after examining the position the language groups took on the election issues, we decided that their deviant lineup on the all-important Liberal support was compatible with the general pattern of responses we observed in relation to the three areas of Private Values, General Issues, and Ethnically Relevant Problems. But it certainly also suggests that the schema is in need of some revision.

The above effort at reconciling what appears to be something of an incongruent set of patterns between the overall effects and evaluations of our respondents, on the one hand, and of their partisan alignments, on the other, may strike the reader as being eccentric on at least two scores: it appears to explain partisan alignments within an excessively short-run perspective – the 1968 election – when Table VII shows that the differences between Party Identification and the 1968 vote were slight; and it fails to draw on the insights into electoral decision-making, and its antecedents, contained in the Michigan canon, the voting studies produced by the Survey Research Center at Ann Arbor. The first impression is illusory: the short-run factors cited in connection with the 1968 election have, with the exception of Mr. Trudeau, been evident in Canada for a very long time, and we simply used the vocabulary of the late 1960s to describe phenomena which have essentially dominated partisan alignments, particularly Liberal support, since the depression and the advent of the Second World War if not before.

Our explanation, although less focused than most of the work of the SRC, nevertheless is compatible with much of it. The context of the present analysis did not allow us to spell out the connection between our data and what has come to be accepted as the explanation of electoral decision-making in political settings like that of Canada. It will be necessary, when the present analysis is expanded, to examine within its framework the concepts and variables generated by the Michigan school and the growing number of scholars associated with it abroad.[30] This exercise is likely to shed further light on why some of the evaluation and affect patterns in our general discussion failed to appear in the support profile of the Liberal party. And this may in turn lead to a greater refinement and/or revision of our overall schema categorizing political perceptions into the three areas outlined above.

CONCLUSION

Review of the Schema

We have sought to gain some insight into cultural differences, particularly as related to politically relevant perceptions, by means of distinguishing between subpopulations in linguistically heterogeneous societies according to the degree to which they speak the major languages. Language use was taken to be a link to the value systems of cultural groups and an indicator of the degree to which a linguistic subpopulation had become identified with the values of one or the other of the two societies comprising Canada. It was assumed that differences would occur in the degree to which linguistic groups share the values of the major cultures, differences varying with the objects to which the values are attached.

Secondly, the common practice of thinking of language use in bilingual societies in dichotomous terms was rejected in favor of a more complex pattern acknowledging the existence of partial language users. We were thus led to establishing a language continuum consisting of pure types at each end, of a partial group associated with each of the pure types, and of a mixed category in the middle only weakly linked to either of the language (and therefore value) systems of their society.

The five types of language users were expected to display greater or lesser differences among themselves with respect to the way they reacted to the world around them and particularly to its political phenomena. A number of predictions was made specifically with respect to the size of the gaps that could be expected between the five groups in relation to three areas: Private Values, General Public Policy and Policy Relevant to Ethnic Relations.

Results of loosely organized exploratory tests of a schema placing the language groups into an anticipated pattern are summarized above, at the end of each relevant section. On the whole they are encouraging in that they confirm the existence of genuine differences between the five language groups on the continuum and in that they support most of the relationships we expected to find. They suggest that it is worthwhile trying to map the positions occupied by linguistic subgroups with respect to one another in various politically relevant areas.

By no means all of our expectations were confirmed, however, both with respect to the positions taken by the pure groups (although here the results were rather impressive) and also to the order in which the five groups lined up on certain clusters of perceptions. The three areas — Private, Public, Ethnically Relevant Public — may provide too crude a grouping of categories and require considerable refinement. It is certainly necessary to depart at least temporarily from this kind of brazen macro-analysis and to select smaller areas of study, much as we have done, again only in a cursory and merely illustrative way, with respect to political alignments. If a series of discrete but extensive subanalyses can fruitfully be attempted (and there is every indication that it can) it should be possible to establish finer subcategories of the three areas. This will either lead to a more complex and finer system of classifying areas within which the relationship in the perceptions of the five language groups will permit easier explanation and possibly reasonably accurate prediction or it may even torpedo an important part of the

John Meisel

conceptual framework within which we have developed our argument. The circular concept applied in the present analysis (see Diagram I), while useful in some respects, does impose artificial and limiting constraints which may become intolerable as the analysis becomes more acceptably refined and may in the end be abandoned for a more supple and multi-dimensional construct.

Additional work also needs to be done on the differences in perceptions between the partial and pure groups. The problem is fairly simple on the English-speaking end of the continuum. The partial anglophones do normally take positions close to the pure groups, but more information is needed about the persistently recurring cases in which they adopt a more extreme stance, in the sense of being further away from the French positions than the pure English.

We were not quite sure what to expect from the partial French: on the one hand it was plausible that they should be socialized, by their exposure to English values, into attitudes and perceptions resembling those of the English-speaking majority and differing somewhat from those of the pure francophones. But it was also possible that their partial contact with English Canada might lead them to a more extreme nationalism than that displayed by their more isolated, and presumably less frequently provoked, pure French-speaking colleagues. The former was usually the case but not always. Our expectations of greater nationalism and extremism among the best-educated and youngest partial francophones were largely disappointed although among the pure French speakers the post-secondary educational group did tend towards more forthrightly nationalist postures than the less well educated. In any event there were enough deviant cases with respect to the relationship between the partial and pure groups at both ends of our continuum to warrant further studies of this problem involving larger numbers of the relevant cases than were present in our national sample.

Implications for Theory and Political Life

Our preoccupation with establishing the use of the analysis of social cleavage in a heterogeneous society and its consequences for political perceptions in terms of a language continuum, and our drawing on heretofore unpublished Canadian data, no doubt deflected us from some of the broader theoretical foundations of this approach. We will not turn to this aspect of our work in this article, but the reader will be aware of the potential relevance of the kind of analysis we wish to encourage for anyone concerned with studying the demands and supports of any given political system or interested in the whole question of system maintenance.

For those concerned more with applied politics, the way of looking at ethnically mixed societies adumbrated above also promises rewards. It provides a kind of warning light which can point to the presence of fissures in multilingual settings. Since it rejects both the false dichotomization of language use and, by focusing on a wide range of perceptions, the overly simple definition of divisions in terms of too few cleavages, it constitutes a realistic means of coming to grips with stress in multilingual and multiethnic polities. The present approach facilitates the identification of the areas and problems creating stress and also of the linguistic (and other) groups involved. It is, therefore, relevant to the policy maker concerned with gaining a better understanding of the problems of his clients.

REFERENCES

Allard E., and Y. Littunen, eds.
1964 *Cleavages, Ideologies and Party Systems* (Helsinki, Westermarck Society).
Carroll, John B.
1968 *Language and Thought* (Englewood Cliffs, N.J.).
Carroll, J. B., ed.
1956 *Language, Thought, and Reality: Selected Writings of Benjamin Lee Whorf* (New York).
Fishman, Joshua A.
1966 'Language Maintenance and Language Shift as a Field of Inquiry', in Fishman, ed. 1966.
Fishman, Joshua A., ed.
1966 *Language Loyalty in the United States* (The Hague, Mouton).
Herman, Simon R.
1966 in Fishman, ed. 1966.
Laponce, J. A.
1969 'Ethnicity, Religion, and Politics in Canada: A Comparative Analysis of Survey and Census Data', in *Quantitative Ecological Analysis of the Social Sciences*, Mattei Dogan and Stein Rokkan, eds. (Cambridge, Massachusetts).
Lenski, G.
1961 *The Religious Factor* (New York, Anchor).
Lieberson, Stanley
1966 'An Extension of Greenberg's Linguistic Diversity Measures', in Fishman, ed. 1966.

Lipset, Seymour M., and Stein Rokkan, eds.
1967   *Party Systems and Voter Alignments* (New York, Free Press).
Mackey, William F.
1966   'The Description of Bilingualism', in Fishman, ed. 1966.
Merritt, Richard L., and Stein Rokkan, eds.
1966   *Comparing Nations* (New Haven, Yale University Press).
A Preliminary Report of the Royal Commission on Bilingualism and Biculturalism (Ottawa, 1965).
Report of the Royal Commission on Bilingualism and Biculturalism, General Introduction, Book I, *The Official Language* (Ottawa, 1967).
Rubin, Joan
1966   'Bilingual Usage in Paraguay', in Fishman, ed. 1966.
Schmidt-Rohr, George
1933   *Mutter Sprache* (Jena).
Stewart, William A.
1966   'A Sociolinguistic Typology for Describing National Multilingualism', in Fishman, ed. 1966.

NOTES

This article was originally a paper presented at the Seventh World Congress of Sociology, Varna, Bulgaria, session on 'Social Structure and Political Alignments', September 15, 1970. Reprinted with permission from John Meisel, *Working Papers on Canadian Politics* (Montreal, London, McGill-Queen's University Press, 1972).

1. The tendency applies equally to distinctions being made between linguistic families in even more multilingual societies but the analysis attempted here, based on only two language groups, will suffice to open up the problem.

2. The research, which started many years ago as a conventional election study, has since assumed larger proportions and is concerned with a variety of mechanisms through which inputs are converted into outputs in political systems. It is supported by a Killam Award of the Canada Council. The data for this article are derived from 2767 interviews of about ninety minutes' duration with a national sample conducted after the 1968 election. Further details about the survey, including a description of the sample design, can be obtained from me. I am grateful for the generous advice of W. P. Irvine and for the competent research assistance of James W. Lightbody.

3. In the aforementioned survey no less than 27 percent answered 'Canada' to the question 'Please tell me from what country most of your ancestors came'. When these 752 individuals were asked 'And before that, where did most of your ancestors come from?' 19 percent (141) still answered 'Canada'.

4. Even some of the most illuminating works give short shrift to cleavages expressed in linguistic forms. Only the most scant and passing attention to this clearly relevant and in some instances critical aspect of social cleavage is to be found, for example, in Lipset and Rokkan, eds. 1967 or in Allardt and Littunen, eds. 1964. In a different idiom, the papers in Merritt and Rokkan, eds. 1966, similarly almost ignore linguistic dimensions. The three collec-

tions of papers cited here are singled out because they are otherwise particularly useful and comprehensive surveys of materials relevant to our present concerns and so offer striking evidence for the view that language factors have been neglected by students of the political consequences of social cleavage. A notable exception to the neglect is Laponce 1969.

5. A good introduction to the vast and rapidly growing literature is to be found in Fishman, ed. 1966; Carroll, ed. 1956; Carroll 1968.

6. *Report of the Royal Commission on Bilingualism and Biculturalism*, General Introduction, Book I, *The Official Languages* 1967: XXXI, XXXIII; and *A Preliminary Report of the Royal Commission on Bilingualism and Biculturalism* 1965:111. Subsequent volumes of the *Report* provide a massive analysis and unique case study of the relation between language and society.

7. Because of their numerical and economic strength, English-speaking Canadians do dominate the country as a whole. In Quebec francophones constitute the majority culture but even here the pull of 'English' values cannot always be avoided.

8. A pioneer study in the early 1930s distinguished between nine 'domains' of language, such as the family, the street, school (instruction and recess), church, etc. See Schmidt-Rohr 1933 and Fishman 1966. The following items (in Fishman, ed. 1966) also edited by Fishman, are fascinating contributions to the literature on the definition of language use: Simon R. Herman 1966; Rubin 1966; Stewart 1966; Lieberson 1966; Mackey 1966.

9. Housewives were coded as speaking the same language at work as at home.

10. The phrase 'testing our hypotheses' may, as will be seen, be too grandiose. For the sake of brevity we shall nevertheless use it occasionally. A methodologically more sophisticated analysis is projected for the future.

11. A rough and ready index of religiosity was constructed, utilizing three criteria: frequency of church (or temple) attendance; proportion of respondent's friends belonging to the same religion as he does; agreement or disagreement with a statement to the effect that too much money was being spent on churches. Details about the indices used here will be published and, in the meantime, can be obtained from me. The highest attainable score of the religiosity index is 11, the lowest 0.

12. See, for example, Lenski 1961, particularly pp. 267–272.

13. These reactions were obtained by asking the respondents to indicate whether they agreed or disagreed with the statements 'Homosexuals should be imprisoned' and 'Canada needs less severe divorce laws'. The answers were coded as follows: Agree strongly 1, Agree mildly 2, No opinion 3, Disagree mildly 4, and Disagree strongly 5, and the means computed for the five language groups and within each, for the usual subgroups (education, age, religion, occupation).

14. The scores run from 0 to 9 and were created on the basis of answers to three questions: (1) 'It seems to be more and more difficult always to obey the law. Some people we talk to feel that a person shouldn't be punished for breaking a law which he believes is against his religion. How about you: do you think a person *should* or *should not* be punished if he breaks a law which he believes is against his religion?' (2) 'What of breaking a law going against some other deeply felt principle but one not related to religion? A

person may feel he has to break a law, for example, to assure the survival of his trade union or even of his own national group. Do you think that under these circumstances a person should or should not be punished if he breaks the law?' (3) Agreement or disagreement with the statement that 'Illegal strikes should be broken up by the police'.

15. The response was given by scoring each group or office with the help of a diagram of a thermometer calibrated from 0 to 100. In coding the responses scores of from 0 to 10 were assigned 1, those from 11 to 20 were coded as 2, etc. A score of 7.8, for example, thus represents a mean 'thermometer reading' in the upper sixties.

16. There are only sixteen cases in this cell, however, and the result must therefore be treated with some caution. It is nevertheless the case that the same individuals comprise the comparable cell in the other three sections of Chart IV where the same results do not obtain. This is a good point at which to mention that, for the sake of not cluttering up the charts and text, the numbers in each cell are not shown. Where they are relevant mention is made either in the text or in the notes.

17. The degree to which the respondents liked or disliked various groups was elicited by means of a thermometer type question, similar to that described in note 15.

18. The statements are part of the battery, mentioned above, which also probed for reactions to homosexuality and divorce. Note 13 indicates how the answers were coded. The statements are: 'Canada would be a better place if all people had the same national origin' and 'Canada would be a better place if all people had the same religion'. It is assumed, in the full knowledge that the assumption is open to challenge, that agreement or disagreement with the statements constitutes a rough indication of religious and ethnic tolerance.

19. The mean score was computed for each language group after the answers were coded as follows: Extremely interested 1; Very interested 2; Fairly interested 3; Not too interested 4; No opinion 5.

20. On another question, seeking a response to the statement that Canada should withdraw its troops from Europe, scored as those in Table V, the results were: A 3.4.; B 3.1; C 2.9; D 2.6; E 2.6.

21. For comparable ratings of other offices see Chart IV.

22. The reactions were obtained by seeking agreement or disagreement to a battery of statements about public issues. Chart II draws an other items in the battery and note 13, above indicates how the responses were coded. The full statements used in Chart VII read: (a) 'Canada should abolish the monarchy', (b) 'Canada's constitution should be changed', and (c) 'Provincial governments should participate at international educational conferences'.

23. The question read as follows: 'Another question often discussed in the election concerned the relations between the governments at Ottawa and Quebec. Some people think that except for the question of language rights Ottawa should resist Quebec's demands for special status. Others say that Quebec has special needs and rights which, in addition to the use of the French language, should be clearly recognized. What are your views? Do you think that Quebec should be *treated exactly like the other provinces* or that it

should *occupy a special position* in the Canadian confederation?'
Ambiguous and nonresponses are excluded from the tabulation.

24. Almost all the interviews were conducted in the second half of 1968. The relevant question was: 'There has been quite a bit of talk recently about the possibility of Quebec separating from the rest of Canada and becoming an independent country. Are you in favor of separation or opposed to it? Please tell me whether you are *strongly in favor* of separation, *slightly in favor, undecided, slightly opposed or strongly opposed* to separation.' The mean score is based on the following coding scheme: Strongly in favor 1; Slightly in favor 2; Undecided 3; Slightly opposed 4; Strongly opposed 5.

25. The scores (with the number of cases in brackets) are: Primary 3.9 (50); Secondary 4.5 (42); Post-secondary 4.4 (22).

26. The relationship between Identification and the vote is not discussed here. The two 'readings' are presented so as to enable the reader to compare what he may consider the Trudeau-dominated vote alongside a somewhat stabler measure.

27. 'One of the things we are interested in is the differences which exist between our federal political parties. Considering everything the parties stand for, would you say that there is a good deal of difference between the parties, some difference, or not much difference?' 'In your opinion, do you think it makes a great deal of difference, some difference, or no difference which political party is in power in Ottawa?' 'Do you think it makes a great deal of difference, some difference, or no difference which party holds office in your provincial legislature?'

28. The scores were coded differently from the earlier thermometer questions. Here the relevant parts of the legend read 41−50 4; 51−60 5; 61−70 6. The question was: 'How much do you like Mr. Trudeau?', etc.

29. Extremely important was scored as 1, Not too important as 4.

30. Since the present research was organized with Survey Research Center studies very much in mind, and indeed with the assistance of several Ann Arbor colleagues, this will not be a difficult task.

Language in East Africa: Linguistic Patterns and Political Ideologies

Pre-independence history created different linguistic situations in Kenya, Tanzania, and Uganda and language differences among these independent nations are being reinforced by official policies arising from their differing political ideologies. Any sociolinguistic study in East Africa must therefore consider the language policies under sixty years of colonialism plus a decade of post-independence language engineering by the three East African governments. Language use patterns, attitudes toward specific languages, and the question of a national/official language are part of the social fabric created by these language policies, past and present. The British colonial language policies were inconsistent and modern language policies in independent East Africa appear uneconomic and at times to bear little relation to social reality and the needs of most of the people. However, present-day language policies in the three nations are firmly rooted in history and are instruments of those political and socioeconomic forces which are dominant in each of the three nations.

This article will consider the sociolinguistic situation in East Africa today in terms of the three most important determining variables. These are (1) the linguistic groupings in each nation, (2) colonial and earlier language history, and (3) present-day social and political developments.

THE LINGUISTIC GROUPINGS

Tanzania, Kenya, and Uganda include basically the same indigenous ethnic groups and might have formed one natural nation had it not been for colonialism's drawing of the present-day borders. Bantu-language-speaking groups dominate the area, representing over two-thirds of the population. Among the larger Bantu groups are the Ganda in Uganda, the Kikuyu in Kenya, and the Sukuma in Tanzania. Swahili, widely used as a *lingua franca* in East Africa, is a Bantu language. Western Nilotic groups are present in all three countries but are numerically significant only in Kenya and Uganda. The Acholi and Langi of Uganda and the Luos of Kenya, who have spilled over into Tanzania, represent the Western Nilotes. Eastern Nilotic groups are also found in all three countries and include the Masai in Kenya and Tanzania and the Iteso in Uganda and Kenya. Some Cushitic-speaking peoples are found in northern Kenya, along the coast, and in an isolated pocket in Tanzania.

But while the three nations share the same linguistic elements, the national borders have established different linguistic proportions within each country. Present-day Tanzania, for example, contains mainly speakers of relatively similar Bantu languages. Estimates of the number of different Bantu languages vary from about 100 to 120 but all scholars agree on the essential point: Bantu groups make up about 95 percent of Tanzania's population.[1] Furthermore only one group, the Sukuma, was large enough to have its own language seriously considered for nationwide use. But the one million Sukuma have been geographically and politically isolated along the shores of Lake Victoria.

Kenya's population is only 63 percent Bantu, but three Bantu Language groups (Kikuyu, Kamba, Luyia) each have more than a million speakers. The Western Nilotic Luos also number more than a million, giving Kenya four competing language groups large enough to prevent any one being accepted as the national language.[2] The Luos naturally resisted suggestions that any of Kenya's three major Bantu Languages be given official national status and they have also resisted learning Swahili, itself a Bantu language. However, there are signs today that Swahili has gradually lost its ethnic or Bantu connotations so that it would be acceptable even to the Luos.[3]

In Uganda about 65 percent of the people speak a Bantu Language. Some 14.5 per cent speak languages in the Western Nilotic group such as Acholi or Lango, while another 11 per cent speak Eastern Nilotic languages. About 5 per cent speak either Madi or Lugbara in the Central Sudanic group of languages. While Eastern and Western Nilotic and the Central Sudanic languages all fall in the Nilo-Saharan family, they are only remotely related and it cannot be assumed that any one language could be chosen to represent northern Uganda, where these non-Bantu languages are spoken.

Except for Luganda, spoken as a first language by 16 percent of Ugandans, none of the country's languages has enough speakers to support a serious claim to national/official status. From a linguistic point of view Luganda could be a serious candidate since it is the Bantu language with the most speakers in a nation with a large Bantu-speaking population.[4] But nonlinguistic criteria rule out Luganda from any national role. Past political and historical events associated with Baganda 'imperialism' give Luganda a sour taste in the mouths of other Ugandans. And, of course, designating a Bantu language the national/official language would give no representation to the one-third of Ugandans whose languages are unrelated to the Bantu group.

Given these three different linguistic situations it is not surprising that Tanzania has chosen Swahili as its national and official language while Kenya and Uganda, with their more complex indigenous linguistic pictures, have carried on with English, their colonial heritage, as an official language. Swahili is recognized as a national language in Kenya but English remains the language of education and government. In Uganda neither Swahili nor any other African language has as yet been seriously considered as a possible replacement for English as the official and/or national language of the nation.[5]

COLONIAL AND EARLIER HISTORY

Tanzania. – It would be a mistake to attribute Swahili's present position in Tanzania merely to the indigenous linguistic situation. Certainly more important was Swahili's spread by trading caravans across what became Tanganyika[6] beginning about 1830 and its use by the Germans as a language of colonial administration from 1890 until World War I. When the British succeeded the Germans as Tanganyika's administrators in 1918 they eagerly accepted the legacy of a Swahili-speaking civil service.[7] After World War II, when Julius Nyerere mobilized the forces of independence in Tanganyika, Swahili was readily at hand for use throughout the territory.

At the outset of the nineteenth century Swahili probably was largely a coastal language, a trading *lingua franca* used from southern Tanganyika to the northern Kenya islands of Lamu and Pate.[8] In the north it was also the medium for religious and later secular poetry written in Arabic script. There is no direct evidence that Swahili was the language of the Arab trading caravans that reached Lake Tanganyika and the Kingdom of the Buganda beyond Lake Victoria by the 1840s, but no other trading language was widespread in the area. Surely Swahili was the likely *lingua franca* used by these caravans from Zanzibar.

Swahili publications in Roman script, including the first grammars, were produced by the nineteenth-century German and British missionaries. By the first decade of the twentieth century Swahili newsletters and magazines were being published by missionaries, government, and even African students and teachers themselves.[9] By then the German colonizers also were making efforts to spread Swahili throughout the area. The Germans envisioned Tanganyika as an efficient and profitable colony and wanted literate Africans, not more expensive Europeans, to be clerks and minor civil servants. The German administrators started with a corps of Swahili-speaking akidas from the Sultan of Zanzibar. They soon had Swahili-speaking Africans as political agents, teachers, and civil servants; founded schools which taught Swahili; and required the missionaries' educational system to produce Swahili-speaking graduates.[10]

When the British assumed the Tanganyika Mandate after World War I, they continued to use Swahili as a means of communication between the local peoples and the government.[11] English did become the language of wider communication and of post-primary education but the British, like the Germans, embraced Swahili for its usefulness and many civil servants learned the language.

When TANU (Tanganyika African National Union) was formed after World War II, it was because so many Tanganyikans could understand and use Swahili that the country could be so quickly organized for political action. President Nyerere used Swahili extensively on his many tours for TANU before independence. The government of Tanzania chose Swahili first as national language in 1964 and then as its official language as well in 1967. Swahili has yet to capture all the prestige English once held in Tanzania, but earlier policies at least ensured that it would be widely known and available for the social leveling task to which the government is now putting it.

Kenya. – Both ambiguity and disparity mark language policy history in Kenya. Since the British took control of Kenya first as a protectorate and then as a crown colony in 1920, periods when language policy was clear and consistent have been few and short. Today ambiguity in language policy persists. The ruling political party of Kenya, KANU (Kenya Africa National Union), declared in 1970 that Swahili should be an official language at least equal in status to English. Since then Swahili has regularly been espoused as the true Kenyan national language but nothing of substance has been done to implement KANU's suggestions and supplant English. English remains the official language and the indicator of high socioeconomic status.[12]

The roots of this pattern of ambiguity and disparity are apparent in the history of Kenya's language policy. Even though Swahili is the native language of Kenya's coast, the area which produced the greatest traditional Swahili literature, Swahili has often been viewed as alien by many Kenyans. First, Swahili reached up-country Kenya not directly from the coast but via the caravan routes from Zanzibar through Tanganyika. Even today up-country Kenyans speak a Swahili based not on Mombasa's Kimvita dialect but on Zanzibar's Kiunguja dialect. It was this Zanzibar dialect which the British accepted as the basis for standard Swahili and spread through Kenya via government notices, school texts, and other official channels. There was also a more general resistance to the spread of Swahili in Kenya than there was in Tanganyika, in part because of the larger size of the linguistic groups in Kenya. Even today the larger linguistic groups in Kenya claim to know less Swahili than do the smaller ones.[13] In addition the influence of Swahili in Kenya was lessened in 1905 when the capital of the colony was moved from Swahili-speaking Mombasa to Nairobi, 300 miles inland near Kikuyu country.

Swahili and the local vernaculars vied as mediums of instruction in Kenya's primary schools until the 1960s, depending on the changing government language policy. Africans themselves were suspicious of Swahili even though it was at times associated with educational opportunity. For it was only primary education which was open to Swahili speakers; the secondary school medium was always to be English and few Africans could expect to enter these English-medium schools. Thus Africans believed they were being educated only to become more useful to the Europeans as servants, laborers, and clerks. Most members of the large settler community in Kenya reinforced Swahili's image as a language for master-servant relationships with their use of a simplified version of the language consisting largely of imperatives.

Still, however low the esteem of Swahili, there were farsighted Africans who recognized early that Swahili was the only language available for reaching across Kenya's ethnic lines. Harry Thuku, a

Kikuyu, began producing a broadsheet newspaper *Tangazo* in 1921.
He makes it clear in the surviving issues that his main concern was
unifying the Africans of Kenya to resist the European encroachment
on African land. For this task he chose Swahili.[14]

European missionaries and educators in Kenya believed that a
child should be taught first in his own language.[15] Swahili was
considered a distracting intermediary between the local languages
and English in introducing the African masses to the fundamentals of
Christianity and western educational values.[16] The difficulty of
providing educational materials in each of Kenya's many vernaculars is obvious. The result was constant policy revision and always a
good deal of disparity between language policy and language practice
in Kenya's educational system. Roughly speaking the vernaculars
were given priority in primary schools up until 1935 and Swahili
then held sway for fifteen years. In the 1950s there was a swing
back to the vernaculars, possibly promoted by British officials who
saw Swahili as an additional unifying force in developing an African
nationalist movement across tribal lines. Finally, in the 1960s
English was becoming a popular choice as a medium of instruction
right from Primary I. In 1970 English was the sole medium of
instruction in at least 60 percent of the schools.

New disparities have appeared in Kenya's language policy since
independence. Swahili was restored to the primary syllabus in the
1960s but it is not always studied seriously because it is not in the
primary school leaving examination, which is written in English.
Despite Swahili's support in Kenya as a symbol of African identification and political integration, there is strong evidence that many
Kenyans recognize that English remains the language of personal
opportunity. Witness this coupling of English and Swahili in a summary of the report of the Kenya Education Commission made in
December 1964:

'The most striking feature of the evidence presented to the commission was, as they themselves remarked, the virtual unanimity of the
witnesses with regard to two basic features of educational practice,
namely, that English should serve as the medium of instruction in
primary schools and that Swahili should be a compulsory subject of
instruction.'[17]

Uganda — The pattern of language policy which exists in Uganda
today emerged very early. Strong support for local vernaculars,

recognition of the high status associated with use of English, and disapproval of Swahili as foreign, non-Christian, and the language of the uneducated have remained the basis of that policy. Uganda schools teach in six vernacular languages and Uganda Radio broadcasts in at least sixteen. Ugandans, including President Idi Amin, hold on to the wish that the country's official language should be a Ugandan language, but English remains unchallenged. And at least publicly President Amin and other Ugandan leaders say Swahili cannot be considered a Ugandan language, whatever its usefulness as a *lingua franca*. (See *Conclusion* for an updating of this situation.)

Even more than Kenya, Uganda was influenced by early missionaries and educators who wanted primary and religious education to be in the child's mother tongue. Yet from the first missionaries concentrated their efforts on Luganda, the language of the Baganda, the largest and most organized group in Uganda.[18] This missionary association with Luganda helped its early spread throughout the Protectorate because reading materials in Luganda were made available. Also, Protectorate officials found the missionary-educated Baganda useful as administrative agents and sent them to posts of authority throughout the country.

Luganda ran into natural local resistance and other vernaculars began to be used for primary instruction throughout Uganda. Today in the sixteen school districts six official school vernaculars are used for instruction from Primary I through IV, with English becoming the medium in Primary V. But Uganda has at least thirty languages and with only six official school vernaculars it is clear that many children start school with a vernacular which is not their mother tongue. About 40 percent of Ugandans are not native speakers of any of the official school vernaculars.[19] In addition many people live outside the district where their own vernacular is the official medium of instruction. This is particularly true in the six districts where Luganda is the school language, for in four of these six another language is the major vernacular. In some urban areas such as Kampala and Jinja English has been tried as a medium from Primary I, but there is no widespread English-medium program in the primary schools as there is in Kenya.

For higher instruction Ugandans have always accepted English. A Ugandan African asked in 1929 by the Joint Select Committee on Closer Union in East Africa which language he preferred answered, 'English, my Lord, which is the key to everything'.[20]

As for Swahili's role in Uganda, as Whiteley wrote, 'In this land of

Christians, (Swahili) was jeopardized from the outset by its association with Islam, a rival and "inferior" religion . . . Whatever merits the language might have had from the administrative point of view, and these were frequently voiced between 1910 and 1920, it is clear that for the Church it was an alien tongue and for the Baganda a thinly veiled threat to their status' (1969:69–70). At the end of the 1920s new opposition to Swahili arose because Ugandans feared its spread might lead to a political union with Kenya and eventual domination of the Protectorate by the Kenya colonists.[21]

The Baganda especially have always opposed granting any official recognition to Swahili because they believe if any African language in Uganda deserves such recognition it is Luganda, their own language.

Swahili, whatever forces have been marshalled against it, has always had some importance as a *lingua franca* in Uganda. It was brought there by the same trading caravans which spread across Tanganyika and then took a northern route west of Lake Victoria. Swahili has become more important as *lingua franca* as migration to the Kampala-Jinja urban area has increased. Especially in ethnically diverse eastern Uganda, Swahili has always had use as a rural *lingua franca* as well.

Special groups in Uganda such as the police and the military used Swahili as a *lingua franca* into the 1950s. Swahili was then even recognized as one of the official school vernaculars, a position it no longer has today. It was not until General Amin came to power in 1971 that it was added to the long list of languages used by Radio Uganda. With Uganda now a military state, Swahili – the unofficial army *lingua franca* – is reported to be much more in evidence. What this particular period in the history of Uganda will mean to Swahili's future there is hard to assess. More people may be using it – because communication with the military often requires Swahili – but its associations may not improve the poor image Swahili has suffered under previously.

Still, whatever Swahili's usage,[22] it is still English that has the prestige. General Amin took power in 1970 knowing little English and as a military man accustomed to speaking a good deal of Swahili. Some speculated he would join the advocates of Swahili as Uganda's official language. He has made radio broadcasts and speeches in Swahili which is more than his predecessors ever did, it is true. But he still expresses his satisfaction at his progress in learning English and uses English officially most of the time. Thus English continues as the official language, limited in the number of Ugandans it can reach until more and better education makes English more widely known, but without a serious challenger.

PRESENT-DAY SOCIAL AND POLITICAL DEVELOPMENTS

Language can be used as a tool of social engineering. In East Africa it is most obviously being put to this use in Tanzania where Swahili has been made not only the national language but also the official language,[23] replacing English in many situations where it functioned under colonial rule. Kenya and Uganda have not altered the status quo of English as the official language and this very fact and the accompanying socioeconomic implications are, in their own way, a form of social engineering.

Social engineering through language policy can operate in two main areas. First, official language choice can effect political integration. Second, it can facilitate or impede socioeconomic integration by opening or closing job opportunities and access to public office.

In Tanzania President Julius Nyerere and his socialist government are trying to shape a truly egalitarian state. Tanzania's leaders say they are trying to return the nation to the traditional values of *ujamaa* (roughly translated as socialism) which it had before colonialization; they claim that in the traditional African society there is no major difference in income between the richest and the poorest. The choice of Swahili as a national/official language is one means of achieving their egalitarian aims.[24]

In social terms, how did Tanzania come to choose Swahili? (a) Since Swahili is not spoken as a first language except on the off-shore islands of Pemba and Zanzibar and in scattered small areas along the coast, the raising of Swahili to preeminence does not represent an advantage to any single group at the expense of other ethnic groups. This is because those who speak Swahili do not share a single ethnic consciousness as a pressure group; therefore, they are not in a position to use Swahili as a tool of power against other Tanzanian ethnic groups.[25] (b) Access to Swahili via primary schooling had been available to all Tanzania Africans for some time. Thus the choice of Swahili promoted linguistic equality. English was accessible only to these who attended more expensive English-medium primary schools or who had gone on to secondary schooling where the medium was English.[26]

In practice, however, simply making Swahili the national language at independence did not usher in an era of egalitarianism. It was not until 1967 when Swahili was made the official as well as national language and a number of substantive changes were made in Tanzanian society that egalitarianism became a practical possibility. These changes were needed for three reasons: (a) Even after independence, when Swahili was espoused as the national language, the wealthier African parents began sending their children to the more expensive English-medium schools. It remained for the government to close this option: in 1967 Swahili was made the medium of all primary schools in Tanzania for citizens. This move cleared up any doubts as to whether a two-class educational system existed; now there was only one medium of instruction and therefore definitely only one class. (b) 1967 was also the year of the Arusha Declaration and President Nyerere's key document on education, *Education for Self-Reliance* (1967). Although he does not refer specifically to Swahili as a tool of egalitarianism in the schools, Nyerere does make clear that he envisions a complete change from the former educational system. Under the colonial legacy, he says, school was 'a place children go to and which they and their parents hope will make it unnecessary for them to become farmers and continue living in villages'. This is a blunt a way of saying that, within the western concept, education is a means of bettering oneself, a means of social mobility. Hand in hand with mobility in most western-oriented societies goes the acquiring of an elitist language or dialect – in the case of the East African framework this means English. The view that education is a means of separating oneself from the masses prevails in Kenya and Uganda. This is certainly one reason why English continues as a medium of instruction in those countries.

Not so in the Tanzania we are building, Nyerere declares. The aim of education must be to return people to their rural homes, not to take them out of them. Education will return them with new useful skills, of course, but skills geared to a rural economy. 'We should not determine the type of things children are taught in primary schools by the things a doctor, engineer, teacher, economist, or administrator needs to know', Nyerere writes in *Education for Self-Reliance*. 'Most of our pupils will never buy any of these things'. What the student should be taught, he says, is 'the skills he ought to acquire and the values he ought to cherish if he or she, is to live happily and well in a socialist and predominantly rural society, and contribute to the improvement of life there. Our sights must be on the majority . . .' (1967:16–17).

With such a view of education it is essential that the language accessible to the people, Swahili, should become the sole medium. Nyerere chose Swahili as a vehicle to break with the individualistically oriented, competitive educational system of the capitalistic world *and* with its language, English. To date, education above the primary level is still in English, except for political education courses in secondary schools and lectures on Swahili itself at the University of Dar es Salaam. Plans call, however, for the gradual introduction of Swahili as a medium at least in secondary schools. Lack of trained teachers and materials stands in the way at the moment.[27]

(c) At about this same time official policy called for a change in patterns of language use in high-status positions. Civil servants were urged to use Swahili for all official business. Today much official business is in fact carried on in Swahili, although in some areas there is a great deal of code-switching between Swahili and English. All of the practical aspects of implementing the policy of promoting Swahili have not been worked out. There still is a serious shortage of Swahili materials for schools; Swahili terminologies have not yet been devised for many technical and scientific fields; Swahili has yet to achieve status as a literary language which the best Tanzanian writers would choose instead of English. Still, Tanzania is actively, if sometimes slowly or even inefficiently, working out these problems. The decision to make Swahili an official language is not just a symbolic one.

The very decision of Tanzania, a poor country even among under-developed nations, to spend part of its meagre resources on a change in language policy is significant. In practical terms, funds spent on producing Swahili textbooks are not available to provide medical dispensaries and other needed services; retaining English as the national language, at least temporarily, would enable Tanzania to use materials already available for its educational effort. It is clear, however, that Tanzania believes its choice of Swahili is necessary within its scheme of social development, which envisions an egalitarian society. Swahili is a leveling language which has unified Tanzania's diverse peoples into one nation. It has opened up opportunities for participation in government and business to many individuals who would have no similar opportunities in a society in which English was the official language. Swahili is being used in Tanzania as a tool of political and socioeconomic integration.

Whether or not Tanzania can in fact shape an egalitarian society is not our subject here. The point we wish to make is that the choice of

Swahili as an official language is not just a nationalistic gesture. The choice represents purposeful use of language as a social and political instrument.

English, which has remained the official language in Kenya and Uganda, has served as a force for political integration in both nations. That is, English has promoted the process of merging subgroup identities into a shared sense of national consciousness.[28] The rationale for choosing English is the same in both nations: a language which is *uniformly less known* throughout the country should have priority as an official language over a language which is well known *if* it is well known by only one section of the community. Choosing English as the official language is 'unfair' in that it is foreign and must be acquired by every citizen outside his home. But the key point is that choosing English is *uniformly* unfair; no one ethnic group is favored. Therefore, no one ethnic group can feel that it is a more integral part of the nation than another group because of official language policy. Thus the official language, and accordingly the nation are as much the birthright of one group as another.[29]

Thus as a neutral leveler in the political arena English is a functional choice in Uganda and Kenya. However, this is true on the macro-political level only. English hardly suffices in either country when we consider the micro-level of political integration and everyday communication between the government and the people. On the macro-level English serves as an adequate symbol to unite the people. But on the practical or micro-level English can function as an interethnic group language only among the relatively highly educated. For example, the Uganda Language Survey of 1968 found in a nationwide sample that only 28 percent of the men and 13 percent of the women claimed to speak any English. No comparable figures are available for Kenya but the percentages are surely not much higher. What this means of course is that English, the official language, cannot be a practical tool in actually communicating with the people.

In Kenya of course Swahili, which is the unofficial national language, can be so used. Therefore, political 'equality' and 'efficiency' in terms of mere communication can be achieved. Uganda perhaps cannot so use Swahili since it is not as widely known there as in Kenya; but how widely known it is does not really matter since Uganda *chooses* not to use Swahili as a political vehicle. Is General Amin thinking of Swahili's potential as a vehicle of political integration and is this why he recently declared it the national language? It

is too soon to say yet since Amin has announced no policies concerning Swahili. Meanwhile, Uganda continues with an inevitable
regionalism in political outlook fostered by the use of a number of
vernaculars for the various nation-to-local communications. This is as
serious a barrier to true nation-making as any overt ethnic chauvin-
ism. The pattern in Uganda has been to solve day-to-day communication problems with proliferating concessions to individual ethnic
groups. Thus, at Independence in 1961 Radio Uganda broadcast in
five languages and in 1970 it broadcast in eighteen.[30] The result is
that fewer nationally oriented programs can be fitted into a schedule
filled with programs each meeting the needs of specific ethnic
groups. News, for example, inevitably becomes distorted by the
linguistic medium itself, with each constituent hearing about national
issues in terms of what its representatives say. Newspapers in Uganda
also reach only small segments of the population. The English language dailies reach the educated; *Taifa Mpya* and the Catholic
Munno, both in Luganda, are read largely by Baganda. There remain
only the Swahili newspapers from Kenya plus government and missionary periodicals in a few of the thirty vernaculars. As Mazrui
noted, 'That part of cultural engineering which is concerned with
nationalizing what is sectional becomes difficult in a situation of
such sectionalized media' (1970:4).

One may well ask if Uganda and Kenya should continue with
English as the official language when it meets so few communication
needs on the micro-level of politics. In Uganda, of course, the choice
of English is admittedly a negative one; there is no alternative
indigenous language to serve national needs. Hostility toward the
Baganda because of their own imperialism and jealousy of their
greater access to education effectively rule out Luganda as a candidate; Swahili's image as the language of the foreign, the rootless, and
the uneducated continues to deny it official status. This situation
may change, however, for despite the Uganda government's failure to
set a realistic language policy, it should not be assumed that a
language policy is not being established. Although many deny
Swahili has a national base in Uganda, the Uganda Language Survey
found it more widely known as a second language than any other
language. In a nationwide survey 52 percent of the men and
18 percent of the women claimed to speak Swahili.[31] And a
1968–70 study I conducted in Kampala, admittedly an ethnically
mixed area where a *lingua franca* would be more widely known,
43 percent of those interviewed said they favored Swahili as

Uganda's national/official language. However, a high percentage indicated they favored having both English and Swahili as national/official languages if given the choice.[32]

In Kenya the choice of English has much less practical linguistic justification than in Uganda. There is after all no question but that Swahili is widely known in Kenya. The 1968—69 Kenya language survey found rural samples where up to 100 percent claimed to know some Swahili. (In most rural samples about 70 percent claimed knowledge of Swahili, and in only two of the twenty samples did less than 35 percent claim it.) The question of why Kenya does not give up English as its official language might well be asked of many nations in Africa. There are, it is true, some African nations where an outside language of wider communication, either English or French, seems the only real possibility. But there are other nations where a local *lingua franca* could serve as an official language. Examples are Senegal where Wolof is widely known, and Zaire where Lingala is widely spoken even if it does not reach every section of the nation.

The answer to this question seems to lie in the matter of socio-economic integration.[33] As Mazrui notes, 'The Promotion of Swahili in Kenya is not — as it might be in Tanzania — inspired by egalitarian imperatives, but more purely by consideration of national integration' (1970:8). While every nation wants as free-flowing a network of communication as possible for political integration, not every nation desires to have the channels of socioeconomic opportunity open to all. These two aims, achieving political integration and the balance of socioeconomic integration, may be in conflict when it comes to setting a language policy.

English may not entirely serve the cause of political integration in Uganda and Kenya. In Uganda various vernaculars have to be used for this purpose on the micro-level of communication; in Kenya mainly Swahili is used. But in terms of socioeconomic integration, English as the official language does effectively serve a purpose: it restricts access to the high status sectors of society to those who command the elite language, English. Truly open socioeconomic integration presupposes increasing mobility across groups within a nation. Such open integration does not exist in Africa, where English or French are the official languages, as long as access to these elite languages is restricted because education is not equally available to all citizens. English and French become barriers between the elite and the masses.

In Kenya Swahili's role as an equalizer is restricted to the political arena. President Kenyatta makes a point of speaking Swahili to address *wananchi* (Swahili for 'citizens' or 'comrades', although its Kenya connotation has come to be 'the masses'). The ruling political party KANU recommended in 1970 that Swahili be made an official language at least equal to English by 1974 and every month some politician somewhere reaffirms KANU's general aim. But no practical steps have been taken to change the present state of affairs.[34]

The *wananchi* themselves know that language policy counts in terms of shillings. They know that until better English education is available to all, or until Swahili becomes the official language, there is little likelihood an open policy of socioeconomic integration will take hold in Kenya.[35] I recently questioned Kenyans in a rural area about whether or not they wanted Swahili as an official language and why. Many favored it and gave their reasons in terms of jobs: those who do not speak English well know that under the present policy the doors of economic opportunity are closed to them.[36]

The love-hate relationship which Kenyans who do not speak English well must almost inevitably have with English, given the present social system, is illustrated in the following examples reported to me during a conversation with one Kenyan university student at his home. First, an example showing the power of English:

'My brother was arrested by the police and sent to the chief for making beer without a license. The chief rejected his plea in our local language that he be forgiven. I then went to the chief's center; Nobody was allowed to go in and there was a policeman at the door. I spoke English to the policeman and said I wanted to see the chief. I was allowed in. It was, I strongly believe, my English that gave me the honor to be allowed in. And it was my English during my talk with the chief, that secured the release of my brother.'

Now, an example showing resentment toward English speakers:

'At a beer party near my home, two boys broke into talk in English. The reaction from the old men was bitter and they said, "Who are those speaking English? Are they back-biting us? They are proud. Push them out!" Although the boys had not been addressing the beer party as such but had been talking only to each other, this use of English was regarded as an insult.'[37]

In Uganda as well, speaking English is the recognized key to socioeconomic advancement. Even the present head of state General Amin, whose best language of wider communication was Swahili before he took power in 1970, has felt it necessary to improve his English and make it his main language of official communication. A study I conducted in Kampala in 1968—70 showed that while Swahili is a highly functional language in Kampala, he who can speak English will do so when socioeconomic status is at stake. Another study I conducted showed that people consider a man's production of English as a good indicator of what job he might hold; but production of Swahili is not a socioeconomic indicator, they judged. Swahili in effect does not count.[38]

CONCLUSION

Since this manuscript was finished in April 1973, two important changes have marked language policy in East Africa. First, as we have noted already in references to this conclusion, General Idi Amin named Swahili the national language of Uganda in August 1973. At the same time he said that English would continue as the official language 'until Kiswahili is developed to a degree that warrants national usage'. Since then, there has been no perceptible change in official usage of Swahili in Uganda. (It is used on Radio Uganda along with a number of other languages but it is not taught in the schools nor used officially in government.)

Second, on July 4, 1974, President Jomo Kenyatta of Kenya and the governing council of Kenya's sole political party, KANU, declared that Swahili would become immediately the only official language of Parliamentary debates. The next day activity began: the Kenya Institute of Public Administration produced a list of parliamentary terms in Swahili and debate in Swahili began; there has been continuous public discussion on the subject with letters to editors, etc. Those against the move mainly protest that not many Members of Parliament know Swahili well enough to use the language for official debate; some said Swahili did not have the lexicon to cover parliamentary topics. A national election to name new Members of Parliament was also announced by KANU at the time of the Swahili pronouncement.

President Kenyatta's decision can be understood in line with the thesis of this article that language policy is tied to social and political policies. In bestowing a new role on Swahili at the same time new elections were called, Kenyatta and KANU could take some of the sting out of opposition candidates' possible criticisms of past policies of the KANU government. KANU is hardly deaf to calls to have an African language as a symbol of Kenya's nationalism, as Swahili's new role attests, KANU candidates can now claim. Further, is not Swahili's new status proof that KANU is moving ahead to create equal opportunities for all Kenyans, KANU supporters can add. This manipulation of Kenyan language policy is an example of a psychologically bold, but practically limited, change being used to bolster the established elite. The replacement of English by Swahili as the official language of Parliament does indeed open up political opportunity to more Kenyans, assuming that many more Kenyans from all socioeconomic strata can speak Swahili competently than can speak English. But it is obvious that the opportunity to serve in Parliament is opportunity only for a few Kenyans; only those persons standing for Parliament will be affected. Socioeconomic opportunities *in general* have been little affected since English, mastered by only the educated few, still remains the key to social mobility. (To date, no changes have been announced to affect the status of English as the medium of instruction in schools and the language of daily government and private business outside of Parliament.) KANU's move, then, should be viewed as a plot to gain support of the masses – on the eve of elections – while little changing access to jobs or the power position of the present government. Making Swahili the official language in Parliament while keeping English in the working world is hardly a policy likely to require widespread changes in language use and in the socioeconomic values attached to English as opposed to Swahili. Policies concerning Swahili, as we have noted, are quite different in Tanzania in both scope and result.

Similarly in Uganda, General Amin's naming of Swahili as Uganda's national language also is a move designed to bolster the establishment; it is not a policy-promoting change. (It could be argued any new role for Swahili may reduce further the role of those in prestige positions in pre-Amin days; however, since English is still the practical key to high socioeconomic status, no positions are being threatened by language policies, at least.) General Amin relies almost entirely on the army for his tenure. Swahili (a Bantu language) is the traditional *lingua franca* of the army in Uganda, even though the army is drawn heavily from the northern non-Bantu areas. It is widely recognized that many of the military know Swahili much better than they know English. One can suggest that Amin granted this 'paper' status to Swahili — with English remaining the official language — as an easy way to reinforce his support from the army. We do know that as recently as September 1972 Amin was quoted in newspapers as saying that a foreign language such as Swahili could never be the national language of Uganda. Something must have changed his mind.

Thus, we can see how language policies are social and political forces in East Africa.[39] What may appear incongruous has its purpose. Given its egalitarian outlook, Tanzania's expenditures to 'equip' Swahili (in terms of texts, trained teachers, general prestige) are logical. In Kenya and Uganda, given the apparent intention in both countries to maintain societies in which socioeconomic mobility is restricted and power stays in the hands of an entrenched few, the choice to continue with an elitist language, English, as the official language is understandable. (It is not, of course, our purpose in this paper to judge such choices, but rather to explain them.)

In Kenya at least, now that Swahili is the official language in Parliament, access to political roles should be open to a wider range of aspirants on the socioeconomic scale. When results from the coming national elections are in, it will be interesting to see if the new Parliament with Swahili as its medium does indeed have a different socioeconomic composition from former Parliaments for which M.P.s were required to pass a test in English in order to stand for office. Time will tell also whether or not this new diglossic situation — linking Swahili officially with politics while the world of offices and education remains with English — can be maintained or will prove too unwieldly.

We should also anticipate that in both Kenya and Uganda it is likely would-be elites will use an African language — probably Swahili — as their symbol to mobilize support for a change in the status quo in the name of African nationalism. History attests to a coupling of local language and nationalism many times over when changes are advocated by those out of power. For the established elite to remain in power and compete successfully with its rivals, it may find it necessary to claim as *its* own a language widely known by the masses, such as Swahili. That is, a widening of Swahili's role in East Africa seems almost inevitable by one group or another. The essential point is to recognize language policies as political and social instruments.[40]

APPENDIX A

Sociolinguistic Research in East Africa

Note: In this brief survey I will mention studies which have been done and give some description of methodology where it is discussed. I will not, however, discuss findings. This is not an exhaustive survey but is designed to give a representative idea of the kind of research which has been undertaken.

The main sociolinguistic research in East Africa since 1968 has been associated with the Survey of Language Use and Language Teaching in Eastern Africa, a Ford Foundation financed project. Under this project individual surveys were conducted in the three East African nations (Tanzania, Kenya, Uganda) and in Ethiopia and Zambia. A team of three full-time researchers undertook these surveys in each country. In addition a number of additional projects were financed by the Survey, some of a sociolinguistic nature. The surveys, each lasting about a year, were conducted mainly between 1968 and 1970.

The findings of the country teams (the Uganda Survey results have been published and the Kenya Survey study appears in Whiteley, ed. 1974) are of a rather basic and general nature. This is almost necessarily so because practically nothing had been done earlier with a socio-linguistic perspective in East Africa.

The Uganda Survey volume is a rather slim one since the illness of one of the three full-time team members kept him from analysing his materials in time for inclusion. The volume does contain a general overview of the Uganda language situation and an analysis of linguistic relationships among Ugandan languages, particularly the Bantu ones, by Professor Peter Ladefoged, the team leader; a study of language in education by Ruth Click; and an article on vernacular teaching by Livingstone Walusimbi.

What causes some children to score higher than others in English reading achievement? This was the most interesting applied socio-linguistics question which the Uganda team attempted to answer. This study by Glick found very little significant correlation between the various factors considered and reading achievement. But at least here we do have an empirical attempt to isolate factors related to language learning which has produced some verifiable data. Twenty rural areas and nine schools in Kampala were surveyed.

The Uganda team also gathered some basic data about the current status of English, Luganda, and Swahili in Uganda, in terms of numbers of persons on a nationwide basis of who claim to know these languages. A sample of about 2,000 was gathered but there is little information in the survey volume about the methodology used and the reported results themselves are rather brief, although some results are reported according to variables such as sex, education, and age.

The only other sociolinguistic studies done in Uganda under Language Survey auspices were two studies by me. The first study surveys language choice in Kampala (C. M. Scotton 1972). It is an analysis of language choice, attitudes about language, and the perception of language choice of others, all with special reference to choosing a *lingua franca*. Data come from a statistically representative 'core' sample which forms a stratified random sample and represents about 25 percent of the heads of households in the areas studied. In addition several smaller, specialized samples were also studied, although they are probably not statistically representative of the groups they come from. While the results from the core sample can only be projected with any confidence for the two areas they represent, I think it reasonable to imply that the results are fairly representative for the male working population of the city of Kampala as a whole.

In presenting the findings I attempted to do two things: (a) summarize and synthesize self-reports gathered from the interviews about language use and attitude while indicating how observations of actual language use compared with these reports; (b) interpret and explain the patterns which arise from the data in terms of a theoretical framework for predicting language choice.

An attempt was made to measure indirectly socioeconomic attitudes toward Swahili and English. The methodology had all respondents in the sample listen to tape recorded descriptions in Swahili by four different persons of the same pictures. Respondents were then asked their opinions about the speaker's Swahili, his probable place of origin, and his probable job. Labov (1966) used a test similar to this. The sample very definitely identified speakers whose Swahili approximated standard Swahili and labeled it as 'better' than the· Swahili of the others. They also had definite and roughly accurate ideas about where speakers came from. But when asked about a speaker's possible occupation many respondents simply said they did not know. In addition many respondents said they believed that every speaker was a teacher, possibly because all speakers were 'teaching' (i.e., describing pictures), although respondents had been told explicitly that the speakers were only doing this because they had been asked to do so for the interview.

A random sample of fifty persons from the core sample of 223 was re-interviewed. This was done to test a hypothesis arising from the findings about responses to the Swahili recordings. As noted, our respondents made no clear correlation between a person's Swahili production and his occupation. What kind of correlations would be made between a speaker's English and the job he might hold? Our hypothesis was that a speaker would be judged on the socioeconomic scale according to his demonstrated English ability. Results of the playing of English recordings confirmed this hypothesis. The same techniques were used as with the Swahili recordings. Respondents made a positive differentiation of the 'best' English speaker from the other three in terms of his English ability and probable job. When the English of the speaker was judged 'good' his job was judged high on the socioeconomic scale; when the English was 'poor' the job was accordingly lower.

This experiment demonstrates the uses which can be made in sociolinguistic research of indirect measurement. I believe our results show that while English production is taken as an indicator of a man's socioeconomic status, production in Swahili is not so used. Direct opinion questioning, with its intervening variables of understanding of the questions, ability to articulate unconscious attitudes, etc., would not have achieved the same reliable and replicable results.

A second study I conducted in Uganda explored the extent to which the psychosociological environment in which speakers of a particular language live effects the source and type of loan words (Scotton 1973). For this study I looked at two noncontiguous dialects of Ateso, one spoken in Uganda and one in neighboring western Kenya but both geographically separated from the standard Ateso-speaking area. In order to get a corpus of loan words in actual use I used the following method: an Ateso speaker from one of the dialect areas made tape recorded interviews of a quota sample in each area. Persons were questioned about their everyday lives, for example, farmers were asked about their crops, etc. No mention was made of interest in loanwords. We then transcribed the interviews and picked out the loanwords. While I do not claim what we obtained was 'natural speech' in our interview situation, still the respondents had no reason not to present us with a 'natural' cross section of the loans they use on everyday topics.

I know of very little other sociolinguistic research which has been conducted in Uganda recently. Richard Pollnac (1973) has studied 'cognitive variability' among the Baganda. His studies deal with semantic groupings made of various objects and the correlation of such groupings with sociocultural variables.

Parkin (1969), who carried out social anthropological field work in Kampala in 1962, did include in his study references to language use as an indicator of social meaning. Using a participant-observer method of research Parkin studied general patterns of social behavior in two Kampala housing estates.

The major recent sociolinguistic work in Kenya is part of the Kenya Language Survey volume which appeared in 1974 (Whiteley, ed.). The Kenya volume contains not only studies by the full-time team members but also a number of other studies conducted by other individuals with survey funding. The late Professor Wilfred Whiteley headed the Kenya team; Barbara Neale and David Parkin were his associates.

Whiteley himself conducted a series of investigations of rural language patterns. Data were collected in a number of ways but mainly through (a) observations by Whiteley himself; (b) surveying by university students who were to make a 100 percent sample of all persons over fifteen in households within a two to five mile radius of their own homes. An overview article by Whiteley (see Whiteley 1974a, 1974b) on the Kenya language situation and several additional articles, including a number of tables, present a variety of data on such subjects as the number of people in the samples who claim to speak Swahili or English; claimed competence in Swahili with several possible gradations; claimed competence in other local vernaculars; and claimed frequency of use of Swahili as compared with English. Survey methodology is not fully ·explained; for example, twenty rural samples are listed but we have no way of knowing just now comparable these 'samples' are in numbers or stratification.

Neale's contribution to the volume (Neale 1974) is several articles on the Kenyan Asian population. Two generations of Asians have been born in Kenya and they numbered about 176,000 in 1968, being concentrated and most visible in Nairobi and Mombasa.

Parkin's contributions to the volume (Parkin 1974a, 1974b, 1974c, 1974d) refer specifically to Nairobi. First, he presents survey findings on language use patterns in two Nairobi housing estates, one 97 percent Kikuyu and the other very ethnically heterogenous. Parkin is particularly interested in patterns of language 'adding' in reference to learning another man's vernacular, as well as more general patterns of use of Swahili and English. Second, Parkin deals in a participant-observer study with the art of language switching, particularly in market-type situations, to gain advantage over one's 'opponent'. Parkin recognizes the influence of socioeconomic values in making language choices, but in this article he stresses the influence of more personal, apparently spontaneous, judgments. He writes:

'. . . we can . . . perceive the speaker making use of a limited number of choices: how should he respond to the use of a particular language; is the use intended to connote "solidarity" or assertiveness; at what state in the conversation is it strategically sound for him to reveal a wider repertoire of languages known by him; what response may be expect in revealing a "new" language?' (Parkin 1974d:191).

A number of chapters on education in Kenya comprise an important part of the survey volume. Rod Hemphill (1974) and Thomas Gorman (1974a, 1974b, 1974c) write on this subject. Gorman's major contribution presents findings from a nationwide study on patterns of language use among school children. Three different samples over the period 1968–70 were taken: a form of cluster sampling, with schools as the sampling unit, reached 2203 students in both rural and urban areas; then a second purposive sample of twenty-seven schools representing 803 children was drawn; finally twenty different classes were interviewed. Gorman's articles include data on such subjects as the claimed Swahili and English competence of mothers and fathers, languages which are favored by parents in the home, claimed point at which children learn both English and Swahili. As did the Uganda Survey, Gorman also tried to correlate English reading comprehension with certain variables such as father's education, initial medium of instruction, etc. And, like the Uganda Survey, Gorman's research found no significant correlation between these factors and English comprehension. Gorman also provides a history of Kenya language policy with particular reference to education.

A number of other writers contributed to the volume: Janet Bujra (1974) studied language use in a predominantly Moslem Nairobi community; Peter Itebete (1974) wrote on the history of the standardization of Luluyia; David Aoko wrote about language use in Independent African churches; John Sharman wrote about comparative Bantu studies and Kenyan languages regarding evidence for point of Bantu dispersal and secondary dispersals.

Berndt Heine conducted an extensive survey on the use of Swahili in western and central Kenya in 1968. His findings are reported in Heine (1970) as well as in other writings. Heine made 1350 interviews in forty-five different localities, and says he gathered material on 15,541 persons.

At present there seems to be little sociolinguistic research going on in either Kenya or Uganda. Because of recent disturbances research in Uganda on any subject has been curtailed. In Kenya John Rhoades is studying beliefs concerning English and Swahili use. He is particularly interested in beliefs about the inappropriate usage of English and Swahili specifically as indicated in jokes. He is studying jokes in Swahili newspapers and statements of language use and humor elicited from a group of secondary school students in the Nairobi area.

James Duran investigated patterns of language use and culture in the town of Lumbwa in western Kenya during the 1971 calendar year. In an unpublished paper, 'The Ecology of Ethnic Groups from a Kenyan Perspective', he discusses the allocation of resources such as land and employment in Lumbwa from the standpoint of ethnicity, with language as one manifestation of ethnicity. Another unpublished paper, 'Non-standard Forms of Swahili in West Central Kenya', describes some characteristics of Swahili as it is spoken in the area and analyzes the ethnic and socioeconomic factors which determine, in part at least, the type of Swahili an individual will speak. Phonological divergences from Standard Swahili are ethnically marked, but the extent to which a person's grammatical production of Swahili differs from the Standard can be related to socioeconomic factors, Duran suggests. Publications on these data are planned in the near future.

A great deal of sociolinguistic research was done during the Tanzania Language Survey, but very little has yet been analyzed and written up. One study which is available is a study of language use in Ilala, an area of the capital city of Dar es Salaam (Barton 1972). Barton studied the relative use of a person's vernacular, Swahili, and English in a number of situations. Five possible determining variables were considered: the muslim: non-muslim distinction, the coast: non-coast distinction (point of origin), the rural: nonrural distinction, sex, and education.

Professor Edgar Polome was country director for Tanzania; Peter

Hill and David Barton were his associates. Hill was most interested in language in education; Barton did studies of language use; Polome himself directed a number of surveys of patterns of language use and also did studies relating to Bantu classification.

Earlier sociolinguistic studies in Tanzania are few. However, both Whiteley (1961) and C. M. Scotton (1965) did descriptive studies on the connotations of certain political words in Swahili vis à vis their meaning in English. Whiteley (1967) also did a study of loanwords in Swahili with some reference to sociological factors influencing the type of words borrowed and the type of person who borrows. Of course, Whiteley also produced several works over the years on general language policy in East Africa, most notably his study of the rise of Swahili as a national language (1969).

M. H. Abdulaziz has written about the Tanzanian language policy (1970) and also about the situation of what he calls triglossia which exists in certain Tanzanian circles where English, Swahili, and the local vernacular all have their own domains (1972).

Anders Andersson (1967) produced a potentially interesting study on attitudes on the part of secondary school children toward English and Swahili. The study also deals with similar attitudes in Ethiopia toward Amharic and English. Unfortunately the study, as it appears, includes little about methods involved in this opinion study nor does it provide much actual analysis of the data.

What problems of conceptualization are inherent in school instruction in a language (English) which is less well known which are not inherent in a better known language (Swahili)? This and related psycholinguistic questions are discussed by Lemon (1972). Lemon tested Tanzanian secondary school students who are bilingual in Swahili and English (in most cases both are second languages) for whom English is presently the medium of instruction. Lemon attempted to test the students' conceptualization of similarities and differences between a given group of foreign countries and between classmates. To put it very briefly, he found that the younger students — with less proficiency in English — could conceptualize 'better' on these subjects in Swahili than in English; the older students — with more command of English — conceptualized 'better' on the topic of foreign countries in English, but did better on the topic of classmates in Swahili (although the older students were more likely to mention personality characteristics about classmates in English than in Swahili).

Lemon concludes that when students use a weaker second

language to construe and differentiate their world, constructs in that language are less meaningful to them than they might be in a better known language. Most researchers would accept this statement but not all would accept implications which Lemon sees in his results. For instance, he says 'the use of English as a medium of instruction could both make it much more difficult for students to attain meaningful concepts in this language and then inhibit them from transfering these concepts into the public language (Swahili) which is used outside the classroom' (1972:13). In fact what Lemon has shown is that students conceptualize more easily in a better known language on certain subjects. The reason – and implications – for this state of affairs has not been shown. Possible intervening variables, such as the use of English for certain topics and Swahili for others (just as in one language a certain style/register is used for certain topics and another style/register for other topics), have not been considered. Still, Lemon's study deals with an important subject which deserves investigation.

APPENDIX B

Possible Directions for Sociolinguistic Research in East Africa

Note: I will discuss very briefly some of the general ways in which I think research can be improved and also outline some possible areas for research. None of my comments applies across the board to all research which has been done in East Africa; I am simply giving my impressions of the *general* situation.

1. Areas which need more attention in terms of theory and methodology:
More attention must be paid simply to formulating goals for research. Too many studies to date have been only descriptive. There is certainly nothing wrong with descriptive studies in themselves; they provide basic data which are necessary before any other type of study can be attempted. Also, their dominance in sociolinguistics in general and East Africa in particular can be rationalized to some extent by the fact that this discipline, particularly in this area, is relatively uncharted.

But too many researchers seem to believe that facts alone are all we are looking for in studying patterns of language use. Facts themselves are of limited value. We need to be more interested in looking at facts *in relation* to other sets of facts. Further, we need attempts to *explain* facts in terms of a theoretical statement.

Research beyond a straight presentation of findings requires more in the way of a research design than do descriptive studies. It requires the formulation of hypotheses which are to be tested and the attempt to fit the findings of the study into some body of theory. Possible determining variables should be proposed and investigated. Both hypotheses particularly concerning relationships between sets of facts and theoretical concepts are lacking in most recent East African sociolinguistic research. Some researchers have attempted to look at their data in terms of determining variables; but even much of this research has been very limited in terms of either (a) the variables it chooses to examine or (b) the set of facts it hopes to explain.

Although one can argue that any imposed 'structure' (such as hypotheses or even a general theory) limits the scope of an investigation adversely, this argument is really applicable only to exploratory studies. While it is true that many basic facts are lacking about patterns of language use in East Africa, general trends have certainly been demonstrated. Therefore, specific hypotheses can and should be formulated and tested.

More attention must be paid to basic methodology. First, many of the studies seem to be based on samples which can hardly stand as representative of any group except themselves. The problems of selecting a truly statistically representative sample anywhere in East Africa are tremendous; enumerations are simply not available, even in the urban areas and any sampler must start from scratch in identifying who constitutes his population. But even given many limitations on the sampling procedures which can be employed, too many sociolinguistic researchers in East Africa — and elsewhere — have been very lax in their procedures. Many fail to report in sufficient detail just what procedures were used in selecting a sample and in the gathering of data. Others seem to think that any collection of speakers can be labelled a 'sample'. Others skew their samples from the start by damaging techniques which have long been recognized in sampling circles as unsatisfactory. For example, in one study the researcher did a random sample in thirty-one houses in his area of study, but how were these thirty-one houses chosen? They were chosen 'simply because either I or one of my assistants has personal links there . . .', writes the researcher. In other cases the researcher seems to exercise very little control over the composition of his sample. In the rural sample collected in the Kenya survey, twenty university students were told to interview every adult over fifteen within a two-to-five mile radius of their own homes. Whiteley himself, who directed this study, admits that the procedure was less than perfect: he pointed out, for example, that male interviewers did not interview all women in their areas and female interviewers showed reluctance to interview all men in their areas. Worse than this, we have no idea how many respondents were missed because they were not home, were uncooperative, etc. Some technique limiting interviewer choice must be employed.

Second, in general only limited use has been made of computer programs in the analysis of data. Few researchers attempted to do more than present cross-tabulations, at best, for much or all of their data. Surely it has been demonstrated in other disciplines that such programs as multiple regression analysis can provide valuable insights for interpreting data.

Third, few research designs can be called imaginative. While it is easier said than done, there is much room for innovation in East African sociolinguistic research both in terms of (a) what set of facts the researcher attempts to explain and (b) what techniques he uses in his study. So far most researchers have been content to study, in its barest form, 'patterns of language use'. This means they ask questions about what languages a person knows and uses and that is about all.

How can this situation be improved on? First, more attention should be paid to constructing questionnaires. Few past researchers have even *commented* on their questionnaires. Many researchers, especially those who are not enamored of survey methods, act as if there is *a* set questionnaire. They suspect the results it produces but they treat the questionnaire as a given quality. Instead we must be more creative about constructing questionnaires, in deciding how to ask questions and which questions can be asked with a hope of obtaining reliable results. Second, new methods of gathering data need to be tried. For example, more attempts should be made to use indirect measurements in conjunction with self-report questionnaires. Indirect measurement devices can include structured observations as well as controlled experiments. Some of the types of experiments used in sociology and psychology can be adapted for use in socio-linguistic research. For example, one way to assess attitudes toward different languages would be to present respondents with either live

or tape-recorded dramatizations which have been constructed so that
language use seems to reflect various social meanings. Respondents
could be questioned about such things as their attitudes toward the
performers — with the assumption that the particular language or
dialect spoken will be taken into account in the respondent's assessment. Third, sociolinguists need to start asking more ambitious
questions. For example, in Nairobi we want to know who speaks
English and who speaks Swahili in *x* situation. But we should also be
attempting to investigate such things as: Do people with similar
socioeconomic profiles (i.e., education, age, ethnic group, etc.) tend
to make truly similar choices? What are the factors which really seem
to determine choice? Just how much of language choice seems to be
individual? Is choice idiosyncratic as does a definite pattern appear in
the choices of a single person?

2. Possible areas for future research
Because of the limited amount of research which has been done, East
Africa is still wide open in terms of possible areas for further
research. There are certain practical limitations in a country such as
Tanzania. Professor Polome, leader of the Tanzania Survey, noted in
discussing the problems his team had to face, Tanzania does not
allow all questions to be asked. 'As a consequence of the irreversible
decision of the Tanzanian government to carry through its policy of
making Swahili the only commonly used language of the nation, a
number of implicit restrictions were imposed upon the survey,'
Polome (1972) noted. He went on to explain, for instance, that 'The
status of Swahili as a national language was not to be questioned'.
Also, 'Extensive studies of attitudes toward Swahili versus English
had to be avoided and the linguistic investigation of the vernaculars
had to be carried out in correlation with their specifically local role
and with the study of interferences between Swahili and Bantu or
non-Bantu dialects' (1972:2).
   Still, in theory here are some of the kinds of studies to which East
Africa lends itself.
   (a) What constitutes a pidgin? Various up-country dialects of
Swahili are spoken all over East Africa, almost all diverging more or
less from the Standard dialect of Zanzibar. Contrary to popular
opinion, most of these dialects are more or less mutually intelligible
with Standard Swahili. But here's the rub: when are dialects *not*
mutually intelligible? What are the determining factors which lead us
to say that a true pidgin has been formed? When does an up-country

form of Swahili cease to become a dialect of Swahili proper and become a pidgin on its own? There is a wealth of data on this subject, particularly in the urban areas where Swahili is heavily spoken by diverse peoples, waiting to be studied. The implications for studies of pidginization and creolization in general seem obvious.

(b) In supposedly homogeneous areas, how much homegeneity is there in fact in terms of ethnic makeup and linguistic usage? In his rural survey in Kenya, Whiteley reported that few areas seem to be truly homogeneous. 'Even in a completely homogeneous group like the Turkana, the few stores in Lodwar are owned by Meru, Kikuyu and Luyia, and a similar diversity characterizes the civil servants stationed there.' (1974:31–32). But what really are the patterns of language use in relatively homogeneous areas? Is a *lingua franca* used? And what languages are used as *lingua francas,* a local or a more widespread language? Do patterns of usage differ in kind or only in degree from those in very heteregeneous areas?

(c) How well do two languages really 'translate'? For example, many people in Nairobi speak a good deal of both Swahili and English in their everyday lives, but with each restricted to its own domains. Put simply, can a person really communicate as effectively in one language as he can in another? Various experiments to answer such questions could be devised. For example, subjects who speak both Swahili and English could be asked to translate various sets of technical directions from one language to another. Differences found could point the way to further research.

(d) How do the styles or registers present in up-country Swahili compare with those present in Swahili as spoken as a first language, in Mombasa, for example? This brings up the entire question of what styles or registers are *available* to a person in his second language. I have noted that even university students do not seem to have a command of English sufficient to allow them easy access to more than one or two styles in English. They have little fluency, for instance, in informal styles. Such a subject could be studied systematically, in terms of how range of style effects the structure of the language as spoken in East Africa and in terms of how it effects the individual's conception of the uses of a particular language.

These are only a few of the types of questions which could be studied in East Africa. They are all of interest because of their implications for sociolinguistic research in general. A multilingual area such as East Africa offers opportunities for investigating many more questions as well.

REFERENCES

Abdulaziz, M. H.
1970 'Tanzania's National Language Policy and the Rise of Swahili Political Culture', in Whiteley 1970:160—178.
1972 'Triglossia and Swahili-English Bilingualism in Tanzania', *Language in Society* 1:197—213.
Andersson, Anders
1967 'Multilingualism and Attitudes, an Explorative-Descriptive Study Among Secondary School Students in Ethiopia and Tanzania, doctoral dissertation (Uppsala, University of Uppsala).
Aoko, David
1974 'Language Use within African Independent Churches of Nairobi', in Whiteley, ed. 1974:253—262.
Barton, David
1972 'Study of Language Use in Ilala', doctoral dissertation (Austin, Texas, University of Texas).
Bujra, Janet
1974 'Pumwani: Language Usage in an Urban Muslim Community', in Whiteley, ed. 1974:217—252.
Cameron, J., and W. A. Dodd
1970 *Society, Schools and Progress in Tanzania* (Oxford, Pergamon Press).
Gorman, Thomas P.
1970a 'Implications of a Choice of Media of Instruction', in Whiteley, ed. 1970:198—220.
1970b 'Language Policy in Kenya', paper presented at the annual conference, Language Association of Eastern Africa, Nairobi.
1971 'A Survey of Educational Language Policy: An Enquiry into Patterns of Language Use and Levels of Attainment among Secondary School Entrants in Kenya', doctoral dissertation (Nairobi, University of Nairobi).
1974a 'Patterns of Language Use among School Children and Their Parents', in Whiteley, ed. 1974:351—396.
1974b 'The Development of Language Policy in Kenya with Particular Reference to the Educational System', in Whiteley, ed. 1974:397—454.
1974c 'The Teaching of Languages at Secondary Level: Some Significant Problems', in Whiteley, ed. 1974:481—543.
Greenberg, Joseph H.
1963 *The Languages of Africa* (Bloomington, Indiana, Indiana University Press).
Heine, Bernd
1970 *Status and Use of African Lingua Francas* (Munchen, Info-Institut für Wirtschaftsforschung).
Hemphill, Rod
1974 'Language Use and Language Teaching in Primary Schools in Kenya', in Whiteley, ed. 1974:455—480.
Itebete, Peter
1974 'Language Standardization in Western Kenya: The Luluyia Experiment', in Whiteley, ed. 1974:87—114.

Labov, William
1966 *The Social Stratification of English in New York City* (Washington, D.C., Center for Applied Linguistics).
Ladefoged, Peter, and Clive Criper
1970 'Linguistic Complexity in Uganda', in Whiteley, ed. 1970:145—159.
Ladefoged, Peter, Clive Criper, and Ruth Glick
1971 *Language in Uganda* (Nairobi, Oxford University Press).
Laitin, David M.
1974 'Language, Politics and Thought: The Somali Experience', doctoral dissertation (University of California, Berkeley).
Lemon, Nigel
1972 'Language and Conceptualization among Secondary School Students', paper presented at the eighth annual conference, East African Universities Social Science Council, Nairobi.
Lucas, Stephen
1972 'The Anthropology of Inequality: Some Sociolinguistic Indices of Domination and Subordination', paper presented at the eighth annual conference, East African Universities Social Science Council, Nairobi.
Mazrui, Ali
1970 'Social Engineering and Language Policy in East Africa', unpublished paper (Kampala, Makerere University).
1972 *Cultural Engineering and Nation-Building* (Evanston, Illinois, Northwestern University Press).
Mchangamwe, A. Bashir
forthcoming 'Swahili in the Schools in Kenya', to appear in volume edited by Faruk Topan (Nairobi, Oxford University Press).
Mhina, George A.
1973 'Another Language Gap that Awaits a Policy Decision', unpublished paper (Dar es Salaam, Institute of Swahili Research).
Mitchell, Sir Philip
1954 *African Afterthoughts* (London, Hutchinson).
Molnos, Angela
1969 *Language problems in Africa: a bibliography, 1946—67.* With special reference in East Africa (Nairobi, East African Research Centre).
Neale, Barbara
1974 'Kenya's Asian Languages', in Whiteley, ed. 1974:69—86.
Nyerere, Julius
1967 *Education for Self-Reliance* (Dar es Salaam, Government Printer).
Parkin, David J.
1969 *Neighbours and Nationals in an African City Ward* (London, Routledge and Kegan Paul).
1970 'Language Choice in Two Kampala Housing Estates', in Whiteley, ed. 1970:347—364.
1974a 'Nairobi: Problems and Methods', in Whiteley, ed. 1974:131—146.
1974b 'Status Factors in Language Adding: Bahati Housing Estate in Nairobi', in Whiteley, ed. 1974:47—158.
1974c 'Language Shift and Ethnicity in Nairobi: The Speech Community of Kaloleni', in Whiteley, ed. 1974:159—166.
1974d 'Language Switching in Nairobi', in Whiteley, ed. 1974:167—216.

Pollnac, Richard B.
1973 'Cognitive Variability and its Sociocultural Correlates among the Baganda', paper presented at the annual conference, American Anthropological Association, New Orleans, November 1973.
Polome, Edgar
1972 'Problems and Techniques of a Sociolinguistics Oriented Survey: The Case of the Tanzania Survey', paper presented at the annual conference, Language Association of Eastern Africa, Nairobi.
Scotton, Carol M.
1965 'Some Swahili Political Words', *Journal of Modern African Studies* 3.4:527−542.
1970a 'Recent trends in language policy in Uganda', paper presented at the annual conference, Language Association of Eastern Africa, Nairobi.
1970b 'The perception of Swahili competence among two groups in Kampala', *Journal of the Language Association of Eastern Africa* 1.1:75−79.
1971 'Towards a sociolinguistic theory of choosing a lingua franca'. *Studies in African Linguistics. Supplement* 2:109−129.
1972 *Choosing a Lingua Franca in an African Capital* (Edmonton, Linguistic Research Inc.).
1973 'Neighbors and Lexical Borrowing: a Study of Two Ateso Dialects', *Language* 49.4:368−382.
forthcoming 'National and Personal Ambition in Language Choice', to appear in festschrift for A. A. Hill (The Hague, Mouton).
Scotton, James F.
1971 'Growth of the Vernacular Press in East Africa: Patterns of Colonial Control', doctoral dissertation (Madison, Wisconsin, University of Wisconsin).
Sharman, John
1974 'Some Uses of Common Bantu', in Whiteley ed. 1974:115−130.
Steere, Bishop Edward
1870 *A Handbook of the Swahili Language as Spoken at Zanzibar* (London, The Sheldon Press).
Walusimbi, Livingstone
1971 'Vernacular Teaching in the Schools', in Ladefoged *et al.* 1971.
Whiteley, W. H.
1961 'Political Concepts and Connotations', *St. Antony's Papers* 10:7−21 (London, Chatto and Windus).
1967 'Loanwords in Linguistic Description: a Case Study from Tanzania', in I. Rauch and C. Scott, eds., *Approaches to Linguistic Methodology* (Madison, Wisconsin, University of Wisconsin Press) pp. 125−143.
1968 'Ideal and Reality in National Language Policy: a Case Study from Tanzania', in J. A. Fishman, C. Ferguson, and J. Das Gupta, eds., *Language Problems of Developing Nations* (New York, John Wiley and Sons) pp. 327−344.
1969 *Swahili, the Rise of a National Language* (London, Methuen).
1970 ed. *Language Use and Social Change* (London, Oxford University Press).
1974 ed. *Language in Kenya* (Nairobi, Oxford University Press).

1974a 'The Classification and Distribution of Kenya's Languages', in Whiteley, ed. 1974:13—59.
1974b 'Some Patterns of Language Use in the Rural Areas of Kenya', in Whiteley, ed. 1974:319—350.
1974c 'Introduction', in Whiteley, ed. 1974:1—9.
Whiteley, W. H.
Wright, Marcia
1965 'Swahili Language Policy 1890—1940', *Swahili* 35.1:40—48.

NOTES

1. The remaining 5 percent of Tanzania's population speaks languages from four different linguistic families. With the Bantu groups representing the Niger-Kordofanian family, this means Tanzania is a nation in which all the language families of Africa are found. The Western Nilotes (represented by the Luo) and the Eastern Nilotes (represented by the Masai) are from the Eastern Sudanic branch of the Nilo-Saharan language family. Sandawe and Hadza are click languages placed in the Khoisan family alongside the South African Hottentot-Bushman languages. Iraqw is a Cushitic language from the Afro-Asiatic family. Mbugu appears to be a Cushitic language with a great deal of borrowing from Bantu. We follow Greenberg (1963) in this classification. All three East African nations have relatively small populations, with the largest language group numbering only somewhat over one million speakers.

2. The Western Nilotic Luos make up about 13 percent of Kenya's population (there are no other Western Nilotes in Kenya); the Eastern Nilotes total about 15 percent (represented by the Masai and the Kalenjin group); and the Cushitics make up 5 percent (represented by the Galla and the Somali). There are only about 60,000 Kenyans at most who speak Swahili as a first language. Over 80 percent of the population of Kenya belongs to the eight largest language groups, that is, they are speakers of Kikuyu, Kikamba, Luluyia, Ekegusii, Myijikenda, Kimeru, Dholuo, or Kalenjin (which is a cover term for the Nandi-Kipsigis group) (Gorman 1970b:1).

3. In 1972—73 I taught in the University of Nairobi Linguistics and African Languages department. Luo students accepted the need to study Swahili but some claimed that requiring them to study the structure of another Bantu language was discriminatory. The fact that all students in the program also had to study a non-Bantu language at some time during their course of study did not lessen the Luo objections.

4. Ladefoged (1971) described the Bantu languages of Uganda as more of a dialect continuum than a string of separate languages.

5. See the conclusion for an updating of this situation.

6. Tanganyika and Zanzibar together were re-named Tanzania in 1964.

7. The Tanganyika Territory Report for 1921, quoted by Wright (1965:46), enthuses over the result of the German language policy in this way: 'Whereas the British official may often have had to risk the mutilation of his instructions to a chief by having to send them verbally, the late German system has made it possible to communicate in writing with every akida and village headman, and in turn to receive from him reports written in Swahili.'

8. See Whiteley (1969) for a detailed description of the early Swahili history.
9. 'Swahili as the Lingua Franca of East Africa', *The Church Overseas* 4(1933): 31.27—29. Referred to in J. F. Scotton 1971:34—35. Names of the newspapers and details are given.
10. Whiteley writes, 'A school was established in Tanga in 1893 to train Africans to occupy places as junior officials, and by 1903 there were eight government schools, twelve local authority schools, and fifteen mission schools. As Swahili was to be the language of the administration, great efforts were made to document it, and scholars like Velten, Seidel, Büttner and others provided the materials on which courses at the Oriental Seminar in Berlin were based. A governor like Rechnenberg (1906—12) spoke the language, and his successor, H. Schnee, had attended courses in Berlin' (1969:59).
11. In continuing to support Swahili in the schools, the British do deserve credit for their stand in Tanganyika since they were going against prevailing educational opinion which generally favored local vernaculars in the lower standards and a language of wider communication in the upper standards (English in the case of East Africa). As Cameron and Dodd write, '. . . in spite of the efforts made from time to time by the voluntary agencies [mainly missionaries] to reverse the policy initiated by the Germans, the British administration steadfastly adhered to it in education . . . Swahili during this period continued to gain ground as the medium of instruction in the primary schools . . . By 1945 the vernaculars had all but disappeared from the educational system — both government and non-government. Thanks to educational policy the future national language was now firmly established' (1970:71). Even as late as 1953 the recommendation of the Binns Mission from England was 'the eventual elimination [of Swahili] from all schools where it is taught as a lingua franca'; the Binns Mission claimed that Swahili 'affected adversely the teaching of both the vernacular and English'. It was against this kind of pressure that the British government in Tanganyika had to stand.
12. See the conclusion for an updating of this situation.
13. In his 1968 survey of the use of Swahili in western and central Kenya Heine (1970) commented on the relatively low percentage of persons among the larger ethnic groups who claimed to know Swahili. He writes, 'Remarkable — and indeed hardly expected — is the low percentage in respect of the Kikuyu tribe. Various reasons can be attributed to this . . . The Kikuyu form the most numerous tribal group in Kenya. As has already been mentioned, a relationship can frequently be observed between the size of an ethnic group and its attitude towards *lingua francas*; the larger the tribe, the stronger the resistance to adoption of a *lingua franca*. This hypothesis is supported by (figures for other ethnic groups on Swahili usage) . . . Whereas . . . the Luhya, one of the largest ethnic groups in Kenya make up a proportion of 58 percent Swahili users, the proportion in the case of the relatively smaller neighboring tribes Teso and Sabaot at 62 percent and 80.2 percent are higher' (1970:100).
14. Harry Thuku in *Tangazo* of February 17, 1922, and March 8, 1922, as referred to in J. F. Scotton 1971:163—166. Scotton reports that in fact it seems the Asian printer of *Tangazo* M. A. Desai was a major force behind

the unity movement, thinking Asians and Africans could unite against the Europeans.

15. It would be a gross oversimplification to claim that all missionaries disliked Swahili. Without the evangelical work in favor of Swahili and the practical work of producing Swahili grammars and dictionaries its spread by formal teaching would have been much slower. And in Kenya, for example, such urban missions as the Salvation Army in Nairobi recognized the need for a *lingua franca* and did use Swahili. See Wright (1965) for details on the missionaries' mixed response to the Tanganyikan government policy favoring Swahili.

16. At the Imperial Education Conference of 1923 two of the six principles agreed upon dealt with the idea that the language 'best known and understood by the child on his entry into school life was, from the educational point of view, the most effective medium of instruction in the preliminary stages of school education'. In 1919 the Director of Education in Kenya had localized this sentiment saying, 'The teaching of Swahili is a waste of time . . . I think teaching in the vernacular is absolutely necessary' (quoted by Gorman 1974b:406).

17. Quoted by Gorman (1974b:442).

18. Whiteley remarks, 'While such studies [of local languages and Luganda in this case] were perhaps, a usual feature of C.M.S. [Church Mission Society] activity, there seems to be no doubt that, as time passed, such knowledge bestowed a gratifying sense of power vis-a-vis the newly arrived Protectorate officials and may well have been a contributory factor to their unwillingness to see Luganda supplanted in any way' (1969:69).

19. Ladefoged *et al.* 1971:99.

20. Joint Select Committee on Closer Union in East Africa, minutes of evidence, Vol. 2, H.M.S.O. 1931:554. Quoted by Whiteley (1969:71).

21. Sir Philip Mitchell, an ex-governor of Kenya and Uganda with forty years' experience in Africa, reports the following incident illustrating the feelings of some Baganda toward Swahili in the earlier part of the century: 'On a visit as governor in 1935 to the Masaka Agricultural Show, Governor Mitchell met Saza Chief Pokino. Not knowing Luganda, Mitchell said so in Swahili and asked Pokino, in Swahili still, if he knew Swahili. Pokino began to say he could speak Swahili, when other Baganda companions — Kabaka, Resident, Catholic bishop — said, 'Of course you can't talk Swahili; you know you can't talk Swahili' (1954:174). Even though Swahili is widely spoken in Kampala and in many parts of Uganda, many still refuse to hear of its obvious wide currency. Parkin, who noted the deaf ears while doing research in 1962, writes, 'The fact that Swahili is spoken on a wide scale in many sectors of Kampala's population causes both surprise and scepticism to those who have not investigated the phenomenon' (1969:19). Not surprisingly it is those of high education, who undoubtedly use little Swahili, whom we find among those who most often discount it as an important language in Uganda. In a May 1971 Radio Uganda panel discussion, a woman of high education complained that Swahili in Uganda was 'the language of prostitutes only' (formerly Baganda women went to Nairobi and Mombasa as prostitutes and nursemaids and returned speaking fluent Swahili). A man on the panel then added (in Luganda), 'Swahili is a

language spoken by swindlers'. And in many parts of up-country Kenya and Uganda someone who is a fluent speaker of Swahili is considered a bit suspect, the implication being that he who speaks Swahili well (i.e., knows foreign ways) has 'been around' a good deal and no doubt has learned devious ways.

22. The sheer number of people in Uganda who claim to speak some Swahili attests to its use there. In a 1968—70 study (C. M. Scotton 1972) conducted in Kampala, where the need for a *lingua franca* is highest, 97 percent of those interviewed claimed to be able to speak some Swahili, although it is true 42 percent said they could only speak it a little. But weighing this against the 24 percent who said they could speak no English at all and the 23 percent who said they could not speak Luganda, one can see the obvious place of Swahili as a *lingua franca*, with or without official status.

23. I distinguish between a national and an official language although one language can certainly be both at once. A national language is that used on various public occasions in a cultural or political display of national unity. An official language is that one directed for use in government business and correspondence and usually used in legislative debate. Sometimes a nation may have regional national or official languages.

24. The use of vernaculars in Tanzania is by no means dying out but the domains in which vernaculars are used are being sharply restricted as more and more Swahili is used. Officially, vernacular domains are being limited by government directives such as that against the teaching of literacy in vernacular languages. Also, religious services are no longer supposed to be held in the vernacular languages. Unofficially, many people are using Swahili where vernaculars used to serve. For example, many of the Chagga who live on the slopes of Mount Kilimanjaro report they use Swahili in everyday conversation with such relations as brothers or sisters although they still use Kichagga with children and elders.

While conducting the Tanzania Language Survey, Polome noted a number of indications of changing patterns of use. He writes, '. . . whereas in Sukumuland most of the Bibles sold until about five years ago were in the local vernacular, a considerable shift to Swahili has taken place quite recently . . . In other areas, like Gogoland, the sale of the Biblé in the local vernacular was practically discontinued. Moreover, many parish priests indicated that in recent years shifts have taken place in their preaching habits; whereas ten years ago they preached essentially in the local vernacular, most of the preaching is done in Swahili nowadays, especially for the younger generation, with occasional translation into the local vernacular for the older population. In many cases this was also due to movement in the population which had brought new people into the area as a result of some economic project . . .' (1972:15). But as both Polome and Barton note, Tanzanians still want their children to learn their own vernaculars alongside Swahili. Students interviewed in teacher training colleges said they would send their children home to their parents to be taught their vernacular and 'to learn who they are' if the children failed to learn the vernacular from their parents. Barton reported, 'One older government officer said that he was ashamed that his children could not understand what was happening if they attended a marriage ceremony or other affair "at home". In each instance it was assumed that the children knew Swahili; only knowledge of the tribal language was in doubt' (chapter 3, 1972:21).

25. However, even though few persons as native speakers of Swahili are in a position to take advantage of Swahili's position, some of those few inevitably do. A paper given at the East African Social Science Conference in December 1972 (Lucas 1972) reported on the linguistic basis of ethnic jealousies and rivalries between the indigenous Bondei people in Tanga many of whom speak Swahili as a first or an almost-first language, and up-country immigrants to the area who have come to work on sisal plantations. The Bondei use the lack of competence in Swahili on the part of the immigrants as a basis of ridicule. Furthermore local Bondei children tend to do better in school, it seems, because of their headstart in Swahili.

26. Until 1967, when Swahili became the medium of instruction in all Tanzanian primary schools (save one or two reserved for children of expatriates), three types of primary schools existed: the Swahili-medium, the English-medium, and the Asian-vernacular medium (Gujarati, Punjabi, and Urdu). All began with different languages but worked toward a common examination in English at the end of eight years. In the second half of the full primary course English replaced both Swahili and the Asian vernaculars as the medium of instruction. Swahili was a subject in those schools where it was not a medium. At the end of 1962 schooling in the Asian vernaculars was stopped and these schools switched over to an English medium (Cameron and Dodd 1970:175).

27. Swahili proponents in Tanzania recognize that the battle to win prestige for Swahili away from English is far from won. They recognize Swahili must become a medium at the higher levels first and use every opportunity to drive home their point. For example, Mhina took this line of argument: '... Some have the feeling that if one is educated through the medium of Kiswahili, then the education he receives is going to be of a lower standard. And in addition to that some say that the educational qualification is not going to be recognized internationally. This assumption is basically wrong ... Is language the yard-stick? How many experts have been employed in this country whose knowledge of both English and Kiswahili is very meagre? These are people who have been educated through their own home languages' (1973:5—6).

28. Ali Mazrui's unpublished paper 'Social Engineering and Language Policy' (1970) is the source of this basic idea.

29. This is true in the abstract only, unfortunately. Past history inevitably has favored some ethnic groups over others in terms of educational opportunities. The fact that missionaries worked first with the Baganda in Uganda, the fact that they settled in up-country areas in Kenya, the fact that the national capitals are located among Baganda-in Uganda and among Kikuyu in Kenya — these are all factors which have given some ethnic groups more access to English. In the student body at the University of Nairobi today, for example, one would be hard put to find even one student from the northern hunting and pastoral ethnic groups to match every twenty students from such groups as the Kikuyu.

30. In 1974 the policy changed and Uganda broadcasted in eleven languages, four of them foreign (English, Swahili, Arabic, and French) and seven of

them Ugandan (Luganda, Madi, Ateso, Lugbara, Kipsabiny, Runyoro-Rutooro).
31. Ladefoged *et al.* 1971:25. Slightly more people speak Luganda than Swahili, but this includes the 16 percent who speak Luganda as a first language.
32. C. M. Scotton 1972:87; 165.
33. Swahili has distinctly neutral socioeconomic connotations in both Kenya and Uganda. This means that a man's production of Swahili does not identify him as having a particular social or economic status. This feature of Swahili, it seems, can both encourage and discourage people from speaking it. In Kampala I found that many people felt 'free' to use Swahili, good or bad, without fearing adverse judgment. They also used Swahili, particularly in non-work situations, to avoid the suspicion that they used English because they were showing off. As one respondent told us, 'If they use Ṣwahili, they cannot be mistaken (as proud)' (C. M. Scotton 1972:120). Also, people do not usually learn to speak English on their own; it is significant that only those in the Kampala sample who studied English in school reported knowing *any* English. But almost all claiming ability in Swahili reported learning it on their own. 'This willingness to "teach yourself Swahili" but not English can be explained, at least in part, by our finding that a speaker's ability in Swahili is hardly used as a socio-economic indicator while his ability in English is' (Scotton 1972:121). In commenting on the Kenyan situation, Whiteley presents the *other* side of the coin of Swahili's neutral socioeconomic image. He claims that in Kenya people often do not use Swahili, especially if they speak it poorly, precisely because speaking Swahili well is not a clue to education or status. He quotes the following comment from a senior administrator and says he believes it represents a widely held view: '. . . no one minds speaking English badly because it is a mark of hard work, initiative, etc., to have tried to learn it at all. A man who corrects one's Swahili may be no better than oneself; this cannot be true of someone who corrects one's English. So . . . those of us who speak Swahili badly are ashamed or shy of speaking it at all .. .' (Whiteley 1974b:344).
34. See the conclusion for an updating of this situation.
35. In his article on 'linguistic gamesmanship' in the Kenya Language Survey volume, Parkin (1974d:207) observes that when several languages are used by both participants in conversations in Nairobi, the switch to English generally signals a claim of high status on the user's part. 'I am . . . referring to the socio-economic prestigious stereotypes with which English is frequently associated', he writes. If the listener then does not reply in English he may be doing it either because his English doesn't measure up to that of the first speaker or because of more idealistic reasons of an egalitarian nature. But whatever his reasons the listener can avoid English by using 'this stereo-typing of English as socially exclusive . . . as a weapon against the language', Parkin notes. 'Swahili is then held up as the "true" national language, freed of colonial implications and of the status divisions brought about by an urban, industrial and monetary complex, and alone likely to express the "fraternity" of all ethnic groups in the nation and the dignity of their political independence. *This powerfully emotive argument underlies many*

of the interesting debates in parliament and press regarding possible national language policy (emphasis mine). Nevertheless, at the personal level in Kenya, the prestigious and socially exclusive stereotype of English remains the dominant one'.

36. A shift from one language to another in the same conversation marks a shift in social meaning, it is generally agreed. The shifts observed in the following illustrate the meaning attached to the use of various languages in Uganda in terms of appropriateness for the place and topic. The conversation took place in the East African post office headquarters in Kampala which at the time, in 1970, was staffed by officers from all three East African countries. 'One of the officers who is from Tanzania came in and greeted his friend from Kenya in Luganda. They conversed for a minute or so in Luganda (of course very poor Luganda and they were only joking) and later on switched to Swahili. Then they started talking about their work in English' (C. M. Scotton 1972:61).

    Whiteley reported the switch to English for status reinforcement in his rural observations in Kenya: 'I have myself been present in Gusii homesteads when a father has switched from Gusii to English in order to quiet his children, and then immediately justify this by reference to the classroom situation, commenting that nowadays children take much more notice of their teachers than they do of their parents. A number of interviewees reported the use of English to give added authority to the user, who in every case is cited as the father . . .' (Whiteley 1974b:330).

37. The poor state of Swahili teaching and, more important, the attitude of the elite toward the value of Swahili is illustrated by the fact that in the school which my son attended in Nairobi, a school where children of high ranking Kenyan officials are also students, only a few children out of my son's Standard VI class of twenty-eight passed the Swahili examination given at the end of their first term. While I personally know some blame can be laid on the teaching methods, surely neither the students nor their parents must take Swahili very seriously if such a state of affairs exists. Swahili has not been made an examinable subject on the examination which determines entry into secondary school; this fact speaks louder than politicians' 'public' praises of Swahili.

38. Many excuse not making Swahili the official language by saying that it is not sufficiently 'developed' yet. These people seem to have the view that for a language to be developed means that it has a large vocabulary and especially words for modern concepts and objects. Swahili has borrowed many words, particularly from Arabic and English, for new concepts and objects; but still, because a Swahili form for something like kinetic energy has not been codified, some think Swahili is not 'developed'. This association of the acceptability of a language with the size of its vocabulary may be due to tendencies in many cultures to judge a man's ability to handle a language not by the ideas he is able to express but by the size of his vocabulary.

39. We already have claimed language policy distinguishes socialistic from capitalistic societies.

    An interesting point to speculate about is what actual *patterns* of language usage tell us about differences *between* various capitalistic societies. There are two aspects to consider, it seems to me: (a) In capitalistic society *x*, is there open communication between all segments of society? That is, do linguistic repertoires overlap so that a company president can and does speak to the porter at his door? In feudalistic societies of course there was not always the possibility of such communication. Nineteenth-century Russia, where the elite spoke French but not much Russian, is the obvious example. Do such societies exist in the world today, one wonders, or is there always a *lingua franca* available — or manufactured in the form of a pidgin — to bridge the communications gap? In all of East Africa of course Swahili is the main *lingua franca* used for such situations. (b) When disparate socioeconomic classes must communicate, which class is it which does the accommodating? That is, does the porter learn the company president's language or vice versa? *And* what are the social implications of the direction of the accommodation? In East Africa the direction is downwards, that is, the elite classes learn Swahili to communicate with the masses; the porter need not know English. It is interesting to note that in immigrant America it was (and is) the porter who had to learn English; accommodation was upwards. What does this say about the society? I would like to put forth very tentatively this interesting hypothesis: when linguistic accommodation is upwards, it signifies a particular form of capitalism in which *upward social mobility* is expected as a distinct possibility. Where accommodation is downwards a more static society is envisioned. Thus the American immigrant porter is expected to learn English because he is expected to not stay in the same place; the possibility of bettering his position exists and learning English is a symbol that he is on his way. The East African porter doesn't bother to learn English because there is no expectation that his circumstances can change.

40. David Laitin (1974) has recently conducted research on a subject similar to that which I treat in this section. Laitin refers to his subject as politico-linguistics, 'the secondary social, economic, and political consequences of legislated language change'. Specifically he is studying the changing situation in Somalia where Somali has just been declared the official language. He notes that as long as English was the official language, it had direct consequences concerning social stratification and societal participation. Having English as the official language meant that students educated in the English school system in the north got most of the better jobs in the government at the expense of those students educated in the Italian school system in the south, or those educated in Arabic, primarily in rural areas. The choice of English meant that in Somalia, where the vast majority of the population does in fact speak Somali, intermediaries were needed for an ordinary citizen to apply for a license, petition the administration, or to have any dealings with the government.

Laitin is interested now in how the social situation will change with Somali as the official language. He is also interested in whether notions about the meaning of various political terms change when the terms are talked about in Somali rather than English?

Trends in Bilingualism in Canada

INTRODUCTION

It is the chief purpose of this article to present an overview of that part of the developing research enterprise which has a direct bearing on issues and policies pertaining to English and French language patterns in Canada. Within that context the special focus is on bilingualism of both the individual and institutional varieties. This is not an exhaustive, annotated survey of relevant research on the subject. Those seeking such detailed information should consult the \excellent bibliography of the International Centre for Research on Bilingualism at Laval University. Furthermore, we restrict discussion to topics in or on the fringe of the sociological domain. Excluded are matters which are in the domains of specialized branches of linguistics, such as lexicography, and of psychology, such as neural or physiological dynamics in language learning and retention.

This article is written at a time when there is a marked surge of interest and activity in language policy and in research. Every week or so new and important materials appear, either in the form of debates and decisions on policy or of studies and 1971 Population Census tabulations which have a bearing on language issues. This means that extensive revision would be required should we attempt a new version of this article every year, a welcome sign of vigor in the research enterprise. To the latter we turn after a brief sketch of the political issues involving language.

NATIONAL UNITY AND LANGUAGE ISSUES

As with any other state, Canada has its burden of internal problems, but it shares with only certain other states the problem of maintaining national unity among two segments, each of which has a world-encompassing international language as a mother tongue. The problem of national unity has been formulated by many political and ideological figures as one of 'keeping Québec in Confederation' by giving French more recognition than it has had in the country as a whole. In concrete terms this is usually stated as the provision for French language education, government services, and mass media content outside the Province of Québec. Most anglophones regard the French language as secure in Québec and in no danger of losing ground, a view which is not shared by many Québecois, as we shall see in a moment. Thus the prevalent view, at least in terms of *public* statements by political leaders about national unity, is that the French should not be regarded as just another ethnic minority group but that they should form one of the 'charter' groups in the country. Large sections of the Canadian public do not subscribe to this view.

The few surveys[1] available on this topic show that in Québec and the Maritime Provinces the 'special' status of the French is acknowledged by the majority of non-French, but that in parts of Ontario, in British Columbia, and particularly in the Prairie Provinces the non-French tend to regard the French in their midst as one among many ethnic minorities of more or less equal status.

To cite only one survey by way of illustration of this point, Table I presents the distribution of responses to a question on the right of the French-speaking citizens to deal with officials in their areas in the French language. In the national sample of 709 the

Table I.   *Response to CIPO Poll #334, March 1969, by Region and English Mother Tongue*[a]

Question 12: 'As you may know, the Federal Government is planning a bill on language rights by which all areas where 10% of the population is French speaking, these citizens should have the right to deal with Federal officials in their area in their own language. Do you approve of this idea or not?'

All mother tongues	Canada	Maritimes	Québec	Ontario	Prairies	British Columbia
Approve	55 (396)	57 (37)	85 (170)	52 (133)	25 (30)	38 (26)
Disapprove	36 (258)	34 (22)	8 (16)	39 (98)	70 (84)	54 (38)
Qualified and don't know	9 (55)	9 (6)	7 (13)	9 (23)	5 (7)	8 (3)

English mother tongue	Canada	Maritimes	Québec	Ontario	Prairies	British Columbia
Approve	45 (187)	58 (35)	71 (10)	50 (101)	22 (20)	43 (21)
Disapprove	47 (194)	32 (19)	14 (2)	43 (86)	71 (63)	49 (24)
Qualified and don't know	8 (33)	10 (6)	14 (2)	7 (15)	7 (6)	8 (4)

[a] From: *Canadian Institute of Public Opinion* (Toronto), made available through Social Science Data Archive, Carleton University, Ottawa.

majority (55%) approved of these French rights. However, if we break the sample down by region and mother tongue we find a disproportionate share of approval accounted for by French mother-tongue respondents and by non-French mother-tongue respondents in Québec and the Maritimes. In fact on the Prairies only 22% of English mother-tongue respondents approve. In Table I we give the regional breakdown by English mother tongue only because the number of French respondents outside Québec and of other mother-tongue (non-French, non-English) respondents outside Ontario and the Prairies are too small to warrant inclusion by region.

That the French are a status minority outside Québec is amply proven by the fact that the granting of certain rights is so often a result of conflict, with the granting regarded as a concession. Conflict over French language rights in Canada has always been the subject of public controversy, that is, has always been politicized. On the other hand it is only since the most recent resurgence of independence movements in Québec that English language rights have become a matter for public debate and special legislation. Until recently public-supported English language schools, the provision of official services in English as well as French and other language rights were taken for granted in the Province of Québec and were not subject to the political bargaining process, being guaranteed statutorily.

However, the French have not had the same statutory guarantees elsewhere in Canada. Because education and the provision of a wide range of public services are under provincial jurisdiction, French language rights outside the Province of Québec have always been problematic. On scores of occasions since Confederation in 1867, francophones outside the province of Québec have won some and have lost some contests over language rights at local and provincial levels.

Such conflict has been a persistent theme running through Canadian history and, in some places, has become almost routinized. Indeed it was the concern for the future of Confederation under the threat of communal conflict which impelled the federal authorities to launch the Royal Commission on Bilingualism and Biculturalism.[2] Many of the recommendations of this massive undertaking are being translated into policies and programs, a brief discussion of which is presented later.

The higher and more inclusive the level of government, the more concern is shown about threats to unity from conflict over language rights and the more readiness there is to take steps to reduce or prevent such conflicts. However, the steps taken, in the form of concrete policies and practices, frequently generate conflict, or make manifest what was latent conflict, at lower levels of the system. Most conflict occurs at the community and institutional levels, involving such units as municipal governments, school boards, work groups, and regional or local representatives of language-group interests. Often some conflict resolution is achieved by parties at this level but increasingly such resolution is being achieved through higher level, extra-community interventions. For instance, in 1972 widely publicized disputes in two Ontario cities over demands from franco-Ontarians for a French high school were only settled when a mediator from Toronto, the provincial capital, carried out successful arbitration. This tendency to higher level intervention is to some extent a result of increasing centralization of educational decision-making at the expense of local control. The topic of changing patterns of conflict over language, as influenced by shifts in loci of decision-making between levels of inclusiveness of governing bodies, begs for careful research.[3] It is not the purpose of this article to go into that topic in depth. We draw attention to it as something to keep in mind when we examine policies and programs that deal with language issues at different levels of Canadian society.

OVERVIEW OF POLICY INITIATIVES

The single most important policy decision of the federal government, following the recommendations of the Royal Commission on Bilingualism and Biculturalism, was the creation of the Official Languages Act in 1969. The post of Commissioner of Official Languages was set up to administer the Act, which also called for the appointment of a Bilingual Districts Advisory Board. Goals of policy at the federal level are not stated negatively as directed simply at conflict management, but rather are stated positively in terms of the development of a model bilingual society and of satisfying the needs of *both* official language groups. However, it is common knowledge that the needs of anglophones have always been more than adequately met. It is only in the Province of Québec where anglophones might soon find themselves in a position occupied by francophones for many generations, and that is having frequently to work, serve, or be served in the other language even in federal institutions. Actually the main thrust of the federal government policy is to generate or increase the extent of French language usage in government agencies for those who use these agencies or are employed in them, with a secondary thrust aimed at fostering French-language education.

In line with these policy aims several types of program have been launched. One concentrates on units under the direct or indirect control of the federal government, such as branches of the civil service, crown corporations, the armed forces, and by various means — selective staffing, French-language learning programs, the creation of bilingual and unilingual French agencies — seeks to increase the use of French as a 'normal' language of work. The principal locale for these programs is Ottawa, the federal capital, although agencies in other parts of the country are also affected. It is hoped that making it possible to work in French in federal agencies will result in the attraction to or retention of more francophones in the federal bureaucracy, a counterforce to the pulls of Québec separatism.

In one respect this type of program is easier to mount than other types: its own agencies are at least officially under the control of the government and decrees issuing therefrom must be acted upon by these agencies. They are accountable, and coercive measures could be used legitimately to bring about changes in them. However, in other respects this type of program is more difficult than others to implement successfully, for at certain points it must run into resistance from groups and individuals whose life styles and careers are threatened by this particular kind of change. The basic norms of language usage at work have been long established, and it requires more than gentle persuasion to change some of them in more than a token way.

Another type of program is more diffuse and is oriented chiefly to those regions where one of the official language groups is present in substantial numbers, but is nevertheless a minority. The major point of this type of program is provision of services to the minority in its own language. A secondary one is the fostering of French-language education and of bilingualism among individuals. An outstanding feature pertaining to this type of program is the policy of setting up what are termed *Bilingual Districts*. One recommendation of the Royal Commission on Bilingualism and Biculturalism was that such districts should be created in those regions where the numerically smaller official language group makes up at least ten percent of the region's population.

Because of the demographic distribution of language groups in Canada, the great majority of these bilingual districts are those involving francophone minorities. The federal government attempts to ensure that services in those agencies under its control are provided at least minimally for both language groups, and through subsidies to foster instruction and cultural expression in the minority language.

In one respect this type of program should meet with less resistance than the type which involves changing the rules about work situations, with all its implications for threatened careers and self-images. The simple provision of services, announcements in the minority language, bilingual signs at airports, and so on should meet with little resistance unless onerous taxation is involved, such as when a French school is to be built from the public funds. On the other hand because the federal government is much confined in so many provincial matters (education, health, labor legislation, etc.), there are stringent limitations on what can be expected from this type of program. For one thing, the federal government may ordain that some of its services be manned and offered in French, but the range of its services is rather narrow and does not touch directly and in a significant way the bulk of the population. For another, in order for the program to work in agencies other than those controlled by the federal government, the cooperation of these agencies is required. Thus influence and persuasion, rather than coercion, must inform strategy in this type of program.

The government takes pains frequently to point out that its policy is not what can be described as 'individual' bilingualism, or the fostering of second-language learning among millions of monoglots. Their policy is described rather as 'institutional' bilingualism, which was distinguished from individual bilingualism in the First Report of the Royal Commission on Bilingualism and Biculturalism:

'A bilingual country is not one where all the inhabitants necessarily have to speak two languages; rather it is a country where the principal public and private institutions must provide services in two languages to citizens, the vast majority of whom may very well be unilingual. The same is true for a bilingual province or a bilingual institution. Consequently, "the existing state of bilingualism" in Canada is not so much a question of the number of bilingual people as of the position of each of the two languages in everyday life and of the opportunities actually offered to each of them.'[4]

While the emphasis is on institutional bilingualism the government

also seeks to foster individual bilingualism, specifically the learning
of French as a second language, hoping that this would increase the
number of persons who are favorably disposed to official bilingualism policy.

The goal of fostering bilingualism in institutions both at the center
and in bilingual districts across the country may seem modest
enough, but what headway has been achieved has been against some
strong currents.[5] Of course it is too early to attempt a systematic
evaluation of how much actual headway has been made, for the
several programs of both types have been in operation for only about
five years. Indeed the Bilingual Districts Advisory Board, set up in
1970, has so far turned in only one Report, recommending that
certain provinces – New Brunswick and Québec – be declared
bilingual districts in their entirety and that selected parts of other
Provinces be so declared.[6]

Also of such recent vintage to preclude serious evaluation are the
policy initiatives of provincial governments pertaining to the official
languages. In some cases these initiatives have been fostered by the
prompting and subsidization of the federal government, which is
prepared to enter into agreements with provinces in the promotion
of minority language survival and bilingualism through second-
language learning.[7] In one case, that of New Brunswick, the provincial initiative in declaring both English and French as official
languages, and in the provision of publicly supported education in
both languages antedated the promptings of the federal government.
Declarations and some legislation in support of bilingualism
minority language rights, especially in the field of education, have
also emanated from the provincial governments of Manitoba and
Ontario. How significant such initiatives are in effecting concrete
change in specific communities it is too early to tell.

The situation of Québec with respect to language policy is different in important respects from that of the other provinces. From the
French point of view the chief problem there has been defined as
making French the normal language of the economic sphere and of
gaining adherents to the francophone population from immigrants
whose mother tongues are neither English nor French, but who tend
in large proportion to augment the anglophone part of the population. From the non-French point of view the problem is defined in
terms of the protection of what language rights are already enjoyed,
rights which they perceive as threatened by the French thrust
towards unilingualism. It is in Québec that language policy and

planning, much of it informed by sound research, is most advanced and taken with most seriousness.[8]

This brief overview of trends in language policies at the federal and provincial levels during the past five years or so points up the movement towards official intervention in the realm of intergroup relations in Canada. Federal and some provincial governments deliberately attempt to foster change in current language practices. As we have said, it is premature to assess how these interventions are faring. However, we can offer suggestions as to the factors which are likely to impede or foster the attainment of official objectives. These factors are derived from what we know — or think we know — about the demographic, sociological, and psychological constraints within which policies and programs must operate. In discussing them we draw upon the corpus of research available to us and offer comments about the state of that research. Before presenting research findings, indeed in order to better evaluate some of these findings, it is necessary to examine the chief source of data and the methodology used by scholars in their studies of language patterns in Canada. Because so many crucial studies have important demographic dimensions and are usually based on the Canadian census of population, we first turn to an examination of that source.

THE NATURE OF THE CANADIAN CENSUS DATA ON ETHNICITY AND LANGUAGE

For a variety of reasons, stemming partly from the officially bilingual nature of Canada and partly from the influx of large numbers of European immigrants at the end of the nineteenth century and the beginning of the twentieth, the Canadian census of population has had a long-standing interest in the ethnic and linguistic characteristics of the Canadian population. It is, therefore, not surprising that a substantial part of the research on bilingualism in Canada has utilized the data from the population census; on the contrary it may be surprising that not more use of the data has been made thus far. Although the questions which appeared in the census schedules do not approach the thorough coverage of linguistic behavior that is advocated by Lieberson (1966), they probably do form the most extensive set of such data available anywhere.

In order to understand the context within which the bilingualism data appear, it is worthwhile to examine the whole array of related questions as they have developed since the census of 1871.

The first question to appear (in 1871) was one asking for the *'racial or ethnic origin' of the people.* In this question, which has appeared in all other censuses except that of 1891, respondents were asked to determine their ancestry through the paternal line. In the 1891 census respondents were subdivided into 'native-born' and 'born outside Canada'; the 'native-born' were subdivided further into 'French-speaking' and 'all others'. The introduction to Volume I justifies this innovation in the census schedule by pointing to the bilingual nature of Canada; whatever the justification might have been, the question was not repeated, so in 1901 we are back to a question on 'origin and nationality'. There are some interesting cues to Canadian history in these census questions and the categories used in the published tables, but to elaborate on these would force us to deviate too much from the topic on hand.

The next question to appear is a question on 'language spoken' in the census of 1901. It appears to be a mixed question which would tap both the 'mother-tongue' and the 'official languages spoken' potential of the population. With regard to mother tongue there is the insistence that the respondent still *speak* the language (Vol. I, p. xx). Language data were only collected for the population five years and over; the published table (appearing at the end of a table dealing with the education of the population) is somewhat difficult to decipher in all details but some information on reported bilingualism can be culled from it.

This 'mixed' version of the language question continues through the census of 1921; for 1911 the question was asked but no tabulation of the findings appears anywhere in the regular volumes. The restrictions on age varied, too: for the 1921 census the question regarding 'languages spoken' refers only to the population ten years and over.

In 1931 we see a refinement of the language question. What heretofore was only one question now gets split into two: one on 'mother tongue' and one on 'official languages spoken'. In the 'mother-tongue' question there is still the requirement that the respondent still *speak* the language. Besides the refinement of the questions themselves (compared with earlier censuses, anyway) the tabulation of the findings is also greatly expanded from 1931 on, so that the 'official language' data appear in a total of five tables, 'mother tongue' in five others, while 'language spoken' (a combination of the 'mother tongue' and 'official languages') has been continued through the 1971 census with remarkably few changes. The only ones worth noting are:

(i) in 1941 the operational definition of 'mother tongue' was changed in the sense that respondents were no longer required to still *speak* the language; it was sufficient for them to *understand* it. This obviously created a discontinuity in the sequence of information especially for native-born Canadians of foreign parentage.

(ii) in 1971 a question was added to the schedule in which respondents were asked which language they spoke most often at home. It is clear that this addition meets the U.N. recommendations for the 1970 Population Censuses regarding language (Shryock *et al.* 1973:276).

Despite the unusually long sequence of language questions and the high quality of the Canadian census data, these questions are open to some criticism. The main critique was raised with regard to the question on ethnic origin in an article by Ryder (1955). The following points are worth noting:

(a) there was no clear definition of the concept of 'origin' until 1951 (466); despite that, respondents appear not to have had any great difficulty answering the question;

(b) bases for the origin categories were color, language, religion or birthplace-cum-nationality;

(c) several of the categories used show large fluctuations from census to census; to a large degree this can be attributed to the changing political situation (470–473);

(d) Ryder postulates that the Canadian data on origin are limited in their utility to the possibility of dividing the Canadian population into four groups: British, French, other whites, and non-whites (476).

Ryder's article stands all by itself as published criticism of the Canadian census data in this area. Strangely enough it continues to be cited by social scientists who use the data on ethnic origin, but virtually no reaction to it is evident on the part of the Canadian census takers. The exception is Krotki's article (1965). Besides the fact that there is a delay of almost exactly a decade between the publication of Ryder's article and Krotki's memorandum, it should be noted that Krotki, aside from labeling the article as a 'milestone' and 'benchmark', does little more than raise some weak objection against it. In some of these cases the objections appear to be based on misunderstandings and/or differences in interpretation.

In short, despite the existence of Ryder's criticisms, the Canadian social science community appears to be satisfied with the ethnic origin data; a favorite strategy appears to be: first Ryder's article gets cited as a caveat, then the analyst proceeds to use the origin data anyway. A common area of usage is that of the linguistic assimilation of French-Canadians; commonly, comparisons between the number of people of French mother tongue and those of French ethnic origin show that the former number is less than the latter. The inference is then drawn that French-Canadians are assimilating. Given the way in which a person's ethnic origin is determined, however, it is possible that the assimilation took place in an earlier generation.

Another problem in the Canadian language data, which is not raised anywhere, lies in the rather peculiar definition of 'mother tongue' both before and after 1941. In either case it is essential that *some* connection between the respondent and the language still exist. Hence it is literally possible, under the Canadian definition, for people to 'change' their mother tongue. And indeed Lieberson suggests that this has occurred to a slight degree in the 1951 to 1961 decade (1966:146—147; 1970:17). Data are not available at present to indicate to what degree this process has been going on in the past; it should be pointed out that the evidence drawn together by Lieberson yields only a 'minimum' value since it only allows estimating the 'net' amount of redefinition of mother tongue rather than the 'gross' which would be the more appropriate value. More serious than that, possibly, is the fact that much of this 'redefining' seems to affect the 'other' mother tongue groups (i.e., those whose mother tongue was neither English nor French).

DEVELOPMENTS IN CANADIAN CENSUS-BASED BILINGUALISM
RESEARCH

Given the lengthy sequence of census data on ethnicity and language characteristics of the Canadian population (as discussed above), it is not surprising that the earliest research efforts in this area were based on the data from the censuses of population. There is indeed a series of census monographs on 'Nativity and Ethnic Origins of the People', dealing with the census data for 1921, 1931, and 1941 respectively.

As the titles suggest, the twin concerns in these monographs were the description of the Canadian population according to the place of birth and to membership in ethnic groups. Obviously both these concerns related directly to the assimilation of immigrants — of which Canada received large numbers in the first half of the twentieth century (see Kalbach [1970, *passim*] for discussions on the impact of immigrants on the Canadian population). Somewhat surprisingly, *no* effort was made in these monographs to study the available data on bilingualism; in fact very few discussions in any of the three studies are pertinent to the analysis of relations between the two 'Charter Groups', i.e., the francophones and the anglophones. To illustrate this, we can briefly summarize the pertinent components of the 1941 monographs: Chapter Nine deals with 'language' in a total of six pages (126–131). The largest portion of the chapter (127–130) deals with those unable to speak *either* official language, while the next largest portion deals with the acquisition of English, respectively French, by people of 'other' mother tongues (130–131). Given the emphasis on the assimilation of immigrants, as noted above, this probably makes eminent sense, but as an element in the study of bilingualism it is clearly not very helpful.

The interest of the Canadian Government in the analysis of the ethnicity and language characteristics of the population declined rather quickly in the years following the World War II: the complete 1941 monograph was only released under restricted distribution in 1965. Furthermore the otherwise fairly extensive 1961 monograph programme did not contain any study regarding ethnicity and/or language characteristics; those monographs which did use breakdowns of the population by ethnicity tended to restrict themselves to the use of the (somewhat suspect) ethnic origin, occasionally supplemented by the use of the (less suspect) mother tongue. In short, the census monographs from 1921 through 1961 provide virtually no details on bilinguals as compared with speakers with one or neither of the official languages.

The 1961 census, however, developed into a major source for studies of Canadian bilingualism by researchers outside the federal government although it is hard to say how much of this research was caused, and/or supported, by the activities of the Royal Commission on Bilingualism and Biculturalism, which started its activities in 1963.

Among the works which have appeared since the publication of the 1961 census, the following deserve special mention: Lieberson's *Language and Ethnic Relations in Canada* (1970) used miscellaneous data sources other than the census (including such items as the telephone guide and employment ads in various newspapers) but the mainstay of the book is formed by the censuses from 1941 through 1961. The two subjects which are discussed extensively in the book are 'causes of bilingualism' and 'mother-tongue maintenance'. In both these topics Lieberson falls back on a general proposition: that '... in virtually any contact setting involving people with different native languages it is necessary for at least one segment to learn to communicate with the other' (1970:249). Lieberson uses a variety of approaches to the problem, utilizing an assortment of data sources and a large number of indices some of which were developed especially for this particular analysis. Despite the wealth of inno-vative ideas the book suffers from some major shortcomings: first, there are several instances where the reported findings are a direct function of the assumptions made; since these assumptions are not always explicitly stated and since, furthermore, Lieberson has a habit of not citing the exact source of his data, the findings suggest a more definitive interpretation than is really warranted. Second, many of the analyses are somewhat superficial, e.g., will remain at the bivariate level. In some of these instances multivariate techniques can show the deficiency, even incorrectness, of the bivariate analysis. Despite the shortcomings, however, the book does represent a landmark in the demographic study of language in Canada.

In several ways Joy's *Languages in Conflict* (1967) forms a contrast to Lieberson's book: while Lieberson worked in the research environment of large American universities Joy worked as a private researcher with an interest in Canada's language situation; while Lieberson works 'from the outside', detached from the Canadian scene, Joy works 'from the inside', i.e., from the federal capital situated on the border of French Canada and containing a large francophone minority. Joy's interest is essentially the geographic dispersion of Canada's francophones and changes therein over time. He uses predominantly data from the censuses of population for 'regions' within the county; these regions are built up from counties and census divisions.

In contrast to the two works mentioned above, where the re-searchers attempt to analyze the language situation in Canada from a neutral, detached point of view, Maheu's *Les Francophones du Canada, 1941–1991* (1970) takes a position with regard to the findings. His analysis is essentially the study of 'rates of assimilation' for francophones from 1941 through 1961, on an age-specific basis, followed by an extrapolation of these rates through 1991. Again the study is based on data from the censuses of population for 1941, 1951, and 1961. In this case data on ethnic origin and mother tongue are used, broken down by province and age group. The shortcomings of this approach become apparent after careful inspection of the analysis: first all the indices used in the extrapolation are based on the question regarding ethnic origin and thus have a somewhat questionable validity; second, the linear extrapolation of three actual data points (1941, 1951, and 1961) to cover three future points (1971, 1981, and 1991) is arbitrary: it is based upon an untestable hypothesis postulating continuation of past trends and it ignores the problem of an increasing standard error of estimate for data points outside the available range. Yet the technique which decomposes shifts in language characteristics by age cohorts warrants further attention.

A final set of research enterprises should be mentioned here: many of the projects commissioned by the Royal Commission on Bilingualism and Biculturalism use data from the census as a base. Most of these studies have not been published at this moment; a listing of projects carried out is supplied on pages 201—212 of Volume I of the Commission's Report. Furthermore selected findings of these projects are presented throughout the other volumes of the Report.

TRENDS IN CENSUS-BASED RESEARCH ON CANADIAN BILINGUALISM

In addition to the observation made above regarding the 'highlights' of this type of research, a few general comments are necessary regarding the overall developments which have taken place.

The first observation one can make is that there is an increased tendency to concentrate on smaller units of analysis. The census monographs studied either the total Canadian population or the populations of provinces and regions. The three major studies mentioned later show a greater variation: Maheu (1970) restricts himself mainly to provinces, with a small section where the proposed bilingual districts are discussed. Joy (1967) has a greater mix, consisting of provinces, counties, and some of the larger cities within the 'bilingual belt'. Lieberson gives an even greater variety, from the total country down to census tracts for the largest cities. This trend is incidentally also evident in several graduate theses written on the topic (e.g., Myles 1970; Kringas 1973; Gryz 1973). It is obvious that this shift to a more detailed analysis has important consequences: it is possible to locate differences within the larger units which would otherwise pass without being noticed. But more importantly it provides a better 'match' between the theoretical underpinnings of most of these studies, which postulate that the efficiency of communication is a major factor in the linguistic behavior of individuals, and the empirical testing of these theories. In other words one can argue that units such as census tracts, cities, and to a lesser degree counties are better proxies for the 'fields of interaction' than are such large units as provinces or the total country. Furthermore the trend toward using smaller units of analysis coincides with a tendency to make more census data at relatively low levels of aggregation available in machine-readable form to interested users. Thus it is now possible to replicate many of Lieberson's analyses using enumeration areas for 1961 and 1971.

This increased utilization of machine-readable data and computer programs for the analysis of those data is probably responsible for the second major development: the use of new and/or more complex modes of analysis. Whereas the census monographs used cross tabulation as their major analytical techniques, the more recent works tend to shift towards the use of correlation and regression analysis. There are beginnings of multivariate analyses in Lieberson's study and, once more, several unpublished theses are utilizing these techniques more thoroughly. For the more geographically oriented researcher there are promising developments in the area of computer mapping (*vide* Taylor and Douglas 1970 for an example of the possibilities of this approach).

Although these developments are of course not unique to the demographic study of language relations, it appears likely that they will have a great impact on the direction of the field, its modes of analysis, and its theoretical orientations.

Before we conclude this section discussing the population census as a data base for the study of bilingualism in Canada, it is worthwhile to summarize some of the main findings which this base has yielded.

DEMOGRAPHIC ASPECTS OF CANADIAN BILINGUALISM

When we look at the series of data on official bilingualism (i.e., the proportion of the population reporting an ability to speak both English and French) we are struck by the *stability* of this bilingualism: the proportions of the population falling into the four categories relating to the question on official language (English only, French only, both, and neither) have remained virtually constant over time. Table II illustrates this stability.

It should be noted that strict comparison cannot be made due to the fact that minimum ages for these tabulations vary from census year to census year. Furthermore the data for 1901 are not com-

Table II. *Ability to Speak the Official Languages, Canada 1901-1971*[a]

	Percent speaking:			
	English only	French only	Both	Neither
1901	64.6	18.2	13.9	3.4
1911	68.0	19.3	7.4	5.2
1921	68.1	13.2	16.7	2.0
1931	69.6	13.6	15.1	1.8
1941	67.2	19.0	12.8	1.0
1951	67.0	19.6	12.3	1.1
1961	67.4	19.1	12.2	1.3
1971	67.1	18.0	13.4	1.5

Notes: (1) Newfoundland included only from 1951 on.
(2) For 1911, 1921, and 1931 data refer only to the population ten years of age and older.
(3) For 1901 data refer only to the population five years of age and older.

[a] From: 1901: *Census of Population,* educational status of persons five years and over, Volume IV, Table XIII.
1911: Lieberson, 1970:32.
1921: *Census of Population,* Volume II, Table 76.
1931: *Census of Population,* Volume I, Table III.
1941: *Census of Population,* Volume IV, Table 12.
1951: *Census of Population,* Volume I, Table 53.
1961: *Census of Population,* Volume I, Part: 2, Table 63.
1971: *Census of Population,* Population by language most often spoken at home and by official language (Advance Bulletin, August, 1973), Table 2.

pletely certain: the data presented in Table II for 1901 are reworked from the original tabulations for which headings were not totally clear. Despite these problems in comparison it is safe to conclude that the proportion of bilinguals has remained remarkably stable. The only exception to this stability is shown by the 1911 data. The reader should note that the 1911 data were *not* found in the census tabulations but in the summary table by Lieberson (1970:32) who, unfortunately, does not give a source for these data. Given that, it is impossible to establish the credibility of the 1911 bilingualism data at this point.

We can analyze the statistics on bilingualism over time in a few other ways:

1. We can look at the degree to which bilingualism is a *regional* phenomenon. For almost all of the preceding censuses data are available by province. Table III gives the available data. It should be noted that data on the (questionable) 1911 census are not included in the table.

Table III. *Percentage of the Population Able to Speak English and French, Canada and Provinces, 1901–1971*[a]

	1901	1921	1931	1941	1951	1961	1971
Canada	13.9	16.7	15.1	12.8	12.3	12.2	13.4
Newfoundland	–	–	–	–	1.1	1.2	1.8
Prince Edward Island	11.5	13.9	11.9	10.8	8.9	7.6	8.2
Nova Scotia	6.6	10.3	7.7	6.9	6.1	6.1	6.7
New Brunswick	13.4	20.8	21.4	18.3	18.6	19.0	21.5
Québec	32.4	38.8	37.1	26.8	25.6	25.5	27.6
Ontario	5.0	8.7	7.0	7.5	7.8	7.9	9.3
Manitoba	5.2	8.4	6.8	7.5	7.5	7.4	8.2
Saskatchewan	–	6.8	5.4	5.2	4.9	4.5	5.0
Alberta	–	6.9	5.2	4.6	4.3	4.3	5.0
British Columbia	3.6	5.4	3.5	2.9	3.4	3.5	4.6

[a] From: *Canada, Census of Population*
    1921: Vol. II, p. 495.
    1931: Vol. I, p. 247.
    1941: Vol. I, p. 257.
    1951: Vol. X, p. 177.
    1961: Vol. VII, 1, p. 9–4.
    1971: Vol. I.3–5, p. 26.

Despite problems of intercensal comparability, the evidence in the table reinforces the point made earlier about the stability of Canadian official bilingualism: rankings in degree of bilingualism by province remain virtually constant despite fluctuations in those degrees of bilingualism themselves. Kendall's tau for adjacent censuses gives values ranging between .89 and 1.00, while Kendall's tau for the two censuses farthest apart has a value of .62. Furthermore the provincial data support Joy's notion of a 'bilingual belt': the degree to which provinces were reported as bilingual tends to decline as one goes farther West and East from the province of Québec (Joy 1967:5).

Further inspection of Table III suggests that bilingualism has remained fairly stable in the three western provinces, has declined in Québec and Prince Edward Island, and has increased in Nova Scotia, New Brunswick, Ontario, and Manitoba. All these changes, however, are quite small when we consider that a seventy-year span is involved, during which millions of immigrants were absorbed, drastic changes in communication and transportation took place, and in general major changes have affected Canada's social structures.

Confirmation about the distribution of bilinguals comes from a new data source, reports from Statistics Canada, published in the form of Education Service bulletins on enrollment in second-language classes. As a result of the federal-provincial agreement of 1970, by which the federal government contributes to the costs of second-language acquisition, a check is maintained on the number of such enrollments in primary and secondary schools across the country. Because the series began in 1970 it is premature to launch an analysis of trends in the extent to which French pupils are enrolled in English-speaking, and non-French pupils in French-speaking classes. However, a comparison of figures for the provinces reveals the pattern of distribution noted above: more than 60% of pupils in Québec and New Brunswick are enrolled in second-language classes; for the remainder of the provinces, considered as a whole, about 37% of pupils receive second-language education in one of the official languages (Statistics Canada 1973).

Another new source of data pertaining to bilingualism from Statistics Canada also throws some light on language among youth. We refer to the 1971 Student Census Study. In this study, carried out in conjunction with the 1971 population census, a sample of 657,450 students in elementary and secondary schools provides information on the following characteristics: mother tongue; facility in both official languages; family size; leisure time activity; part-time work; and geographical mobility. The sample was drawn from the twenty largest metropolitan areas in Canada. This implies a limitation on the utility of the results for those parts of Canada where the French are much under-represented in metropolitan areas. The case of New Brunswick is particularly noteworthy here for the samples include only one metropolitan area, St. John, with a proportion of only 7% of French mother tongue, while the proportion for the Province as a whole is 34%.[9]

The question in the Student Census Study of special relevance to this section has to do with language facility and is worded as follows:

'Can you speak English or French well enough to conduct a conversation? (Check: English only, French only; both English and French; neither English nor French)'

The instructions given on the questionnaire are as follows:

'Do not report a language studied at school unless you can conduct a conversation in it. By this we mean being able to carry on a conversation of some length on a variety of topics.'

Table IV. *Proportion Student Census Sample with Facility in English and French Compared with Proportion of Total Population Bilingual, Census, 1971*[a]

	% bilingual, Canadian population, 1971	% bilingual, Student Census, 1971
Canada	13.4	12.3
Newfoundland	1.8	3.1
Nova Scotia	6.7	4.7
Québec	27.6	28.9
Ontario	9.3	12.5
Prairie Provinces	5.8	7.0
British Columbia	4.6	6.6

[a] From: 1971 Student Census of Canada (Kassirer, forthcoming) and Advance Information Bulletin, Population by Official Language, 1971 Census, Statistics Canada.

Note: New Brunswick is omitted from the table because of lack of adequate representation of French mother tongue in the Student Census Study. Prince Edward Island is omitted because it was not included in the Student Census Study.

Responses to this question reveal the same profile of the distribution of bilingualism as that presented above. If we leave out those provinces for which the metropolitan area sample seriously underestimates the francophone population, Table IV reveals the pattern of a gradient of decline in bilingualism correlated with distance from Québec.

The Student Census data suggest that bilingualism is growing among the school age population, especially among those of English mother tongue, for in every province or region except one (Nova Scotia) the proportion of students who are bilingual exceeds that of the total population bilingual. However, we must interpret these figures with caution. For one thing, the selectivity factor in the Student sample possibly over-represents the English mother tongue bilinguals, because it does not include those who have dropped out of high school and it could be that those who complete the upper grades are more likely than those who do not to have acquired a second language.

2. The other way to analyze trends in official bilingualism since the beginning of the twentieth century is to investigate the differences in the degree to which various groups have tended to become (or report themselves as) bilingual. It can be asserted that in virtually all bilingual societies one of the groups involved tends to be much more bilingual than the other group(s), in the sense that a higher proportion of its members will report itself as bilingual than does the remainder of the population. Assertions of this kind have been made with regard to such countries as South Africa, Finland, and Canada. In the Canadian case it is fairly quickly evident that it is the francophones who are the main 'supporters' of bilingualism.

When we try to study the degrees to which English-Canadians and French-Canadians have been bilingual, according to the censuses of population, we find to our dismay that most of the necessary information has never been tabulated. Furthermore most of the existing tabulations involve the 'ethnic origin' variable which, as we have noted before, presents some unpleasant complications. The only case where bilingualism was reported by mother tongue was in the 1901 census, where table headings are not very clear.

For the censuses from 1941 on, however, we have used a technique first worked out by Burton Hurd and further developed by Lieberson (1966). The method involves estimation of frequencies in cells in the cross tabulation between mother tongue and official languages spoken, where we are only given the marginal frequencies and can make some assumptions about the retention of mother tongues. The technique allows one to calculate a minimum and a maximum value for the degree of bilingualism for the two main mother-tongue groups. Adopting Lieberson's convention of assuming the *maximum* value as the best estimate of the bilingualism for persons of English mother tongue, and the minimum value for those of French mother tongue (Lieberson 1970:100), we obtained the figures reported in Table V.

Table V. *Percent Bilingual, by Mother Tongue and by Ethnic Origin, Canada, 1901-1971*

	By mother tongue		By ethnic origin	
	English	French	English	French
1901	4.0	38.1	–	–
1921	–	–	4.8	50.8
1931	–	–	4.2	45.1
1941	4.6	35.0	4.0	38.0
1951	4.8	32.6	3.8	31.0
1961	5.6	31.9	4.0	30.1
1971	7.6	33.1	–	–

It is obvious that indeed French-Canadians have been the largest 'supporters' of bilingualism in Canada, at least since 1901. It is also obvious that we had a rather 'stable' bilingualism from 1901 through 1961 – at least if we use the estimates based on mother tongue. For that period, there are evidently slight increases in English bilingualism accompanied by slight decreases in French bilingualism. It looks, however, as though the 1961–1971 decade contains some 'turning point' in which the declining trend in French bilingualism reversed itself and the English bilingualism increased by more than it had done in the preceding sixty years.

To specify further where the increases occurred we extended the analysis to the provincial level. Table VI gives the estimates of bilingualism by mother tongue for the three most bilingual provinces – Québec, New Brunswick, and Ontario – for the last three censuses.

Inspection of those data allows us to hypothesize that the large jump in English bilingualism is largely attributable to the increase in

Table VI. *Percent Bilingual, by Mother Tongue, for Québec, New Brunswick, and Ontario, 1951-1971* [a]

	Québec		New Brunswick		Ontario	
	English	French	English	French	English	French
1951	40.4	24.3	3.6	46.6	2.6	76.9
1961	46.5	23.8	4.0	46.8	3.4	77.6
1971	59.1	24.6	5.1	53.2	5.5	80.7

[a] From: 1951: Volume II, Tables 19 and 22.
        1961: Volume I, Table 96.
        1971: *Statistics Canada Daily*.

Québec (from 46.5% in 1961 to 59.1% in 1971), whereas the moderate increase in French bilingualism is due to increases in bilingualism among French mother-tongue speakers in Ontario and New Brunswick. In short it would appear that the increase in bilingualism in the 1961–1971 intercensal decade is largely due to increases in bilingualism among provincial minorities.

Further insights in these processes of language maintenance and language shift may be obtained if we combine the data on 'mother tongue', 'official language', and 'language spoken most often in the home'. It should be remembered that this last question was asked for the first time in the 1971 census; an advance bulletin appeared in August 1973.

If we make the following assumptions:

(a) all persons classified as 'French only' (official language) had French as their mother tongue;
(b) all persons classified as 'bilingual' (official language) use either English or French as their home language,

then we can develop the columns in Table VII:

(i) we obtain the number of bilinguals of French mother tongue (using assumption a above);
(ii) we decompose these French mother-tongue bilinguals into those using French resp. English as home language (using assumption b above).

Table VII. *Decomposition of French Mother-Tongue Bilinguals by Language Spoken Most Often in the Home, by Province, Canada 1971*[a]

	FMT (1)	FOL (2)	FB (3) = (1-2)	FHL (4)	FBFHL (5) = (4-2)	FBEHL (6) = (3-5)
Nfdld	3,640	510	3,130	2,295	1,785	1,345
PEI	7,365	675	6,690	4,405	3,730	2,960
NS	39,335	4,185	35,150	27,220	23,035	12,115
NB	215,725	100,985	114,740	199,085	98,100	16,640
Qué	4,867,250	3,668,015	1,199,235	4,870,105	1,202,090	b)
Ont	482,040	92,845	389,195	352,465	259,620	129,575
Man	60,545	5,020	55,525	39,600	34,580	20,945
Sask	31,605	1,825	29,780	15,930	14,105	15,675
Alta	46,500	3,305	43,195	22,695	19,390	23,805
BC	38,035	1,775	36,260	11,505	9,730	26,530

Abbreviations:
FMT   French Mother Tongue
FOL   French (only) Official Language
FB   Bilinguals of French Mother Tongue
FHL   French Home Language
FBFHL   Bilinguals of French Mother Tongue, with French as Home Language
FBEHL   Bilinguals of French Mother Tongue, with English as Home Language
[a] From: Census of Population (Advance Bulletin, August 1973), Table 2.
[b] Denotes 'negative number'.

Inspection of Tables VII and VIII suggests that, in addition to the imbalance in second-language acquisition by language group (as was noted before), there is a pattern in the degree to which francophone bilinguals are using English as their home language. We find again a correlation with the distance from Québec: the further away from Québec, the larger the proportion of francophone bilinguals which is using English as home language. Apparently the francophones in the extreme eastern and western provinces are in an advanced stage of language shift. It should be noted, by the way, that the negative number for the province of Québec is a function of the original assumptions and thus suggests that, for that province, at least one of the basic assumptions is not tenable. In any case it is as though francophones in many locations far from Québec are in a stage of bilingualism characteristic of most immigrant groups, a stage identified by Fishman as one of mother-tongue displacement, where even the mother tongue is mediated by English (Fishman 1972:115). The implications for programs seeking to foster French usage and bilingualism are obvious.

We have seen that data from Statistics Canada are becoming in-

Table VIII.   *Percent of French Mother-Tongue Bilinguals Outside
Québec with English* or *French as Language Most Often
Spoken at Home, by Province, Canada 1971*[a]

Province	Mother tongue French bilinguals	% speaking mostly French at home	% speaking mostly English at home
Newfoundland	3,640	57.0	43.0
P.E.I.	7,365	55.8	44.2
Nova Scotia	39,335	65.5	34.5
New Brunswick	215,725	85.4	14.6
Ontario	482,040	66.7	33.3
Manitoba	60,545	62.2	37.8
Saskatchewan	31,605	47.3	52.7
Alberta	46,500	44.8	55.2
British Columbia	38,035	26.8	73.2

a For sources see Table VI.

creasingly useful to students of language patterns. Some improvement would be welcome in the provision of cross tabulations from
the Vital Statistics files with those of the population census. For
instance, we can make cross tabulations between such matters as
intermarriage and ethnic origin as well as religion, but cannot do the
same for intermarriage and language, a key concern in the study of
bilingualism and language shift.

NON-DEMOGRAPHIC STUDIES

The trend discussed earlier towards the study of language practices in
the context of smaller units than Canada as a whole or very large
regional groupings, such as provinces, has its counterpart in non-
demographic studies based on data sources other than the census.
These studies focus on the behavior and attitudes of people in
settings involving interaction between anglophones, francophones,
and bilinguals. One set of these studies is experimental, using controlled small group research techniques. The most prolific center for
these studies is the Department of Psychology at McGill University,
where for more than a decade W. E. Lambert and his associates have
been probing in the areas of motivation for second-language learning.
language usage and stereotyping, ethnic identity and the like.[10]

Because the findings from this ongoing enterprise are so many and varied, limitation of space prevents an accounting of them here. However, we can say that if we were to range experimental research along a continuum of optimism-pessimism with reference to the potential for harmonious and effective bilingual and bicultural interaction, we would place the results of this group's research near the optimistic end (e.g., Simard and Taylor 1973).

A major limitation of controlled small group experiments from a sociological point of view is lack of fit between the experimental situations and interactional settings outside the laboratory. Significant factors associated with these interactional settings cannot be accounted for and must be treated as given in the controlled experiment. An important study which attempts to combine some of the controllable features of the experimental variety with features of the 'real' world outside the laboratory is widely known as the St. Lambert experiment (Lambert and Tucker 1972). An English-speaking school in a Montreal suburb converted to French as the language of instruction while retaining its English-speaking pupils as clientele. Over a period of about five years psychologists observed the experiment closely, carrying out frequent tests on the pupils whom they discovered acquired a very good knowledge of French without their immersion in that language producing negative effects on their knowledge of English or on their performance in the demanding subject of mathematics.

A quick survey of the research situation indicates that it is probably in the field of bilingual education in Canada that major advances are most likely to be made in research which is of equal relevance to linguistics, psychology, and sociology.[11] This interdisciplinary thrust is especially evident in the research program of the International Centre for Research in Bilingualism at Laval University. In his most recent works Mackey, a leading scholar at that Centre, draws attention to the need for taking into account in a systematic fashion the sociocultural contexts in which particular programs of bilingual education take place, and not just the schools. Of special value is his typology of bilingual education based on the relationship between the learner's home language and the language of instruction; the aims, type and media of instruction; the relationship between the language of the home and that of environing units, such as neighborhood, city, region; and the status of the languages involved in the situation, whether these are of wide or narrow usage, national or international and so on (Mackey 1970).

Another set of studies involves the observation of language behavior in 'natural' settings, such as factories, offices, stores, neighborhoods. The pioneer and now veteran leader in fostering this approach in Canada is Everett C. Hughes. In a recent article Hughes (1970:115) reminisces about ideas he had more than a generation ago, ideas which if pursued by many who had been inspired by this distinguished scholar would have resulted in a much larger corpus of institutional studies than we now have on hand:

'My proposal, once made but not carried out, was to train an army of observers to pick up language cues quickly and send them to observe a large sample of places where people meet in various roles to carry out transactions, and to record choice and use of language. They were also to have initiated transactions in various situations and to have noted the reactions. Such a study would have included detailed observation of the characteristic linguistic encounters inside various institutions.'

It would be gratifying to report that scholarly research on 'linguistic encounters' in institutions has produced a respectable literature which permits generalization about linguistic patterns and processes and comparison among bilingual institutions. However, while there are several studies which report on patterns of language use — English in this sphere, French in that — there is very little at the microsociological level on the *dynamics* of language use among francophones and anglophones in interaction with one another. The most useful generalizations on this topic are from the pen of Hughes himself and are the results of his own experiences and those of some of his students. Only one of his generalizations is cited here (1970:104):

'Thus, there are essentially two kinds of communication. One is horizontal, among people of the same level, either inside the same organization or reaching out into the large world. The other is vertical, predominantly downward, but also sometimes upward. The choice of language for each kind of communication will depend upon what will be effective as between the parties to the language transactions. Given the large French population, horizontal communication in French characterizes many transactions. In the delivery of professional services such as medicine, religion, social services, and education, all parties to the transaction are often of one language.

There are two sets of institutions in all these fields: one French-speaking, the other, English. English dominates in industrial vertical communication downward from the top, and out into the larger world of international transactions. But there is a strong movement to change the situation. It is by no means certain what the future division of linguistic labor will be.'

The Report of the Gendron Commission, on the position of the French language in Québec, appeared just as this article was completed and we have not been able to incorporate its findings in any detail here. However, the findings, based on careful research, confirm the generalizations of Hughes and fill many of the gaps in our information about language use in various institutions, at least for the Province of Québec (Government of Québec, Report of the Commission, Vol. I).

The great majority of studies mentioned so far treat language usage as a dependent variable, the thing to be explained, or as an indicator of something else, such as ethnic assimilation. However, language also requires *performance* in social settings and performance is a social act with consequences other than purely linguistic ones. The research enterprise has not come to grips with this kind of question in institutional settings, except for the experimental work mentioned earlier (see especially Simard and Taylor 1973). A good field for such research would be the new structures of government and the armed forces, such as French Language Units and Bilingual Units.

Language *affiliation* has been used as an independent variable in only a few studies. A most notable recent one is that of John Meisel (1972 and *infra*), where the attempt is made to discover differences in political attitudes and values according to the language characteristics of five language groups which he labels pure English, partial English, mixed, partial French, and pure French. Indeed important differences were found and Meisel shows how using language rather than ethnic origin as an independent variable in research on attitudes and values provides insights both for theoretical formulations and policy analysis in multilingual societies.

One research sector of both political and academic significance which requires more intensive systematic research is the differential 'consumption' by anglophones, francophones, and bilinguals of mass media offerings and the differential experiences of one in the other group's culture and language. Meisel's study, incidentally, contains some relevant findings on this issue although it is not a central one in his work. The aforementioned Government of Québec Commission of Inquiry (Gendron) provides some good recent survey material for Québec and some studies carried out for the Royal Commission on Bilingualism and Biculturalism contain relevant materials on the topic, but much of the latter is out of date (Royal Commission, Vol I, Appendix 4,5; Mousseau-Glazer 1972). Of much value would be up-to-date studies on cultural consumption and participation outside Québec for the various language groupings.

CONCLUSIONS

In the matter of the relations between anglophones and franco-phones as members of distinctive language categories, and in some cases of distinctive cultures, policy issues are becoming more clearly defined. Given the remarkable data base provided by the Canadian census of population and the research facilities and personnel in the country, it might have been expected that Canada would for a long time have been a world leader in the provision of research based findings to inform policy making at home and to add significantly to the corpus of data for the study of multilingual societies all over the world. Actually the research effort has been more modest than it might have been.

We have suggested that two reasons help explain lacks in language-couched research pertaining to the anglophone-francophone situations: one, the official concern with the absorption of immigrants, and second, the related concern with ethnic group integration and assimilation. Both concerns were shared with the United States, although the latter does not have the Canadian linguistic dualism to go along with its ethnic pluralism and perhaps the relative lack of language-focused social science research in Canada reflects this American influence. However, as we have pointed out, there are signs of an upswing in language-focused research in Canada, involving several disciplines. One reason for the upswing is the research-generating process launched by governmental Commissions of Inquiry for Canada as as whole and for Québec. We have tried to indicate the directions in which the research thrusts are going and to locate some of the strengths and weaknesses in the research enter-prise.

Needless to say, studies of relations between the English and

French in Canada need not be language-focused in order to be useful and many worthy studies, not reviewed here, have been conducted within the ethnic-relations framework without paying special attention to language factors as such; others have used vital statistics as a focus (natural increase, intermarriage, etc.) and have produced important insights for our knowledge of anglophone-francophone relations. A good case in point during the past decade is Nathan Keyfitz's article 'Canadians and Canadiens' (1963), although many others could be cited.

REFERENCES

Berry, J. W., and G. J. S. Wilde
1972 *Social Psychology: The Canadian Context* (Toronto, McClelland and Stewart).
Bilingual Districts Advisory Board
1971 *Recommendations of the Bilingual Districts Advisory Board, 1971* (Ottawa, Information Canada, March).
Commissioner of Official Languages
1973 *Second Annual Report, 1971–72* (Ottawa, Information Canada).
Department of the Secretary of State
1973 *Federal-Provincial Programme of Cooperation for the Development of Bilingualism* (Ottawa, May).
Fishman, Joshua A.
1972 *The Sociology of Language* (Rowley, Newbury House).
Gendron, Jean-Denis
1972 See Government of Québec.
Government of Québec
1972 *Report of the Commission of Inquiry on the Position of the French Language and on Language Rights in Québec:* Bk I *The Language of Work,* Bk II *Language Rights,* Bk III *Ethnic Groups* (Québec). (Gendron Commission).
Gryz, Zbigniew
1973 'Assimilation: Language Shift Among French-Canadians', unpublished M. A. thesis (Ottawa, Carleton University, Department of Sociology and Anthropology).
Hughes, E. C.
1970 'The Linguistic Division of Labor in Industrial and Urban Societies', in *Georgetown University Monograph Series on Languages and Linguistics,* 103–119 (Washington, D.C., Georgetown University) (Reprinted in J. A. Fishman, ed., *Readings in the Sociology of Language,* Vol. II [The Hague, Mouton, 1972])
Hurd, E. C.
1937 *Racial Origins and Nativity of the Canadian People* (*Census Monograph* no. 4) (Ottawa, Queen's Printer).

790   Frank G. Vallee and John de Vries

Jackson, John D.
  1966 'French-English Relations in an Ontario Community', *Canadian Review of Sociology-Anthropology* 3:3. 117–132 (August).
Joy, R. J.
  1967 *Languages in Conflict* (Ottawa, published by the author). (Reprinted as *Languages in Conflict: The Canadian Experience* [Toronto, McClelland and Stewart Limited, 1972]).
Kalbach, W. E.
  1970 *The Impact of Immigration on Canada's Population* (*1961 Census Monograph*) (Ottawa Dominion Bureau of Statistics).
Keyfitz, Nathan
  1963 'Canadians and Canadiens', *Queen's Quarterly* 70:2. 163–182.
Kringas, P. R.
  1973 'Is Assimilation Inevitable: A Case Study of Social and Residential Mobility', unpublished M.A. thesis (Ottawa, Carleton University, Department of Sociology and Anthropology).
Krotki, Karol
  1965 'Some Comments on Norm Ryder's Article on Ethnic Origin', in *Dominion Bureau of Statistics Technical Memorandum* 3 (August).
Lambert, W. E., and R. Gardner
  1972 *Attitudes and Motivation in Second Language Learning* (Rowley, Newbury House Publishers, Inc.)
Lambert, W. E., and G. R. Tucker
  1972 *Bilingual Education of Children, The St-Lambert Experiment* (Rowley, Newbury House Publishers, Inc.).
Lieberson, Stanley
  1966 'Language Questions in Censuses', *Sociological Inquiry* 36:262–279.
  1970 *Language and Ethnic Relations in Canada* (Toronto, John Wiley and Sons).
Mackey, W. F.
  1970 'A Typology of Bilingual Education', *Foreign Language Annals* 3:4. 596–608 (May).
Maheu, Robert
  1970 *Les Francophones du Canada 1941–1991* (Québec, Editions Parti Pris).
Meisel, John
  1972 *Working Papers on Canadian Politics* (Montreal and London, McGill-Queen's University Press).
Myles, J. F.
  1970 'Community Determinants of Language Assimilation Among the French-Canadians', unpublished thesis (Ottawa, Carleton University, Department of Sociology and Anthropology).
Ontario Institute for Studies in Education
  1973 'The Activities Related to Minority Groups in the Educational System' (The Office of the Coordinator of Research and Development Studies, University of Toronto, January).
Royal Commission on Bilingualism and Biculturalism (Ottawa)
  1965 'A Preliminary Report of the Royal Commission on Bilingualism and Biculturalism'.

1967 Book I, *The Official Languages.*
1968 Book II, *Education.*
1969 Book III, *The Work World,* Sections A and B.
1970 Book IV, *The Cultural Contribution of the Other Ethnic Groups.*
1970 Book V, *The Federal Capital.*
1970 Book VI, *Voluntary Associations.*
Ryder, N. B.
1955 'The Interpretation of Origin Statistics', *Canadian Journal of Economics and Political Science* 21:466—479.
Simard, Lise M., and D. M. Taylor
1973 'The Potential for Bicultural Communication in a Dyadic Situation', *Canadian Journal of Behavioural Science* 5:3. 211—225 (May).
Shryock, Henry, and Jacob S. Siegel and Associates
1973 *The Methods and Materials of Demography* (Washington, D.C., United States Bureau of the Census, Second Printing).
Social Research Group, The
1965 'A Study of Interethnic Relations in Canada', Unpublished Report to the Royal Commission on Bilingualism and Biculturalism (Ottawa).
Statistics Canada
1973 'Minority Language Education, 1970—71 & 1972—73', *Education Division Service Bulletin* W 4.
   Census of Population, Canada, various volumes from 1901 to 1971.
forthcoming 'Sociocultural Characteristics of Elementary & Secondary School Students in Canada, 1971', Eve Kassirer, ed.
Taylor, D. R. F., and D. H. Douglas
1970 *A Computer Atlas of Ottawa-Hull* (Department of Carleton University, Ottawa, second edition).

NOTES

1. The chief source upon which the following statements are based is the Canadian Institute of Public Opinion (CIPO), a few of whose polls have included questions pertaining to French language rights and bilingualism. During the past decade or so the following polls have included questions relevant to the topic: 305 (November 1963); 312 (June 1965); 334 (March 1969); 353 (May 1972); 359 (May 1973). Data from these surveys were made available to us through the Social Science Data Archive, Carleton University, Ottawa. Another survey whose findings support the conclusion about regional and mother-tongue differences in attitudes to French language rights is the Social Research Group 1965.
2. The publications of this Commission most pertinent to this article are 1967, General Introduction, Book I, *The Official Languages;* 1968, Book II, *Education;* 1969, Book III, *The Work World.*
3. Historians have treated the topic of language conflict in Canada, the most numerous of their studies pertaining to provincial disputes late in the nineteenth and early in the twentieth century in Manitoba and Ontario. The paucity of sociological studies on the topic is perhaps a reflection of the tendency in ethnic studies to focus on the processes of accommodation and

assimilation, leaving that of conflict to the periphery. A notable exception is Jackson 1966, an excellent case study of French-English language conflict and the process of institutionalization of such conflict in an Ontario community.

4. Report of the Royal Commission on Bilingualism and Biculturalism, Book I 1967: xxviii.

5. Several hindrances to the implementation of the Official Languages Act are mentioned in Commissioner of Official Languages 1973. Of special note are the unrealistic fears of monoglots and the bureaucratic process itself.

6. *Bilingual Districts Advisory Board,* 1971. The second Report of this Board was presented in the Fall of 1973.

7. For details of these federal-provincial programs see *Federal-Provincial Programme of Cooperation for the Development of Bilingualism* 1973.

8. This article was on the verge of completion when the publication was announced of the Report of what has come to be called the Gendron Commission, after its head, Jean-Denis Gendron. The full title of the Commission is as follows: *The Commission of Inquiry on the Position of the French Language and on Language Rights in Québec.* We have not had the opportunity to digest the many findings and recommendations of this Commission, but we can say that the Reports of the Commission are informed by excellent research from several fields of social science and law, most of it carried out especially for the Commission. The Reports are in three volumes as follow: *Language of Work, The Position of the French Language in Québec,* and *The Ethnic Groups.*

9. Reports on this study have yet to be published but we have been given access to the data in manuscript form. The references we use are from Eve Kassirer (forthcoming). Of special interest is Chapter II, by Eve Kassirer, 'Second-Language Facility'.

10. A great many publications have appeared reporting the findings of these studies. An excellent summary and up-dating will be found in Lambert and Gardner 1972. See also section on 'Canadian Dualism' in Berry and Wilde 1972:45–202.

11. For instance, a variety of research projects have been launched by the *Ontario Institute for Studies in Education* on Franco-Ontarians and bilingualism. A list of these projects and publications will be found in 'Activities Related to Minority Groups in the Educational System', issued by the Office of the Coordinator of Research and Development Studies, Ontario Institute for Studies in Education, University of Toronto, January 1973. Another source for information on this particular line of research is the *Annual Reports,* with their attached publication lists, of the International Centre for Research on Bilingualism, Laval University.

Addenda

A Graduate Program
in the Sociology of Language

This volume and its companion, *Advances in the Creation and Revision of Writing Systems* bring to a close the self-imposed task which I set for myself a decade ago (1963), during my year as a fellow of the Center for Advanced Study in the Behavioral Sciences (Stanford, California). At that time, while completing *Language Loyalty in the United States* and while in the midst of planning a long-range program of empirical and theoretical research, I undertook to develop a graduate training program for the sociology of language as well as the appropriate texts. At that time neither the one nor the other existed, in the United States or elsewhere. The first issue of this decision (*Readings in the Sociology of Language*) was itself conceived at the Center. Since that time it has been my rare good fortune to be associated for several years with two graduate programs in the sociology of language, one at Yeshiva University in New York and the other at The Hebrew University in Jerusalem, as well as to be associated with a number of others in a visiting capacity of one type or another. These associations have enabled me to define, test, and revise both my graduate training notions as well as the text materials that I prepared or selected to accompany them.

I do not mean to imply by any of the foregoing that yet other and better text materials are not needed in the sociology of language, but, rather, that for the time being I have prepared all that I can (and, perhaps, more than I should) and that others must now step in and contribute where they find gaps in the field.

As Table I reveals, my basic notion has been that the sociology of language was itself an interdisciplinary field and, as such, one that needed to be pursued in conjunction with its two parent disciplines, not to mention any one of a number of its other related fields. The American pattern of graduate work, providing as it does for three or

Table I. *Graduate Training Program in the Sociology of Language*

Core I: Linguistics[1]	Core II: Sociology of Language[2]
(24 credits)	*(24 credits)*
Introduction	Introduction
Syntax	Psychology of Language
Phonology	Language Attitudes
Theories of Grammar	Language and National Identity
Field Methods	Language Planning
Comparative	Sociolinguistic Research Methods
Historical	Sociology of Bilingualism
Conversational Analysis	Seminar: Sociolinguistic Theories
Seminar in Linguistics	Seminar: Applied Sociology of Language

Core III: Sociology

(24 credits)
Eight courses with emphasis on sociological theory and social research methods, including up to three courses in anthropology, political science, economics and/ or history.

[1] Including demonstrated reading knowledge of two pertinent foreign languages.
[2] Including doctoral seminar (no credit) and two course-related research apprenticeships (no credit) dealing with both sociological and linguistic data.

more years of full-time, broadly gauged and yet rather well-defined study, is of course the underlying (and often unstated) assumption on which a program such as this is based. In the Israeli and, more generally, in much of the European framework of graduate work, it is the master's degree alone which is well-defined while the doctorate is largely left to the individual requirements that professors care to impose on their advanced students. The latter framework is, therefore, typically more specialized in that students have little if any opportunity for interdisciplinary study or research experience during their relatively brief period of study for the master's degree. Nevertheless, via a combination of prerequisite requirements prior to admission to master's work, plus supplementary requirements after admission to doctoral work proper, a program essentially like the American one can also be implemented.

The rebirth of the sociology of language occurred in the United States at a time of plentiful research funds and training fellowships. As a result, it was relatively painless for universities to offer the specialized and expensive courses and training opportunities upon which it depended. During periods of plenty, interdisciplinary programs are hailed for their experimental, pioneering, and stimulating qualities. Some will even venture that such programs come closer than do traditional departmental approaches to paralleling the 'true state' in the 'real world' of the subject matter or problems to which they are devoted. However, when the fat years are followed by lean ones, as they inevitably seem to be, interdisciplinary problems are the first to be sacrificed. They quickly appear to have no well-established protectors who would claim them as their own natural and legitimate offspring. Universities must be extremely impoverished, indeed, to cut out one department or another, but it takes only a minor budgetary scare to declare an interdisciplinary program to be a luxury. As a result, it is my definite advice that the courses and faculty of programs in the sociology of language must all also have their definite homes in one or both of the parent discipline departments. The courses listed above are all of such a nature as to make such dual citizenship possible and to enrich any 'standard' department of linguistics and/or sociology in the process, by strengthening or offering course work of interest and importance far beyond the limits of sociology or language *per se.*

The entire enterprise in which I have engaged during the prior ten years has benefited immeasurably from the fact that program building, textbook preparing, and other 'pedagogic' efforts (whether directed at students, colleagues, and/or administrators) were carried on in constant fruitful interaction with basic and applied research. It is, therefore, my strong conviction that students too should be trained in this way, so that study, research, application, and evaluation can be seen and experienced as the necessary continuum that they constitute, rather than as a series of separate and isolated status-related concerns. I have gone out of my way, as a result, whether in connection with *Language Loyalty in the United States, Bilingualism in the Barrio, Language Planning Processes,* or (currently) *The Sociology of English as an Additional Language,* and *The Sociology of Bilingual Education,* to involve as many students as possible in study design, data collection, data analysis, data interpretation, and report writing. I have also tried to be just as helpful as I could with respect to the publication of their joint efforts, often via professional journals and books, or most recently via a journal expressly for student research (*Language Behavior Papers*). It is my view that whatever *I* need in order to facilitate and stimulate my work is also needed by and for my students in order to facilitate and stimulate theirs. We are colleagues in a joint enterprise and that should extend (and it definitely *has* extended) even to the revision of the training program shown above.

It should be the aim of a graduate training program in the sociology of language to develop that field, as well as to cultivate its interdisciplinary ties. Competence in the sociology of language is not something that good linguistics programs or good sociology programs can develop or train for incidentally to their main pursuits. Interdisciplinary fields are not 'picked up' en route to other goals. Indeed, they are harder to master than are corresponding disciplinary fields, precisely because of their broader and less traditional nature.

The view of some linguists that they and their students are qualified to engage in sociolinguistic enterprises because they are 'interested in conversations' or because they have 'studied or taught anthropology', or because they are 'language and area specialists in . . .', is no less ludicrous than would be the claim of sociologists to engage in linguistic (or even in sociolinguistic) enterprises on the basis of such qualifications. After a decade in which I have pursued the sociology of language from one topic to the next, from one discipline to another, and from one continent to another, I am more and more impressed with what remains to be known, and more and more dubious of claims that the field can be theoretically and methodologically mastered or enlightened from a monodisciplinary base or via incidental forays therefrom.

NOTE

Published simultaneously in this volume and in *Advances in the Creation and Revision of Writing Systems*, J. A. Fishman, ed. The Hague, Mouton Publishers ('Contributions to the Sociology of Language', Vol. 8), 1976.

The Development of the Sociology of Language and Its Social Implications*

The recent emergence in the middle 1960s and subsequent rapid development of the sociology of language as a new interdisciplinary field in the United States represents a very notable social phenomenon worthy of some reflection.

For example, why has this field emerged and found such an echo at this time and not earlier or later? Is it presently organized, socially and conceptually, in a manner indicating some degree of autonomy and persistence or is it likely to be only a passing fad? What issues currently characterize the field and do they reveal hints as to its likely direction in the future?

In this brief discussion I will present a few preliminary considerations of these questions. Although its focus will be primarily on the situation of sociolinguistics in the United States, it is hoped that this emphasis will not be entirely ethnocentric but rather instructive because it was there that this field received relatively earlier and stronger development than in other countries to which it is now rapidly expanding.

The complex set of questions raised by the appearance of sociolinguistics in the United States can be grouped roughly under three general headings which will be taken up in turn: (1) What are the

---

* This essay is an expanded and updated English version of the Introduction to Rolf Kjolseth u. Fritz Sack (eds.) *Zur Soziologie der Sprache: Ausgewaehlte Beitraege vom 7. Weltkongress der Soziologie in Varna, Bulgarien, September 14–19, 1970* (Towards a Sociology of Language: Selected Contributions from the Seventh World Congress of Sociology in Varna, Bulgaria. September 14–19, 1970); published as a special anthology edition of the *Kölner Zeitschrift für Soziologie und Sozialpsychologie* (Westdeutscher Verlag, March, 1972, 350 pp.), with an appended bibliography of 890 topically subdivided items prepared by the senior editor.

social and intellectual origins of the sociology of language?, (2) What is the sociology of language, i.e., how is it presently constituted?, and (3) In what directions is the sociology of language likely to develop?

1. ON THE ORIGINS OF THE SOCIOLOGY OF LANGUAGE

Certainly it will take a careful empirical study in the sociology of knowledge to give anything like an adequate answer to questions concerning the social origins of the sociology of language, and there is little question but that those who work in this field could well benefit from the better understanding of their place in society which such a study might make possible.

Hymes (1967a:634) has suggested the need for the sociology of knowledge to study 'the development of the profession (of linguistics) and the ideological aspect of its theoretical assumptions'.

No less needed is such a study of the recent emergence and current structure of the sociology of language.

However, in the absence of any such study at the present time, for purposes of suggestion, it may be useful to propose some dimensions of the social context which may have contributed greatly to the successful emergence and current sustenance of the sociology of language.

Initially, one can assume that the successful emergence of any new discipline is a response to new conditions, both sociopolitical and academic. In other words, a description of the emergence of a new field which emphasizes only intellectual factors (Shuy and Fasold, 1971) is likely to be quite insufficient. Therefore, if socioeconomic factors seem to require new disciplines in order to meet emerging needs, but the necessary intellectual development is not forthcoming, it is difficult to see the development of a field. In the same way, if there are new intellectual developments which are not supported by socioeconomic factors, it is difficult to see how such a field of thought can gain the support necessary for its sustenance.

In other words, social problems may arise for which no solutions can be found, and conversely, solutions may be found which are not applied or implemented. Finally, it would be both tenuous and unreasonable to suppose that socioeconomic conditions or intellectual developments are in principle either independent or dependent variables.

In the specific context of the question, 'Why did the sociology of language emerge so robustly in the mid 1960s in the United States?', a cursory examination of the situation suggests a number of inter- acting factors.

First of all, in complex, stratified societies (and almost all societies with which we are familiar in depth would appear to fall into this category) many social differences are language-linked, that is, language plays an important role in the differential social distribution of positive and negative social values of both a material and symbolic nature. Such a differential distribution is, of course, not necessarily seen as linked to language nor necessarily viewed as a 'problem'. Rather it may simply be taken for granted and considered un- changeable. The transformation of covert conflicts of interest into overt social issues is a social accomplishment, and, at any point in time, only a few matters of covert conflict will become transformed into specific social issues while the remainder will remain covert.

Thus, for example, it happens that while poverty continues to exist for long periods of time in a society, in a certain period it may be 'discovered', and then later 'disappear' from social consciousness as an issue, only, at some later date to be 're-discovered' again. This is exactly what has recently happened in the United States. Further- more, in addition to the 're-discovery' of poverty, matters pertaining to education as well as 'development' have come to be viewed as social issues and hence targets of governmental programs. Most notable of all, and particularly relevant for the discussion here, is the further fact that all three phenomena (poverty, education, and 'development') are currently seen as being related in one way or another to questions of language differences within and between social groupings.

Consider the matter of education. Perhaps because formal educa- tion is so often seen in the popular view as a principal modality by which the differential distribution of advantages (and hence dis- advantages) is achieved within society, recently organized dis- advantaged groups such as the Blacks and the Chicanos (Mexican- Americans) have looked to the schools — where a great deal of curricular emphasis is placed on the acquisition of certain language skills — as an important focus for their concerns. One now hears, for example, that schools with significant concentrations of disadvan- taged cultural, ethnic, and linguistic minorities are characterized by a 'massive reading failure' (Labov 1971a). Yet, a 'massive reading failure' has probably been typical of school for as long as mass compulsory education has been in existence. The difference is that this is now focused upon as an issue and a problem rather than simply as the way things are. Certainly the Black civil rights movement is related to this transformation in important ways. Or, to take another example, one now hears demands for bilingual education programs for linguistically distinct minorities within the United States, whereas not too long ago such a proposal was quite inconceivable as bilingualism and biculturalism were essentially conceived of as maladies – and certainly no school system could 'responsibly' participate in the perpetration of a 'malady'. Again, the transformation is not conceivable without taking into consideration – among a host of other factors – the recent social movements which have been achieved among linguistic minorities in the United States.

Governments do not simply manage conflicts. Rather the role of government is to demonstrate or at least create the impression or illusion of its capacity to respond to those few matters which have come to be defined as social issues and problems among significant numbers of those constituencies which the administration feels it must – for its own survival – take into account. At the present time we therefore find governmental institutions on both the state and federal levels quite deeply involved in promoting research and programs in response to these matters of presently defined concern.

Actually, government support for language-related research in the United States has a long history. For example, as Regna Darnell (1969, 1970) has shown in a recent unpublished dissertation, during the latter part of the nineteenth century, when Native Americans (Indians) were the overriding foreign policy issue in the United States, the government was the primary source of financial support for research on Indian languages and Indian beliefs with regard to property and its ownership. This government support lasted only as long as Native Americans were a primary foreign policy issue. As soon as they were pacified and re-located the support dried up. As Darnell shows, it was during this period of support that anthropology became a professional academic discipline in the United States.

And, as Bolinger (1967) points out, it was in the wake of World War II, when faced with the administration of far-flung areas, that the government passed the National Defense Education Act which contributed strong support for research and instruction related to languages useful in the administration of the new regions.

Much more recently, with the development of new supra-national forms of economic organization, the whole question of regional and national 'development' has arisen and there appears to be a well-articulated awareness that many of the problems involved are related to language. That is, an important part of an economic development program is seen as involving what might be called the establishment of a 'linguistic infra-structure', i.e., a common language of wider communication among numerous vernacular groups. Surveys of vernacular languages, contrastive analyses between them and the language of the developing power, and research on more effective methods of second-language instruction are all the order of the day.

Furthermore, several world powers appear to be in a form of competition in this regard, each seeking to find more effective ways for its language to gain hegemony as the dominant language of wider communication in different 'developing' areas of the world. One also thinks of the competition for primacy among the working languages of the European Common Market.

In summary, when one views some of the principal topical foci for current investigations in the sociology of language, one must recognize that these areas are not simply 'intrinsically' interesting but are related to large and pervasive social issues as currently conceived. This raises some rather deep and problematic issues for any reflective sociology of language which must concern itself not only with the fascinations of particular topics, but, as I have suggested with regard to the example of current bilingual education programs in the United States (Kjolseth 1971), sociolinguistics must also weight the actual social consequences brought about by the products of its investigations as applied (and misapplied) by others in different social roles and with different vested interests. In the same vein, Fishman, speaking in the context of language planning asks 'Who has what to gain and what to lose by what language policy decisions?' (Fishman 1971a:294). Simple answers are not possible and frequently require sophisticated sociolinguistic investigation. Again, a reflective rather than narrowly technocratic sociolinguistic is called for.

Thus the sociology of language is becoming a 'policy science'. On the one hand, because the problems to which it is responding are large and pervasive issues which will be with us for some time, indications are that socioeconomic interests will contribute to its continuing support and probably to its growth in the future. However, this very development and support raises many difficult questions of both an ethical and political nature with which the sociology of language will probably have to come to terms in the rather near future.

2. THE SOCIOLOGY OF LANGUAGE AS AN INTELLECTUAL
   REVOLUTION

Socioeconomic support for the sociology of language is, in and of itself, hardly sufficient for the emergence of that discipline. If the traditional linguistic and social sciences were considered adequate for responding to the above social issues, it would be difficult to see a reason for the existence of a new field such as contemporary sociology of language.

Indeed, it is largely due to the limitations of these antecedent disciplines, stemming from overly narrow and restrictive specialization, that the sociology of language has emerged as a response.

Probably all new disciplines in history are viewed as interdisciplinary during their early phases, for they appear in and between the already existing intellectual groupings. Frequently in such periods of intellectual development and change — or what Kuhn (1962) calls scientific revolutions, profound discontinuities develop between the traditional and the new orientation towards a phenomenon. This is indeed the contemporary situation of the sociology of language for, with quite remarkable speed, it has made great advances in all of those characteristics by which any distinct discipline distinguishes itself from its neighbors. Four particularly salient or relevant criteria in terms of which a distinct discipline can be identified are: (1) a distinct manner of defining its particular subject matter, (2) a specialized language or set of constructs by means of which it defines and analyzes its subject matter, (3) distinctive hypotheses and questions to which it addresses itself which are not being asked by neighboring disciplines, and (4) a particular and distinctive set of methods which are applied in seeking answers to these questions. On all of these counts the sociology of language manifests basic differences from the disciplines out of which it has sprung and it may, therefore, be useful to comment briefly upon them in order to give a few concrete illustrations of the kind of conceptual revolution which contemporary sociology of language involves. In doing this, the conceptual framework of the sociology of language can be contrasted simultaneously with its 'parent' disciplines.

Definition of Subject Matter: 'Language' — While traditional descriptive linguistics has essentially conceived of language as *langue,* i.e., as a single homogeneous system, the sociology of language addresses itself to functionally differentiated language varieties (Fishman, ed. 1971, Chapter 20) as elements or subsystems within complex linguistic repertoires of individuals, groups, social categories, or communities (Gumperz 1964).

Psychology has viewed language as 'non-componentialized, noncontextualized' language competence (Fishman, ed. 1971:561) in contrast to the sociology of language which defines language behavior as essentially contextualized or situated behavior involving a number of socially significant varieties subject to multiple levels of normative constraint.

Sociology has tended to utilize common-sense definitions of language and viewed it as a generally homogeneous phenomenon within social groups and categories, whereas the sociology of language views it as an important means by which intra-group as well as inter-group differentiation is articulated.

Therefore common to all the 'parent' disciplines has been a generally homogeneous, noncontextual conception of a group's language, in direct and profound contrast to the sociolinguistic definition which identifies natural language behavior as essentially heterogeneous, or variable, and situationally contextualized. As Labov (1971b, 469) has noted, 'variation is an *inherent* property of the linguistic situation . . . homogeneity, if it existed, would no doubt be dysfunctional, and would give way to more heterogeneous language forms. The *major* theoretical move required is to abandon the identification of structure with homogeneity' [emphasis added].

Some Basic Constructs Used to Define 'Language' — Operating with a conception of linguistic form isolated from social-situational context, traditional descriptive linguistics has relied heavily upon the notion of grammaticality. Yet, as Hymes (1967a, 639–40) has commented, 'A child from whom any and all of the grammatical sentences of a language might come with equal likelihood would be of course a social monster'. Consequently the sociology of language operates with a much broader construct, namely, the situational appropriateness of differing language varieties.

Psychology has also focused on the notion of linguistic competence as opposed to performance and usually conceived of competence as roughly equivalent to automaticity. But sociolinguists, concerned as they are with normal speech behavior and its situational variability, have come to feel, as does Labov (1971b:468), that:

'It is now evident . . . that the primary purpose of this distinction (competence vs. performance) has been to help the linguist exclude data which he finds inconvenient to handle — that is to further the restricted definition of linguistics set out by Chomsky in *Aspects* (1965, 3). As a whole, the distinction between competence and performance has never proven to be particularly helpful for our work, and it becomes more and more unclear as we consider its general implications.'

Traditional sociology, while it perhaps has the most to offer in the way of future contributions to the sociology of language (Hymes 1967a), has in the past operated with a number of terms such as role, stratification, ethnicity, etc., which have been formulated in isolation from language variables, thereby permitting only a 'grossly correlational approach' (Hymes 1967a: 639) between linguistic and social categories. On the other hand, the sociology of language has developed a much more integrated view of the interaction of speech and social setting (Hymes 1967b) as well as a number of new constructs of a higher order such as speech networks (Gumperz 1964, 1967a), speech domains (Fishman 1964, 1966, 1967a, 1971b), and value clusters (Fishman 1971b).

In general, because traditional descriptive linguistics, psychology, and sociology have tended to view language in a less differentiated manner, and because they have generally isolated language phenomena from situational contexts of actual everyday usage, they, in contrast with the sociology of language, have tended to develop constructs which are both more formal and more isolated from the social contexts of actual language use.

Leading Premises, Hypotheses, and Questions — Descriptive linguistics, 'positing the functional equivalence . . . of all languages' (Hymes 1967a: 633), has tended to greatly restrict its inquiries to the referential function of language (Hymes 1967:663). This could not be more diametrically opposed to the premises of the sociology of language, which assumes that actual, situated language use may fulfill not only different functions in different settings, but multiple functions within any particular setting. Furthermore, the referential function of language is not assigned a priori primacy in terms of its social salience or significance. Rather, it is assumed that the relative significance of reference to the other situational functions must be empirically determined. In the area of multilingualism, descriptive linguistics has traditionally sought to determine how 'unnatural' inter-group contact between 'normally pure' (and invariant) languages has 'interfered' with the internal ideal-typical structure of either or both. Or, as Fishman (ed. 1971:561) puts it, 'the linguist has traditionally seen his task in relation to bilingualism, as being similar to that of a housewife looking for smears of wet paint. He asks what phonetic, lexical, or grammatical structures of language X have rubbed off on language Y and vice versa'. This view has not been without pervasive negative social consequences, for as Fishman (1971:577, footnote 10) notes, 'Language "educators" who are most concerned with teaching pure, contextually lifeless varieties have become particularly enamored of the concept of "interference" and have most fully exploited its inherently proscriptive implications'.

Psychologists have shared this concern of the descriptive linguists and devoted most of their inquiries to the question of the 'costs' to the individual of bi- or plura-lingualism, attempting to determine its effects on the subject's intelligence, educability, adjustment, associations, etc. Such inquiries stem from the premise that man is 'normally' monolingual. Additionally, in the course of all this psychological research, it is noteworthy that it has 'yielded neither an explicit model of bilingual functioning nor the same componential sophistication as is found in connection with psychological exploration of other behaviors such as intelligence or learning' (Fishman, ed. 1971: 557).

In contrast to both descriptive linguistics and psychology, the sociology of language — because it does not posit language as normally a single, pure, homogenous system and because it does not assume that language contact is 'unnatural' — is free to follow a paradigmatically distinct set of inquiries which Fishman (1965; 1972a; Fishman, ed. 1971) has formulated as, who speaks what language variety to whom, where, when about what topics and with what individual intents and social consequences? Additionally, because of the use of the construct 'language variety' this general query is equally relevant whether the investigator is concerned with situations where entirely different (e.g., national) languages are employed or where different varieties within some popularly conceived 'language' are used.

Finally, the emphasis of traditional sociological inquiry has been into the principal *inter*-group variations in language use, primarily because it has not had the linguistic sophistication necessary for identifying *intra*-group differences in language use, but also because, like linguistics and psychology, it has considered multilingual individuals as 'unnatural' and therefore unstable. It has, therefore, tended to focus upon 'marginal' individuals who have served as communicators between groups and sought to determine their other 'unique' characteristics and discover signs of their 'assimilation' into one or the other of the groups between which they move (Fishman, ed. 1971: Chapter 20).

The sociology of language, on the other hand, cannot share with sociology the belief in the priority of this type of inquiry in part because in the sense of distinct languages over half of the world's population is characterized by stable intra-group bi- and multilingualism (MacNamara, ed. 1967), and, in the sense of functionally distinct language varieties within languages, certainly all of the world's population is for all practical purposes so characterized.

Rather, a main concern of the sociology of language is into the social-contextual rules of appropriateness which govern an individual's selection between language varieties in different speech settings.

In general, then, the parent disciplines' typical inquiries share certain restrictions: principally that all posit some form of overly monolithic and simplified set of norms as a benchmark against which their data gain significance in terms of the degree to which it conforms or deviates. The typical type of query orienting sociolinguistic investigation diametrically differs from this, for it makes such norms problematic and hence something which must be inductively derived from empirical inquiry. This leads directly into the final set of characteristics (methods) in terms of which the weaknesses of the parent disciplines can be illustratively contrasted with the sociolinguistic approach.

Methods for Generating Data and Analytical Procedures — The validity of work in structural linguistics has been severely restricted by the nature of the data upon which it has relied. In Labov's (1971a, 41) characterization:

'Traditionally and obviously, historical linguistics is based on the evidence of literary texts, which survive by the grace of various happy historical accidents. To this material, the dialectologist and anthropologist added the evidence obtained by direct questioning of informants. . . . Thus whether we like it or not, the major current of linguistic research in the past four decades has carried us further away from the speech of everyday life.'

At least four characteristics of informant's data weaken their possible validity: (1) we usually do not have a basis for assessing the informant's range of communicative competence, (2) we usually do not know and cannot determine the informant's representativity, (3) it is usually self-report data *about* language behavior rather than actual language behavior, and (4) the investigator himself rarely has sufficient time in the field and hence the communicative competence necessary to validly interpret the social significance of the field data collected. The analytical procedures to which these anecdotal data are typically subjected merely compound their weakness. Labov (1971b:46) notes in this regard that:

'One of the serious limitations of current generative grammar is . . . in the mode of work, and the relation of the analyst to the data . . . The now accepted paradigm is to develop an idea on the basis of a few examples, without any serious consideration of what would happen if all the available data were treated in this way . . . To lean parasitically upon generative grammar for theoretical support will inevitably lead to a rejection of the data themselves.'

In other words, to anecdotal evidence one adds formal deductive reasoning frequently of a transformational type even though 'The categorical rules of generative grammar, for example, are no better adapted to deal with the actual use of language than the categorical statements of the structural linguists of the 1940s' (Labov 1971b:463).

Most of psychology's language data, on the other hand, have been generated under experimental conditions. At first blush one might feel that this type of data would tend to be more valid. However, this is far from true for at least two interrelated reasons: (1) they are contextfree, that is, their context is not isomorphic with everyday speech settings, and (2) the social structure of the psychological experiment tends to produce shifts in the language varieties of the subject. Concerning the first point, how can we possibly know to what degree the subject's language performance is simply a product of the experimental setting (experimenter and/or experiment effects)? And, concerning the latter weakness, Labov's (1971a:44) insight, based on considerable research is particularly relevant, namely, that shifted forms of speech are the least regular and hence make generalization suspect even within the limiting context of the experiment itself.

Again, as in the case of linguistics, the analytical procedures to which these psychological data are subjected tend to compound their weaknesses since they strive for the development of quite limited norms of standardization for establishing comparisons.

Traditional sociological procedures of generating and collecting language data do not show much improvement over the others, for although sampling techniques may be carefully applied it is usually to the easiest form of data available: self-reports — sometimes collected by the investigator himself, but more frequently collected by others (e.g., census data) even though, as Fishman (1971b, 564) notes, the warnings concerning the weaknesses of this kind of data 'go back 40 years' to the work of Kloss (1929). Fishman (ed., 1971:5) summarizes this situation by pointing out that such data have not 'been sufficiently contextualized to either recognize or yield societal patterns with respect to the functional allocation of codes', and notes that these difficulties are in no way overcome with traditional sociological modes of analysis where 'probability theory replaces sociological theory for the study of communication' (Fishman, ed. 1971:564). Hymes (1967a:640) states it this way:

'A mechanical amalgamation of standard linguistics and standard sociology is not likely to suffice. . . Adding a speechless sociology to a sociology-free linguistics can yield little better than post-hoc attempts at correlation between accounts from which the heart of the relevant data will be missing.'

The sociology of language, conscious of the above weaknesses in data collection and analysis in all of the 'parent' disciplines, has been careful in its selection from among existing methods and has developed new methods in a concerted effort to improve the validity of its data and strengthen its generalizations. Perhaps because it is a new discipline, less bound by tradition, it can more freely draw on a number of methods chosen to fit the particular problem being addressed (e.g., participant observation, direct observation, survey techniques, etc.). Methodological 'triangulation' is frequent and concern with construct validity checks is prominent as is shown in Fishman's (ed. 1971) attention to 'domains'. In general, sensitivity to the limitations of self-report data, either as a measure of attitudes towards language varieties and their users, or as an indicator of actual language use, is pronounced when not sufficiently contextualized. As a result, there is great interest in procedures for recording and sampling actual language use *in situ*.

If the sociology of language's approach to data collection is multi-method, its approach to data analysis tends to be multi-level (Fishman 1972a) and its purpose is 'to identify the rules, patterns, purposes, and consequences of language use and to account for their interrelations' (Hymes 1967a:639). Furthermore, it is understood that speech events are ordered by several simultaneous levels of norms, some of which are operative on the micro-level of speech acts and role relationships, while others govern the domains and networks of which the former are a part. Consequently, heuristic considerations and the particular formulation of any particular investigation will determine which level or levels may be emphasized in analysis.

In summary, the sociology of language can be viewed as an integrated, interdisciplinary, multi-method, and multi-level approach to the study of natural, sequenced, and socially situated language behavior. Its thoroughgoing paradigmatic distinctiveness from neighboring disciplines gives it all the character of an intellectual or conceptual revolution vis á vis the 'parent' disciplines, in response to whose overly restrictive specializations it has developed as a new and broad approach to language *in* society. As such, one can fully expect it to prove useful to all the disciplines from which it has sprung. When one remembers that the sociology of language only began to gain impetus around 1965, it is amazing that it has already developed so far — and its conceptual and methodological advances show no signs of slackening.

3. THE SOCIAL ORGANIZATION OF THE SOCIOLOGY OF LANGUAGE

Still the survival and vitality of any field of study require not only a distinctive conceptual and methodological view; equally important to its existence and persistence are various forms of supporting social organization.

Therefore, this brief overview of the contemporary field of the sociology of language would be entirely lacking if it did not pay some attention to its institutional dimensions. These will now be touched upon briefly under four general headings arranged in order of generally increasing degree of institutionalization, namely: (1) publications, (2) programs at professional meetings, (3) teaching and training programs, and (4) research organizations.

Publications — Different genres of publications are useful indicators of the degree of conceptual and social organization which has been achieved within any particular scientific community. In general we may distinguish individual publications, for example, articles and books, from those which require larger scale group organization, such as newsletters and journals.

While the appearance of separate articles in different journals may have been seen as indicating the recognition of certain topics, it is with the appearance of anthologies, readers, and similar collections that these topics become grouped and ordered into a subject area. Such a level of organization is still quite pre-theoretical. However, when trend reports and position papers begin to appear, the subject area is tending towards becoming a field and this transformation is extended with the publication of integrative studies with a paradigmatic or theoretical character and the appearance of exemplary studies. Finally, with the emergence of textbooks, one can suspect that the field is becoming an autonomous discipline. This progression from topic to discipline paralleling that of isolated journal articles to textbooks (and the successive intermediate phases), is, of course, only an ideal-typical scheme. In the real world considerable overlapping of the phases is likely and in the case of the sociology of language, we indeed find some of this.

Readers, Anthologies, and Collections, with certain exceptions such as the special journal issue of Ferguson and Gumperz (1960) and the exemplary study of Haugen (1953), one can take 1964 as the year in which publications began to appear grouping topics and collecting papers in a way which heralded the sociology of language as a field of study. Particularly notable were two sociolinguistic journal issues (ed. Hymes 1964a and Gumperz and Hymes 1972) and Hymes' (editor) remarkably extensive collection, *Language in Culture and Society* (1964b). The scant eight years since this beginning has been followed by a steady flow of special journal issues and readers plus a surge of position papers and paradigmatic statements. For example, in addition to the journal issues on general sociolinguistics of Lieberson (ed. 1966) and Ewton and Ornstein (ed. 1970), special journal issues have been devoted to sociolinguistic perspectives on problems of bilingualism (MacNamara, ed. 1967), linguistic-cultural differences and education (Aarons, ed. 1969), social science methodology (Deutscher 1969) and migration and language maintenance and shift (Fishman, ed. 1971). The development of the field has also been greatly stimulated by Bright's (ed. 1966) collection of papers from the SSRC's 1964 conference on sociolinguistics and by Fishman's (ed. 1968) *Readings in the Sociology of Language.*

Prior to the end of the decade Hymes and Bittle (1967c) published a collection of studies focusing on ethnolinguistic concerns and Fishman *et al.* (eds.) contributed *Language Problems of Developing Nations* (1968). But if the publication of special journal issues in the 1964—1972 period and of anthologies and collections in the 1964—1969 period is characterized as a steady flow, the publication of anthologies and readers in the 1970—1972 period would have to be termed a virtual flood — for there are at least a dozen of note which have either already appeared or are presently in press. In 1972 alone, three general readers appeared, edited by Fishman (1972a), Gumperz and Hymes (1972), and Giglioli (1972). Four collections focusing on various aspects of bilingualism had already appeared (Alatis, 1970, Anderson and Boyer, eds. 1970, and John and Horner 1971 and Kelly, 1969). Also of recent appearance are volumes which bring a sociolinguistic perspective to bear on problems of poverty (Williams 1970), pidginization and creolization of languages (Hymes, ed. 1971), and language planning (Rubin and Jernudd, eds. 1971). And there are the more recent collections dealing with children's acquisition of language (Mackey and Andersson 1973; Ferguson and Slobin, eds. 1973), and language and education (Cazden *et al.* 1972).

Also of note is the recent series edited by Anwar Dil and published by Stanford University Press wherein separate volumes are dedicated to the most outstanding papers of several sociolinguists such as Haugen, Lambert, Ervin-Tripp, Gumperz, Ferguson, and Fishman.

For persons who were teaching courses in or related to the sociology of language prior to 1964, the lack of available materials presented a great problem. However, by the end of the decade this problem had been cast aside and, as the above developments make clear, at the present time one has a wide range of choice from among both general and topically focused collections.

Position Papers and Trend Reports — Position papers generally have as their general goal either defining the general characteristics of the field and describing what types of approaches fall inside and outside its domain or giving a general view of the work which has been or needs to be done in the field. We find, for example, Hymes (1964) and later Gumperz (1967b) and Labov (1971a) emphasizing the importance of examining language behavior within its situational context, Grimshaw (1966) and Hymes (1967a) pointing to the importance of social science concerns generally and sociological

interests in particular in order to prevent the sociology of language
slipping back into a narrowly defined linguistic view, Fishman
(1967a) specifying the principal differences between older
approaches to the sociology of language and its new emphasis,
Ervin-Tripp (1969) reviewing the insights and accomplishments of
micro-sociolinguistics, and Fishman (1967a, 1972b) and Luckmann
(1969) presenting reviews of both its micro and macro levels. To this
one might add some review articles which have surveyed the state of
development of sociolinguistics in Great Britain (Dinneen 1971),
Australia (Kaldor 1968) and the USSR (Lencek 1971).

Conceptual, Paradigmatic, and Theoretical Papers — Equally important for the transformation of a collection of topics from a loose
subject area into a more carefully defined field of study are those
papers which either introduce new constructs or develop existing
ones, and present typologies, or develop paradigms; all of these help
to draw together several topical studies into an integrated conceptual
whole. Gumperz (1962; 1964; 1967b) has contributed a number of
papers in which the important constructs of language variety and
linguistic repertoire have been introduced and developed. Ferguson's
(1959) useful concept of diglossia has been imaginatively applied by
Fishman (1967b) to more precisely interrelate the individual and
social dimensions of bilingualism. Of particular importance to the
integration of micro- and macro-sociolinguistic investigations is the
construct of domain which Fishman (1966; 1971b; ed. 1971) has put
forward in a number of publications dealing not only with its
definition but he has also shown its role in particular types of
analyses and demonstrating empirical means by which its validity can
be checked. Paradigmatic statements, which are capable of integrating large areas of data, are especially important to the conceptual
constitution of a field and two are particularly worthy of note here,
namely Hymes' (1964, 1967a) etic model for identifying the
principal dimensions of speech settings, and Fishman's (1965; 1972a;
1972b; ed. 1971: 557–582; 1972b; 1972) paradigmatic set of
questions identifying the main social dimensions involved in studying
the functional distribution of speech varieties in society. Because
Hymes' paradigm primarily applies to the micro level, and Fishman's
emphasizes more macro processes, the two are — happily — quite
complementary.

Exemplary Studies and Texts — If one understands exemplary texts as book-length studies which present useful illustrations of design, data collection, analysis, and interpretation of sociolinguistic projects, a number of good examples can be cited such as Haugen's (1953) early study of language maintenance and shift among Norwegians in the United States, as well as his (Haugen 1966) investigation into language conflict and planning efforts in Norway. Fishman's *Language Loyalty in the United States* (1966) offers a very broad range analysis of the language maintenance efforts of a number of immigrant language groups. Finally, especially relevant because of their methodological and theoretical sophistication are Labov's *The Social Stratification of English in New York City* (1966) and Fishman's *Bilingualism in the Barrio* (ed. 1971).

Both because the sociology of language is such a new field and because methodological and theoretical innovations have proceeded so rapidly, one might expect that it is still too early for any textbooks to have appeared. Nevertheless one, Fishman's *Sociolinguistics: A Brief Introduction* (1971b), has already appeared in English and been translated into both Dutch and French and his *Sociology of Language* (1972b) was published shortly thereafter.

Organized (Organizational) Publications — As can be seen in the bibliographic sections at the end of this article, sociolinguistics has had a newsletter which bears its name since 1968, published by the Research Committee on Sociolinguistics of the International Sociological Association and an inter-American organization (PILEI) has begun a similar publication. Furthermore, with increasing frequency information and resource centers as well as abstracting and reprint services have begun collecting and making materials available under the headings of sociology of language and.sociolinguistics. Publishers, moreover, have begun to initiate field related series such as one on the sociology of language which Fishman is editing for Mouton. Finally, and this is a real landmark in the social as well as the intellectual organization of the field, two journals quite specifically for the field have been organized. The first, which began appearing in April 1972 is titled *Language in Society,* edited by Dell Hymes and published by Cambridge University Press. The second, the *International Journal of the Sociology of Language* appeared in 1974 under the general editorship of Joshua A. Fishman and is published by Mouton Publishers, The Hague.

Professional Meetings and Conferences — Steps toward increasing institutionalization of the sociology of language are indicated by the organization of special program sessions within conferences of regional, national, and international professional associations for linguistics and the various social sciences. We find special sessions devoted to the sociology of language beginning with the 1966 meeting of the American Anthropological Association and followed by similar sessions at the meetings of the American Sociological Association and the American Psychological Association, where sessions on sociolinguistics have now become a regular part of their yearly meetings.

Underlying such programs we find the formation of research committees of scholarly organizations and one in particular has played an especially seminal role, namely, the Committee on Socio-linguistics of the U.S. Social Science Research Council (SSRC) which was begun in 1963 with C. A. Ferguson as chairman (Ferguson 1965) and is presently headed by Dell Hymes and Alan Grimshaw. Among its many accomplishments one can note the instrumental role it played in encouraging the above-mentioned conference programs, its introduction of sociolinguistics into the programs of summer Linguistic Institutes in the United States since 1964, the organization of a number of work groups and study seminars on special topical areas within the field, and the stimulation of a short conference immediately following the Fourth World Congress of Sociology in Evian. This last event then led to the formation of the Committee on Sociolinguistics of the International Sociological Association (RCS-ISA) which prepared the first ISA program on sociolinguistics held at the World Congress of Sociology in Varna, Bulgaria. A selection of those papers was published subsequently as the first German language reader in sociolinguistics (Kjolseth and Sack 1971). The RCS-ISA in turn has initiated a cooperative undertaking with the Association International de la Linguistique Appliqué (AILA) which has (1972) stimulated the formation of an AILA Commission on Sociolinguistics with Norman Denison of the London School of Economics as its taskmaster and the preparation, in cooperation with the RCS-ISA, of a program on sociolinguistics for the quadrennial AILA meeting which took place in Copenhagen in the summer of 1972. A selection of these papers focusing upon applied socio-linguistic concerns is now available in book form (Verdoodt, 1974). AILA also helped organize a three-week post-graduate international summer seminar on sociolinguistics in 1974 in Belgium. In addition, the RCS-ISA aided the Sociolinguistics Section of the USSR Academy of Sciences' Institute of Linguistics in planning an international congress on sociolinguistics which took place in the summer of 1974 in Moscow. This has been followed by an extensive RCS-ISA program on sociolinguistics at the regular quadrennial ISA World Congress of Sociology in the summer of 1974 at Toronto. Also of note is the present existence of a planning group in the Federal Republic of Germany which is laying the groundwork for the organization of a committee on sociolinguistics within the German Sociological Association. In the spring of 1973 this group organized an international conference on speech act theory at the University of Bielefeld, West Germany. And in 1974 a Catalan sociolinguistics group was formed.

These developments clearly demonstrate the extensive degree to which the social organization of the sociology of language is spreading to countries outside the U.S. and becoming cross-nationally integrated at the same time through more international organizations.

Teaching and Training Programs – Parallel to all of the developments which have been mentioned so far, the period under discussion has witnessed a great increase in the number of universities at which courses in the sociology of language are being offered. Indeed courses have proliferated to such an extent that it is difficult to gain an overview and one of the current projects of the RCS-ISA is to conduct an international survey on the matter, initial reports of which have already appeared in recent numbers of the Committee's Newsletter. In the United States alone, although it is presently impossible to enumerate all those universities offering courses in the sociology of language and although there is still a lack of agreement on the criteria for what might be called a training center, there are, nevertheless, a number of universities which clearly have effective programs such as Pennsylvania, Georgetown, Yeshiva, Indiana, Berkeley, and Stanford. Such a list is obviously not complete and the number will certainly continue to grow. Finally, it is interesting that (to my knowledge) nowhere are there currently plans for the formation of special departments of sociolinguistics. Whether or not this is desirable, or even possible, would be difficult to ascertain at the present time.

Independent Research Institutes – Although there are presently no independent research institutes fully dedicated to sociolinguistic concerns, a number do have special sections or programs with such a focus. Several of these research institutes are connected with universities, especially those mentioned above as training centers. In addition, there is, of course, the Center for Applied Linguistics in Washington which has played a central role in organizing a number of sociolinguistic research projects such as those reported on in its urban language series, as well as helping to organize conferences such as the Conference on Child Language (Mackey and Andersson 1973) held in November 1971 in Chicago.

In summary, this all too brief and incomplete survey of a few of the current characteristics of the field of the sociology of language indicates that paralleling its rapid conceptual development has been an equally impressive proliferation of supportive social-organizational forms, which, when taken jointly and added to the socioeconomic considerations mentioned at the outset of this essay, persuasively back up the assertion that the interdisciplinary field of sociolinguistics has become an important and well-established social fact.

Nevertheless, a critical examination of the field suggests that its social-organizational dimension is presently one of the weaker parts of the whole, for, in general, although there are many organizational forms which support the field, most of them are quite reversable. Research committees of most professional societies are usually given limited mandates for specified periods of time. For example, the Committee on Sociolinguistics of the SSRC was scheduled to die a natural death in 1972 because it had fulfilled its original mandate of making sociolinguistics known as a field and bringing together scholars from diverse social sciences. At the Georgetown roundtable meetings in March 1972, a group considered the possibility and desirability of developing a new mandate and the Committee has now been continued with a renewed mandate and expanded membership.

Similarly, the research committees of the ISA operate on the basis of limited mandates which are periodically reviewed, and the same is true for most committees of national and international professional associations. The principle is, of course, a good one for it prevents inactive, fossilized committees from persisting

Also quite reversable are current course offerings which frequently follow academic fashions and special programs within research institutes which can be expediently dropped as the social definitions of priorities change.

Because of these factors, the social definition of issues and problems as language-linked by socioeconomic interest groups within societies is crucial. This situation also makes any predictions about the likely future of the field particularly difficult — although one can surmise a few probable problems and trends, and it is to this that I will now turn.

4. FUTURE DIRECTIONS

In the opinion of this writer, the conceptual core of the sociology of language has now become sufficiently well-developed and integrated so that it is now relatively easy to identify the conceptual and topical concerns which lie near the center or on the several margins between the field itself and the many neighboring disciplines of the social sciences and humanities. This is a happy development for it would seem that its consequence will be to create a tolerant atmosphere in which forays into many new areas of investigation will be seen not as threatening but rather as enriching for the field.

However, among persons now active within the field, two rather radically opposed positions can be found concerning the desired future of sociolinguistics. On the one hand Hymes (1966: 12) proposes that 'In my own view . . . sociolinguistics (is) an inter-disciplinary field which has the possibility of becoming a basic science' with its own integrity and 'a degree of autonomy'. On the other side is the position which holds that when sociolinguistics comes of age it will be synonymous with 'good' linguistics, sociology, or psychology, depending upon the original disciplinary identification of the speaker. Fishman has referred to these as the 'self-annulling prophecies'. There is no question but that the sociology of language has already made very important contributions to all its 'parent' and related disciplines and will continue to do so. As all of the social sciences rely heavily upon data generated in or abstracted from one form or another of speech situation, sociolinguistics is a broad contributor to general methodology. Furthermore, its payoffs for theory (e.g., social process analysis) and topical concerns (e.g., stratification, education, language learning, second-language instruction, language planning and development, ethnicity, etc.) is no less broad. The issue is therefore not, Can and will sociolinguistics contribute to the several social sciences?, but How will this harvest be most productively encouraged?

To me it seems that those who support the 'self-annulling

prophecy' overlook the qualitative difference between part and whole. Or, to use a metaphor, if each of the parent disciplines celebrates the maturation of the tree of sociolinguistics by tearing off those pieces which it finds most interesting while the trunk is no longer cultivated, then, while the initial reaping may be momentarily useful to all participants there will not be anything to harvest the following year. Naturally such a development would be quite in the spirit of the ever-more-fractured specialization and reductionism which has been so characteristic of science for the last three-quarters of a century. However, it would also be diametrically opposed to the leading idea out of which the field was born, namely, *away* from specialization towards interdisciplinary integration. It is inconceivable that a parcelled-out sociology of language will be able to produce and accomplish anything like what it will be able to achieve as an integrated whole. In any event, this debate is now coming to the fore and its results will undoubtedly have great consequences for the future course of sociolinguistics.

Another problem which the field faces involves the complex interrelationships between its premises and constructs on the one hand and its recruitment of scholars and forms of social organization and support on the other. While no form of human activity is 'value-free', scientific activity must strive to make its values explicit and attempt to anticipate the social uses and consequences which its products may generate in the hands of other interest groups. Clearly such complex issues cannot be taken up here. However, precisely because the sociology of language is so useful and has so many implications for applied concerns, one must recognize that this carries with it both productive and destructive potential. What the sociology of language becomes in the future may therefore greatly depend upon whether these possibilities come to be understood or are dismissed as issues meriting serious consideration.

Finally, in order to concretize these problems, attention may be drawn to the specific dangers of ethnocentrism and the possibility of becoming a handmaiden to unanalyzed interest groupings which typically faces all sciences — including the sociology of language. Although awareness of these dangers is a beginning point, the search for solutions and alternatives can be very difficult and it would be pretentious to propose any formula. However, it would seem almost obvious that it is in the self-interest of sociolinguistics to systematically recruit into the field persons from more diverse socioeconomic, linguistic, cultural, and disciplinary backgrounds as one way of tempering intra-societal forms of ethnocentrism. Furthermore, the organization of sociolinguistics on an international level should be considerably extended as, among other things, a possible antidote to national ethnocentrism. However, this offers no panacea since 'cooperation' between intra- and intersocietal interest groupings frequently serves only as a euphemism for forms of dominance and co-optation. Deep conceptual and theoretical differences often can not be reduced to some common denominator. If one recognizes this, a pluri-centric, multi-method, multi-level approach would appear to be more realistic for the sociology of language. Its realization remains a task for the future.

BIBLIOGRAPHY

Aarons, Alfred C., ed.
　1969　Linguistic-Cultural Differences and American Education, *The Florida FL Reporter* 7:1.
Alatis, James E., ed.
　1970　*Bilingualism and Language Contact: Anthropological, Linguistic Psychological, and Sociological Aspects* (Washington, D.C., Georgetown University Press).
Andersson, Theodore, and Mildred Boyer, eds.
　1970　*Bilingual Schooling in the United States*, 2 vols. (Washington, D.C., U.S. Government Printing Office).
Bolinger, Dwight
　1967　*Aspects of Language* (New York, Harcourt, Brace and World).
Bright, William, ed.
　1966　*Sociolinguistics: Proceedings of the UCLA Sociolinguistics Conference, 1964* (The Hague, Mouton).
Cazden, C. B., Vera P. John, and Dell Hymes, eds.
　1972　*Functions of Language in the Classroom* (New York, Columbia University Teacher's College Press).
Chomsky, Noam
　1965　*Aspects of a Theory of Syntax* (Cambridge, Mass., M.I.T. Press).
Darnell, Regna
　1969　'The Development of American Anthropology 1879—1920: From the Bureau of American Ethnology to Franz Boas', unpublished Ph.D. dissertation (University of Pennsylvania).
　1970　'The Professionalization of American Anthropology: A Case Study in the Sociology of Knowledge', paper presented at the 7th World Congress of Sociology, Varna, Bulgaria, September.
Deutscher, Irwin, ed.
　1969　'On Language and Conduct', *Sociological Focus* 3(2).
Dinneen, Francis P., S. J.
　1971　'Linguistics in Great Britain in the Sixties: Perspectives for the Seven-

ties', in *Linguistics: Developments of the Sixties — Viewpoints for the Seventies*, Richard J. O'Brien, S. J., ed. (Washington, D.C., Georgetown University Press) pp. 125—143.

Ervin-Tripp, Susan M.
  1969 'Sociolinguistics', in *Advances in Experimental Social Psychology*, Vol. 4, Leonard Berkowitz, ed. (New York, Academic Press).

Ewton, Ralph W., Jr., and Jacob Ornstein, eds.
  1970 *Studies in Language and Linguistics, 1969—70* (El Paso, Texas, Texas Western Press).

Ferguson, Charles A.
  1959 'Diglossia', *Word* 15:325—340 (New York).
  1965 'Directions in Sociolinguistics, Report on an Interdisciplinary Seminar', *SSRC Items* 19(1): 1—4.

Ferguson, Charles H., and John J. Gumperz, eds.
  1960 'Linguistic Diversity in South Asia: Studies in Regional, Social and Functional Variation', *International J. of American Linguistics* 4(1).

Ferguson, C. A., and D. I. Slobin, eds.
  1973 *Studies on Child Language Development* (New York, Holt, Rinehart and Winston).

Fishman, Joshua A.
  1964 'Language Maintenance and Language Shift as a Field of Inquiry', *Linguistics* 9: S. 32—70.
  1965 'Who Speaks What Language to Whom and When', *La linguistique* 2: 67—88.
  1966 *Language Loyalty in the United States* (The Hague, Mouton).
  1967a 'A Sociology of Language (A Review of J. O. Hertzler, *A Sociology of Language*, New York: Random House, 1965)', *Language* 43(2): 586—604.
  1967b 'Bilingualism With and Without Diglossia: Diglossia With and Without Bilingualism', *Journal of Social Issues* 23(2): 29—38.
  1971a 'The Impact of Nationalism on Language Planning: Some Comparisons Between Early 20th Century Europe and Subsequent Developments in South and South East Asia', in *Can Languages be Planned?* Joan Rubin and Bjorn Jernudd, eds. (Honolulu, Hawaii, East-West Center Press).
  1971b *Sociolinguistics: A Brief Introduction* (Rowley, Mass., Newbury House). [Dutch edition: *Taalsociologie* (Bruxelles, Labor 1970); French edition: *Sociolinguistique* (Bruxelles, Labor 1971).]
  1972a 'The Sociology of Language: An Interdisciplinary Social Science Approach to Sociolinguistics', in *Advances in the Sociology of Language* J. A. Fishman, ed. (The Hague, Mouton). (Also published under the same title by Newbury House, Rowley, Mass.).
  1972b 'The Links Between Micro- and Macro-Sociolinguistics in the Study of Who Speaks That Language to Whom and When,' in *Directions in Sociolinguistics.* John J. Gumperz and Dell Hymes, eds. (New York, Holt, Rinehart and Winston).

Fishman, Joshua A., ed.
  1968 *Readings in the Sociology of Language* (The Hague, Mouton).
  1971 *Bilingualism in the Barrio* (Bloomington, Indiana, and The Hague, University of Indiana Press and Mouton).

The sociology of language and its social implications   823

1972   *Advances in the Sociology of Language* (The Hague, Mouton).

Fishman, Joshua A., *et al.*, eds.
1968   *Language Problems of Developing Nations* (New York, John Wiley and Sons, Inc.).

Giglioli, Pier Paolo, ed.
1972   *Language in Context* (London, Penguin).

Grimshaw, Allen
1966   'Directions for Research in Sociolinguistics: Suggestions of A Non-Linguist Sociologist', *Sociological Inquiry* 36(2): 319—322.

Gumperz, John J.
1962   'Types of Linguistic Communities', *Anthropological Linguistics* 4(1): 28—40.
1964   'Linguistic and Social Interaction in Two Communities', *American Anthropologist* 66:2.37—53.
1967a 'The Linguistic Markers of Bilingualism', *J. of Social Issues* 23(2): 48—57.
1967b 'Language and Communication', *The Annals of the American Academy of Political and Social Science* 364:219—231.

Gumperz, John J., and Dell Hymes, eds.
1972   *Directions in Sociolinguistics: The Ethnography of Communication* (New York, Holt, Rinehart, and Winston).

Haugen, Einar
1953   *The Norwegian Language in America: A Study in Bilingual Behavior*, 2 Vols. (Philadelphia, Pa., The University of Pennsylvania Press).
1966   *Language Planning and Language Conflict: The Case of Modern Norwegian* (Cambridge, Mass., Harvard University Press).

Hymes, Dell
1964   'Toward Ethnographics of Communication', *American Anthropologist* 66:6:2. 1—34.
1966   'Report on Teaching and Training in Sociolinguistics', unpublished manuscript, November 1.
1967a 'Why Linguistics Needs the Sociologist', *Social Research* 34:632—47.
1967b 'Models of the Interaction of Language and Social Setting', *Journal of Social Issues* 23(2): 8—28.

Hymes, Dell ed.
1964a 'Directions in (Ethno-) Linguistic Theory', *American Anthropologist* 66:3:1. 6—56.
1964b *Language in Culture and Society: A Reader in Linguistics and Anthropology* (New York, Harper and Row).
1971   *Pidginization and Creolization of Languages: Proceedings of a Conference Held at the University of the West Indies, 1968* (Cambridge, Mass., Cambridge University Press).

Hymes, Dell, and William E. Bittle, eds.
1967   *Studies in Southwestern Ethnolinguistics: Meaning and History in Language of the American Southwest* (= Studies in General Anthropology 3). (The Hague, Mouton).

John, Vera, and Vivian Horner
1971   *Early Childhood Bilingual Education* (New York, Modern Language Association).

Kaldor, Susan
  1968 'Sociolinguistics in Australia', *Language Sciences* 3 (Dec.) 3—6.
Kelly, L. G.
  1969 *Description et mesure du bilinguisme: un colloque international,*
         Université de Moncton, 6—14 juin 1967/Description and Measurement
         of Bilingualism: An International Seminar, University of Moncton, June
         6—14, 1967 (Toronto, University of Toronto Press).
Kjolseth, Rolf
         'Bilingual Education Programs in the United States — For Assimilation
         or Pluralism?' Paper originally presented in the section on 'Sociological
         Perspectives on Bilingual Education' in the Sociolinguistics Program at
         the Seventh World Congress of Sociology, Varna, Bulgaria, Sept.
         14—19, 1970. Revised version published (in German): 'Zweisprachige
         Erziehungsprogramme in den Vereinigten Staaten: Assimilation oder
         Pluralismus?', in Rolf Kjolseth und Fritz Sack (Hrsg.) *Zur Soziologie*
         der Sprache: Ausgewaehlte Beitraege vom 7. Weltkongress der
         Soziologie (= *Sonderheft 15 der Koelner Zeitschrift fuer Soziologie und*
         Sozialpsychologie) (Opladen, Westdeutscher Verlag, 1971) pp. 251—
         275. Revised and reprinted in English: 'Bilingual Education Programs in
         the United States: For Assimilation or Pluralism?', in Bernard Spolsky,
         ed. *The Language Education of Minority Children* (Rowley, Mass.,
         Newbury House Publishers, 1972) pp. 94—121. Reprinted: 'Bilingual
         Education Programs in the United States: For Assimilation or
         Pluralism?', in Paul R. Turner, ed. *Bilingualism in the Southwest*
         (Tucson, Arizona, The University of Arizona Press, 1973) pp. 3—27.
Kloss, H.
  1929 'Sprachtabellen als Grundlage für Sprachstatistik, Sprachenkarten und
         für eine allgemeine Soziologie der Sprachgemeinschaften', *Vierteljahr-*
         schrift für Politik und Geschichte 7(1): 103—117.
Kuhn, Thomas
  1962 *The Structure of Scientific Revolutions* (Chicago, University of Chicago
         Press).
Labov, William
  1966 *The Social Stratification of English in New York City* (Washington,
         D.C., Center for Applied Linguistics).
  1971a 'The Place of Linguistic Research in American Society', in *Linguistics in*
         the 1970's (Pre-Publication edition), Center for Applied Linguistics, ed.
         (Washington, D.C., Center for Applied Linguistics) pp. 41—70.
  1971b 'The Notion of "System" in Creole Languages', in *Pidginization and*
         Creolization of Languages, Dell Hymes, ed. (London, Cambridge
         University Press) pp. 447—472.
Lencek, Rado
  1971 'Problems in Sociolinguistics in the Soviet Union', in *Linguistics:*
         Developments of the Sixties — Viewpoints for the Seventies, Richard
         J. O'Brien, S. J., ed. (Washington, D.C., Georgetown University Press)
         pp. 269—301.
Lieberson, Stanley, ed.
  1966 'Explorations in Sociolinguistics', *Sociological Inquiry* 36(2).

Luckmann, Thomas
   1969   'Soziologie der Sprache', in *Handbuch der empirischen Sozialforschung*,
         Rene Koenig, ed. Vol. 4. (Stuttgart) pp. 1050—1101.
Mackey, William F., and Theodore Andersson, eds.
   1973   *Bilingualism in Early Childhood* (Rowley, Mass., Newbury House).
MacNamara, John, ed.
   1967   'Problems of Bilingualism', *The Journal of Social Issues* 23(2).
Rubin, Joan, and Bjorn Jernudd, eds.
   1971   *Can Language be Planned?* (Honolulu, Hawaii, East-West Center Press).
Shuy, Roger, and Ralph Fasold
   1971   'Contemporary Emphases in Sociolinguistics', in *Linguistics: Develop-
         ments of the Sixties — Viewpoints for the Seventies*, Richard
         J. O'Brien, S. J., ed. (Washington, D.C., Georgetown University Press)
         pp. 185—197.
Sociolinguistics Newsletter Research Committee on Sociolinguistics, International
         Sociological Association, ed. Subscriptions: Jon Driessen Scholars Press,
         University of Montana, Missoula, Montana 59801, U.S.A.
Verdoodt, A, ed.
   1974   Applied Sociolinguistics (Association Internationale de Linguistique
         Appliqué, Third Congress, Copenhagen 1972: Proceedings Volume 2:
         Applied Sociolinguistics). (Heidelberg, Julius Groos Verlag).
Williams, Frederick, ed.
   1970   *Language and Poverty: Perspectives on a Theme* (Chicago, Markham
         Publishing Co.)

Index

social change, VII—IX, 67, 82, 157—
158, 162, 164—165, 180, 181,
182, 187, 199, 304—309, 323,
409, 436—437, 439, 441—445,
447, 448, 471, 607—608,
616—617, 621, 665, 667, 675,
727, 728, 732, 735, 736, 759
social dialect, 12, 13—14, 42, 69,
148
socio-cultural background, 4, 5, 10,
14, 24, 35, 36, 41, 44, 47,
49—50, 55, 57—65 *passim*,
71—82 *passim*, 129—145 passim, 153—171 *passim*, 181—
188 *passim*, 199, 201, 207,
213, 217, 228—239, 242—256
passim, 265, 286, 304—309,
323—324, 327—328, 358, 360,
372, 382, 403, 405, 407—408,
417—418, 424, 429, 431, 438,
445, 449, 455, 466, 483, 497,
506—507, 509, 522, 546, 636,
640, 643—644, 648, 655—657,
674—676, 681—683, 686—690,
693, 706—708, 710, 716, 724,
731, 740, 742, 766, 785, 787—
788, 812
see also ethnicity, folklore, Jews,
linguistic determinism, nationalism, *Weltanschauung*
sociolinguistic situation, 11, 16, 19,
38, 39, 42, 47, 49, 53, 58, 64,
66, 69, 72, 75, 78, 122, 131—
132, 133, 135, 141, 142, 143,
146, 155, 159, 171—174, 180,
192—193, 206, 209, 247, 252,
280, 286, 320, 322, 324, 364,
365, 375, 385, 394—396, 403,
406, 417, 425, 427, 428, 435—
440, 445, 450, 451, 463—465,
473, 489, 511—512, 517,
521—522, 544, 547, 549, 553,
570, 572, 639, 650, 653, 656,
667—668, 712—715, 719, 722,
725—736 *passim*, 755, 757—
759, 778
sociolinguistic studies, 6, 9, 10, 50,
59, 60—62, 67, 77, 81, 153—

154, 180, 182, 186, 187—189,
386—387, 500, 506, 509—510,
588, 590, 624, 636, 653—658,
659, 666, 740—752, 768, 770,
784, 786, 787, 795—798,
799—825
origins of, 800—803
patterns of, 744—752, 774—775,
785, 811—819
philosophy of, 804—811, 819—
820
publications in, 811—815
techniques of, 61—62, 114, 739,
742, 746, 747, 773
sociological factors, 3, 9, 10, 37, 44,
50, 60, 61, 72, 79, 129—149,
153, 154, 187—189, 378—379,
402, 423, 432, 478, 562, 746,
785, 789, 792, 795, 801, 803,
814
Somali, 470, 759—760
Sorbian, 18, 21, 42, 430, 432, 434,
456
-German, 21
South Africa, 425
South America, 3, 20, 187, 194, 195,
206, 226, 233, 252, 261
see also individual countries
South Asian English, 477—551
South Australia, 118, 120
Southwestern U.S., 10, 14, 59, 74,
78
Soviet Union, 189, 194, 204—206,
213, 226, 230—239 *passim*,
246, 252, 262, 323, 403, 418,
421, 426, 439
Spain, 434, 471
Spanish
in bilingual context, 10, 11, 12,
13, 14, 15, 65, 75, 78, 390,
463, 652, 656
as minority language, 19, 33, 34,
37, 42, 52, 59, 72, 73, 74, 77,
78, 191, 195—211 *passim*, 223,
246, 259, 632
teaching of, 22
words in American Indian, 14, 41
spelling, 12, 26, 142, 188, 241, 342,